Presenting the Third Edition of Siegel and Welsh's Best-Seller

Concise CORE coverage of juvenile delinquency that gets your students' attention!

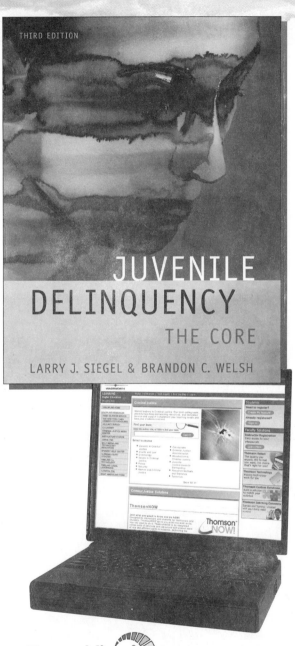

THIRD EDITION

JUVENILE DELINQUENCY
THE CORE

LARRY J. SIEGEL & BRANDON C. WELSH

Juvenile Delinquency: The Core presents the theories, policies, and latest research of this dynamic, constantly evolving field in one value-priced, student-friendly paperback! Praised as much for its authority and balance as it is for the authors' ability to engage students in the juvenile delinquency course, this brief book is an exceptional value. Siegel and Welsh help students understand the nature of delinquency and its causes and correlates, as well as current strategies being used to control or eliminate its occurrence. You'll find much that's new in this important revision:

► A **NEW** *Case Profile* opens each chapter! These real-life, chapter-opening stories of at-risk youths are revisited within the chapter and linked to chapter concepts. *See page P-2.*

► **NEW** and updated topics—recent legal cases, research studies, policy initiatives, and more are included throughout! *See page P-3.*

► *Focus on Delinquency* and *Preventing and Treating Delinquency* boxes—featuring many **NEW** topics—give students opportunities for critical thinking and reflection. *See page P-4.*

► INNOVATIVE study tools guide students through every chapter—illustrating, clarifying, and reinforcing the material. *See page P-5.*

THOMSON
™
WADSWORTH

ExamView®
Assessment Suite

Power Lecture

Value-priced!
Accompanied by an interactive, information-packed website and other innovative instructor and student resources.
See P-6 through P-8 for details.

Preview

NEW *Case Profiles* reinforce chapter content with fascinating, real-life stories of at-risk youths

Provided by professionals working in the juvenile justice system, this edition's new *Case Profiles* will intrigue your students with the circumstances, challenges, and eventual successes of fourteen at-risk youths who have worked their way out of delinquency. For example, in Chapter 7, "The Family and Delinquency," the *Case Profile* explores the plight of Joey Williams, who entered the child welfare system at the age of nine when it was discovered that he and his younger sister were being sexually assaulted by their stepfather.

CASE PROFILE Joey's Story

Joey Williams entered the child welfare system at the age of nine, when it was discovered that he and his younger sister and brother were being sexually abused by their stepfather. The children had also been experiencing neglect due to a lack of sufficient resources in the family; they often went without food or proper clothing. Joey's mother struggled to provide structure for the children, but she was also facing many of her own personal problems. All three of the children were acting out and having difficulties in school. When Joey's stepfather was incarcerated, the child welfare system placed the children in separate foster homes and began to provide services for the family with the goal of returning the children to their mother's home. Joey had a difficult time adjusting to foster care and being separated from his family.

Joey's return to his family. She did not comply with those recommendations however.

As Joey approached his seventeenth birthday, the professionals involved in his case began to prepare for him to exit the juvenile system. He had not committed any more law violations. His siblings had been able to return home to their mother, and it was also decided that Joey, with significant family supports and interventions, would also be able to return home. The family entered intensive therapy, which utilized a "wrap-around" approach that focused on family [...] and on the positive aspects of their situation. The [...] service model shifts the focus away from a [...] pathologies and weaknesses and works with them [...] on their assets, skills, and resources.

[...] Joey's family, there were many things going well. [...] some assistance getting a few items to meet [...] basic needs, but overall, they were doing much [...] the areas of employment and housing. Joey re-[...] correct combination of medications, appropriate [...] and support to enable him to live at home again. [...] he always had a passion for music, as part of his re-[...] into the family home, the wrap-around funds [...] to purchase guitar lessons for him, providing [...] and a positive and creative outlet. Joey, his family, [...] team of professionals involved with his case worked [...] very closely for a period of six months. The transi-[...] was difficult at times, but ultimately successful. [...] for his GED and worked hard to accomplish his [...] goals. The younger siblings also began to show [...] improvement and Joey became a role model in his [...] Joey is doing well today, has a full-time job, and has [...] any further problems with the law.

[...]ysfunction is a key ingredient in the development [...]ually lead to long-term social problems.[1] Interac-[...], and between siblings, provide opportunities for [...]cial behavior patterns.[2] Even kids who are predis-posed toward delinquency, because of personality traits, such as low self-control and impulsive personality, may find their life circumstances improved and their involve-ment with antisocial behavior diminished if they are exposed to positive and effective parenting.[3]

Good parenting lowers the risk of delinquency for children living in high-crime areas. Research shows they are able to resist the temptation of the streets if they re-ceive fair discipline and support from parents who provide them with positive role models.[4] However, children in affluent families who are being raised in a household characterized by abuse and conflict, or whose parents are absent or separated, will still

THE FAMILY AND DELINQUENCY **151**

LOOKING BACK TO JOEY'S STORY

Considering the above mentioned family influences on delinquency, which do you think had the greatest impact on Joey's misbehaviors? Is it possible to single out one factor or do they all contribute?

LOOKING BACK TO JOEY'S STORY

What should be done in situations where juveniles of similar ages engage in sexual contact? Should they be charged criminally or is there a better alternative?

LOOKING BACK TO JOEY'S STORY

What is the responsibility of a parent when his child is removed from their home? What should happen in situations where parents are not following the juvenile court-ordered recommendations?

Thought-provoking *Looking Back* boxes link the *Case Profiles* to chapter topics
As students progress through the chapter, *Looking Back* boxes revisit the chapter-opening *Case Profile* with questions that ask students to think critically about chapter topics as they relate to the *Case Profile*.

Case Profiles

Cutting-edge material and new research give students a real-world look at juvenile delinquency

JUVENILE VICTIMIZATION

victimization
A person who has suffered direct, or threatened, physical, emotional, or financial harm as a result of being the target of a criminal act.

Juveniles are also victims of crime, and data from victim surveys can help us understand the nature of juvenile **victimization**. One source of juvenile victimization data is the result of an ongoing cooperative effort of the Bureau of Justice Statistics of the U.S. Department of Justice and the U.S. Census Bureau called the National Crime Victimization Survey (NCVS).[84] The NCVS is a household survey of victims of criminal behavior that measures the nature of the crime and the characteristics of victims.

The total annual sample size of the NCVS has been about forty thousand households, containing about seventy-five thousand individuals. The sample is broken down into subsamples of ten thousand households, and each group is interviewed twice a year. The NCVS has been conducted annually for more than fifteen years.

Victimization in the United States

The NCVS provides estimates of the total number of personal contact crimes (assault, rape, robbery) and household victimizations (burglary, larceny, vehicle theft). The survey indicates that currently about 23 million criminal incidents occur each year. Being the target or victim of rape, robbery, or assault is a terrible burden,

CHAPTER 12

Police Work with Juveniles

ported by surveys that ... or more years of education, co... tion.[22] In sum, the school ex... shaping the direction of an adolescent's life c...

school failure
Failing to achieve success in school can result in frustration, anger, and reduced self-esteem, which may contribute to delinquent behavior.

School Failure and Delinquency

Although there is general agreement that **school failure** and delinquency are related, some questions remain concerning the nature and direction of this relationship. There are actually three independent views on the association:

1. School failure is a direct cause of delinquent behavior. Children who fail at school soon feel frustrated and rejected. Believing they will never achieve success through conventional means, they seek out like-minded companions and together engage in antisocial behaviors. Educational failure evokes negative responses from important people in the child's life, including teachers, parents, and prospective employers. These reactions help solidify feelings of inadequacy, and in some cases, lead to a pattern of chronic delinquency.

2. School failure leads to emotional and psychological problems that are the actual cause of antisocial behavior. Academic failure reduces self-esteem and reduced self-esteem is an immediate cause of delinquency. Studies using a variety of measures of academic competence and self-esteem demonstrate that good students have a better attitude about themselves than poor students; low self-esteem has been found to contribute to delinquent behavior.[23] The association then runs from school failure to low self-concept to delinquency.

3. School failure and delinquency share a common cause. Both are caused by another condition so that although it appears that school failure precedes and causes delinquency the association is actually false and spurious. For example, prior substance abuse leads to both delinquency and school failure.

Andrew, a high school dropout, waits for his friends outside his old campus, Hollywood High School in Los Angeles. Some critics charge that California's high school dropout problem has been underestimated, with more accurate figures showing that only half of the African American, Hispanic, and American Indian students in the state are earning regular high school diplomas. Education experts are calling for greater accountability over the high number of dropouts instead of the current emphasis on test scores. What can be done to keep kids in school? Should high school dropouts be allowed to serve in the military?

Correlates of School Failure

Despite disagreement over the direction the relationship takes, there is little argument that delinquent behavior is influenced by educational experiences. A number of factors have been linked to school failure; the most prominent are discussed in the next sections.

Respected, accurate, and always meticulous in their search for the latest important research, Siegel and Welsh infuse this edition with the most current theories of the causes and correlates of juvenile delinquency, research studies, and policy issues affecting the field today. A few highlights:

▶ Juvenile victimization—including new information on the victim-offender relationship (Chapter 2).

▶ Individual, sociological, and developmental views of delinquency, including new research findings in each of these three key areas (Chapters 3, 4, and 5).

▶ Paths to delinquency—a new section discussing this critical topic (Chapter 5).

▶ Gender differences in cognition and socialization, and a new section on early puberty and victimization (Chapter 6).

▶ The legacy of divorce—including updated material on parental deviance, and the association between mothers' employment and children's delinquency (Chapter 7).

▶ "No Child Left Behind"—new coverage of this controversial program and new measures designed to reduce school crime (Chapter 9).

▶ Juvenile drug use—the latest findings and recent trends from three national surveys (Chapter 10).

▶ Juvenile justice—new evaluation studies on the effectiveness of a comprehensive strategy (Chapter 11).

▶ Police work with juveniles—new findings on what works, including results from the National Research Council panel on police effectiveness (Chapter 12).

Important legal cases showcasing juvenile delinquency issues

In *Juvenile Law in Review* boxes, as well as throughout this book's narrative, students will find discussion of major court cases that address key juvenile delinquency issues. A newly added *Juvenile Law in Review* in Chapter 9 focuses on a case about drug testing in an Oklahoma school district.

Intriguing boxed material focuses students on key issues, including prevention and treatment

Throughout this book, Siegel and Welsh examine current strategies and major initiatives by the police, courts, and within communities. Nearly two dozen *Focus on Delinquency* and *Preventing and Treating Delinquency* boxes throughout the book give students an insightful look at these issues.

For example, a new *Focus on Delinquency* topic in this edition, "Human Trafficking and the Sexual Exploitation of Children," discusses the many forms of human trafficking, contributing factors, and the troubling trend of "sexual tourism." Another new *Focus on Delinquency* box, "The Chicken or the Egg?" looks at the provocative question which comes first, bad parents or bad kids?

Preventing and Treating Delinquency boxes examine major policy initiatives and programs in juvenile justice. Topics include "Drug Abuse Resistance Education (D.A.R.E)," "Boston's Operation Ceasefire," and "Teen Courts."

Focus on Delinquency

Human Trafficking and the Sexual Exploitation of Children

Human trafficking includes all forms of transportation of women and girls (as well as young boys) through the use of force, abduction, fraud, and/or commercial exploitation. Trafficking activities include recruiting individuals, transporting and transferring them from their home country or region to other transshipment points and to destination countries, receiving such trafficked persons and keeping them in custody or housing them.

Many forms of trafficking exist. Young girls and women are common targets of commercial sexual exploitation. They may be forced into prostitution and other sexual activities such as the production of pornography. There are accounts of women being forced to service thirty men a day and children trapped in pornography rings. Others become human containers in the

are often poor and aspire to a better life. They may be forced, coerced, deceived, and psychologically manipulated into industrial or agricultural work, marriage, domestic servitude, organ donation, or sexual exploitation. Although victims often come from poorer countries, the market for labor and sex is found in wealthier countries or in countries that, while economically poor, cater to the needs of citizens from wealthy countries, of corporations, or of tourists.

While some individuals are trafficked directly for purposes of prostitution or commercial sexual exploitation, other trafficked persons and even those trafficked for legitimate work may become victims of interpersonal violence. Women trafficked for domestic work in wealthy countries or laborers trafficked for construction, logging, factory or farm work, are vulnerable to exploitation by their employers. Individuals trafficked for the labor purposes are usually unfamiliar with their new location and the language spoken there. They often lack formal education and do not know

Preventing and Treating Delinquency

Drug Abuse Resistance Education (D.A.R.E.)

The most widely known drug education program, Drug Abuse Resistance Education (D.A.R.E.), is an elementary school course designed to give students the skills they need to resist peer pressure to experiment with tobacco, drugs, and alcohol. It is unique because it employs uniformed police officers to carry the anti-drug message to the children before they enter junior high school. The program focuses on five major areas:

- Providing accurate information about tobacco, alcohol, and drugs
- Teaching students techniques to resist peer pressure
- Teaching students to respect the law and law enforcers
- Giving students ideas for alternatives to drug use
- Building the self-esteem of students

The D.A.R.E. program is based on the concept that the young students need specific analytical and social skills to resist peer pressure and "say no" to drugs. Instructors work with children to raise their self-esteem, provide them with decision-making tools, and help them identify positive alternatives to substance abuse.

The D.A.R.E. approach has been adopted widely since it was founded in 1983. D.A.R.E. America indicates that the program is now taught in almost 80 percent of school districts

Changing the D.A.R.E. Curriculum

Although national evaluations and independent reviews have questioned the validity of D.A.R.E. and many communities have discontinued its use—due in part to the program not meeting U.S. Department of Education effectiveness standards—it is still widely employed in school districts around the country. To meet criticism head-on, D.A.R.E. began testing a new curriculum for middle and high school programs, known as "Take Charge of Your Life." The new program is aimed at older students and relies more on having them question their assumptions about drug use than on listening to lectures on the subject. The new program will work largely on changing social norms, teaching students to question whether they really have to use drugs to fit in with their peers. Emphasis will shift from fifth-grade students to those in the seventh grade and a booster program will be added in ninth grade, when kids are more likely to experiment with drugs. Police officers will now serve more as coaches than as lecturers, encouraging students to challenge the social norm of drug use in discussion groups. Students also will do more role-playing in an effort to learn decision-making skills. There will also be an emphasis on the role of media and advertising in shaping behavior. The new curricula is undergoing tests in a total of 83 high schools and 122 middle schools in six large cities—half the schools will continue using the curriculum they do now, and the other half will use the new D.A.R.E. program—so that the new curriculum may be scientifically evaluated. Early [stu]dy results suggest that the new curriculum is being delivered [as] designed and is reaching the highest risk youth.

CRITICAL THINKING

Do you believe that an education program such as D.A.R.E. can turn kids away from drugs, or are the reasons for teenage drug use so complex that a single school-based program is doomed to fail?
If you ran D.A.R.E., what experiences would you give to the children? Do you think it would be effective to have current or ex-addicts address classes about how drugs influenced their lives?

INFOTRAC COLLEGE EDITION RESEARCH
For more information on the enhanced D.A.R.E. program, [g]o InfoTrac College Edition and read "Enhanced D.A.R.E. Pro[gra]m More Effective for Adolescent Boys," *Brown University* [Ch]*ild and Adolescent Behavior Letter* 19:1 (April 2003).

NEW DIRECTIONS IN PREVENTING DELINQUENCY

Primary Prevention Efforts: Early Childhood

Delinquency prevention refers to intervening in a young person's life prior to engagement in a delinquent act. In some instances, prevention means helping kids develop defenses to help them resist the crime-promoting elements in their immediate environment. In other instances, it can mean helping experienced offenders who have already been involved in antisocial behaviors develop the skills that can enable them to resist delinquency and a delinquent way of life. An understanding of prevention is critical to the field of juvenile delinquency, because efforts to explain and understand why kids commit crime would exist in a vacuum if they could not provide a blueprint for eliminating, controlling, or preventing youth crime.

Traditionally, delinquency prevention efforts are divided into three types: primary prevention, secondary prevention, and tertiary prevention.

- *Primary prevention* focuses on improving the general well-being of individual children through such measures as providing access to health care services and education or modifying conditions in the physical environment, such as removing abandoned vehicles and improving the appearance of neighborhood buildings.
- *Secondary prevention* involves intervening with children and young people who are viewed as being at high risk for becoming juvenile offenders. Secondary

from delinquency-producing forces in the family and community. Later in the text, secondary and tertiary efforts will be examined independently.

PRIMARY PREVENTION

All of the theoretical models of delinquency we have discussed in the preceding chapters suggest that the seeds of delinquency are planted early in life. Although some people may begin their offending career relatively late—in their later teen years or even early adulthood—it appears that the majority of the most serious delinquents experience antisocial episodes much earlier, in their early adolescence or before. Given this finding, primary prevention programs are often aimed at positively influencing the early risk factors or "root causes" of delinquency. Early risk factors may include structural factors such as poverty and residency in a lower-class neighborhood, socialization issues such as inadequate parental supervision and harsh or inconsistent discipline, and individual or trait issues such as a high level of hyperactivity or impulsiveness. Consequently, primary prevention interventions are often multidimensional, targeting more than one risk factor at a time. This approach attacks delinquency on a number of different fronts, including cognitive development, child skills training, and family support. What are some of the directions being explored to deliver primary prevention before the onset of a delinquent career?

New Directions in Preventing Delinquency essays, located at the end of selected chapters, explore three levels of efforts being made to prevent delinquency: programs designed to help kids avoid delinquent behaviors, programs aimed at kids who are at risk for delinquency, and programs attempting to help kids who have committed delinquent acts.

Helping students retain the material, think critically, and apply what they learn

What Does This Mean to Me?

"Bully for You!"

Research indicates that more than 80 percent of school kids say their behavior includes physical aggression, social ridicule, teasing, name calling, and issuing threats over the previous thirty days. Some kids seem proud of being bullies and think their behavior, no matter how destructive, is just having fun at another's expense. Many of us have been the targets of bullies, but felt unsure of how to cope with the problem. If you told the teacher or your parents you were a wimp; if you did nothing you remained a target.

1. Did you ever find yourself having to confront this dilemma, and if so what did you do to solve the problem?
2. Do you believe there is a link between being the victim of bullying and engaging in school violence? The Columbine shooters were believed to be targets of bullying. Could this have been the spark that caused them to snap?

The Causes of School Crime

What are the suspected causes of school violence? Research indicates that they may be found at the individual, school, and community level.

School Level Causes Schools with a high proportion of students behind grade level in reading, with many students from families on welfare, and located in a community with high unemployment, crime, and poverty rates, are also at risk for delinquency.[47] Research shows that the perpetrators and victims of school crime cannot be neatly divided into separate groups and that many offenders have been victims of delinquency themselves.[48] It is possible that school-based crimes have "survival value": striking back against a weaker victim is a method of regaining lost possessions or self-respect.[49]

Research also shows that school climate—the social and educational atmosphere of a school—is

Featuring personalized, experiential learning activities and self-assessments, *What Does This Mean to Me?* boxes help students recognize risk factors contributing to delinquency and examine these important issues by using their life experiences as a starting point.

APPLYING WHAT YOU HAVE LEARNED

Fourteen-year-old Daphne A., a product of the city's best private schools, lives with her wealthy family in a fashionable neighborhood. Her father is an executive at a local financial services conglomerate and earns close to a million dollars per year. Daphne, however, is always in trouble at school, and teachers report she is impulsive and has poor self-control. At times she can be kind and warm, but on other occasions she is obnoxious, unpredictable, insecure, and demanding of attention. She is overly self-conscious about her body and has a drinking problem.

Despite repeated promises to get her life together, Daphne likes to hang out at night in a local park, drinking with neighborhood kids. On more than one occasion she has gone to the park with her friend Chris G., a quiet boy with his own personal problems. His parents have separated and he is prone to severe anxiety attacks. He has been suspended from school, and diagnosed with depression, for which he takes two drugs—an antidepressant and a sedative.

One night, the two met up with Michael M., a forty-four-year-old man with a long history of alcoholism. After a night of drinking, a fight broke out and Michael was stabbed, his throat cut, and his body dumped in a pond.

Soon after the attack, Daphne called 911, telling police that a friend "jumped in the lake and didn't come out." Police searched the area and found the slashed and stabbed body in the water; the body had been disemboweled in an attempt to sink it. When the authorities traced the call, Daphne was arrested, and she confessed to police that she had helped Chris murder the victim.

During an interview with court psychiatrists, Daphne admits she participated in the killing, but cannot articulate what caused her to get involved. She had been drinking and remembers little of the events. She said she was flirting with Michael and Chris stabbed him in a jealous rage. She speaks in a flat, hollow voice and shows little remorse for her actions. It was a spur-of-the-moment thing, she claims, and after all it was Chris who had the knife and not she. Later, Chris claims that Daphne instigated the fight, egged him on, taunting him that he was too scared to kill someone. Chris says that Daphne, while drunk, often talked of killing an adult because she hates older people, especially her parents.

If Daphne is tried as a juvenile, she can be kept in institutions until she is seventeen; the sentence could be expanded to age twenty-one, but only if she is a behavior problem in

282 CHAPTER 11

Found at the end of every chapter, fascinating *Applying What You Have Learned* scenarios offer students many opportunities to role-play as professionals in various decision-making roles. For example:

▶ "You have just been appointed by the governor as the chairperson of the newly formed group charged with overhauling the state's juvenile justice system . . ."

▶ "As a juvenile court judge, you are forced to make a tough decision during a hearing . . ."

▶ "You are a state legislator who is a member of the subcommittee on juvenile justice . . ."

CHAPTER OBJECTIVES
After reading this chapter you should:

1. Know what is meant by the term *official delinquency.*
2. Understand how the FBI's Uniform Crime Report (UCR) is compiled.
3. Be familiar with recent trends in juvenile delinquency.
4. Understand how self-report data are collected and what they say about juvenile crime.
5. Recognize the factors that affect the juvenile crime rate.
6. Be aware of gender patterns in delinquency.
7. Appreciate the factors that cause racial differences in delinquency.
8. Be able to debate the issue of class position and delinquency.
9. Be aware of the debate over the role age plays in delinquency.
10. Understand the concept of the chronic persistent offender.
11. Be familiar with the relationship between childhood and victimization.

21

✓ CHECKPOINTS

■ Choice theory maintains that delinquency is rational and can be prevented by punishment that is sufficiently severe and certain.

■ Delinquents who choose crime must evaluate the characteristics of a target to determine its suitability.

■ Routine activities theory suggests that delinquent acts are a function of motivated offenders, lack of capable guardians, and availability of suitable targets.

■ General deterrence models are based on the fear of punishment. If punishments are severe, swift, and certain, then would-be delinquents would choose not to risk breaking the law.

■ Specific deterrence aims at reducing crime through the application of severe punishments. Once offenders experience these punishments they will be unwilling to repeat their delinquent activities.

■ Situational crime prevention efforts are designed to reduce or redirect crime by making it more difficult to profit from illegal acts.

Plus these study tools in every chapter

▶ *Chapter Objectives* at the beginning of each chapter are reinforced by chapter-end *Summary* lists.

▶ *Checkpoints* at strategic points throughout each chapter clarify key concepts.

▶ *Concept Summaries* visually reinforce key theories and other important topics.

▶ *Questions for Discussion,* which often ask students to project their understanding onto real-life scenarios, further reinforce chapter material.

SUMMARY

■ Official delinquency refers to youths who are arrested.
■ Arrest data come from the FBI's Uniform Crime Report (UCR), an annual tally of crimes reported to police by citizens.
■ The FBI gathers arrest statistics from local police departments. From these, it is possible to determine the number of youths who are arrested each year, along with their age, race, and gender.

■ Disagreement also exis[...]
class position and delinquency. Some hold that adolescent crime is a lower-class phenomenon, whereas others see it throughout the s[...]
methodology have obs[...]
relationship. However[...]
lower-class youths are[...]
criminal acts.
■ There is general agreem[...]
decline with age. Some[...]

Concept Summary **3.1** **Delinquency Prevention Methods**

Method	Central Premise	Technique
General deterrence	Kids will avoid delinquency if they fear punishment.	Make punishment swift, severe, and certain.
Specific deterrence	Delinquents who are punished severely will not repeat their detention.	Use harsh punishments, such as a stay in secure offenses.
Situational crime	Make delinquency more difficult and less profitable.	Harden targets, use prevention surveillance, street lighting.

critical thinking

Companion Website for *Juvenile Delinquency: The Core*
www.thomsonedu.com/criminaljustice/siegel

This information- and activity-rich site includes:

▶ Concept Builders—three-step modules that (1) briefly review a key chapter concept, (2) apply the concept to a real-world scenario, and (3) challenge students to apply the concept with a related essay question.

▶ Tutorial quizzing for each chapter.

▶ Links to juvenile delinquency and other criminal justice sites, flash cards, and glossary—all organized by textbook chapter.

▶ The Instructor's Companion Website, which contains chapter outlines, chapter objectives, chapter summaries, lecture suggestions, a downloadable *Instructor's Resource Manual*, sample syllabus, and Microsoft® PowerPoint® images.

reality, many youths from affluent families choose digent adolescents are law abiding. For example, pears to be a senseless act motivated by grinding p tion. However, economic hopelessness cannot be th substance abuse of millions of middle-class users, high school and go on to college. These kids are the desire for physical gratification, peer group ac efits. They choose to break the law, because, despi lieve that taking drugs and drinking provide more try into substance abuse is facilitated by their perc encourage drug use onal choice model b

To read a selection from Cesare Beccaria's *On Crime and Punishment*, go to the website www.thomsonedu.com/criminaljustice/siegel.

To learn more about the causes of alcoholism, go to the **National Council on Alcoholism and Drug Dependence, Inc. (NCADD)**, a group that advocates prevention, intervention, research, and treatment of alcoholism and other drug addictions, via www.thomsonedu.com/criminaljustice/siegel.

Web links in the margins throughout every chapter encourage online research.

NEW! Careers in Criminal Justice Website
Access to this password-protected site is available for packaging with the textbook.
The website includes video testimonials from a variety of CJ professionals, Interest Assessment, a Career Planner, and Links for Reference.

InfoTrac® College Edition with InfoMarks™
Available packaged with the textbook.
This extensive, easily searchable database features full-length articles from thousands of academic journals and periodicals.

WebTUTOR™ ToolBox
WebTutor™ ToolBox
Available on Blackboard® and WebCT®
Easy and efficient to use, **WebTutor™** ToolBox combines course management with content from this text's information-rich Companion Website. You can use **ToolBox** as is—or customize the program with web links, images, and other resources.

Current Perspectives: Readings from InfoTrac College Edition: Juvenile Justice
Available packaged with the textbook. Includes access to InfoTrac College Edition!
This reader, edited by James Chriss of Cleveland State University, draws from both popular and academic sources to provide students with a detailed, current look at the juvenile justice system today. 0-495-12995-X

Online connections

Essential resources to lighten your teaching load

PowerLecture: A One-Stop PowerPoint® Tool
An easy-to-use digital library and presentation resource
0-495-38284-1

This instructor resource includes Microsoft® PowerPoint® lecture slides with graphics from the text, making it easy for you to assemble, edit, publish, and present custom lectures for your course. **PowerLecture** also includes video-based polling and quiz questions that can be used with the **JoinIn™ Student Response System,** and integrates **ExamView®** testing software for customizing tests of up to 250 items that can be delivered in print or online. Finally, all of your media teaching resources in one place!

Instructor's Resource Manual
Updated Comprehensive
0-495-38282-5

This exceptional resource includes Learning Objectives, a detailed Chapter Summary, Chapter Outline, Key Terms with Definitions, Classroom Discussion Questions, and Student Activities for every text chapter. The Test Bank section includes multiple-choice, true/false, fill-in-the-blank, and essay questions for each chapter, saving you countless hours of test preparation. Each question in the Test Bank has been carefully reviewed by experienced criminal justice instructors for quality, accuracy, and content coverage. Our *Instructor Approved* seal, which appears on the front cover, is our assurance that you are working with an assessment and grading resource of the highest caliber. **ExamView®** testing software, which contains all Test Bank questions electronically, is included on **PowerLecture** and also available as a separate item (0-495-38283-3).

JoinIn™ Student Response System featuring TurningPoint®
Transform every lecture into an interactive experience
0-495-38286-8

▶ **Includes book-specific content** created especially for use with personal response systems and your choice of several leading keypad systems.

▶ **With just a click on a handheld device,** students respond to multiple-choice questions, short polls, interactive exercises, and peer review questions. You can take attendance, collect student demographics to better assess student needs, and administer quizzes without collecting paper or grading.

▶ **NEW! Video clips from current ABC® News stories!** Students view the videos and "click" their responses to onscreen questions. **JoinIn Student Response System** tallies the responses and presents the results on screen.

Please consult your Thomson Wadsworth representative for details or visit **http://www.thomsonedu.com/tlc** and select **JoinIn Student Response System** from the drop-down menu under "Technology Product."

The Wadsworth Criminal Justice Video Library
A great selection of new and historic footage

▶ **ABC® Videos for Criminal Justice**—current and historic news

▶ **Wadsworth Custom Videos for Criminal Justice**

▶ **Oral History Project Video Series**

▶ **Court TV Videos**—One-hour videos presenting seminal and high-profile cases

▶ **A&E American Justice**—Forty videos to choose from on a variety of criminal justice topics

▶ **Films for the Humanities**—A selection of nearly 200 criminal justice-related videos

For more information and a list of offerings, visit **www.thomsonedu.com/criminaljustice/media_center.**

Tools that help students excel in your course

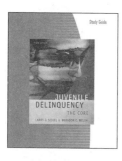

NEW! Thomson Audio Study Products for Siegel & Welsh's _Juvenile Delinquency: The Core_
Students simply load these files into their digital music players and they can review course material while walking to class, driving, working out—whenever it's impossible or inconvenient to read! Audio files for each chapter of this textbook include key concept reviews and vocabulary materials—enabling students to test their knowledge with quiz questions, as well as listen to a brief overview reflecting the major themes of each chapter. **Thomson Audio Study Products** give today's busy students a quick, convenient, and enjoyable way to study. Students can select the chapters they wish to purchase at **www.thomsonedu.com.**

Study Guide
Thoroughly updated
0-495-38281-7
This engaging _Study Guide_ is designed to ensure that students get the most out of both their text and their classroom experience. The Learning Objectives, detailed Chapter Summaries, Chapter Outlines, and Key Terms with Definitions, which allow students to conduct an in-depth review of the material at their own pace, are followed by a series of multiple-choice, true/false, fill-in-the-blank, and short response questions, which students can then use to assess their knowledge.

Writing and Communicating for Criminal Justice
0-495-00041-8
Including articles on writing skills, along with basic grammar review and a survey of verbal communication on the job, this useful guide gives students an introduction to academic, professional, and research writing in criminal justice.

Due to contractual reasons, certain ancillaries are available only in higher education or U.S. domestic markets. Minimum purchases may apply to receive the ancillaries at no charge. For more information, please contact your local Thomson sales representative.

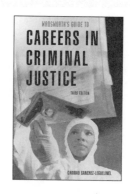

Wadsworth's Guide to Careers in Criminal Justice, Third Edition
0-495-13038-9
by Caridad Sanchez-Leguelinel, John Jay College of Criminal Justice.
The author provides a brief introduction to the exciting and diverse field of criminal justice. Students learn about opportunities in law enforcement, courts, and corrections—and how to get those jobs!

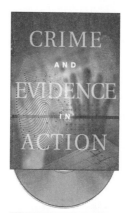

Crime and Evidence in Action CD-ROM
Includes an accompanying website
0-534-61531-7
Contains essential tools to practice investigation techniques! Students make decisions as a patrol officer, detective, prosecutor, defense attorney, judge, corrections officer, and parole officer.

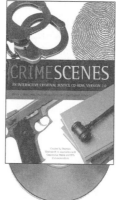

Crime Scenes 2.0: An Interactive Criminal Justice CD-ROM
0-534-56831-9
The six vignettes included on this CD-ROM enable students to play various roles as they explore all aspects of the criminal justice system, including policing, investigation, courts, sentencing, and corrections.

Tools to help with online study— available packaged with this textbook:

▶ InfoTrac® College Edition Student Guide for Criminal Justice: **0-534-24719-9**

▶ InfoTrac® College Edition Exercises for Criminal Justice: **0-534-55900-X**

▶ Internet Activities for Criminal Justice, Third Edition: **0-495-10442-6**

▶ The Criminal Justice Internet Investigator, Third Edition: **0-534-56832-7**

JUVENILE
DELINQUENCY
The Core

THIRD EDITION

JUVENILE DELINQUENCY
The Core

LARRY J. SIEGEL
University of Massachusetts, Lowell

BRANDON C. WELSH
University of Massachusetts, Lowell

THOMSON

WADSWORTH

Australia • Brazil • Canada • Mexico • Singapore • Spain • United Kingdom • United States

THOMSON

WADSWORTH

Juvenile Delinquency: The Core, Third Edition
Larry J. Siegel, Brandon C. Welsh

Senior Acquisitions Editor, Criminal Justice: Carolyn Henderson Meier
Development Editor: Shelley Murphy
Assistant Editor: Rebecca Johnson
Technology Project Manager: Amanda Kaufmann
Marketing Manager: Terra Schultz
Marketing Assistant: Emily Elrod
Marketing Communications Manager: Tami Strang
Project Manager, Editorial Production: Jennie Redwitz
Creative Director: Rob Hugel
Art Director: Vernon Boes
Print Buyer: Becky Cross

Permissions Editor: Bob Kauser
Production Service: Linda Jupiter, Jupiter Productions
Text Designer: Adrienne Bosworth
Photo Researcher: Linda Rill
Copy Editor: Tricia Lawrence
Proofreader: Mary Kanable
Indexer: Medea Minnich
Illustrator: John and Judy Waller
Cover Designer: Yvo Riezebos Design
Cover Image: © Graham Dean/Corbis
Compositor: Pre-PressPMG
Text and Cover Printer: Edwards Brothers, Incorporated

Library of Congress Control Number: 2006937999

ISBN-13: 978-0-495-09542-2

ISBN-10: 0-495-09542-7

Thomson Higher Education
10 Davis Drive
Belmont, CA 94002-3098
USA

For more information about our products, contact us at:
Thomson Learning Academic Resource Center
1-800-423-0563

For permission to use material from this text or product, submit a request online at
http://www.thomsonrights.com.

Any additional questions about permissions can be submitted by e-mail to **thomsonrights@thomson.com.**

About the Authors

LARRY J. SIEGEL was born in the Bronx in 1947. While attending City College of New York in the 1960s he was swept up in the social and political currents of the time. He became intrigued with the influence contemporary culture had on individual behavior: Did people shape society or did society shape people? He applied his interest in social forces and human behavior to the study of crime and justice. After graduating CCNY, he attended the newly opened program in criminal justice at the State University of New York at Albany, earning both his M.A. and Ph.D. degrees there. After completing his graduate work, Dr. Siegel began his teaching career at Northeastern University, where he was a faculty member for nine years. After leaving Northeastern, he held teaching positions at the University of Nebraska–Omaha and Saint Anselm College in New Hampshire. He is currently a professor at the University of Massachusetts, Lowell. Dr. Siegel has written extensively in the area of crime and justice, including books on juvenile law, delinquency, criminology, and criminal procedure. He is a court-certified expert on police conduct and has testified in numerous legal cases. The father of four and grandfather of three, Larry Siegel and his wife Terry now reside in Bedford, New Hampshire, with their two cockapoos, Watson and Cody.

BRANDON C. WELSH was born in Canada. He received his undergraduate and M.A. degrees at the University of Ottawa and his Ph.D. from Cambridge University in England. Dr. Welsh is currently an associate professor of criminology at the University of Massachusetts, Lowell. He teaches graduate and undergraduate courses on crime prevention, juvenile delinquency, and evidence-based policing. His research interests focus on the prevention of crime and delinquency and the economic analysis of crime prevention programs. Dr. Welsh has published extensively in these areas, and is an author or editor of six books.

Brief Contents

Contents

Preface

Jesse James Hollywood (his real name) never held a job, but he was able to purchase, by age nineteen, an expensive home in West Hills, California, and a Mercedes. His place became a popular spot for local kids who came and went at all hours of the day. Jesse was a well-liked guy, an outgoing kid who, despite being short in stature, was an excellent athlete. How was Jesse able to do all this? By becoming a very successful high-volume marijuana dealer.

Jesse's world began to unravel when he came up with a scheme to obtain the money owed him by drug customer Benjamin Markowitz. Jesse and some of his cohorts concocted a plan to kidnap Benjamin and hold him for ransom until someone paid up. Things went awry when Jesse and his friends could not locate Benjamin and instead abducted his fifteen-year-old stepbrother Nicholas. Unaware of the danger he faced, Nicholas spent several days socializing and partying with his captors. Hollywood concluded he could not release Nick after he talked to attorneys and found out that the penalty for kidnapping was life in prison. So on August 8, 2000, Nick Markowitz was made to walk a mile into Los Padres National Forest and was shot nine times with a high-powered assault rifle. Buried in a shallow grave, his body was discovered four days later by hikers. Although his accomplices were tried and convicted in the case, Hollywood escaped and became the subject of an international manhunt. His mug shot was plastered on the FBI's website and he became one of the youngest men ever to be on the FBI's Ten Most Wanted Fugitives list. Jesse wound up in Brazil, where he used fake papers that identified him as Michael Costa Giroux, a native of Rio de Janeiro. He lived a comfortable life in Brazil, teaching English and having a home in a fashionable neighborhood, when he was arrested in November of 2005 and sent back to California for trial. The latest twist in the case happened on October 6, 2006, when lead prosecutor Ron Zonen was prevented from participating in the case because of his involvement as a consultant in the film *Alpha Dog*, starring Bruce Willis, Justin Timberlake, and Sharon Stone, which is based on the case.

What can cause the behavior of someone like Jesse James Hollywood? He grew up in an affluent family and seemed popular and successful. How could he have become involved in an awful, violent crime? What are the forces that drive such kids to engage in theft and violence, to take drugs, and to vandalize schools? How can such delinquent acts be prevented?

Inexplicable incidents of violence occur all too frequently in schools, homes, and public places. Teen gangs can be found in most major cities and now contain more than 750,000 members. Hundreds of thousands of youths are the victims of serious neglect and sexual and physical abuse each year. It is not surprising, considering the concern with the problems of youth, that courses on juvenile delinquency have become popular offerings on the nation's college campuses. We have written *Juvenile Delinquency: The Core* to help students understand the nature of juvenile delinquency and its cause and correlates, as well as the current strategies being used to control or eliminate its occurrence. Our text also reviews the legal rules that have been set down to either protect innocent minors or control adolescent misconduct: Can children be required to submit to drug testing in school? Can teachers search suspicious students or use corporal punishment as a method of discipline? Should children be allowed to testify on closed-circuit TV in child abuse cases?

Because the study of juvenile delinquency is a dynamic, ever-changing field of scientific inquiry, and because the theories, concepts, and processes of this area of study are constantly evolving, we have updated *Juvenile Delinquency: The Core* to reflect the changes that have taken place in the study of delinquent behavior during the past few years. This new edition includes a review of recent legal cases, research studies, and policy initiatives. It aims to provide a groundwork for the study of juvenile delinquency by analyzing and describing the nature and extent of delinquency, the suspected causes of delinquent behavior, and the environmental influences on youthful misbehavior. It also covers what most experts believe are the critical issues in juvenile delinquency and analyzes crucial policy issues, including the use of pretrial detention, waiver to adult court, and restorative justice programs.

GOALS AND OBJECTIVES OF THIS TEXT

Our primary goals in writing this edition remain the same as in previous editions:

1. To be as objective as possible, presenting the many diverse views and perspectives that characterize the study of juvenile delinquency and reflect its interdisciplinary nature. We take no single position nor espouse a particular viewpoint or philosophy.

2. To maintain a balance of research, theory, law, policy, and practice. It is essential that a text on delinquency not be solely a theory book without presentation of the juvenile justice system; likewise, such a text should also contain discussion on current policies that closely examines related legal issues and cases.

3. To be as thorough and up to date as possible. We have attempted to include the most current data and information available.

4. To make the study of delinquency interesting as well as informative. We want to encourage interest in the study of delinquency so that readers will pursue the study of it on an undergraduate or graduate level.

We have tried to provide a text that is scholarly and informative, comprehensive yet interesting, well organized and objective, yet provocative and thought provoking.

ORGANIZATION OF THE TEXT

The third edition of *Juvenile Delinquency: The Core* has 14 chapters:

- **Chapter 1, Childhood and Delinquency** contains extensive material on the history of childhood and the legal concept of delinquency and status offending. This material enables students to understand how the concept of adolescence evolved over time and how that evolution influenced the development of the juvenile court and the special status of delinquency.
- **Chapter 2, The Nature and Extent of Delinquency** covers the measurement of delinquent behavior as well as trends and patterns in teen crime, and also discusses the correlates of delinquency, including race, gender, class, age, and chronic offending.
- **Chapter 3, Individual Views of Delinquency: Choice and Trait** reviews individual-level views of the cause of delinquency, including choice, biological, and psychological theories.
- **Chapter 4, Sociological Views of Delinquency** looks at theories suggesting that economic, cultural, and environmental influences control delinquent behavior. These include structure, process, reaction, and conflict theories.

- **Chapter 5, Developmental Views of Delinquency** covers developmental theories of delinquency, including such issues as the onset, continuity, paths, and termination of delinquent careers.
- **Chapter 6, Gender and Delinquency** explores the sex-based differences that are thought to account for the gender patterns in the delinquency rate.
- **Chapter 7, The Family and Delinquency** covers the influence of families on children and delinquency. The concept of child abuse is covered in detail and the steps in the child protection system are reviewed.
- **Chapter 8, Peers and Delinquency: Juvenile Gangs and Groups** reviews the effects peers have on delinquency and the topic of teen gangs.
- **Chapter 9, Schools and Delinquency** looks at the influence of schools and the education process as well as delinquency within the school setting.
- **Chapter 10, Drug Use and Delinquency** reviews the influence drugs and substance abuse has on delinquent behavior and what is being done to reduce teenage drug use.
- **Chapter 11, The History and Development of Juvenile Justice** presents extensive coverage on the emergence of state control over children in need and the development of the juvenile justice system. It also covers the contemporary juvenile justice system, the major stages in the justice process, the role of the federal government in the juvenile justice system, an analysis of the differences between the adult and juvenile justice system, and extensive coverage of the legal rights of children.
- **Chapter 12, Police Work with Juveniles** discusses the role of police in delinquency prevention. It covers legal issues such as major court decisions on searches and *Miranda* rights of juveniles. It also contains material on race and gender effects on police discretion as well as efforts by police departments to control delinquent behavior.
- **Chapter 13, Juvenile Court Process: Pretrial, Trial, and Sentencing** examines the juvenile court process, contains information on plea bargaining in juvenile court, the use of detention and transfer to adult jails, an analysis of the critical factors that influence the waiver decision, and discussions regarding the juvenile trial and sentencing.
- **Chapter 14, Juvenile Corrections: Probation, Community Treatment, and Institutionalization** reviews material on probation and other community dispositions including restorative justice programs, and secure juvenile corrections with emphasis on legal issues such as right to treatment and innovative aftercare and reentry programs.

WHAT'S NEW IN THIS EDITION

- New **Case Profiles** open each chapter of the text. These vignettes are provided by real professionals working in the juvenile justice system and describe the circumstances, challenges, and eventual successes of fourteen "at-risk" youths who have worked their way out of delinquency. The success stories are then tied to the material within the chapters through thought-provoking critical thinking "Looking Back . . ." boxes.
- Additional coverage of changes in the treatment of status offenders, parental responsibility laws, and curfews has been added to chapter 1. The most recent data on child well-being, housing, health care, and education have been added, as well as new information on programs to reduce the number of status offenders in local juvenile courts.
- Chapter 2 updates recent trends and patterns in delinquency and juvenile victimization. It contains new information on the victim-offender relationship and new sections on the compatibility of juvenile delinquency data sources and the time and place of delinquency.

- New research findings on crime as problem solving, false expectations and delinquency, mental illness and delinquency, twin studies, conduct disorders, disruptive behavior disorder, diet and delinquency, and the genetic basis of delinquency have been added to chapter 3.

- Chapter 4 covers the most recent developments in social theory. We have added new research on collective efficacy and community change, and a new boxed feature on Elijah Anderson's concept of the "code of the streets," a widely cited view of the interrelationship of culture and behavior.

- A new section on the paths to delinquency has been added to chapter 5, as well as a review of the work of John Laub and Robert Sampson to track down members of the original Glueck research cohort.

- New data on gender differences in cognition and socialization is included in chapter 6, as well as a new section on early puberty and victimization. And two new Focus on Delinquency boxes have been added to this chapter: the first covers human trafficking and sexual exploitation of children; the second discusses "honor killing" crimes common in traditional societies in the Middle East, Southwest Asia, India, China, and Latin America, where violence against women and girls by family members or relatives is provoked by the belief that an individual's or family's honor has been threatened by the actual or perceived sexual misconduct of the female.

- In chapter 7 we have updated the material on the legacy of divorce, including the effects of divorce and parental deviance. The newest data on child abuse and sexual abuse have been added, as well as a new section on the association between mothers' employment and children's delinquency. We also include a new Focus on Delinquency box entitled "The Chicken or the Egg?" that looks at a provocative question: Which comes first, bad parents or bad kids?

- Chapter 8 contains a new feature box examining the problem of drug-dealing gangs in southwest Texas, the latest data on gang membership, and new material on gang migration and immigration. A new Preventing and Treating Delinquency box looks at gang control efforts in the city of Miami, Florida.

- To chapter 9 we have added new coverage of the No Child Left Behind program and new measures designed to reduce school crime. A new Juvenile Law in Review feature discusses the important case of *Board of Education of Independent School District No. 92 of Pottawatomie County et al. v. Earls et al.* regarding the issue of drug testing in schools.

- We present the latest findings on juvenile drug use today in chapter 10, and included are recent trends from three national surveys. We have expanded the coverage of the use and control of methamphetamines, and added new material reviewing the most up-to-date evidence on what works to reduce juvenile drug use. Also included in chapter 10 is a new section on the "harm reduction" approach to minimizing the harmful effects of drug use, as well as expanded coverage of the "War on Drugs."

- In chapter 11 we present new evaluation studies on the effectiveness of a comprehensive juvenile justice strategy. We have also expanded the coverage of juvenile drug courts and teen courts and provided up-to-date commentaries from leading experts on the future of juvenile justice.

- Chapter 12 brings together the latest findings on what works when it comes to police efforts to prevent juvenile crime, including results from the National Research Council panel on police effectiveness and replications of Operation Ceasefire. We have also updated the material on juveniles' attitudes toward police and added a new section on police and procedural justice.

- Expanded coverage of juvenile court personnel, up-to-date statistics on juvenile court case flow, and new material on diversion are now included in chapter 13. We also provide the latest research and statistics on transfers to adult court and review the new Supreme Court ruling on the juvenile death penalty.

- Chapter 14 presents up-to-date information on disproportionate minority confinement, new trends in juvenile probation and incarceration, and new material on the mental health needs of incarcerated youth. The latest research findings on what works in treating juvenile offenders is reviewed, along with new studies on the economics of treating violent juvenile offenders. There is expanded coverage of juvenile aftercare and a new section on juvenile reentry.

IN-TEXT LEARNING TOOLS

The text contains the following pedagogical features designed to help students learn and comprehend the material:

Chapter Outline and Objectives Each chapter begins with an outline and a list of chapter objectives.

Case Profiles Each chapter now opens with a new vignette describing a real case of an at-risk youth who worked his or her way out of delinquency. These true success stories are then tied to the material within the chapters through thought-provoking critical thinking boxes.

Prevention Features Because preventing delinquency is an important element of the study of delinquency, the text includes three extensive sections entitled **New Directions in Preventing Delinquency**, which describe three levels of efforts being made to prevent delinquency. The first essay on primary prevention explains how programs are designed to help kids avoid delinquent behaviors before they actually get involved in delinquency. The second, on secondary prevention, reviews programs aimed at kids at risk for delinquency because of personal or social problems. And the third prevention essay, on tertiary prevention, discusses those programs attempting to help kids who have committed delinquent acts and are involved in the juvenile justice system.

Concept Summaries These are visual aids used throughout the text to help students review material and key concepts in an organized fashion.

Checkpoints Within-chapter summaries of key points from preceding sections serve to remind students to check their comprehension and retention of important concepts before going on to the next section of the chapter.

What Does This Mean to Me? These are short, yet provocative discussions designed to help students understand risk factors contributing to delinquency. These boxes intend to provoke student interest, interaction, and analysis through more applied and personalized learning opportunities.

Focus on Delinquency As in previous editions, these boxed inserts focus attention on topics of special importance and concern. For example, in chapter 11, a Focus on Delinquency feature discusses the similarities and differences between juvenile and adult justice systems.

Juvenile Law in Review Some chapters include boxes discussing major Supreme Court cases that influence and control the juvenile justice system. For example, *In re Gault*, which defines the concept of due process for youthful offenders, is discussed in a box in chapter 13.

Preventing and Treating Delinquency These boxed features examine major policy initiatives and programs in juvenile justice. For example, the box in chapter 4 tells about Homeboy Industries, founded by a Jesuit priest in Los Angeles to help young people who want to leave gangs and join conventional society.

Web Links In the margins of every chapter are links to websites that can be used to help students enrich their understanding of important issues and concepts found within the text.

Chapter Summary Each chapter ends with a summary list of key concepts from the chapter. These correlate with the objectives stated at the beginning of the chapter.

Applying What You Have Learned Found at the end of each chapter, these features present hypothetical cases for the student to analyze based on his or her understanding of the chapter materials.

Doing Research on the Web These present material found in articles on InfoTrac College Edition and the Internet, and are designed to lead students to find answers to the case presented in the preceding application feature.

Key Terms Key terms are set out and defined in a **Running Glossary** placed in the text margins where the concepts are introduced. They are also listed with page references at the end of each chapter, and in the comprehensive **Glossary** at the end of the book.

Discussion Questions Each chapter ends with a series of thought-provoking discussion questions.

ANCILLARIES

A number of supplements are provided by Thomson Wadsworth to help instructors use *Juvenile Delinquency: The Core,* Third Edition in their courses and to help students prepare for exams. Available to qualified adopters. Please consult your local sales representative for details.

For the Instructor

ExamView® (Windows/Macintosh) Create, deliver, and customize tests and study guides (both print and online) in minutes with this easy-to-use assessment and tutorial system. ExamView offers both a Quick Test Wizard and an Online Test Wizard that guide you step by step through the process of creating tests, while the unique WYSIWYG capability allows you to see the test you are creating on the screen exactly as it will print or display online. You can build tests of up to 250 questions using up to 12 question types. Using ExamView's complete word processing capabilities, you can enter an unlimited number of new questions or edit existing questions. The updated test bank includes the following for each chapter: 30 multiple-choice questions, 25 true-false questions, 20 fill-in-the-blank questions, and 5 essay questions.

Instructor's Resource Manual The already extensive *Instructor's Resource Manual* has been completely revised and updated for the new edition by Dr. Paulina Ruf of Lenoir-Rhyne College. It includes Learning Objectives, a detailed Chapter Summary, a Chapter Outline, Key Terms with Definitions, Classroom Discussion Questions, and Student Activities for every text chapter. The Test Bank portion includes 30 multiple-choice questions, 25 true-false questions, 20 fill-in-the-blank questions, and 5 essay questions for each chapter, saving you countless hours of test preparation. Each question in the Test Bank has been carefully reviewed by experienced criminal justice instructors for quality, accuracy, and content coverage. Our Instructor Approved seal, which appears on the front cover, is our assurance that you are working with an assessment and grading resource of the highest caliber.

Power Lecture for Siegel/Welsh's *Juvenile Delinquency: The Core,* Third Edition This instructor resource includes Microsoft® PowerPoint® lecture slides with graphics from the text, making it easy for you to assemble, edit, publish, and present custom lectures for your course. The PowerLecture CD also includes video-based polling and quiz questions that can be used with the JoinIn on TurningPoint personal response system, and integrates ExamView testing software for customized tests of up to 250 items that can be delivered in print or online. Finally, all of your media teaching resources in one place!

JoinIn™ on TurningPoint® Spark discussion and assess your students' comprehension of chapter concepts with interactive classroom quizzes and background polls developed specifically for use with this edition of *Juvenile Delinquency: The Core*. Also available are polling/quiz questions that enable you to maximize the educational benefits of the ABC® News video clips we custom-selected to accompany this textbook. Thomson Wadsworth's exclusive agreement with TurningPoint lets you run our tailor-made Microsoft PowerPoint slides in conjunction with the "clicker" hardware of your choice. Enhance how your students interact with you, your lecture, and each other.

WebTutor™ ToolBox on Blackboard® and WebCT® A powerful combination: easy-to-use course management tools for whichever program you use—WebCT or Blackboard—with content from this text's rich companion website, all in one place. You can use ToolBox as is, from the moment you log on—or, if you prefer, customize the program with web links, images, and other resources.

Wadsworth Criminal Justice Video Library So many exciting new videos—so many great ways to enrich your lectures and spark discussion of the material in this text! A list of our unique and expansive video program follows. Or, visit **www.thomsonedu.com/criminaljustice/media_center/index.html** for a complete, up-to-the-minute list of all of Wadsworth's video offerings—many of which are also available in DVD format—as well as clip lists and running times. The library includes these selections and many others:

- *ABC* Videos: Featuring short, high-interest clips from current news events specially developed for courses including Introduction to Criminal Justice, Criminology, Corrections, Terrorism, and White-Collar Crime, these videos are perfect for use as discussion starters or lecture launchers to spark student interest. The brief video clips provide students with a new lens through which to view the past and present, one that will greatly enhance their knowledge and understanding of significant events and open up to them new dimensions in learning. Clips are drawn from such programs as *World News Tonight*, *Good Morning America*, *This Week*, *PrimeTime Live*, *20/20*, and *Nightline*, as well as numerous ABC News specials and material from the Associated Press Television News and British Movietone News collections.
- *Wadsworth Custom Videos for Criminal Justice*: Produced by Wadsworth and Films for the Humanities, these videos include short (five- to ten-minute) segments that encourage classroom discussion. Topics include white-collar crime, domestic violence, forensics, suicide and the police officer, the court process, the history of corrections, prison society, and juvenile justice.
- *Court TV*: One-hour videos presenting seminal and high-profile cases, such as the interrogations of Michael Crowe and serial killer Ted Bundy, as well as crucial and current issues such as cyber crime, double jeopardy, and the management of the prison on Riker's Island.
- *A&E American Justice*: Forty videos to choose from, on topics such as deadly force, women on death row, juvenile justice, strange defenses, and Alcatraz.
- *Films for the Humanities*: Nearly 200 videos to choose from on a variety of topics such as elder abuse, supermax prisons, suicide and the police officer, the making of an FBI agent, domestic violence, and more.

- *Oral History Project*: Developed in association with the American Society of Criminology, the Academy of Criminal Justice Society, and the National Institute of Justice, these videos will help you introduce your students to the scholars who have developed the criminal justice discipline. Compiled over the last several years, each video features a set of Guest Lecturers—scholars whose thinking has helped to build the foundation of present ideas in the discipline.

The Wadsworth Criminal Justice Resource Center www.thomsonedu.com/criminaljustice Designed with the instructor in mind, this website features information about Thomson Wadsworth's technology and teaching solutions, as well as several features created specifically for today's criminal justice student. Supreme Court updates, timelines, and hot-topic polling can all be used to supplement in-class assignments and discussions. You'll also find a wealth of links to careers and news in criminal justice, book-specific sites, and much more.

For the Student

Study Guide *Juvenile Delinquency: The Core* is accompanied by a robust *Study Guide*, prepared by Michael Fischer of Norfolk State University, that has been designed to ensure students get the most out of the text as well as their classroom experience. The Learning Objectives, detailed Chapter Summaries, Chapter Outlines, and Key Terms with Definitions, which allow students to conduct an in-depth review of the material at their own pace, are followed by a series of multiple-choice, true-false, fill-in-the-blank, and short response questions that students can then use to assess their knowledge.

iAudio Study Guide Students can study anytime and anywhere they want using Thomson's iAudio for *Juvenile Delinquency: The Core*. Our exclusive iAudio content, which can be downloaded to any MP3 player, includes a review of all key terms and concepts, as well as a summary of the chapter. With this unique supplement, students can quiz themselves on each chapter's vocabulary and key concepts as they go or review important material before tests—even if they don't have their textbook on hand or aren't at their desk.

Current Perspectives: Readings from InfoTrac® College Edition: Juvenile Justice This reader, edited by James Chriss of Cleveland State University and available when packaged with this text, draws from both popular and academic sources to provide students with a detailed, up-to-the-minute look at the juvenile justice system today. Along with the reader, students receive access to InfoTrac College Edition and can create their own online reader in InfoTrac College Edition using InfoMarks.

Wadsworth's Guide to Careers in Criminal Justice, Third Edition This handy guide, compiled by Caridad Sanchez-Leguelinel of John Jay College of Criminal Justice, gives students information on a wide variety of career paths, including requirements, salaries, training, contact information for key agencies, and employment outlooks.

Writing and Communicating for Criminal Justice This book contains articles on writing skills, along with basic grammar review and a survey of verbal communication on the job, that will give students an introduction to academic, professional, and research writing in criminal justice. The voices of professionals who have used these techniques on the job will help students see the relevance of these skills to their future careers.

ACKNOWLEDGMENTS

We gratefully acknowledge the work of our colleagues who reviewed the previous edition and made important suggestions for improvements:

Michael P. Brown, Ball State University

G. David Curry, University of Missouri, St. Louis

Noelle Fearn, Washington State University

David F. Machell, Western Connecticut State University

Michael S. Penrod, Kirkwood Community College

Don Sebo, High-Tech Institute

We also thank the reviewers who have helped us in the previous two editions of *Juvenile Delinquency: The Core*: Bruce Berg, California State University, Long Beach; Sue Bourke, University of Cincinnati; Jerald C. Burns, Alabama State University; Ann Butzin, Owens State Community College; John R. Cross, Oklahoma State University; Patricia Grant, Virginia Commonwealth University; Julia Glover Hall, Drexel University; Eric L. Jensen, University of Idaho; Brendan Maguire, Western Illinois University; Jane Kravitz Munley, Luzern County Community College; Brian A. Perusek, Lakeland Community College; Rebecca D. Peterson, University of Texas, San Antonio; Cheryl Tieman, Radford University; Shela Vanness, University of Tennessee at Chattanooga; Charles M. Vivona, SUNY College at Old Westbury; and Lisa Hutchinson Wallace, University of Alaska, Fairbanks.

The preparation of this text would not have been possible without the aid of our Editor, Carolyn Henderson Meier, who is patient, competent, and terrific, to say the least. Shelley Murphy is the world's most wonderful Development Editor. What would we do without her? We don't even want to think about it! We are indebted to Debra Borquist, Department of Social Work, University of Wisconsin–Whitewater, who worked so hard to locate and summarize the real-world case studies we have added to this edition of the text. We also appreciate the efforts of the entire Wadsworth Criminal Justice team on our behalf: Terra Schultz, Marketing Manager; Rebecca Johnson, Assistant Editor; Amanda Kaufmann, Technology Project Manager; and Beth McMurray, Editorial Assistant. And we give special thanks to our terrific and supportive Production Manager, Jennie Redwitz, and fabulous Production Editor, Linda Jupiter, without whom this volume would never have been published. Tricia Lawrence, copy editor, was a pleasure to work with; Mary Kanable, proofreader, has an excellent eye; and Medea Minnich, indexer, did a very thorough job. And Linda Rill, our photo editor, to put it simply, is just the best.

Larry Siegel
Brandon Welsh

The authors and editors are grateful for the contributions from the following individuals, which formed the Case Profiles that open each chapter of *Juvenile Delinquency: The Core,* Third Edition:

Christian Sharpe, El Paso Human Services, Colorado, contributed the case profiles for chapters 1 and 7. Mr. Sharpe has been an Adolescent Intake and Crisis Intervention Worker at the program for nine years. He strives to focus on individual and family strengths with his clients.

Audrey Conn, MSSW, contributed the case profile for chapter 2. Ms. Conn has worked with children in the Special Needs Adoption Unit in Wisconsin for three years. She strives to place children in permanent homes and often works with teens already involved or on the verge of entering the juvenile justice system. She also makes a significant effort to provide culturally competent services to her families.

Gary Keifenheim, Family and Children's Services, Brooklyn Park, Minnesota, contributed the case profile for chapter 3. Mr. Keifenheim has been a Youth Services Supervisor at the program for twenty-two years. Please visit www.fcsmn.org for more information about their programs.

Kristel Tatus, Delinquency Social Worker, Dane County Department of Human Services, Madison, Wisconsin, contributed the case profile for chapter 4. Ms. Tatus has been with the department for seven years.

Paula Shore, LCSW, MSW, has worked with both juvenile and adult offenders in New Jersey for over twenty-seven years. She was employed in a rural community as a Crisis Intervention Counselor for the county Family Court program when she encountered Kia, the individual whose case profile appears in chapter 5.

Excell Williams, LSW, contributed the case profile for chapter 6. A social worker for many years, he started his professional career working in a teen drop-in center in Aurora, Illinois.

Marlia Moore, MPA, contributed the case profile for chapter 8. Ms. Moore worked as an Intensive Supervision Counselor for many years in a large midwestern city. The court-ordered program worked with adolescents involved in the juvenile justice system, some of which were gang affiliated. The program utilized several strategies to assist young people in danger of going to juvenile correctional facilities.

Yorel Lashley, Drum Power, New York City, contributed the case profile for chapter 9. Mr. Lashley has been involved with at-risk youth for over ten years. He is a professional percussionist and is the president of Drum Power, which has programs in seven schools in the New York area. For more information on their programs visit www.mydrumpower.com.

Angela Bahr, MSW, contributed the case profile for chapter 10. Ms. Bahr was employed as a Clinical Therapist for a community mental health agency in an impoverished community in rural Illinois. The mental health/substance abuse treatment center worked primarily with individuals and families receiving medical assistance.

Sheri Gatts, Program Director for Youth Services of Wisconsin's Youth Court, contributed the case profile for chapter 11. Ms. Gatts coordinates several teen courts throughout Dane County that provide for local teens to participate in their own communities.

Dr. Richard Larkin (Rico) shares his own story as a case profile in chapter 12 to pay honor to his mother, as well as to the community that tried to provide him with a safe environment and an education.

Ann Obderbecke, BA, MSSW, in-home family therapist in a small community outside of Denver, Colorado, contributed the case profile for chapter 13. Her program works with adolescents involved in the juvenile justice system and utilizes Functional Family Therapy, an evidence-based practice that involves working with families in three phases. Ms. Obderbecke has been a social worker since 1997 and began working in the mental health arena in 2003. She reports that her program sees a 30 percent to 50 percent reduction in recidivism utilizing this model, and that the clinicians feel more successful utilizing this strategy.

Debra Borquist, MSSW, contributed the case profile for chapter 14. Ms. Borquist has been a social worker for over fifteen years, working in the areas of child protection, juvenile delinquency, and children's mental health.

Childhood and Delinquency

© Larry Towell/Magnum Photos

CHAPTER OBJECTIVES

After reading this chapter you should:

1. Be familiar with the problems of youth in American culture.
2. Be able to discuss the concept of adolescence and risk taking.
3. Develop an understanding of the history of childhood.
4. Be familiar with the concept of *parens patriae.*
5. Be able to discuss development of a special status of minor offenders.
6. Know what is meant by the terms *juvenile delinquent* and *status offender.*
7. Be able to describe the differences between delinquency and status offending.
8. Be able to discuss what is meant by *parental responsibility laws.*
9. Be familiar with juvenile curfew laws.
10. Identify the efforts being made to reform status offense laws.

Aaliyah's Story

Aaliyah Parker ran away from home at the age of seventeen. She struggled with family issues and felt she could no longer live with her mother, stepfather, and younger siblings in their California home. Arriving in Colorado with no family support, no money, and no place to live, she joined other runaway adolescents, homeless on the streets. Aaliyah began using drugs and was eventually arrested and detained at a juvenile detention center for possession of methamphetamines and providing false information to a police officer. At only five feet, seven inches tall and weighing only ninety-five pounds, Aaliyah was an addict—her health and quality of life were suffering greatly.

When Aaliyah entered the juvenile justice system she was a few months from turning eighteen. Due to issues of jurisdiction, budget concerns, and Aaliyah's age, system administrators encouraged the case worker assigned to Aaliyah to make arrangements for her to return to her family in California. After interviewing her at length about her situation and need for treatment, the case worker could see that Aaliyah had a strong desire to get her life back on track. She needed assistance, but the cost of her treatment would be over three thousand dollars per month, and the county agency's budget was already stretched. Despite objections from administrators, the case worker remained a strong advocate for Aaliyah, convincing them of the harsh reality she would face back at home without first receiving drug treatment. The case worker's advocacy on her behalf, combined with her own motivation to get her life together, compelled the department to agree to pay for Aaliyah's treatment program, but only until she turned eighteen. She was transported from the juvenile detention center to a ninety-day drug and alcohol treatment program where she was able to detoxify her body and engage in intensive counseling. The program also provided family therapy through phone counseling for Aaliyah's mother, allowing the family to reconnect.

Despite this renewed contact, returning home was not an option for Aaliyah.

Nearing the end of the program, Aaliyah was again faced with being homeless, but she was determined not to return to the streets. She needed an environment where she could make new friends who did not use drugs, and where she could be supported in her sobriety. Because of her age, the county department of human services had to close the case and could no longer assist her with housing or an aftercare program. The caseworker provided Aaliyah with some places to call, but she would have to be her own advocate.

Aaliyah contacted a group home run by a local church that takes runaway adolescents through county placements and provides a variety of services for clients and their families. In Aaliyah's case, no funding was available, so she contacted the therapist at the group home and explained her situation. Initially, they indicated that they would not be able to assist her, but Aaliyah was persistent and determined to find a quality living environment for herself. She continued to contact professionals at the group home to plead her case and was eventually successful. Aaliyah entered the group home, was able to get her high school diploma, and eventually enrolled in an independent living program that assisted her in finding a job and getting her own apartment. Aaliyah has remained in contact with her juvenile case worker. Although she has struggled with her sobriety on occasion, she has been able to refrain from using methamphetamines and is now at a healthy weight. Her case worker continues to encourage Aaliyah and has been an ongoing source of support, despite the fact that the client file was closed several years ago. Aaliyah's success can be credited to the initial advocacy of her case worker, the effective interventions, and to the strong determination demonstrated by this young woman.

There are now more than 70 million children under age eighteen in the United States many who share some of the same problems as Aaliyah. Though, down from a peak of 36 percent at the end of the baby boom, in 1964, minors still make up more than 25 percent of the population.[1] Children are projected to remain a substantial percentage of the total population, expected to reach 80 million or about 24 percent of the population in 2020.[2] The present generation of adolescents has been described as cynical, preoccupied with material acquisitions, and uninterested in creative expression.[3] By age eighteen they have spent more time in front of a television set than in the classroom; each year they may see up to one thousand rapes, murders, and assaults on TV.

In the 1950s, teenagers were reading comic books, but now they are watching TV shows and movies that rely on graphic scenes of violence as their main theme. Today teens are listening to rap CDs, such as 50 Cent's "In da Club," and Kanye West's "Gold-digger," whose sexually explicit lyrics routinely describe substance abuse and promiscuity. How will this exposure affect them? Should we be concerned? Maybe we should. A recent study by Steven Martino and his colleagues found that kids who listen to music with a sexual content are much more likely to engage in precocious sex than adolescents whose musical tastes run to the Mormon Tabernacle Choir and the "Sound of Music."[4]

THE ADOLESCENT DILEMMA

The problems of American society have had a significant effect on our nation's youth. Adolescence is a time of trial and uncertainty, a time when youths experience anxiety, humiliation, and mood swings. During this period, the personality is still developing and is vulnerable to a host of external factors. Adolescents also undergo a period of rapid biological development. During just a few years' time, their height, weight, and sexual characteristics change dramatically. A hundred and fifty years ago girls matured sexually at age sixteen, but today they do so at twelve-and-a-half years of age. Although they may be capable of having children as early as fourteen, many youngsters remain emotionally immature long after reaching biological maturity. At age fifteen, a significant number of teenagers are unable to meet the responsibilities of the workplace, the family, and the neighborhood. Many suffer from health problems, are underachievers in school, and are skeptical about their ability to enter the workforce and become productive members of society.

In later adolescence (ages sixteen to eighteen), youths may experience a crisis that psychologist Erik Erikson described as a struggle between ego identity and role diffusion. **Ego identity** is formed when youths develop a firm sense of who they are and what they stand for; **role diffusion** occurs when youths experience uncertainty and place themselves at the mercy of leaders who promise to give them a sense of identity they cannot mold for themselves.[5] Psychologists also find that late adolescence is dominated by a yearning for independence from parental control.[6] Given this mixture of biological change and desire for autonomy, it isn't surprising that the teenage years are a time of conflict with authority at home, at school, and in the community.

Youth in Crisis

Problems in the home, the school, and the neighborhood have placed a significant portion of American youths at risk. Youths considered at risk are those who engage in dangerous conduct, such as drug abuse, alcohol use, and precocious sexuality. Although it is impossible to determine precisely the number of **at-risk youths** in the United States, one estimate is that 25 percent of the population under age seventeen, or about 18 million youths, are in this category.[7] The teen years bring many new risks—including some that are life-threatening. Each year almost fourteen thousand Americans ages fifteen to nineteen lose their lives in such unexpected incidents as motor vehicle accidents, homicide, and suicide. It is estimated that three-quarters of teen deaths are due to preventable causes, yet little is being done to reduce the death rate.[8] The most pressing problems facing American youth revolve around five issues.[9]

Poverty According to watchdog group, the Children's Defense Fund, almost 37 million people living in America can be classified as poor, 13 million of them children.[10] Today, real incomes are falling and poverty in the United States is more prevalent now than in the late 1960s and early 1970s, and has escalated rapidly since 2000. For every five children living in poverty, three are in "extreme poverty," a term describing families living at less than one-half of the poverty level (see Figure 1.1). This means that these families have to get by on less than $7,500 a year, or $20 a day. Working hard and

ego identity
According to Erik Erikson, ego identity is formed when persons develop a firm sense of who they are and what they stand for.

role diffusion
According to Erik Erikson, role diffusion occurs when youths spread themselves too thin, experience personal uncertainty, and place themselves at the mercy of leaders who promise to give them a sense of identity they cannot develop for themselves.

at-risk youths
Young people who are extremely vulnerable to the negative consequences of school failure, substance abuse, and early sexuality.

What Does This Mean to Me?

Older, But Wiser

"When I was a boy of fourteen, my father was so ignorant I could hardly stand to have the old man around. But when I got to be twenty-one, I was astonished at how much he had learned in seven years" (Mark Twain, "Old Times on the Mississippi," *Atlantic Monthly*, 1874).

Do you agree with Mark Twain? When you look back at your adolescence are you surprised at how much you thought you knew then and how little you know now? Did you do anything that you now consider silly and immature? Of course, as they say, "Hindsight is always 20/20." Maybe there is a benefit to teenage rebellion. For example, would it make you a better parent knowing firsthand about all the trouble your kids get into and why they do?

Formed in 1985, the **Children's Rights Council (CRC)** is a national nonprofit organization based in Washington, D.C., that works to ensure children meaningful and continuing contact with both their parents and extended family, regardless of the parents' marital status. Find this website by going to www.thomsonedu.com/criminaljustice/siegel.

playing by the rules is not enough to lift families out of poverty: even if parents work full-time at the federal minimum wage, the family still lives in poverty.[11]

Hundreds of studies have documented the association between family poverty and children's health, achievement, and behavior impairments.[12] Children who grow up in low-income homes are less likely to achieve in school and less likely to complete their schooling than children with more affluent parents.

Health Problems Receiving adequate health care is another significant concern for American youth. There are some troubling signs. For the first time in our nation's history, the life expectancy for children may be *less* than that of their parents. More than 9 million children in the United States lack health insurance and budget cuts threaten many child health programs.[13] As might be expected, children who are not healthy, especially those who live in lower-income families and children from ethnic and minority backgrounds, are subject to illness and early mortality. Recently, the infant mortality rate rose for the first time in more than forty years, and is now seven per one thousand births. The United States currently ranks twenty-fifth in the world among industrialized nations in preventing infant mortality, and the percent of children born at low birth weight has increased.[14]

Family Problems Divorce strikes about half of all new marriages and many families sacrifice time with each other to afford more affluent lifestyles. A national study sponsored by National Center for Health Statistics found that the probability of a first marriage ending in separation or divorce within five years is 20 percent. If the couple is not married, but lives together, the odds of breaking up within five years jumps to 49 percent. After ten years, the probability of a first marriage ending is 33 percent, compared with 62 percent for cohabitations.[15]

As families undergo divorce, separation, and breakup, kids are often placed in foster care. About 800,000 kids spend some time in foster care each year and the daily

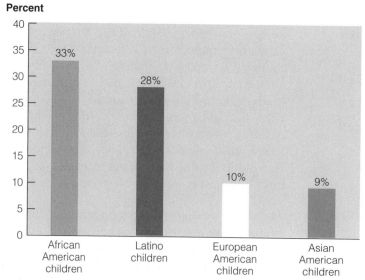

Figure 1.1 **Children in Poverty**

Source: S. Fass and N. K. Cauthen, "Who Are America's Poor Children?" (New York: National Center for Children in Poverty, Columbia University Mailman School of Public Health, 2005. Available at: www.nccp.org/pub_cpt05b.html (accessed November 15, 2006).

count is about 500,000. Children of color are significantly overrepresented in foster care; although African American children make up 16 percent of the nation's children, they make up 35 percent of children in foster care.[16]

These social conditions have a significant impact on kids. Children are being polarized into two distinct economic groups: those in affluent, two-earner, married-couple households and those in poor, single-parent households.[17] Kids whose parents divorce may increase their involvement in delinquency, especially if they have a close bond with the parent who is forced to leave.[18]

Substandard Living Conditions Many children live in substandard housing—such as high-rise, multiple-family dwellings—which can have a negative influence on their long-term psychological health.[19] Adolescents living in deteriorated urban areas are prevented from having productive and happy lives. Many die from random bullets and drive-by shootings. Some adolescents are homeless and living on the street, where they are at risk of drug addiction and sexually transmitted diseases (STDs), including AIDS. Today about one-third of U.S. households with children have one or more of the following three housing problems: physically inadequate housing, crowded housing, or housing that costs more than 30 percent of the household income.[20]

🌐 There are, in fact, a number of organizations dedicated to improving educational standards in the United States. The **Eisenhower National Clearinghouse's** mission is to identify effective curriculum resources, create high-quality professional development materials, and disseminate useful information and products to improve K–12 mathematics and science teaching and learning. Find this website by going to www.thomsonedu.com/criminaljustice/siegel.

Inadequate Education The U.S. educational system seems to be failing many young people. We are lagging behind other developed nations in critical areas, such as science and mathematics. The rate of *retention* (being forced to repeat a grade) is far higher than it should be. Retention rates are associated with another major problem: dropping out. As Figure 1.2 shows, there are fewer kids dropping out of school today than thirty years ago. Yet, more than 10 percent of minority youths never finish high school; the Hispanic drop-out rate is almost five times the European American rate.

Why the discrepancy? Poor minority-group children attend the most underfunded schools, receive inadequate educational opportunities, and have the fewest opportunities to achieve conventional success.

Considering that youth are at risk during the most tumultuous time of their lives, it comes as no surprise that they are willing to engage in risky, destructive behavior.

Maria Sanchez, shown here with her family, lives in Starr County, Texas, one of the poorest communities in the United States. Do you think there is a relationship between delinquency and growing up in an area with high levels of substandard housing and high rates of poverty?

© Lara Jo Regan/Getty Images

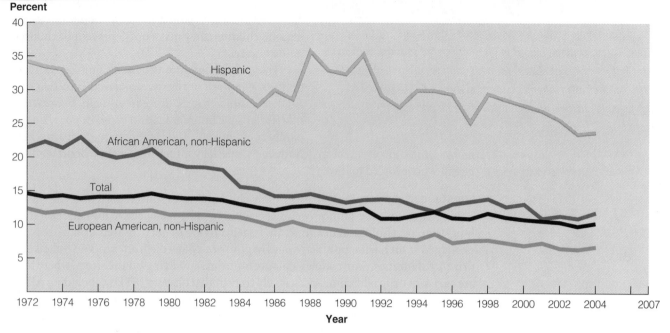

Source: U.S. Department of Education. National Center for Educational Statistics, The Condition of Education 2006 (NCES 2006-071), 2006. Available at: http://nces.ed.gov/fastfacts/display.asp?id=16 (accessed November 16, 2006).

Is There Reason for Hope?

Despite the many hazards faced by teens, there are some bright spots on the horizon. Teenage birthrates nationwide have declined substantially during the past decade, with the sharpest declines among African American girls. Over the past decade, the teen birthrate has dropped significantly and so has the teen abortion rate. These data indicate that more young girls are using birth control and practicing safe sex. Fewer children with health risks are being born today than in 1990. This probably means that fewer women are drinking or smoking during pregnancy and that fewer are receiving late or no prenatal care. In addition, since 1990 the number of children immunized against disease has increased.

Education is still a problem area, but more parents are reading to their children, and math achievement is rising in grades four through twelve. And more kids are going to college. Enrollment in degree-granting institutions increased (21 percent), from 14.3 million to 17.3 million during the past decade. Much of the growth was in female enrollment; the number of men enrolled rose 16 percent, whereas the number of women increased by 25 percent.[21]

There are also indications that youngsters may be rejecting hard drugs. Teen smoking and drinking rates remain high, but fewer kids are using heroin and crack cocaine and the numbers of teens who report cigarette use has been in decline since the mid-1990s.[22] Although these are encouraging signs, many problem areas remain, and the improvement of adolescent life continues to be a national goal.

 The mission of the **Children's Defense Fund** is to "leave no child behind" and ensure every child a healthy start, a head start, a fair start, a safe start, and a moral start in life and a successful passage to adulthood with the help of caring families and communities. The CDF tries to provide a strong, effective voice for kids who cannot vote, lobby, or speak for themselves. Find this website by going to www.thomsonedu.com/criminaljustice/siegel.

THE STUDY OF JUVENILE DELINQUENCY

juvenile delinquency
Participation in illegal behavior by a minor who falls under a statutory age limit.

The problems of youth in modern society are an important subject for academic study. This text focuses on one area of particular concern: **juvenile delinquency**, or criminal behavior engaged in by minors. The study of juvenile delinquency is important both because of the damage suffered by its victims and the problems faced by its perpetrators.

About 1.5 million youths under age eighteen are arrested each year for crimes ranging from loitering to murder.[23] Though most juvenile law violations are minor, some young offenders are extremely dangerous and violent. More than seven hundred thousand youths belong to street gangs. Youths involved in multiple serious criminal acts, referred to as *repeat,* or ***chronic juvenile offenders***, are considered a serious social problem. State juvenile authorities must deal with these offenders while responding to a range of other social problems, including child abuse and neglect, school crime and vandalism, family crises, and drug abuse. In addition, research shows that teens engage in many other risky behaviors:

- 10% had driven a car or other vehicle when they had been drinking alcohol
- 18% had carried a weapon
- 43% had drunk alcohol
- 20% had used marijuana
- 36% had been in a physical fight
- 8% had attempted suicide
- 53% of high school students had engaged in sexual intercourse
- 37% of sexually active high school students had not used a condom at last sexual intercourse
- 2% had injected an illegal drug
- 23% of high school students have smoked cigarettes during the past thirty days
- 80% had not eaten five portions of fruits and vegetables during the past week
- 67% did not attend physical education classes daily
- 13% were overweight[24]

LOOKING BACK TO AALIYAH'S STORY

Many juvenile delinquents commit crimes while under the influence of alcohol or drugs or because they are addicted and need to support their habit. If this is the case, should these juveniles be court ordered into a treatment program? Why/ Why not? What can be done to prevent alcohol and drug abuse in the teen population?

Clearly, there is an urgent need for strategies to combat juvenile delinquency. But formulating effective strategies demands a solid understanding of the causes of delinquency. Is it a function of psychological abnormality? A reaction against destructive social conditions? The product of a disturbed home life? Does serious delinquent behavior occur only in urban areas among lower-class youths? Or is it spread throughout the social structure? What are the effects of family life, substance abuse, school experiences, and peer relations?

The study of delinquency also involves the analysis of the **juvenile justice system**—the law enforcement, court, and correctional agencies designed to treat youthful offenders. How should police deal with minors who violate the law? What are the legal rights of children? What kinds of correctional programs are most effective with delinquent youths? How useful are educational, community, counseling, and vocational development programs? Is it true, as some critics claim, that most efforts to rehabilitate young offenders are doomed to failure?[25] The reaction to juvenile delinquency frequently divides the public. People want to insulate young people from a life of crime and drug abuse. Research suggests that a majority still favor policies mandating rehabilitation of offenders.[26] Evidence also exists that many at-risk youths can be helped successfully with the proper treatment.[27] However, many Americans are wary of teenage hoodlums and gangs. How can we control their behavior? Should we embrace a "get tough" policy in which violent teens are locked up? Or should we continue to treat delinquents as troubled teens who need a helping hand? Many juvenile court judges today base their sentencing decisions on the need to punish offenders and are more concerned about protecting the rights of victims of crime

Governor Rod Blagojevich speaks at Springman Middle School to promote his Governor's Safe Games Illinois Act, which would ban the sale or rental of sexually explicit or violent video games to minors. Can such measures reduce the incidence of violent juvenile crime? Does game playing make kids more violent or is violent behavior a function of psychological abnormality? Or a reaction against destructive social conditions? Or the product of a disturbed home life?

© Tim Boyle/Getty Images

than rehabilitating juveniles.[28] Concerned with the treatment of children, the Supreme Court has banned the death penalty for children until they reach age eighteen.[29] Should the juvenile justice system be more concerned about the long-term effects of punishment? Can even the most violent teenager one day be rehabilitated?

In summary, the scientific study of delinquency requires understanding the nature, extent, and cause of youthful law violations and the methods devised for their control. We also need to study environmental and social issues, including substance abuse, child abuse and neglect, education, and peer relations. All of these aspects of juvenile delinquency will be discussed in this text. We begin, however, with a look back to the development of the concept of childhood and how children were first identified as a unique group with their own special needs and behaviors.

THE DEVELOPMENT OF CHILDHOOD

paternalistic family
A family style wherein the father is the final authority on all family matters and exercises complete control over his wife and children.

Treating children as a distinct social group with special needs and behavior is a relatively new concept. Only for the past 350 years has any formal mechanism existed to care for even the neediest children. In Europe during the Middle Ages (A.D. 700–1500), the concept of childhood as we know it today did not exist. In the **paternalistic family** of the time, the father exercised complete control over his wife and children.[30] Children who did not obey were subject to severe physical punishment, even death.

Custom and Practice in the Middle Ages

During the Middle Ages, as soon as they were physically capable, children of all classes were expected to take on adult roles. Boys learned farming or a skilled trade such as masonry or metalworking; girls aided in food preparation or household maintenance.[31] Some peasant youths went into domestic or agricultural service on the estates of powerful landowners or became apprenticed in trades or crafts.[32] Children of the landholding classes also assumed adult roles at an early age. At age seven or eight, boys born to landholding families were either sent to a monastery or cathedral school or were sent to serve as squires, or assistants, to experienced knights. At age twenty-one, young men of the knightly classes received their own knighthood and returned home to live with their parents. Girls were educated at home and married in their early teens. A few were taught to read, write, and do sufficient mathematics to handle household accounts in addition to typical female duties, such as supervising servants.

Some experts, most notably Philippe Aries, have described the medieval child as a "miniature adult" who began to work and accept adult roles at an early age and were treated with great cruelty.[33] In his work, *Medieval Children* (2003), historian Nicholas Orme disagrees with this standard vision. Orme finds that the medieval mother began to care for her children even before their delivery. Royal ladies borrowed relics of the Virgin Mary from the Church to protect their unborn children, whereas poorer women used jasper stones or drawings of the cross, which were placed across their stomachs to ensure a healthy and uneventful birth. Parents associated their children's birthdays with a saint's feast day. As they do today, children devised songs, rhymes, and games. Some used cherry pits and hazelnuts in their games. They had toys, including dolls, and even mechanical toys made for royalty.[34]

Child Rearing and Discipline In many families, especially the highborn, newborns were handed over to *wet nurses* who fed and cared for them during the first two years of life; parents had little contact with their children. Discipline was severe. Young children of all classes were subjected to stringent rules and regulations. Children were beaten severely for any sign of disobedience or ill temper, and many would be considered abused by today's standards. Children were expected to undertake responsibilities early in their lives, sharing in the work of siblings and parents. Those thought to be suffering from disease or retardation were often abandoned to churches, orphanages, or foundling homes.[35]

The impersonal relationship between parent and child can be traced to the high mortality rates of the day. Parents were reluctant to invest emotional effort in relationships that could so easily end because of violence, accident, or disease. Many believed that children must be toughened to ensure their survival, and close family relationships were viewed as detrimental to this process. Also, because the oldest male child was the essential player in a family's well-being, younger male and female siblings were considered liabilities.

The Development of Concern for Children

Throughout the seventeenth and eighteenth centuries, a number of developments in England heralded the march toward the recognition of children's rights. Among them were changes in family style and child care, the English Poor Laws, the apprenticeship movement, and the role of the chancery court.[36]

Changes in Family Structure Family structure began to change after the Middle Ages. Extended families, which were created over centuries, gave way to the nuclear family structure with which we are familiar today. It became more common for marriage to be based on love rather than parental consent and paternal dominance. This changing concept of marriage from an economic arrangement to an emotional commitment also began to influence the way children were treated. Although parents still rigidly disciplined their children, they formed closer ties and had greater concern for the well-being of their offspring.

Grammar and boarding schools were established in many large cities during this time.[37] Children studied grammar, Latin, law, and logic. Teachers often ruled by fear. Students were beaten for academic mistakes as well as for moral lapses. Such brutal treatment fell on both the rich and the poor throughout all levels of educational life, including boarding schools and universities. This treatment abated in Europe during the Enlightenment, but it remained in full force in Great Britain until late in the nineteenth century.

Toward the close of the eighteenth century, the work of such philosophers as Voltaire, Rousseau, and Locke launched a new age for childhood and the family.[38] Their vision produced a period known as the Enlightenment, which stressed a humanistic view of life, freedom, family, reason, and law. These new beliefs influenced the family. The father's authority was tempered, discipline became more relaxed, and the expression of affection became more commonplace. Upper- and middle-class families began to devote attention to child rearing, and the status of children was advanced.

As a result of these changes, children began to emerge as a distinct group with independent needs and interests. Serious questions arose over the treatment of children in school. Restrictions were placed on the use of the whip, and in some schools academic assignments or the loss of privileges replaced corporal punishment. Despite such reforms, punishment was still primarily physical, and schools continued to mistreat children.

Poor Laws

Poor Laws As early as 1535, the English passed statutes known as **Poor Laws**.[39] These laws allowed for the appointment of overseers to place destitute or neglected children as servants in the homes of the affluent, where they were trained in agricultural, trade, or domestic services. The Elizabethan Poor Laws of 1601 created a system of church wardens and masters who, with the consent of justices of the peace, identified vagrant, delinquent, and neglected children and put them to work. Often this meant placing them in poorhouses or workhouses or apprenticing them to masters.

The Apprenticeship Movement Apprenticeship existed throughout almost the entire history of Great Britain.[40] Under this practice, children were placed in the care of adults who trained them in specific skills, such as being a blacksmith or a farrier (a shoer of horses). *Voluntary apprentices* were bound out by parents or guardians in exchange for a fee. Legal authority over the child was then transferred to the apprentice's master. The system helped parents avoid the costs and responsibilities of child rearing. *Involuntary apprentices* were compelled by the legal authorities to serve a master until they were twenty-one or older. The master–apprentice relationship was similar to the parent–child relationship in that the master had complete authority over the apprentice and could have agreements enforced by local magistrates.

chancery courts

Court proceedings created in fifteenth-century England to oversee the lives of highborn minors who were orphaned or otherwise could not care for themselves.

parens patriae

The power of the state to act on behalf of the child and provide care and protection equivalent to that of a parent.

Chancery Court Throughout Great Britain in the Middle Ages, **chancery courts** were established to protect property rights and seek equitable solutions to disputes and conflicts. Eventually, its authority was extended to the welfare of children in cases involving the guardianship of orphans. This included safeguarding their property and inheritance rights and appointing a guardian to protect them until they reached the age of majority.

The courts operated on the proposition that children were under the protective control of the king; thus, the Latin phrase **parens patriae** was used, which refers to the role of the king as the father of his country. The concept was first used by English kings to establish their right to intervene in the lives of the children of their vassals.[41] In the famous 1827 case *Wellesley v. Wellesley,* a duke's children were taken away from him in the name and interest of *parens patriae,* because of his scandalous behavior.[42] Thus, the concept of *parens patriae* became the theoretical basis for the protective jurisdiction of the chancery courts acting as part of the Crown's power. As time passed, the monarchy used *parens patriae* more and more to justify its intervention in the lives of families and children.[43]

The chancery courts did not have jurisdiction over children charged with criminal conduct. Juveniles who violated the law were handled through the regular criminal court system. Nonetheless, the concept of *parens patriae* grew to refer primarily to the responsibility of the courts and the state to act in the best interests of the child.

This engraving shows the 1877 arrest of a juvenile delinquent—with his mother begging the arresting officer for his release. Until the twentieth century, little distinction was made between adult and juvenile offenders. Both were eligible to be arrested, tried, sent to prison, and punished in the same manner. Children could be treated with extreme cruelty at home, at school, and by the law with few consequences for the perpetrators.

✔ CHECKPOINTS

■ The problems of American youth have become a national concern and an important subject of academic study.

■ There are more than 70 million youths in the United States, and the number is expected to rise.

■ American youth are under a great deal of stress. They face poverty, family problems, urban decay, inadequate education, teen pregnancy, and social conflict.

■ The concept of a separate status of childhood has developed slowly over the centuries.

■ Early family life was controlled by parents. Punishment was severe and children were expected to take on adult roles early in their lives.

■ With the start of the seventeenth century came greater recognition of the needs of children. In Great Britain, the chancery court movement, the Poor Laws, and the apprenticeship programs greatly affected the lives of children.

■ In colonial America, many of the characteristics of English family living were adopted.

■ In the nineteenth century, neglected, delinquent, and dependent or runaway children were treated no differently than criminal defendants. Children were often charged and convicted of crimes.

Childhood in America

While England was using its chancery courts and Poor Laws to care for children in need, the American colonies were developing similar concepts. The colonies were a haven for people looking for opportunities denied them in England and Europe. Along with the adult early settlers, many children came not as citizens, but as indentured servants, apprentices, or agricultural workers. They were recruited from workhouses, orphanages, prisons, and asylums that housed vagrant and delinquent youths.[44]

At the same time, the colonists themselves produced illegitimate, neglected, and delinquent children. The initial response to caring for such children was to adopt court and Poor Law systems similar to those in England. Poor Law legislation requiring poor and dependent children to serve apprenticeships was passed in Virginia in 1646 and in Massachusetts and Connecticut in 1673.[45]

It was also possible, as in England, for parents to voluntarily apprentice their children to a master for care and training. The master in colonial America acted as a surrogate parent, and in certain instances apprentices would actually become part of the family. If they disobeyed their masters, they were punished by local tribunals. If masters abused apprentices, courts would make them pay damages, return the children to the parents, or find new guardians for them. Maryland and Virginia developed an orphans' court that supervised the treatment of youths placed with guardians. These courts did not supervise children living with their natural parents, leaving intact parents' rights to care for their children.[46]

By the beginning of the nineteenth century, the apprenticeship system gave way to the factory system, and the problems of how to deal with dependent youths increased. Early settlers believed hard work, strict discipline, and education were the only reliable methods for salvation. A child's life was marked by work alongside parents, some schooling, prayer, more work, and further study. Work in the factories, however, often placed demands on child laborers that they were too young to endure. To alleviate this problem, the *Factory Act* of the early nineteenth century limited the hours children were permitted to work and the age at which they could begin to work. It also prescribed a minimum amount of schooling to be provided by factory owners.[47] This and related statutes were often violated, and conditions of work and school remained troublesome issues well into the twentieth century. Nevertheless, the statutes were a step in the direction of reform.

Controlling Children

In the United States, as in England, moral discipline was rigidly enforced. Stubborn child laws were passed that required children to obey their parents.[48] It was not uncommon for children to be whipped if they were disobedient or disrespectful to their families. Children were often required to attend public whippings and executions, because these events were thought to be important forms of moral instruction. Parents referred their children to published writings on behavior and expected them to follow their precepts carefully. The early colonists, however, viewed family violence as a sin, and child protection laws were passed as early as 1639 (in New Haven, Connecticut).

These laws expressed the community's commitment to God to oppose sin, but offenders usually received lenient sentences.[49] Although most colonies adopted a protectionist stance, few cases of child abuse were actually brought before the courts.

For more information on the early history of childhood and the development of education, go to "Factors Influencing the Development of the Idea of Childhood in Europe and America," by Jim Vandergriff. Find this website by going to www.thomsonedu.com/criminaljustice/siegel.

This neglect may reflect the nature of life in extremely religious households. Children were productive laborers and respected by their parents. In addition, large families provided many siblings and kinfolk who could care for children and relieve the burden on parents.[50] Another view is that although many children were harshly punished, in early America the acceptable limits of discipline were so high that few parents were charged with assault. Any punishment that fell short of maiming or permanently harming a child was considered within the sphere of parental rights.[51] ✔ Checkpoints

THE CONCEPT OF DELINQUENCY

Until the twentieth century, little distinction was made between adult and juvenile offenders. Although judges considered the age of an offender when deciding on punishment, both adults and children were eligible for prison, corporal punishment, and even the death penalty. In fact, children were treated with extreme cruelty at home, at school, and by the law.[52]

Over the years this treatment changed as society became sensitive to the special needs of children. Beginning in the mid-nineteenth century, there was official recognition that children formed a separate group with their own special needs. In New York, Boston, and Chicago, groups known as **child savers** were formed to assist children. They created community programs to service needy children and lobbied for a separate legal status for children, which ultimately led to development of a formal juvenile justice system. The child-saving movement will be discussed more fully in Chapter 11.

Delinquency and *Parens Patriae*

The current treatment of juvenile delinquents is a by-product of this developing national consciousness of children's needs. The designation *delinquent* became popular at the onset of the twentieth century when the first separate juvenile courts were instituted. The child savers believed that treating minors and adults equally violated the humanitarian ideals of American society. Consequently, the emerging juvenile justice system operated under the *parens patriae* philosophy. Minors who engaged in illegal behavior were viewed as victims of improper care at home. Illegal behavior was a sign that the state should step in and take control of the youths before they committed more serious crimes. The state should act in the **best interests of the child**. Children should not be punished for their misdeeds, but instead should be given the care necessary to control wayward behavior. It makes no sense to find children guilty of specific crimes, such as burglary or petty larceny, because that stigmatizes them as thieves or burglars. Instead, the catchall term *juvenile delinquency* should be used, because it indicates that the child needs the care and custody of the state.

The Legal Status of Delinquency

The child savers fought hard for a legal status of juvenile delinquent, but the concept that children could be treated differently before the law can actually be traced to the British legal tradition. Early British jurisprudence held that children under the age of seven were legally incapable of committing crimes. Children between the ages of seven and fourteen were responsible for their actions, but their age might be used to excuse or lighten their punishment. Our legal system still recognizes that many young people are incapable of making mature judgments and that responsibility for their acts should be limited. Children can intentionally steal cars and know that the act is illegal, but they may be incapable of fully understanding the consequences of their behavior. Therefore, the law does not punish a youth as it would an adult, and it sees youthful misconduct as evidence of impaired judgment.

Today, the legal status of *juvenile delinquent* refers to a minor child who has been found to have violated the penal code. Most states define *minor child* as an individual who falls under a statutory age limit, most commonly seventeen years of age (see Exhibit 1.1).

child savers
Nineteenth-century reformers who developed programs for troubled youth and influenced legislation creating the juvenile justice system; today some critics view them as being more concerned with control of the poor than with their welfare.

delinquent
Juvenile who has been adjudicated by a judicial officer of a juvenile court as having committed a delinquent act.

best interests of the child
A philosophical viewpoint that encourages the state to take control of wayward children and provide care, custody, and treatment to remedy delinquent behavior.

Age 15 Connecticut, New York, North Carolina

Age 16 Georgia, Illinois, Louisiana, Massachusetts, Michigan, Missouri, New Hampshire, South Carolina, Texas, Wisconsin

Age 17 Alabama, Alaska, Arizona, Arkansas, California, Colorado, Delaware, District of Columbia, Florida, Hawaii, Idaho, Indiana, Iowa,

Kansas, Kentucky, Maine, Maryland, Minnesota, Mississippi, Montana, Nebraska, Nevada, New Jersey, New Mexico, North Dakota, Ohio, Oklahoma, Oregon, Pennsylvania, Rhode Island, South Dakota, Tennessee, Utah, Vermont, Virginia, Washington, West Virginia, Wyoming

Source: Howard Snyder and Melissa Sickmund, Juvenile Offenders and Victims, 2006 (Pittsburgh: National Center for Juvenile Justice, 2006).

LOOKING BACK TO AALIYAH'S STORY

Teens close to the age of eighteen like Aaliyah may be too old for the juvenile justice system, but too young for the adult system. What should be done with juveniles who are close to eighteen years when they receive a delinquency charge? Should something be done to bridge the gap between the juvenile justice system and the adult criminal justice system?

Juveniles are usually kept separate from adults and receive different treatment under the law. Most large police departments employ officers whose sole responsibility is delinquency. Every state has some form of juvenile court with its own judges, probation department, and other facilities. Terminology is also different. Adults are *tried* in court; children are *adjudicated*. Adults can be *punished*; children are *treated*. If treatment is mandated, children can be sent to secure detention facilities, but they cannot normally be committed to adult prisons.

Children also have a unique legal status. A minor apprehended for a criminal act is usually charged with being a juvenile delinquent, regardless of the offense. These charges are confidential, and trial records are kept secret. The purpose of these safeguards is to shield children from the stigma of a criminal conviction and to prevent youthful misdeeds from becoming a lifelong burden.

Each state defines juvenile delinquency differently, setting its own age limits and boundaries. The federal government also has a delinquency category for youngsters who violate federal laws, but typically allows the states to handle delinquency matters.

Legal Responsibility of Youths

In our society the actions of adults are controlled by two types of law: criminal law and civil law. Criminal laws prohibit activities that are injurious to the well-being of society, such as drug use, theft, and rape; criminal legal actions are brought by state authorities against private citizens. In contrast, civil laws control interpersonal or private activities and legal actions are usually initiated by individual citizens. Contractual relationships and personal conflicts (torts) are subjects of civil law. Also covered under civil law are provisions for the care of people who cannot care for themselves—for example, the mentally ill, the incompetent, and the infirm.

Today juvenile delinquency falls somewhere between criminal and civil law. Under *parens patriae*, delinquent acts are not considered criminal violations. The legal action against them is similar (though not identical) to a civil action that, in an ideal situation, is based on their **need for treatment**. This legal theory recognizes that children who violate the law are in need of the same treatment as are law-abiding citizens who cannot care for themselves.

Delinquent behavior is treated more leniently than adult misbehavior, because the law considers juveniles to be less responsible for their behavior than adults. Compared with adults, adolescents are believed to

- have a stronger preference for risk and novelty;
- be less accurate in assessing the potential consequences of risky conduct;

need for treatment
The criteria on which juvenile sentencing is based. Ideally, juveniles are treated according to their need for treatment and not for the seriousness of the delinquent act they committed.

- be more impulsive and more concerned with short-term consequences;
- have a different appreciation of time and self-control; and
- be more susceptible to peer pressure.[53]

Even though youths have a lesser degree of legal responsibility, like adults they are subject to arrest, trial, and incarceration. Their legal predicament has prompted the courts to grant children many of the same legal protections conferred on adults accused of criminal offenses. These include the right to consult an attorney, to be free from self-incrimination, and to be protected from illegal searches and seizures.

Although most children who break the law are considered salvageable and worthy of community treatment efforts, there are also violent juvenile offenders whose behavior requires a firmer response. Some state authorities have declared that these hard-core offenders cannot be treated as children and must be given more secure treatment that is beyond the resources of the juvenile justice system. This recognition has prompted the policy of **waiver**—also known as **bindover** or **removal**—that is, transferring legal jurisdiction over the most serious juvenile offenders to the adult court for criminal prosecution. To the chagrin of reformers, waived youth may find themselves serving time in adult prisons.[54] So although the *parens patriae* concept is still applied to children whose law violations are considered not to be serious, the more serious juvenile offenders can be treated in a manner similar to adults.

waiver (also known as bindover or removal)
Transferring legal jurisdiction over the most serious and experienced juvenile offenders to the adult court for criminal prosecution.

STATUS OFFENDERS

A child can also become subject to state authority for committing actions that would not be considered illegal if committed by an adult. Conduct that is illegal only because the child is underage is known as a **status offense**. Exhibit 1.2, showing the status offense law of Maryland, is representative of this type of statute. Eleven states classify these youths using the term *child in need of supervision,* whereas the remainder use terms such as *unruly child, incorrigible child,* or *minor in need of supervision.*[55] The court can also exercise control over dependent children who are not being properly cared for by their parents or guardians.

State control over a child's noncriminal behavior supports the *parens patriae* philosophy, because it is assumed to be in the best interests of the child. Usually, a status offender is directed to the juvenile court when it is determined that his parents are unable or unwilling to care for or control him and that the adolescent's behavior is self-destructive or harmful to society. Each year approximately 150,000 youths are sent to juvenile court as status offenders.[56]

A historical basis exists for status offense statutes. It was common practice early in the nation's history to place disobedient or runaway youths in orphan asylums, residential homes, or houses of refuge.[57] When the first juvenile courts were established

status offense
Conduct that is illegal only because the child is underage.

Exhibit 1.2	Status Offense Law: Maryland

(d) Child. "Child" means an individual under the age of 18 years.

(e) Child in need of supervision. "Child in need of supervision" is a child who requires guidance, treatment, or rehabilitation and: (1) Is required by law to attend school and is habitually truant; (2) Is habitually disobedient, ungovernable, and beyond the control of the person having custody of him; (3) Deports himself so as to injure or endanger himself or others; or (4) Has committed an offense applicable only to children.

Source: Maryland Courts and Judicial Proceedings Code Ann. § 3-8A-01 (2002).

in Illinois, the Chicago Bar Association described part of their purpose as follows:

> *The whole trend and spirit of the [1889 Juvenile Court Act] is that the State, acting through the Juvenile Court, exercises that tender solicitude and care over its neglected, dependent wards that a wise and loving parent would exercise with reference to his own children under similar circumstances.*[58]

Until relatively recently, however, almost every state treated status offenders and juvenile delinquents alike, referring to them either as **wayward minors** or delinquent children. A trend begun in the 1960s has resulted in the creation of separate status offense categories that vary from state to state: children, minors, persons, youths, or juveniles in need of supervision (CHINS, MINS, PINS, YINS, or JINS). The purpose is to shield noncriminal youths from the stigma attached to the juvenile delinquent label and to signify that they have special needs and problems (see Concept Summary 1.1). But even where there are separate legal categories for delinquents and status offenders, the distinction between them has become blurred. Some noncriminal conduct may be included in the definition of delinquency, and some less serious criminal offenses occasionally may be labeled as status offenses.[59] In some states the juvenile court judge may substitute a status offense for a delinquency charge.[60] This possibility can be used to encourage youths to admit to the charges against them in return for less punitive treatment.

The Status Offender in the Juvenile Justice System

Separate status offense categories may avoid some of the stigma associated with the delinquency label, but they have little effect on treatment. Youths in either category can be picked up by the police and brought to a police station. They can be petitioned to the same juvenile court, where they have a hearing before the same judge and come under the supervision of the probation department, the court clinic, and the treatment staff. At a hearing, status offenders may see little difference between the treatment they receive and the treatment of the delinquent offenders sitting across the room. Although status offenders are usually not detained or incarcerated with delinquents, they can be transferred to secure facilities if they are considered uncontrollable.

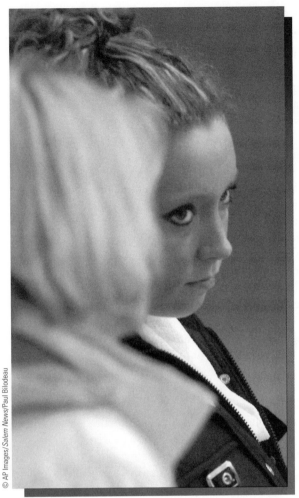

Status offenses include running away from home, being disobedient, and engaging in behavior forbidden to minors, such as drinking. This cheerleader from Danvers High School in Massachusetts is shown at a court hearing after she was arrested for having allegedly shown up drunk for a football playoff game with archrival Walpole High.

wayward minors
Early legal designation of youths who violate the law because of their minority status; now referred to as status offenders.

 Concept Summary **1.1**

Treatment of Juveniles

	Juvenile Delinquents	Status Offenders
Act	Burglary, shoplifting, robbery	Truancy, running away, disobedient
Injured party	Crime victim	Themselves, their family
Philosophy	*Parens patriae*	Best interests of the children
Legal status	Can be detained in secure confinement	Must be kept in nonsecure shelter
Is there resulting stigma?	Yes	Yes

What should happen with teens who run away from home? This is considered a status offense but many communities do not charge runaways or require them to be involved in the juvenile justice system. Do you agree with this? Should something more be done and if so, what?

Office of Juvenile Justice and Delinquency Prevention (OJJDP)
Branch of the U.S. Justice Department charged with shaping national juvenile justice policy through disbursement of federal aid and research funds.

To learn more about the efforts to remove status offenders from secure lockups, check out **Gwen A. Holden and Robert A. Kapler, "Deinstitutionalizing Status Offenders: A Record of Progress."** Find this website by going to www.thomsonedu.com/criminaljustice/siegel.

Aiding the Status Offender

Efforts have been ongoing to reduce the penalties and stigma borne by status offenders. In 1974, the U.S. Congress passed the Juvenile Justice and Delinquency Prevention Act (JJDPA) that provides the major source of federal funding to improve states' juvenile justice systems. Under the JJDPA and its subsequent reauthorizations, in order to receive federal funds, states were and are required to remove status offenders from secure detention and lockups in order to insulate them from more serious delinquent offenders. The act created the **Office of Juvenile Justice and Delinquency Prevention (OJJDP)**, which was authorized to distribute grants and provide support to those states that developed alternate procedural methods.[61] Title III of the JJDPA, referred to as the Runaway and Homeless Youth Act (RHYA) of 1974, provides funds for nonsecure facilities where status offenders who need protection can receive safe shelter, counseling, and education until an effective family reunion can be realized.[62]

This has been a highly successful policy, and the number of status offenders kept in secure pretrial detention has dropped significantly during the past three decades. Nevertheless, juvenile court judges in many states can still detain status offenders in secure lockups if the youths are found in contempt of court. The act that created the OJJDP was amended in 1987 to allow status offenders to be detained for violations of valid court orders.[63] At last count, more than forty states were in compliance with the OJJDP mandate and were eligible for receiving federal funds.[64]

Changes in the treatment of status offenders reflect the current attitude toward children who violate the law. On the one hand, there appears to be a movement to severely sanction youths who commit serious offenses and transfer them to the adult court. On the other hand, a great effort has been made to remove nonserious cases from the official agencies of justice and place these youths in community-based treatment programs.

Reforming Status Offense Laws

For more than thirty years national crime commissions have called for limiting control over status offenders.[65] In 1976 the National Advisory Commission on Criminal Justice Standards and Goals, created by the federal government to study the

Catie, 15, is seen at the Renfrew Center, a clinic for eating disorders in Coconut Creek, Florida. Catie started cutting herself after meals in the seventh grade. She has carved designs into her flesh, such as the Japanese symbol for pain. Kids like Catie may need the help of the juvenile justice system, yet they are not really delinquents or status offenders. A few states have attempted to eliminate status offense laws and treat these youths as neglected or dependent children, giving child protective services the primary responsibility for their care.

© AP Images/Lauren Greenfield/VII

Mayor Frank Melton (right) speaks with reporters on June 20, 2006, at City Hall in Jackson, Mississippi, telling them that he plans to issue a civil emergency proclamation to enforce a stricter curfew and hold parents accountable for their children's criminal acts. Can such measures reduce delinquency in high-crime areas?

© AP Images/Rogelio V. Solis

🌐 Do curfew laws work in reducing the rate of youth crime? To find out, visit the website of the **Justice Policy Institute** by going to www.thomsonedu. com/criminaljustice/siegel.

✔ CHECKPOINTS

■ The concept of delinquency was developed in the early twentieth century.

■ Before that, criminal youths and adults were treated in almost the same fashion.

■ A group of reformers, referred to as child savers, helped create a separate delinquency category to insulate juvenile offenders from the influence of adult criminals.

■ The separate status of juvenile delinquency is based on the *parens patriae* philosophy, which holds that children have the right to care and custody and that, if parents are not capable of providing that care, the state must step in to take control.

■ Delinquents are given greater legal protection than adult criminals and are shielded from stigma and labels.

■ More serious juvenile cases may be waived to the adult court.

■ Juvenile courts also have jurisdiction over noncriminal status offenders.

■ Status offenses are illegal only because of the minority status of the offender.

crime problem, opted for the nonjudicial treatment of status offenders by arguing that the only conduct that should warrant family court intervention is conduct that is clearly self-destructive or otherwise harmful to the child. The commission suggested that juvenile courts confine themselves to controlling five status offenses: habitual truancy, repeated disregard for parental authority, repeated running away, repeated use of intoxicating beverages, and delinquent acts by youths under the age of ten.[66]

These calls for reform prompted a number of changes. Kentucky, for example, has amended its status offense law in order to eliminate vague terms and language. Instead of labeling a child who is "beyond control of school" as a status offender, the state is now required to show that the student has repeatedly violated "lawful regulations for the government of the school," with the petition describing the behaviors "and all intervention strategies attempted by the school."[67] A few states, including Maine, Delaware, and Idaho, have attempted to eliminate status offense laws and treat these youths as neglected or dependent children, giving child protective services the primary responsibility for their care.

There is serious debate over the liberalization of status offense laws. Some juvenile court judges believe that reducing judicial authority over children will limit juvenile court jurisdiction to hard-core offenders and constrain its ability to help youths before they commit serious antisocial acts.[68] Their concerns are fueled by research that shows that many status offenders, especially those who are runaways living on the streets, often have serious emotional problems and engage in self-destructive behaviors ranging from substance abuse to self-mutilation; they have high rates of suicide.[69] Consequently, some jurisdictions have resisted weakening status offense laws and gone in the opposite direction by mandating that habitual truants and runaways be placed in secure detention facilities, and if found to be in need of supervision, placed in secure treatment facilities. There has been a call for greater rather than less control over wayward youth, a policy that has spawned both curfew laws and parental responsibility laws, discussed in the Preventing and Treating Delinquency feature.

Although this debate will not end soon, we cannot lose sight of the fact that a majority of youths engage in some status offenses.[70] Illegal acts such as teen sex and substance abuse have become commonplace. Does it make sense, then, to have the juvenile court intervene in cases when no criminal act occurred? The predominant view today is that many status offenders and delinquents share similar problems, and that both categories should fall under the jurisdiction of the juvenile court.

✔ Checkpoints

Increasing Social Control over Juveniles and Their Parents

Those in favor of retaining the status offense category point to society's responsibility to care for troubled youths. Others maintain that the status offense should remain a legal category so that juvenile courts can force a youth to receive treatment. Although it is recognized that a court appearance can produce stigma, the taint may be less important than the need for treatment. Many state jurisdictions, prompted by concern over serious delinquency, have enacted laws that actually expand social control over juveniles.

Curfew Laws

Beginning in 1990, a number of states created or amended curfew laws aimed at restricting the opportunity kids have for getting in trouble. A survey of seventy-seven large U.S. cities found that fifty-nine of them have such laws. Each year about sixty thousand youths are arrested for curfew violations and there number is considered responsible for the decade long increase in the status offender population in juvenile court. As of yet, there is little conclusive evidence that curfews have a significant impact on youth crime rates. Evaluations of the benefits of curfews yield mixed results. Andra Bannister and her associates surveyed more than four hundred police agencies and found that most had curfew ordinances in effect for several years. In the vast majority of cases, police felt that curfew was an effective tool to control vandalism, graffiti, nighttime burglary, and auto theft. Those jurisdictions that did not have curfew laws reported that their absence was a result of political objections rather than perceived ineffectiveness. However, although this research is supportive of curfews, other efforts, such as the national survey by Ken Adams, have found that juvenile arrests and juvenile crime do not seem to decrease significantly during curfew hours. Some research efforts have even found that, after curfews were implemented, victimizations increased significantly during noncurfew hours. This indicates that, rather than suppressing delinquency, curfews merely shift the time of occurrence of the offenses. Some studies have found that strict enforcement of curfew laws actually increases juvenile crime rates. The failure of curfews to control crime coupled with their infringement on civil rights prompted the American Civil Liberties Union to condemn the practice and say in part:

> *Curfews are just the latest in a long line of misguided anti-crime strategies that divert public attention from the real root causes of crime. The fact is that such laws are empty political gestures: they will do nothing to make our streets safer. It is absurd to think that any teenager who is selling drugs or carrying a gun—crimes that could lead to years in prison— would rush home at 11:00 to avoid violating curfew, or that this same teenager won't have a false ID. And certainly any crime that would be committed after midnight can just as easily be committed earlier. In fact, most juvenile crimes are committed right after school, between 3:00 and 6:00 P.M.*

Disciplining Parents

Since the early twentieth century, there have been laws aimed at disciplining parents for *contributing to the delinquency of a minor*. The first of these was enacted in Colorado in 1903, and today all states have some form of statute requiring parents to take some responsibility for their children's misbehavior. All states make it either mandatory or discretionary for the juvenile court to require a parent or guardian to pay at least part of the support costs for a child who is adjudicated delinquent and placed out of the home. Even when the payment is required, however, payment is based on the parent's financial ability to make such payments. During the past decade, approximately one-half of the states enacted or strengthened existing parental liability statutes that make parents criminally liable for the actions of their delinquent children. Such laws allow parents to be sanctioned in juvenile courts for behaviors associated with their child's misbehavior. Some states (Florida, Idaho, Virginia) require parents to reimburse the government for the costs of detention or care of their children. Others (Maryland, Missouri,

SUMMARY

- The study of delinquency is concerned with the nature and extent of the criminal behavior of youths, the causes of youthful law violations, the legal rights of juveniles, and prevention and treatment.
- The problems of American youths have become an important subject of academic study. Many children live in poverty, have inadequate health care, and suffer family problems.
- Adolescence is a time of taking risks, which can get kids into trouble.
- Our modern conception of a separate status for children is quite different than in the past. In earlier times, relationships between children and parents were remote.

Punishment was severe, and children were expected to take on adult roles early in their lives.
- With the start of the seventeenth century came greater recognition of the needs of children. In Great Britain, the chancery court movement, Poor Laws, and apprenticeship programs helped reinforce the idea of children as a distinct social group. In colonial America, many of the characteristics of English family living were adopted.
- In the nineteenth century, delinquent and runaway children were treated no differently than criminal defendants.
- During this time, however, increased support for the *parens patriae* concept resulted in steps to reduce the responsibility of children under the criminal law.

Oklahoma) demand that parents make restitution payments—for example, paying for damage caused by their children who vandalized a school. All states except New Hampshire have incorporated parental liability laws in their statutes, although most recent legislation places limits on recovery at somewhere between $250 (Vermont) and $15,000 (Texas); the average is $2,500. Other states (Colorado, Texas, Louisiana) require parents as well as children to participate in counseling and community service activities.

Parents may also be held civilly liable, under the concept of *vicarious liability,* for the damages caused by their child. In some states, parents are responsible for up to $300,000 in damages; in others the liability cap is $3,500 (sometimes homeowner's insurance covers at least some of liability). Parents can also be charged with civil negligence if they should have known of the damage a child was about to inflict but did nothing to stop them—for example, when they give a weapon to an emotionally unstable youth. Juries have levied awards of up to $500,000 in such cases. Since 1990 there have been more than eighteen cases in which parents have been ordered to serve time in jail, because their children have been truant from school.

Some critics charge that these laws contravene the right to due process, because they are unfairly used only against lower-class and minority parents. As legal scholar Elena Laskin points out, imposing penalties on these parents may actually be detrimental. Fining a delinquent's mother removes money from someone who is already among society's poorest people. If a single mother is sent to jail, it leaves her children, including those who are not delinquent, with no parent to raise them; the kids may become depressed, and lose concentration and sleep. Even if punishment encourages the parent to take action, it may be too late, because by the time a parent is charged with violating the statute, the child has already committed a crime, indicating that any damaging socialization by the parent has already occurred. Despite these problems, surveys indicate that the public favors parental responsibility laws.

CRITICAL THINKING

1. Does punishing parents for the behavior of their children violate their rights to be free from vague and undefined punishments? Should children be punished for the behavior of their parents? (They were in the Middle Ages.) Should a husband be held responsible for the actions of his wife or a wife for her husband?
2. At what age should a child be subject to a curfew law? Should the cutoff be sixteen, seventeen, or eighteen?

INFOTRAC COLLEGE EDITION RESEARCH

To learn more about these issues, use "curfew laws" in a key word search on InfoTrac College Edition. Also read Elena Laskin, "How Parental Liability Statutes Criminalize and Stigmatize Minority Mothers," *American Criminal Law Review* 37:1195–1217 (2000).

Sources: Eve Brank and Victoria Weisz, "Paying for the Crimes of Their Children: Public Support of Parental Responsibility," *Journal of Criminal Justice 32*:465–475 (2004); Kenneth Adams, "The Effectiveness of Juvenile Curfews at Crime Prevention," ANNALS *of the American Academy of Political and Social Science 587*:136–159 (2003); Linda Szymanski, "Parental Support Obligation of Institutionalized Delinquents," *NCJJ Snapshot 6.6* (Pittsburgh, PA: National Center for Juvenile Justice, 2001); Andra Bannister, David Carter, and Joseph Schafer, "A National Police Survey on the Use of Juvenile Curfews," *Journal of Criminal Justice 29*:233–240 (2001); Jerry Tyler and Thomas Segady, "Parental Liability Laws: Rationale, Theory, and Effectiveness," *Social Science Journal 37*:79–98 (2000); Elena Laskin, "How Parental Liability Statutes Criminalize and Stigmatize Minority Mothers," *American Criminal Law Review 37*:1195–1217 (2000); Mike Reynolds, Ruth Seydlitz, and Pamela Jenkins, "Do Juvenile Curfew Laws Work? A Time-Series Analysis of the New Orleans Law," *Justice Quarterly* (2000); William Ruefle and Kenneth Mike Reynolds, "Curfews and Delinquency in Major American Cities," *Crime and Delinquency 41*:347–363 (1995); Gilbert Geis and Arnold Binder, "Sins of Their Children: Parental Responsibility for Juvenile Delinquency," *Notre Dame Journal of Law, Ethics, and Public Policy 5*:303–322 (1991).

- The concept of delinquency was developed in the early twentieth century. Before that time, criminal youths and adults were treated in almost the same fashion. A group of reformers, referred to as *child savers,* helped create a separate delinquency category to insulate juvenile offenders from the influence of adult criminals.
- The status of juvenile delinquency is still based on the *parens patriae* philosophy, which holds that children have the right to care and custody and that if parents are not capable of providing that care, the state must step in to take control.
- Juvenile courts also have jurisdiction over noncriminal status offenders, whose offenses (truancy, running away, sexual misconduct) are illegal only because of their minority status.

- Some experts have called for an end to juvenile court control over status offenders, charging that it further stigmatizes already troubled youths. Some research indicates that status offenders are harmed by juvenile court processing. Other research indicates that status offenders and delinquents are quite similar.
- There has been a successful effort to separate status offenders from delinquents and to maintain separate facilities for those who need to be placed in a shelter care program.
- The treatment of juveniles is an ongoing dilemma. Still uncertain is whether young law violators respond better to harsh punishments or to benevolent treatment.

ego identity, p. 3
role diffusion, p. 3
at-risk youths, p. 3
juvenile delinquency, p. 6
chronic juvenile offenders, p. 7
juvenile justice system, p. 7
paternalistic family, p. 8

Poor Laws, p. 10
chancery courts, p. 10
parens patriae, p. 10
child savers, p. 12
delinquent, p. 12
best interests of the child, p. 12
need for treatment, p. 13

waiver, bindover, removal, p. 14
status offense, p. 14
wayward minors, p. 15
Office of Juvenile Justice and
    Delinquency Prevention (OJJDP),
    p. 16

QUESTIONS FOR DISCUSSION

1. Is it fair to have a separate legal category for youths? Considering how dangerous young people can be, does it make more sense to group offenders on the basis of what they have done rather than on their age?

2. At what age are juveniles truly capable of understanding the seriousness of their actions? Should juvenile court jurisdiction be raised or lowered?

3. Is it fair to institutionalize a minor simply for being truant or running away from home? Should the jurisdiction of status offenders be removed from juvenile court and placed with the state's department of social services or some other welfare organization?

4. Should delinquency proceedings be secretive? Does the public have a right to know who juvenile criminals are?

5. Can a "get tough" policy help control juvenile misbehavior, or should *parens patriae* remain the standard?

6. Should juveniles who commit felonies such as rape or robbery be treated as adults?

APPLYING WHAT YOU HAVE LEARNED

You have just been appointed by the governor as chairperson of a newly formed group charged with overhauling the state's juvenile justice system. One primary concern is the treatment of status offenders—kids who have been picked up and charged with being runaways, sexually active, truant from school, or unmanageable at home. Under existing status offense statutes, these youth can be sent to juvenile court and stand trial for their misbehaviors. If the allegations against them are proven valid, they may be removed from the home and placed in foster care or even in a state or private custodial institution.

Recently, a great deal of media attention has been given to the plight of runaway children who live on the streets, take drugs, and engage in prostitution. At an open hearing, advocates of the current system argue that many families cannot provide the care and control needed to keep kids out of trouble and that the state must maintain control of at-risk youth. They contend that many status offenders have histories of drug and delinquency problems and are little different from kids arrested on criminal charges; control by the juvenile court is necessary if the youths are ever to get needed treatment.

Another vocal group argues that it is a mistake for a system that deals with criminal youth also to handle troubled adolescents, whose problems usually are the result of child abuse and neglect. They believe that the current statute should be amended to give the state's department of social welfare (DSW) jurisdiction over all noncriminal youths who are in need of assistance. These opponents of the current law point out that, even though status offenders and delinquents are held in separate facilities, those who run away or are unmanageable can be transferred to more secure correctional facilities that house criminal youths. Furthermore, the current court-based process, where troubled youths are involved with lawyers, trials, and court proceedings, helps convince them that they are "bad kids" and social outcasts.

- Should status offenders be treated differently than juvenile delinquents?
- Should distinctions be made between different types of status offenders? That is, are runaways different from truants?
- Are these behavioral problems better handled by a social service or mental health agency than a juvenile court?
- What recommendations would you make to the governor?

DOING RESEARCH ON THE WEB

For reports on deinstitutionalization and respite care for status offenders, and to read about the problems of high-risk kids, go to the website **www.thomsonedu.com/criminaljustice/siegel**.

The Nature and Extent of Delinquency

© Jim Goldberg/Magnum Photos

CHAPTER OBJECTIVES

After reading this chapter you should:

1. Know what is meant by the term *official delinquency*.
2. Understand how the FBI's Uniform Crime Report (UCR) is compiled.
3. Be familiar with recent trends in juvenile delinquency.
4. Understand how self-report data are collected and what they say about juvenile crime.
5. Recognize the factors that affect the juvenile crime rate.
6. Be aware of gender patterns in delinquency.
7. Appreciate the factors that cause racial differences in delinquency.
8. Be able to debate the issue of class position and delinquency.
9. Be aware of the debate over the role age plays in delinquency.
10. Understand the concept of the chronic persistent offender.
11. Be familiar with the relationship between childhood and victimization.

Jamesetta was born in a poor, urban neighborhood. As her parents struggled with substance abuse, poverty, and unemployment, Jamesetta suffered both physical and sexual abuse before being placed in foster care at the age of five. By the age of nine, Jamesetta was shoplifting, skipping school, and violating curfew. At age thirteen, she physically assaulted her foster mother and entered the juvenile justice system with charges of disorderly conduct and being a habitual delinquent. Her foster home placement was terminated and Jamesetta was sent to live with her aunt, uncle, and six cousins. It wasn't long before her relatives began to have additional concerns that Jamesetta was exhibiting sexualized behavior, "sneaking around" with her seventeen-year-old boyfriend, staying out all night, and being disrespectful. They felt she was out of control.

Jamesetta had been ordered by the Juvenile Court to cooperate with her family's household rules, attend school on a regular basis, have no further law violations, complete twenty-five hours of community service, and pay restitution for the shoplifting, but she refused to cooperate with any of the programs or services, continuing to come and go as she pleased. The family was receiving support from Jamesetta's intensive supervision program counselor, as well as a family therapist, but during the second month of placement with her relatives, at the age of fourteen, Jamesetta disclosed that she was pregnant and planning to keep her baby. The program counselor and other professionals involved in Jamesetta's case had to work with her and her family to re-evaluate their plan.

Jamesetta was enrolled in a school specifically designed to support teens who are pregnant or already parenting, where in addition to her academic studies to complete high school, she would receive help from parenting classes, independent living courses, and relationship counseling. Jamesetta also received services from a neighborhood intervention program that focused on providing structure and accountability for her through counselors and daily group meetings to encourage her. Even with these additional supports and interventions, Jamesetta continued to have status offenses. She skipped school, didn't come home on time, and would not follow household rules; however, she did not have any further law violations.

Jamesetta continued living with her aunt and uncle, and did eventually complete her community service and restitution payment. After the baby was born, Jamesetta began to understand the consequences of her actions. With continued services and support from her counselors, she started following the rules and expectations of her family. Upon taking responsibility to find the necessary medical and child care for her daughter, Jamesetta found employment, a position in retail, and started planning for her future. Despite being at high risk for dropping out of school, Jamesetta was able to complete her high school education and have a positive view of her future. The team of involved professionals continued to provide the needed supports and encouraged Jamesetta to make good decisions for both herself and her new baby. She still struggles at times, but has remained free of further law violations.

High-risk kids such as Jamesetta get involved in more than 1 million serious illegal acts each year. Who commits delinquent acts, and where are they most likely to occur? Is the juvenile crime rate increasing or decreasing? Are juveniles more likely than adults to become the victims of crime? To understand the causes of delinquent behavior and to devise effective means to reduce its occurrence, we must seek answers to these questions.

Delinquency experts have devised a variety of methods to measure the nature and extent of delinquency. We begin with a description of the most widely used sources of data on crime and delinquency. We also examine the information these resources furnish on juvenile crime rates and trends. These data sources will then be used to provide information on the characteristics of adolescent law violators.

OFFICIAL STATISTICS

Each year the U.S. Justice Department's **Federal Bureau of Investigation (FBI)** compiles information gathered by police departments on the number of criminal acts reported by citizens and the number of persons arrested.[1] This information is published in the annual **Uniform Crime Report (UCR)**, which is the most widely used source of national crime and delinquency statistics.

The UCR is compiled from statistics sent to the FBI from more than seventeen thousand police departments. It groups offenses into two categories. **Part I offenses**, include homicide and non-negligent manslaughter, forcible rape, robbery, aggravated assault, burglary, larceny, arson, and motor vehicle theft. Police record every reported incident of these offenses and report them on a quarterly basis to the FBI. Data are broken down by city, county, metropolitan area, and geographical divisions. In addition, the UCR provides information on individuals who have been arrested for these and all other criminal offenses, including vandalism, liquor law violations, and drug trafficking. These are known as **Part II offenses**. The arrest data are presented by age, sex, and race.

The UCR uses three methods to express crime data. First, the number of crimes reported to the police and arrests made are expressed as raw figures (for instance, 16,692 murders occurred in 2005). Second, crime rates per 100,000 people are computed. That is, when the UCR indicates that the murder rate was 5.6 in 2005, it means that almost 6 people in every 100,000 were murdered between January 1 and December 31, 2005. This is the equation used:

$$\frac{\text{Number of Reported Crimes}}{\text{Total U.S. Population}} \times 100{,}000 = \text{Rate per } 100{,}000$$

Third, the FBI computes changes in the number and rate of crime over time. Murder rates increased 3.5 percent between 2004 and 2005, and the number of murders increased by about 500.

Crime Trends in the United States

As measured by the UCR, crime rates increased gradually following the 1930s until the 1960s, when the growth rate became much greater. The homicide rate, which had actually declined from the 1930s to the 1960s, also began a sharp increase that continued through the 1970s.

In 1981 the number of index crimes rose to about 13.4 million and then began a consistent decline until 1984, when police recorded 11.1 million crimes. By the following year, however, the number of crimes once again began an upward trend, so that by 1991 police recorded about 15 million crimes. Since then the number of crimes has been in decline; Figure 2.1 illustrates crime rate trends between 1960 and 2005, the last data available. Although the general crime rates did not increase in 2005, violent crimes, especially murder, ticked upward and continued to do so during the first half of 2006. Although this recent increase in violence is disturbing, it is too soon to tell whether it is the beginning of a new long-term trend or a single year aberration.

Figure 2.1   **Crime Rate Trends**

Rate per 1,000 population

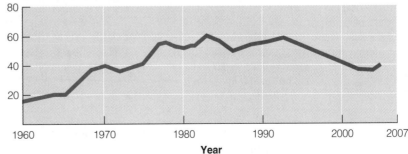

Source: FBI, *Crime in the United States*, 2005, Table 1. Available at: www.fbi.gov/ucr/05cius/data/table_01.htm (accessed December 24, 2006).

Shaping Delinquency Trends

Crime experts have identified a variety of social, economic, personal, and demographic factors that influence crime rate trends. Although crime experts are still uncertain about how these factors affect these trends, directional change seems to be associated with changes in crime rates.

Age

Because teenagers have extremely high crime rates, crime experts view changes in the population age distribution as having the greatest influence on crime trends: As a general rule, the crime rate follows the proportion of young males in the population. Kids who commit a lot of crime early in childhood are also likely to continue to commit crime in their adolescence and into adulthood. More teens in the population means a higher crime rate. The number of juveniles should be increasing over the next decade, and some crime experts fear that this will signal a return to escalating crime rates. However, the number of senior citizens is also expanding, and their presence in the population may have a moderating effect on crime rates (seniors do not commit much crime), offsetting the effect of teens.

Economy/Jobs

There is debate over the effect the economy has on delinquency rates. It seems logical that when the economy turns down, people (especially those who are unemployed) will become more motivated to commit theft crimes. Kids who find it hard to get after school jobs or find employment after they leave school may be motivated to seek other forms of income such as theft and drug dealing. As the economy heats up, delinquency rates should decline because people can secure good jobs; why risk breaking the law when there are legitimate opportunities? Recent (2006) research by Thomas Arvanites and Robert Defina found that the delinquency rate drop in the 1990s could be linked to a strong economy.

However, some experts believe that a poor economy may actually help lower delinquency rates because it actually limits the opportunity kids have to commit crime: Unemployed parents are at home to supervise children and guard their possessions, and because there is less money to spend, people have fewer valuables worth stealing. Moreover, law-abiding people do not begin to violate the law just because there is an economic downturn.

Although the effect of the economy on delinquency rates is still in question, it is possible that over the long haul, a strong economy will help lower delinquency rates, whereas long periods of sustained economic weakness and unemployment may eventually lead to increased rates. Crime skyrocketed in the 1930s during the Great Depression; crime rates fell when the economy surged for almost a decade during the 1990s. Also, economic effects may be localized: People in one area of the city are doing well, but people living in another part of town may be suffering unemployment. The economic effect on the delinquency rates may vary by neighborhood or even by street.

Social Malaise

As the level of social problems increases—such as single-parent families, dropout rates, racial conflict, and teen pregnancies—so do delinquency rates. Delinquency rates are correlated with the number of unwed mothers in the population. It is possible that children of unwed mothers need more social services than children in two-parent families. As the number of kids born to single mothers increases, the child welfare system will be taxed and services depleted. The teenage birth rate has trended downward in recent years, and so have delinquency rates.

Racial conflict may also increase delinquency rates. Areas undergoing racial change, especially those experiencing a migration of minorities into predominantly European American neighborhoods, seem prone to significant increases in their delinquency rate. European Americans in these areas may be using violence to protect what they view as their home turf. Racially motivated crimes actually diminish as neighborhoods become more integrated and power struggles are resolved.

Abortion

In a controversial work, John J. Donohue III and Steven D. Levitt found empirical evidence that the recent drop in the delinquency rate can be attributed to the availability of legalized abortion. In 1973, *Roe v. Wade* legalized abortion nationwide. Within a few years of *Roe v. Wade*, more than 1 million abortions were being performed annually, or roughly one abortion for every three live births. Donohue and Levitt suggest that the delinquency rate drop, which began approximately eighteen years later, in 1991, can be tied to the fact that at that point the first groups of potential offenders affected by the abortion decision began reaching the peak age of criminal activity. The researchers found that states that legalized abortion before the rest of the nation were the first to experience decreasing delinquency rates and that states with high abortion rates have seen a greater drop in delinquency since 1985.

It is possible that the link between delinquency rates and abortion is the result of three mechanisms: (1) selective abortion on the part of women most at risk to have children who would engage in delinquent activity, (2) improved child-rearing or environmental circumstances, because women are having fewer children, and (3) absence of unwanted children who stand the greatest risk of delinquency. If abortion were illegal, they find, delinquency rates might be 10 to 20 percent higher than they currently are with legal abortion.

Understandably, Donohue and Levitt's views has sparked considerable controversy and continued research. One recent (2006) effort by Carter Hay and Michelle Evans found that children unwanted by their mothers do in fact commit more delinquency than children who were "wanted" or planned.

However, the effect was only modest and temporary: By their late teens and twenties, unwanted kids commit as much crime as their "wanted" brothers and sisters, a finding that seems to contradict Donohue and Levitt.

Guns

The availability of firearms may influence the delinquency rate, especially the proliferation of weapons in the hands of teens. Surveys of high school students indicate that between 6 and 10 percent carry guns at least some of the time. Guns also cause escalation in the seriousness of delinquency. As the number of gun-toting students increases, so does the seriousness of violent delinquency: A schoolyard fight may well turn into murder.

Gangs

Another factor that affects delinquency rates is the explosive growth in teenage gangs. Surveys indicate that there are about 750,000 gang members in the United States. Boys who are members of gangs are far more likely to possess guns than non-gang members; criminal activity increases when kids join gangs.

Drug Use

Some experts tie increases in the violent delinquency rate between 1980 and 1990 to the crack epidemic, which swept the nation's largest cities, and to drug-trafficking gangs that fought over drug turf. These well-armed gangs did not hesitate to use violence to control territory, intimidate rivals, and increase market share. As the crack epidemic has subsided, so has the violence in New York City and other metropolitan areas where crack use was rampant. A sudden increase in drug use, on the other hand, may be a harbinger of future increases in the delinquency rate.

Media

Some experts argue that violent media can influence the direction of delinquency rates. The introduction of home video players, DVDs, cable TV, computers, and video games coincided with increasing teen violence rates. Perhaps the increased availability of media violence on these platforms produced more aggressive teens? Watching violence on TV may be correlated with aggressive behaviors, especially when viewers have a pre-existing tendency toward delinquency and violence. Research shows that the more kids watch TV, the more often they get into violent encounters.

Juvenile Justice Policy

Some law enforcement experts have suggested that a reduction in delinquency rates may be attributed to adding large numbers of police officers and using them in aggressive police practices aimed at reducing gang membership, gun possession, and substance abuse.

It is also possible that tough laws such as waiving juveniles to adult courts or sending them to adult prisons can affect crime rates. The fear of punishment may inhibit some would-be delinquents, and tough laws place a significant number of chronic juvenile offenders behind bars, lowering delinquency rates.

CRITICAL THINKING

Although juvenile delinquency rates have been declining in the United States, they have been increasing in Europe. Is it possible that factors that correlate with delinquency rate changes in the United States have little utility in predicting changes in other cultures? What other factors may increase or reduce delinquency rates?

INFOTRAC COLLEGE EDITION RESEARCH

Gang activity may have a big impact on delinquency rates. To find out the influence of gangs in other nations, read this article: Rob White and Ron Mason, "Youth Gangs and Youth Violence: Charting the Key Dimensions," *Australian and New Zealand Journal of Criminology* 39:54–70 (2006).

Sources: Carter Hay and Michelle Evans, "Has Roe v. Wade Reduced U.S. Crime Rates?: Examining the Link Between Mothers' Pregnancy Intentions and Children's Later Involvement in Law-Violating Behavior," *Journal of Research in Crime and Delinquency* 43:36–66 (2006); Thomas Arvanites and Robert Defina, "Business Cycles and Street Crime," *Criminology* 44:139–164 (2006); David Fergusson, L. John Horwood, and Elizabeth Ridder, "Show Me the Child at Seven: The Consequences of Conduct Problems in Childhood for Psychosocial Functioning in Adulthood," *Journal of Child Psychology & Psychiatry & Allied Disciplines* 46:837–849 (2005); Fahui Wang, "Job Access and Homicide Patterns in Chicago: An Analysis at Multiple Geographic Levels Based on Scale-Space Theory," *Journal of Quantitative Criminology* 21:195–217 (2005); Gary Kleck and Ted Chiricos, "Unemployment and Property Crime: A Target-Specific Assessment of Opportunity and Motivation as Mediating Factors," *Criminology* 40:649–680 (2002); Steven Levitt, "Understanding Why Crime Fell in the 1990s: Four Factors That Explain the Decline and Six That Do Not," *Journal of Economic Perspectives* 18:163–190 (2004); Jeffrey Johnson, Patricia Cohen, Elizabeth Smailes, Stephanie Kasen, and Judith Brook, "Television Viewing and Aggressive Behavior During Adolescence and Adulthood," *Science* 295:2468–2471 (2002); Brad Bushman and Craig Anderson, "Media Violence and the American Public," *American Psychologist* 56:477–489 (2001); Steven Messner, Lawrence Raffalovich, and Richard McMillan, "Economic Deprivation and Changes in Homicide Arrest Rates for White and Black Youths, 1967–1998: A National Time-Series Analysis," *Criminology* 39:591–614 (2001); John Laub, "Review of the Crime Drop in America," *American Journal of Sociology* 106:1820–1822 (2001); John J. Donohue III and Steven D. Levitt, "The Impact of Legalized Abortion on Crime," *Quarterly Journal of Economics* 116:379–420 (2001); Robert O'Brien, Jean Stockard, and Lynne Isaacson, "The Enduring Effects of Cohort Characteristics on Age-Specific Homicide Rates, 1960–1995," *American Journal of Sociology* 104:1061–1095 (1999).

These data indicate that crime rates ebb and flow and are rarely constant. Experts believe that social, economic, and individual factors all influence the direction crime rates take. The factors that help explain the upward and downward movement in crime rates are discussed in the Focus on Delinquency feature on page 24.

Measuring Official Delinquency

disaggregated
To break down a variable into its constituent parts in order to better understand its association with another variable.

Because the UCR arrest statistics are **disaggregated** (broken down) by suspect's age, they can be used to estimate adolescent delinquency. Juvenile arrest data must be interpreted with caution, however. First, the number of teenagers arrested does not represent the actual number of youths who have committed delinquent acts. Some offenders are never counted, because they are never caught. Others are counted more than once because multiple arrests of the same individual for different crimes are counted separately in the UCR. Consequently, the total number of arrests does not equal the number of people who have been arrested. Put another way, if 2 million arrests of youths under eighteen years of age were made in a given year, we could not be sure if 2 million individuals had been arrested once or if five hundred thousand chronic offenders had been arrested four times each. In addition, when an arrested offender commits multiple crimes, only the most serious one is recorded. Therefore, if 2 million juveniles are arrested, the number of crimes committed is at least 2 million, but it may be much higher.

Despite these limitations, the nature of arrest data remains constant over time. Consequently, arrest data can provide some indication of the nature and trends in juvenile crime. What does the UCR tell us about delinquency?

Official Delinquency In 2005 (the latest data available), about 14 million arrests were made, or about 5,000 per 100,000 population. Of these, about 2 million were for serious Part I crimes and 12 million for less serious Part II crimes.

In 2005, juveniles were responsible for about 380,000 Part I arrests, including 16 percent of the Part I violent crime arrests and about 26 percent of the property crime arrests (see Table 2.1). Because kids ages fourteen through seventeen who account for almost all underage arrests constitute only about 6 percent of the population, these data show that teens account for a significantly disproportionate share of all arrests.

It is often difficult to measure the full extent of delinquency, because many acts are not included in the UCR. Here, a young man is escorted past his family after a court appearance on a charge of making a false bomb threat while boarding a flight. Would this act be reported to the FBI's program?

© AP Images/Michael Dwyer

Table 2.1 Persons Arrested, by Age

	Under 15	Under 18	Over 18
Serious violent crime	5%	16%	79%
Serious property crime	9%	26%	65%
Total all crimes	5%	15%	80%

Source: FBI, *Crime in the United States, 2005.* Available at: www.fbi.gov/ucr/05cius/data/table_38.html (accessed November 15, 2006).

About 1.2 million juvenile arrests were made in 2005 for Part II offenses. Included in this total were 81,000 arrests for running away from home, 148,000 for disorderly conduct, 138,000 for drug-abuse violations, and 104,000 for curfew violations. In all, about 1.5 million juveniles are now arrested each year.

Juvenile Delinquency Trends Juvenile delinquency continues to have a significant influence on the nation's overall crime statistics. The juvenile arrest rate began to climb in the 1980s, peaked during the mid-1990s, and then began to fall; it has since been in decline. Even the teen murder rate, which had remained stubbornly high, has undergone a decline during the past few years.[2] For example, 1,700 youths were arrested for murder in 1997, a number that by 2005 had declined by almost half (to about 900). Similarly, 3,800 juveniles were arrested for rape in 1997, and about 2,900 in 2005. However, although juvenile violence rates have declined over the past ten years, there was disturbingly, a recent uptick in juvenile violent crime arrests: Arrests of juveniles (under eighteen years of age) for murder climbed 20 percent in 2005 compared with 2004 arrest data; for robbery, arrests of juveniles rose 11.4 percent over the same two-year period.

What factors account for change in the crime and delinquency rate? This is the topic of the Focus on Delinquency box "Shaping Delinquency Trends" on page 24.

What the Future Holds Some experts, such as criminologist James A. Fox, predict a significant increase in teen violence if current population trends persist. The nation's teenage population will increase by 15 percent, or more than 9 million, between now and 2010; the number in the high-risk ages of fifteen to seventeen will increase by more than 3 million, or 31 percent. There are approximately 53 million school-age children in the United States, many younger than ten—more than we have had for decades. Although many come from stable homes, others lack stable families and adequate supervision; these are some of the children who will soon enter their prime crime years.[3]

In contrast, economist Steven Levitt believes that even though teen crime rates may eventually rise, their influence on the nation's total crime rate may be offset by the growing number of relatively crime-free senior citizens.[4] Levitt also believes that punitive policies, such as putting more kids behind bars and adding police, may help control delinquency. One problem on the horizon remains the maturation of "crack babies," who spent their early childhood years in families and neighborhoods ravaged by crack cocaine. Coupled with a difficult home environment, these children may turn out to be extremely prone to delinquency activity, producing the increase in the delinquency predicted by James A. Fox.[5]

Of course both Fox's and Levitt's prognostications, predictions, and forecasts are based on contemporary conditions that can change at any time due to the sudden emergence of war, terrorism, social unrest, economic meltdown, and the like. Although the number of adolescents in the population may shape crime rates under current conditions, the mere fact of a large juvenile population may have less of an impact serious social and economic conditions emerge in the future.[6]

ARE THE UCR DATA VALID?

Questions have been raised about the validity and accuracy of UCR's "official" crime data. Victim surveys show that less than half of all victims report the crime to police. This is especially problematic in delinquency research, because juveniles are less likely to report crimes than adults. Moreover, they are unlikely to report crimes to which they are most vulnerable: crimes committed by peers that occur on school grounds.[7] Because official data are derived entirely from police records, we can assume that a significant number of crimes are not accounted for in the UCR. There are also concerns that police departments make systematic errors in recording crime data or manipulate the data in order to give the public the impression that they are highly effective crime fighters.[8]

Using official arrest data to measure delinquency rates is particularly problematic. Arrest records count only adolescents who have been *caught*, and these youths may be different from those who evade capture. Victimless crimes, such as drug and alcohol use, are significantly undercounted using this measure. Another problem is that arrest decision criteria vary among police agencies. Some police agencies practice full enforcement, arresting all teens who violate the law, whereas others follow a policy of discretion that encourages unofficial handling of juvenile matters through social service agencies.

Although these questions are troubling, the problems associated with collecting and verifying the official UCR data are consistent and stable over time. This means that, although the absolute accuracy of the data can be questioned, the trends and patterns they show are probably reliable. In other words, we cannot be absolutely sure about the actual number of adolescents who commit crimes, but it is likely that the teen crime rate has been in a significant decline.

The National Incident-Based Reporting System (NIBRS)

The FBI is currently instituting a new program that collects data on each reported crime incident. Instead of submitting statements of the kinds of crime that individual citizens reported to the police and summary statements of resulting arrests, the new program will require local police agencies to provide at least a brief account of each incident and arrest, including the incident, victim, and offender information. Under NIBRS, law enforcement authorities will provide information to the FBI on each criminal incident involving forty-six specific offenses, including the eight Part I crimes, that occur in their jurisdiction; arrest information on the forty-six offenses plus eleven lesser offenses is also provided in NIBRS. These expanded crime categories would include numerous additional crimes, such as blackmail, embezzlement, drug offenses, and bribery; this would allow a national database on the nature of crime, victims, and criminals to be developed. So far, twenty-two states have implemented their NIBRS program and twelve others are in the process of finalizing their data collections. When this new UCR program is fully implemented and adopted across the nation, it should provide significantly better data on juvenile crime than exists today.

SELF-REPORTED DELINQUENCY

Official statistics are useful for examining general trends, but they cannot tell us how many youth commit crime but are never arrested. Nor do they reveal much about the personality, attitudes, and behavior of individual delinquents. To get information at

self-reports
Questionnaire or survey technique that asks subjects to reveal their own participation in delinquent or criminal acts.

this level, criminologists have developed alternative sources of delinquency statistics, with the most commonly used source being **self-reports** of delinquent behavior.

Self-report studies are designed to obtain information from youthful subjects about their violations of the law. They can be administered in a variety of settings with a variety of subject groupings: Youths arrested by police may be interviewed at the station house; an anonymous survey can be distributed to every student in a high school; boys in a detention center may be asked to respond to a survey; or youths randomly selected from the population of teenagers can be questioned in their homes.

The typical self-report survey is designed to measure behavior across all segments of the population. They provide information on offenders who have never been arrested and are therefore not part of the official data. They also measure behavior that is rarely detected by police, such as drug abuse, because their anonymity allows youths freely to describe their illegal activities. Surveys can also include items measuring personality characteristics, behavior, and attitudes.

Table 2.2 shows one format for self-report questions. Youths are asked to indicate how many times they have participated in illegal or deviant behavior. Other formats allow subjects to record the precise number of times they engaged in each delinquent activity. Note that the reporting period is limited to the previous twelve months here, but some surveys question lifetime activity.

Questions not directly related to delinquent activity are often included in self-report surveys. Information may be collected on self-image; intelligence; personality; attitudes toward family, friends, and school; leisure activities; and school activities. Self-report surveys also gather information on family background, social status, race, and sex. Reports of delinquent acts can be correlated with this information to create a much more complete picture of delinquent offenders than official statistics can provide.

Self-Report Validity Criminologists have used self-report studies of delinquency for more than sixty years.[9] They are a valuable source of information on the activities of youths who have had contact with the juvenile justice system as well as on the **dark figures of crime**—that is, those who have escaped official notice. However, some question of their validity still remains. Responses may be embellished by some subjects who wish to exaggerate the extent of their deviant activities, and understated by others who want to shield themselves from possible exposure. Recent (2006) research by David Kirk shows that some kids with an official arrest record deny legal involvement, whereas others who remain arrest-free report having an official record. Why would adolescents claim to have engaged in antisocial behaviors, such as getting arrested or using drugs, when in fact they had not? One reason is that they may live

dark figures of crime
Incidents of crime and delinquency that go undetected by police.

Table 2.2	Self-Report Survey Sample

Please indicate how often in the past twelve months you did each act. (Check the best answer.)

	Never did act	One time	2–5 times	6–9 times	10+ times
Stole something worth less than $50	_____	_____	_____	_____	_____
Stole something worth more than $50	_____	_____	_____	_____	_____
Used cocaine	_____	_____	_____	_____	_____
Was in a fight	_____	_____	_____	_____	_____
Carried a weapon such as a gun or a knife	_____	_____	_____	_____	_____
Fought someone using a weapon	_____	_____	_____	_____	_____

in a subculture that requires kids to be tough rule breakers unafraid of conventional authority. Kids may fear that they would be taunted or harassed if anyone found out they were not really "experienced" delinquents.[10]

Research also shows that the accuracy and validity of responses may differ between serious versus petty offenders: kids will remember armed robberies and rapes better than they do minor assaults and altercations.[11] Muddled-headed substance abusers may have a tougher time accounting for their prior misbehavior than clear-thinking burglars.[12]

Other factors that influence self-report validity are age, criminal history, recentness of the reported event, IQ, education level, and variety of criminal acts. Despite these caveats, some of the most recent research supports the validity of the self-report method with both occasional and committed delinquents, for example, gang members.[13]

What Self-Report Data Show

Most self-report studies indicate that the number of children who break the law is far greater than official statistics would lead us to believe.[14] In fact, when truancy, alcohol consumption, petty theft, and recreational drug use are included in self-report scales, delinquency appears to be almost universal. The most common offenses are truancy, drinking alcohol, using a false ID, shoplifting or larceny under five dollars, fighting, using marijuana, and damaging the property of others. In Chapter 10, self-report data will be used to gauge trends in adolescent drug abuse.

Researchers at the University of Michigan's Institute for Social Research (ISR)[15] conducted an annual national self-report survey, called Monitoring the Future (MTF), that involved a sample of about three thousand youths. Table 2.3 contains some of the data from the most recent MTF survey.

A surprising number of these *typical* teenagers reported involvement in serious criminal behavior: about 12 percent reported hurting someone badly enough that the victim needed medical care (6 percent said they did it more than once); about 29 percent reported stealing something worth less than fifty dollars, and another 10 percent stole something worth more than fifty dollars; 28 percent reported shoplifting; 11 percent had damaged school property.

Self-report data can be used to gauge the extent of gang membership in areas where gangs are not assumed to exist. Here, Robert Ryales (front) and Thaddeus Manzano, both 16, stand in the front door of Ryales' house in A Pocono Country Place, a gated community near Tobyhanna, Pennsylvania, on April 10, 2006. A few doors down, police say a reputed Crip gang member stabbed a reputed Blood gang member. Authorities say gang members from New York City and its suburbs have quietly taken up residence in some of the private, gated communities of the Poconos, where they can stake out new drug turf with little interference from municipal or state police.

© AP Images/David Kidwell

Table 2.3 Survey of Criminal Activity of High School Seniors

Crime	Total	Percentage Engaging in Offenses — Committed More Than Once
Set fire on purpose	4	2
Damaged school property	12	6
Damaged work property	7	4
Auto theft	5	3
Auto part theft	4	2
Break and enter	26	13
Theft, less than $50	27	15
Theft, more than $50	9	5
Shoplift	25	13
Gang fight	19	8
Hurt someone badly enough to require medical care	12	5
Used force to steal	4	2
Hit teacher or supervisor	3	2
Participated in serious fight	12	5

Source: *Monitoring the Future, 2005* (Ann Arbor, MI: Institute for Social Research, 2005).

 To find out more about the **Institute for Social Research**, go to the website www.thomsonedu.com/criminaljustice/siegel.

CHECKPOINTS

■ The FBI's Uniform Crime Report is an annual tally of crime reported to local police departments; it is the nation's official crime data.

■ Crime rates peaked in the early 1990s and have been in decline ever since.

■ The murder rate has undergone a particularly steep decline though it picked up between 2004 and 2005.

■ A number of factors influence delinquency trends, including the economy, drug use, availability of guns, and crime control policies.

■ During the past decade, the number of youths arrested for delinquent behavior has also declined, including a significant decrease in those arrested for violent offenses.

■ However, there was a recent upswing in juvenile violence between 2004 and 2005.

■ Self-report surveys ask respondents about their criminal activity.

■ They are useful in measuring crimes such as drug usage that are rarely reported to police.

■ Self-reports show us that a significant number of kids engage in criminal acts, far more than is measured by the arrest data.

■ It is difficult to gauge future trends. Some experts forecast an increase in juvenile crime, whereas others foresee a long-term decline in the crime rate.

If the MTF data are accurate, the juvenile crime problem is much greater than official statistics would lead us to believe. There are approximately 40 million youths between the ages of ten and eighteen. Extrapolating from the MTF findings, this group accounts for more than 100 percent of all the theft offenses reported in the UCR. More than 3 percent of high school students said they had used force to steal (which is the legal definition of a robbery). At this rate, high school students alone commit 1.2 million robberies per year. In comparison, the UCR tallies about 400,000 robberies for all age groups in 2005. Over the past decade, the MTF surveys indicate that with a few exceptions, self-reported teenage participation in theft, violence, and damage-related crimes seems to be more stable than the trends reported in the UCR arrest data.

There is also some question about the accuracy of self-report data. Reporting practices differ between racial, ethnic, and gender groups. One study found that even though girls are generally more willing to report drug use than boys, Hispanic girls tend to *underreport* substance abuse. Such gender-cultural differences in self-reporting can skew data and provide misleading results.[16] ✔ Checkpoints

Are the Data Sources Compatible?

Each source of crime data has strengths and weaknesses. The FBI survey contains data on the number and characteristics of people arrested, information that the other data sources lack. It is also the source of information on particular crimes such as murder, which no other data source can provide.[17] Although used extensively, the UCR omits the many crimes that victims choose not to report to police, and relies on the reporting accuracy of individual police departments.

Self-report data include unreported crime missed by the UCR and also contains important information on the personal characteristics of victims. However, the data in the MTF and similar surveys consist of estimates made from relatively limited samples of the total U.S. population, so that even narrow fluctuations in the rates of some crimes can have a major impact on findings. It also relies on personal recollections that may be inaccurate. Self-reports do not include data on important crime patterns, including murder.

Self-report surveys provide useful information, because questions on delinquent activity are often supplemented with items measuring the personal characteristics of offenders, such as their attitudes, values, beliefs, and psychological profiles. It can also be used to measure drug and alcohol abuse; this data is not included in the UCR. Yet, at their core, self-reports rely on the honesty of criminal offenders and drug abusers, a population not generally known for accuracy and integrity.

Although their tallies of delinquency are certainly not in synch, the patterns and trends they measure are often quite similar: when the UCR shows a drop in illegal activity, so too do self-report studies.[18] They both generally agree about the personal characteristics of serious delinquents (i.e., age and gender) and where and when delinquency occurs (i.e., urban areas, nighttime, and summer months). And because the measurement problems inherent in both sources are consistent over time they are reliable indicators of changes and fluctuations in delinquency rates.

CORRELATES OF DELINQUENCY

An important aspect of delinquency research is measurement of the personal traits and social characteristics associated with adolescent misbehavior. If, for example, a strong association exists between delinquent behavior and family income, then poverty and economic deprivation must be considered in any explanation of the onset of adolescent criminality. If the delinquency-income association is not present, then other forces may be responsible for producing antisocial behavior. It would be fruitless to concentrate delinquency control efforts in areas such as job creation and vocational training if social status were found to be unrelated to delinquent behavior. Similarly, if only a handful of delinquents are responsible for most serious crimes, then crime control policies might be made more effective by identifying and treating these offenders. The next sections discuss where and when relationship between delinquency and the characteristics of gender, race, social class, and age.

The Time and Place of Delinquency Most delinquent acts occur during the warm summer months of July and August. Weather may affect delinquent behavior in a number of different ways. During the summer, teenagers are out of school and have greater opportunity to commit crime. Homes are left vacant more often during the summer, making them more vulnerable to property crimes. Weather may also have a direct effect on behavior: as it gets warmer kids get more violent.[19] However, some experts believe if it gets too hot, over 85 degrees, the frequency of some violent acts such as sexual assault will begin to decline.[20]

There are also geographic differences in the incidence of delinquent behaviors. Large urban areas have by far the highest juvenile violence rates; rural areas have the lowest. Typically, the western and southern states have had consistently higher delinquency rates than the Midwest and Northeast that has been linked to differences in cultural values, population makeup, gun ownership, and economic differences.

Gender and Delinquency

With a few exceptions, males are significantly more delinquent than females. The teenage gender ratio for serious violent crime is approximately four to one, and for property crime approximately two to one, male to female.

The only exception to this pattern is arrests for being a runaway: Girls are more likely than boys to be arrested as runaways. There are two possible explanations for this. Girls could be more likely than boys to run away from home or police may view the female runaway as the more serious problem and therefore more likely to process girls through official justice channels. This may reflect paternalistic attitudes toward girls, who are viewed as likely to "get in trouble" if they are on the street.

Girls are increasing their involvement in violence at a faster pace than boys, and it is no longer surprising when young women commit armed robberies and murders. Police say 15-year-old Holly Harvey (right) and 16-year-old Sandy Ketchum of Fayetteville, Georgia, were involved in a romantic relationship and that Harvey's grandparents had tried to keep them apart. The two are accused of stabbing to death Harvey's grandparents. Harvey had a list inked on her arm that read, "Kill, keys, money, jewelry." Harvey pleaded guilty to two counts of malice murder and was sentenced to two consecutive life sentences. Sandy Ketchum was sentenced to three life terms for murder and armed robbery, to be served concurrently.

© AP Images/WSB-TV Channel 2

Between 1995 and 2005, during a period of rapidly declining crime rates, the number of arrests of male delinquents decreased about 28 percent, whereas the number of female delinquents arrested declined by half as much (14 percent). The average girl today is actually "less delinquent" than her older sisters.

Self-report data also seem to show that the incidence of female delinquency is much higher than believed earlier, and that the most common crimes committed by males are also the ones most female offenders commit.[21] Table 2.4 shows the percentages of male and female high school seniors who admitted engaging in delinquent acts during the past twelve months in the latest MTF survey. As the table indicates, about 35 percent of boys and 22 percent of girls admit to shoplifting; 16 percent of boys and 7 percent of girls said they stole something worth more than fifty dollars, and 18 percent of boys and 6 percent of girls said they hurt someone badly enough

Table 2.4 Percentage of High School Seniors Admitting to at Least One Offense During the Past 12 Months, by Gender

Delinquent Acts	Males	Females
Serious fight	13	9
Gang fight	22	16
Hurt someone badly	18	6
Used a weapon to steal	5	1
Stole less than $50	33	22
Stole more than $50	16	7
Shoplift	35	22
Breaking and entering	30	22
Arson	5	1
Damaged school property	17	7

Source: *Monitoring the Future, 2005* (Ann Arbor, MI: Institute for Social Research, 2005).

that they required medical care. Over the past decade, girls have increased their self-reported delinquency, whereas boys report somewhat less involvement. Because the relationship between gender and delinquency rate is so important, this topic will be discussed further in Chapter 6.

Although these trends indicate that gender differences in the crime rate may be eroding, some experts, such as Darrell Steffensmeier and his associates, remain skeptical. They believe that female arrest trends may be explained more by changes in police activity than in criminal activity: Police today may be more willing to arrest girls for crimes than ever before.[22] What appears to be increases in female delinquency may be a function of police activity rather than changes in behavior patterns.

Race and Delinquency

There are approximately 41 million European American and 9 million African American youths ages five to seventeen, a ratio of about five to one. Yet racial minorities are disproportionately represented in the arrest statistics (see Exhibit 2.1).

The official statistics show that minority youths are arrested for serious criminal behavior at a rate that is disproportionate to their representation in the population. To many delinquency experts, this pattern reflects discrimination in the juvenile justice system. In other words, African American youths are more likely to be formally arrested by the police, who, in contrast, will treat European American youths informally. One way to examine this issue is to compare the racial differences in self-reported data with those found in the official delinquency records. Given the disproportionate numbers of African Americans arrested, charges of racial discrimination would be supported if we found little difference between the number of self-reported minority and European American crimes.

Early researchers found that the relationship between race and self-reported delinquency was virtually nonexistent.[23] This suggests that racial differences in the official crime data may reflect the fact that African American youths have a much greater chance of being arrested and officially processed.[24] Self-report studies also suggest that the delinquent behavior rates of African American and European American teenagers are generally similar and that differences in arrest statistics may indicate discrimination by police.[25] The MTF survey, for example, generally shows that offending differences between African American and European American youths are marginal.[26] However, some experts warn that African American youths may underreport more serious crimes, limiting the ability of self-reports to be a valid indicator of racial differences in the crime rate.[27]

Exhibit 2.1 Racial Trends in the Arrest Data

- About 70 percent of all persons arrested were European American, 30 percent were African American

- About 60 percent of persons arrested for violent crime were European American, 40 percent African American

- About 70 percent of persons arrested for property crime were European American, 30 percent African American.

- African American juveniles composed about half of all juveniles arrested in 2005 for violent crime and about one-third of all juveniles arrested for property crime.

- European American juveniles composed about 68 percent of all juveniles arrested in 2005, 67 percent of juveniles arrested for property crime, and about half of all those arrested for violent crime.

Source: FBI, *Uniform Crime Reports, 2005.* Available at: www.fbi.gov/ucr/05cius/arrests/index.html (accessed November 15, 2006).

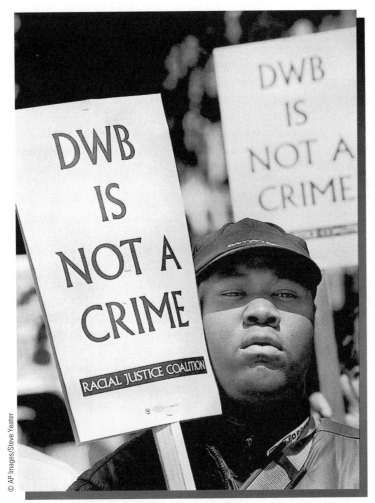

Some experts believe that racial differences in the juvenile arrest rate are a function of police officer bias. Although African American and European American juveniles commit crimes at the same rate, the former are much more likely to get arrested and maintain an official record. Lonnell McGhee of Oakland, California, listens to speakers at a rally against racial profiling at the state capitol in Sacramento, California. Hundreds of others were there to show support for SB1389, the so-called "DWB Bill," or "Driving While Black/Brown Bill."

© AP Images/Steve Yeater

Bias Effects How can the disproportionate number of African American youngsters arrested for serious crimes be explained? One view is that it is a result of bias by the police and courts. Minority group members are more likely to be formally arrested than European Americans.[28] According to the racial threat theory, as the size of the African American population increases, the perceived threat to the European American population increases, resulting in a greater amount of social control imposed against African Americans by police.[29] Police will then routinely search, question, and detain all African American males in an area if a violent criminal has been described as "looking or sounding Black"; this is called *racial profiling.* African American youth who develop a police record are more likely to be severely punished if they are picked up again and sent back to juvenile court.[30] Consequently, the racial discrimination that is present at the early stages of the justice system ensures that minorities receive greater punishments at its conclusion.[31]

Juvenile court judges may see the offenses committed by African American youths as more serious than those committed by European American offenders. Consequently, they are more likely to keep minority juveniles in detention pending trial in juvenile court than they are European American youth with similar backgrounds.[32] European American juveniles are more likely to receive lenient sentences or have their cases dismissed their cases.[33] As a result, African American youths are more likely to get an official record.

According to this view then, the disproportionate number of minority youth who are arrested is less a function of their involvement in serious crime and more the result of the race-based decision making that is found in the juvenile justice system.[34] Institutional racism by police and the courts is still an element of daily life in the African American community, a factor that undermines faith in social and political institutions and weakens confidence in the justice system.[35]

Race Matters The other point of view holds that although evidence of racial bias does exist in the justice system, there is enough correspondence between official and self-report data to conclude that racial differences in the crime rate are real.[36] If African American youths are arrested at a disproportionately high rate for crimes, such as robbery and assault, it is a result of actual offending rates rather than bias on the part of the criminal justice system.[37]

If they exist, how can racial differences in the delinquency rate be explained? One view is that racial differentials are tied to the social and economic disparity suffered by African American youths. Too many are forced to live in the nation's poorest areas that suffer high crime rates.[38] Many African American youth are forced to attend essentially segregated schools that are underfunded and deteriorated, a condition that increases the likelihood of their being incarcerated in adulthood.[39] The burden of social and economic marginalization has weakened the African American family structure. When families are weakened or disrupted, their ability to act as social control agents is compromised.[40]

Even during times of economic growth, lower-class African Americans are left out of the economic mainstream, causing a growing sense of frustration and failure.[41] As a result of being shut out of educational and economic opportunities enjoyed by the rest of society, this population may be prone, some believe, to the lure of illegitimate gain and criminality. However, even among at-risk African American kids growing up in communities characterized by poverty, high unemployment levels, and single-parent households, those who do live in stable families with reasonable incomes and educational achievement are much less likely to engage in violent behaviors than those lacking family support.[42] Consequently, racial differences in the delinquency rate would evaporate if the social and economic characteristics of racial minorities were improved to levels currently enjoyed by European American, and if African American kids could enjoy the same vocational and educational privileges.[43]

In summary, official data indicate that African American youths are arrested for more serious crimes than European Americans. However, self-report studies show that the differences in the rates of delinquency between the races are insignificant. Therefore, some experts believe that official differences in the delinquency rate are an artifact of bias in the justice system: police are more likely to arrest and courts are more likely to convict young African Americans.[44] To those who believe that the official data have validity, the participation of African American youths in serious criminal behavior is generally viewed as a function of their socioeconomic position and the racism they face.

www If you want to learn more about race-related issues in America, go to the NAACP website via www.thomsonedu.com/criminaljustice/siegel.

Social Class and Delinquency

Defining the relationship between economic status and delinquent behavior is a key element in the study of delinquency. If youth crime is purely a lower-class phenomenon, its cause must be rooted in the social forces that are found solely in lower-class areas: poverty, unemployment, social disorganization, culture conflict, and alienation. However, if delinquent behavior is spread throughout the social structure, its cause must be related to some non-economic factor: intelligence, personality, socialization, family dysfunction, educational failure, or peer influence. According to this line of reasoning, providing jobs or economic incentives would have little effect on the crime rate because the root cause of delinquency would be found in the individual and not his or her socioeconomic status.

At first glance, the relationship between class and crime seems clear. Youths who lack wealth or social standing are the most likely to use criminal means to achieve their goals. Communities that lack economic and social opportunities produce high levels of frustration. Kids who live in these areas believe that they can never compete socially or economically with adolescents being raised in more affluent areas. They may turn to criminal behavior for monetary gain and psychological satisfaction.[45] Family life is disrupted in these low-income areas, and law-violating youth groups thrive in a climate that undermines and neutralizes adult supervision.[46]

Research on Social Class and Delinquency The social class–delinquency relationship was challenged by pioneering self-report studies, specifically those that revealed no direct relationship between social class and the commission of delinquent acts.[47] Instead, socioeconomic class was related to the manner of official processing by police, court, and correctional agencies.[48] In other words, although both poor and affluent kids get into fights, shoplift, and take drugs, only the indigent are likely to be arrested and sent to juvenile court.[49] This finding casts doubt on the assumption that poverty and lower-class position is a significant cause of delinquent behavior.

Those who fault self-report studies point to the inclusion of trivial offenses—for example, using a false ID—in most self-report instruments. Although middle- and upper-class youths may appear to be as delinquent as those in the lower class, it is because they engage in significant amounts of such status offenses. Lower-class youths are more likely to engage in serious delinquent acts.[50]

In sum, there are those experts who believe that antisocial behavior occurs at all levels of the social strata. Other experts argue that, although some middle- and upper-class youths engage in some forms of minor illegal activity and theft offenses, it is under-class youth who are responsible for the majority of serious delinquent acts.[51] The prevailing wisdom is that kids who engage in the most serious forms of delinquency (for example, gang violence) are more likely to be members of the lower class.

To get information on the **economic status of America's children**, go to the federal government's website via www.thomsonedu.com/criminaljustice/siegel.

Age and Delinquency

It is generally believed that age is inversely related to criminality: as people age, the likelihood that they will commit crime declines.[52] Official statistics tell us that young people are arrested at a disproportionate rate to their numbers in the population, and this finding is supported by victim surveys. As you may recall, youths ages fourteen through seventeen make up about 6 percent of the total U.S. population, but account for about 15 percent for all arrests. In contrast, adults age fifty and older, who make up slightly less than a third of the population, account for only about 6 percent of arrests. Figure 2.2 shows that even though the number of arrests has been in decline, the peak age for arrest remains the teen years.

Why Age Matters What is the true association between age and crime? One view is that the relationship is constant: regardless of race, sex, social class, intelligence, or any other social variable, people commit less crime as they age.[53] This is referred to as the *aging-out process*, sometimes called *desistance from crime* or *spontaneous remission*. According to this viewpoint, even the most chronic juvenile offenders will commit less crime as they age.[54] Because almost everyone eventually ages out of crime, it is difficult to predict or identify the relatively few offenders who will continue to commit crime as they travel through their life course.[55]

aging-out process (also known as desistance from crime or spontaneous remission)
The tendency for youths to reduce the frequency of their offending behavior as they age; aging out is thought to occur among all groups of offenders.

There are also experts who disagree with the concept of spontaneous remission. They suggest that age is one important determinant of crime, but that other factors directly associated with a person's lifestyle, such as peer relations, also affect offending rates.[56] The probability that a person will become a persistent career criminal is influenced by a number of personal and environmental factors.[57] Evidence exists, for example, that the **age of onset** of a delinquent career has an important effect on its length: those who demonstrate antisocial tendencies at a very early age are more likely to commit more crimes for a longer period of time. This is referred to as the *developmental view of delinquency*.

age of onset
Age at which youths begin their delinquent careers; early onset is believed to be linked with chronic offending patterns.

In summary, some criminologists believe youths who get involved with delinquency at a very early age are most likely to become career criminals. These researchers believe age is a key determinant of delinquency.[58] Those opposed to this view find that all people commit less crime as they age and that because the relationship between age and crime is constant, it is irrelevant to the study of delinquency.[59]

LOOKING BACK TO JAMESETTA'S STORY

As Jamesetta grew older, she was less involved in criminal activity. Discuss the reasons for the "aging-out" process and apply them to this case example.

Why Does Crime Decline with Age? Although there is certainly disagreement about the nature of the aging-out process, there is no question that people commit less crime as they grow older. Delinquency experts have developed a number of reasons for the aging-out process:

Figure 2.2 **Relationship Between Age and Serious Crime Arrests**

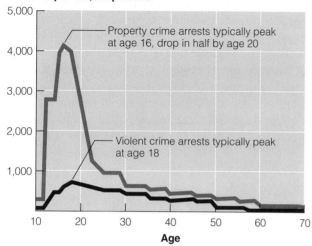

Arrest rate per 100,000 persons

Property crime arrests typically peak at age 16, drop in half by age 20

Violent crime arrests typically peak at age 18

Age

Source: FBI, *Uniform Crime Report, 2005*. Available at: www.fbi.gov/ucr/05cius/data/table_38.html (accessed December 24, 2006).

■ *Growing older means having to face the future.* Young people, especially the indigent and antisocial, tend to "discount the future."[60] Why should they delay gratification when faced with an uncertain future?

■ *With maturity comes the ability to resist the "quick fix" to their problems.*[61] Research shows that some kids may turn to crime as a way to solve the problems of adolescence, loneliness, frustration, and fear of peer rejection. As they mature, conventional means of problem solving become available. Life experience helps former delinquents seek out nondestructive solutions to their personal problems.[62]

■ *Maturation coincides with increased levels of responsibility.* Petty crimes are risky and exciting social activities that provide adventure in an otherwise boring world. As youths grow older, they take on new responsibilities that are inconsistent with criminality.[63] For example, young people who marry, enlist in the armed services, or enroll in vocational training courses are less likely to pursue criminal activities.[64]

■ *Personalities can change with age.* As youths mature, rebellious youngsters may develop increased self-control and be able to resist antisocial behavior.[65]

■ *Young adults become more aware of the risks that accompany crime.* As adults, they are no longer protected by the relatively kindly arms of the juvenile justice system.[66]

Of course, not all juvenile criminals desist as they age; some go on to become chronic adult offenders. Yet even they slow down as they age. Crime is too dangerous, physically taxing, and unrewarding, and punishments too harsh and long lasting, to become a way of life for most people.[67]

Most experts believe crime declines with age. One reason is that maturity brings new responsibilities, such as marriage and parenthood, which reduce the opportunity to commit crime.

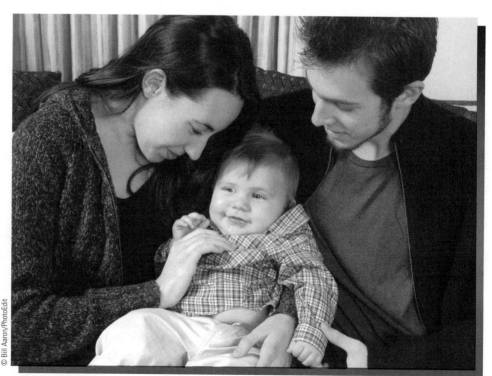

© Bill Aaron/PhotoEdit

CHRONIC OFFENDING: CAREERS IN DELINQUENCY

Although most adolescents age out of crime, a relatively small number of youths begin to violate the law early in their lives (early onset) and continue at a high rate well into adulthood (persistence).[68] The association between early onset and high-rate persistent offending has been demonstrated in samples drawn from a variety of cultures, time periods, and offender types.[69] These offenders are resistant to change and seem immune to the effects of punishment. Arrest, prosecution, and conviction do little to slow down their offending careers. These *chronic offenders* are responsible for a significant amount of all delinquent and criminal activity.

Current interest in the delinquent life cycle was prompted in part by the "discovery" in the 1970s of the **chronic juvenile** (or delinquent) **offender**. According to this view, a relatively small number of youthful offenders commit a significant percentage of all serious crimes, and many of these same offenders grow up to become chronic adult criminals.

Chronic offenders can be distinguished from other delinquent youths. Many youthful law violators are apprehended for a single instance of criminal behavior, such as shoplifting or joyriding. Chronic offenders begin their delinquent careers at a young age (under ten years, referred to as early onset), have serious and persistent brushes with the law, and may be excessively violent and destructive. They do not age out of crime, but continue their law-violating behavior into adulthood.[70] Most research shows that early, repeated delinquent activity is the best predictor of future adult criminality.

A number of research efforts have set out to chronicle the careers of serious delinquent offenders. The next sections describe these initiatives.

Delinquency in a Birth Cohort

The concept of the chronic career offender is most closely associated with the research efforts of Marvin Wolfgang.[71] In 1972, Wolfgang, Robert Figlio, and Thorsten Sellin published a landmark study, *Delinquency in a Birth Cohort*. They followed the delinquent careers of a cohort of 9,945 boys born in Philadelphia from birth until they reached age eighteen. Data were obtained from police files and school records. Socioeconomic status was determined by locating the residence of each member of the cohort and assigning him the median family income for that area. About one-third of the boys (3,475) had some police contact. The remaining two-thirds (6,470) had none. Those boys who had at least one contact with the police committed a total of 10,214 offenses.

The most significant discovery of Wolfgang and his associates was that of the so-called chronic offender. The data indicated that 54 percent (1,862) of the sample's delinquent youths were repeat offenders. The repeaters could be further categorized as non-chronic recidivists and **chronic recidivists**. *Non-chronic recidivists* had been arrested more than once but fewer than five times. In contrast, the 627 boys labeled *chronic recidivists* had been arrested five times or more. Although these offenders accounted for only 18 percent of the delinquent population (6 percent of the total sample), they were responsible for 52 percent of all offenses. Known today as the "chronic 6 percent," this group perpetrated 71 percent of the homicides, 82 percent of the robberies, and 64 percent of the aggravated assaults (see Figure 2.3).

Arrest and juvenile court experience did little to deter chronic offenders. In fact, the greater the punishment, the more likely they were to engage in repeat delinquent behavior. Strict punishment also increased the probability that further court action would be taken. Two factors stood out as encouraging recidivism: the seriousness of the original offense and the severity of the punishment. The researchers concluded that efforts of the juvenile justice system to eliminate delinquent behavior may be futile.

chronic juvenile offenders (also known as chronic delinquent offenders, chronic delinquents, or chronic recidivists) Youths who have been arrested four or more times during their minority and perpetuate a striking majority of serious criminal acts; this small group, known as the "chronic 6 percent," is believed to engage in a significant portion of all delinquent behavior; these youths do not age out of crime but continue their criminal behavior into adulthood.

chronic recidivists A youth who has been arrested five times or more before age eighteen.

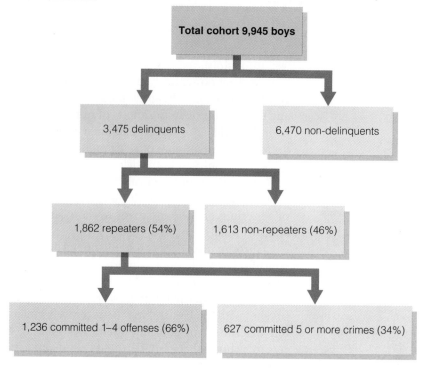

Figure 2.3 **Distribution of Offenses in the Philadelphia Cohort**

Source: Marvin Wolfgang, Robert Figlio, and Thorsten Sellen, *Delinquency in a Birth Cohort* (Chicago: University of Chicago Press, 1972).

LOOKING BACK TO JAMESETTA'S STORY

What childhood risk factors did Jamesetta have regarding the possibility of becoming a persistent delinquent? How was this avoided? What can be done to reduce chronic offending among at-risk youth?

Wolfgang and his colleagues conducted a second cohort study with children born in 1958 and substantiated the finding that a relatively few chronic offenders are responsible for a significant portion of all delinquent acts.[72] Wolfgang's results have been duplicated in a number of research studies conducted in locales across the United States and also in Great Britain.[73] Some have used the records of court-processed youths and others have employed self-report data.

Stability in Crime: From Delinquent to Criminal

Do chronic juvenile offenders grow up to become chronic adult criminals? One study that followed a 10 percent sample of the original Pennsylvania cohort (974 subjects) to age thirty found that 70 percent of the "persistent" adult offenders had also been chronic juvenile offenders. Chronic juvenile offenders had an 80 percent chance of becoming adult offenders and a 50 percent chance of being arrested four or more times as adults.[74] Paul Tracy and Kimberly Kempf-Leonard conducted a follow-up study of all the subjects in the second 1958 cohort. By age twenty-six, Cohort II subjects were displaying the same behavior patterns as their older peers. Kids who started their delinquent careers early, committed a violent crime, and continued offending throughout adolescence were most likely to persist in criminal behavior as adults. Delinquents who began their offending careers with serious offenses or who quickly increased the severity of their offending early in life were most likely to persist in their criminal behavior into adulthood. Severity of offending rather than frequency of criminal behavior had the greatest impact on later adult criminality.[75]

These studies indicate that chronic juvenile offenders continue their law-violating careers as adults, a concept referred to as the **continuity of crime**. Kids who are disruptive as early as age five or six are most likely to exhibit disruptive behavior throughout adolescence.[76]

What Causes Chronic Offending?

Research indicates that chronic offenders suffer from a number of personal, environmental, social, and developmental deficits, as shown in Exhibit 2.2. Other research studies have found that involvement in criminal activity (for example, getting arrested before age fifteen), relatively low intellectual development, and parental drug involvement were key predictive factors for future chronic offending.[77] Measurable problems in learning and motor skills, cognitive abilities, family relations, and other areas also predict chronicity.[78] Youthful offenders who persist are more likely to abuse alcohol, become economically dependent, have lower aspirations, and have a weak employment record.[79] Apprehension and punishment seem to have little effect on their offending behavior. Youths who have long juvenile records will most likely continue their offending careers into adulthood.

Policy Implications

Efforts to chart the life cycle of crime and delinquency will have a major influence on both theory and policy. Rather than simply asking why youths become delinquent or commit antisocial acts, theorists are charting the onset, escalation, frequency, and cessation of delinquent behavior. Research on delinquent careers has also influenced policy. If relatively few offenders commit a great proportion of all delinquent acts and then persist as adult criminals, it follows that steps should

CHECKPOINTS

■ Official arrest statistics, victim data, and self-reports indicate that males are significantly more delinquent than females. In recent years, however, the female delinquency rate appears to be increasing faster than that for males.

■ Although the true association between class and delinquency is still unknown, the official data tell us that delinquency rates are highest in areas with high rates of poverty.

■ African American youths are arrested for a disproportionate number of delinquent acts, such as robbery and assault, whereas European American youths are arrested for a disproportionate share of arson and alcohol-related violations.

■ Some criminologists suggest that institutional racism, such as police profiling, accounts for the racial differences in the delinquency rate. Others believe that high African American delinquency rates are a function of living in a racially segregated society.

■ Kids who engage in the most serious forms of delinquency are more likely to be members of the lower class.

■ Delinquency rates decline with age. As youthful offenders mature, the likelihood that they will commit offenses declines.

■ Not all juvenile criminals desist as they age; some go on to become chronic adult offenders.

■ Chronic offenders commit a significant portion of all delinquent acts.

■ Age of onset has an important effect on a delinquent career: those who demonstrate antisocial tendencies at a very early age are more likely to commit more crimes for a longer duration.

| Exhibit 2.2 | Childhood Risk Factors for Persistent Delinquency |

Individual Factors

- Early antisocial behavior
- Emotional factors, such as high behavioral activation and low behavioral inhibition
- Poor cognitive development
- Low intelligence
- Hyperactivity

School and Community Factors

- Failure to bond to school
- Poor academic performance
- Low academic aspirations
- Living in a poor family
- Neighborhood disadvantage
- Disorganized neighborhoods
- Concentration of delinquent peer groups
- Access to weapons

Family Factors

- Parenting
- Maltreatment
- Family violence
- Divorce
- Parental psychopathology
- Familial antisocial behaviors
- Teenage parenthood
- Family structure
- Large family size

Peer Factors

- Association with deviant peers
- Peer rejection

Source: Gail Wasserman, Kate Keenan, Richard Tremblay, John Coie, Todd Herrenkohl, Rolf Loeber, and David Petechuk, "Risk and Protective Factors of Child Delinquency," *Child Delinquency Bulletin Series* (Washington, DC: Office of Juvenile Justice and Delinquency Prevention, 2003).

LOOKING BACK TO JAMESETTA'S STORY

Family problems may be a key determinate of chronic offending. Families can also be a great resource for delinquent teens who otherwise would be placed in the foster care system. How did such support influence Jamesetta's success? What do relatives need from the system to help them parent these often difficult teenagers?

be taken to limit their criminal opportunities.[80] One approach is to identify persistent offenders at the beginning of their offending careers and provide early treatment.[81] This might be facilitated by research aimed at identifying traits (for example, impulsive personalities) that can be used to classify high-risk offenders.[82] Because many of these youths suffer from a variety of problems, treatment must be aimed at a broad range of educational, family, vocational, and psychological problems. Focusing on a single problem, such as a lack of employment, may be ineffective.[83] ✔ **Checkpoints**

JUVENILE VICTIMIZATION

victimization
A person who has suffered direct, or threatened, physical, emotional, or financial harm as a result of being the target of a criminal act.

Juveniles are also victims of crime, and data from victim surveys can help us understand the nature of juvenile **victimization**. One source of juvenile victimization data is the result of an ongoing cooperative effort of the Bureau of Justice Statistics of the U.S. Department of Justice and the U.S. Census Bureau called the National Crime Victimization Survey (NCVS).[84] The NCVS is a household survey of victims of criminal behavior that measures the nature of the crime and the characteristics of victims.

The total annual sample size of the NCVS has been about forty thousand households, containing about seventy-five thousand individuals. The sample is broken down into subsamples of ten thousand households, and each group is interviewed twice a year. The NCVS has been conducted annually for more than fifteen years.

Victimization in the United States

The NCVS provides estimates of the total number of personal contact crimes (assault, rape, robbery) and household victimizations (burglary, larceny, vehicle theft). The survey indicates that currently about 23 million criminal incidents occur each year. Being the target or victim of rape, robbery, or assault is a terrible burden, and one that can have considerable long-term consequences. If we translate the value of pain, emotional trauma, disability, and risk of death into dollar terms, the cost is $450 billion, or $1,800 for every person in the United States.[85] At first glance these figures seem overwhelming, but victimization rates are stable or declining for most crime categories.

Many of the differences between NCVS data and official statistics can be attributed to the fact that victimizations are frequently not reported. Less than half of all violent crime victimizations and 40 percent of all property crime victimizations are reported to the police.

Young Victims NCVS data indicate that young people are much more likely to be the victims of crime than adults. The chance of victimization declines with age. The difference is particularly striking when we compare teens under age nineteen with people over age sixty-five: teens are more than fifteen times as likely to become victims than their grandparents. The data also indicate that male teenagers have a significantly higher chance than females of becoming victims of violent crime, and that African American youth have a greater chance of becoming victims of violent crimes than European Americans of the same age.[86]

✔ CHECKPOINTS

■ The National Crime Victimization Survey (NCVS) samples about seventy-five thousand people annually in order to estimate the total number of criminal incidents, including those not reported to police.

■ Males are more often the victims of delinquency than females.

■ Younger people are more often targets than older people.

■ African American rates of violent victimization are much higher than European American rates. Crime victimization tends to be intraracial.

■ Self-report data show that a significant number of adolescents become crime victims. The NCVS may underreport juvenile victimization.

Aging and Wisdom

The research tells us that delinquency declines with age and this book mentions a number of possible reasons for the current "crime drop." Even those of us who did some wild things in our youth behave more responsibly as we get older. But it is difficult, even for us, to understand why this change occurs. The cause might be purely physical: as people age, most become physically weaker. Even professional athletes have to retire in their thirties; the forty-plus athlete is a rare bird. Or it may be social: all of our old friends who use to be "party animals" are now married with children.

1. Have you changed since your high school days? Do you feel responsibility and maturity setting in? In other words, are you slowly turning into your parents?
2. If so, what do you think is the cause: changes in you or changes in your environment?

Juveniles are much more likely to become crime victims than adults. They have a more dangerous lifestyle, which places them at risk for crime. They spend a great deal of time in one of the most dangerous areas in the community, the local school, and hang out with the most dangerous people, fellow teenagers!

The Victims and Their Criminals

NCVS data can also tell us something about the relationship between victims and offenders. This information is available because victims of violent personal crimes, such as assault and robbery, can identify the age, sex, and race of their attackers.

In general, teens tend to be victimized by their peers. A majority of teens were shown to have been victimized by other teens, whereas victims age twenty and over identified their attackers as being twenty-one or older. However, people in almost all age groups who were victimized by *groups* of offenders identified their attackers as teenagers. Violent crime victims report that a disproportionate number of their attackers are young, ranging in age from sixteen to twenty-five.

The data also tell us that victimization is intraracial (that is, within race). European American teenagers tend to be victimized by European American teens, and African American teenagers tend to be victimized by African American teens.

Most teens are victimized by people with whom they are acquainted, and their victimization is more likely to occur during the day. In contrast, adults are more often victimized by strangers, and at night. One explanation for this pattern is that youths are at greatest risk from their own family and relatives. (Chapter 8 deals with the issue of child abuse and neglect.) Another possibility is that many teenage victimizations occur at school, in school buildings, or on school grounds. ✔ Checkpoints

Despite some sensational cases, the number of children abducted or murdered by strangers is less than commonly thought. However, when a young child is victimized, the impact can devastate an entire community. Kidnap victim Carlie Brucia, 11, is shown being led away by an unidentified man February 1, 2004. This image was taken by an exterior motion-sensor surveillance camera at a car wash. Carlie's body was found five days after she was abducted. On December 1, 2005, Joseph Smith, a Florida auto mechanic, was sentenced to death for her rape and murder. This tragic case sadly shows the vulnerability of children to predatory criminals.

© Photo by Sarasota County Sheriff's Office via Getty Images

18:21:41 02/01/2004

SUMMARY

■ Official delinquency refers to youths who are arrested.

■ Arrest data come from the FBI's Uniform Crime Report (UCR), an annual tally of crimes reported to police by citizens.

■ The FBI gathers arrest statistics from local police departments. From these, it is possible to determine the number of youths who are arrested each year, along with their age, race, and gender.

■ About 1.5 million youths are arrested annually.

■ After a long increase in juvenile crime, there has been a decade decrease in the number of juveniles arrested for nonviolent and violent crimes.

■ Dissatisfaction with the UCR prompted criminologists to develop other means of measuring delinquent behavior. Self-reports are surveys in which subjects are asked to describe their misbehavior. Although self-reports indicate that many more crimes are committed than are known to the police, they also show that the delinquency rate is rather stable.

■ The factors that are believed to shape and control teen delinquency rates include gang activity, drug abuse, and teen gun ownership, abortion rates, economy, punishment, and social conditions.

■ Delinquents are disproportionately male, although female delinquency rates are rising faster than those for males.

■ Minority youth are overrepresented in the delinquency rate, especially for violent crime. Experts are split on the cause of racial differences. Some believe they are a function of system bias, others see them as representing actual differences in the delinquency rate.

■ Disagreement also exists over the relationship between class position and delinquency. Some hold that adolescent crime is a lower-class phenomenon, whereas others see it throughout the social structure. Problems in methodology have obscured the true class-crime relationship. However, official statistics indicate that lower-class youths are responsible for the most serious criminal acts.

■ There is general agreement that delinquency rates decline with age. Some experts believe this phenomenon is universal, whereas others believe a small group of offenders persist in crime at a high rate. The age-crime relationship has spurred research on the nature of delinquency over the life course.

■ Delinquency data show the existence of a chronic persistent offender who begins his or her offending career early in life and persists as an adult. Wolfgang and his colleagues identified chronic offenders in a series of cohort studies conducted in Philadelphia.

■ Ongoing research has identified the characteristics of persistent offenders as they mature, and both personality and social factors help us predict long-term offending patterns.

■ The National Crime Victimization Survey (NCVS) is an annual national survey of the victims of crime that is conducted by agencies of the federal government.

■ Teenagers are much more likely to become victims of crime than are people in other age groups.

KEY TERMS

Federal Bureau of Investigation (FBI), p. 23

Uniform Crime Report (UCR), p. 23

Part I offenses, p. 23

Part II offenses, p. 23

disaggregated, p. 26

self-reports, p. 29

dark figures of crime, p. 29

aging-out process, desistance, spontaneous remission, p. 37

age of onset, p. 37

chronic juvenile offenders, p. 39

chronic recidivists, p. 39

continuity of crime, p. 41

victimization, p. 42

QUESTIONS FOR DISCUSSION

1. What factors contribute to the aging-out process?

2. Why are males more delinquent than females? Is it a matter of lifestyle, culture, or physical properties?

3. Discuss the racial differences found in the crime rate. What factors account for differences in the African American and European American crime rates?

4. Should kids who have been arrested more than three times be given mandatory incarceration sentences?

5. Do you believe that self-reports are an accurate method of gauging the nature and extent of delinquent behavior?

As a juvenile court judge you are forced to make a tough decision during a hearing: whether a juvenile should be waived to the adult court. It seems that gang activity has become a way of life for residents living in local public housing projects. The "Bloods" sell crack, and the "Wolfpack" controls the drug market. When the rivalry between the two gangs exploded, sixteen-year-old Shatiek Johnson, a Wolfpack member, shot and killed a member of the Bloods; in retaliation, the Bloods put out a contract on his life. While in hiding, Shatiek was confronted by two undercover detectives who recognized the young fugitive. Fearing for his life, Shatiek pulled a pistol and began firing, fatally wounding one of the officers. During the hearing, you learn that Shatiek's story is not dissimilar from that of many other children raised in tough housing projects. With an absent father and a single mother who could not control her five sons, Shatiek lived in a world of drugs, gangs, and shootouts long before he was old enough to vote. By age thirteen, Shatiek had been involved in the gang-beating death of a homeless man in a dispute over ten dollars, for which he was given a one-year sentence at a youth detention center and released after six months. Now charged with a crime that could be considered first-degree murder if committed by an adult, Shatiek could—if waived to the adult court—be sentenced to life in prison.

At the hearing, Shatiek seems like a lost soul. He claims he thought the police officers were killers out to collect the bounty put on his life by the Bloods. He says that killing the police officer was an act of self-defense. The DA confirms that the victim was in fact a known gang assassin with numerous criminal convictions. Shatiek's mother begs you to consider the fact that her son is only sixteen years old, that he has had a very difficult childhood, and that he is a victim of society's indifference to the poor.

Would you treat Shatiek as a juvenile and see if a prolonged stay in a youth facility could help this troubled young man, or would you transfer (waive) him to the adult justice system? Does a sixteen-year-old like Shatiek deserve a second chance? Is Shatiek's behavior common among adolescent boys or unusual and disturbing?

DOING RESEARCH ON THE WEB

To help you answer these questions and to learn more about gang membership, go to **www.thomsonedu.com/criminaljustice/ siegel** to access the federal site for the National Criminal Justice Reference service, a U.N. site that offers important information, and a site on a private treatment center.

Individual Views of Delinquency: Choice and Trait

© Mika/zefa/Corbis

CHAPTER OBJECTIVES

After reading this chapter you should:

1. Know the difference between choice and trait theories.
2. Understand the concept of criminal choice.
3. Be familiar with the concept of routine activities.
4. Be able to discuss the pros and cons of general deterrence.
5. Recognize what is meant by the term *specific deterrence*.
6. Understand the concept of situational crime prevention.
7. Know the biochemical, neurological, and genetic factors linked to delinquency.
8. Understand the psychodynamic model of delinquency.
9. Understand why, according to the behavioral perspective, watching violent media causes violent behaviors.
10. Be familiar with the term *psychopath*.
11. Recognize the issues linking intelligence to delinquency.

Sixteen-year-old Eric Peterson's parents divorced when he was very young; there had been a history of domestic violence in his Minnesota family. Eric, an only child, was diagnosed with attention-deficit/hyperactivity disorder (ADHD) at the age of eight, and also was suffering from reading and math deficiencies. Diagnosed with learning disabilities, Eric had challenges at school and was struggling academically.

About a year ago, Eric's mother became extremely concerned about his behavior, both at home and at school. Eric was acting aggressively at school and had been involved in several fights. Although his teachers were understanding, some were openly concerned about his sudden hostility and believed he posed a threat to the safety of the other children; he was on the verge of expulsion. At home Eric was defiant, refused to obey his mother's rules, and was often verbally abusive. He made verbal threats toward his mother and damaged property in their home. Part of Eric's problem might have been linked to his expanding substance abuse. He had a history of smoking marijuana on a regular basis. Although he had recently completed a drug and alcohol assessment and treatment program, his drug use persisted.

Sensing that a crisis was about to explode, Eric's mother got in contact with Family and Children's Services of Minnesota and requested assistance. After completing their initial assessment, Family and Children's Services provided Eric and his mother with family therapy and individual counseling. The family received treatment to address the issues at home and to try to provide support for them both. Eric's mother was given help with establishing rules and creating consequences for misbehavior. Eric participated in individual counseling to address his anger issues. During these sessions, Eric admitted that in addition to being physically aggressive toward his mother and peers at school, he was also physically abusing his girlfriend. Eric was honest about his behavior and indicated a desire to stop the abuse. He did not blame others for his behavior and took responsibility for his actions, an attitude that bolstered his counselor's belief that he could be helped by a proper treatment regime.

Eric was referred to the Adolescent Domestic Abuse Program, a unique counseling program for boys ages thirteen through seventeen who are physically abusive or intimidating to a family member or dating partner. The program involves ten weeks of group counseling with other young men who have also been involved in this type of violent behavior. The treatment protocol includes a family counseling component to help stop the abuse and help the family heal. Eric made an excellent connection with the group facilitator and worked very hard to address his behavior.

In this instance, the Adolescent Domestic Abuse Program proved to be a successful treatment milieu: Eric was able to stop his abusive behavior and create a better life for himself and his family. He has gone on to assist other teens stop the cycle of domestic violence by becoming a regular speaker and volunteer at the Adolescent Domestic Abuse Program and at local schools. Eric has also graduated from high school and has even started college classes. His goal: to work with troubled teens and set them on the path to a better life, just like the one he took himself.

choice theory
Holds that youths will engage in delinquent and criminal behavior after weighing the consequences and benefits of their actions; delinquent behavior is a rational choice made by a motivated offender who perceives that the chances of gain outweigh any possible punishment or loss.

Eric's involvement in antisocial behavior may reflect personal, individual level problems. Considering stories such as Eric's, some delinquency experts question whether the root cause of juvenile misbehavior can be found among social factors, such as poverty and neighborhood conflict. Are delinquents really a "product of their environment" or are they troubled individuals beset by personal, emotional, and/or physical problems? If social and economic factors alone can determine behavior, how is it that many youths residing in dangerous neighborhoods live law-abiding lives? According to the U.S. Census Bureau, more than 37 million Americans live in poverty, yet the vast majority do not become delinquents and criminals.[1] Research indicates that relatively few youths in any population, even the most economically disadvantaged, actually become hard-core, chronic delinquents.[2] The quality of neighborhood and family life may have little impact on the choices individuals make.[3]

Views of delinquency that focus on the individual can be divided into two categories. One position, referred to as **choice theory**, suggests that offenders are rational decision makers who choose to engage in antisocial activity because they believe their actions will be beneficial. Whether they join a gang, steal cars, or sell drugs, their delinquent acts are motivated by the belief that crime can be a relatively risk-free way to better their situation, make money, and have fun. They have little fear of getting caught. Some have fantasies of riches, and others may enjoy the excitement produced by criminal acts such as beating up someone or stealing a car.

The second view, referred to as **trait theory**, suggests that delinquent acts, such as the behaviors that Eric was getting involved in, are the product of personal problems and conditions. Many forms of delinquency, such as substance abuse and violence, appear more impulsive than rational, and these behaviors may be inspired by aberrant physical or psychological traits. Although some youths may choose to commit crime because they desire conventional luxuries and power, others may be driven by abnormalities, such as hyperactivity, low intelligence, biochemical imbalance, or genetic defects.

Choice and trait theories are linked, because they both focus on an individual's mental processes and behavioral reactions. They suggest that each person reacts to environmental and social circumstances in a unique fashion. Faced with the same set of conditions, one person will live a law-abiding life, whereas another will use antisocial or violent behavior to satisfy his or her needs. Choice theorists suggest that the delinquent freely chooses antisocial behaviors to satisfy needs, whereas trait theorists argue that the choice of antisocial behavior is shaped by mental and physical traits.

CHOICE THEORY

trait theory
Holds that youths engage in delinquent or criminal behavior due to aberrant physical or psychological traits that govern behavioral choices; delinquent actions are impulsive or instinctual rather than rational choices.

free will
The view that youths are in charge of their own destinies and are free to make personal behavior choices unencumbered by environmental factors.

utilitarian
A person who believes that people weigh the benefits and consequences of their future actions before deciding on a course of behavior.

classical criminology
Holds that decisions to violate the law are weighed against possible punishments and to deter crime the pain of punishment must outweigh the benefit of illegal gain; led to graduated punishments based on seriousness of the crime (let the punishment fit the crime).

The first formal explanations of crime held that human behavior is a matter of choice. It was assumed that people had **free will** to choose their behavior and that those who violated the law were motivated by greed, revenge, survival, or hedonism. More than two hundred years ago, **utilitarian** philosophers Cesare Beccaria and Jeremy Bentham argued that people weigh the consequences of their actions before deciding on a course of behavior.[4] Their writings formed the core of what used to be called **classical criminology** and is now referred to as *rational choice theory* (or more simply *choice theory*).

Choice theory holds that the decision to violate the law comes after a careful weighing of the benefits and costs of criminal behaviors. Most potential law violators would cease their actions if the pain associated with a behavior outweighed the gain; conversely, law-violating behavior seems attractive if the rewards seem greater than the punishment.[5] Delinquents are not the product of a "bad environment" or life. They choose to commit crime because they find violating the law attractive and not because they are a product of a "broken home" or troubled family.[6]

According to the choice view, youths who decide to become drug dealers compare the benefits, such as cash to buy cars and other luxury items, with the penalties, such as arrest followed by a long stay in a juvenile facility. Many have "learned" the drug trade from more experienced adult criminals who show them the "ropes"—how to avoid detection by camouflaging their activities within the bustle of their daily lives. They sell crack while hanging out in a park or shooting hoops in a playground. They try to act normal, having a good time, anything not to draw attention to themselves and their business.[7] If they take their "lessons" to heart and become accomplished dealers, they may believe that they cannot be caught and even when they do they can avoid severe punishments. They may know or hear about criminals who make a significant income from their illegal activities and want to follow in their footsteps.[8]

THE RATIONAL DELINQUENT

The view that delinquents *choose* to violate the law remains a popular approach to the study of delinquency. According to this view, delinquency is not merely a function of social ills, such as lack of economic opportunity or family dysfunction. In

To read a selection from **Cesare Beccaria's** *On Crime and Punishment*, go to the website www.thomsonedu.com/criminaljustice/siegel.

To learn more about the causes of alcoholism, go to the **National Council on Alcoholism and Drug Dependence, Inc. (NCADD)**, a group that advocates prevention, intervention, research, and treatment of alcoholism and other drug addictions, via www.thomsonedu.com/criminaljustice/siegel.

reality, many youths from affluent families choose to break the law, and most indigent adolescents are law abiding. For example, at first glance drug abuse appears to be a senseless act motivated by grinding poverty and a sense of desperation. However, economic hopelessness cannot be the motivating force behind the substance abuse of millions of middle-class users, many of whom plan to finish high school and go on to college. These kids are more likely to be motivated by the desire for physical gratification, peer group acceptance, and other social benefits. They choose to break the law, because, despite the inherent risks, they believe that taking drugs and drinking provide more pleasure than pain. Their entry into substance abuse is facilitated by their perception that valued friends and family members endorse and encourage drug use and abuse substances themselves.[9] Subscribers to the rational choice model believe the decision to commit a specific type of crime is a matter of personal decision making; hence, the term *rational choice.*

Choosing Delinquent Acts

The focus of choice theory is on the *act,* not on the offender. The concepts of delinquent and delinquency are considered separate: delinquents are youth who maintain the propensity to commit delinquent acts; delinquency is an event during which an adolescent chooses to violate the law.[10] They carefully choose targets and their behavior is systematic and selective. Teen burglars seem to choose targets based on their value, freshness, and resale potential. A relatively new piece of electronic gear, such as Apple's iPod, may be a prime target, because it has not yet saturated the market and still retains high value.[11]

Delinquents do not like to travel to commit crimes. Familiarity with an area gives kids a ready knowledge of escape routes; this is referred to as their "awareness space."[12] A familiar location allows them to blend in, not look out of place, and not get lost when returning home with their loot.[13]

Rational delinquents are not immune from the dangers of their "profession." Even if youths have a delinquent propensity and are motivated to commit crimes, they may not do so if the opportunity to is restricted or absent. They may want to break into a home, but are frightened off by a security system, guard dog, or gun-toting owner. In contrast, the least-motivated adolescent may turn to crime if the rewards are very attractive, the chance of apprehension small, and the punishment tolerable. Why a child has the propensity to commit delinquent acts is an issue quite distinct from the reasons a delinquent decides to break into a particular house one day or to sell narcotics the next. A number of personal factors are linked to the decision to choose delinquency:

Economic Need/Opportunity Some kids are motivated by economic needs. Kids who use drugs, for example, may increase their delinquent activities proportionate to the costs of their habit. As the cost of their drug habit increases, the lure of illegal profits becomes overwhelmingly attractive.[14] Kids may choose delinquency because they believe they have little chance of becoming successful in the conventional world. They view drug dealing and car thefts as their ticket to a better life.

Problem Solving Kids may choose crime as a means to solve personal problems and show their competence. Delinquent acts are an ideal mechanism for displaying courage and fearlessness

Do delinquents choose to commit illegal acts? The evidence shows that most do and that delinquency is a matter of planning as well. Andrew Elisha Staley, a teenager accused of burning a U.S. flag on the Fourth of July, is released after spending nine days in custody. It would be difficult to believe that an act such as flag burning is not planned.

to one's running mates. What could be a better way for kids to show how tough they are than being able to get into a gang fight with their buddies? Rather than creating overwhelming social problems, a delinquent way of life may help kids overcome the problems and stresses they face in their daily lives. Some turn to substance abuse to increase their sense of personal power, to become more assertive, and to reduce tension and anxiety. Some kids embrace deviant lifestyles, such as joining a gang, in order to compensate for their feelings of social powerlessness. Engaging in risky behavior helps them to feel alive and competent.[15]

False Expectations   Some kids have the false belief that "crime pays." They may admire older criminals who have made "big scores" and seem to be quite successful at crime. They get the false impression that crime is an easy way to make a big buck.[16] In reality, the rewards of crime are often quite meager. When Steven Levitt and Sudhir Alladi Venkatesh studied the financial rewards of being in a drug gang, they found that despite enormous risks to their health, life, and freedom, average gang members earned slightly more than what they could in the legitimate labor market (about six to eleven dollars per hour).[17] Why then did they stay in the gang? Members believed that there was a strong potential for future riches if they earned a "management" position (that is, gang leaders earned a lot more than mere members). In this case, the rational choice to commit crime is structured by the adolescent's perception that they can make a lot of money in the future by being a successful gang member as opposed to the limited opportunities available in the legitimate world.[18]

Opportunity   Choosing delinquency may be directly associated with the opportunity to commit crime. Kids who are granted a lot of time socializing with peers are more likely to engage in deviant behaviors, especially if their parents are not around to supervise or control their behavior.[19] Teenage boys may have the highest crime rates, because they, rather than girls, have the freedom to engage in unsupervised socialization.[20] Girls who are physically mature and have more freedom without parental supervision are more likely to have the opportunity to engage in antisocial acts than their less mature peers.[21]

If opportunity influences choice, can providing kids with "character-building" activities—such as a part-time job after school—reduce their involvement in delinquency? Research shows that adolescent work experience may actually increase antisocial activity rather than limit its occurrence. Kids who get jobs may be looking for an easy opportunity to acquire cash to buy drugs and alcohol; after-school jobs may attract teens who are more impulsive than ambitious.[22] At work, the opportunity to socialize with deviant peers combined with lack of parental supervision increases criminal motivation.[23] Although some adults may think that providing teens with a job will reduce their criminal activity ("idle hands are the devil's workshop") many qualities of the work experience—autonomy, increased social status among peers, and increased income—may neutralize the positive effects of working. If providing jobs is to have any positive influence on kids, the jobs must in turn provide a learning experience and support academic achievement.[24]

Routine Activities

If the motivation to commit delinquent acts is a constant, why do delinquency rates rise and fall? Why are some areas more delinquency-ridden than others? To answer these questions, some choice theorists believe that attention must be paid to the *opportunity to commit delinquent acts.*[25]

According to **routine activities theory**, developed by Lawrence Cohen and Marcus Felson, the volume and distribution of **predatory crimes** (violent crimes against

routine activities theory
The view that crime is a "normal" function of the routine activities of modern living; offenses can be expected if there is a motivated offender and a suitable target that is not protected by capable guardians.

predatory crimes
Violent crimes against persons and crimes in which an offender attempts to steal an object directly from its holder.

persons and crimes in which an offender attempts to steal an object directly from its holder) in a particular area and at a particular time is influenced by the interaction of three variables: the availability of *suitable targets* (such as homes containing easily saleable goods), the absence of *capable guardians* (such as homeowners, police, and security guards), and the presence of *motivated offenders* (such as unemployed teenagers)[26] (see Figure 3.1).

This approach gives equal weight to opportunity and propensity: the decision to violate the law is influenced by opportunity and the greater the opportunity, the greater the likelihood of delinquency.[27]

Lack of Capable Guardians Kids will commit crimes when they believe their actions will go undetected by guardians, such as police, security guards, neighbors, teachers, or homeowners. They choose what they consider safe places to commit crimes and to buy and sell drugs.[28]

Research does show that crime levels are relatively low in neighborhoods where residents keep a watchful eye on their neighbors' property.[29] Delinquency rates trend upward as the number of adult caretakers (guardians) who are at home during the day decreases. With mothers at work and children in day care, homes are left unguarded, becoming vulnerable targets. In our highly transient society, the traditional neighborhood, in which streets are monitored by familiar guardians, such as family members, neighbors, and friends, has been vanishing and replaced by anonymous housing developments.[30] Potential thieves look for these unguarded neighborhoods in order to plan their break-ins and burglaries.[31]

Suitable Targets The availability of suitable targets, such as DVD and CD players, cell phones, digital cameras, jewelry, and cash, will increase crime rates. Research has generally supported the fact that the more wealth a home contains, the more likely it is to be a crime target. As the value of goods such as mobile phones and camcorders

Figure 3.1   **Routine Activities Theory Helps Explain Fluctuations in the Delinquency Rate**

Lack of capable guardians
- Police officers
- Homeowners
- Security systems

Motivated offenders
- Teenage boys
- Unemployed
- Addict population

Delinquency

Suitable targets
- Costly jewelry
- Expensive cars
- Easily transportable goods

declines because of production efficiency and retail competition so too does the motivation to steal them; burglary rates may be influenced by re-sale values.[32] And even if they contain valuable commodities, private homes and/or public businesses may be considered off-limits if they are well protected by capable guardians and efficient security systems.[33]

Motivated Offenders Routine activities theory also links delinquency rates to the number of kids in the population who are highly motivated to commit crime. If social forces increase the motivated population, then delinquency rates may rise. For example, if the number of teenagers in a given population exceeds the number of available part-time and after-school jobs, the supply of motivated offenders may increase.[34] As the "crack epidemic" of the 1980s waned the delinquency rate dropped, because crack addicts are highly motivated offenders.

CHOICE THEORY AND DELINQUENCY PREVENTION

If delinquency is a rational choice and a routine activity, then delinquency prevention is a matter of convincing potential delinquents that they will be punished for committing delinquent acts, punishing them so severely that they never again commit crimes, or making it so difficult to commit crimes that the potential gain is not worth the risk. The first of these strategies is called *general deterrence,* the second *specific deterrence,* and the third *situational crime prevention.* Let's look at each of these strategies in more detail.

General Deterrence

general deterrence
Crime control policies that depend on the fear of criminal penalties, such as long prison sentences for violent crimes; the aim is to convince law violators that the pain outweighs the benefit of criminal activity.

The **general deterrence** concept holds that the choice to commit delinquent acts can be controlled by the threat of punishment. The concept is simple: People will commit crime if they believe they will be successful in their criminal endeavor.[35]

If people believe illegal behavior will result in severe sanctions, they will choose not to commit crimes.[36] If kids believed that their illegal behavior would result in apprehension and punishment, then only the truly irrational would commit delinquent acts.[37]

A guiding principle of deterrence theory is that the more severe, certain, and swift the punishment, the greater the deterrent effect.[38] Even if a particular delinquent act carries a very severe punishment, there will be relatively little deterrent effect if most kids do not believe they will be caught. Conversely, even a mild sanction may deter crime if kids believe punishment is certain.[39] So if the justice system can convince would-be delinquents that they will be caught—these youths may decide that delinquency simply does not pay.[40] One approach has been to put more cops on the street and having them aggressively enforce the law. Proactive, aggressive law enforcement officers who quickly get to the scene of the crime may help deter delinquent activities.[41]

Deterrence and Delinquency Traditionally, juvenile justice authorities have been reluctant to incorporate deterrence-based punishments on the ground that they interfere with the *parens patriae* philosophy. Children are punished less severely than adults, limiting the power of the law to deter juvenile crime. However, during the 1990s the increase in teenage violence, gang activity, and drug abuse prompted a reevaluation of deterrence strategies. Some juvenile courts have shifted from an emphasis on treatment to an emphasis on public safety.[42] Police began to focus on particular problems in their jurisdiction rather than to react after a crime occurred.[43] They began to use aggressive tactics to deter membership in drug-trafficking gangs.[44] Some police officers were sent into high schools undercover to identify and arrest student drug dealers.[45]

Another deterrent effort was to toughen juvenile sentencing codes and make it easier to waive juveniles to the adult court. In addition, legislators have passed more restrictive juvenile codes, and the number of incarcerated juveniles continues to increase. To those who advocate a "get tough" approach to juvenile crime, these efforts have had a beneficial effect: the overall delinquency rate declined as the threat of punishment increased.

Can Delinquency Be Deterred? On the surface, deterrence appears to have benefit, but there is reason to believe that the benefit is limited. Although delinquency rates have declined during a period when deterrence measures are in vogue, it does not necessarily mean that kids were deterred from crime. As you may recall, other social factors in play during the same period may have explained the drop, including lower rates of drug abuse, reduced teen pregnancy, and a strong economy.

Because deterrence strategies are based on the idea of a "rational" offender, they may not be effective when applied to young people. It is possible that punishment may bring defiance rather than deterrence in a teen population not known for its reasonableness. Minors tend to be less capable of making mature judgments, and many younger offenders are unaware of the content of juvenile legal codes. A deterrence policy (e.g., mandatory waiver to the adult court for violent crimes) will have little effect on delinquency rates of kids who are not even aware these statutes exist.[46] It seems futile, therefore, to try to deter delinquency through fear of legal punishment. Teens seem more fearful of being punished by their parents or of being the target of disapproval from their friends than they are of the police.[47]

LOOKING BACK TO ERIC'S STORY

Dating and relationship violence can start at a very early age. What can be done to deter dating violence? What should happen to teens involved in this type of behavior? Should they be charged criminally? Why or why not?

Juveniles often commit crimes in groups, a process called co-offending, and peer pressure can outweigh the deterrent effect of the law. Here, at a sixteenth birthday party in Arlington, Virginia, kids are getting drunk even though their parents are home and periodically supervising the party.

© AP Images/Lauren Greenfield/VII

What Does This Mean to Me?

Does Punishment Work?

To some experts and pundits, if delinquency is punished severely kids will not risk committing delinquent acts. Consider this statement by Texas congressman Lamar Smith, an advocate of sending juveniles to adult court:

> It is commonsense public policy when states pass laws that allow or require violent juveniles to be transferred to adult courts. I strongly believe that we can no longer tolerate young people who commit violent crimes simply because of their age. Young people have the ability to decide between right and wrong, as the vast majority of us do every day. But those youths who choose to prey on other juveniles, senior citizens, merchants, or homeowners will be held responsible. If that choice results in confinement in an adult prison system, perhaps youths who have a propensity to commit violent crimes will think twice before acting.

1. Do you think that sending kids to adult prisons will really deter others from committing crimes?
2. What do you recommend be done to stop or deter delinquency?
3. Do you think kids who commit crime really have the capacity to "think twice" before they act?
4. Can you remember ever being in a situation where you felt forced to break the law because of peer pressure, when being afraid of the consequences had no real effect on your behavior?

Source: Lamar Smith, "Sentencing Youths to Adult Correctional Facilities Increases Public Safety," *Corrections Today* 65:20 (April 2003).

It is also possible that experience with crime dampens an adolescent's fear of punishment, thus neutralizing its deterrent effect. One recent research effort by Greg Pogarsky and his associates found that getting arrested had little deterrent effect on youth and that kids who were experienced offenders were the ones most likely to continue committing crime. As the old saying goes, "the best predictor of future behavior is past behavior." One reason may be that the crime-prone youths, ones who have a long history of delinquency, may not be influenced by the deterrent effect of the law, because they know that crimes provide immediate gratification, whereas the threat of punishment is far in the future.[48] Kids who have already committed delinquent acts in the past may maintain a risk-taking personality that is less likely to be impacted by the threat of punishment and more immune from the moral dilemmas caused by crime (i.e., it's bad to steal and attack) than kids who have so far remained delinquency free.

It is also possible that for the highest-risk group of young offenders—teens living in economically depressed neighborhoods—the deterrent threat of formal sanctions may be irrelevant. Inner-city youngsters may not have internalized the norms that hold that getting arrested is wrong. They have less to lose if arrested; they have a limited stake in society and are not worried about their future. They also may not connect their illegal behavior with punishment, because they see many people committing crimes and not getting caught or being punished.

Research also shows that many juvenile offenders are under the influence of drugs or alcohol, a condition that might impair their decision-making ability.[49] Similarly, juveniles often commit crimes in groups, a process called **co-offending**, and peer pressure can outweigh the deterrent effect of the law.

In summary, according to deterrence theory, it is possible to reduce or eliminate delinquent behavior by convincing youth that they will be apprehended and punished for their future misbehaviors. Deterring delinquency through the fear of punishment seems to. Deterrence may be of limited value in controlling delinquency, because children may neither fully comprehend the seriousness of their acts nor appreciate their consequences.[50]

co-offending
Committing criminal acts in groups.

Specific Deterrence

It stands to reason that if delinquents truly are rational and commit crimes because they see them as beneficial, they will stop offending if they are caught and severely punished. What rational person would recidivate after being exposed to an arrest, court appearance, and incarceration in an unpleasant detention facility, with the promise of more to come? According to the concept of **specific deterrence**, if young offenders are punished severely, the experience will convince them not to repeat their illegal acts. Juveniles are punished by state authorities with the understanding that their ordeal will deter future misbehavior.

Although the association between punishment and desistance seems logical, there is little evidence that punitive measures alone deter future delinquency. There are research studies that show that arrest and conviction may under some circumstances lower the frequency of re-offending, a finding that supports specific deterrence.[51] However, other

specific deterrence
Sending convicted offenders to secure incarceration facilities so that punishment is severe enough to convince them not to repeat their criminal activity.

studies indicate that punishment has little real effect on re-offending and in some instances may actually increase the likelihood that first-time offenders will commit new crimes (recidivate).[52] Kids who are placed in a juvenile justice facility are just as likely to become adult criminals as those treated with greater leniency.[53] In fact, a history of prior arrests, convictions, and punishments has proven to be the best predictor of re-arrest among young offenders released from correctional institutions. Rather than deterring future offending, punishment may encourage it.[54]

Why does punishment encourage rather than reduce delinquency? According to some experts, institutionalization cuts youths off from pro-social supports in the community, making them more reliant on deviant peers. Incarceration may also diminish chances for successful employment, reducing access to legitimate opportunities. This might help explain why delinquency rates can still increase even though incarceration rates remain quite high.

The experience of punishment itself may motivate some adolescents to re-offend. The use of mandatory sentences for some crimes means that all youths who are found to have committed those crimes must be institutionalized; first offenders may then be treated the same as chronic recidivists. These novice offenders are then packed into overcrowded facilities with experienced violent juveniles and consequently suffer significant and irrevocable harm from their experience. Punishment strategies may stigmatize kids and help lock offenders into a delinquent career.

Kids who are punished may also believe that the likelihood of getting caught twice for the same type of crime is remote: "Lightning never strikes twice in the same spot," they may reason; no one is that unlucky.[55]

Although some researchers have found that punishment may reduce the frequency of future offending, the weight of the evidence suggests that being punished for a delinquent act has little impact on recidivism.[56]

Situational Crime Prevention

According to the concept of **situational crime prevention**, in order to reduce delinquent activity, planners must be aware of the characteristics of sites and situations that are at risk to crime; the things that draw or push kids toward these sites and

situational crime prevention
A crime prevention method that relies on reducing the opportunity to commit criminal acts by making them more difficult to perform, reducing their reward, and increasing their risks.

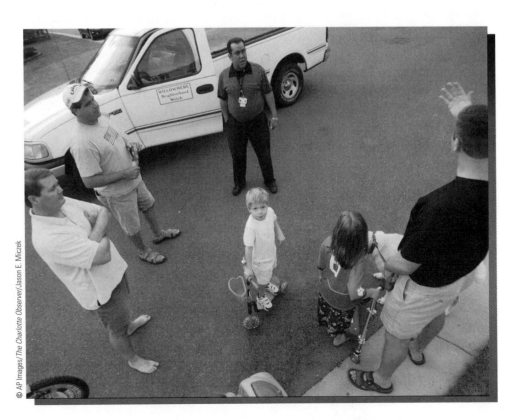

Willie Wahnon (top center) chats with Willowmere homeowners Dave Powlen (left) Randy Abrams (second from left) and Mark Ellis (right) as he patrols the Charlotte, North Carolina, neighborhood on September 15, 2006. Wahnon, a retired New York City transit employee, started his patrol after several homes were vandalized. Can the presence of guardians convince kids not to commit crime?

© AP Images/*The Charlotte Observer*/Jason E. Miczek

situations; what equips potential delinquents to take advantage of illegal opportunities offered by these sites and situations; and what constitutes the immediate triggers for delinquent actions.[57] Delinquency can be neutralized if (1) potential targets are carefully guarded, (2) the means to commit crime are controlled, and (3) potential offenders are carefully monitored. Desperate people may contemplate crime, but only the truly irrational will attack a well-defended, inaccessible target and risk strict punishment. **Situational crime prevention** strategies are designed to make it so difficult to commit delinquent acts that would-be offenders will be convinced the risks are greater than the rewards.[58] Rather than deterring or punishing individuals, they aim to reduce opportunities to commit delinquent acts. This can be accomplished by:

- Increasing the effort to commit delinquent acts
- Increasing the risks of delinquent activity
- Reducing the rewards attached to delinquent acts
- Increasing the shame of committing a delinquent act
- Reduce provocations that produce delinquent acts
- Remove excuses for committing a delinquent act

LOOKING BACK TO ERIC'S STORY

If you were the assigned juvenile probation officer, what would you recommend to the judge regarding rules of supervision and services for Eric? What are the goals you would like to accomplish?

Increasing the effort of delinquency might involve *target-hardening techniques,* such as placing unbreakable glass on storefronts. Some successful target-hardening efforts include installing a locking device on cars that prevents drunken drivers from starting the vehicle (the Breath Analyzed Ignition Interlock Device).[59] Access can be controlled by locking gates and fencing yards.[60] Facilitators of crime can be controlled by banning the sale of spray paint to adolescents in an effort to cut down on graffiti, or putting ID photos on credit cards to reduce their value if stolen.

Increasing the risks of delinquency might involve improving lighting, creating neighborhood watch programs, controlling building exits, installing security systems, or increasing the number of security officers and police patrols. The installation of street lights may convince would-be burglars that their entries will be seen and reported.[61] Closed-circuit TV cameras have been shown to reduce the amount of car theft from parking lots, also reducing the need for higher-cost security personnel.[62]

Reducing the rewards of delinquency could include strategies, such as making car radios removable so they can be kept in the home at night, marking property so it is more difficult to sell when stolen, and having gender-neutral phone listings to discourage obscene phone calls. Tracking systems help police locate and return stolen vehicles. Increasing shame might include efforts to publish the names of some offenders in the local papers.

Because delinquent acts are often the result of extreme provocation, it might be possible to reduce delinquency rates by creating programs that reduce conflict. Posting guards outside schools at closing time might prevent childish taunts from escalating into full-blown brawls. Anti-bullying programs that have been implemented in schools are another method of reducing provocation.

Some delinquents neutralize their responsibility for their acts by learning to excuse their behavior by saying things like

Can all delinquent acts be rational? Tracy Hart holds a photo of him and his wife, Michelle Hart, who was killed when a vehicle crashed into their Hampton, Virginia, home. A 12-year-old boy and a 14-year-old boy are accused of stealing a Jeep from a convenience store to go joy riding, then losing control and crashing into the house. While the theft of the car was a rational act, could the boys have foreseen its consequences?

© AP Images/*Daily Press*/Sangjib Min

Delinquency Prevention Methods

Method	Central Premise	Technique
General deterrence	Kids will avoid delinquency if they fear punishment.	Make punishment swift, severe, and certain.
Specific deterrence	Delinquents who are punished severely will not repeat their detention.	Use harsh punishments, such as a stay in secure offenses.
Situational crime	Make delinquency more difficult and less profitable.	Harden targets, use prevention surveillance, street lighting.

hot spot
A particular location or address that is the site of repeated and frequent criminal activity.

crackdown
A law enforcement operation that is designed to reduce or eliminate a particular criminal activity through the application of aggressive police tactics, usually involving a larger than usual contingent of police officers.

✔ **CHECKPOINTS**

■ Choice theory maintains that delinquency is rational and can be prevented by punishment that is sufficiently severe and certain.

■ Delinquents who choose crime must evaluate the characteristics of a target to determine its suitability.

■ Routine activities theory suggests that delinquent acts are a function of motivated offenders, lack of capable guardians, and availability of suitable targets.

■ General deterrence models are based on the fear of punishment. If punishments are severe, swift, and certain, then would-be delinquents would choose not to risk breaking the law.

■ Specific deterrence aims at reducing crime through the application of severe punishments. Once offenders experience these punishments they will be unwilling to repeat their delinquent activities.

■ Situational crime prevention efforts are designed to reduce or redirect crime by making it more difficult to profit from illegal acts.

"I didn't know that was illegal" or "I had no choice." It might be possible to reduce delinquency by eliminating excuses. For example, vandalism may be reduced by setting up brightly colored trash containers that help eliminate the excuse, "I just didn't know where to throw my trash." Reducing or eliminating excuses in this way also makes it physically easy for people to comply with laws and regulations, thereby reducing the likelihood they will choose crime.

Hot Spots and Crackdowns One type of situational crime prevention effort targets locales that are known to be the scene of repeated delinquent activity. By focusing on a **hot spot**—a shopping mall, public park, or housing project—law enforcement efforts can be used to crack down on persistent youth crime. A police task force might target gang members who are street-level drug dealers by using undercover agents and surveillance cameras in known drug-dealing locales. Unfortunately, these efforts have not often proven to be successful mechanisms for lowering crime and delinquency rates.[63] **Crackdowns** seem to be an effective short-term strategy, but their effect begins to decay once the initial shock effect wears off.[64] Crackdowns also may displace illegal activity to areas where there are fewer police.

Although these results are discouraging, delinquency rates seem to be reduced when police officers combine the use of aggressive problem solving with community improvement techniques (increased lighting, cleaned vacant lots) to fight particular crimes in selected places.[65] One recent initiative by the Dallas Police Department to aggressively pursue truancy and curfew enforcement resulted in lower rates of gang violence.[66]

Concept Summary 3.1 summarizes these three methods of delinquency prevention and control.

Do Delinquents Choose Crime?

Although the logic of choice theory seems plausible, before we can accept its propositions several important questions need to be addressed. First, why do some poor and desperate kids choose to break the law, whereas others who live in the same neighborhoods manage to live law-abiding lives? Conversely, why do affluent suburban youths choose to break the law when they have everything to lose and little to gain?

Choice theorists also have difficulty explaining seemingly irrational crimes, such as vandalism, arson, and even drug abuse. To say a teenager painted swastikas on a synagogue after making a "rational choice" seems inadequate. Is it possible that violent adolescents—such as Dylan Klebold and Eric Harris, who on April 20, 1999, killed thirteen and wounded twenty-one classmates at Columbine High School—were "rational" decision makers, or was their behavior the product of twisted minds? To assume they made a "rational choice" to kill their classmates seems ill advised.

In summary, choice theory helps us to understand delinquent events and victim patterns. However, the question remains, why are some adolescents motivated to commit crime whereas others in similar circumstances remain law abiding? Why do some kids choose crime over legal activities? The remaining sections of this chapter present some possible explanations. ✔ **Checkpoints**

TRAIT THEORIES: BIOSOCIAL AND PSYCHOLOGICAL VIEWS

To get detailed information on the **Columbine tragedy**, go to the website www.thomsonedu.com/criminaljustice/siegel.

Choice theorists would have us believe that young people select crime after weighing the benefits of delinquent over legal behavior. Teens may decide to commit a robbery if they believe they will make a good profit, have a good chance of getting away, and even if caught, stand little chance of being severely punished. Conversely, they will forgo criminal activities if they see a lot of cops around and come to the conclusion they will get caught and punished. Their choice is both rational and logical.

A number of experts think this model is incomplete. They believe it is simplistic to infer that all youths choose crime simply because the advantages outweigh the risks. If that were the case, how could one explain profitless crimes, such as violence or vandalism? These experts argue that behavioral choices are a function of an individual's mental and physical makeup. Most law-abiding youths have traits that keep them within conventional society. In contrast, youths who choose to engage in antisocial behavior manifest abnormal mental and physical traits that influence their choices. When they commit crime, their behavior is shaped by these uncontrollable mental and physical traits.

The *source* of behavioral control, therefore, is one of the main differences between trait and choice theories. Although both views focus on the individual, the choice theorist views delinquents as rational and self-serving decision makers. The trait theorist views their "decisions" as a by-product of uncontrollable personal traits or experiences. To a choice theorist, reducing the benefits of crime by increasing the likelihood of punishment will lower the crime rate. Because trait theorists question whether delinquents are rational decision makers, they focus more on the treatment of abnormal mental and physical conditions as a method of delinquency reduction. In the next sections, the primary components of trait theory are reviewed.

The Origins of Trait Theory

The first attempts to discover why criminal tendencies develop focused on biological traits present at birth. This school of thought is generally believed to have originated with the Italian physician Cesare Lombroso (1835–1909).[67] Known as the father of criminology, Lombroso developed the theory of **criminal atavism**.[68] He found that delinquents manifest physical anomalies that make them similar to our primitive ancestors. These individuals are throwbacks to an earlier stage of human evolution. Because of this link, the "born criminal" has such traits as enormous jaws, strong canines, a flattened nose, and supernumerary teeth (double rows, as in snakes). Lombroso made statements such as: "[I]t was easy to understand why the span of the arms in criminals so often exceeds the height, for this is a characteristic of apes, whose forelimbs are used in walking and climbing."[69]

Contemporaries of Lombroso refined the notion of a physical basis of crime. Raffaele Garofalo (1851–1934) shared Lombroso's belief that certain physical characteristics indicate a criminal nature.[70] Enrico Ferri (1856–1929), a student of Lombroso, accepted the biological approach to explaining criminal activity, but he attempted to interweave social factors into his explanation.[71] The English criminologist

criminal atavism
The idea that delinquents manifest physical anomalies that make them biologically and physiologically similar to our primitive ancestors, savage throwbacks to an earlier stage of human evolution.

Charles Goring (1870–1919) challenged the validity of Lombroso's research and claimed instead that delinquent behaviors bore a significant relationship to "defective intelligence."[72] Consequently, he advocated that criminality could best be controlled by regulating the reproduction of families exhibiting abnormal traits, such as "feeblemindedness."[73]

The early views that portrayed delinquent behavior as a function of a single biological trait had a significant impact on American criminology; biocriminologists helped develop a science of "criminal anthropology."[74] Eventually, these views evoked criticism for their unsound methodology. Many trait studies used captive offender populations and failed to compare experimental subjects with control groups.[75] These methodological flaws make it impossible to determine if biological traits produce delinquency. It is equally plausible that police are more likely to arrest the mentally and physically abnormal. By the middle of the twentieth century, biological theories had fallen out of favor.

Contemporary Trait Theory

For most of the twentieth century, most delinquency research focused on social factors, such as poverty and family life. However, a small group of researchers kept alive the biological approach.[76] Some embraced *sociobiology*, a perspective suggesting that behavior will adapt to the environment in which it evolved.[77] Creatures of all species are influenced by their innate need to survive and dominate others. Sociobiology revived interest in a biological basis for crime. If biological (genetic) and psychological (mental) makeup controls all human behavior, it follows that a person's genes should determine whether he or she chooses law-violating or conventional behavior.[78]

Trait theorists argue that a combination of personal traits and environmental influences produce individual behavior patterns. People with pathological traits, such as abnormal personality or a low IQ, may have a heightened risk for crime over the life course.[79] This risk may be elevated by environmental stresses, such as poor family life, educational failure, and exposure to delinquent peers. The reverse may also apply: a supportive environment may counteract adverse biological and psychological traits.[80]

According to contemporary trait theorists, individual deficits by themselves do not cause delinquency. However, possessing suspect individual traits may make a child more susceptible to the delinquency-producing factors in the environment. An adolescent suffering from a learning disability may have an increased risk of school failure; those who fail at school are at risk to commit delinquent acts. Learning disabilities alone, therefore, are not a cause of delinquency and only present a problem when they produce school failure. Programs to help learning-disabled kids achieve in school will prevent later delinquent involvements.

Today trait theory can be divided into two separate branches: the first, most often called biosocial theory, assumes that the cause of delinquency can be found in a child's physical or biological makeup, and the second points the finger at psychological traits and characteristics.

 For a complete list of the **crime-producing physical traits identified by Lombroso**, go to the website www.thomsonedu.com/criminaljustice/siegel.

BIOSOCIAL THEORIES OF DELINQUENCY

biosocial theory
The view that both thought and behavior have biological and social bases.

The first branch of trait theory—**biosocial theory**—focuses on the association between biological makeup, environmental conditions, and antisocial behaviors. As a group, these theories suggest that kids who exhibit abnormal biological traits also have difficulty adjusting to the social environment. Their adjustment problems make normal social relations challenging. Because their biological inadequacy makes them socially dysfunctional, they are vulnerable to crime producing stimulus in the environment. Three areas of biological functioning are suspect: biochemical makeup, neurological function, and genetic history.

Biochemical Factors

One area of concern is the suspected relationship between antisocial behavior and biochemical makeup.[81] Adolescents may be exposed to damaging chemical contaminants from the point of conception when their mothers ingest harmful substances during pregnancy.[82] Maternal alcohol abuse during gestation has long been linked to prenatal damage and subsequent antisocial behavior in adolescence.[83] Lead exposure also begins in the womb due to mother's consumption of foods, such as seafood that are high in lead content.[84] A number of research studies have confirmed that lead ingestion may be a direct cause of antisocial behaviors.[85]

Another view is that abnormal body chemistry is an indirect cause of antisocial behavior through its association with abnormal psychological and mental conditions. Research conducted over the past decade shows that an over- or undersupply of certain chemicals and minerals, including sodium, mercury, potassium, calcium, amino acids, and/or iron, can lead to depression, hyperactivity, cognitive problems, intelligence deficits, memory loss, or abnormal sexual activity; these conditions have been associated with crime and delinquency.[86] Attention-deficit/hyperactivity disorder (ADHD), believed to be a precursor of delinquent behaviors, has been linked to the presence of excessive iron (see later in this chapter for more on ADHD).[87]

Diet and Delinquency There is evidence that a child's diet may influence his or her behavior through its impact on body chemistry. Either eliminating harmful substances or introducing beneficial ones into the diet can reduce the threat of antisocial behaviors.[88]

A recent review of existing research on the association between diet and delinquency was recently released in Great Britain.[89] The report found that the combination of nutrients most commonly associated with good mental health and well-being is as follows:

- Polyunsaturated fatty acids (particularly the omega-3 types found in oily fish and some plants)
- Minerals, such as zinc (in whole grains, legumes, meat and milk); magnesium (in green leafy vegetables, nuts, and whole grains); and iron (in red meat, green leafy vegetables, eggs, and some fruit)
- Vitamins, such as folate (in green leafy vegetables and fortified cereals); a range of B vitamins (whole grain products, yeast, and dairy products); and antioxidant vitamins, such as C and E (in a wide range of fruits and vegetables)

People eating diets that lack one or more of this combination of polyunsaturated fats, minerals, and vitamins, and/or contain too much saturated fat (or other elements, including sugar and a range of food and agricultural chemicals) seem to be at higher risk of developing the following conditions:

- Attention-deficit/hyperactivity disorder (ADHD)
- A range of depressive conditions
- Schizophrenia
- Dementia, including Alzheimer's disease

The survey found that we are eating too much saturated fat, sugar, and salt and not enough vitamins and minerals. This type of diet not only fuels obesity, cardiovascular disease, diabetes, and some cancers, but may also be contributing to rising rates of mental ill-health and antisocial behavior.

A number of research studies have found a link between diet and aggressive behavior patterns. In some cases, the relationship is direct; in others, a poor diet may compromise individual functioning, which in turn produces aggressive behavior responses. A poor diet may inhibit school performance, and children who fail at school are at risk for delinquent behavior and criminality. Student misbehavior levels have been reduced in controlled experiments in which school age subjects were provided with improved diets and provided with nutritional supplements.[90]

Hormonal Levels Antisocial behavior allegedly peaks in the teenage years, because hormonal activity is then at its greatest level. It is possible that increased levels of testosterone are responsible for excessive violence among teenage boys. Adolescents who experience more intense moods, anxiety, and restlessness also have the highest crime rates.[91] Research has shown that hormonal sensitivity may begin very early in life if the fetus is exposed to abnormally high levels of testosterone. This may trigger a heightened response to the release of testosterone at puberty. Although testosterone levels may appear normal, the young male is at risk for overly aggressive behavior.[92] Females may be biologically protected from deviant behavior in the same way they are immune from some diseases that strike males.[93] Girls who have high levels of testosterone or are exposed to testosterone in utero may become more aggressive in adolescence.[94] Chapter 6 further discusses hormonal activity as an explanation of gender differences in delinquency.

Neurological Dysfunction

Another focus of biosocial theory is the neurological—or brain and nervous system—structure of offenders. It has been suggested that children who manifest behavioral disturbances may have neurological deficits, such as damage to the hemispheres of the brain; this is sometimes referred to as **minimal brain dysfunction (MBD)**.[95] Impairment in brain functioning may be present at birth, produced by factors such as low birth weight, brain injury during pregnancy, birth complications, and inherited abnormalities. Brain injuries can also occur later in life as a result of brutal beatings or sexual abuse by a parent. According to research conducted by Dr. Martin Teicher of the McLean Hospital in Massachusetts, emotional trauma, such as child abuse, can actually cause adverse physical changes in the brain, and these deformities can lead to depression, anxiety, and other serious emotional conditions.[96]

Children who experience neurological deficits at birth also suffer from a number of antisocial traits throughout their life course. Research has even linked this type of deficit to becoming a habitual liar.[97] Kids who suffer from this sort of impairment are more likely to become criminals as adults.[98] Clinical analysis of convicted murderers has found that a significant number had suffered head injuries as children that resulted in neurological impairment.[99] In an important study by Adrian Raine, researchers looked at the medical histories of 4,269 Danish males born between 1959 and 1961. By age eighteen, boys whose mothers had experienced birth complications and who had also experienced maternal rejection later in life were more than twice as likely to commit a violent crime than boys who did not experience birth trauma and maternal rejection. Raine concluded that birth complications and maternal rejection seemed to predispose offenders to some kinds of criminal offenses.[100]

The form of brain dysfunction most often linked to delinquency is attention-deficit/hyperactivity disorder (ADHD), the topic of the following Focus on Delinquency feature.

minimal brain dysfunction (MBD)
Damage to the brain itself that causes antisocial behavior injurious to the individual's lifestyle and social adjustment.

LOOKING BACK TO ERIC'S STORY

Eric had been diagnosed with ADHD. Could his aggressive behavior have a biological basis? If so, how would you deal with his behavior?

learning disabilities (LD)
Neurological dysfunctions that prevent an individual from learning to his or her potential.

Learning Disabilities The relationship between **learning disabilities (LD)** and delinquency has been highlighted by studies showing that arrested and incarcerated children have a far higher LD rate than do children in the general population. Although approximately 10 percent of all youths have some form of learning disorder, estimates of LD among adjudicated delinquents range from 26 to 73 percent.[101] There are two possible explanations for the link between learning disabilities and delinquency.[102] One view, known as the *susceptibility rationale,* argues that the link is caused

ADHD: Attention-Deficit/Hyperactivity Disorder

Many parents have noticed that their children do not pay attention to them—they run around and do things in their own way. Sometimes this inattention is a function of age; in other instances it is a symptom of a common learning disability referred to as attention-deficit/hyperactivity disorder (ADHD), a condition in which a child shows a developmentally inappropriate lack of attention, distractibility, impulsivity, and hyperactivity. The various symptoms of ADHD are listed in the following lists.

Symptoms of ADHD

Lack of Attention
- Frequently fails to finish projects
- Does not seem to pay attention
- Does not sustain interest in play activities
- Cannot sustain concentration on schoolwork or related tasks
- Is easily distracted

Impulsivity
- Frequently acts without thinking
- Often calls out in class
- Does not want to wait his or her turn
- Shifts from activity to activity
- Cannot organize tasks or work
- Requires constant supervision in school line or while playing games

Hyperactivity
- Constantly runs around and climbs on things
- Shows excessive motor activity while asleep
- Cannot sit still; is constantly fidgeting
- Does not remain in his or her seat in class
- Is constantly on the go, like a "motor"
- Has difficulty regulating emotions
- Has difficulty getting started
- Has difficulty staying on track
- Has difficulty adjusting to social demands

Estimates of ADHD in the general population range from 3 percent to 12 percent, but it is much more prevalent in adolescents, where some estimates reach as high as one-third of the population. Children from any background can develop ADHD, but it is five to seven times more common in boys than girls. It does not affect intelligence, and ADHD children often show considerable ability with artistic endeavors. More common in the United States than elsewhere, ADHD tends to run in families, and there is some suggestion of an association with a family history of alcoholism or depression.

Cause

No one is really sure how ADHD develops, but some psychologists believe it is tied to dysfunction in a section of the lower portion of the brain known as the *reticular activating system*. This area keeps the higher brain centers alert and ready for input. There is some evidence that this area is not working properly in ADHD kids and that their behavior is really the brain's attempt to generate new stimulation or arousal to maintain alertness. Other suspected origins are neurological damage to the frontal lobes of the brain, prenatal stress, and even food additives and chemical allergies. Some experts suggest that the condition might be traced to the neurological effects of abnormal levels of the chemicals dopamine and norepinephrine.

by side effects of learning disabilities, such as impulsiveness and inability to take social cues. In contrast, the *school failure rationale* assumes that the frustration caused by poor school performance will lead to a negative self-image and acting-out behavior.

Psychologist Terrie Moffitt has evaluated the literature on the connection between LD and delinquency and concludes that it is a significant correlate of persistent antisocial behavior (or conduct disorders).[103] She finds that neurological symptoms, such as LD and MBD, correlate highly with early onset of deviance, hyperactivity, and aggressiveness.[104] And there is new evidence that the factors that cause learning disabilities are also highly related to substance abuse, which may help explain the learning disability–juvenile delinquency connection. The National Center on Addiction and Substance Abuse at Columbia University recently released findings that show how learning disabilities are linked to substance abuse:

- Risk factors for adolescent substance abuse are very similar to the behavioral effects of learning disabilities—reduced self-esteem, academic difficulty, loneliness, depression, and the desire for social acceptance. Thus, learning disabilities may indirectly lead to substance abuse by generating the types of behavior that typically lead adolescents to abuse drugs.

Effects

ADHD may result in poor school performance, including a high dropout rate, bullying, stubbornness, mental disorder, and a lack of response to discipline; these conditions are highly correlated with delinquent behavior. Children with ADHD are more likely to use illicit drugs, alcohol, and cigarettes in adolescence and are more likely to be arrested, to be charged with a felony, and to have multiple arrests than non-ADHD youths. There is also evidence that ADHD youths who also exhibit early signs of MBD and conduct disorder (e.g., fighting) are the most at risk for persistent antisocial behaviors continuing into adulthood.

A series of research studies link ADHD to the onset and continuance of a delinquent career and increased risk for antisocial behavior and substance abuse in adulthood. Joseph Biederman and colleagues conducted a ten-year longitudinal study of more than one hundred boys with ADHD. By age twenty-one, ADHD youth were at an elevated risk for antisocial, addictive, mood, and anxiety disorders. Kids with ADHD subjects exhibited higher levels of psychopathology over the life course despite the fact that 93 percent had received treatment for the disorder at some point during their lives. Of those, 86 percent had received both medication and counseling, whereas 6 percent received medication alone and 1 percent received counseling alone.

Treatment

ADHD children are most often treated by giving them doses of stimulants, most commonly Ritalin and Dexedrine (or dextroamphetamine), which, ironically, help these children control their emotional and behavioral outbursts. The anti-manic, anticonvulsant drug Tegretol has also been used effectively. New treatment techniques featuring behavior modification and drug therapies are constantly being developed to help children who have attention or hyperactivity problems.

CRITICAL THINKING

Considering that many ADHD kids engage in antisocial behaviors, should those diagnosed with the condition be closely monitored by the school system? Would that be fair to the majority of ADHD kids, who never violate the law? Would paying special attention to the ADHD population stigmatize them and actually encourage their law-violating behaviors?

INFOTRAC COLLEGE EDITION RESEARCH

Use "Attention Deficit Hyperactivity Disorder" as a key word search on InfoTrac College Edition.

Sources: Joseph Biederman, Michael Monuteaux, Eric Mick, Thomas Spencer, Timothy Wilens, Julie Silva, Lindsey Snyder, and Stephen Faraone, "Young Adult Outcome of Attention Deficit Hyperactivity Disorder: A Controlled 10-Year Follow-Up Study," *Psychological Medicine* 36:167–179 (2006); Aldis Putninö, "Substance Use Among Young Offenders: Thrills, Bad Feelings, or Bad Behavior?" *Substance Use & Misuse* 41:415–422 (2006); Molina Pelham, Jr., "Childhood Predictors of Adolescent Substance Use in a Longitudinal Study of Children with ADHD," *Journal of Abnormal Psychology* 112:497–507 (2003); Peter Muris and Cor Meesters, "The Validity of Attention Deficit Hyperactivity and Hyperkinetic Disorder Symptom Domains in Nonclinical Dutch Children," *Journal of Clinical Child & Adolescent Psychology* 32:460–466 (2003); D. R. Blachman and S. P. Hinshaw, "Patterns of Friendship Among Girls with and without Attention Deficit/Hyperactivity Disorder," *Journal of Abnormal Child Psychology* 30:625–640 (2002); Terrie Moffitt and Phil Silva, "Self-Reported Delinquency, Neuropsychological Deficit, and History of Attention Deficit Disorder," *Journal of Abnormal Child Psychology* 16:553–569 (1988); Karen Harding, Richard Judah, and Charles Gant, "Outcome-Based Comparison of Ritalin Versus Food Supplement–Treated Children with AD/HD," *Alternative Medicine Review* 8:319–330 (2003).

- A child with a learning disability is twice as likely to suffer attention deficit disorder (ADD) as a member of the general population, and there is a high incidence of ADD among individuals who abuse alcohol and drugs. It is known that as many as half of those suffering ADD self-medicate with drugs and alcohol.

- Children who are exposed to alcohol, tobacco, and drugs in the womb are at higher risk for various developmental disorders, including learning disabilities. Furthermore, a mother who uses drugs while pregnant may be a predictor that the child will grow up in a home with a parent who is a substance abuser. This too will increase the risk that the child will abuse drugs or alcohol himself.[105]

Despite this evidence, the learning disability–juvenile delinquency link has always been controversial. It is possible that the LD child may not be more susceptible to delinquent behavior than the non-LD child and that the link may be an artifact of bias in the way LD children are treated at school or by the police. LD youths are more likely to be arrested, and if petitioned to juvenile court, they bring with them a record of school problems that may increase the likelihood of their being sent to juvenile court.

Arousal Theory It has long been suspected that adolescents may engage in crimes such as shoplifting and vandalism, because they offer the thrill of "getting away with it."[106] Is it possible that thrill seekers have some form of abnormal brain functioning? Arousal theorists believe that some people's brains function differently in response to environmental stimuli. We all seek to maintain an optimal level of arousal: too much stimulation leaves us anxious, and too little makes us feel bored. However, there is variation in the way children's brains process sensory input. Some nearly always feel comfortable with little stimulation, whereas others require a high degree of environmental input to feel comfortable. The latter group becomes "sensation seekers," who seek out stimulating activities that may include aggressive behavior.[107] The factors that determine a person's level of arousal are not fully understood. Suspected sources include brain chemistry and brain structure. Another view is that adolescents with low heart rates are more likely to commit crimes, because they seek out stimulation to increase their arousal to normal levels.[108]

Genetic Influences

It has been hypothesized that some youths inherit a genetic configuration that predisposes them to aggression.[109] In the same way that people inherit genes that control height and eye color, biosocial theorists believe antisocial behavior characteristics and mental disorders also may be passed down. According to this view, (1) antisocial behavior is inherited, (2) the genetic makeup of parents is passed on to children, and (3) genetic abnormality is linked to a variety of antisocial behaviors.[110] Early theories suggested that proneness to delinquency ran in families. However, most families share a similar lifestyle as well as a similar gene pool, making it difficult to determine whether behavior is a function of heredity or the environment.

Parental Deviance If criminal tendencies are inherited, then the children of criminal parents should be more likely to become law violators than the offspring of conventional parents. A number of studies have found that parental criminality and deviance do, in fact, powerfully influence delinquent behavior.[111] Some of the most important data on parental deviance were gathered by Donald J. West and David P. Farrington as part of the long-term Cambridge-Somerville Youth Survey. These cohort data indicate that a significant number of delinquent youths have criminal

Arousal theorists believe that some people's brains function differently in response to environmental stimuli. We all seek to maintain an optimal level of arousal: too much stimulation leaves us anxious, and too little makes us feel bored. Zaryus "Enforcer Rude Boy" Moore, 15, dances on top of a car in front of fellow members of the Remnant krumping dance crew, during a dance session in south central Los Angeles. Krumping is a high-energy, clowning dance style born out of hip-hop and other influences such as African dance, and is intended to be an alternative to street violence. Can socially acceptable activities such as krumping provide a level of arousal that can substitute for deviant forms of behavior?

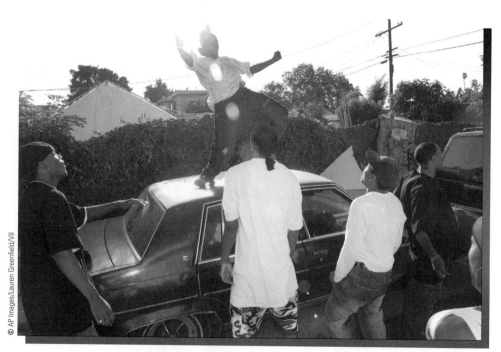

© AP Images/Lauren Greenfield/VII

fathers.[112] Whereas 8 percent of the sons of noncriminal fathers eventually became chronic offenders, about 37 percent of boys with criminal fathers were multiple offenders.[113] In another important analysis, Farrington found that one type of parental deviance—schoolyard aggression or bullying—may be both inter- and intragenerational. Bullies have children who bully others, and these second-generation bullies grow up to father children who are also bullies, in a never-ending cycle.[114]

Farrington's findings are supported by some recent data from the Rochester Youth Development Study (RYDS), a longitudinal analysis that has been monitoring the behavior of a thousand area youths since 1988. RYDS researchers have also found an intergenerational continuity in antisocial behavior: criminal fathers produce delinquent sons who grow up to have delinquent children themselves.[115]

In sum, there is growing evidence that crime is intergenerational: criminal fathers produce criminal sons who then produce criminal grandchildren. It is possible that at least part of the association is genetic.[116]

Twin Studies One method of studying the genetic basis of delinquency is to compare twins to non-twin siblings. If crime is an inherited trait, identical twins should be quite similar in their behavior because they share a common genetic makeup. Because twins are usually brought up in the same household, however, any similarity in their delinquent behavior might be a function of environmental influences and not genetics. To guard against this, biosocial theorists have compared the behavior of identical, monozygotic (MZ) twins with fraternal, dizygotic (DZ) twins; the former have an identical genetic makeup, whereas the latter share only about 50 percent of their genes. Studies conducted on twin behavior detected a significant relationship between the criminal activities of MZ twins and a much lower association between those of DZ twins.[117] About 60 percent of MZ twins share criminal behavior patterns (if one twin was criminal, so was the other), whereas only 30 percent of DZ twins are similarly related.[118] Among relevant findings:

- There is a significantly higher risk for suicidal behavior among monozygotic twin pairs than dizygotic twin pairs.[119]

- Differences in concordance between MZ and DZ twins have been found in tests measuring psychological dysfunctions, such as conduct disorders, impulsivity, and antisocial behavior.[120]

- MZ twins are closer than DZ twins in such crime relevant measures as level of aggression and verbal skills.[121]

- Both members of MZ twin pairs who suffer child abuse are more likely to engage in later antisocial activity more often than DZ pairs.[122]

Although this seems to support a connection between genetic makeup and delinquency, it is also true that MZ twins are more likely to look alike and to share physical traits than DZ twins, and they are more likely to be treated similarly. Shared behavior patterns may therefore be a function of socialization and not heredity.

One famous study of twin behavior still under way is the Minnesota Study of Twins Reared Apart, which is part of the Minnesota Twin Family Study. This research compares the behavior of MZ and DZ twin pairs who were raised together with others who were separated at birth and in some cases did not even know of the other's existence. The study shows some striking similarities in behavior and ability for twin pairs raised apart. An MZ twin reared away from a co-twin has about as good a chance of being similar to the co-twin in terms of personality, interests, and attitudes as one who has been reared with the co-twin. The conclusion: similarities between twins are due to genes, not to the environment[123] (see Exhibit 3.1).

Adoption Studies Another way to determine whether delinquency is an inherited trait is to compare the behavior of adopted children with that of their biological parents. If the criminal behavior of children is more like that of their biological parents

To learn more about twin research, go to the **Minnesota Twin Family Study, "What's Special About Twins to Science?"** website via www.thomsonedu.com/criminaljustice/siegel.

| Exhibit 3.1 | **Findings from the Minnesota Study of Twins Reared Apart** |

- If you are a DZ twin and your co-twin is divorced, your risk of divorce is 30 percent. If you are an MZ twin and your co-twin is divorced, your risk of divorce rises to 45 percent, which is 25 percent above the rates for the Minnesota population. Because this was not true for DZ twins, we can conclude that genes do influence the likelihood of divorce.

- MZ twins become *more* similar with respect to abilities, such as vocabularies and arithmetic scores as they age. As DZ (fraternal) twins get older they become less similar in these traits.

- A P300 is a tiny electrical response (a few millionths of a volt) that occurs in the brain when a person detects something that is unusual or interesting. For example, if a person were shown nine circles and one square, a P300 brain response would appear after seeing the square because it's different. Identical (MZ) twin children have very similar-looking P300s. By comparison, children who are fraternal (DZ) twins do not show as much similarity in their P300s. These results indicate that the way the brain processes information may be greatly influenced by genes.

- An EEG is a measure of brain activity or brain waves that can be used to monitor a person's state of arousal. MZ twins tend to produce strikingly similar EEG spectra; DZ twins show far less similarity.

Source: University of Minnesota–Twin Cities, Department of Psychology, *Minnesota Study of Twins Reared Apart.* Available at: www.psych.umn.edu/psylabs/mtfs/special.htm (accessed November 21, 2006).

(whom they have never met) than that of their adoptive parents (who brought them up), it would indicate that the tendency toward delinquency is inherited.

Studies of this kind have generally supported the hypothesis that there is a link between genetics and behavior.[124] Adoptees share many of the behavioral and intellectual characteristics of their biological parents despite the conditions found in their adoptive homes. Genetic makeup is sufficient to counteract even extreme conditions, such as malnutrition and abuse.[125] Some of the most influential research in this area has been conducted by Sarnoff Mednick. In one study, Mednick and Bernard Hutchings found that although only 13 percent of the adoptive fathers of a sample of delinquent youths had criminal records, 31 percent of their biological fathers had criminal records.[126] Analysis of a control group's background indicated that about 11 percent of all fathers have criminal records. Hutchings and Mednick were forced to conclude that genetics played at least some role in creating delinquent tendencies.[127]

In sum, twin studies and adoption studies provide some evidence that delinquent-producing traits may be inherited. Concept Summary 3.2 reviews the biological basis of delinquency.

 Concept Summary 3.2

Biological Views of Delinquency

Theory	Major Premise	Focus
Biochemical	Delinquency, especially violence, is a function of diet, vitamin intake, hormonal imbalance, or food allergies.	Explains irrational violence. Shows how the environment interacts with personal traits to influence behavior.
Neurological	Delinquents often suffer brain impairment, as measured by the EEG. ADHD and minimal brain dysfunction are related to antisocial behavior.	Explains the relationship between child abuse and delinquency. May be used to clarify the link between school problems and delinquency.
Genetic	Criminal traits and predispositions are inherited. The criminality of parents can predict the delinquency of children.	Explains why only a small percentage of youth in a high-crime area become chronic offenders.

PSYCHOLOGICAL THEORIES OF DELINQUENCY

Some experts view the cause of delinquency as psychological.[128] After all, most behaviors labeled delinquent seem to be symptomatic of some psychological problem. Psychologists point out that many delinquent youths have poor home lives; destructive relationships with neighbors, friends, and teachers; and conflicts with authority figures. These relationships seem to indicate a disturbed personality. Furthermore, studies of incarcerated youths indicate that their personalities are marked by antisocial characteristics. And because delinquent behavior occurs among youths in every racial, ethnic, and socioeconomic group, psychologists view it as a function of mental disturbance, rather than of social factors such as alienation and poverty. Many delinquents do not manifest significant psychological problems, but enough do to give clinicians a powerful influence on delinquency theory.

Because psychology is a complex discipline, more than one psychological perspective on crime exists. Three prominent psychological perspectives on delinquency are psychodynamic theory, behavioral theory, and cognitive theory.[129] Figure 3.2 outlines these perspectives.

Psychodynamic Theory

psychodynamic theory
Branch of psychology that holds that the human personality is controlled by unconscious mental processes developed early in childhood.

According to the **psychodynamic theory**, which originated with the Austrian physician Sigmund Freud (1856–1939), law violations are a product of the subconscious personality formed early in life.[130] The theory argues that the personality contains three major components. The *id* is the unrestrained, pleasure-seeking component with which each child is born. The *ego* develops through the reality of living in the

Figure 3.2   **Psychological Perspectives on Delinquency**

Theory	Cause
Psychodynamic (psychoanalytic)	**Intrapsychic processes** • Unconscious conflicts • Childhood traumas • Family abuse • Neurosis • Psychosis
Behavioral	**Learning processes** • Past experiences • Stimuli • Rewards and punishments
Cognitive	**Information processing** • Thinking • Problem solving • Scripts • Moral development

world and helps restrain the id's need for immediate gratification. The *superego* develops through interactions with parents and others and represents the conscience and the moral rules that are shared by most adults.

All three segments of the personality operate simultaneously. The id dictates needs and desires, the superego counteracts the id by fostering feelings of morality, and the ego evaluates the reality of a position between these two extremes. If these components are balanced, the individual can lead a normal life. If one aspect of the personality becomes dominant at the expense of the others, however, the individual exhibits abnormal personality traits. Furthermore, the theory suggests that an imbalance in personality traits caused by a traumatic early childhood can result in long-term psychological difficulties. For example, if parents fail to help the child develop his or her superego adequately, the child's id may become dominant. The absence of a strong superego results in inability to distinguish clearly between right and wrong. Later, the youth may demand immediate gratification, lack sensitivity for the needs of others, act aggressively and impulsively, or demonstrate psychotic symptoms. Antisocial behavior may result from conflict or trauma occurring early in a child's development, and delinquent activity may become an outlet for these feelings.

Disorders and Delinquency According to Freud's version of psychodynamic theory, people who experience anxiety and fear they are losing control are suffering from a form of *neurosis* and are referred to as *neurotics*. People who have lost control and are dominated by their id are known as *psychotics*; their behavior may be marked by hallucinations and inappropriate responses.

Psychosis takes many forms, the most common being *schizophrenia*, a condition marked by illogical thought processes, distorted perceptions, and abnormal emotional expression. According to the classical psychoanalytic view, the most serious types of antisocial behavior might be motivated by psychosis, whereas neurotic feelings would be responsible for less serious delinquent acts and status offenses.[131]

Contemporary psychologists no longer use the term *neuroses* to describe all the various forms of unconscious conflict. It is more common to refer to specific types of disorders, including *anxiety disorder, mood disorder, sleep disorder*, and so on. Among these is **bipolar disorder**, in which moods alternate between periods of wild elation and deep depression.[132]

The Psychodynamic Tradition and Delinquency How do psychodynamic theorists explain delinquency? Erik Erikson speculated that many adolescents experience a life crisis in which they feel emotional, impulsive, and uncertain of their role and purpose.[133] He coined the phrase **identity crisis** to denote this period of inner turmoil. Erikson's approach might characterize the behavior of youthful drug abusers as an expression of confusion over their place in society, inability to direct their behavior toward useful outlets, and perhaps, dependence on others to offer solutions to their problems.

Psychologists view youth crime as a result of unresolved internal conflict. Some children, especially those who have been abused or mistreated, may experience unconscious feelings of fear and hatred. Others are driven by an unconscious desire to be punished for prior sins, either real or imaginary. They may violate the law to gain attention or punish their parents. If these conflicts cannot be reconciled, regression occurs and the id becomes dominant. This regression accounts for a great number of mental diseases, and in many cases it may be related to criminal behavior.[134] The psychodynamic view is supported by research that shows that juvenile offenders suffer from a disproportionate amount of mental health problems and personality disturbance.[135] Violent youths have been clinically diagnosed as "overtly hostile," "explosive or volatile," "anxious," and "depressed."[136] Research efforts have found that juvenile offenders who engage in serious violent crimes often suffer from some sort of mental disturbance, such as depression.[137]

bipolar disorder
A psychological condition producing mood swings between wild elation and deep depression.

identity crisis
Psychological state, identified by Erikson, in which youth face inner turmoil and uncertainty about life roles.

Another psychodynamic view is that delinquents are unable to control their impulsive drives. Perhaps because they suffered unhappy experiences in childhood or had families that could not provide proper care, they have weak egos and are unable to cope with conventional society.[138] In its most extreme form, delinquency may be viewed as a form of psychosis that prevents delinquent youths from appreciating the feelings of victims or controlling their need for gratification.[139] Research shows that some delinquents exhibit indications of such psychological abnormalities as schizophrenia, paranoia, and obsessive behaviors; female offenders seem to have more serious mental health symptoms and psychological disturbances than male offenders.[140]

Mental Disorders and Crime According to the psychodynamic approach, criminal behavior is a function of unconscious mental instability and turmoil. Offenders may suffer from a garden variety of mood and/or behavior disorders rendering them histrionic, depressed, antisocial, or narcissistic.[141] Some have been diagnosed with some form of mood disorders characterized by disturbance in expressed emotions.

Children with **oppositional defiant disorder (ODD)**, for example, experience an ongoing pattern of uncooperative, defiant, and hostile behavior toward authority figures that seriously interferes with day-to-day functioning. Symptoms of ODD may include frequent loss of temper, constant arguing with adults; defying adults or refusing adult requests or rules; deliberately annoying others; blaming others for mistakes or misbehavior; being angry and resentful; being spiteful or vindictive; swearing or using obscene language; or having a low opinion of yourself.[142]

Children who are diagnosed with **conduct disorder (CD)**, have great difficulty following rules and behaving in a socially acceptable way.[143] They are often viewed by other children, adults, and social agencies as severely antisocial. Research shows that they are frequently involved in such activities as bullying, fighting, committing sexual assaults, and behaving cruelly toward animals.

It is also possible that antisocial behavior is a consequence of inability to cope with feelings of oppression or depression. Research shows that kids who are clinically depressed are more likely to engage in a garden variety of delinquent acts, whereas nondepressed kids tend to specialize in violent or theft crimes.[144] Some suffer from alexithymia, a deficit in emotional cognition that prevents people from being aware of their feelings or being able to understand or talk about their thoughts and emotions; they seem robotic and emotionally dead.[145] Others may suffer from eating disorders and are likely to use fasting, vomiting, and drugs to lose weight or to keep from gaining weight.[146]

For kids who suffer from such psychological deficits, delinquency may actually produce positive psychic results: it helps youths feel independent; gives them the possibility of excitement and the chance to use their skills and imagination; provides the promise of gain; allows them to blame others (the police) for their predicament; and gives them a chance to rationalize their sense of failure ("If I hadn't gotten into trouble, I could have been a success").[147]

The psychodynamic approach places heavy emphasis on the family's role. Antisocial youths frequently come from families in which parents are unable to provide the controls that allow children to develop the personal tools they need to cope with the world.[148] Their destructive behavior may actually be a call for help. In fact, some psychoanalysts view delinquent behaviors as motivated by an unconscious urge to be punished. These children, who feel unloved, assume the reason must be their own inadequacy; hence, they deserve punishment.

Although this evidence is persuasive, the association between mental disturbance and delinquency is unresolved. It is possible that any link is caused by some intervening variable or factor:

- Psychologically troubled youth do poorly in school and school failure leads to delinquency.[149]
- Psychologically troubled youth have conflict-ridden social relationships that make them prone to commit delinquent acts.[150]

oppositional defiant disorder (ODD)
A psychological condition with symptoms including an ongoing pattern of uncooperative, defiant, and hostile behavior toward authority figures that seriously interferes with day-to-day functioning.

conduct disorder (CD)
A psychological disorder characterized by difficulty following rules and behaving in a socially acceptable way.

- Kids who suffer child abuse are more likely to have mental anguish and commit violent acts; child abuse is the actual cause of both problems.[151]
- Living in a stress-filled urban environment may produce symptoms of both mental illness and crime.[152]

It is also possible that the link is spurious and caused by the treatment of the mentally ill: The police may be more likely to arrest the mentally ill, giving the illusion that they are crime-prone.[153] However, some recent research by Paul Hirschfield and his associates gives only mixed support to this view. Although some mental health problems increase the risk of arrest, others bring out more cautious or compassionate police responses that may result in treatment rather than arrest.[154] Further research is needed to clarify this important relationship.

Behavioral Theory

Not all psychologists agree that behavior is controlled by unconscious mental processes determined by relationships early in childhood. Behavioral psychologists argue that personality is learned throughout life during interaction with others. Based primarily on the work of the American psychologist John B. Watson (1878–1958), and popularized by Harvard professor B. F. Skinner (1904–1990), **behaviorism** concerns itself with measurable events rather than unobservable psychic phenomena.

behaviorism
Branch of psychology concerned with the study of observable behavior rather than unconscious processes; focuses on particular stimuli and responses to them.

Behaviorists suggest that individuals learn by observing how people react to their behavior. Behavior is triggered initially by a stimulus or change in the environment. If a particular behavior is reinforced by some positive reaction or event, that behavior will be continued and eventually learned. However, behaviors that are not reinforced or are punished will be extinguished. For example, if children are given a reward (dessert) for eating their entire dinner, eventually they will learn to eat successfully. Conversely, if children are punished for some misbehavior, they will associate disapproval with that act and avoid that behavior.

Social Learning Theory Some behaviorists hold that learning and social experiences, coupled with values and expectations, determine behavior. This is known as **social learning theory**. The most widely read social learning theorists are Albert Bandura, Walter Mischel, and Richard Walters.[155] They hold that children will model their behavior according to the reactions they receive from others; the behavior of adults, especially parents; and the behavior they view on television and in movies (see Focus on Delinquency, "Violent Media/Violent Behavior?" on page 72). If children observe aggression and see that it is approved or rewarded, they will likely react violently during a similar incident. Eventually, they will master the techniques of aggression and become more confident that their behavior will bring tangible rewards.[156]

social learning theory
The view that behavior is modeled through observation either directly through intimate contact with others or indirectly through media; interactions that are rewarded are copied, whereas those that are punished are avoided.

Social learning suggests that children who grow up in homes where violence is a way of life may learn to believe that such behavior is acceptable. Even if parents tell children not to be violent and punish them if they are, the children will model their behavior on the observed violence. Thus, children are more likely to heed what parents *do* than what they *say*. By middle childhood, some children have already acquired an association between their use of aggression against others and the physical punishment they receive at home. Often their aggressive responses are directed at other family members. The family may serve as a training ground for violence, because the child perceives physical punishment as the norm during conflict situations.[157]

Adolescent aggression is a result of disrupted dependency relations with parents. This refers to the frustration a child feels when parents provide poor role models and hold back affection. Children who lack close ties to their parents may have little opportunity or desire to model themselves after them or to internalize their standards.

In the absence of such internalized controls, the child's frustration is likely to be expressed in a socially unacceptable fashion, such as aggression.

Cognitive Theory

A third area of psychology that has received increasing recognition in recent years is **cognitive theory**. Psychologists with a cognitive perspective focus on mental processes.

The pioneers of this school were Wilhelm Wundt (1832–1920), Edward Titchener (1867–1927), and William James (1842–1920). This perspective contains several subgroups. Perhaps the most important of these for delinquency theory is the one that is concerned with how people morally represent and reason about the world.

Jean Piaget (1896–1980), founder of this approach, hypothesized that reasoning processes develop in an orderly fashion, beginning at birth and continuing until age twelve and older.[158] At first, during the *sensorimotor stage*, children respond to the environment in a simple manner, seeking interesting objects and developing their reflexes. By the fourth and final stage, the *formal operations stage*, they have developed into mature adults who can use logic and abstract thought.

Lawrence Kohlberg applied this concept to issues in delinquency.[159] He suggested that there are stages of moral development during which the basis for moral decisions changes. It is possible that serious offenders have a moral orientation that differs from that of law-abiding citizens. Kohlberg classified people according to the stage at which their moral development has ceased to grow. In his studies, the majority of delinquents were revealed as having a lack of respect for the law and a personality marked by self-interest; in contrast, non-offenders viewed the law as something that benefits all of society and were willing to honor the rights of others.[160] Subsequent research has found that a significant number of non-delinquent youths displayed higher stages of moral reasoning than delinquents and that engaging in delinquent activities leads to reduced levels of moral reasoning, which in turn produces more delinquency in a never-ending loop.[161]

Information Processing Cognitive theorists who study information processing try to explain antisocial behavior in terms of perception and analysis of data. When people make decisions, they engage in a sequence of thought processes. First, they encode information so it can be interpreted. Then, they search for a proper response and decide on the most appropriate action. Finally, they act on their decision.[162] Law violators may lack the ability to perform cognitive functions in a normal and orderly fashion.[163] Some may be sensation seekers who are constantly looking for novel experiences, whereas others lack deliberation and rarely think through problems. Some may give up easily, whereas others act without thinking when they get upset.[164]

Adolescents who use information properly and can make reasoned decisions when facing emotion-laden events are best able to avoid antisocial behavior.[165] In contrast, delinquency-prone adolescents may have cognitive deficits and use information incorrectly when they make decisions.[166] They have a distorted view of the world that shapes their thinking and colors their judgments. These youths view crime as an appropriate means to satisfy their immediate personal needs, which take precedence over more distant social needs, such as obedience to the law.[167] They have difficulty making the "right" decision while under stress. As a result of their faulty calculations, they pursue behaviors that they perceive as beneficial and satisfying, but that turn out to be harmful and detrimental.[168] They may take aggressive action, because they wrongly believe that a situation demands forceful responses when it actually does not. They find it difficult to understand or sympathize with other people's feelings and emotions, which leads them to blame their victims for their problems.[169] Thus, the sexual offender believes their target either "led them on" or secretly wanted the encounter to occur.[170]

One reason for this may be that they are relying on mental "scripts" learned in early childhood that tell them how to interpret events, what to expect, how they should react, and what the outcome of the interaction should be.[171] Hostile children may have learned improper scripts by observing how others react to events; their own parents' aggressive, inappropriate behavior would have considerable impact. Some may have had early, prolonged exposure to violence (such as child abuse), which in-

Violent Media/Violent Behavior?

One aspect of social learning theory that has received a great deal of attention is the belief that children will model their behavior after characters they observe on TV or see in movies. Many parents are concerned about the effects of their children's exposure to violence in the mass media. Often the violence is of a sexual nature, and some experts fear there is a link between sexual violence and viewing pornography.

Children are particularly susceptible to TV imagery. It is believed that many children consider television images to be real, especially if the images are authoritatively presented by an adult (as in a commercial). Some children, especially those considered "emotionally disturbed," may be unable to distinguish between fantasy and reality when watching TV shows. Children begin frequent TV viewing at 2.5 years of age and continue at a high level during the preschool and early school years. But what do they watch? Marketing research indicates that adolescents ages eleven to fourteen rent violent horror movies at a higher rate than any other age group; adolescents also use older peers and siblings or apathetic parents to gain access to R-rated films. Even children's programming is saturated with violence. It is estimated that the average child views eight thousand TV murders before finishing elementary school.

Media-Violence Linkage

A number of hypotheses have been formulated to explain the media-violence linkage:

- Media *violence* influences specific areas of the brain, including the precuneus, posterior cingulate, amygdala, inferior parietal, and prefrontal and premotor cortex of the right hemisphere region. These areas of the brain are involved in the regulation of emotion, arousal and attention, episodic memory encoding and retrieval, and motor programming. Extensive viewing may result in a large number of aggressive scripts stored in long-term memory in the posterior cingulate, which can then be used as a guide for social behavior.
- Observing media violence promotes negative attitudes, such as suspiciousness and the expectation that the viewer will become involved in violence. Those who watch television frequently view aggression and violence as common, socially acceptable behavior.
- Media violence allows aggressive youths to justify their behavior. Rather than causing violence, television may help violent youths rationalize their behavior as socially acceptable.
- Extensive and repeated exposure to media violence desensitizes kids to real world violence thereby increasing aggression by removing normal inhibitions against aggression.
- Media violence may disinhibit aggressive behavior, which is normally controlled by other learning processes. Disinhibition takes place when adults are viewed as being rewarded for violence and when violence is seen as socially acceptable. This contradicts previous learning experiences in which violent behavior was viewed as wrong.

Testing the Link

A number of methods have been used to measure the effect of TV viewing on violent behavior. One method is to expose groups of people to violent TV shows in a laboratory setting and compare them to control groups who viewed nonviolent programming; observations have also been made at playgrounds, athletic fields, and residences. Other experiments require individuals to answer attitude surveys after watching violent TV shows. Still another approach is to use aggregate measures of TV viewing, that is, the number of violent TV shows on the air during a given period is compared to crime rates during the same period.

Most evaluations of experimental data indicate that watching violence on TV is correlated with aggressive behaviors. In one of the most important recent studies, L. Rowell Huesmann and his associates found that children ages six to nine who watched more violent television displayed more aggressive behavior than their peers. Brad Bushman and his colleagues at the University of Michigan contacted 329 of these children fifteen years after they had participated in the Huesmann study. Now as adults, those same children who had viewed violent shows in their adolescence continued to behave

creases their sensitivity to slights and maltreatment.[172] Oversensitivity to rejection by their peers is a continuation of sensitivity to rejection by their parents.[173] Violence becomes a stable behavior, because the scripts that emphasize aggressive responses are repeatedly rehearsed as the child matures. When they attack victims, they may believe they are defending themselves, even though they are misreading the situation.[174] They may have a poor sense of time, leaving them incapable of dealing with social problems in an effective manner.[175]

Cognitive Treatment Treatment based on information processing acknowledges that people are more likely to respond aggressively to a provocation when thoughts stir feelings of anger. Cognitive therapists attempt to teach people to control aggressive impulses by experiencing provocations as problems demanding a solution rather than as in a violent and aggressive manner. Boys who liked violent television shows grew into men who were significantly more likely to have pushed, grabbed, or shoved their wives or others whom they found insulting. They were also much more likely to be convicted of a crime. Ironically, women who watched violent shows as children reported being punched, beaten, or choked as adults at a rate over four times the rate of women who did not watch violent programs.

Rethinking the Media-Violence Link

Though this evidence is persuasive, the relationship between TV viewing and violence is still uncertain. A number of critics say the evidence does not support the claim that TV viewing is related to antisocial behavior. Some assert that experimental results are short-lived. Children may have an immediate reaction to viewing violence on TV, but aggression is extinguished once the viewing ends. Although experiments do show that children act aggressively in a laboratory setting after watching violent TV shows, that does not mean they will actually commit rape and assault. And although Huesmann showed that kids who watch violent TV grow up to be violent adults, it is also possible that they would have been violent even if they had not watched TV at all. Violence-prone children like to watch violent TV shows, and not the other way around. It is also possible that children are able to watch inappropriate violent media because their parents are ineffectual and do not monitor their viewing habits. Poor parental supervision and not violent media is the actual cause of teen aggression.

Aggregate data are also inconclusive. Little evidence exists that areas that have high levels of violent TV viewing also have rates of violent crime that are above the norm. Millions of children watch violence yet fail to become violent criminals. And even if a violent behavior–TV link could be established, it would be difficult to show that antisocial people develop aggressive traits merely from watching TV.

CRITICAL THINKING

1. Should TV shows with a violent theme be prohibited from being aired on commercial TV before 9 P.M.? If you say yes, would you broadcast the national news?

2. Even if a violence-TV link could be established, is it not possible that aggressive, antisocial youths may simply enjoy watching TV shows that support their personal behavioral orientation, in the same way that science fiction fans flock to *Star Wars* and *Star Trek* films?

INFOTRAC COLLEGE EDITION RESEARCH

Use "media violence" as a key term on InfoTrac College Edition in order to learn more about the association between observing violence on TV and in movies and personal involvement in antisocial behaviors.

Sources: Bruce Bartholow, Brad Bushman, and Marc Sestir, "Chronic Violent Video Game Exposure and Desensitization to Violence: Behavioral and Event-Related Brain Potential Data," *Journal of Experimental Social Psychology* 42:532–539 (2006); Jon Fridrik Sigurdsson, Gisli Gudjonsson, Atli Vidar Bragason, Elsa Kristjansdottir, and Inga Dora Sigfusdottir, "The Role of Violent Cognition in the Relationship Between Personality and the Involvement in Violent Films and Computer Games," *Personality & Individual Differences* 41:381–392 (2006); René Weber, Ute Ritterfeld, and Klaus Mathiak, "Does Playing Violent Video Games Induce Aggression? Empirical Evidence of a Functional Magnetic Resonance Imaging Study," *Media Psychology* 8:39–60 (2006); John Murray, et.al. "Children's Brain Activations While Viewing Televised Violence Revealed by MRI," *Media Psychology* 8:25–37 (2006); Dimitri Christakis, Frederick Zimmerman, David DiGiuseppe, and Carolyn McCarty, "Early Television Exposure and Subsequent Attentional Problems in Children," *Pediatrics* 113:708–713 (2004); L. Rowell Huesmann, Jessica Moise-Titus, Cheryl-Lynn Podolski, and Leonard Eron, "Longitudinal Relations Between Children's Exposure to TV Violence and Their Aggressive and Violent Behavior in Young Adulthood: 1977–1992," *Developmental Psychology* 39:201–221 (2003); Brad Bushman and Craig Anderson, "Media Violence and the American Public," *American Psychologist* 56:477–489 (2001); Edward Donnerstein and Daniel Linz, "The Question of Pornography," *Psychology Today* 20:56–59 (1986); Joyce Sprafkin, Kenneth Gadow, and Monique Dussault, "Reality Perceptions of Television: A Preliminary Comparison of Emotionally Disturbed and Nonhandicapped Children," *American Journal of Orthopsychiatry* 56:147–152 (1986); UCLA Center for Communication Policy, *Television Violence Monitoring Project* (Los Angeles: University of California Press, 1995); Wendy Wood, Frank Wong, and J. Gregory Chachere, "Effects of Media Violence on Viewers' Aggression in Unconstrained Social Interaction," *Psychological Bulletin* 109:371–383 (1991).

insults requiring retaliation. Programs teach problem-solving skills that may include self-disclosure, listening, following instructions, and using self-control.[176] Areas for improvement include (1) coping and problem-solving skills; (2) relationships with peers, parents, and other adults; (3) conflict resolution and communication skills; (4) decision-making abilities; (5) pro-social behaviors, including cooperation with others and respecting others; and (6) awareness of feelings of others (empathy).[177]

Personality and Delinquency

Personality can be defined as the stable patterns of behavior, including thoughts and emotions, which distinguish one person from another.[178] Personality reflects characteristic ways of adapting to life's demands. The way we behave is a function of how our personality enables us to interpret events and make appropriate choices.

More than fifty years ago, Sheldon and Eleanor Glueck identified a number of personality traits that characterize delinquents:

self-assertiveness	extraversion
defiance	ambivalence
impulsiveness	feeling unappreciated
narcissism	distrust of authority
suspicion	poor personal skills
destructiveness	mental instability
sadism	hostility
lack of concern for others	resentment

This research is representative of the view that delinquents maintain a distinct personality whose characteristics increase the probability that they will be antisocial and that their actions will involve them with agents of social control, ranging from teachers to police.[179] Callous, unemotional traits in very young children can be a warning sign for future psychopathy and antisocial behavior.[180]

Following the Glueck effort, researchers have continued to examine the personality traits of delinquents, finding that many are impulsive individuals with short attention spans.[181] Among the most well known efforts was psychologist Hans Eysenck's identification of two traits he closely associates with antisocial behavior: **extraversion** and **neuroticism**.[182] Extraverts are impulsive individuals who lack the ability to examine their own motives; those high in neuroticism are anxious and emotionally unstable.[183] Youths who are both neurotic and extraverted often lack insight and are highly impulsive. They act self-destructively, for example, by abusing drugs, and are the type of offender who will repeat their criminal activity over and over.[184]

The Antisocial Personality It has also been suggested that delinquency may result from a syndrome interchangeably referred to as the **antisocial**, **psychopathic**, or **sociopathic personality**. Although no more than 3 percent of male offenders may be classified as antisocial, it is possible that a large segment of persistent offenders share this trait.[185]

extraversion
Impulsive behavior without the ability to examine motives and behavior.

neuroticism
A personality trait marked by unfounded anxiety, tension, and emotional instability.

psychopathic personality (also known as sociopathic or antisocial personality)
A person lacking in warmth, exhibiting inappropriate behavior responses, and unable to learn from experience; the condition is defined by persistent violations of social norms, including lying, stealing, truancy, inconsistent work behavior, and traffic arrests.

People with antisocial personalities lack affect and remorse even when they commit horrific crimes. Brendan Dassey, 16, is escorted into a Manitowoc County, Wisconsin courthouse on May 26, 2006. Dassey was accused of murder and sexual assault after admitting to investigators that he and his uncle, Steven Avery, raped and killed 25-year-old photographer Teresa Halbach and then burned her body in a fire pit. Dassey has since recanted his confession.

Antisocial youths exhibit low levels of guilt and anxiety and persistently violate the rights of others. Although they may exhibit charm and be highly intelligent, these mask a disturbed personality that makes them incapable of forming enduring relationships.[186] Frequently involved in such deviant behaviors as truancy, lying, and substance abuse, antisocial people lack the ability to empathize with others. From an early age, the antisocial person's home life was filled with frustration and quarreling. Consequently, throughout life the antisocial youth is unreliable, unstable, and demanding.

Youths diagnosed as being clinically antisocial are believed to be thrill seekers who engage in destructive behavior. Some may become almost addicted to thrill seeking, resulting in repeated and dangerous risky behaviors.[187] Some become gang members and participate in violent sexual escapades to compensate for a fear of responsibility and an inability to maintain relationships.[188] Delinquents have been described as sensation seekers who desire an extraverted lifestyle, including partying, drinking, and having a variety of sexual partners.[189]

The Origins of Antisocial Personality A number of factors contribute to the development of antisocial personalities. One source may be family dysfunction and include having an emotionally disturbed parent, parental rejection during childhood, and inconsistent or overly abusive discipline.[190] Another possibility is that psychopaths may have brain-related physical anomalies that cause them to process emotional input differently than non-psychopaths.[191] Another view is that antisocial youths suffer from lower levels of arousal than the general population. Consequently, they may need greater-than-average stimulation to bring them up to comfortable levels.[192] Psychologists have attempted to treat antisocial youths by giving them adrenaline, which increases their arousal levels.

Intelligence and Delinquency

Early criminologists thought that if they could determine which individuals were less intelligent, they might be able to identify potential delinquents before they committed socially harmful acts.[193] Psychologists began to measure the correlation between IQ and crime by testing adjudicated juvenile delinquents. Delinquent juveniles were believed to be substandard in intelligence and thus inclined to commit more crimes than more intelligent persons. Thus, juvenile delinquents were used as a test group around which numerous theories about intelligence were built.

Nature Theory When IQ tests were administered to inmates of prisons and juvenile training schools early in the twentieth century, a large proportion of the inmates scored low on the tests. Henry Goddard found in 1920 that many institutionalized persons were "feebleminded" and concluded that at least half of all juvenile delinquents were mental defectives.[194] In 1926, William Healy and Augusta Bronner tested a group of delinquents in Chicago and Boston and found that 37 percent were subnormal in intelligence.[195] They concluded that delinquents were five to ten times more likely to be mentally deficient than non-delinquent boys. These and other early studies were embraced as proof that a correlation existed between innate low intelligence and deviant behavior. IQ tests were believed to measure genetic makeup, and many psychologists accepted the predisposition of substandard individuals toward delinquency. This view is referred to as the **nature theory** of intelligence.

Nurture Theory In the 1930s, more culturally sensitive explanations of behavior led to the **nurture theory**. Nurture theory argues that intelligence is not inherited and that low-IQ parents do not necessarily produce low-IQ children.[196] This view holds that intelligence must be viewed as partly biological, and primarily sociological. Nurture theorists discredit the notion that people commit crimes because they have low IQs. Instead, they postulate that environmental stimulation from parents, schools,

nature theory
The view that intelligence is inherited and is a function of genetic makeup.

nurture theory
The view that intelligence is determined by environmental stimulation and socialization.

peer groups, and others create a child's IQ level and that low IQs result from an environment that also encourages delinquent behavior.[197] It was reasoned that if educational environments could be improved, the result might be both an elevation in IQ scores and a decrease in delinquency.[198]

Rethinking IQ and Delinquency The relationship between IQ and delinquency is controversial because it implies that a condition is present at birth that accounts for delinquent behavior throughout the life cycle and that this condition is not easily changed. Research shows that measurements of intelligence taken in infancy are good predictors of later IQ.[199] By implication, if delinquency is not spread evenly through the social structure, neither is intelligence.

Some social scientists actively dispute that any association actually exists. As early as 1931, Edwin Sutherland evaluated IQ studies of criminals and delinquents and found evidence disputing the association between intelligence and criminality.[200] His findings did much to discredit the notion that a strong relationship exists between IQ and criminality, and for many years the IQ-delinquency link was ignored. Sutherland's research has been substantiated by a number of contemporary studies that find that IQ has a negligible influence on behavior.[201]

Those who still believe in an IQ-delinquency link refer to a study by Travis Hirschi and Michael Hindelang, who, after conducting a statistical analysis of IQ and delinquency data, concluded that "the weight of evidence is that IQ is more important than race and social class" for predicting delinquency.[202] They argued that a low IQ increases the likelihood of delinquent behavior through its effect on school performance. Youths with low IQs do poorly in school, and school failure is highly related to delinquency. Their conclusions have also been supported by a number of research efforts.[203]

Even those experts who believe that IQ influences delinquent behavior are split on the structure of the associations. Some believe IQ has an *indirect influence* on delinquency. For example, children with low IQs are more likely to engage in delinquent behavior because low IQ leads to school failure, and educational underachievement is associated with delinquency.[204] Even high-risk youths are less likely to become delinquents if they have relatively high IQs; low IQ increases the probability of a delinquent career.[205] The relationship between IQ and delinquency has been found to be consistent after controlling for class, race, and personality traits.[206]

Some experts believe IQ may have a *direct influence* on delinquency. The key linkage is the ability to manipulate abstract concepts. Low intelligence limits adolescents' ability to "foresee the consequences of their offending and to appreciate the feelings of victims."[207] Therefore, youths with limited intelligence are more likely to misinterpret events, take risks, and engage in harmful behavior. ✔ **Checkpoints**

CRITIQUING TRAIT THEORY VIEWS

Trait theories have been criticized on a number of grounds. One view is that the research methodologies they employ are invalid. Most research efforts use adjudicated or incarcerated offenders. It is difficult to determine whether findings represent the delinquent population or merely those most likely to be arrested. For example, some critics have described heredity studies as "poorly designed, ambiguously reported, and exceedingly inadequate in addressing the relevant issues."[208] Some critics also fear that trait-theory research can be socially and politically damaging. If an above-average number of indigent youths become delinquent offenders, can it be assumed that the less affluent are genetically inferior? This conclusion is unacceptable to many social scientists in light of what is known about race, gender, and class bias.

Defenders counter that trait theorists do not ignore environmental and social factors.[209] For example, some kids may have emotional and psychological problems that place them at a disadvantage, limit their chances of success, and heighten their

Psychological Views

Theory	Major Premise	Focus
Psychodynamic	The development of the unconscious personality early in childhood influences behavior for the rest of a person's life. Criminals have weak egos and damaged personalities.	Explains the onset of delinquency and why crime and drug abuse cut across class lines.
Behavioral	Kids commit delinquent acts when they model their behavior after others they see being rewarded for the same acts. Behavior is reinforced by rewards and extinguished by punishment.	Explains the role of significant others in the delinquency process. Shows how family life and media can influence crime and violence.
Cognitive	Individual reasoning processes influence behavior. Reasoning is influenced by the way people perceive their environment.	Shows why delinquent behavior patterns change over time as people mature and develop their reasoning powers. May explain the aging-out process.

feelings of anger and frustration. If their family is affluent, they will have the resources available to treat these problems; a less affluent family would lack the economic means and the institutional support needed to counteract these potentially destructive traits. Delinquency rate differences may then result from differential access to opportunities either to commit crime or to receive the treatment needed to correct developmental problems.

Concept Summary 3.3 reviews the psychological basis of delinquency.

TRAIT THEORY AND DELINQUENCY PREVENTION

Trait theory perspectives on delinquency suggest that prevention efforts should be directed at strengthening a youth's home life and relationships. If parents cannot supply proper nurturing, discipline, nutrition, and so on, the child cannot develop properly. Whether we believe that delinquency has a biosocial basis, a psychological basis, or a combination of both, it is evident that prevention efforts should be oriented to reach children early in their development.

County welfare agencies and private treatment centers offer counseling and other mental health services to families referred by schools, welfare agents, and court authorities. In some instances, intervention is focused on a particular family problem that has the potential for producing delinquent behavior—for example, alcohol and drug problems, child abuse, or sexual abuse. In other situations, intervention is oriented toward developing the self-image of parents and children or improving discipline in the family.

Some programs utilize treatment regimens based on specific theories (such as behavioral modification therapies). For example, the Decisions to Actions program in Kincheloe, Michigan, is organized around cognitive-behavioral restructuring of children's personalities. Its main focus is changing attitudes and beliefs associated with improper feelings and behaviors. Youths are taught to identify poor decision making and to explore the thinking behind "bad" decisions. They also are taught relapse prevention techniques that enable them to manage their emotions and behavior better. The ten-week program includes an assessment, meetings between the youths and mentors, victim empathy sessions where convicted felons speak with the youths, and team-building exercises.[210]

In addition, individual approaches have been used to prevent adjudicated youths from engaging in further criminal activities. Incarcerated and court-adjudicated youths are now almost universally given some form of mental and physical evaluation before they begin their correctional treatment. Such rehabilitation methods as

Because they are based on physical and psychological conditions, treatment programs based on trait theory can involve youth at a very early age. Mesa, Arizona preschool teacher Venus Leopold steps in to help find a solution for preschoolers (from left) Landon Hunt, Itzel Montero, and Allen Jiminez, who all want to use the same toy telephone during class. By setting the stage in preschool, educators believe these children can lead a new generation of kids who won't turn into bullies or allow themselves to be bullied.

psychological counseling and psychotropic medication (drugs like Ritalin) are often prescribed. In some instances, rehabilitation programs are provided through drop-in centers that service youths who are able to remain in their homes; more intensive programs require residential care. The creation of such programs illustrates that agents of the juvenile justice system believe that many delinquent youths and status offenders have psychological or physical problems and that their treatment can help reduce repeat criminal behavior. Faith in this approach suggests widespread agreement that delinquency can be traced to individual pathology.

The influence of psychological theory on delinquency prevention has been extensive, and programs based on biosocial theory have been dormant for some time. However, institutions are beginning to sponsor projects designed to study the influence of diet on crime and to determine whether regulating metabolism can affect behavior. Such efforts are relatively new and untested. Similarly, schools are making an effort to help youths with learning disabilities and other developmental problems. Delinquency prevention efforts based on biocriminological theory are still in their infancy.

Some questions remain about the effectiveness of individual treatment as a delinquency prevention technique. Little hard evidence exists that clinical treatment alone can prevent delinquency or rehabilitate delinquents. Critics still point to the failure of the Cambridge-Somerville Youth Study as evidence that clinical treatment has little value. In that effort, 325 high-risk youths were given intensive counseling, and their progress was compared with a control group that received no special attention. An evaluation of the project by Joan and William McCord found that the treated youths were more likely to become involved in law violation than the untreated controls.[211] By implication, the danger is that the efforts designed to help youths may actually stigmatize them, hindering their efforts to live conventional lives.

Critics argue that the more we try to help youths, the more likely they will be to see themselves as different, or as troublemakers.[212] Such questions have led to prevention efforts designed to influence the social as well as the psychological world of youths (see chapters 4 and 5). Both choice and trait theories have been embraced by conservatives because they focus on personal characteristics and traits rather than on the social environment. Both theoretical positions agree that delinquency can be prevented by dealing with the youths who engage in crime, not by transforming the social conditions associated with youth crime. In contrast, more liberal delinquency experts view the environment as the main source of delinquency.

SUMMARY

- Criminological theories that focus on the individual can be classified in two groups: choice theories and trait theories.
- Choice theory holds that people have free will to control their actions. Delinquency is a product of weighing the risks of crime against its benefits. If the risk is greater than the gain, people will choose not to commit crimes.
- One way of creating a greater risk is to make sure that the punishments associated with delinquency are severe, certain, and fast.
- Routine activities theory maintains that a pool of motivated offenders exists and that these offenders will take advantage of suitable targets unless they are heavily guarded.
- General deterrence theory holds that if delinquents are rational, an inverse relationship should exist between punishment and crime. The harsher, more certain, and swifter the punishment, the more likely it will deter delinquency.
- General deterrence assumes that delinquents make a rational choice before committing delinquent acts.
- Research has not indicated that deterrent measures actually reduce the delinquency rate.
- Specific deterrence theory holds that the delinquency rate can be reduced if offenders are punished so severely that they never commit crimes again.
- There is little evidence that harsh punishments reduce the delinquency rate, perhaps because most delinquents are not severely punished.
- Choice theorists agree that if the punishment for delinquency could be increased, the delinquency rate might fall. One method is to transfer youths to the criminal courts or to grant the adult justice system jurisdiction over serious juvenile cases. Similarly, some experts advocate incapacitation for serious juvenile offenders—for example, long-term sentences for chronic delinquents.
- Situational crime prevention strategies aim to reduce opportunities for crime to take place. By imposing obstacles that make it difficult to offend, such strategies strive to dissuade would-be offenders.

- Trait theories hold that delinquents do not choose to commit crimes freely but are influenced by forces beyond their control.
- The two types of current trait theory are biosocial and psychological.
- One of the earliest branches of biosocial theory was biological theory, formulated by Cesare Lombroso, who linked delinquency to inborn traits. Following his lead were theories based on genetic inheritance and body build. Although biological theory was in disrepute for many years, it has recently re-emerged.
- Biochemical factors linked to delinquency include diet, hormones, and blood chemistry.
- Neurological factors include brain damage and ADHD.
- Some experts believe that delinquent tendencies may be inherited. Studies use twins and adoptees to test this theory.
- Psychological theories include the psychodynamic model, which links antisocial behaviors to unconscious emotions and feelings developed in early childhood.
- The behavioral perspective emphasizes that children imitate the behavior they observe personally or view on television or in movies. Children who are exposed to violence and see it rewarded may become violent as adults.
- Cognitive psychology is concerned with how people perceive the world. Criminality is viewed as a function of improper information processing or lack of moral development.
- Psychopaths are people with a total lack of concern for others. They may commit the most serious violent crimes.
- Intelligence has also been related to delinquency. Some studies claim to show that delinquents have lower IQs than non-delinquents.
- Many delinquency prevention efforts are based on psychological theory. Judges commonly order delinquent youths to receive counseling. Recently, some delinquent offenders have been given biochemical therapy.

KEY TERMS

choice theory, p. 47
trait theory, p. 48
free will, p. 48
utilitarians, p. 48
classical criminology, p. 50
routine activities theory, p. 50
predatory crimes, p. 52
general deterrence, p. 54
co-offending, p. 54
specific deterrence, p. 54
situational crime prevention, p. 55

hot spot, p. 57
crackdown, p. 57
criminal atavism, p. 58
biosocial theory, p. 59
minimal brain dysfunction (MBD), p. 61
learning disabilities (LD), p. 61
psychodynamic theory, p. 67
bipolar disorder, p. 68
identity crisis, p. 68
oppositional defiant disorder (ODD), p. 69

conduct disorder (CD), p. 69
behaviorism, p. 70
social learning theory, p. 70
cognitive theory, p. 71
extraversion, p. 74
neuroticism, p. 74
psychopathic personality, sociopathic personality, antisocial personality, p. 74
nature theory, p. 75
nurture theory, p. 75

1. Are all delinquent acts psychologically abnormal? Can there be "normal" crimes?

2. How would you apply psychodynamic theory to delinquent acts such as shoplifting and breaking and entering a house?

3. Can delinquent behavior be deterred by the threat of punishment? If not, how can it be controlled?

4. Do you think that watching violence on TV and in films encourage youths to be aggressive and antisocial?

5. Do beer advertisements that feature attractive, scantily dressed young men and women encourage drinking? If they do not encourage people to drink, why bother advertising? If suggestive advertising works in getting people to buy beer, then why shouldn't suggestive violence encourage kids to be violent?

6. Discuss the characteristics of psychopaths. Do you know anyone who fits the description?

APPLYING WHAT YOU HAVE LEARNED

You are a state legislator who is a member of the subcommittee on juvenile justice. Your committee has been asked to redesign the state's juvenile code, because of public outrage over serious juvenile crime.

At an open hearing, a professor from the local university testifies that she has devised a surefire test to predict violence-prone delinquents. The procedure involves brain scans, DNA testing, and blood analysis. Used with samples of incarcerated adolescents, her procedure has been able to distinguish with 90 percent accuracy between youths with a history of violence and those who are exclusively property offenders. The professor testifies that, if each juvenile offender were tested with her techniques, the violence-prone career offender could easily be identified and given special treatment. Their scores could be kept on a registry and law enforcement agencies notified of the offenders' whereabouts.

Opponents argue that this type of testing is unconstitutional, because it violates the Fifth Amendment protection against self-incrimination and can unjustly label nonviolent offenders. Any attempt to base policy on biosocial makeup seems inherently wrong and unfair. Those who favor the professor's approach maintain that it is not uncommon to single out the insane or mentally incompetent for special treatment and that these conditions often have a biological basis. It is better that a few delinquents be unfairly labeled than have seriously violent offenders be ignored until it is too late.

- Is it possible that some kids are born to be delinquents? Or do kids "choose" crime?
- Is it fair to test kids to see if they have biological traits related to crime even if they have never committed a single offense?
- Should special laws be created to deal with the "potentially" dangerous offender?
- Should offenders be typed on the basis of their biological characteristics?

DOING RESEARCH ON THE WEB

To get more information on DNA testing, the American Civil Liberties Union's stance on personal privacy rights of Americans in the age of technology, and the DNA registry now operated by Alaska, go to **www.thomsonedu.com/criminaljustice/siegel** and surf to the federal sites for the National Criminal Justice Reference Service and the Office of Juvenile Justice and Delinquency Prevention.

Sociological Views of Delinquency

© Christopher Anderson/Magnum Photos

CHAPTER OBJECTIVES

After reading this chapter you should:

1. Know what is meant by the term *social disorganization.*

2. Understand the relationship between neighborhood fear, unemployment, social change, and lack of cohesion and delinquent behavior patterns.

3. Be familiar with the concept of strain and anomie.

4. Comprehend the elements of general strain theory and the concept of negative affective states.

5. Understand how cultural deviance creates a breeding ground for gangs and law-violating groups.

6. Know the social processes that have been linked to delinquency.

7. Be able to differentiate between learning and control theories.

8. Identify the elements of labeling and stigma that reinforce delinquency.

9. Recognize the role that criticism plays in creating an environment that breeds antisocial behaviors.

10. Be familiar with the social programs that have been designed to improve neighborhood conditions, help children be properly socialized, and reduce conflict.

Jay Simmons, the youngest of six children, was living with his family in an impoverished community when he entered the juvenile justice system. Growing up in a tough urban neighborhood took an early toll on Jay and his family. Around the age of eleven, his problems were becoming more evident at home and school. He was absent from school on a regular basis, often stayed out all night with friends, and was eventually arrested on retail theft charges. Jay's parents were struggling to find permanent housing and faced being homeless, so Jay was voluntarily placed in foster care. A teacher at his school took a strong interest in Jay and offered to care for him until his parents could again meet his needs. The family continued to have contact with Jay and hoped to have him return home when their situation improved.

A smart young man with many positive attributes, Jay was an engaging person and a talented athlete who excelled in school sports. Many adults could see great potential in him, but Jay's criminal activity continued. His foster parents became increasingly concerned that they could not provide the care and treatment Jay needed. In a short period of time Jay was arrested on two more violations for disorderly conduct and battery while becoming involved in fights at school. He was at risk for being placed in a more secure living environment. While in juvenile court for his delinquent behavior, Jay was sentenced to community supervision and probation. After an initial assessment, Jay's probation officer made formal dispositional recommendations to the court.

Although his foster parents had established clear rules for him, Jay felt torn between his old way of life and the new possibilities. Because of his family's issues of poverty, health concerns, unemployment, and homelessness, he had been very independent prior to his involvement with the juvenile justice system, doing what he wanted, staying in different places with different people much of the time. Jay now struggled with the new rules and expectations. He missed some of his initial appointments with his probation officer and continued to skip school. There were also concerns that Jay was drinking alcohol and becoming involved in gang activities.

Jay's probation officer, family, and foster parents encouraged him to follow the court-ordered recommendations and understand the consequences of his behavior. He developed a very strong relationship with his foster parents,

who were direct and honest with Jay about their concerns, often confronting him and contacting his coach, social workers, and parents about his behavior. The Substitute Care Unit at the local human services agency provided valuable support to Jay, his family, and foster parents during these difficult times, making home and school visits, trying to help maintain his placement in the foster home, and encouraging him to make good decisions. The team of professionals, coaches, and parents remained in close contact regarding Jay's behavior, as well as his academic progress. This level of parental involvement and teamwork made a huge impact on Jay and held him more accountable for his choices. He began to see his own potential and the need to make changes for his life.

Accountability was a key ingredient to Jay's success. He attended a retail theft group to address his criminal behavior and to encourage him to take responsibility for his actions. The program brings together eight to ten teenagers who have been involved in retail thefts with volunteers from the community, store security personnel, and a program leader. With fellow group members Jay would discuss the nature of his crimes, why they are wrong, the impact on victims, and how to prevent future delinquent acts by making better choices. The group participants and family members also met with a group facilitator to discuss the juvenile court process and what parents can expect if their children have further delinquencies, providing valuable information to the parents and a forum to ask questions and learn about other resources. Jay was also held accountable by being required to complete fifteen hours of community service. He worked with the Youth Restitution Program and was assigned a counselor who would help him locate volunteer opportunities and verify his participation.

Jay's involvement with a variety of programs and the many caring adults in his life made a significant difference for him. He continued to excel in sports and began to work harder in school. Although Jay never returned to his parental home, with the support of his foster parents he did remain in close contact with his family and they regularly attended activities together. With a new vision for his life, Jay started thinking seriously about going to college. He successfully completed his court-ordered programs, stayed out of trouble, eventually graduating from high school and receiving a full athletic scholarship to attend college.

Jay's story is not atypical; however, unlike Jay, many troubled youths are not able to turn their lives around. Delinquents often live in tough urban environments in families torn apart and in stress. Although there may be some factors related to delinquent behavior at the individual level, the majority of delinquency experts believe that the key to understanding delinquent behavior lies in the social environment. Many delinquents are indigent and desperate, not calculating or evil. A good number grew up in deteriorated parts of town and lack the social support and economic resources familiar to more affluent members of society. Understanding delinquent behavior, then, may require consideration of how these destructive social forces impact on human behavior.

Explanations of delinquency as an individual-level phenomenon fail to account for the consistent social patterns in delinquency. If violence is related to some individual level biochemical or chromosomal abnormality, then how can the following facts be explained:

- Some areas of the city have much higher crime and delinquency rates than others.
- Large cities have more crime problems than rural towns.
- Inner-city areas have higher delinquency rates than suburban areas.
- Some states and regions of the country have higher crime and delinquency rates than others.

These social facts contradict individual level theories, discussed in chapter 3, which maintain that the cause of delinquency can be traced to some personal choice, trait, or personality characteristic. It is unlikely that all people with physical or mental problems live in one section of town or in one area of the country. Why would kids in the far west choose crime more often than kids in the Midwest or New England? Yet, delinquency rates are higher in some sections of the country than in others. Some individual-level theorists believe that viewing violent TV shows can cause aggression. Yet adolescents in rural and suburban areas watch the same shows and movies as kids who live in the city. If the media causes violence, how can we explain urban-rural delinquency rate differences? If violence has a biological or psychological origin, should it not be distributed more evenly throughout the social structure, as opposed to being concentrated in certain areas?

SOCIAL FACTORS AND DELINQUENCY

What are the critical social factors believed to cause or affect delinquent behaviors?

- *Interpersonal interactions.* Social relationships with families, peers, schools, jobs, criminal justice agencies, and the like, may play an important role in shaping behavioral choices.[1] Inappropriate and disrupted social relations have been linked to crime and delinquency.[2]

- *Community ecological conditions.* Social scientists have noted the harm suffered by residents of deteriorated inner-city areas, wracked by poverty, decay, fear, and despair, extends from an increase in poor health to higher risk of criminal victimization.[3] Not surprisingly, these areas are the home of delinquent gangs and groups. Because these areas often have high violence rates, neighborhood kids are exposed to a constant stream of antisocial behaviors, which makes them susceptible to associating with violent peers and becoming the victim of violent crimes.[4] Even when neighborhood disadvantage and poverty are taken into account, the more often children are exposed to violence within their residential community the more likely they are to become violent themselves.[5]

- *Social change.* Political unrest and mistrust, economic stress, and family disintegration are social changes that have been found to precede sharp increases in crime rates. Conversely, stabilization of traditional social institutions typically precedes crime rate declines.[6]

- *Socioeconomic status.* The government estimates that there are now 37 million Americans living in poverty, defined as a family of four earning about twenty thousand dollars per year, who have scant, if any, resources and suffer socially and economically as a result. Today, the poorest fifth (20 percent) of all U.S. households receive 3.5 percent of the country's aggregate income, the smallest share ever. In contrast, the top fifth (20 percent) of households receive more than 50 percent of all income, a record high; the top 5 percent collect more than 20 percent of all household income, the most in history.[7]

    It seems logical that people on the lowest rung of the economic ladder will have the greatest incentive to commit crime: they may be enraged by their lack of economic success or simply financially desperate and disillusioned. In either instance, delinquency, despite its inherent dangers, may appear an attractive alternative to a life of indigence. Economic influences may be heightened by the rapid advance in technology: kids who lack the requisite social and educational training have found the road to success almost impassable. A lack of opportunity for upward mobility may make drug dealing and other crimes an attractive solution for socially deprived, but economically enterprising people.[8]

- *Racial Disparity.* The consequences of racial disparity take a toll on youth. Poverty rates among minority groups are still double that of European Americans.[9] The share of young African American men without jobs has climbed relentlessly especially among the most at risk groups: more than 70 percent of African American male high school dropouts in their twenties were jobless—that is, unable to find work, not seeking it, or incarcerated, compared with 34 percent of European American and 19 percent of Hispanic dropouts. Even when high school graduates were included, half of African American men in their twenties were jobless. Minorities face other social problems. More than 20 percent of young African American men are incarcerated. By their mid-thirties, six in ten African American men who had dropped out of school had spent time in prison; in the inner cities, more than half of all African American men do not finish high school.[10]

All of these social problems and conditions take a toll on American youth and may help turn them toward antisocial behaviors. In this chapter we will review the most prominent social theories of delinquency that are based on the effects of social

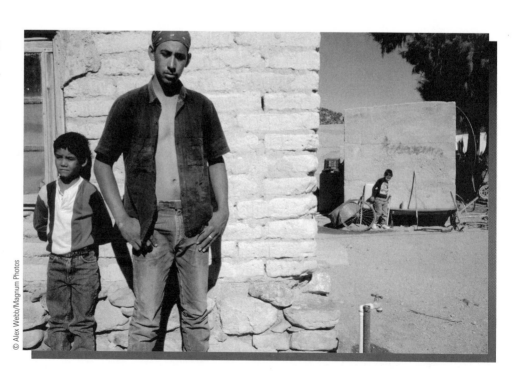

In Candelaria, TX (population 55), a remote town on the border of Texas and Mexico, necessities like water are hard to come by. Poverty rates among minority groups are still double that of whites. How does growing up in conditions of limited socioeconomic resources impact on behavior?

© Alex Webb/Magnum Photos

problems and social relations. They are divided into three main groups: (1) *social structure theories* hold that delinquency is a function of a person's place in the economic structure; (2) *social process theories* view delinquency as the result of a person's interaction with critical elements of socialization; and (3) *critical theories* consider delinquent behavior to be a result of economic deprivation caused by the inequities of the capitalist system of production.

SOCIAL STRUCTURE THEORIES

culture of poverty
The view that lower-class people form a separate culture with their own values and norms, which are sometimes in conflict with conventional society.

underclass
Group of urban poor whose members have little chance of upward mobility or improvement.

truly disadvantaged
According to William Julius Wilson, those people who are left out of the economic mainstream and reduced to living in the most deteriorated inner-city areas.

In 1966, sociologist Oscar Lewis coined the phrase **culture of poverty** to describe the crushing burden faced by the urban poor.[11] According to Lewis, the culture of poverty is marked by apathy, cynicism, helplessness, and mistrust of institutions, such as police and government. Mistrust of authority prevents the impoverished from taking advantage of the few conventional opportunities available to them. The result is a permanent **underclass** whose members have little chance of upward mobility or improvement. This extreme level of economic and social hardship has been related to psychological maladjustment: people who live in poverty are more likely to suffer low self-esteem, depression, and loneliness.[12]

Nowhere are urban problems more pressing than in the inner-city neighborhoods that experience constant population turnover as their more affluent residents move to stable communities or suburbs. Social conditions have actually worsened in some urban areas during the past decade.[13] As a city becomes *hollowed out,* with a deteriorated inner core surrounded by less devastated communities, delinquency rates spiral upward.[14] Those remaining are forced to live in communities with poorly organized social networks, alienated populations, and high crime.[15] Members of the urban underclass, typically minority group members, are referred to by sociologist William Julius Wilson as the **truly disadvantaged**.[16]

LOOKING BACK TO JAY'S STORY

How do poverty and homelessness affect children? Do you think they are related to delinquent behavior? How did Jay's home life affect his childhood in both positive and negative ways? How important do you believe it was to Jay's success that his biological parents remained active in his life?

The impoverished are deprived of a standard of living enjoyed by most other citizens, and their children suffer from much more than financial hardship. They attend poor schools, live in substandard housing, and lack good health care. More than half of families in poverty are fatherless and husbandless; many are supported entirely by government aid. Instead of increasing government aid to the needy, states have limited the eligibility for public assistance.

Neighborhoods that provide few employment opportunities are the most vulnerable to predatory crime. Unemployment destabilizes households, and unstable families are more likely to produce children who choose aggression as a means of dealing with limited opportunity. Lack of employment opportunity also limits the authority of parents, reducing their ability to influence children. Because adults cannot serve as role models, the local culture is dominated by gangs whose members are both feared and respected. Predatory crime increases to levels that cannot easily be controlled by police. Hundreds of studies have documented the association between family poverty and children's health, achievement, and behavior.[17] Children who live in extreme poverty or who remain poor for extended periods of time exhibit the worst outcomes.[18] The cycle of poverty can lead to a variety of adverse outcomes, including life- and health-endangering conditions. Providing adequate care to children under these circumstances can be an immense undertaking.

 To read the transcript of an interview with **Dr. William Julius Wilson**, go to the website www.thomsonedu.com/criminaljustice/siegel.

This view of delinquency is both *structural* and *cultural.* It holds that delinquency is a consequence of the inequalities built into the social structure and the cultural values that form in inner-city, poverty areas. Even youths who receive the loving support of family members are at risk of delinquency if they suffer from social disadvantage.[19]

The **social structure theories** tie delinquency rates to both socioeconomic structural conditions (e.g., poverty, chronic unemployment, neighborhood deterioration) and cultural values (e.g., gang culture). Areas that experience high levels of poverty and social disorganization and also maintain deviant cultural values will also have high delinquency rates. Residents of such areas view conventional social values, such as hard work and getting an education skeptically. They believe that they can never be part of the American Dream.

All social structure theorists are linked in their belief that social conditions control behavior choices. However, there are different interpretations of the nature of the interaction between social structure and individual behavior choices. Three prominent views stand out: social disorganization, anomie/strain, and cultural deviance.

Social Disorganization

The concept of **social disorganization** was first recognized early in the twentieth century by sociologists Clifford Shaw and Henry McKay. These Chicago-based scholars found that delinquency rates were high in what they called **transitional neighborhoods**—areas that had changed from affluence to decay. Here, factories and commercial establishments were interspersed with private residences. In such environments, teenage gangs developed as a means of survival, defense, and friendship. Gang leaders recruited younger members, passing on delinquent traditions and ensuring survival of the gang from one generation to the next, a process referred to as **cultural transmission**. While mapping delinquency rates in Chicago, Shaw and McKay noted that distinct ecological areas had developed what could be visualized as a series of concentric zones, each with a stable delinquency rate (see Figure 4.1).[20] The areas of heaviest delinquency concentration appeared to be the poverty-stricken, transitional, inner-city zones. The zones farthest from the city's center were the least prone to delinquency. Analysis of these data indicated a stable pattern of delinquent activity in the ecological zones over a sixty-five-year period.[21]

According to the social disorganization view, a healthy, organized community has the ability to regulate itself so that common goals (such as living in a crime-free area) can be achieved; this is referred to as **social control**.[22] Those neighborhoods that become *disorganized* are incapable of social control, because they are wracked by deterioration and economic failure; they are most at risk for delinquency.[23] Social control can come in a variety of forms including formal (e.g., police, courts, government agencies) and informal (e.g., parents, neighbors) sources. In areas where social control remains high, children are less likely to become involved with deviant peers and engage in problem behaviors.[24] Social institutions like schools and churches can work effectively in maintaining order. Neighbors work together to control problem kids and keep police in the community.

In contrast, children who reside in disorganized neighborhoods live in an environment absent of social control. Their involvement with conventional social institutions, such as schools and after-school programs, is either absent or

Figure 4.1 **Shaw and McKay's Concentric Zones Map of Chicago**

3.5 3.8 3.7 4.1 5.8 7.5 9.7 12.9 24.5 Loop Lake Michigan

I II III IV V VI VII VIII IX

Note: Arabic numerals represent the rate of male delinquency.

Source: Clifford R. Shaw, *Delinquency Areas* (Chicago: University of Chicago Press, 1929), p. 99.

Figure 4.2 Percentages of Youths Aged 12 to 17 Engaging in Past Year Violent Behavior, by Family Income Relative to Federal Poverty Threshold

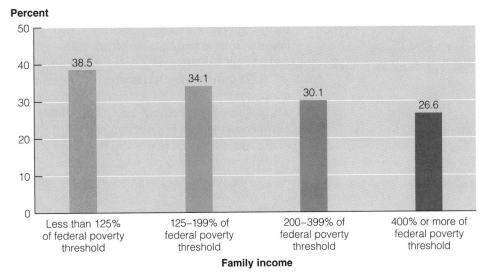

Percent

Less than 125% of federal poverty threshold	38.5
125–199% of federal poverty threshold	34.1
200–399% of federal poverty threshold	30.1
400% or more of federal poverty threshold	26.6

Family income

Source: National Survey on Drug Use and Health (NSDUH). Youth Violence and Illicit Drug Use, 2006. Available at: www.oas.samhsa.gov/2k6/youthCiolence/youthViolence.htm.

---

social disorganization
Neighborhood or area marked by culture conflict, lack of cohesiveness, a transient population, and insufficient social organizations; these problems are reflected in the problems at schools in these areas.

transitional neighborhood
Area undergoing a shift in population and structure, usually from middle-class residential to lower-class mixed use.

cultural transmission
The process of passing on deviant traditions and delinquent values from one generation to the next.

social control
Ability of social institutions to influence human behavior; the justice system is the primary agency of formal social control.

relative deprivation
Condition that exists when people of wealth and poverty live in close proximity to one another; the relatively deprived are apt to have feelings of anger and hostility, which may produce criminal behavior.

gentrified
The process of transforming a lower-class area into a middle-class enclave through property rehabilitation.

blocked, which puts them at risk for recruitment into gangs.[25] Because informal and formal avenues of social control have become frayed, kids are given a free hand to mix with deviant peers.[26] As a result poor kids are more likely to engage in drug use and violence than the affluent. A recent federal survey found that kids who live at or below the poverty level are much more likely to engage in violent behavior than those whose families earn above the poverty line (Figure 4.2).[27]

These problems are stubborn and difficult to overcome. Sometimes, when an attempt is made to revitalize a disorganized neighborhood by creating institutional support programs such as community centers and better schools, the effort may be countered by the ongoing drain of deep-rooted economic and social deprivation.[28] Even in relatively crime-free rural areas, areas that are disorganized as a result of residential instability, family disruption, and changing ethnic composition have relatively high rates of delinquent behavior and youth violence.[29]

A number of concepts define contemporary social disorganization theory.

Relative Deprivation According to the concept of **relative deprivation**, in communities where the poor and the wealthy live relatively close to one another, kids who feel they are less well off than others begin to form negative self-feelings and hostility, a condition that motivates them to engage in delinquent and antisocial behaviors.[30] This feeling of relative deprivation fuels the frustration that eventually produces high delinquency rates.

Community Change Some impoverished areas are being rehabilitated or **gentrified,** going from poor, commercial, or transient to stable, residential, and affluent. Other formerly affluent communities are becoming rundown. As the manufacturing economy is sent overseas, formerly affluent areas may experience job loss and a permanent change in their socioeconomic climate. Minority neighborhoods are especially hard hit by the loss of relatively high-paid manufacturing jobs and their replacement with a relatively low-paid service economy. Such change may foreshadow increases in substance abuse and drug-related arrests.[31]

Communities on the downswing are likely to experience increases in the number of single-parent families, changes in housing from owner- to renter-occupied units, a loss of semiskilled and unskilled jobs, and the growth in the numbers of discouraged, unemployed workers who are no longer seeking jobs. These communities also tend to develop mixed-use areas in which commercial and residential properties stand side by side, an ecological development that increases the opportunity to commit crime.[32] Poverty becomes highly concentrated as people become despondent and employment opportunities non-existent.[33] Urban areas marked by concentrated poverty become isolated and insulated from the social mainstream and more prone to gangs and juvenile deliquency.[34]

As communities deteriorate, those who can move to more affluent neighborhoods to improve their lifestyles.[35] Because of racial differences in economic well-being, those "left behind" are all too often minority citizens.[36] The remaining European American population may feel threatened as the percentage of minorities in the community increases and they are forced to compete with them for jobs and political power.[37] As racial prejudice increases, the call for "law and order" aimed at controlling the minority population grows louder.[38]

Community Fear Disorganized neighborhoods suffer social incivility—trash and litter, graffiti, burned-out buildings, drunks, vagabonds, loiterers, prostitutes, noise, congestion, angry words. Having parks and playgrounds where teens hang out and loiter may contribute to fear.[39] As fear increases, quality of life deteriorates.[40] Residents become convinced that their neighborhood is dangerous and in decline.[41] They become fearful and wary and try not to leave their homes at night.

Fear of teen crime is much higher in disorganized neighborhoods than in affluent suburbs.[42] Residents have little confidence that the police can do anything to counter the drug dealers and gangs that terrorize the neighborhood.[43] The police are believed to ignore crime and when they do take action to use excessive force against neighborhood kids.[44] Residents tell others of their experiences, spreading the word that the neighborhood is dangerous. Businesses avoid these areas and neighbors try to move out and relocate to other, safer areas. As people and businesses leave, the neighborhood becomes even more destabilized and crime rates soar. Neighborhood kids may adjust psychologically by taking risks and discounting the future; teenage birth rates soar, and so do violence rates.[45] As delinquency rates rise, so does fear.[46]

In fear-ridden transitional neighborhoods where residents are trying to get out as fast as possible, social institutions cannot mount an effective social control effort.[47] Because the population is transient, interpersonal relationships tend to be superficial. Neighbors don't know each other and can't help each other out. Social institutions such as schools and religious groups cannot work effectively in a climate of mistrust. Social control efforts are weak and attenuated.[48] When community social control efforts are blunted, crime rates increase, further weakening neighborhood cohesiveness.[49] As cohesiveness declines, fear increases, which reduces community cohesion and thwarts the ability of its institutions to exert social control over its residents.[50] Figure 4.3 shows this neverending cycle.

When fear grips a neighborhood, people may seek to flee to safer environments, undermining the area's human capital. A woman walks past graffiti in an alley where residents say gang members congregate in Irvington, New Jersey. State and local police swept through this block, arresting six people and painting over gang graffiti in what they promised would be a sustained crackdown on street gangs in one of New Jersey's deadliest cities.

Community Cohesion In contrast to disorganized areas, cohesive communities have high levels of social control and social integration; people know one another and develop interpersonal ties.[51] They experience a relatively low crime rates and

Figure 4.3 The Cycle of Social Disorganization

Poverty
- Development of isolated lower-class areas
- Lack of conventional social opportunities
- Racial and ethnic discrimination

Social disorganization
- Breakdown of social institutions and organizations such as school and family
- Lack of informal and formal social control

Erosion of traditional values
- Development of gangs, groups
- Peer group replaces family and social institutions

Limited collective efficacy
- Absence of informal social control
- Weekend institutional social control

Development of criminal areas
- Neighborhood becomes crime-prone
- Stable pockets of crime develop
- Lack of external support and investment

Cultural transmission
Adults pass norms (focal concerns) to younger generation, creating stable lower-class culture

Criminal careers
Most youths age out of delinquency, marry, and raise families, but some remain in life of crime

collective efficacy
A process in which mutual trust and a willingness to intervene in the supervision of children and help maintain public order creates a sense of well-being in a neighborhood and helps control antisocial activities.

strain
A condition caused by the failure to achieve one's social goals.

anomie
Normlessness produced by rapidly shifting moral values; according to Merton, anomie occurs when personal goals cannot be achieved using available means.

have the strength to restrict substance abuse and criminal activity.[52] Residents of these areas develop a sense of **collective efficacy**: mutual trust and a willingness to intervene in the supervision of children and help maintain public order.[53] Communities that are able to maintain collective efficacy can utilize their local institutions—businesses, stores, schools, churches, and social service and volunteer organizations—to control crime.[54] These institutions can be effective in helping kids avoid gang membership, thereby lowering neighborhood crime rates.[55] Residents in these areas enjoy a better life because the fruits of cohesiveness can be better education, health care, and housing opportunities.[56]

The benefits of collective efficacy can trickle down to the family level. Parents in these areas are able to call on neighborhood resources to help control their children; single mothers do not have to face the burden of providing adequate supervision alone.[57] In neighborhoods with high levels of collective efficacy, parents are better able to function and effectively supervise their children. Confident and authoritative parents are able to prevent kids from joining gangs and getting involved in delinquent behavior.[58]

Anomie/Strain

Inhabitants of a disorganized inner-city area feel isolated, frustrated, ostracized from the economic mainstream, hopeless, and eventually angry. These are all signs of what sociologists call **strain**. How do these feelings affect criminal activities? To relieve strain, indigent people may achieve their goals through deviant methods, such as theft or drug trafficking, or they may reject socially accepted goals and substitute more deviant goals, such as being tough and aggressive.

Strain theorists view crime as a direct result of lower-class frustration and anger. Strain is limited in affluent areas because educational and vocational opportunities are available. In disorganized areas, strain occurs, because legitimate avenues for success are all but closed.

It was Robert Merton (1910–2003), one of America's preeminent sociologists, who adopted the concept of strain to explain crime and delinquency. Merton argued that although most people share common values and goals, the means for legitimate economic and social success are stratified by socioeconomic class. Upper-class kids have ready access to good education and prestigious jobs; kids in the lower class rarely have such opportunities. Without acceptable means for obtaining success, individuals feel social and psychological strain; Merton called this condition **anomie**. Consequently, these youths may either (1) use deviant methods to achieve their goals (for example, stealing money) or (2) reject socially accepted goals and substitute deviant ones (for example, becoming drug users or alcoholics). Feelings of anomie or strain are not typically found in middle- and upper-class communities, in which education and prestigious occupations are readily obtainable. In lower-class areas, however, strain occurs because legitimate avenues for success are closed. Considering the economic stratification of U.S. society, anomie predicts that crime will prevail in lower-class culture, which it does.[59]

General Strain Theory Merton's view focuses on the strain that builds up when lower-class kids become frustrated because they lack the means for achieving their personal goals. In his **general strain theory**, sociologist Robert Agnew argues that there are actually more sources of strain than Merton realized (see Figure 4.4).[60]

general strain theory
Links delinquency to the strain of being locked out of the economic mainstream, which creates the anger and frustration that lead to delinquent acts.

1. *Strain caused by failure to achieve positively valued goals.* This type of strain will occur when youths aspire to wealth and fame, but assume that such goals are impossible to achieve. Also falling within this category is the strain that occurs when individuals compare themselves with peers who seem to be doing a lot better, or when youths believe they are not being treated fairly by a parent or a teacher. Such perceptions may result in reactions ranging from running away from the source of the problem to lowering the benefits of others through physical attacks or vandalism of their property. For example, the student who believes he is being "picked on" unfairly by a teacher slashes the tires on the teacher's car for revenge.

2. *Strain as the removal of positively valued stimuli.* Strain may occur because of the loss of a positively valued stimulus.[61] Sometimes, the loss of a girlfriend or boyfriend can produce strain, as can the death of a loved one, moving to a new neighborhood, or the divorce or separation of parents.[62] Loss of positive stimuli may lead to delinquency as the adolescent tries to prevent the loss, retrieve what has been lost, obtain substitutes, or seek revenge against those responsible for the loss. A child who experiences parental separation or divorce early in his life may seek out deviant peers to help fill his emotional needs and in so doing increase his chances of delinquency.[63]

3. *Strain as the presentation of negative stimuli.* Strain may also be caused by negative stimuli. Included in this category are such pain-inducing social interactions as child abuse, criminal victimization, school failure, and stressful events, ranging from verbal threats to air pollution. For example, children who are abused at home may take their rage out on younger children at school or become involved in violent delinquency.[64]

negative affective states
Anger, depression, disappointment, fear, and other adverse emotions that derive from strain.

According to Agnew, adolescents engage in delinquency as a result of **negative affective states**—the anger, frustration, fear, and other adverse emotions that derive from strain. The greater the intensity and frequency of strain experienced, the greater their impact and the more likely they are to cause delinquency. Even though some

Figure 4.4 **Elements of General Strain Theory**

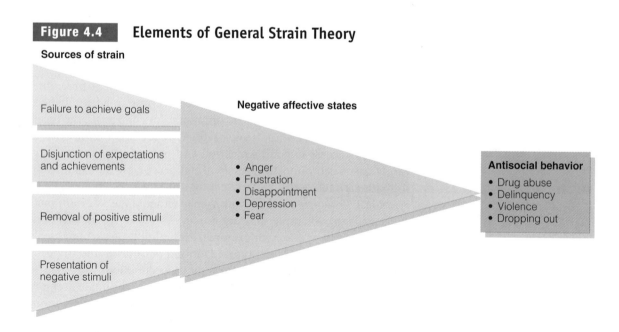

Sources of strain

Failure to achieve goals

Disjunction of expectations and achievements

Removal of positive stimuli

Presentation of negative stimuli

Negative affective states
- Anger
- Frustration
- Disappointment
- Depression
- Fear

Antisocial behavior
- Drug abuse
- Delinquency
- Violence
- Dropping out

According to Agnew, strain can provoke negative affective states and lead to violent behaviors. Scott Dyleski (middle) is escorted out of court as he walks by his attorney, Ellen Leonida (left) moments after his sentencing in Martinez, California, September 26, 2006. Dyleski was convicted of murdering the wife of defense attorney and TV legal analyst Daniel Horowitz and sentenced to life in prison without parole. Dyleski was 16 when he bludgeoned and stabbed neighbor Pamela Vitale, 45, in an apparent attempt to cover up a scheme in which he used stolen credit cards to buy marijuana-growing equipment.

© AP Images/Dan Rosenstrauch, Pool

LOOKING BACK TO JAY'S STORY

Initially, Jay struggled with rules and expectations. His team worked with him to help him establish and accomplish his goals. What types of things could you say to a juvenile who is in this situation? How would you try to motivate a teen in trouble with the law?

kids are better able to cope with strain, other kids, especially those with an explosive temperament, low tolerance for adversity, poor problem-solving skills, and who are overly sensitive or emotional, are more likely to feel its effect.[65] As their perception of strain increases, so too does their involvement in antisocial behaviors.[66]

Research supports many of Agnew's claims: kids who report feelings of stress and anger are more likely to interact with delinquent peers and engage in criminal behaviors;[67] people who fail to meet success goals are more likely to engage in illegal activities.[68]

In sum, kids who feel strain because of stress, disappointment, and anger are more likely to engage in delinquent behaviors.[69] To relieve their feelings of frustration, they may join deviant groups and gangs whose law-violating activities produce even more strain and pressures, which result in even more crime.[70]

Agnew himself has recently found evidence that experiencing violent victimization and anticipating future victimization are associated with antisocial behavior.[71] This finding indicates not only that strain is produced by actual experiences, but that it may result from anticipated ones.

Cultural Deviance Theory

cultural deviance theory
Links delinquent acts to the formation of independent subcultures with a unique set of values that clash with the mainstream culture.

The third structural theory, **cultural deviance theory**, holds that delinquency is a result of youths' desire to conform to lower-class neighborhood cultural values that conflict with those of the larger society. Lower-class values include being tough, never showing fear, living for today, and disrespecting authority. In a socially disorganized neighborhood, conventional values, such as honesty, obedience, and hard work, exist, but are hard to achieve. They exist side by side with lower-class values that stress being tough, using your wits, and defying authority. Conventional values may make little sense to a youth whose role models may include the neighborhood gun runner, drug dealer, or pimp. Those adolescents who share lower-class values and admire criminals, drug dealers, and pimps may find it difficult to also conform to the middle-class values that impress authority figures such as teachers or employers. They experience

The Code of the Streets

A widely cited view of the interrelationship of culture and behavior is Elijah Anderson's concept of the "code of the streets." He sees that life circumstances are tough for the "ghetto poor"—lack of jobs that pay a living wage, stigma of race, fallout from rampant drug use and drug trafficking, and alienation and lack of hope for the future. Living in such an environment places young people at special risk of crime and deviant behavior.

There are two cultural forces running through the neighborhood that shape their reactions. *Decent values* are taught by families committed to middle-class values and representing mainstream goals and standards of behavior. Although they may be better off financially than some of their street-oriented neighbors, they are generally "working poor." They value hard work and self-reliance and are willing to sacrifice for their children; they harbor hopes that their sons and daughters will achieve a better future. Most go to church and take a strong interest in education. Some see their difficult situation as a test from God and derive great support from their faith and from the church community.

In opposition, *street values*, those of "the streets," are born in the despair of inner-city life and are in opposition to those of mainstream society. The street culture has developed what Anderson calls a *code of the streets*, which are a set of informal rules setting down both proper attitudes and ways to respond if challenged. If the rules are violated, there are penalties and sometimes violent retribution.

At the heart of the code is the issue of respect—loosely defined as being treated "right." The code demands that disrespect be punished or else hard-won respect will be lost. With the right amount of respect, a person can avoid "being bothered" in public. If he is bothered, not only may he be in physical danger, but he has been disgraced or "dissed" (disrespected). Some forms of dissing, such as maintaining eye contact for too long, may seem pretty mild. But to street kids who live by the code, these actions become serious indications of the other person's intentions and a warning of imminent physical confrontation.

These two orientations—decent and street—socially organize the community. Their co-existence means that kids who are brought up in "decent" homes must be able to successfully navigate the demands of the "street" culture. Even in decent families, parents recognize that the code must be obeyed or at the very least "negotiated"; it cannot simply be ignored.

The Respect Game

Young men in poor inner-city neighborhoods build their self-image on the foundation of *respect*. Having "juice" (as respect is sometimes called on the street) means that they can take care of themselves even if it means resorting to violence. For street youth, losing respect on the street can be damaging and dangerous. Once they have demonstrated that they can be insulted, beaten up, or stolen from, they become an easy target. Kids from "decent" families may be able to keep their self-respect by getting good grades or a scholarship. Street kids do not have that luxury. With nothing to fall back on, they cannot walk away from an insult. They must retaliate with violence.

One method of preventing attacks is to go on the offensive. Aggressive, violence-prone people are not seen as "easy prey." Robbers do not get robbed, and street fighters are not the favorite targets of bullies. A youth who communicates an image of not being afraid to die and not being afraid to kill gives himself a sense of power on the street.

Anderson's work has been well received by the criminological community. A number of researchers have found that Anderson's observations seem valid. There is a link between living in a deteriorated neighborhood, family values, and adopting the code of the street and those who adopt the code are more likely to engage in violent behaviors.

CRITICAL THINKING

1. Does the code of the street, as described by Anderson, apply in the neighborhood in which you were raised? That is, is it universal?
2. Is there a form of "respect game" being played out on college campuses? If so, what is the substitute for violence?

 INFOTRAC COLLEGE EDITION RESEARCH
Go to InfoTrac College Edition and use "street culture" in a key word search.

Sources: Elijah Anderson, *Code of the Street: Decency, Violence, and the Moral Life of the Inner City* (New York: Norton, 2000); idem., "Violence and the Inner-City Street Code," in *Violence and Children in the Inner City*, ed. Joan McCord (New York: Cambridge University Press, 1998), pp. 1–30; idem., "The Code of the Streets," *Atlantic Monthly 273*:80–94 (May 1994); Timothy Brezina, Robert Agnew, Francis T. Cullen, and John Paul Wright, "The Code of the Street: A Quantitative Assessment of Elijah Anderson's Subculture of Violence Thesis and Its Contribution to Youth Violence Research," *Youth Violence and Juvenile Justice 2*:303–328 (2004); Eric Stewart and Ronald Simons, "Structure and Culture in African American Adolescent Violence: A Partial Test of the 'Code of the Street' Thesis," *Justice Quarterly 23*:1–33 (March 2006).

culture conflict
When the values of a subculture clash with those of the dominant culture.

a form of **culture conflict** and are rendered incapable of achieving success in a legitimate fashion; as a result, they join together in gangs and engage in behavior that is malicious and negativistic.[72] Sociologist Elijah Anderson has studied this dilemma in his research on the "code of the streets." This concept is explored in the Focus on Delinquency feature.

Both legitimate and illegitimate opportunities are closed to youths in the most disorganized inner-city areas.[73] Consequently, they may join violent gangs to defend their turf, displaying their bravery and fighting prowess.[74] Instead of aspiring to be "preppies" or "yuppies," they want to be considered tough and street-smart.

Youths living in disorganized areas consider themselves part of an urban underclass whose members must use their wits to survive or they will succumb to poverty, alcoholism, and drug addiction.[75] Exploitation of women abounds in a culture wracked by limited opportunity. Sexual conquest is one of the few areas open to lower-class males for achieving self-respect. The absence of male authority figures contributes to the fear that marriage will limit freedom. Peers heap scorn on anyone who allows himself to get "trapped" by a female, fueling the number of single-parent households. Youths who are committed to the norms of this deviant subculture are also more likely to disparage agents of conventional society, such as police and teachers.[76] By joining gangs and committing crimes, lower-class youths are rejecting the culture that has already rejected them; they may be failures in conventional society, but they are the kings and queens of the neighborhood.

SOCIAL PROCESS THEORIES: SOCIALIZATION AND DELINQUENCY

socialization
The process of learning the values and norms of the society or the subculture to which the individual belongs.

Not all sociologists believe that merely living in an impoverished, deteriorated, lower-class area is determinant of a delinquent career. Instead, they argue that the root cause of delinquency may be traced to learning delinquent attitudes from peers, becoming detached from school, or experiencing conflict in the home. Although social position is important, **socialization** is considered to be the key determinant of behavior. If the socialization process is incomplete or negatively focused, it can produce an adolescent with a poor self-image who is alienated from conventional social institutions.

Socialization is the process of guiding people into acceptable behavior patterns through information, approval, rewards, and punishments. It involves learning the techniques needed to function in society. Socialization is a developmental process

After finishing her graveyard shift at Bremerton Health and Rehabilitation Center, Julie Cone quizzes her son, Mason, 7, on his homework at their South Kitsap, Washington, home before he heads off to school. According to social process theories, kids with parents that guide and socialize them with an eye toward conventional behavior are insulated from delinquency.

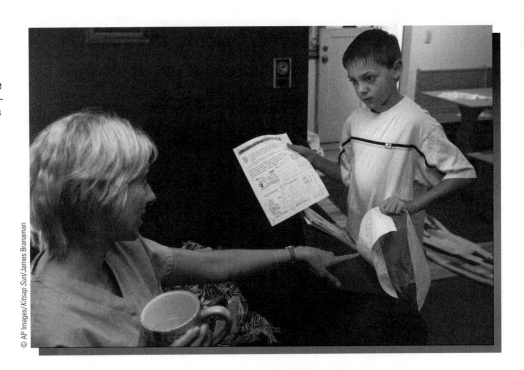

© AP Images/*Kitsap Sun*/James Branaman

■ The social structure view is that position in the socioeconomic structure influences the chances of becoming a delinquent.

■ Poor kids are more likely to commit crimes, because they are unable to achieve monetary or social success in any other way.

■ Kids who live in socially disorganized areas commit crime because the forces of social control have broken down.

■ Strain occurs when kids experience anger over their inability to achieve legitimate social and economic success.

■ The best-known strain theory is Robert Merton's theory of anomie, which describes what happens when people have inadequate means to satisfy their goals.

■ Robert Agnew's general strain theory holds that strain has multiple sources.

■ Cultural deviance theories hold that a unique value system develops in lower-class areas; lower-class kids approve of behaviors, such as being tough and having street smarts.

parental efficacy
Parents are said to have parental efficacy when they are supportive and effectively control their children in a non-coercive fashion.

LOOKING BACK TO JAY'S STORY

When juveniles are involved in the justice system, the issue of placement is always of concern. In this case, Jay was placed in foster care due to his parental situation. Jay developed an excellent relationship with his foster family, but there were some very difficult times. Do you agree with Jay's foster parents' parenting techniques? What would you do to help support a child in a foster care placement? What types of services and/or supports are needed for foster parents and for the children placed in their care?

---

that is influenced by family and peers, neighbors, teachers, and other authority figures.

Early socialization experiences have a lifelong influence on self-image, values, and behavior. Even children living in the most deteriorated inner-city environments will not get involved in delinquency if their socialization experiences are positive.[77] After all, most inner-city youths do not commit serious crimes, and relatively few of those who do become career criminals.[78] More than 14 million youths live in poverty, but the majority of those do not become chronic offenders. Simply living in a violent neighborhood does not produce violent children; research shows that family, peer, and individual characteristics play a large role in predicting violence in childhood.[79] Only those who experience improper socialization are at risk for crime.

✔ Checkpoints

Research consistently shows a relationship between the elements of socialization and delinquency. The primary influence is the family. When parenting is inadequate, a child's maturational processes will be interrupted and damaged. Children who grow up in homes where parents use severe discipline, yet lack warmth and involvement in their lives, are prone to antisocial behavior.[80] Children, both males and females, both African American or European American, who experience abuse, neglect, or sexual abuse are believed to be more crime prone and suffer from other social problems, such as depression, suicide attempts and self-injurious behaviors.[81] In contrast, parents who are supportive and effectively control their children in a non-coercive fashion are more likely to raise children who refrain from delinquency; this is referred to as **parental efficacy**.[82] Delinquency will be reduced if parents provide the type of structure that integrates children into the family, while giving them the ability to assert their individuality and regulate their own behavior.[83]

The family-crime relationship is significant across racial, ethnic, and gender lines and is one of the most replicated findings in the criminological literature.[84]

The literature linking delinquency to poor school performance and inadequate educational facilities is extensive. Youths who feel that teachers do not care, who consider themselves failures, and who drop out of school are more likely to become involved in a delinquent way of life than adolescents who are educationally successful. Though national dropout rates are in decline, more than 10 percent of Americans ages sixteen to twenty-four have left school permanently without a diploma; of these more than 1 million withdrew before completing tenth grade. There are still ethnic racial gaps in graduation rates. Students from historically disadvantaged minority groups (American Indian, Hispanic, African American) have little more than a 50:50 chance of finishing high school with a diploma.[85]

Still another suspected element of deviant socialization is peer group relations. Youths who become involved with peers who engage in antisocial behavior and hold antisocial attitudes may be deeply influenced by negative peer pressure.[86] Both in the United States and abroad, kids who feel alienated and alone may become involved with others who share their disaffection.[87] Being a social outcast causes them to hook up with friends who are dangerous and get them into trouble.[88] Once acquired, deviant peers may sustain or amplify antisocial behavior trends and amplify delinquent careers.[89] In contrast, having pro-social friends who are committed to conventional success may help shield kids from crime producing inducements in their environment.[90]

The effect of delinquent peers is so powerful that they may even neutralize the beneficial effect of potentially productive activities such as after-school jobs. Research shows that rather than reducing delinquency, both formal and informal

What Does This Mean to Me?

Tools That Can Make a Difference

When you think about your community, what organization might you start, or volunteer to assist, that could enhance children's lives and help prevent gang violence and delinquency? Consider, for example, these:

- A peer-support hotline—to address issues and questions about gangs, drugs, crime, and personal problems.
- Preventive education programs—skits and workshops dealing with suicide, child abuse, teen pregnancy, and AIDS presented at shopping malls, schools, and community centers.
- Improvement projects for neighborhoods—to encourage children and young people to participate in projects to clean up graffiti and improve neighborhoods.
- Learning public life skills—programs might include public speaking, planning, and active listening.
- Organizing young people for social change—volunteers work with children and young people to organize so that their voices can be heard.

Do you think these would work? What others might you suggest?

(e.g., summer jobs) can promote crime if they involve unsupervised involvement with peers.[91] Politicians who advocate spending government money to fund after-school jobs for kids should realize that the money earned will be spent on bling, drugs, and alcohol instead of funding a college education trust![92] Jobs do little to reduce delinquency and in some instances may accelerate involvement in antisocial activities.

Sociologists believe that the socialization process affects delinquency in three different ways.

- *Learning.* Delinquency may be learned through interaction with other people. By interacting with deviant peers, parents, neighbors, and relatives, kids may learn both the techniques of crime and the attitudes necessary to support delinquency. According to this view, because they learn to comimit crimes, children who are born "good" learn to be "bad" from others.

- *Control.* Delinquency may result when life circumstances weaken the attachment a child has to family, peers, school, and society. Because their bonds to these institutions are severed, some adolescents feel free to exercise antisocial behavior. This view assumes that people are born "bad" and then must be taught to control themselves through the efforts of parents and teachers.

- *Reaction.* Some kids are considered winners by others; they are admired and envied. Others are labeled as "troublemakers," "losers," or "punks." They are stigmatized and find themselves locked out of conventional society and into a deviant or delinquent way of life. This view holds that kids are born neither bad nor good, but become what they are through the reactions of others.

Each of these views is discussed in the following sections.

Social Learning Theories

social learning theories
Posit that delinquency is learned through close relationships with others; assert that children are born "good" and learn to be "bad" from others.

Social learning theories hold that children living in even the most deteriorated areas can resist inducements to crime if they have *learned* proper values and behaviors. Delinquency, by contrast, develops by learning the values and behaviors associated with criminal activity. Kids can learn deviant values from their parents, relatives, or peers. Social learning can involve the techniques of crime (how to hot-wire a car) as well as the psychological aspects (how to deal with guilt). The former are needed to commit crimes, whereas the latter are required to cope with the emotional turmoil that follows.

differential association theory
Asserts that criminal behavior is learned primarily in interpersonal groups and that youths will become delinquent if definitions they learn in those groups that are favorable to violating the law exceed definitions favorable to obeying the law.

The best-known social learning theory is Edwin Sutherland's **differential association theory**.[93] Sutherland believed that as children are socialized, they are exposed to and learn pro-social and antisocial attitudes and behavior from friends, relatives, parents, and so on. A pro-delinquency definition might be "don't get mad, get even" or "only suckers work for a living" (see Figure 4.5). Simply put, if the pro-delinquency definitions they have learned delinquent attitudes and definitions are vulnerable to choosing criminal behaviors over conventional ones.[94] The pro-delinquency definitions will be particularly influential if they come from significant

Figure 4.5 Social Learning Theory of Delinquency

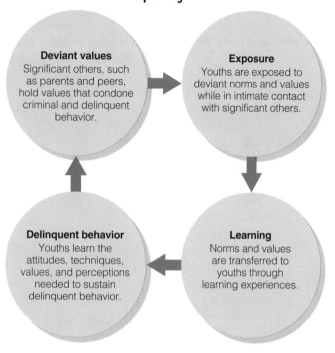

Deviant values
Significant others, such as parents and peers, hold values that condone criminal and delinquent behavior.

Exposure
Youths are exposed to deviant norms and values while in intimate contact with significant others.

Delinquent behavior
Youths learn the attitudes, techniques, values, and perceptions needed to sustain delinquent behavior.

Learning
Norms and values are transferred to youths through learning experiences.

LOOKING BACK TO JAY'S STORY

What do you think is the purpose or goal of having Jay complete community service hours? What might this help teach him? How does it benefit the community?

others, such as parents or peers, and are frequent and intense. Some kids may meet and associate with criminal "mentors," who teach them how to be successful criminals and gain the greatest benefits from their criminal activities.[95]

In contrast, if a child is constantly told by her parents to be honest and never harm others, and is brought up in an environment in which people "practice what they preach," then she will have learned the necessary attitudes and behaviors to allow her to avoid environmental inducements to delinquency.

Social Control Theories

Social control theories suggest that the cause of delinquency resides in the strength of the relationships a child forms with conventional individuals and groups. Those who are socialized to have close relationships with their parents, friends, and teachers will develop a positive self-image and the ability to resist the lure of deviant behaviors. They develop a strong commitment to conformity that enables them to resist pressures to violate the law. If, however, their bonds to society become fractured or broken, youths will feel free to violate the law because they are not worried about jeopardizing their social relationships (see Figure 4.6).

The most prominent control theory is the one developed by sociologist Travis Hirschi.[96] In his classic book *Causes of Delinquency,* Hirschi set out the following arguments:

According to social control theory, strengthening a youth's bond to society helps insulate her from delinquent behaviors. New Mexico Youth ChalleNGe cadets work on a landscaping project to beautify a street median in Roswell, February 2006. Created by the New Mexico National Guard, Youth ChalleNGe provides a military setting for at-risk youth to gain an education, develop social responsibility, and strengthen their bonds to society.

© AP Images/*Roswell Daily Record*/Andrew Poertner

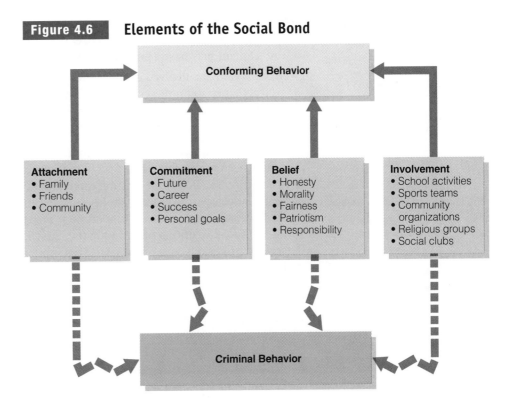

Figure 4.6   Elements of the Social Bond

Conforming Behavior

Attachment
• Family
• Friends
• Community

Commitment
• Future
• Career
• Success
• Personal goals

Belief
• Honesty
• Morality
• Fairness
• Patriotism
• Responsibility

Involvement
• School activities
• Sports teams
• Community organizations
• Religious groups
• Social clubs

Criminal Behavior

social control theories
Posit that delinquency results from a weakened commitment to the major social institutions (family, peers, and school); lack of such commitment allows youths to exercise antisocial behavioral choices.

social bond
Ties a person to the institutions and processes of society; elements of the bond include attachment, commitment, involvement, and belief.

- All people have the potential to commit crimes—for example, under-age drinking—because they are pleasurable.
- People are kept in check by their social bonds or attachments to society.
- If these social bonds are weakened, kids are able to engage in antisocial, but personally desirable behaviors.

Hirschi argues that the **social bond** a person maintains with society contains four main elements.

- *Attachment* to parents, peers, and schools
- *Commitment* to the pursuit of conventional activities, such as getting an education and saving for the future
- *Involvement* in conventional activities, such as school, sports, and religion
- *Belief* in values, such as sensitivity to the rights of others and respect for the legal code

If any or all of these elements of the social bond weaken, kids are free to violate the law. The boy who is not attached to his parents may also lack commitment to his future. It is unlikely that he will be involved in conventional activities, such as sports, school, or church. It is also likely that he will not believe in conventional values, such as "honesty," "hard work," and "discipline." Because he does not have to worry what his parents or teachers think about him or about how his behavior will affect his future, he is free to engage in unconventional activities, such as shoplifting, substance abuse, and precocious sex. It really doesn't matter if he gets caught, he has little to lose.

Hirschi's vision of delinquency causation is one of the most influential of recent times. There is a significant amount of research evidence that supports his ideas:

- Positive social attachments help control delinquency.[97]
- Kids who are detached from the educational experience are at risk of criminality.[98]
- Kids who do well and are committed to school are less likely to engage in delinquent acts.[99]

Figure 4.7 **Labeling Theory**

Initial delinquent act
Youths commit crimes for a number of reasons.

▼

Detection by the justice system
Arrest is influenced by racial, economic, and power relations.

▼

Decision to label
Some youths are labeled "official" delinquents by police and court authorities.

▼

Creation of a new identity
Those labeled are known as troublemakers, criminals, and so on, and are shunned by conventional society.

▼

Acceptance of labels
Labeled youths begin to see themselves as outsiders (secondary deviance, self-labeling).

▼

Deviance amplification
Stigmatized youths are now locked into criminal careers.

stigmatized
People who have been negatively labeled as a result of their participation, or alleged participation, in deviant or outlawed behaviors.

labeling theory
Posits that society creates deviance through a system of social control agencies that designate (or label) certain individuals as delinquent, thereby stigmatizing them and encouraging them to accept this negative personal identity.

■ Kids who are attached to their families are less likely to get involved in a deviant peer group and consequently less likely to engage in criminal activities.[100] Family attachment may have a greater impact on boys rather than girls.[101]

■ Youths who are involved in conventional leisure activities, such as supervised social activities and noncompetitive sports, are less likely to engage in delinquency than those who are involved in unconventional leisure activities and unsupervised, peer-oriented social pursuits.[102]

Although many research efforts support Hirschi's ideas, some important questions have been raised about his views. For example, Hirschi argues that commitment to future success, such as an exciting career, reduces delinquent involvement. What about the adolescent who wants to be a success, but fails to achieve what he desires; would the resulting strain make him crime-prone?[103] Questions have also been raised about the social relations of delinquents. Hirschi portrays them as "lone wolves," detached from family and friends, whereas some critics believe that delinquents do maintain close peer group ties.[104] In fact, there is some evidence that drug abusers maintain even more intimate relations with peers than do non-abusers.[105] Hirschi would counter that what appears to be a close friendship is really a relationship of convenience—"Birds of a feather flock together." Do you really believe that gang boys have close relationships and "bond" with one another?

Despite these questions, Hirschi's vision of control has remained one of the most influential models of delinquency for the past twenty-five years.

Social Reaction Theories

Another group of delinquency experts believes that the way *society* reacts to individuals and the way *individuals* react to society determines individual behavior. Becoming **stigmatized**, or labeled, by agents of social control, including official institutions, such as the police and the courts, and unofficial institutions, such as parents and neighbors, creates and sustains delinquent careers.[106]

According to this view, also known as **labeling theory**, kids may violate the law for a variety of reasons, including poor family relationships, peer pressure, psychological abnormality, and so on. Regardless of the original cause, if their deviant behavior is detected and punished, the result is a negative label that can follow them throughout life. These labels include "juvenile delinquent," "mentally ill," "junkie," and many more. Although the original cause of the misbehavior is important, it is the labeling process that transforms the youngsters' identity. Without the label and stigma they might be able to return to a conventional lifestyle; with it, they are locked forever into a delinquent way of life.

Labeling Effects The degree to which a youngster is perceived as deviant may affect their treatment at home and at school. Parents may consider them a bad influence on younger brothers and sisters. Neighbors may tell their children to avoid the "troublemaker." Teachers may place them in classes reserved for students with behavior problems, minimizing their chances of obtaining higher education.

Beyond these results, and depending on the visibility of the label and the manner in which it is applied, youths will have an increasing commitment to delinquent careers. They may seek out others who are similarly labeled, for example, joining delinquent gangs and groups. Involvement with these new found delinquent peers increase their involvement in delinquent activities and helps further enmesh them in criminality.[107]

As the labeled teen gets further involved in his new deviant peer group and increases the frequency of their deviant activities they face renewed condemnation from law enforcement officers, teachers, and other authority figures. This new round of labeling strengthens their commitment to antisocial behavior. The labeled teens may begin to view themselves as "outcasts," abandoned by society. They may actually join others begin to see themselves as "troublemakers" and "screw-ups." Thus, through a process of identification and sanctioning, re-identification, and increased

self-labeling
The process by which a person who has been negatively labeled accepts the label as a personal role or identity.

self-fulfilling prophecy
Deviant behavior patterns that are a response to an earlier labeling experience; youths act out these social roles even if they were falsely bestowed.

critical theories
The view that inter-group conflict, borne out of the unequal distribution of wealth and power, is the root cause of delinquency.

CHECKPOINTS

■ Some experts believe that delinquency is a function of socialization.

■ People from all walks of life have the potential to become delinquents if they maintain destructive social relationships with families, schools, peers, and neighbors.

■ Social learning theory stresses that kids learn both how to commit crimes and the attitudes needed to support the behavior.

■ People learn criminal behaviors as much as they learn conventional behavior.

■ Social control theory analyzes the failure of society to control antisocial tendencies.

■ All people have the potential to become delinquents, but their bonds to conventional society prevent them from violating the law.

■ Labeling theory (also known as social reaction theory) maintains that negative labels produce delinquent careers.

■ Labels create expectations that the labeled person will act in a certain way; labeled people are always watched and suspected.

sanctioning, the young offender is transformed. They are no longer children in trouble; they are "delinquents," and they accept that label as a personal identity—a process called **self-labeling** (see Figure 4.7).[108]

Labeling Ceremonies Labels are often applied in formal "ceremonies" that are designed to impress their target with the gravity and seriousness of his or her offenses. Sanctioning ceremonies, such as school disciplinary hearings, are aimed at not only at punishing transgressions, but also serve as rituals to impress the mischief makers both with the seriousness of their behavior and the communities outrage over their misconduct.[109] They ought to be "ashamed" at what they did! The effect of this process is a *durable negative label and an accompanying loss of status.* The labeled deviant becomes a social outcast who should be prevented from enjoying higher education, well-paying jobs, and other societal benefits. Because this label is "official," few question the accuracy of the assessment. People who may have been merely suspicious now feel justified in their assessments: "I always knew he was a bad kid."

A good example of the labeling ceremony occurs in juvenile courts. Here offenders find (perhaps for the first time) that authority figures consider them incorrigible outcasts who must be separated from the law-abiding members of society. To reach that decision, the judge relies on the testimony of witnesses—parents, teachers, police officers, social workers, and psychologists—who may testify that the offender is unfit to be part of conventional society.[110] As the label *juvenile delinquent* is conferred on offenders, their identities may be transformed from kids who have done something bad to "bad kids."[111] This process has been observed in the United States and abroad, indicating that the labeling process is universal.[112] Kids who perceive that they have been negatively labeled by significant others, such as peers and teachers, are also more likely to self-report delinquent behavior and adopt a deviant self-concept.[113] The labeling process helps create a **self-fulfilling prophecy.**[114] If children continually receive negative feedback from parents, teachers, and others whose opinion they take to heart, they will interpret this rejection as accurate. Their behavior will begin to conform to the negative expectations; they will become the person that others perceive them to be ("Teachers already think I'm stupid, so why should I bother to study?"). The self-fulfilling prophecy leads to a damaged self-image and an increase in antisocial behaviors.[115]

The labeling perspective can offer important insights:

■ It identifies the role played by social control agents in the process of delinquency causation; delinquent behavior cannot be fully understood if the agencies empowered to control it are ignored.

■ It recognizes that delinquency is not a pathological behavior; it focuses on the social interactions that shape behavior.

■ It distinguishes between delinquent acts and delinquent careers and shows that they must be treated differently.[116]

Labeling theory, then, may help explain the onset and continuation of a delinquent career. It clarifies why some youths continue down the path of antisocial behavior (they are self-labeled), whereas most are able to desist from crime (they are stigma-free). ✔ Checkpoints

CRITICAL THEORY

According to **critical theory**, society is in a constant state of internal conflict, and different groups strive to impose their will on others. Those with money and power succeed in shaping the law to meet their needs and to maintain their interests. Those adolescents whose behavior cannot conform to the needs of the power elite are defined as delinquents and criminals.

Those in power use the justice system to maintain their status while keeping others subservient: men use their economic power to subjugate women; members of the majority want to stave off the economic advancement of minorities; capitalists want to reduce the power of workers to ensure they are willing to accept low wages. Critical thinkers are deeply concerned about the current state of the American political system and the creation of what they consider to be an American empire abroad. Their concern stems from recent events ranging from the war in Iraq to the efforts to penalize immigrants and close the borders.[117] The conservative agenda, they believe, calls for the dismantling of welfare and health programs, lowering of labor costs through union busting, tax cuts that favor the wealthy, ending affirmative action, and reducing environmental control and regulation. Racism still pervades the American system and manifests itself in a wide variety of social practices ranging from the administration of criminal justice to the "whitening" of the teaching force because selection of teachers, even in minority communities, rests upon a racially skewed selection process.[118] Critical theory thus centers around a view of society in which an elite class uses the law as a means of meeting threats to its status. The ruling class is a self-interested collective whose primary interest is self-gain.[119]

Law and Justice

Critical theorists view the law and the justice system as vehicles for controlling the have-not members of society; legal institutions help the powerful and rich to impose their standards of good behavior on the entire society. The law protects the property and physical safety of the haves from attack by the have-nots, and helps control the behavior of those who might otherwise threaten the status quo. The ruling elite draws the lower middle class into this pattern of control, leading it to believe it has a stake in maintaining the status quo. According to critical theory, the poor may or may not commit more crimes than the rich, but they certainly are arrested more often. Police may act more forcefully in areas where class conflict creates the perception that extreme forms of social control are needed to maintain order. It is not surprising to critical theorists that complaints of police brutality are highest in minority neighborhoods.[120] Police misbehavior, which is routine in minority neighborhoods, would never be tolerated in affluent European American areas. Consequently, a deep-seated hostility is generated among members of the lower class toward a social order that they may neither shape nor share in.[121]

The Cause of Delinquency

Critical theorists view delinquency as a normal response to the conditions created by capitalism.[122] In fact, the creation of the legal category *delinquency* is a function of the class consciousness that occurred around the turn of the century.[123] In *The Child Savers*, Anthony Platt documented the creation of the delinquency concept and the role played by wealthy child advocates in forming the philosophy of the juvenile court. Platt believed that the real goal was to maintain order and control while preserving the existing class system.[124] He and others have concluded that the turn-of-the-century child advocates were powerful citizens who aimed to control the behavior of disenfranchised youths.[125]

Critical theorists still view delinquent behavior as a function of the capitalist system's inherent inequity. They argue that capitalism accelerates the trend toward replacing human labor with machines so that youths are removed from the labor force and prevented from getting meaningful, high-paying jobs.[126] Social control agencies such as schools prepare youths for placement in the capitalist system by presenting them with behavior models that will help them conform to later job expectations. For example, rewards for good schoolwork correspond to the rewards a manager uses with

The conflict view of delinquency is rooted in the political philosophy of **Karl Marx.** To learn more about Marx's viewpoints, go to the website www. thomsonedu.com/criminaljustice/siegel.

Social Theory

Theory	Core Premise	Focus
Social disorganization	Crime is a product of transitional neighborhoods that manifest social disorganization and value conflict. The conflicts and problems of urban social life and communities, including fear, unemployment, deterioration, and siege mentality, influence crime rates	Identifies why crime rates are highest in lower-class areas. Points out the factors that produce the delinquency.
Strain	People who adopt the goals of society but lack the means to attain them seek alternatives, such as crime.	Points out how competition for success creates conflict and crime. Suggests that social conditions and not personality can account for crime. Can explain middle- and upper-class crime.
Cultural deviance	Obedience to the norms of their lower-class culture puts people in conflict with the norms of the dominant culture.	Identifies the aspects of lower-class life that produce street crime. Creates the concept of culture conflict.
Social learning	People learn to commit delinquent acts through exposure to others who hold deviant values and engage in deviant behaviors.	Explains why some "at-risk" kids do not become delinquents. Accounts for the effects of parental deviance on kids.
Social control	A person's bond to society prevents him or her from violating social rules. If the bond weakens, the person is free to commit delinquent acts.	Explains the onset of delinquency; can apply to both middle- and lower-class crime. Explains its theoretical constructs adequately so it can be measured. Has been empirically tested.
Social reaction	People enter into law-violating careers when they are labeled for their acts and organize their personalities around the labels.	Explains the role of society in creating deviance. Explains why some juvenile offenders do not become adult criminals. Develops concepts of criminal careers.
Critical theory	Crime is a function of class conflict. The law is defined by people who hold social and political power. The capitalist system produces delinquency.	Accounts for class differentials in the delinquency rate. Shows how class conflict influences behavior.

employees. In fact, most schools are set up to reward youths who show promise in self-discipline and motivation and are therefore judged likely to perform well in the capitalist system. Youths who are judged inferior as potential job prospects are kept out of the system and wind up in delinquent roles.

Concept Summary 4.1 summarizes the various sociological theories of delinquency.

SOCIAL THEORY AND DELINQUENCY PREVENTION

Each of the various branches of social theory has had an impact on delinquency prevention activities and programs. The following sections describe a few of these efforts.

Social Structure Theory and Delinquency Prevention

The decade of the 1960s was the heyday of delinquency prevention programs based on social structure theory. The approach seemed compatible with the policies of the Kennedy (New Frontier) and Johnson (Great Society/War on Poverty) administrations. Delinquency prevention programs received copious federal funding. The most ambitious of these was the New York City–based Mobilization for Youth (MOBY). Funded by more than $50 million, MOBY attempted an integrated approach to community development. MOBY created employment opportunities in the community, coordinated social services, and sponsored social action groups such as tenants' committees, legal action services, and voter registration. But MOBY died for lack of funding amid questions about its utility and use of funds. The most prominent contemporary manifestation of a program based on social structure theory is Operation Weed and Seed, the federal multilevel action plan for revitalizing communities.[127] The concept of this program is that no single approach can reduce crime rates and that social service and law enforcement agencies must cooperate to be effective. Therefore, there are four basic elements in this plan: law enforcement; community policing; prevention, intervention, and treatment; and neighborhood restoration. The last element, neighborhood restoration, is the one most closely attached to social structure theory because it is designed to revitalize distressed neighborhoods and improve the quality of life in the target communities. The neighborhood restoration element focuses on economic development activities, such as economic opportunities for residents, improved housing conditions, enhanced social services, and improved public services in the target area. Programs are being developed that will improve living conditions; enhance home security; allow for low-cost physical improvements; develop long-term efforts to renovate and maintain housing; and provide educational, economic, social, recreational, and other vital opportunities. A key feature is the fostering of self-worth and individual responsibility among community members.

Social Process Theories and Delinquency Prevention

Social process theories suggest that delinquency can be prevented by strengthening the socialization process. Some are aimed at improving self-image, an outcome that may help kids develop revamped identities and desist from crime. With

According to social process theory, negative labels produce delinquency, whereas positive ones may help kids improve their self-image and resist the temptation of law-violating behaviors. Cecelia "Kiki" Gil, 15, of Cody, Wyoming, gives her horse a treat at the Reaching Hands Ranch on October 6, 2006. The ranch teaches responsibility and trust to at-risk youth and holds classes in a different sort of classroom—a barnyard—using rescued horses. Can such positive reinforcement counteract the effect of negative labels?

© AP Images/Powell Tribune/Gib Mathers

LOOKING BACK TO JAY'S STORY

In Jay's case his family struggled with poverty, homelessness, and unemployment issues. Jay was skipping school, using alcohol, committing crimes, and possibly involved with gangs. How would you design a delinquency prevention program to assist youth dealing with these types of concerns in their families? What are the main elements of your program? What are the expectations for the involved clients? What are the goals of your program and how would you measure success?

proper treatment, former offenders are able to cast off their damaged identities and develop new ones. As a result, they develop an improved self-concept that reflects the positive reinforcement they receive while in treatment.[128] One approach has been to help social institutions improve their outreach. Educational programs have been improved by expanding preschool programs, developing curricula relevant to students' lives, and stressing teacher development. Counseling and remedial services have been aimed at troubled youth.

Prevention programs have also been aimed at strengthening families in crisis. Because attachment to parents is a cornerstone of all social process theories, developing good family relations is an essential element of delinquency prevention. Programs have been developed that encourage families to help children develop the positive self-image necessary to resist the forces promoting delinquency.[129]

Prevention programs have also focused on providing services for youngsters who have been identified as delinquents or pre-delinquents. Such services usually include counseling, job placement, legal assistance, and more. Their aim is to reach out to troubled youths and provide them with the skills necessary to function in their environment before they get into trouble with the law.

In addition to these local efforts, the federal government has sponsored several delinquency-prevention efforts using the principles of social process theory. These include vocational training programs, such as the Comprehensive Employment Training Act, as well as educational enrichment programs, such as Head Start for preschoolers.

Reducing Stigma and Labeling

Some prevention programs have attempted to limit the interface of youths with the juvenile justice system in order to reduce the effects of labeling and stigma. One approach has been to divert youths from official processing at the time of their initial contact with police. The usual practice is to have police refer children to treatment facilities rather than to the juvenile court. In a similar vein, children who are petitioned to juvenile court may be eligible for alternative programs rather than traditional juvenile justice processing. For example, restitution programs allow children to pay back the victims of their crimes for the damage (or inconvenience) they have caused instead of receiving an official delinquency label.

If a youth is found delinquent, efforts are being made to reduce stigma by using alternative programs, such as boot camp or intensive probation monitoring. Alternative community-based sanctions are substituted for state training schools, a policy known as **deinstitutionalization**. Whenever possible, anything producing stigma was to be avoided, a philosophy referred to as *non-intervention*.

deinstitutionalization
Removing juveniles from adult jails and placing them in community-based programs to avoid the stigma attached to these facilities.

The federal government has been a prime mover in the effort to divert children from the justice system. The Office of Juvenile Justice and Delinquency Prevention has sponsored numerous diversion and restitution programs. In addition, it made one of its priorities the removal of juveniles from adult jails and the discontinuance of housing status offenders and juvenile delinquents together. These programs were designed to limit juveniles' interaction with the justice system, reduce stigma, and make use of informal treatment modalities. (Chapter 14 covers diversion and deinstitutionalization in detail.)[130]

Critical Theories and Delinquency Prevention

If conflict is the source of delinquency, then conflict resolution may be the key to its demise. This is the aim of **restorative justice**, an approach that relies on non-punitive strategies for delinquency control.[131] The restorative justice movement has a number of origins. Negotiation, mediation, and peacemaking have been part of the dispute resolution process in European and Asian communities for centuries.[132] Native American and Native Canadian people have long used participation of community members in the adjudication process (sentencing circles, panels of elders).[133] Members of the U.S. peacemaking movement have also championed the use of non-punitive alternatives to justice.

Restoration involves turning the justice system into a healing process rather than a distributor of retribution. Most people involved in offender-victim relationships actually know one another or are related. Restorative justice attempts to address the issues that produced conflict between these people rather than to treat one as a victim deserving sympathy and the other as a delinquent deserving punishment. Rather than choose whom to punish, society should try to reconcile the parties.[134]

Gordon Bazemore and his associates have suggested that centered on the principle of BARJ or *Balanced and Restorative Justice*.[135] BARJ attempts to link community protection and victims' rights. Offenders must take responsibility for their actions, a process that can increase self-esteem and decrease recidivism.[136] In contrast, over-reliance on punishment can be counterproductive.[137] According to BARJ, the juvenile justice system should give equal weight to:

1. Holding offenders accountable to victims, *Offender Accountability* refers specifically to the requirement that offenders "make amends" for the harm resulting from their crimes by repaying or restoring losses to victims and the community

2. Providing competency development for offenders in the system so they can pursue legitimate endeavors after release. *Competency Development*, the rehabilitative goal for intervention, requires that people who enter the justice system should exit the system more capable of being productive and responsible in the community,

3. Ensuring community safety. The *Community Protection* goal explicitly acknowledges and endorses a long-time public expectation—a safe and secure community.

The BARJ approach means that juvenile justice policies and priorities should seek to address each of the three goals in *each case* and that *system balance* should be pursued. The goal of achieving balance suggests that no one objective take precedence over any other without creating a system that is "out of balance" and implies that efforts to achieve one goal (e.g., offender accountability) should not hinder efforts to achieve other goals.

BARJ is founded on the belief that justice is best served when the victim, community and offender are viewed as equal clients of the justice system who will receive fair and balanced attention, be actively involved in the justice process, and gain tangible benefits from their interactions with the justice system.

To counteract the negative effects of punishment, restorative justice programs for juveniles typically involve diversion from the court process, reconciliation between offenders and victims, victim advocacy, mediation programs, and sentencing circles, in which crime victims and their families are brought together with offenders and their families in an effort to formulate a sanction that addresses the needs of each party. Concept Summary 4.2 summarizes the principles of restorative justice. Restorative justice programs will be discussed further in Chapter 14.

Crime and delinquency are fundamentally a violation of people and interpersonal relationships.	Victims and the community have been harmed and are in need of restoration. Victims include the target of the offense but also include family members, witnesses, and the community at large. Victims, offenders, and the affected communities are the key stakeholders in justice. The state must investigate crime and ensure safety, but it is not the center of the justice process. Victims are the key, and they must help in the search for restoration, healing, responsibility, and prevention.
Violations create obligations and liabilities.	Offenders have the obligation to make things right as much as possible. They must understand the harm they have caused. Their participation should be as voluntary as possible; coercion is to be minimized.
Restorative justice seeks to heal and put right the wrongs.	Victims' needs are the focal concern of the justice process. Safety is a top priority, and victims should be empowered to participate in determining their needs and case outcomes. The exchange of information between victim and offender should be encouraged; when possible, face-to-face meetings might be undertaken. There should be mutual agreement over imposed outcomes. Offenders' needs and competencies need to be addressed. Healing and reintegration are emphasized; isolation and removal from the community are restricted.

SUMMARY

- Social structure theories hold that delinquent behavior is an adaptation to conditions that predominate in lower-class environments.
- The social disorganization view suggests that economically deprived areas lose their ability to control the behavior of residents. Gangs flourish in these areas.
- Delinquency is a product of the socialization mechanisms in a neighborhood: unstable neighborhoods have the greatest chance of producing delinquents. Factors such as fear, unemployment, change, and lack of cohesion help produce delinquent behavior patterns.
- Strain theories hold that lower-class youths may desire legitimate goals but their unavailability causes frustration and deviant behavior.
- Robert Merton linked strain to anomie, a condition caused when there is a disjunction between goals and means.
- In his general strain theory, Robert Agnew identifies two more sources of strain: the removal of positive reinforcements and the addition of negative ones. He shows how strain causes delinquent behavior by creating negative affective states, and he outlines the means adolescents employ to cope with strain.
- Cultural deviance theory maintains that the result of social disorganization and strain is the development of independent subcultures whose members hold values

in opposition to mainstream society. These subcultures are the breeding grounds for gangs and law-violating groups.

- Social process theories hold that improper socialization is the key to delinquency. One branch, called learning theories, holds that kids learn deviant behaviors and attitudes during interaction with family and peers.
- Control theories suggest that kids are prone to delinquent behavior when they have not been properly socialized and lack a strong bond to society. Without a strong bond they are free to succumb to the lure of delinquent behavior. Labeling and stigma may also reinforce delinquency. Kids who receive negative labels may internalize them and engage in self-labeling. This causes a self-fulfilling prophecy, which breeds even more deviant behaviors and locks kids into a delinquent way of life.
- Critical theory views delinquency as an inevitable result of the class and racial conflict that pervades society. Delinquents are members of the "have-not" class that is shut out of the mainstream. The law benefits the wealthy over the poor.
- Social views of delinquency have had a great deal of influence on social policy. Programs have been designed to improve neighborhood conditions, help children be properly socialized, and reduce conflict.

culture of poverty, p. 85
underclass, p. 85
truly disadvantaged, p. 85
social structure theories, p. 86
social disorganization, p. 87
transitional neighborhood, p. 87
cultural transmission, p. 87
social control, p. 87
relative deprivation, p. 87
gentrified, p. 87

collective efficacy, p. 89
strain, p. 89
anomie, p. 89
general strain theory, p. 90
negative affective states, p. 90
cultural deviance theory, p. 91
culture conflict, p. 92
socialization, p. 93
parental efficacy, p. 94
social learning theories, p. 95

differential association theory, p. 95
social control theories, p. 97
social bond, p. 97
stigmatized, p. 98
labeling theory, p. 98
self-labeling, p. 99
self-fulfilling prophecy, p. 99
critical theories, p. 99
deinstitutionalization, p. 103
restorative justice, p. 104

QUESTIONS FOR DISCUSSION

1. Is there a transitional neighborhood in your town or city?

2. Is it possible that a distinct lower-class culture exists?

3. Have you ever perceived anomie? What causes anomie? Is there more than one cause of strain?

4. How does poverty cause delinquency?

5. Do middle-class youths become delinquent for the same reasons as lower-class youths?

6. Does relative deprivation produce delinquency?

APPLYING WHAT YOU HAVE LEARNED

You have just been appointed as a presidential adviser on urban problems. The president informs you that she wants to initiate a demonstration project in a major city aimed at showing that the government can do something to reduce poverty, crime, and drug abuse. The area she has chosen for development is a large inner-city neighborhood with more than a hundred thousand residents. The neighborhood suffers from disorganized community structure, poverty, and hopelessness. Predatory delinquent gangs run free and terrorize local merchants and citizens. The school system has failed to provide opportunities and education experiences sufficient to dampen enthusiasm for gang recruitment. Stores, homes, and public buildings are deteriorated and decayed. Commercial enterprise has fled the area, and civil servants are reluctant to enter the neighborhood. There is an uneasy truce among the various ethnic and racial groups that populate the area. Residents feel that little can be done to bring the neighborhood back to life.

You are faced with suggesting an urban redevelopment program that can revitalize the area and eventually bring down the crime rate. You can bring any element of the public and private sector to bear on this rather overwhelming problem—including the military! You can also ask private industry to help in the struggle, promising them tax breaks for their participation.

- Do you believe that living in such an area contributes to high delinquency rates? Or is poverty merely an excuse and delinquency a matter of personal choice?
- What programs do you feel could break the cycle of urban poverty?
- Would reducing the poverty rate produce a lowered delinquency rate?
- What role does the family play in creating delinquent behaviors?

DOING RESEARCH ON THE WEB

Before you answer, you may want to learn more about Operation Weed and Seed, the federal office most involved in community development projects designed to reduce delinquency, and about Canada's National Crime Prevention Strategy, which aims to reduce crime and victimization by tackling crime before it happens. They can be found through the website **www.thomsonedu.com/criminaljustic/siegel.**

To read about a program in Minneapolis, go to InfoTrac College Edition and read Judith Martin and Paula Pentel, "What the Neighbors Want: The Neighborhood Revitalization Program's First Decade," *Journal of the American Planning Association* 68:435–449 (2002). To find out more, use "community crime prevention" in a key word search.

Developmental Views of Delinquency

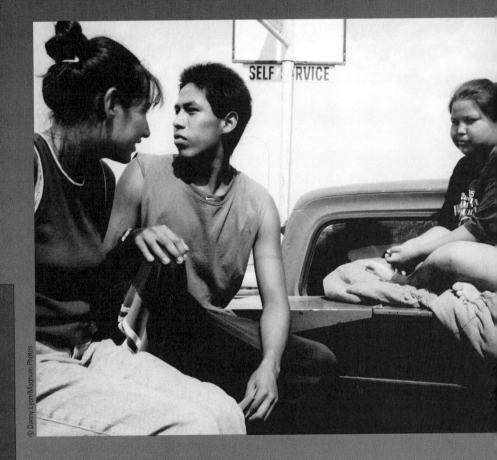

© Danny Lyon/Magnum Photos

CHAPTER OBJECTIVES

After reading this chapter you should:

1. Be familiar with the concept of *developmental theory.*
2. Know the factors that influence the life course.
3. Recognize that there are different pathways to delinquency.
4. Be familiar with the *turning points* in delinquency.
5. Be able to discuss the influence of social capital on delinquency.
6. Know what is meant by a *latent trait.*
7. Be able to discuss Gottfredson and Hirschi's general theory of crime.
8. Be familiar with the concepts of impulsivity and self-control.

Kia was born in Vietnam and moved to the United States when he was eleven. He had been having problems at school, and when he was fourteen years old the teachers at his middle school referred him to the Family Court Crisis Intervention Program. The program was established to provide a one-time intervention with young people on the verge of getting a more serious referral to the juvenile justice system. The philosophy of the program is to provide short-term assessment and intervention, and any further necessary services are referred out to other community resources and supports. Many of the referrals to this program are for adolescents involved with issues of truancy, running away, and family relationship concerns. Although to the community Kia's behaviors did not rise to the level of "delinquent," the adults in his life were very concerned for him. He was verbally aggressive toward both his female peers and teachers—verbally abusive, disrespectful, and threatening. School interventions were attempted to address these concerns, but to no avail. Kia was at risk for school disciplinary action, and possible involvement in the juvenile justice system.

The counselor made an appointment to meet with Kia and his parents, during which the family was asked a series of questions regarding the current concerns and situation, family background, relationships, and history. It was revealed that Kia's parents had moved to the United States several years prior to Kia, and that his grandmother had raised Kia for many years in Vietnam until the family could afford to bring their six children to America. This separation had created a significant disruption for the family, but no one had ever talked with the children about why their parents had to leave for the United States without them. The counselor realized during the assessment that much of what the parents were explaining was new information to Kia, and he seemed eager to hear their explanation.

Kia's parents explained that they had worked hard for many years to be able to have the children join them and that they missed their children a great deal, but felt they had no other choice. They wanted to provide a safe home for their children with a multitude of opportunities that they believed were available in the United States, in the hopes that the children would transition easily, feel appreciative, and be academically successful. His mother cried and expressed her sadness in leaving the children and being separated for so many years. Kia's parents expressed their love for him and their desire for him to feel important in their lives.

After this session with the counselor, things began to change for Kia and his family. They began to see that Kia had felt rejected and abandoned by his parents, and was also struggling to assimilate in the new country. Because his parents had never explained to him their reasons for the separation, Kia had believed his parents did not care about him. The one-time intervention offered by the crisis intervention program was very beneficial to Kia and his family. Kia's negative behaviors at school significantly diminished.

developmental theory
The view that criminality is a dynamic process, influenced by social experiences as well as individual characteristics.

life course theory
A developmental theory that focuses on changes in behavior as people travel along the path of life and how these changes affect crime and delinquency.

Kia's story jibes with the view that the roots of children's misbehavior can be traced to a time much earlier in childhood, and are the culmination of a long history of improper development. They seek the answer to such questions as: Why is it that some kids become delinquents and then abandon the delinquent way of life as they mature, whereas others persist in criminality into their adulthood? Why do some offenders escalate their delinquent activities, whereas others decrease or limit their law violations? Why do some offenders specialize in a particular delinquency, whereas others become generalists? Why do some criminals reduce delinquent activity and then resume it once again? Research now shows that some offenders begin their delinquent careers at a very early age, whereas others begin later. How can early- and late-onset criminality be explained? Focusing attention on these questions has produced what is known as the **developmental theory** of crime and delinquency, a view that looks at the onset, continuity, and termination of a delinquent career.

There are actually two distinct developmental views. The first, referred to as the **life course theory,** suggests that delinquent behavior is a dynamic process, influenced by individual characteristics as well as social experiences, and that the factors that cause antisocial behaviors change dramatically over a person's life span.

However, although their position is growing increasingly popular, the life course theorists are challenged by another group of scholars who suggest that human

Interested in the **concept of human development**? Access the United Nations' website by going to www.thomsonedu.com/criminaljustice/siegel.

development is controlled by a "master trait" that remains stable, unchanging, throughout a person's lifetime. As people travel through their life course this trait is always there, directing their behavior. Because this master trait is enduring, the ebb and flow of delinquent behavior is shaped less by personal change and more by the impact of external forces such as delinquent opportunity. For example, delinquency may increase when an adolescent joins a gang that provides him with more opportunities to steal, take drugs, and attack others. In other words, the *propensity* to commit delinquent acts is constant, but the *opportunity* to commit them is constantly fluctuating. Concept Summary 5.1 summarizes the main points of the life course and **latent trait theories**.

THE LIFE COURSE VIEW

latent trait theory
The view that delinquent behavior is controlled by a "master trait," present at birth or soon after, that remains stable and unchanging throughout a person's lifetime.

According to the life course view, even as toddlers people begin relationships and behaviors that will follow them into adolescence and beyond. As children they must learn to conform to social rules and function effectively in society. Later they are expected to begin thinking about careers, leave their parents' home, find permanent relationships, and eventually marry and begin their own families.[1] These transitions are expected to take place in an orderly fashion, beginning with finishing school, entering the workforce, getting married, and having children.

Some kids, however, are incapable of maturing in a reasonable and timely fashion because of family, environmental, or personal problems. In some cases transitions can occur too early—for example, when adolescents engage in precocious sex. In other cases transitions may occur too late, as when a student fails to graduate on time because of bad grades or too many incompletes. Sometimes disruption of one trajectory can harm another. Having a child while still a teenager is likely to disrupt educational and career development. These negative life experiences can become cumulative: as kids acquire more personal deficits, the chances of acquiring additional ones increases.[2] So the boy who experiences significant amounts of anger in early adolescence is the one who is more likely to become involved in antisocial behavior as a teen and to mature into a depressed adult who abuses alcohol.[3]

Disruptions in life's major transitions can be destructive and ultimately promote criminality. Those who are already at risk because of socioeconomic problems or family dysfunction are the most susceptible during these awkward transitions. The cumulative impact of these disruptions sustains criminality from childhood into adulthood.

Because a transition from one stage of life to another can be a bumpy ride, the propensity to commit delinquent acts is neither stable nor constant; it is a *developmental process*. A positive life experience may help some

 LOOKING BACK TO KIA'S STORY

What are the special problems of immigrant kids and how may they contribute to negative life experiences?

Concept Summary 5.1   **Life Course Versus Latent Trait Theories**

Life Course Theory
- People have multiple traits: social, psychological, economic.
- People change over the life course.
- Family, job, peers influence behavior.
- Criminal careers are a passage.
- Personal and structural factors influence crime.
- Informal social controls affect behavior.
- People can stop and restart their criminal careers.

Latent Trait Theory
- People have a master trait: personality, intelligence, genetic makeup.
- People do not change, criminal opportunities change; maturity brings fewer opportunities.
- Early social control and proper parenting can reduce criminal propensity.
- Change does not affect criminal propensity.
- Criminal propensity remains stable over the life course.

kids desist from delinquency for a while, whereas a negative one may cause them to resume their activities. Delinquent careers are also said to be *interactional*, because people are influenced by the behavior of those around them, and in turn, they influence the behavior of others. For example, a girl who is constantly in trouble may be rejected by her friends, which causes her to (a) seek antisocial friends and (b) increase her involvement in antisocial behavior, which (c) causes even more rejection.

Life course theories also recognize that as people mature the factors that influence their behavior undergo change. At first, family relations may be most influential; in later adolescence, school and peer relations predominate; in adulthood, vocational achievement and marital relations may be the most critical influences. For example, antisocial children who are in trouble throughout their adolescence may manage to find stable work and maintain intact marriages as adults; these life events help them desist from delinquency. In contrast, the less fortunate adolescents who develop arrest records and get involved with the wrong crowd may find themselves limited to menial jobs, never find a stable partner, and continue to be at risk for criminal careers into their adulthood.

The Glueck Research

One of the cornerstones of recent life course theories has been renewed interest in the research efforts of Sheldon and Eleanor Glueck. While at Harvard University in the 1930s, the Gluecks popularized research on the life cycle of delinquent careers. In a series of longitudinal research studies, they followed the careers of known delinquents to determine the factors that predicted persistent offending.[4] The Gluecks made extensive use of interviews and records in their elaborate comparisons of delinquents and non-delinquents.[5]

The Gluecks' research focused on early onset of delinquency as a harbinger of a delinquent career: "The deeper the roots of childhood maladjustment, the smaller the chance of adult adjustment."[6] They also noted the stability of offending careers: children who are antisocial early in life are the most likely to continue their offending careers into adulthood.

The Gluecks identified a number of personal and social factors related to persistent offending. The most important of these factors was family relations, considered in terms of quality of discipline and emotional ties with parents. The adolescent raised in a large, single-parent family of limited economic means and educational achievement was the most vulnerable to delinquency.

The Gluecks did not restrict their analysis to social variables. When they measured such biological and psychological traits as body type, intelligence, and personality, they found that physical and mental factors also played a role in determining behavior. Children with low intelligence, a background of mental disease, and a powerful (mesomorph) physique were the most likely to become persistent offenders.

LOOKING BACK TO KIA'S STORY

Why was it important for the counselor to ask about this family's story in relation to their culture, background, and decision-making processes? How can these factors impact an adolescent's development?

LIFE COURSE CONCEPTS

A number of key concepts help define the life course view. We describe a few of the most critical concepts in this section.[7]

Age of Onset

early onset
The view that kids who begin engaging in antisocial behaviors at a very early age are the ones most at risk for a delinquency career.

The seeds of a delinquent career are planted early in life (preschool); **early onset** of deviance strongly predicts more frequent, varied, and sustained criminality later in life.[8] Most of these early onset delinquents begin their careers with disruptive behavior, truancy, cruelty to animals, lying, and theft.[9] They also appear to be more violent than their less precocious peers.[10] Because symptoms appear early in life, it is not

A key element of developmental theory is that kids begin their offending careers early in life. Maribel Cuevas (left), 11, arrives at juvenile court in Fresno, California, under the charge of assault with a deadly weapon for throwing a rock at a boy during a water balloon fight. The girl's lawyers reached a deal that allowed her to escape confinement time.

© AP Images/Gary Kazanjian

The Murray Research Center at Radcliffe College sponsors an ongoing "Crime Causation Study: Unraveling Juvenile Delinquency 1940–1963," based on the work of the Gluecks. Find this website by going to www.thomsonedu.com/criminaljustice/siegel.

adolescent-limited offenders
Offenders who follow the most common delinquent trajectory, in which antisocial behavior peaks in adolescence and then diminishes.

life course persister offenders
One of the small group of offenders whose delinquent career continues well into adulthood.

surprising that teacher's evaluations of children during their public school years have been found to be a significant predictor of troublesome and aggressive behavior in adulthood.[11] The earlier the onset, the more likely a kid will engage in serious delinquency and for a longer period of time. Studies of the juvenile justice system show that many incarcerated youth began their offending careers very early in life and that a significant number had engaged in heavy drinking and drug abuse by age ten or younger.[12]

What causes some kids to begin offending at an early age? Research shows that poor parental discipline and monitoring seem to be a key to the early onset of criminality and that these influences may follow kids into their adulthood. The psychic scars of childhood are hard to erase.[13]

Adolescent-Limited Offenders Versus Life Course Persister Offenders

But not all persistent offenders begin at an early age. Some begin their journey at different times.[14] Some stay out of trouble in adolescence and do not violate the law until their teenage years. A few even skip antisocial behavior in their childhood and adolescence altogether and begin their offending career in adulthood.[15]

Psychologist Terrie Moffitt, has studied this phenomenon and her research shows that delinquents can be divided into two groups: **adolescent-limited offenders** and **life course persister offenders**.[16]

Adolescent-limited offenders get involved with antisocial activities early in life and then begin to phase out of their delinquent behaviors as they mature. These kids may be considered "typical teenagers" who get into minor scrapes and engage in what might be considered rebellious teenage behavior with their friends, such as recreational drug use.[17]

In contrast, life course persister offenders remain high-rate offenders into young adulthood.[18] They combine family dysfunction with severe neurological problems that predispose them to antisocial behavior patterns. These problems can be the result of maternal drug abuse, poor nutrition, or exposure to toxic agents such as lead. Life course persister offenders may have lower verbal ability and suffer hyperactivity, which inhibits reasoning skills, learning ability, and school

pseudomaturity
Characteristic of life course persister offenders, who tend to engage in early sexuality and drug use.

achievement. They display a negative or impulsive personality and seem particularly impaired on spatial and memory functions.[19] They seem to mature faster and engage in early sexuality and drug use, referred to as **pseudomaturity**.[20] Individual traits then rather than environment seem to have the greatest influence on life course persistence.[21]

Life course persister offenders are more likely to suffer the consequences of their behavior than adolescent-limited offenders. Follow-up studies show that these persistent young offenders have a mortality rate far higher than the general population with violence being a not uncommon cause of early death.[22]

Problem Behavior Syndrome (PBS)

problem behavior syndrome (PBS)
A cluster of antisocial behaviors that may include family dysfunction, substance abuse, smoking, precocious sexuality and early pregnancy, educational underachievement, suicide attempts, sensation seeking, and unemployment, as well as delinquency.

The life course view is that delinquency is but one of many social problems faced by at-risk youth. Referred to collectively as **problem behavior syndrome (PBS)**, these behaviors include family dysfunction, substance abuse, smoking, precocious sexuality and early pregnancy, educational underachievement, suicide attempts, sensation seeking, and unemployment (see Exhibit 5.1).[23] People who suffer from one of these conditions typically exhibit many symptoms of the others.[24] Research has found the following problem behaviors cluster together:

- Youths who drink in the late elementary school years, who are aggressive, and who have attention problems are more likely to be offenders during adolescence.

- Youths who are less attached to their parents and school and have antisocial friends are more likely to be offenders.

- Youths from neighborhoods where drugs are easily available are more likely to be offenders during adolescence.[25]

- Juvenile delinquents with conduct disorder who have experienced and observed violence, who have been traumatized, and who suffer from a wide spectrum of psychopathology also have high rates of suicidal thoughts and attempts.[26]

- Delinquents exhibit a complex combination of externalizing behaviors including conduct disorder, attention-deficit/hyperactivity disorder [ADHD], drug abuse, familial and interpersonal difficulties, such as conflict with parents, and low intelligence.[27]

People who exhibit one of these conditions typically exhibit many of the others.[28] All varieties of delinquent behavior, including violence, theft, and drug offenses, may be part of a generalized PBS, indicating that all forms of antisocial behavior have similar developmental patterns.[29]

Exhibit 5.1   **Problem Behavior Syndrome**

Personal Characteristics
- Substance abuse
- Suicide attempts
- Early sexuality
- Sensation seeking
- Early parenthood
- Accident proneness
- Medical problems
- Mental disease
- Anxiety
- Eating disorders (bulimia, anorexia)

Social Characteristics
- Family dysfunction
- Unemployment
- Educational underachievement
- School misconduct

Environmental Characteristics
- High-delinquency area
- Disorganized area
- Racism
- Exposure to poverty

Multiple Pathways

Life course theorists recognize that delinquents may travel more than a single road in their delinquent career. Some are chronic offenders, whereas others may commit delinquent acts only once or twice; some increase their activities as they age, whereas others de-escalate their antisocial behaviors.[30] Some may specialize in a single type of delinquent act, such as selling drugs, whereas others may engage in a variety of delinquent acts.

Rolf Loeber and his associates have identified three distinct paths to a delinquent career (see Figure 5.1).[31]

1. The **authority conflict pathway** begins at an early age with stubborn behavior. This leads to defiance (doing things one's own way, disobedience) and then to authority avoidance (staying out late, truancy, running away).
2. The **covert pathway** begins with minor, underhanded behavior (lying, shoplifting) that leads to property damage (setting nuisance fires, damaging property). This behavior eventually escalates to more serious forms of criminality, ranging

authority conflict pathway
Pathway to delinquent deviance that begins at an early age with stubborn behavior and leads to defiance and then to authority avoidance.

covert pathway
Pathway to a delinquent career that begins with minor under-handed behavior, leads to property damage, and eventually escalates to more serious forms of theft and fraud.

To read highlights of the **Pittsburgh Youth Study** directed by Rolf Loeber, go to the website www.thomsonedu.com/criminaljustice/siegel.

The **Program of Research on the Causes and Correlates of Delinquency**, sponsored by the federal government, coordinates longitudinal projects that are often referred to in this text. Find this website by going to www.thomsonedu.com/criminaljustice/siegel.

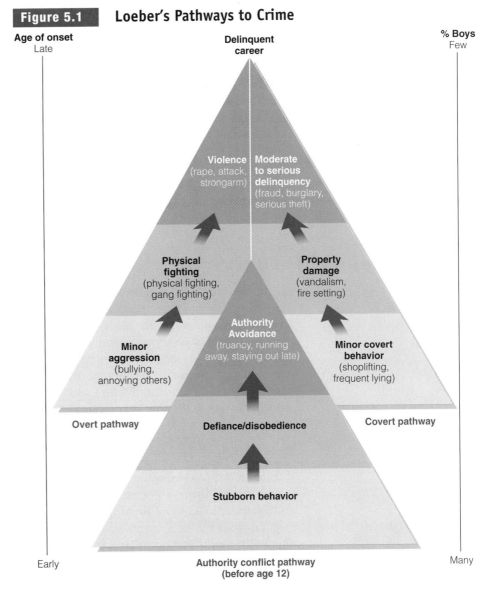

Figure 5.1 **Loeber's Pathways to Crime**

Source: "Serious and Violent Offenders," *Juvenile Justice Bulletin*, May 1998, p. 1.

overt pathway
Pathway to a delinquent career
that begins with minor aggression,
leads to physical fighting, and
eventually escalates to violent
delinquency.

from joyriding, pocket picking, larceny, and fencing to passing bad checks, using stolen credit cards, stealing cars, dealing drugs, and breaking and entering.

3. The **overt pathway** escalates to aggressive acts beginning with aggression (annoying others, bullying), leading to physical (and gang) fighting and then to violence (attacking someone, forced theft).

Not all youth travel down a single path. Some are stubborn, lie to teachers and parents, are schoolyard bullies, and commit petty thefts. Those who travel more than one path are the most likely to become persistent offenders as they mature.

Continuity of Crime and Delinquency

Another aspect of developmental theory is *continuity of crime and delinquency*: the best predictor of future criminality is past criminality. Children who are repeatedly in trouble during early adolescence will generally still be antisocial in their middle teens; kids who are delinquent in their mid-teens are the ones most likely to commit crime as adults.[32] Research shows that kids who persist engage in more aggressive acts and are continually involved in theft offenses and aggression. As they emerge into adulthood, persisters report less emotional support, lower job satisfaction, distant peer relationships, and more psychiatric problems than those who desist.[33]

Early delinquent activity is likely to be sustained, because these offenders seem to lack the social survival skills necessary to find work or to develop the interpersonal relationships they need to allow them to drop out of delinquency. Delinquency may be *contagious*: kids at risk for delinquency may be located in families and neighborhoods in which they are constantly exposed to deviant behavior. Having brothers, fathers, neighbors, and friends who engage in and support their activities reinforces their deviance.[34]

As they mature, delinquents may continue to be involved in antisocial behavior. But even if they aren't, they are still at risk for a large variety of adult social behavior problems. There are gender differences in the effect. For males, the path runs from delinquency to problems at work and substance abuse. For females, antisocial behavior in youth leads to relationship problems, depression, a tendency to commit suicide, and poor health in adulthood.[35] ✔ **Checkpoints**

✔ **CHECKPOINTS**

■ Pioneering criminologists Sheldon and Eleanor Glueck tracked the onset and termination of delinquent careers.

■ Life course theories look at such issues as the onset of delinquency, escalation of offenses, continuity of delinquency, and desistance from delinquency.

■ The concept of problem behavior syndrome suggests that criminality may be just one of a cluster of social, psychological, and physical problems.

■ There is more than one pathway to delinquency.

■ Adolescent-limited offenders begin offending late and age out of delinquency. Life course persister offenders exhibit early onset of delinquency that persists into adulthood.

LIFE COURSE THEORIES

An ongoing effort has been made to track persistent offenders over their life course.[36] The early data seem to support what is already known about delinquent career patterns: juvenile offenders are likely to become adult criminals; early onset predicts more lasting delinquency; and chronic offenders commit a significant portion of all delinquent acts.[37] Based on these findings, criminologists have formulated a number of systematic theories that account for onset, continuance, and desistance from delinquency. Robert Sampson and John Laub's age-graded theory, a principle life course model, is set out in detail below.

Age-Graded Theory

If there are various pathways to crime and delinquency, are there various trails back to conformity? In an important 1993 work, *Crime in the Making*, Robert Sampson and John Laub identified **turning points** in a delinquent career.[38] Reanalyzing the original Glueck data, they found that the stability of delinquent behavior can be affected by events that occur later in life, even after a chronic delinquent career has been established. They also believe that formal and informal social controls restrict criminality and that delinquency begins early in life and continues over the life course.

turning points
Critical life events, such as career
and marriage, which may enable
adult offenders to desist from
delinquency.

Sampson and Laub's age-graded theory posits that the key influences on behavior change over the life course. At first, families are critical. In adolescence, the peer group is the most important influence on behavior. In adulthood, marriage and work shape people's lives.

Turning Points Sampson and Laub's most important contribution is identifying the life events that enable adult offenders to desist from delinquency. Two critical turning points are career and marriage.

- *Adolescents who are at risk for delinquency can live conventional lives if they can find good jobs or achieve successful careers.* Their success may hinge on a lucky break. Even those who have been in trouble with the law may turn from delinquency if employers are willing to give them a chance despite their records. Serving in the military also helps kids achieve success and leave deviant pathways.

- *Adolescents who have had significant problems with the law are also able to desist from delinquency if, as adults, they become attached to a spouse who supports and sustains them, regardless of their past.*[39] Spending time in marital and family activities reduces exposure to deviant peers, which reduces the opportunity to become involved in delinquent activities.[40] People who cannot sustain secure marital relations are less likely to desist from delinquency.

Social Capital A cornerstone of age-graded theory is the influence of **social capital** on behavior. Social scientists recognize that people build social capital—positive relations with individuals and institutions that are life sustaining. Social capital, which includes the resources accessed through interpersonal connections and relationships, is as critical to individuals (and to social groups, organizations, and communities) in obtaining their objectives as is human capital, or what a person (or organization) actually possesses.[41]

Although building financial capital improves the chances for economic success, building social capital supports conventional behavior and inhibits deviant behavior (see Figure 5.2).[42] Recent research by Ross Macmillan and his colleagues supports the influence of social capital on family functioning: children whose mothers were initially poor, but escaped from poverty were no more likely to develop behavior problems than children from more affluent households. Gaining social capital then may help erase some of the original damage caused by its absence.[43]

As they travel the life course, kids who accumulate social capital can knife off from a deviant path. If they can find love, enter into a successful marriage, and enter a rewarding career, they accumulate social capital that will enhance their stature, create

social capital
Positive relations with individuals and institutions, as in a successful marriage or a successful career, that support conventional behavior and inhibit deviant behavior.

Figure 5.2   Sampson and Laub's Age-Graded Theory

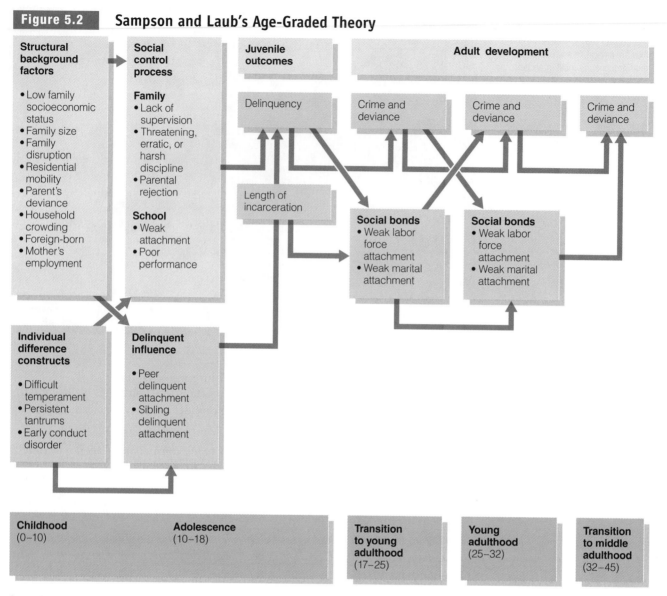

Source: Robert Sampson and John Laub, *Crime in the Making: Pathways and Turning Points Through Life* (Cambridge, MA: Harvard University Press, 1993), pp. 244–245.

feelings of self-worth, and encourage others to trust them. Social capital inhibits delinquency by creating a stake in conformity: Why risk a successful marriage? Why commit crime when you are doing well at your job? The relationship is reciprocal. If people are chosen to be employees, they return the favor by doing the best job possible; if they are chosen as spouses, they blossom into devoted partners.

In contrast, losing or wasting social capital increases both personal deficits and the likelihood of getting involved in delinquency. For example, moving to a new city reduces social capital by closing people off from long-term relationships.[44] Losing social capital has a cumulative effect, and as kids develop more and more disadvantages the likelihood of their entering a delinquent and criminal career increases.[45]

Testing Age-Graded Theory   Several indicators support the validity of age-graded theory.[46] Research shows that children who are raised in two-parent families are more likely to grow up to have happier marriages than children whose parents were divorced or never married.[47] This finding suggests that the marriage-delinquency association may be intergenerational: if people with marital problems are more delinquency-prone, their children will also suffer a greater long-term risk of marital failure and antisocial activity.

Evidence now shows that once begun, delinquent career trajectories can be reversed if life conditions improve, an outcome predicted by age-graded theory.[48] Youths who accumulate social capital in childhood (for example, by doing well in school or having a tightly knit family) are also the most likely to maintain steady work as adults. In addition, people who are unemployed or underemployed report higher delinquent participation rates than employed men.[49] Several areas still need to be explored. Does a military career actually help reduce future criminality? Recent research by John Paul Wright and his colleagues found that Vietnam veterans significantly increased their involvement in substance abuse once they returned home. Considering the strong association between drug abuse and crime, their research sheds some doubt on whether all types of military service can be beneficial as Laub and Sampson suggest. Future research may want to focus on individual experiences in the military and their effect on subsequent civilian behavior.[50]

As predicted by age-graded theory, delinquent youth who enter the military, serve overseas, and receive veterans' benefits enhance their occupational status (social capital) while reducing delinquent involvement.[51] In contrast, people who are self-centered and present-oriented are less likely to accumulate social capital and more prone to committing delinquent acts.[52]

Laub and Sampson are now conducting an important follow-up to their original research: they are finding and interviewing the survivors from the original Glueck research. These two researchers have located the survivors, the oldest subject being seventy years old and the youngest sixty-two! The results of their research are examined in the following Focus on Delinquency feature. ✔ Checkpoints

CHECKPOINTS

■ Life course theories attempt to integrate social, personal, and environmental factors into detailed explanations of the onset and persistence of delinquent careers.

■ According to age-graded theory, building social capital and strong social bonds reduces the likelihood of long-term deviance. As people go through their life course the factors that influence their behavior undergo change.

■ Successful marriage and military service can help people desist.

■ Building social capital can help erase the damage caused by its absence.

THE LATENT TRAIT VIEW

latent trait
A stable feature, characteristic, property, or condition, such as defective intelligence or impulsive personality, which makes some people delinquency-prone over the life course.

In a popular 1985 book, *Crime and Human Nature*, two prominent social scientists, James Q. Wilson and Richard Herrnstein, argued that personal traits, such as genetic makeup, intelligence, and body build, operate in tandem with social variables that include poverty and family function. Together these factors influence people to "choose delinquency" over non-delinquent behavioral alternatives.[53]

Following their lead, David Rowe, D. Wayne Osgood, and W. Alan Nicewander proposed the concept of **latent traits**. Their model assumes that a number of people in the population have a personal attribute or characteristic that controls their inclination or propensity to commit delinquent acts.[54] This disposition, or latent trait, is either present at birth or established early in life, and it remains stable over time. Suspected latent traits include defective intelligence, impulsive personality, genetic abnormalities, the physical-chemical functioning of the brain, and environmental influences on brain function, such as drugs, chemicals, and injuries.[55] Those who carry one of these latent traits are in danger of becoming career criminals; those who lack the traits have a much lower risk. Latent traits should affect the behavioral choices of all people equally, regardless of their gender or personal characteristics.[56]

According to this latent trait view, the *propensity* or inclination to commit delinquency is stable, but the *opportunity* to commit delinquency fluctuates over time. People age out of delinquency, because, as they mature, there are simply fewer opportunities to commit such acts and greater inducements to remain "straight." They may marry, have children, and obtain jobs. The former delinquents' newfound adult responsibilities leave them little time to hang with their friends, abuse substances, and get into scrapes with the law.

Assume, for example, that a stable latent trait such as low IQ causes some people to commit delinquent acts. Teenagers have more opportunity to do so than adults, so at every level of intelligence, adolescent delinquency rates will be higher. As they mature, however, teens with both high and low IQs will commit less delinquency, because their adult responsibilities provide them with fewer opportunities to do so. Thus, latent trait theories integrate concepts usually associated with trait theories

Tracking Down the 500 Delinquent Boys in the New Millennium

Why are some delinquents destined to become persistent criminals as adults? To find out, John Laub and Robert Sampson located the survivors of the delinquent sample first collected by Sheldon and Eleanor Glueck. The oldest is now seventy years old and the youngest is sixty-two.

The interviews showed that that delinquency and other forms of antisocial conduct in childhood are strongly related to adult delinquency and drug and alcohol abuse. Former delinquents also suffer consequences in other areas of social life, such as school, work, and family life: They are far less likely to finish high school than are non-delinquents and subsequently are more likely to be unemployed, receive welfare, and experience separation or divorce as adults.

In their latest research, Laub and Sampson address a key question posed by life course theories: Is it possible for former delinquents to turn their lives around as adults? The researchers found that most antisocial children do not remain antisocial as adults. Of men in the study cohort who survived to fifty years of age, 24 percent had no arrests for delinquent acts of violence and property (predatory delinquency) after age seventeen (6 percent had no arrests for total delinquency); 48 percent had no arrests for predatory delinquency after age twenty-five (19 percent for total delinquency); 60 percent had no arrests for predatory delinquency after age thirty-one (33 percent for total delinquency); and 79 percent had no arrests for predatory delinquency after age forty (57 percent for total delinquency). Laub and Sampson concluded that desistance from delinquency is the norm and that most, if not all, serious delinquents desist from delinquency.

Why Do Delinquents Desist?

Laub and Sampson's earlier research indicated that building social capital through marriage and jobs was the key component of desistance from delinquency. In this new round of research, however, Laub and Sampson found out more about long-term desistance by interviewing fifty-two men as they approached age seventy. The follow-up showed a dramatic drop in criminal activity as the men aged: Between seventeen and twenty-four years of age, 84 percent of the subjects had committed violent crimes; in their thirties and forties, that number dropped to 14 percent; it fell to 3 percent as the men reached their sixties and seventies. Property crimes and alcohol- and drug-related crimes showed significant decreases. The researchers found that the former delinquents who desisted from crime were rooted in structural routines and had strong social ties to family and community. They found that one important element for "going straight" is the "knifing off" of individuals from their immediate environment, offering the men a new script for the future. Joining the military can provide this knifing-off effect, as can marriage or changing one's residence. One former delinquent (age sixty-nine) told them:

I'd say the turning point was, number one, the Army. You get into an outfit, you had a sense of belonging, you made your friends. I think I became a pretty good judge of character. In the Army, you met some good ones, you met some foul balls. Then I met the wife. I'd say probably that would be the turning point. Got married, then naturally, kids come. So now you got to get a better job, you got to make more money. And that's how I got to the Navy Yard and tried to improve myself.

Former delinquents who "went straight" were able to put structure into their lives. Structure often led the men to disassociate from delinquent peers, reducing the opportunity to get into trouble. Getting married, for example, may limit the number of nights available to "hang with the guys." As one wife of a former delinquent said, "It is not how many beers you have, it's who you drink with." Even multiple offenders who did time in prison were able to desist with the help of a stabilizing marriage.

(such as personality and temperament) and concepts associated with rational choice theories (such as delinquent opportunity and suitable targets).

Although there are a number of latent trait–type theories of crime and delinquency, the most well known is the general theory of crime.

General Theory of Crime

general theory of crime (GTC)
A developmental theory that modifies social control theory by integrating concepts from biosocial, psychological, routine activities, and rational choice theories.

Michael Gottfredson and Travis Hirschi's **general theory of crime (GTC)** modifies and redefines some of the principles articulated in Hirschi's social control theory (see chapter 4) by integrating the concepts of control with those of biosocial, psychological, routine activities, and rational choice theories.[57]

The Act and the Offender In their general theory of crime, Gottfredson and Hirschi consider the delinquent offender and the delinquent act as separate concepts.

- Delinquent acts, such as robberies or burglaries, are illegal events or deeds that people engage in when they perceive them to be advantageous. For example, burglaries are typically committed by young males looking for cash, liquor, and entertainment; the delinquency provides "easy, short-term gratification."[58]

Former delinquents who can turn their life around, who have acquired a degree of maturity by taking on family and work responsibilities, and who have forged new commitments are most likely to make a fresh start and find new direction and meaning in life. It seems that men who desisted changed their identity as well, and this, in turn, affected their outlook and sense of maturity and responsibility. The ability to change did not reflect delinquency "specialty": Violent offenders followed the same path as property offenders.

Although many former delinquents desisted from delinquency, they still faced the risk of an early and untimely death. Thirteen percent ($N = 62$) of the delinquent subjects as compared to 6 percent ($N = 28$) of the non-delinquent subjects died unnatural deaths, such as by violence, cirrhosis of the liver caused by alcoholism, poor self-care, and suicide. By sixty-five years of age, 29 percent ($N = 139$) of the delinquent and 21 percent ($N = 95$) of the non-delinquent subjects had died from natural causes. Frequent involvement in delinquency during adolescence and alcohol abuse were the strongest predictors of an early and unnatural death. So, while many troubled youths are able to reform, their early excesses may haunt them across their life span.

Policy Implications

Laub and Sampson found that youth problems—delinquency, substance abuse, violence, dropping out, teen pregnancy—often share common risk characteristics. Intervention strategies, therefore, should consider a broad array of antisocial, criminal, and deviant behaviors and not limit the focus to one subgroup or delinquency type. Because criminality and other social problems are linked, early prevention efforts that reduce delinquency will probably also reduce alcohol abuse, drunk driving, drug abuse, sexual promiscuity, and family violence. The best way to achieve these goals is through four significant life-changing events: marriage, joining the military, getting a job, and changing one's environment or neighborhood. What appears to be important about these processes is that they all involve, to varying degrees, the following items: a knifing off of the past from the present; new situations that provide both supervision and monitoring as well as new opportunities of social support and growth; and new situations that provide the opportunity for transforming identity. Prevention of delinquency must be a policy at all times and at all stages of life.

CRITICAL THINKING

1. Do you believe that the factors that influenced the men in the original Glueck sample are still relevant for change, for example, a military career?
2. Would it be possible for men such as these to join the military today?
3. Do you believe that some sort of universal service program might be beneficial and help people turn their lives around?

INFOTRAC COLLEGE EDITION RESEARCH

Read a review of Laub and Sampson's *Crime in the Making* at Roland Chilton, "Crime in the Making: Pathways and Turning Points through Life," *Social Forces* 74:357 (September 1995).

To learn more about the concept of "social capital," use it as a key word term in InfoTrac College Edition.

Sources: John Laub and Robert Sampson, *Shared Beginnings, Divergent Lives: Delinquent Boys to Age 70* (Cambridge, MA: Harvard University Press, 2003); John Laub and Robert Sampson, "Understanding Desistance from Delinquency," in *Delinquency and Justice: An Annual Review of Research*, vol. 28, ed. Michael Tonry (Chicago: University of Chicago Press, 2001), pp. 1–71; John Laub and George Vaillant, "Delinquency and Mortality: A 50-Year Follow-Up Study of 1,000 Delinquent and Nondelinquent Boys," *American Journal of Psychiatry* 157:96–102 (2000).

- ■ Delinquency is rational and predictable. Kids break the law when it promises rewards with minimal threat of pain. Therefore, the threat of punishment can deter delinquency: if targets are well guarded, and guardians are present, delinquency rates will diminish.

- ■ Delinquent offenders are predisposed to commit crimes. However, they are not robots who commit crimes without restraint; their days are also filled with conventional behaviors, such as going to school, parties, concerts, and church. But given the same set of delinquent opportunities, such as having a lot of free time for mischief and living in a neighborhood with unguarded homes containing valuable merchandise, delinquency-prone kids have a much higher probability of violating the law than do non-delinquents. The propensity to commit delinquent acts remains stable throughout a person's life; change in the frequency of delinquent activity is purely a function of change in opportunity.

By recognizing that there are stable differences in people's propensity to commit delinquent acts, the GTC adds a biosocial element to the concept of social control. The biological and psychological factors that make people impulsive and delinquency-prone may be inherited or may develop through incompetent or absent parenting.

self-control
Refers to a person's ability to exercise restraint and control over his or her feelings, emotions, reactions, and behaviors.

impulsive
Lacking in thought or deliberation in decision making. An impulsive person lacks close attention to details, has organizational problems, is distracted and forgetful.

Recent research shows that children who suffer anoxia (i.e., oxygen starvation) during the birthing process are the ones most likely to lack self-control later in life, supporting Gottfredson and Hirschi's contention that impulsivity may have a biological basis.[59]

What Makes People Delinquency-Prone? What, then, causes people to become excessively delinquency-prone? Gottfredson and Hirschi attribute the tendency to commit delinquent acts to a person's level of **self-control**. Low self-control develops early in life and remains stable into and through adulthood.[60] People with limited self-control tend to be **impulsive**; they are insensitive to other people's feelings, physical (rather than mental), risk takers, shortsighted, and nonverbal.[61] They have a "here and now" orientation and refuse to work for distant goals; they lack diligence, tenacity, and persistence. Impulsive people tend to be adventuresome, active, physical, and self-centered. As they mature, they often have unstable marriages, jobs, and friendships.[62] People lacking self-control are less likely to feel shame if they engage in deviant acts and more likely to find them pleasurable.[63] They are also more likely to engage in dangerous behaviors that are associated with criminality[64] (see Figure 5.3).

Because those with low self-control enjoy risky, exciting, or thrilling behaviors with immediate gratification, they are more likely to enjoy delinquent acts, which require stealth, agility, speed, and power, than conventional acts, which demand long-term study and cognitive and verbal skills. And because they enjoy taking risks, they are more likely to get involved in accidents and suffer injuries than people who maintain self-control.[65] As Gottfredson and Hirschi put it, they derive satisfaction from "money without work, sex without courtship, revenge without court delays."[66] Many of these individuals who have a propensity for committing delinquent acts also engage in other behaviors, such as smoking, drinking, gambling, reckless driving, and illicit sexuality.[67] Although these acts are not illegal, they too provide immediate, short-term gratification. Exhibit 5.2 lists the elements of impulsivity, or low self-control.

According to latent trait theories, delinquent propensity varies among people. Walter Stawarz IV (center) is escorted to the courtroom in Beaver, Pennsylvania. Stawarz, 16, was charged as an adult with attempted homicide, reckless endangerment, and aggravated assault for allegedly beating 15-year-old Jeremy Delon along the Ohio River in Hopewell Township. Police accused Stawarz of beating Delon around the time the teenagers attempted to buy some marijuana.

© AP Images/The Beaver County Times/Sylvester Washington Jr.

Figure 5.3   The General Theory of Crime

Delinquent Offender

Impulsive personality
- Physical
- Insensitive
- Risk-taking
- Short-sighted
- Nonverbal

Low self-control
- Poor parenting
- Deviant parents
- Lack of supervision
- Active
- Self-centered

Weakening of social bonds
- Attachment
- Involvement
- Commitment
- Belief

Delinquent Opportunity
- Presence of gangs
- Lack of supervision
- Lack of guardianship
- Suitable targets

Delinquent Act
- Delinquency
- Smoking
- Drinking
- Underage sex
- Crime

Gottfredson and Hirschi trace the root cause of poor self-control to inadequate child-rearing practices. Parents who are unwilling or unable to monitor a child's behavior, to recognize deviant behavior when it occurs, and to punish that behavior, will produce children who lack self-control. Children who are not attached to their parents, who are poorly supervised, and whose parents are delinquent or deviant themselves are the most likely to develop poor self-control. In a sense, lack of self-control occurs naturally when steps are not taken to stop its development.[68] It comes as no shock to life course theorists when research shows that antisocial behavior runs in families and that having delinquent relatives is a significant predictor of future misbehaviors.[69]

Gottfredson and Hirschi claim that self-control theory can explain all varieties of delinquent behavior and all the social and behavioral correlates of delinquency. That is, such widely disparate delinquent acts as burglary, robbery, embezzlement, drug dealing, murder, rape, and running away from home all stem from a deficiency in self-control. Likewise, gender, racial, and ecological differences in delinquency rates can be explained by discrepancies in self-control: If male delinquency rates are higher than female delinquency rates, it is the result of males having lower levels of self-control than females.

LOOKING BACK TO KIA'S STORY

Gottfredson and Hirschi question whether people really change in their criminal propensity. But Kia seemed to change because of his counselor's intervention. How would they explain his transformation?

Supporting the GTC

Following the publication of *A General Theory of Crime*, dozens of research efforts tested the validity of Gottfredson and Hirschi's theoretical views. One approach involves identifying indicators of impulsiveness and self-control to determine whether

Exhibit 5.2   Elements of Impulsivity: Signs That a Person Has Low Self-Control

- Insensitive
- Physical
- Shortsighted
- Nonverbal
- Here-and-now orientation
- Unstable social relations
- Enjoys deviant behaviors
- Risk taker
- Refuses to work for distant goals
- Lacks diligence
- Lacks tenacity
- Adventuresome
- Self-centered
- Shameless
- Imprudent
- Lacks cognitive and verbal skills
- Enjoys danger and excitement

scales measuring these factors correlate with measures of delinquent activity. A number of studies conducted both in the United States and abroad have shown that delinquent kids score much higher on scales measuring impulsivity than non-delinquent youth.[70] When Alexander Vazsonyi and his associates analyzed self-control and deviant behavior with samples drawn from a number of different countries (Hungary, Switzerland, the Netherlands, the United States, and Japan). They found that low self-control is significantly related to antisocial behavior and that the association can be seen regardless of culture or national settings.[71]

There is also research showing that the patterns of antisocial behavior found in groups of youth offenders mimics those predicted by Gottfredson and Hirschi.[72] One such effort found that those delinquents who begin their offending career at an early age and become "life course persister offenders" are also the ones to be lacking in self-control.[73] Another found that victims have lower self-control than non-victims. Impulsivity predicts both the likelihood that a person will engage in criminal behavior and the likelihood that the person will become a victim of crime. These patterns are all predicted by the GTC.[74]

By integrating the concepts of socialization and criminality, Gottfredson and Hirschi help explain why some people who lack self-control can escape criminality, and conversely, why some people who have self-control might not escape criminality. People who are at risk, because they have impulsive personalities, may forgo delinquent careers because there are no opportunities to commit delinquent acts; instead, they may find other outlets for their impulsive personalities. In contrast, if the opportunity is strong enough, even people with relatively strong self-control may be tempted to violate the law; the incentives to commit delinquent acts may overwhelm their self-control.

Criticisms and Questions Although the GTC seems persuasive, several questions and criticisms remain to be answered. Among the most important are the following:

1. *Circular reasoning.* Some critics argue that the theory involves circular reasoning.

   How do we know when people are impulsive? When they commit crime? Are all criminals impulsive? Of course, or else they would not have broken the law![75]

2. *Personality disorder.* It is possible that a lack of self-control is merely a symptom of some broader, underlying personality disorder, such as an antisocial personality, that produces delinquency. Other personality traits such as low self-direction (the tendency not to act in one's long-term benefit) may be a better predictor of criminality than impulsivity or lack of self-control.[76]

3. *Ecological-individual differences.* The GTC also fails to address individual and ecological patterns in the delinquency rate. For example, if delinquency rates are higher in Los Angeles than in Albany, New York, can it be assumed that residents of Los Angeles are more impulsive than residents of Albany? Gottfredson and Hirschi might argue that there are more delinquent opportunities in Los Angeles, hence the delinquency rate difference.

4. *Racial and gender differences.* Although distinct gender differences in the delinquency rate exist, there is little evidence that males are more impulsive than females.[77] Some research efforts have found gender differences in the association between self-control and crime; the theory predicts no such difference should occur.[78] Girls seem more deeply influenced by their delinquent boyfriends than boys are by their delinquent girlfriends.[79] Differences in impulsivity and self-control alone may not be able to explain differences in male and female offending rates.[80] Similarly, Gottfredson and Hirschi explain racial differences in the delinquency rate as a failure of child-rearing practices in the African American community.[81] In so doing, they overlook issues of institutional racism, poverty, and relative deprivation, which have been shown to have a significant impact on delinquency rate differentials.

5. *People change and so does their level of self-control.* The general theory assumes that delinquent propensity does not change; opportunities change. However, social scientists recognize that behavior shaping factors that are dominant in early adolescence, for example, peer group, may fade and be replaced by others, for example, the nuclear family, in adulthood.[82] Personality also undergoes change and so does its impact on antisocial behavior.[83] It is not surprising then that research efforts show that the stability in self-control predicted by Gottfredson and Hirschi may be an illusion.[84] As kids mature the focus of their lives likewise changes and they may be better able to control their impulsive behavior.[85] In one recent research effort, Thomas Winfree and his associates noted a significant change in level of self-control as youths mature.[86]

Influence of External Factors Gottfredson and Hirschi discount the influence of outside factors: low self-control produces delinquency notwithstanding the characteristics of the adolescent's social world. However, research indicates that an adolescent's social world mediates the influence of self-control on crime.[87] Social cultural factors have been found to make an independent contribution to criminal offending patterns.[88] Kids who lack self-control and who live in high crime areas may be more inclined to antisocial activities than youth with similar levels of self-control who reside in areas that work to maintain collective efficacy and that are relatively crime-free.[89]

As associations with these external factors (e.g., family relations, peer interactions, and school performance) vary over time, so too does their influence on self-control. Even impulsive kids commit less crime if they are able to strengthen their ties to their parents and friends and improve their social bonds.[90] One recent analysis by Callie Burt and her associates found that kids whose parents improved their parenting skills over time experienced (1) an increase in self-control and (2) a subsequent decrease in the level of their delinquent activities. Also helping to reduce low self-control was developing positive relationships with teachers and reducing exposure to deviant peers. The Burt research is a direct rebuttal of Hirschi and Gottfredson's core premise that once acquired low self-control is hard to shake.[91]

1. *Modest relationship.* Some research results support the proposition that self-control is a causal factor in delinquent and other forms of deviant behavior, but that the association is quite modest.[92] Low self-control alone cannot predict the onset of a delinquent or deviant career.

External factors may influence the behavior of at-risk kids, insulating them from delinquency even if they have a high propensity to commit crime. Here, children volunteer to dance before having a traditional Thanksgiving dinner for approximately seven hundred south Los Angeles parents and children at A Place Called Home, which provides at-risk youth ages 8 to 20 with a secure, positive family environment. Can such programs reduce delinquent involvement and counteract criminal propensity?

CHECKPOINTS

■ Latent trait theories assume a physical or psychological trait makes some people delinquency-prone.

■ Opportunity to commit delinquency varies; latent traits remain stable.

■ The general theory of crime says an impulsive personality is key.

■ Impulsive people have low self-control and a weak bond to society.

■ Impulsive people often cannot resist delinquent opportunities.

2. *Cross-cultural differences.* Some evidence shows that law violators in other countries do not lack self-control, indicating that the GTC may be culturally limited.[93] Behavior that may be considered imprudent in one culture may be socially acceptable in another, and therefore, cannot be viewed as "lack of self-control."[94]

Although questions like these remain, the strength of the general theory lies in its scope and breadth; it attempts to explain all forms of delinquency and deviance, from lower-class gang delinquency to sexual harassment in the business community.[95] By integrating concepts of delinquent choice, delinquent opportunity, socialization, and personality, Gottfredson and Hirschi make a plausible argument that all deviant behaviors may originate at the same source. Continued efforts are needed to test the GTC and establish the validity of its core concepts. It remains one of the key developments of modern criminological theory. ✔ **Checkpoints**

EVALUATING THE DEVELOPMENTAL VIEW

The developmental view is that a delinquent career must be understood as a passage along which people travel, that it has a beginning and an end, and that events and life circumstances influence the journey. The factors that affect a delinquent career may include structural factors, such as income and status; socialization factors, such as family and peer relations; biological factors, such as size and strength; psychological factors, including intelligence and personality; and opportunity factors, such as free time, inadequate police protection, and a supply of easily stolen merchandise.

Life course theories emphasize the influence of changing interpersonal and structural factors—that is, people change along with the world they live in. Latent trait theories assume that an individual's behavior is linked less to personal change than to changes in the surrounding world.

These perspectives differ in their view of human development. Do people constantly change, as life course theories suggest, or are they more stable, constant, and changeless, as the latent trait view indicates? Are the factors that produce criminality different at each stage of life, as the life course view suggests, or does a master trait— for example, impulsivity or self-control—steer the course of human behavior?

It is also possible that these two positions are not mutually exclusive and each may make a notable contribution to understanding the onset and continuity of a delinquent career. For example, recent research by Bradley Entner Wright and his associates found evidence supporting both latent trait and life course theories.[96] Their research, conducted with subjects in New Zealand, indicates that low self-control in childhood predicts disrupted social bonds and delinquent offending later in life, a finding that supports latent trait theory. They also found that maintaining positive social bonds helps reduce criminality and that such bonds could even counteract the effect of low self-control. Latent traits are an important influence on delinquency, but Wright's findings indicate that social relationships that form later in life appear to influence delinquent behavior "above and beyond" individuals' pre-existing characteristics.[97] This finding may reflect the fact that there are two classes of criminals: a less serious group who are influenced by life events, and a more chronic group whose latent traits insulate them from any positive pro-social relationships.[98]

Developmental Theory and Delinquency Prevention

There have been a number of policy-based initiatives based on premises of developmental theory. These typically feature multisystemic treatment efforts designed to provide at-risk kids with personal, social, educational, and family services. For example, one program found that an intervention that promotes academic success, social competence, and educational enhancement during the elementary grades can reduce risky sexual practices and their accompanying health consequences in early adulthood.[99]

Other programs are now employing multidimensional strategies and are aimed at targeting children in preschool through the early elementary grades in order to alter the direction of their life course. Many of the most successful programs are aimed at strengthening children's social-emotional competence and positive coping skills and suppressing the development of antisocial, aggressive behavior.[100] Research evaluations indicate that the most promising multicomponent crime and substance abuse prevention programs for youths, especially those at high risk, are aimed at improving their developmental skills. They may include a school component, an after-school component, and a parent-involvement component. All of these components have the common goal of increasing protective factors and decreasing risk factors in the areas of the family, the community, the school, and the individual.[101] For example, the Boys and Girls Clubs and School Collaborations' Substance Abuse Prevention Program includes a school component called SMART (skills mastery and resistance training) Teachers, an after-school component called SMART Kids, and a parent-involvement component called SMART Parents. Each component is designed to reduce specific risk factors in the children's school, family, community, and personal environments.[102]

SUMMARY

- Life course theories argue that events that take place over the life course influence delinquent choices.
- The cause of delinquency constantly changes as people mature. At first, the nuclear family influences behavior; during adolescence, the peer group dominates; in adulthood, marriage and career are critical.
- There are a variety of pathways to delinquency: some kids are sneaky, others hostile, and still others defiant.
- According to the concept of problem behavior syndrome, delinquency may be just one of a variety of social problems, including health, physical, and interpersonal troubles.
- Sampson and Laub's age-graded theory holds that the social sources of behavior change over the life course. People who develop social capital are best able to avoid antisocial entanglements. Important life events, or turning points, enable adult offenders to desist from delinquency. Among the most important are getting married and serving in the military.

- Latent trait theories hold that some underlying condition present from birth or soon after controls behavior. Suspect traits include low IQ, impulsivity, and personality structure. This underlying trait explains the continuity of offending, because, once present, it remains with a person throughout the lifetime.
- The General Theory of Crime, developed by Gottfredson and Hirschi, integrates rational choice theory concepts. People with latent traits choose delinquency over nondelinquency; the opportunity for delinquency mediates their choice.
- According to the General Theory of Crime, impulsive people have low self-control, and a weak bond to society; they often cannot resist criminal opportunities.
- Programs that are based on developmental theory are typically multidimensional and multifaceted.

KEY TERMS

developmental theory, p. 108
life course theory, p. 108
latent trait theory, p. 109
early onset, p. 110
adolescent-limited offender, p. 111
life course persister offender, p. 111

pseudomaturity, p. 112
problem behavior syndrome (PBS), p. 112
authority conflict pathway, p. 113
covert pathway, p. 113
overt pathway, p. 114

turning points, p. 114
social capital, p. 115
latent trait, p. 117
General Theory of Crime (GTC), p. 118
self-control, p. 120
impulsive, p. 120

1. Do you consider yourself a holder of "social capital?" If so, what form does it take?

2. A person gets a 1600 on the SAT. Without knowing this person, what personal, family, and social characteristics must he or she have? Another person becomes a serial killer. Without knowing this person, what personal, family, and social characteristics must he or she have? If "bad behavior" is explained by multiple problems, is "good behavior" explained by multiple strengths?

3. Do you believe there is a "latent trait" that makes a person delinquency-prone, or is delinquency a function of environment and socialization?

4. Do you agree with Loeber's multiple pathways model? Do you know people who have traveled down those paths?

APPLYING WHAT YOU HAVE LEARNED

Luis Francisco is the leader of the Almighty Latin Kings and Queens Nation. He was convicted of murder in 1998 and sentenced to life imprisonment plus forty-five years. Luis Francisco's life has been filled with displacement, poverty, and chronic predatory delinquency. The son of a prostitute in Havana, at the age of nine he was sent to prison for robbery. He had trouble in school, and teachers described him as having attention problems; he dropped out in the seventh grade. On his nineteenth birthday in 1980, he emigrated to the United States and soon became a gang member in Chicago, joining the Latin Kings. After moving to the Bronx, he shot and killed his girlfriend in 1981. He fled to Chicago and was not apprehended until 1984. Sentenced to nine years for second-degree manslaughter, Luis Francisco ended up in a New York prison, where he started a prison chapter of the Latin Kings. As King Blood Inka, First Supreme Crown, Francisco ruled the two thousand Latin Kings in and out of prison. Disciplinary troubles erupted when some Kings were found stealing from the organization. Infuriated, King Blood wrote to his street lieutenants and ordered their termination. Federal authorities, who had been monitoring Francisco's mail, arrested thirty-five Latin Kings. The other thirty-four pled guilty; only Francisco insisted on a trial, where he was found guilty of conspiracy to commit murder.

Explain Luis's behavior patterns from a developmental perspective. How would a latent trait theorist explain his escalating delinquent activities?

DOING RESEARCH ON THE WEB

Do you think that a repeat offender like Luis Francisco could ever turn his life around and reenter society? It may prove more difficult than you think. To learn about some of the obstacles he would face, go to InfoTrac College Edition and read Devah Pager, "The Mark of a Criminal Record," *American Journal of Sociology* 108:937–977 (2003).

To read more about reentry problems on a website maintained by the federal government's Office of Justice Programs, go to www.thomsonedu.com/criminaljustice/siegel.

Primary Prevention Efforts: Early Childhood

Delinquency prevention refers to intervening in a young person's life prior to engagement in a delinquent act. In some instances, prevention means helping kids develop defenses to help them resist the crime-promoting elements in their immediate environment. In other instances, it can mean helping experienced offenders who have already been involved in antisocial behaviors develop the skills that can enable them to resist delinquency and a delinquent way of life. An understanding of prevention is critical to the field of juvenile delinquency, because efforts to explain and understand why kids commit crime would exist in a vacuum if they could not provide a blueprint for eliminating, controlling, or preventing youth crime.

Traditionally, delinquency prevention efforts are divided into three types: primary prevention, secondary prevention, and tertiary prevention.

- *Primary prevention* focuses on improving the general well-being of individual children through such measures as providing access to health care services and education or modifying conditions in the physical environment, such as removing abandoned vehicles and improving the appearance of neighborhood buildings.
- *Secondary prevention* involves intervening with children and young people who are viewed as being at high risk for becoming juvenile offenders. Secondary programs involve provision of neighborhood youth programs designed to help such kids avoid involvement with gangs, drugs, and delinquency.
- *Tertiary prevention* focuses on intervening with juveniles who have already committed delinquent acts and have been adjudicated delinquent in juvenile court. These youth are placed in substance abuse treatment programs, anger management programs, group counseling, and so on. Here, the goal is to reduce repeat offending or recidivism.

In this section, we will discuss elements of primary prevention—those efforts that are aimed at providing children with an atmosphere in which they can develop and grow in a positive manner and become insulated from delinquency-producing forces in the family and community. Later in the text, secondary and tertiary efforts will be examined independently.

PRIMARY PREVENTION

All of the theoretical models of delinquency we have discussed in the preceding chapters suggest that the seeds of delinquency are planted early in life. Although some people may begin their offending career relatively late—in their later teen years or even early adulthood—it appears that the majority of the most serious delinquents experience antisocial episodes much earlier, in their early adolescence or before. Given this finding, primary prevention programs are often aimed at positively influencing the early risk factors or "root causes" of delinquency. Early risk factors may include structural factors such as poverty and residency in a lower-class neighborhood, socialization issues such as inadequate parental supervision and harsh or inconsistent discipline, and individual or trait issues such as a high level of hyperactivity or impulsiveness. Consequently, primary prevention interventions are often multidimensional, targeting more than one risk factor at a time. This approach attacks delinquency on a number of different fronts, including cognitive development, child skills training, and family support. What are some of the directions being explored to deliver primary prevention before the onset of a delinquent career?

HELPING FAMILIES CARE FOR CHILDREN'S HEALTH AND WELL-BEING

Delinquency theorists of all persuasions recognize that a positive home environment is a key element in a child's successful development. Because a supportive and loving home is so important for the successful development of a child, prevention programs are often aimed at improving family well-being. These programs are designed to help parents care for their children's health and general well-being, instill in their children positive values such as honesty and respect for others, and nurture pro-social behaviors.

One of the most important types of family-based programs to prevent juvenile delinquency involves the provision of home visitation by experienced and trained human resource personnel.[1] One of the best-known home visitation programs is the Prenatal/Early Infancy Project (PEIP), which was started in Elmira, New York.[2] This program has three broad objectives:

1. To improve the outcomes of pregnancy.
2. To improve the quality of care that parents provide to their children (and their children's subsequent health and development).
3. To improve the women's own personal life-course development (completing their education, finding work, and planning future pregnancies).[3]

The program provides nurse home visiting services to teenage, Medicaid-eligible, and first-time mothers. Prenatal and postpartum home visiting is available for the mother and for the child. Home visiting for routine health guidance is available to the child for two years after birth. Prenatal and postpartum home visiting services are made by County Health Department Maternal Child Health (MCH) nurses upon referral from physicians, hospitals, local departments of social services, and other service providers. The MCH program provides prenatal, postpartum, and health guidance assessment and intervention to high-risk clients. MCH nurses also are able to provide skilled services to ill pediatric client through the Certified Home Health Agency. There are no restrictive criteria for entry into the program.

The program targeted first-time mothers-to-be who were under nineteen years of age, unmarried, or poor. In all, four hundred women were enrolled in the program. These mothers-to-be received home visits from nurses during pregnancy and then during the first two years of their child's life. Each home visit lasted about one and a quarter hours, and the mothers were visited on average every two weeks. The home visitors gave advice to the young women about child care, infant development, and the importance of eating properly and avoiding smoking and drinking during pregnancy.

Several cost-benefit analyses show that the benefits of this program outweighed its costs for the higher risk mothers. Peter Greenwood and his colleagues measured benefits to the government or taxpayer (welfare, education, employment, and criminal justice), whereas Steven Aos and his colleagues measured a somewhat different range of benefits to the government (education, public assistance, substance abuse, teen pregnancy, child abuse and neglect, and criminal justice), as well as tangible benefits to crime victims. Both reported that for every dollar spent on the program, benefits were about three to four times greater; $4.06 according to Greenwood and his colleagues and $2.88 according to Aos and his colleagues.[4]

There are many other home visitation programs across the United States. In the early 1990s, Hawaii became the first state to offer free home visits for all new mothers. A small number of other states, with Colorado at the forefront, have more recently implemented more intensive, but targeted versions of home visiting programs with the aim of eventually providing universal coverage.[5] It is difficult to say with much certainty how effective home visitation services are in preventing delinquency. The claim can, however, be made that home visitation can be very effective in reducing child abuse and neglect and child injuries and in improving the lives of families, particularly young mothers.[6] These too are very important benefits.

IMPROVING PARENTING SKILLS

Some programs aim to prevent delinquency in the long run by helping parents improve their parenting skills. This is another form of family support that has shown some success in preventing juvenile delinquency. Although the main focus of parent training programs is on the parents, many of these programs also involve children in an effort to improve the parent-child bond. One of the most famous parenting skills programs, the Oregon Social Learning Center (OSLC), is based on the assumption that many parents do not know how to deal effectively with their children, sometimes ignoring their behavior and at other times reacting with explosive rage. Some parents discipline their children for reasons that have little to do with the children's behavior, instead reflecting their own frustrations. The OSLC program uses behavior modification techniques to help parents acquire proper disciplinary methods. Parents are asked to select several behaviors for change and to count the frequency of their occurrence. OSLC personnel teach social skills to reinforce positive behaviors and constructive disciplinary methods to discourage negative ones. Incentive programs are initiated in which a child can earn points for desirable behaviors. Points can be exchanged for allowance, prizes, or privileges. Parents are also taught disciplinary techniques that stress firmness and consistency, rather than "nattering" (low-intensity behaviors, such as scowling or scolding) or explosive discipline, such as hitting or screaming. One important technique is the "time-out," in which the child is removed for brief isolation in a quiet room. Parents are taught the importance of setting rules and sticking to them. A number of evaluation studies show that improving parenting skills can lead to reductions in juvenile delinquency.[7] A Rand study found that parent training costs about one-twentieth what a home visit program costs and is more effective in preventing serious crimes.[8]

Another effort known as Preparing for the Drug Free Years (PDFY) is designed to aid parents on many fronts that include teaching parents about the risk and protective factors for substance abuse and helping them to develop skills for establishing and communicating clear behavioral expectations, monitoring their children's behavior and enforcing norms, reducing family conflict, promoting child involvement, and strengthening family bonds. The PDFY program has been carried out in a group format and was fairly short in duration, involving five weekly parenting sessions each lasting about two hours. Children were involved in one of the sessions. Evaluations show that kids going through the program had experienced a significantly slower rate of increase in delinquency and substance abuse compared to the control group.[9]

PROVIDING BETTER NUTRITION

Some trait theorists believe that prevention efforts might best be served by altering the biochemical factors, such as poor nutrition, that have been linked to the onset of delinquent behavior. For example, in one study researchers led by Adrian Raine looked at the long-term effects of a two-year diet enrichment program in which kids were placed at only three years old.[10] One hundred randomly selected children were placed in the program, which provided nutritious lunches, physical exercise, and enhanced education. They were then compared with a control group who did not participate in the program. By age seventeen, kids who had been malnourished before they entered the nutrition program had higher scores on physical and psychological well-being than malnourished kids who had not been in the program. By age twenty-three, the malnourished kids who had been in the program twenty years earlier still did better on personality tests and had lower levels of self-reported crimes than the malnourished children who had not been placed in the program. Overall, the results showed that providing children with nutritious diets and enriched environments is associated with greater mental health and reduced antisocial activities later in life.

HELPING KIDS PREPARE FOR SCHOOL

In addition to helping parents become more effective caregivers, primary prevention programs focus on helping kids get ready for the school experience. Preschool is typically provided to children ages three to five years. These are the formative years of brain development; more learning takes place during this developmental stage than at any other stage over the life course. Low intelligence and school failure are important risk factors for juvenile delinquency.[11] For these reasons, highly structured,

cognitive-based preschool programs offer young children an important start in life.

One of the most widely admired preschool programs is the Perry Preschool in Ypsilanti, Michigan. Started in the mid-1960s, it provides disadvantaged children with a program of educational enrichment supplemented with weekly home visits. The Perry formula is that a good preschool program can help children in poverty make a better start in their transition from home to community and thereby set more of them on the path to becoming economically self-sufficient, socially responsible adults.[12] The Perry program provides high-quality, active-learning programming administered by professional teachers who have worked in the field for two years. The educational approach is focused on supporting the development of the children's cognitive and social skills through individualized teaching and learning. Its success is largely due to the following components:

- A developmentally appropriate curriculum that views children as active, self-initiated learners
- Small classrooms of twenty children and at least two staff, which allows a more supervised and supportive learning environment
- Staff who are trained in early childhood development and education, who receive supervision and ongoing instruction, and who actively communicate with parents
- Sensitivity to the non-educational needs of disadvantaged children and their families, which includes providing meals and recommending other social service agencies
- Ongoing monitoring and evaluation of both teachers' activities and children's behaviors and development

The kids who went through the Perry program have been closely monitored. The most recent follow-up of the original Perry children, now age forty, found that the program continued to make an important difference in the lives of the participants Compared to a control group, program group members had significantly fewer lifetime arrests for violent, drug and property crimes. Improvements were also recorded in many other important life course outcomes such as higher levels of schooling, better records of employment, and higher annual incomes. A cost-benefit analysis found that Perry produced just over seventeen dollars of benefit per dollar of cost, with most of this savings returned to the general public—in the form of savings in crime, education, and welfare, and increased tax revenue.[13]

Mixed Programs

Some programs provide a mixture of services ranging from heath care to parenting skill improvement. The CODAC Family Health Promotion (FHP) program is a primary prevention program that offers a variety of interventions to children ages three through eight and to their families. The program offers children developmentally appropriate activities in child care, school, and recreation to help develop resiliency skills. Parents are encouraged to become involved in activities that enable them to increase protective factors. Participants requiring treatment services will receive them onsite. The central feature of the FHP is the family services team that serves as the integrating force of the program. Specific program activities include the following:

- Training in resiliency and protective factors is provided to parents through home visitation. These visits occur once a month during the first year, twice a month during the second year, and as needed during the third year.
- Parent advisory council meetings.
- The *S.T.E.P. Curriculum* workshop series.
- Support groups.
- Family weekend activities.
- Training of school personnel on the *Building Me* program curricula and cultural competence.
- Implementation of the *Building Me* curriculum at the Connie Chambers Early Childhood Education Center.
- Transportation to the program.
- Art therapy sessions.

The target population for FHP is predominantly Hispanic/Latino. The risk group is mixed and includes latchkey children, children who live in poverty, children who have substance-abusing parents, and children who have been physically, sexually, or psychologically abused.[14]

CAN PRIMARY PREVENTION WORK?

The success of these and other primary prevention programs seems to indicate that they can be effective in reducing the incidence of delinquency. However, their effectiveness often rests in their targeting of important individual- and family-level risk factors for delinquency, such as low intelligence, impulsiveness, and inconsistent and poor parenting. Even if these problems can be identified, families may be required to get involved in a package of child- and parent-centered interventions that target multiple risk factors ranging from mental health to educational enrichment.[15] A number of program evaluations, including the Great Smoky Mountains Study of Youth in North Carolina, the Patterns of Care program in San Diego, California, and the Southwestern Pennsylvania Costs of Services in Medicaid Study, have found that the first step toward obtaining effective treatment is to provide families with access to mental health and other social services. Research from these studies shows that the delay between detecting problems, and the families' ability to obtain treatment is still extremely low. For primary prevention ultimately to be successful, effective mechanisms must be developed for obtaining timely, specialized help that, although costly, will provide long-term savings by helping children avoid involvement in antisocial behavior and its legal consequences.

Gender and Delinquency

© Manoocher Geghati/AFP/Getty Images

CHAPTER OBJECTIVES

After reading this chapter you should:

1. Be familiar with the changes in the female delinquency rate.
2. Understand the cognitive differences between males and females.
3. Be able to discuss the differences in socialization between boys and girls and how this may affect their behavior.
4. Understand the psychological differences between the sexes.
5. Be able to discuss the early work on gender, delinquency, and human traits.
6. Know the elements contemporary trait theorists view as the key to understanding gender differences, such as psychological makeup and hormonal differences.
7. Know how socialization is thought to affect delinquency rates.
8. Discuss the views of contemporary socialization theorists.
9. Know what the term *liberal feminism* refers to.
10. Discuss how critical feminists view female delinquency and describe Hagan's power-control theory.
11. Be familiar with how the treatment girls receive by the juvenile justice system differs from the treatment of boys.

Laticia, a fifteen-year-old female of African descent, was referred to the teen center for her involvement in a gang-related physical assault. According to Laticia, she "beat the girl down," because she had publicly disrespected Laticia's gang and friends. Laticia was fighting and having significant behavioral issues in school. When she was referred to the teen center by juvenile court, she had not attended school for several months and had little positive direction in her life. Standing nearly six feet tall and weighing close to three hundred pounds, she was aggressive and intimidating to many people in her life. Even some school personnel felt intimidated by Laticia, and because she had threatened a number of teachers and was often suspended for unruly behavior they were glad she dropped out. Laticia was difficult to get to know, and seemingly hostile most of the time, which made counseling her a challenge. Teen counselors would have to work hard to build her trust and to engage her in the program.

Upon the referral to the teen drop-in program, Laticia resisted involvement in the teen drop-in program. One counselor in particular, who had significant experience with similar situations, made it his mission to assist her. Looking beyond her exterior and striving to make a positive connection with her, he engaged Laticia in the program by focusing on her positive attributes, as well as standing firm on the code of conduct at the center. He discovered that Laticia's mother worked three jobs to support the family and that her father was not in her life. Despite her mother's hard work, the children were neglected in many ways and their basic needs were rarely met. It was also suspected that their mother was physically abusive to the children. Laticia was generally responsible for taking care of her many siblings, which she resented.

And she often acted out because she herself was not receiving the attention she needed. Because of her larger size, she also felt rejected by males her own age, reporting that they would "sleep" with her, but never wanted to date her on a longer-term basis. Laticia's counselor tried to help her understand that she needed to focus on respecting herself and that her negative behaviors were not the way to get her needs met. He spent a lot of time trying to help her gain insight in order to deconstruct her negative belief system, and to address her negative self-image.

The program provided group sessions to address Laticia's anger management issues, relationships and unhealthy sexual activity, and criminal and gang involvement. In addition, Laticia participated in a group to complete her court-ordered requirement for community services. Lastly, the program coordinated a field trip to a maximum-security female prison, which made a significant impression on Laticia. It helped her to face the reality of where her behavior could lead if she did not make better life choices.

Laticia continued attending the center even after she had completed the requirements of the juvenile court, a significant advantage of this particular program. The relationship Laticia established with her primary counselor continued for many years. They often visited with each other and he became somewhat of a parental figure in her life. Laticia returned to school and achieved a level of success that surprised everyone involved with her case. She tried to make better relationship decisions and had no further delinquency referrals. Laticia graduated from high school and was able to continue her education at the local community college.

To early delinquency experts, the female offender was an aberration who engaged in crimes that usually had a sexual connotation—prostitution, running away (which presumably leads to sexual misadventure), premarital sex, and crimes of sexual passion (killing a boyfriend or a husband).[1] Criminologists often ignored female offenders, assuming that they rarely violated the law, or if they did, that their illegal acts were status-type offenses. Female delinquency was viewed as emotional or family-related, and such problems were not an important concern of criminologists. In fact, the few "true" female delinquents were sexual oddities whose criminal activity was a function of having masculine traits and characteristics, a concept referred to today as the **masculinity hypothesis**.[2]

Contemporary interest in the association between gender and delinquency has surged, fueled by observations that although the female delinquency rate is still much lower than the male rate, it is growing, both in the United States and abroad at a faster

masculinity hypothesis
View that women who commit crimes have biological and psychological traits similar to those of men.

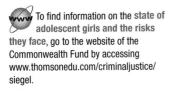

LOOKING BACK TO LATICIA'S STORY

Laticia is described as being very big and strong. How does her size and strength jibe with the masculinity hypothesis?

pace than male delinquency. Australian sociologist Kerry Carrington reports that young women represent the fastest growing population within juvenile justice systems around the world. In Canada, for instance, the number of young women charged with criminal offences has more than tripled during the past two decades; in England, the gender gap has also narrowed, with the ratio of delinquent boys to delinquent girls declining from 7:1 during the 1960s to 5:1 today; a similar pattern of rising adolescent female crime rates is evident in Australia.[3]

The types of delinquent acts that young women engage in today also seem quite similar to those of young men. Larceny and aggravated assault, the crimes for which most young men are arrested, are also the most common offenses for which females are arrested. There is evidence that girls get more heavily involved in gangs and gang violence.[4] Gone are the days when criminologists portrayed female delinquents as "fallen women" who were exploited by men and involved in illicit sexual activities. Research now indicates, ironically, that boys rather than girls are more likely to be arrested for sexually related offenses, such as prostitution. When David Finkelhor and Richard Ormrod analyzed national arrest data, they found that juvenile prostitution offenders known to police were more often male (61 percent) than female (39 percent), a greater disproportion than among adult prostitution offenders (53 percent male and 47 percent female).[5]

Another reason for the interest in gender studies is that conceptions of gender differences have changed. A feminist approach to understanding crime is now firmly established. The result has been an increased effort to conduct research that would adequately explain differences and similarities in male and female offending patterns.

This chapter provides an overview of gender factors in delinquency. We first discuss some of the gender differences in development and how they may relate to the gender differences in offending rates. Then we turn to some explanations for these differences: (1) the trait view, (2) the socialization view, (3) the liberal feminist view, and (4) the critical feminist view.

 To find information on the **state of adolescent girls and the risks they face**, go to the website of the Commonwealth Fund by accessing www.thomsonedu.com/criminaljustice/siegel.

GENDER DIFFERENCES IN DEVELOPMENT

Do gender differences in development, including socialization, cognition, and personality pave the way for future differences in misbehaving?[6] It is possible that the traits that produce delinquency may exist as early as infancy, when infant girls show greater control over their emotions, whereas boys are more easily angered and depend more on inputs from their mothers.[7]

Socialization Differences

Psychologists believe that differences in the way females and males are socialized affect their development. Males learn to value independence, whereas females are taught that their self-worth depends on their ability to sustain relationships. Girls, therefore, run the risk of losing themselves in their relationships with others, whereas boys may experience a chronic sense of alienation. Because so many relationships go sour, females also run the risk of feeling alienated, because of the failure to achieve relational success.[8]

Although there are few gender differences in aggression during the first few years of life, girls are socialized to be less aggressive than boys and are supervised more closely.[9] Differences in aggression become noticeable between ages three and six, when children are socialized into organized groups, such as the daycare center. Males are more likely to display physical aggression, whereas females display relational aggression—for example, by excluding disliked peers from play groups.[10]

As they mature, girls learn to respond to provocation by feeling anxious, unlike boys, who are encouraged to retaliate.[11] It is not surprising that fathers are more likely

© ACE Stock Limited/Alamy

Why do males and females behave differently? Some experts believe that socialization affects development. Males learn to value independence, whereas females are taught that their self-worth depends on their ability to sustain relationships. If their relationships go sour, girls may place blame, whereas boys may experience a chronic sense of alienation.

to teach boys about using and maintaining weapons. Self-report studies show that boys are three times as likely to report hunting or shooting with a family member than girls.[12]

Overall, women are much more likely to feel distressed than men.[13] Although females get angry as often as males, many have been taught to blame themselves for such feelings. Females are, therefore, much more likely than males to respond to anger with feelings of depression, anxiety, and shame. Females are socialized to fear that anger will harm relationships; males are encouraged to react with "moral outrage," blaming others for their discomfort.[14]

Cognitive Differences

There are also cognitive differences between males and females starting in childhood. The more replicated findings about gender difference in cognitive performance suggest female superiority on visual-motor speed and language ability and male superiority on mechanical and visual-spatial tasks.[15] Put another way, males excel in tasks that assess the ability to manipulate visual images in working memory, whereas females do better in tasks that require retrieval from long-term memory and the acquisition and use of verbal information.[16] Gender group strengths found in the early school years become more established at adolescence and remain stable through adulthood.[17]

Girls learn to speak earlier and faster, and with better pronunciation, most likely because parents talk more to their infant daughters than to their infant sons. A girl's verbal proficiency enables her to develop a skill that may later help her deal with conflict without resorting to violence.[18] When faced with conflict, women might be more likely to attempt to negotiate, rather than to respond passively or resist physically, especially when they perceive increased threat of harm or death.[19]

When girls are aggressive, they are more likely than boys to hide their behavior from adults; girls who "bully" others are less likely than boys to admit their behavior.[20] Girls are shielded by their moral sense, which directs them to avoid harming others. Their moral sensitivity may counterbalance the effects of family problems.[21] Females display more self-control than males, a factor that has been related to criminality.[22]

In most cases cognitive differences are small, narrowing, and usually attributed to cultural expectations. When given training, girls can increase their visual-spatial skills. However, differences still exert a penalty on young girls. For example, performance on the mathematics portion of the Scholastic Aptitude Test (SAT) still favors males: twice as many boys as girls attain scores over 500 and thirteen times as many boys as girls attain scores over 700.[23]

LOOKING BACK TO LATICIA'S STORY

Laticia got in trouble when she beat a girl who had publicly disrespected Laticia's gang and friends. Did Laticia's perceptions of disrespect lead to the fight? Is this a good example of how cognition influences delinquency?

Personality Differences

Girls are often stereotyped as talkative, but research shows that in many situations boys spend more time talking than girls do. Females are more willing to reveal their feelings and more likely to express concern for others. Females are more

Gender Differences

	Females	**Males**
Socialization	Sustain relationships.	Are independent.
	Are less aggressive.	Are aggressive.
	Blame self.	Externalize anger.
Cognitive	Have superior verbal ability.	Have superior visual/spatial ability.
	Speak earlier.	Are better at math.
	Have better pronunciation.	
	Read better	
Personality	Have lower self-esteem.	Have high self-esteem.
	Are self-aware.	Are materialistic.
	Have better attention span.	Have low attention span.

concerned about finding the "meaning of life" and less interested in competing for material success.[24] Males are more likely to introduce new topics and to interrupt conversations.

Adolescent females use different knowledge than males and have different ways of interpreting their interactions with others. These gender differences may have an impact on self-esteem and self-concept. Research shows that, as adolescents develop, male self-esteem and self-concept rise, whereas female self-confidence is lowered.[25] One reason is that girls are more likely to stress about their weight and be more dissatisfied with the size and shape of their bodies.[26] Young girls are regularly confronted with unrealistically high standards of slimness that make them extremely unhappy with their own bodies; it is not surprising that the incidence of eating disorders, such as *anorexia* and *bulimia* have increased markedly in recent years. Psychologist Carol Gilligan uncovered an alternative explanation for this decline in female self-esteem: as girls move into adolescence, they become aware of the conflict between the positive way they see themselves and the negative way society views females. Many girls respond by "losing their voices"—that is, submerging their own feelings and accepting the negative view of women conveyed by adult authorities.[27]

Concept Summary 6.1 discusses these various gender differences.

What Causes Gender Differences?

Why do these gender differences occur? Some experts suggest that gender differences may have a biological origin: males and females are essentially different. They have somewhat different brain organizations; females are more left brain–oriented and males more right brain–oriented. (The left brain is believed to control language; the right, spatial relations.)[28] Others point to the hormonal differences between the sexes as the key to understanding their behavior.

© Ed Quinn/Corbis

Girls learn to respond to provocation by feeling anxious and depressed. Their anxiety may lead to psychological turmoil, sometimes manifested in eating conditions such as anorexia or bulimia. Jennifer Shortis, a young Massachusetts girl, developed anorexia and wasted away from 124 pounds to just 70 pounds. After more than $100,000 in anorexia-related treatment, she is now on the road to recovery.

Another view is that gender differences are a result of the interaction of socialization, learning, and enculturation. Boys and girls may behave differently, because they have been exposed to different styles of socialization, learned different values, and had different cultural experiences. It follows, then, that if members of both sexes were equally exposed to the factors that produce delinquency, their delinquency rates would be equivalent.[29] According to psychologist Sandra Bem's **gender-schema theory**, our culture polarizes males and females by forcing them to obey mutually exclusive gender roles, or "scripts." Girls are expected to be "feminine," exhibiting sympathetic and gentle traits. In contrast, boys are expected to be "masculine," exhibiting assertiveness and dominance. Children internalize these scripts and accept gender polarization as normal. Children's self-esteem becomes wrapped up in how closely their behavior conforms to the proper sex role stereotype. When children begin to perceive themselves as either *boys* or *girls* (which occurs at about age three), they search for information to help them define their role; they begin to learn what behavior is appropriate for their sex.[30] Girls are expected to behave according to the appropriate script and to seek approval of their behavior: Are they acting as girls should at that age? Masculine behavior is to be avoided. In contrast, males look for cues from their peers to define their masculinity; aggressive behavior may be rewarded with peer approval, whereas sensitivity is viewed as non-masculine.[31]

See the What Does This Mean to Me? feature on this page for an interesting perspective on the issue of sexual harassment.

gender-schema theory
A theory of development that holds that children internalize gender scripts that reflect the gender-related social practices of the culture. Once internalized, these gender scripts predispose the kids to construct a self-identity that is consistent with them.

 The mission of the **National Council for Research on Women** is to enhance the connections among research, policy analysis, advocacy, and innovative programming on behalf of women and girls. Visit their website by going to www.thomsonedu.com/criminaljustice/siegel.

GENDER DIFFERENCES AND DELINQUENCY

Regardless of their origin, gender distinctions may partly explain the significant gender differences in the delinquency rate. Research conducted in the United States and abroad have found that the factors that direction the trajectories of male delinquency are quite different than those that influence female delinquency. Among males, early offending is highly correlated with later misbehavior, whereas females take on a more haphazard criminal career path: females are more likely to be influenced by current levels of social support than they are by their early history of antisocial behavior.[32] Males seem more aggressive and less likely to form attachments to others, which are factors that might help them maintain their crime rates over their life span. Males view aggression as an appropriate means to gain status. Boys are also more likely than girls to socialize with deviant peers, and when they do, they display personality traits that make them more susceptible to delinquency.

This pattern fits within the two cultures view that suggests that girls and boys differ in their social behavior largely because their sex-segregated peer groups demand behaviors, for example, aggression, which may not be characteristic of them in other social situations.[33] What is typically assumed to be an inherent difference in antisocial behavior tendencies may actually be a function of peer socialization differences. The fact that young boys perceive their roles as being more dominant than young girls may be a function of peer pressure. Male perceptions of power, their ability to have freedom and hang with their friends, help explain gender differences in personality.[34]

While socialization may be a strong force, inherent gender differences in cognition, personality and biology still seem to play a role in shaping in-

What Does This Mean to Me?

Sexual Harassment

Can gender differences in perception shape the perception of sexual harassment? Research now shows that males and females both generally agree that sexual coercion and sexual propositions constitute sexual harassment. Yet males do not think that sex-stereotyped jokes are a form of harassment, whereas females do; females think that repeated requests for dates after a refusal constitute harassment, whereas males think there is nothing wrong with asking girls out again and again. It is not surprising to discover that females perceive that sexual harassment has occurred in situations where males find no wrongdoing.

1. Do you think that these different perceptions are biologically related or a matter of socialization?
2. (For women): Have you ever been in a situation where you felt yourself being sexually harassed by a male who thought he was doing nothing wrong?
3. (For men): Have you ever been accused of sexual harassment by a woman you know even though you personally felt you did nothing wrong?

CHECKPOINTS

■ Female delinquency was considered unimportant by early delinquency experts because girls rarely committed crime, and when they did it was sexual in nature.

■ Interest in female delinquency has risen because the female crime rate has been increasing, whereas the male rate is in decline.

■ There are distinct gender patterns in development that may explain crime rate differences.

■ Girls are socialized to be less aggressive than boys.

■ Girls read better and have better verbal skills than boys.

■ Gender differences may have both biological and social origins.

■ The female proportion of the delinquency rate has grown at a faster pace than that of males during the past twenty-five years.

■ Though males still are arrested more often than females, the intergender patterns of delinquency are remarkably similar.

 A number of institutes at major universities are devoted to the **study of women's issues**. You can visit the site of the one at the University of Michigan by accessing www.thomsonedu.com/criminaljustice/siegel.

terpersonal interactions, including aggression, and cannot be totally discounted.[35] Cognitive and personality differences are magnified when children internalize gender-specific behaviors. Boys who aren't tough are labeled sissies. Girls are expected to form closer bonds with their friends and to share feelings.

Gender Patterns in Delinquency

As we noted in chapter 2, males, both adults and juveniles, are arrested far more often than females. Today males account for about 76 percent of the total number of arrests and 82 percent of all serious violent crime arrests. For the most violent crimes the differences are even more striking: Only 90 girls were arrested on murder charges in 2005 compared to more than 800 boys. One reason for the gender disparity in lethal violence is that males and females display differences in the victims they target and the weapons they use. The typical male juvenile kills a friend or acquaintance with a handgun during an argument. In contrast, the typical female is as likely to kill a family member as an acquaintance and is more likely to use a knife. Both males and females tend to kill males—generally their brothers, fathers, or friends.

While the differences are still significant, over time the gender gap has been narrowing and the ratio of male-female juvenile arrests is much smaller today than thirty years ago. And not only is the gap between the ratio of male-to-female arrests narrowing, but so too is the difference in the type and pattern of delinquent acts. The Monitoring the Future self-report study also shows that patterns of male and female criminality appear to be converging. Self-report data indicate that the rank-ordering of male and female deviant behaviors is similar. The illegal acts most common for boys—petty larceny, using a false ID, and smoking marijuana—are also the ones most frequently committed by girls.[36]

Why do these differences occur, and why are girls increasing their involvement in delinquent activities at a faster pace than boys? The wide range of opinions on these questions will be presented in the remaining sections of this chapter. ✔ Checkpoints

ARE FEMALE DELINQUENTS BORN THAT WAY?

There is a long tradition of tracing gender differences in delinquency to traits that are uniquely male or female. The argument that biological and psychological differences between males and females can explain differences in crime rates is not a new one. The earliest criminologists focused on physical characteristics believed to be precursors of crime.

Early Biological Explanations

With the publication in 1895 of *The Female Offender,* Lombroso (with William Ferrero) extended his work on criminality to females.[37] Lombroso maintained that women were lower on the evolutionary scale than men, more childlike and less intelligent.[38] Women who committed crimes could be distinguished from "normal" women by physical characteristics—excessive body hair, wrinkles, and an abnormal cranium, for example.[39] In appearance, delinquent females appeared closer to men than to other women. The masculinity hypothesis suggested that delinquent girls had excessive male characteristics.[40]

Lombrosian thought had a significant influence for much of the twentieth century. Delinquency rate differentials were explained in terms of gender-based differences. For example, in 1925, Cyril Burt linked female delinquency to menstruation.[41] Similarly, William Healy and Augusta Bronner suggested that males' physical superiority enhanced their criminality. Their research showed that about 70 percent of the delinquent girls they studied had abnormal weight and size, a finding that supported the "masculinity hypothesis."[42]

So-called experts suggested that female delinquency goes unrecorded, because the female is the instigator rather than the perpetrator.[43] Females first use their sexual

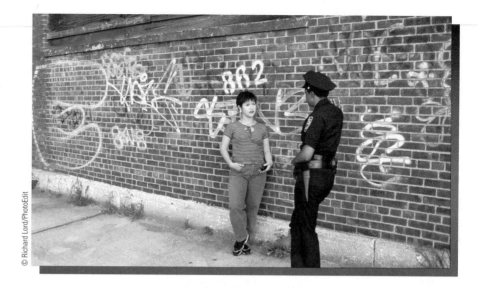

According to the chivalry hypothesis, male police officers are less likely to arrest female offenders than male offenders because they have been socialized to be solicitous to women. As the percentage of women entering police work increases, the effects of chivalry may decline, serving to increase the female arrest rate.

chivalry hypothesis (also known as paternalism hypothesis) The view that low female crime and delinquency rates are a reflection of the leniency with which police treat female offenders.

To read more about the **chivalry hypothesis and how it relates to gang-related delinquency**, go to the website by accessing www.thomsonedu.com/criminaljustice/siegel.

charms to instigate crime and then beguile males in the justice system to obtain deferential treatment. This observation, referred to as the **chivalry hypothesis**, holds that gender differences in the delinquency rate can be explained by the fact that female criminality is overlooked or forgiven by male agents of the justice system. Those who believe in the chivalry hypothesis point to data showing that even though women make up about 20 percent of arrestees, they account for less than 5 percent of inmates. Police and other justice system personnel may be less willing to penalize female offenders than male offenders.[44]

Early Psychological Explanations

Psychologists also viewed the physical differences between males and females as a basis for their behavior differentials. Sigmund Freud maintained that girls interpret their lack of a penis as a sign that they have been punished. Boys fear that they can be punished by having their penis cut off, and thus learn to fear women. From this conflict comes *penis envy,* which often produces an inferiority complex in girls, forcing them to make an effort to compensate for their "defect." One way to compensate is to identify with their mothers and accept a maternal role. Also, girls may attempt to compensate for their lack of a penis by dressing well and beautifying themselves.[45] Freud also claimed that "if a little girl persists in her first wish—to grow into a boy—in extreme cases she will end as a manifest homosexual, and otherwise she will exhibit markedly masculine traits in the conduct of her later life, will choose a masculine vocation, and so on."[46]

At mid-century, psychodynamic theorists suggested that girls are socialized to be passive, which helps explain their low crime rate. However, this condition also makes some females susceptible to being manipulated by men; hence, their participation in sex-related crimes, such as prostitution. A girl's wayward behavior, psychoanalysts suggested, was restricted to neurotic theft (kleptomania) and overt sexual acts, which were symptoms of personality maladaption.[47]

According to these early versions of the psychoanalytic approach, gender differences in the delinquency rate can be traced to differences in psychological orientation. Male delinquency reflects aggressive traits, whereas female delinquency is a function of repressed sexuality, gender conflict, and abnormal socialization.

Contemporary Trait Views

Contemporary biosocial and psychological theorists have continued the tradition of attributing gender differences in delinquency to physical and emotional traits. These theorists recognize that it is the interaction of biological and psychological traits with the social environment that produces delinquency.

Early Puberty/Precocious Sexuality Early theorists linked female delinquency to early puberty and **precocious sexuality**. According to this view, girls who experience an early onset of physical maturity are most likely to engage in antisocial behavior.[48] Female delinquents were believed to be promiscuous and more sophisticated than male delinquents.[49] Linking female delinquency to sexuality was responsible, in part, for the view that female delinquency is symptomatic of maladjustment.[50]

Equating female delinquency purely with sexual activity is no longer taken seriously, but early sexual maturity has been linked to other problems, such as a higher risk of teen pregnancy and sexually transmitted diseases.[51] Empirical evidence suggests that girls who reach puberty at an early age are at the highest risk for delinquency.[52] One reason is that "early bloomers" may be more attractive to older adolescent boys, and increased contact with this high-risk group places the girls in jeopardy for antisocial behavior. Research shows that young girls who date boys three or more years older are more likely to engage in precocious sex, feel pressured into having sex and engage in sex while under the influence of drugs and/or alcohol than girls who date more age-appropriate boys.[53]

Girls who are more sexually developed relative to their peers are more likely to socialize at an early age and to get involved in deviant behaviors, especially "party deviance," such as drinking, smoking, and substance abuse. Early puberty is most likely to encourage delinquent activities that occur in the context of socializing with peers and having romantic relationships with boys.[54] The delinquency gap between early and late bloomers narrows when the latter group reaches sexual maturity and increases in exposure to boys.[55] Biological and social factors seem to interact to postpone or accelerate female delinquent activity.

Hormonal Effects As you may recall from chapter 3, some biosocial theorists link antisocial behavior to hormonal influences.[56] One view is that hormonal imbalance may influence aggressive behavior. For example, changes in the level of the hormone *cortisol*, which is secreted by the adrenal glands in response to any kind of physical or psychological stress, has been linked to conduct problems in young girls.[57] Another view is that excessive amounts of male hormones (androgens) are related to delinquency. The androgen most often related to antisocial behavior is testosterone.[58] In general, females who test higher for testosterone are more likely to engage in stereotypical male behaviors.[59] Females who have low androgen levels are less aggressive than males, whereas those who have elevated levels will take on characteristically male traits, including aggression.[60]

Some females who are overexposed to male hormones in utero may become "constitutionally masculinized." They may develop abnormal hair growth, large musculature, low voice, irregular menstrual cycle, and hyperaggressive behavior. Females exposed to male hormones in utero are more likely to engage in aggressive behavior later in life.[61]

Premenstrual Syndrome Early biotheorists suspected that premenstrual syndrome (PMS) was a direct cause of the relatively rare instances of female violence: "For several days prior to and during menstruation, the stereotype has been that 'raging hormones' doom women to irritability and poor judgment—two facets of premenstrual syndrome."[62] The link between PMS and delinquency was popularized by Katharina Dalton, whose studies of Englishwomen led her to conclude that females are more likely to commit suicide and be aggressive and otherwise antisocial before or during menstruation.[63]

Today there is conflicting evidence on the relationship between PMS and female delinquency. Research shows that a significant number of incarcerated females committed their crimes during the premenstrual phase, and also that a small percentage of women appear vulnerable to cyclical hormonal changes that make them more prone to anxiety and hostility.[64] Although this evidence is persuasive, the true relationship between crime and the female menstrual cycle still remains unknown.[65] There is a causal dilemma: while it is possible that the stress associated with menstruation produces crime, it is also possible that the stress of antisocial behavior produces early menstruation.[66]

Aggression According to some biosocial theorists, gender differences in the delinquency rate can be explained by inborn differences in aggression.[67] Some psychologists believe that males are inherently more aggressive a condition that appears very early in life, before socialization can influence behavior.

Gender-based differences in aggression have been developing for millions of years reflect the dissimilarities in the male and female reproductive systems. Males are more aggressive, because they wish to possess as many sex partners as possible to increase their chances of producing offspring. Females have learned to control their aggressive impulses, because having multiple mates does not increase their chances of conception. Instead, females concentrate on acquiring things that will help them rear their offspring, such as a reliable mate who will supply material resources.[68]

Contemporary Psychological Views

Because girls are socialized to be less aggressive than boys, it is possible that the young women who do get involved in antisocial and violent behavior are suffering from some form of mental anguish or abnormality. Girls are also more likely than boys to be involved in status offenses, such as running away and truancy, behaviors that suggest underlying psychological distress.

Research indicates that antisocial adolescent girls do suffer a wide variety of psychiatric problems and have dysfunctional and violent relationships.[69] Incarcerated adolescent female offenders have more acute mental health symptoms and psychological disturbances than male offenders.[70] Female delinquents score high on psychological tests measuring such traits as psychopathic deviation, schizophrenia, paranoia, and psychasthenia (a psychological disorder characterized by phobias, obsessions, compulsions, or excessive anxiety).[71] Clinical interviews indicate that female delinquents are significantly more likely than males to suffer from mood disorders, including any disruptive disorder, major depressive disorder, and separation anxiety disorder.[72] For example, serious female delinquents have been found to have a relatively high incidence of callous-unemotional (CU) traits, an affective disorder described by a lack of remorse or shame, poor judgment, failure to learn by experience, and chronic lying.[73] In sum, there are some experts who believe that female delinquents suffer from psychological deficits ranging from lack of self-control to serious impairments.[74]

SOCIALIZATION VIEWS

Socialization views are based on the idea that a child's social development may be the key to understanding delinquent behavior. If a child experiences impairment, family disruption, and so on, the child will be more susceptible to delinquent associations and criminality.

Linking crime rate variations to gender differences in socialization is not a recent phenomenon. In a 1928 work, *The Unadjusted Girl*, W. I. Thomas suggested that some girls who have not been socialized under middle-class family controls can become impulsive thrill seekers. According to Thomas, female delinquency is linked to the "wish" for luxury and excitement. Inequities in social class condemn poor girls from demoralized families to using sex as a means to gain amusement, pretty clothes, and other luxuries. Precocious sexuality makes these girls vulnerable to older men, who lead them down the path to decadence.[75]

Socialization and Delinquency

Scholars concerned with gender differences in crime are interested in the distinction between the lifestyles of males and females. Girls may be supervised more closely than boys. If girls behave in a socially disapproved fashion, their parents may be more likely to notice. Adults may be more tolerant of deviant behavior in boys and expect boys to act tough and take risks.[76] Closer supervision restricts the opportunity for

To read about the **socialization of female delinquents**, go to the website www.thomsonedu.com/criminaljustice/siegel.

crime and the time available to mingle with delinquent peers. It follows, then, that the adolescent girl who is growing up in a troubled home and lacks supervision may be more prone to delinquency.[77]

Focus on Socialization In the 1950s, a number of researchers began to focus on gender-specific socialization patterns. They made three assumptions about gender differences in socialization: families exert a more powerful influence on girls than on boys; girls do not form close same-sex friendships, but compete with their peers; and female criminals are primarily sexual offenders. First, parents are stricter with girls because they perceive them as needing control. In some families, adolescent girls rebel against strict controls. In others, where parents are absent or unavailable, girls may turn to the streets for companionship. Second, girls rarely form close relationships with female peers, because they view them as rivals for males who would make eligible marriage partners.[78] Instead, girls enter into affairs with older men who exploit them, involve them in sexual deviance, and father their illegitimate children.[79] The result is prostitution, drug abuse, and marginal lives. Their daughters repeat this pattern in a never-ending cycle of exploitation.

> ### LOOKING BACK TO LATICIA'S STORY
>
> *Laticia and her counselor visited with each other often and he became somewhat of a parental figure in her life. Does such a relationship provide a substitute for parental relations?*

Contemporary Socialization Views

Investigators continue to support the view that female delinquents have more dysfunctional home lives than male offenders.[80] One focus is the effects of abuse on behavior. Girls seem to be more deeply affected than boys by child abuse, and the link between abuse and female delinquency seems stronger than it is for male delinquency.[81] These experiences take a toll on their behavior choices: research shows that girls who are the victims of child sexual abuse and physical abuse are the ones most likely to engage in violent and nonviolent criminal behavior.[82] Their predicament has long-term consequences. Some are placed outside the home early in childhood, because of family breakdown and their own conduct problems. Institutionalization does little to help matters. Those sent away are much more likely to develop criminal records as adults than similarly troubled girls who manage to stay with their families throughout their childhood.[83]

Girls may be forced into a life of sexual promiscuity, because their sexual desirability makes them a valuable commodity for families living on the edge. There are cases of young girls being "lent out" to drug dealers so their parents or partners can get high. Girls on the streets are encouraged to sell their bodies, because they have little else of value to trade.[84] Meda Chesney-Lind, a prominent feminist scholar, has described this association: "Young women on the run from homes characterized by sexual abuse and parental neglect are forced, by the very statutes designed to protect them, into the life of an escaped convict."[85] Many of these girls may find themselves pregnant at a very young age. Physical and sexual abuse and the toll it takes on young girls is not unique to any one culture. As the following Focus on Delinquency shows girls in developing nations may become the victims of one particularly vile form of exploitation: human trafficking and sexual exploitation.

© Cleo Photography/PhotoEdit

According to contemporary socialization views, if a girl grows up in an atmosphere of sexual tension, where hostility exists between her parents or where the parents are absent, she likely will turn to outside sources for affection and support. In their reaction to loneliness, frustration, and parental hostility, girls begin to engage in the same activities as boys: staying out late at night, drinking, partying, and riding around with their friends.

Human Trafficking and the Sexual Exploitation of Children

Human trafficking includes all forms of transportation of women and girls (as well as young boys) through the use of force, abduction, fraud, and coercion for the purpose of sexual and/or commercial exploitation. Trafficking activities include recruiting individuals, transporting and transferring them from their home country or region to other transshipment points and to destination countries, receiving such trafficked persons and keeping them in custody or housing them.

Many forms of trafficking exist. Young girls and women are common targets of commercial sexual exploitation. They may be forced into prostitution and other sexual activities such as the production of pornography. There are accounts of women being forced to service thirty men a day and children trapped in pornography rings. Others become human containers in the transportation of drugs through forced ingestion of condoms or other containers of illegal substances. Labor servitude can be found in nearly every area of industry. Young girls have been forced to work in sweatshops, factories, agricultural fields, and fisheries. Victims may work long hours in unpleasant, unsanitary, or dangerous conditions for low wages, sometimes unable to take breaks or leave the facility. In some instances debts may be passed on to other family members or even entire villages from generation to generation, creating a constant supply of indentured servants for traffickers.

How common is the practice? While data is unreliable, estimates of the amount of people trafficked internationally each year range from six hundred thousand men, women, and children to 1.2 million children alone. The United States is not immune: The CIA issued a report in 2000 estimating that forty-five thousand to fifty thousand individuals were trafficked into the United States annually. Despite the differences in these numbers, it is undeniable that a huge amount of trafficking in humans occurs around the globe.

Contributing Factors

Human trafficking is facilitated by the global economy and relaxation of corporate boundaries. They young female victims are often poor and aspire to a better life. They may be forced, coerced, deceived, and psychologically manipulated into industrial or agricultural work, marriage, domestic servitude, organ donation, or sexual exploitation. Although victims often come from poorer countries, the market for labor and sex is found in wealthier countries or in countries that, while economically poor, cater to the needs of citizens from wealthy countries, of corporations, or of tourists.

While some individuals are trafficked directly for purposes of prostitution or commercial sexual exploitation, other trafficked persons and even those trafficked for legitimate work may become victims of interpersonal violence. Women trafficked for domestic work in wealthy countries or laborers trafficked for construction, logging, factory or farm work, are vulnerable to exploitation by their employers. Individuals trafficked for the labor purposes are usually unfamiliar with their new location and the language spoken there. They often lack formal education and do not know about the human and legal resources that could help them. For these reasons, individuals are vulnerable to the violence of exploitation.

Sex Tourism

Sex tourism is a booming business and many men from wealthy nations engage in sexual activities with trafficked individuals by travelling to destinations where women and children are prostituted. One area of particular concern is child prostitution that flourishes along the German-Czech border. Girls (and boys) hang out near petrol stations, bus stops and restaurants on the connecting roads between the two nations. Within towns, they are found in parks, in front of supermarkets and the entrances of gambling halls and houses, and at the railway station. In some areas, the children wait for tourists in cars or by windows. Small babies and children up to six years of age are usually offered to tourists by women. Children older than seven years are usually accompanied by a male adolescent or an adult. Small children can be seen addressing German men asking if they want sex or begging for money or food. Many of the children get inside the cars of German tourists and drive away with them. Older children from eight years on negotiate prices and sexual

Socialization and Gangs There is a significant body of literature linking abusive home lives to gang participation and crime. Joan Moore's analysis of gang girls in East Los Angeles found that many came from troubled homes. Sixty-eight percent of the girls she interviewed were afraid of their fathers, and 55 percent reported fear of their mothers.[86] Many of the girls reported that their parents were overly strict and controlling, despite the fact that they engaged in criminality themselves. Moore also details accounts of sexual abuse; about 30 percent of the girls reported that family members had made sexual advances.[87] Emily Gaarder and Joanne Belknap's interviews with young women sent to adult prisons indicated that most had endured prolonged sexual abuse and violence. One of their subjects named Lisa, a young European American woman was serving time for attempted murder. Lisa had used drugs, alcohol, and joined gangs to escape the pain and troubles of her home life. Her mother was an alcoholic, and her father a convicted rapist. She had been sexually and physically abused by her stepfather from the ages of nine to eleven. Soon after, Lisa began skipping school, started using alcohol, and took acid. She joined a gang when she was services. The men usually drive with their victim to a place they are familiar with, and where they will not be observed. These places may be on the outskirts of a town, in nearby forests, near parks, in isolated garages or empty side-streets. Or the abusers go with their victims—sometimes accompanied by a pimp—to a nearby flat.

Many of the children were raped or sexually abused before they became involved in commercial sexual exploitation. Poverty, sexual abuse, and family obligation are the main reasons given by children for entering into prostitution. The children usually receive between five to twenty-five euros in payment. Sometimes they just receive sweets. Some sex tourists take the children for a meal or give financial support to their families.

Can Sex Trafficking Be Controlled?

Controlling human trafficking and sex tourism has proven to be difficult. Some countries have recently written laws to prevent their citizens from engaging in sexual activities with minors while travelling outside of their own country. These laws try to deter sex tourism, making travellers reconsider their actions as a result of the consequences. However, enforcement of these laws may prove challenging due to jurisdiction and proof, so that the practice continues unabated in many parts of the world. The United States passed the Trafficking Victims Protection Act of 2000 and then strengthened it with 2003 and 2005 revisions. Included in the bills was a $360-million funding package—an expansion of the Operation Innocence Lost program, a nationwide initiative that helps law enforcement agents pursue sex traffickers and child prostitution rings. The federal laws created several new crimes, including human trafficking, sex trafficking, forced labor, and document servitude, which involves the withholding or destruction of identity or travel documents as a means of controlling young women. They outlawed psychological manipulation, which means that traffickers can be prosecuted if they cause victims to believe that they would be harmed if they resist. Provisions of the 2005 Act provide state and local law enforcement with new tools to target demand and investigate and prosecute sex *trafficking*. Whether or

not these measures will prove sufficient to reduce the sexual exploitation of children remains to be seen.

CRITICAL THINKING

1. How would you reduce the incidence of human trafficking? Would you punish the sex tourists as felons? Can anything be done to protect young girls from sexual predators?
2. Does pornography on the Internet increase interest in sex with underage females and should there be greater controls placed on Internet viewing?

 INFOTRAC COLLEGE EDITION RESEARCH
Use "sex tourism" and "human trafficking" in key word searches on InfoTrac College Edition.

Sources: Linda Williams and Jennifer Ngo, "Human Trafficking," In Claire M. Renzetti and Jeffrey I. Edelson, eds., *Encyclopedia of Interpersonal Violence* (Thousand Oaks, CA: Sage Publications, 2007, in press); NA, "Remedying the Injustices of Human Trafficking Through Tort Law," *Harvard Law Review 119*:2574–2595 (2006); Cathrin Schauer, Children in Street Prostitution—Report from the German-Czech Border (publication by ECPAT Germany, UNICEF Germany, Horlemann Editors, Bad Honnef, 2003). Available at: www.childcentre.info/projects/exploitation/germany/dbaFile11447.doc (accessed November 21, 2006); International Office of Migration (IOM), *Journeys of Jeopardy: A Review of Research on Trafficking on Women and Children in Europe* (Publication No. 11, 2002). Available at: www.iom.int/documents/publication/en/mrs%5F11%5F2002.pdf and www.iom.int/jahia/Jahia/pid/8/Servlet SearchPublication?event=detail&id=5112 (accessed November 21, 2006); UNICEF. (n.d.). *Factsheet: Trafficking*. Available at: www.unicef.org/protection/files/trafficking.pdf (accessed January 15, 2006); U.S. Department of State. *Trafficking in Persons Report* (Washington, DC: US Department of State, 2005). Available at: www.state.gov/g/tip/rls/tiprpt/2005/ (accessed November 21, 2006); United Nations Population Fund (UNFPA): *Trafficking in Human Misery*. Available at: www.unfpa.org/gender/violence1.htm (accessed December 21, 2006); UNESCO Trafficking Project. Available at: www.unescobkk.org/culture/trafficking (accessed November 21, 2006).

twelve. "They were like a family to me," she told Gaarder and Belknap. "But I became involved in a lot of stuff. . . . I got high a lot, I robbed people, burglarized homes, stabbed people, and was involved in drive-bys." At age fifteen, she stabbed a woman in a fight. She is serving seven to fifteen years for the crime. She made this statement:

> I had just gotten out of this group home. The lady I stabbed had been messing with my sister's fiancé. This woman [had] a bunch of my sister's stuff, like her stereo and VCR, so me, my sister, her fiancé, and my boyfriend went over to pick up the stuff. We were all getting high beforehand. When we got to the house, my sister and I went in. . . . They [her sister and the victim] started fighting over him, and I started stabbing her with a knife. I always carried a knife with me because I was in a gang.[88]

Girls are expected to follow narrowly defined behavioral patterns. In contrast, it is not unusual for boys to stay out late, drive around with friends, or get involved in other unstructured behaviors linked to delinquency. If in reaction to loneliness and parental hostility, girls engage in the same "routine activities" as boys (staying out late, partying, and riding around with friends), they run the risk of engaging in similar types of delinquent behavior.[89]

The socialization approach holds that a poor home life is likely to have an even more damaging effect on females than on males. Because girls are less likely than boys to have close-knit peer associations, they are more likely to need close parental relationships to retain emotional stability. In fact, girls may become sexually involved with boys to receive support from them, a practice that tends to magnify their problems.

In summary, the socialization approach holds that family interaction is the key to understanding female delinquency. If a girl grows up in an atmosphere of sexual tension, where hostility exists between her parents, or where her parents are absent, she is likely to turn to outside sources for support. In contrast, a strong bond to parents may help insulate girls from social forces that produce delinquency.[90]

LIBERAL FEMINIST VIEWS

The feminist movement has, from its origins, fought to help women break away from their traditional roles and gain economic, educational, and social advancement. There is little question that the women's movement has revised the way women perceive their roles in society, and it has altered the relationships of women to many social institutions.

liberal feminism
Asserts that females are less delinquent than males, because their social roles provide them with fewer opportunities to commit crimes; as the roles of girls and women become more similar to those of boys and men, so too will their crime patterns.

Liberal feminism has influenced thinking about delinquency. According to liberal feminists, females are less delinquent than males, because their social roles provide fewer opportunities to commit crime. As the roles of women become more similar to those of men, so will their crime patterns. Female criminality is motivated by the same influences as male criminality. According to Freda Adler's *Sisters in Crime* (1975), by striving for independence women have begun to alter the institutions that had protected males in their traditional positions of power.[91] Adler argued that female delinquency would be affected by the changing role of women. As females entered new occupations and participated in sports, politics, and other traditionally male endeavors, they would also become involved in crimes that had heretofore been male-oriented; delinquency rates would then converge. She noted that girls were becoming increasingly involved in traditionally masculine crimes such as gang activity and fighting.

Adler predicted that the women's movement would produce steeper increases in the rate of female delinquency, because it created an environment in which the roles of girls and boys converge. She also assumed that the changing female role would produce female criminals who are similar to their male counterparts.[92]

Support for Liberal Feminism

A number of studies support the feminist view of gender differences in delinquency.[93] More than twenty years ago, Rita James Simon explained how the increase in female criminality is a function of the changing role of women. She claimed that as women were empowered economically and socially, they would be less likely to feel dependent and oppressed. Consequently, they would be less likely to attack their traditional targets: their husbands, their lovers, or even their own children.[94] Instead, their new role as breadwinner might encourage women to engage in traditional male crimes, such as larceny and car theft.

Simon's view has been supported in part by research showing a significant correlation between the women's rights movement and the female crime rate.[95] If 1966 is used as a jumping-off point (because the National Organization for Women was founded in that year), there are indications that patterns of serious female crime (robbery and auto theft) correlate with indicators of female emancipation (the divorce rate and participation in the labor force). Although this research does not prove that female crime is related to social change, it identifies behavior patterns that support that hypothesis.

In addition to these efforts, self-report studies support the liberal feminist view by showing that gender differences in delinquency are fading; that is, the delinquent acts committed most and least often by girls are nearly identical to those reported most and least often by boys.[96] The pattern of female delinquency, if not the extent, is now similar to that of male delinquency, and with few exceptions the factors that seem to motivate both male and female criminality seem similar.[97]

As the sex roles of males and females have become less distinct, their offending patterns have become more similar. Girls may be committing crimes to gain economic advancement and not because they lack parental support. Both of these patterns were predicted by liberal feminists.

LOOKING BACK TO LATICIA'S STORY

Laticia graduated from high school and was able to continue her education at the local community college. Did her social achievement, illustrated by her educational success, help turn her life around, as predicated by liberal feminists?

CRITICAL FEMINIST VIEWS

critical feminists
Hold that gender inequality stems from the unequal power of men and women and the subsequent exploitation of women by men; the cause of female delinquency originates with the onset of male supremacy and the efforts of males to control females' sexuality.

A number of writers take a more critical view of gender differences in crime. These **critical feminists** believe gender inequality stems from the unequal power of men and women in society and the exploitation of females by fathers and husbands; in a patriarchal society women are a "commodity" like land or money.[98] Female delinquency originates with the onset of male supremacy (*patriarchy*), the subordination of women, male aggression, and the efforts of men to control females sexually.[99] Women's victimization rates decline as they are empowered socially, economically, and legally.[100]

Critical feminists focus on the social forces that shape girls' lives.[101] They attempt to show how the sexual victimization of girls is often a function of male socialization and that young males learn to be exploitive of women. James Messerschmidt, an influential feminist scholar, has formulated a theoretical model to show how misguided concepts of "masculinity" flow from the inequities built into "patriarchal capitalism." Men dominate business in capitalist societies, and males who cannot function well within its parameters are at risk for crime. Women are inherently powerless in such a society, and their crimes reflect their limited access to both legitimate and illegitimate opportunity.[102] It is not surprising that research surveys have found that 90 percent of adolescent girls are sexually harassed in school, with almost 30 percent reporting having been psychologically pressured to "do something sexual," and 10 percent physically forced into sexual behaviors.[103]

According to the critical feminist view, male exploitation acts as a trigger for female delinquent behavior. Female delinquents recount being so severely harassed at school that they were forced to carry knives. Some reported that boyfriends—men sometimes in their thirties—who "knew how to treat a girl" would draw them into criminal activity, such as drug trafficking, which eventually entangled them in the justice system.[104]

When female adolescents run away and use drugs, they may be reacting to abuse at home or at school. Their attempts at survival are then labeled delinquent.[105] Research shows that a significant number of girls who are victims of sexual and other forms of abuse will later engage in delinquency.[106] All too often, school officials ignore complaints made by female students. Young girls therefore may feel trapped and desperate.

CHECKPOINTS

■ There are a variety of views on why girls become delinquent and why there are gender differences in the crime rate.

■ At one time it was believed that girls were naturally less aggressive and female criminals were a biological aberration.

■ Some experts still believe that hormonal differences can explain why males are more aggressive.

■ Some experts believe that males are more aggressive, because they have evolved that way to secure mates.

■ Under some circumstances females may act more aggressively than males.

■ Some experts believe that girls have been socialized to be less violent.

■ Female delinquents may be the product of a destructive home life, rebelling against abusive parents.

■ The liberal feminist view is that girls did not have the same opportunities to commit crime as boys and that rising female crime rates represent changing life circumstances.

■ Critical feminists see female delinquency as a function of male domination and abuse.

Crime and Patriarchy

A number of theoretical models have attempted to use a critical or Marxist feminist perspective to explain gender differences in delinquency. For example, in *Capitalism, Patriarchy, and Crime*, Marxist James Messerschmidt argues that capitalist society is characterized by both patriarchy and class conflict. Capitalists control workers, and men control women, both economically and biologically.[107] This "double marginality"

According to power-control theory, as more families become egalitarian, with both parents sharing equal roles and having equal authority, children's roles will become more homogenous. When sons and daughters are treated equally, their behavior will take on similar patterns. This may cause juveniles like Alice Blair, shown here listening to coach Russ Wilson during a huddle, October 22, 2005, in Paint Creek, Texas, will take on what has been considered a traditional male role. Blair plays defense on the school's six-person football team.

© AP Images/Matt Slocum

 For more than twenty years, the **Center for Research on Women** has been at the forefront of research in which the central questions are shaped by the experiences and perspectives of women. Its website can be accessed by going to www.thomsonedu.com/criminaljustice/siegel.

power-control theory
Holds that gender differences in the delinquency rate are a function of class differences and economic conditions that influence the structure of family life.

egalitarian families
Husband and wife share power at home; daughters gain a kind of freedom similar to that of sons and their law-violating behaviors mirror those of their brothers.

explains why females in a capitalist society commit fewer crimes than males: they are isolated in the family and have fewer opportunities to engage in elite deviance (white-collar and economic crimes); they are also denied access to male-dominated street crimes. Because capitalism renders women powerless, they are forced to commit less serious crimes, such as abusing drugs.

John Hagan and his associates have speculated that gender differences in delinquency are a function of class differences that influence family life. Hagan, who calls his view **power-control theory**, suggests that in traditional paternalistic families, fathers assume the role of breadwinners and mothers have menial jobs or remain at home.[108] Mothers are expected to control the behavior of their daughters while granting greater freedom to sons. The parent-daughter relationship can be viewed as a preparation for the "cult of domesticity," which makes daughters' involvement in delinquency unlikely.

In **egalitarian families**—in which the husband and wife share similar positions of power at home and in the workplace—daughters gain a kind of freedom that reflects reduced parental control. These families produce daughters whose law-violating behaviors mirror those of their brothers. Ironically, these kinds of relationships also occur in households with absent fathers. Hagan and his associates found that when both fathers and mothers hold equally valued managerial positions the similarity between the rates of their daughters' and sons' delinquency is greatest. Therefore, middle-class girls are most likely to violate the law, because they are less closely controlled than lower-class girls. Female delinquency rates have risen because more mothers now work and more families are therefore egalitarian. ✔ Checkpoints

GENDER AND THE JUVENILE JUSTICE SYSTEM

Gender differences not only have an effect on crime patterns, but also may have a significant impact on the way children are treated by the juvenile justice system. Several feminist scholars argue that girls are not only the victims of injustice at home, but also risk being victimized by agents of the justice system.

Are girls "victims" of the juvenile justice system? Meda Chesney-Lind's well-regarded research found that police are more likely to arrest female adolescents for sexual activity and to ignore the same behavior among male delinquents.[109] Girls were also more likely to be sent to a detention facility before trial, and the length of their detention averaged three times that of boys.

Girls are far more likely than boys to be picked up by police for status offenses and are more likely to be kept in detention for such offenses.[110] Girls, more than boys, are still disadvantaged if their behavior is viewed as morally incorrect by government officials or if they are considered beyond parental control.[111] Research conducted by John MacDonald and Meda Chesney-Lind found that the juvenile justice system still categorizes female offenders into two distinct groups: girls who momentarily strayed from the "good girl" path and are therefore deserving of solicitous, humanitarian treatment, and dangerously wayward girls who have serious problems and must therefore be kept under strict control lest they stray further.[112]

Girls may also be feeling the brunt of the more punitive policies now being used in the juvenile justice system. For example, when Chesney-Lind and Vickie Paramore analyzed data from the city and county of Honolulu they found that tougher juvenile justice standards meant that more cases were being handled formally in the juvenile justice system.[113] While girls are actually committing fewer violent crimes, they are more likely to become enmeshed in the grasp of the juvenile justice system. Once in the system, they may receive fewer benefits and services than their male counterparts. Institutionalized girls report that they are given fewer privileges and less space, equipment, programs, and treatment than institutionalized boys.[114]

Girls may still be subject to harsh punishments if they are considered dangerously immoral. Girls are significantly more likely to be arrested on status offense charges than boys.[115] However, the arrest rates for girls show that girls are charged with status offenses more often than boys, because some of the behaviors they are participating in are considered negative when perpetrated by a female, but would not gain official attention if engaged in by a male.[116] There still appears to be an association between male standards of "beauty" and sexual behavior: criminal justice professionals may look on attractive girls who engage in sexual behavior more harshly, overlooking some of the same behaviors in less attractive girls. In some jurisdictions, girls are still being incarcerated for status offenses, because their behavior does not measure up to concepts of "proper" female behavior.[117] Even though girls are still less likely to be arrested than boys, those who fail to measure up to stereotypes of proper female behavior are more likely to be sanctioned than male offenders.[118]

Why do these differences persist? The reason may be because correctional authorities continue to subscribe to stereotyped beliefs about the needs of young girls. Writing with Randall Shelden, Meda Chesney-Lind found that court officials and policymakers still show a lack of concern about girls' victimization and instead are more concerned with controlling their behavior than addressing the factors that brought them to the attention of the juvenile justice system in the first place.[119]

SUMMARY

- The relationship between gender and delinquency has become a topic of considerable interest to criminologists.
- At one time, attention was directed solely at male offenders and the rare female delinquent was considered an oddity. The nature and extent of female delinquent activities have changed, and girls are now engaging in more frequent and serious illegal activity.
- Sociologists and psychologists recognize that there are differences in attitudes, values, and behavior between boys and girls.

- There are cognitive differences. Females process information differently than males do and have different cognitive and physical strengths. These differences may, in part, explain gender differences in delinquency.
- Girls are socialized differently, which causes them to internalize rather than externalize anger and aggression.
- There are also psychological differences between the sexes. Girls may actually be at risk for a greater level of mental anguish than boys.
- There are a number of different views of female delinquency.

- Trait views are concerned with biological and psychological differences between the sexes. Early efforts by Cesare Lombroso and his followers placed the blame for delinquency on physical differences between males and females. Girls who were delinquent had inherent masculine characteristics.
- Contemporary trait theorists view girls' psychological makeup and hormonal and physical characteristics as key to their delinquent behavior.
- Socialization has also been identified as a cause of delinquency. Males are socialized to be tough and aggressive, females to be passive and obedient.
- Early socialization views portrayed the adolescent female offender as a troubled girl who lacked love at home and supportive peer relations.
- These theories treated female delinquents as sexual offenders whose criminal activities were linked to destructive relationships with men.
- Contemporary socialization views continue to depict female delinquents as being raised in hellish homes where they are victims of sexual and physical abuse.
- More recent views of gender and delinquency incorporate the changes brought about by the women's movement. Liberal feminists argue that, as the roles of women change, so will their crime patterns. Although a number of studies support this view, some theorists question its validity. The female crime rate has increased, and female delinquency patterns now resemble those of males, but the gender gap has not narrowed after more than two decades.
- Critical feminists view female delinquency as a function of patriarchy and the mistreatment and exploitation of females in a male-dominated society.
- Hagan's power-control theory helps us understand why these differences exist and whether change may be coming.
- The treatment girls receive by the juvenile justice system has also been the subject of debate. Originally, it was thought that police protected girls from the stigma of a delinquency label. Contemporary criminologists charge, however, that girls are discriminated against by agents of the justice system.

KEY TERMS

masculinity hypothesis, p. 132
gender-schema theory, p. 136
chivalry hypothesis, p. 138

precocious sexuality, p. 139
liberal feminism, p. 144
critical feminists, p. 145

power-control theory, p. 146
egalitarian families, p. 146

QUESTIONS FOR DISCUSSION

1. Are girls delinquent for different reasons than boys? Do girls have a unique set of problems?
2. As sex roles become more homogenous, do you believe female delinquency will become identical to male delinquency in rate and type?
3. Does the sexual double standard still exist?
4. Are lower-class girls more strictly supervised than upper- and middle-class girls? Is control stratified across class lines?
5. Are girls the victims of unfairness at the hands of the justice system, or do they benefit from "chivalry?"

APPLYING WHAT YOU HAVE LEARNED

As the principal of a northeastern junior high school, you get a call from a parent who is disturbed, because he has heard a rumor that the student literary digest plans to publish a story with a sexual theme. The work is written by a junior high school girl who became pregnant during the year and underwent an abortion. You ask for and receive a copy of the narrative.

The girl's story is actually a cautionary tale of young love that results in an unwanted pregnancy. The author details the abusive home life that led her to engage in an intimate relationship with another student, her pregnancy, her conflict with her parents, her decision to abort, and the emotional turmoil that the incident created. She tells students to use contraception if they are sexually active and recommends appropriate types of birth control. There is nothing provocative or sexually explicit in the work.

Some teachers argue that girls should not be allowed to read this material, because it has sexual content from which they must be protected, and that in a sense it advocates defiance of parents. Also, some parents may object to a story about precocious sexuality because they fear it may encourage their children to "experiment." Such behavior is linked to delinquency and drug abuse. Those who advocate publication believe that girls have a right to read about such important issues and decide on their own course of action.

- Should you force the story's deletion, because its theme is essentially sexual and controversial?
- Should you allow publication, because it deals with the subject matter in a mature fashion?
- Do you think reading and learning about sexual matters encourages or discourages experimentation in sexuality?

- Should young girls be protected from such material? Would it cause them damage?
- Inequalities still exist in the way boys and girls are socialized by their parents and treated by social institutions. Do these gender differences also manifest themselves in the delinquency rate? What effect do gender roles have on behavior choices?

DOING RESEARCH ON THE WEB

To help you answer these questions and to find out more information on the gender of status offenders, go to the website **www.thomsonedu.com/criminaljustice/siegel**. Once there, go to the website for *Hazelwood School District et al. v. Kuhlmeier et al.* and other landmark cases; go also to the National Scholastic Press Association and the high school journalism website to read more about school news and censorship issues.

The Family and Delinquency

© Eli Reed/Magnum Photos

CHAPTER OBJECTIVES

After reading this chapter you should:

1. Be familiar with the link between family relationships and juvenile delinquency.

2. Understand the complex association between family breakup and delinquent behavior.

3. Understand why families in conflict produce more delinquents than those that function harmoniously.

4. Know the association between inconsistent discipline and supervision and juvenile crime.

5. Be able to discuss how parental and sibling misconduct influences delinquent behaviors.

6. Define the concept of *child abuse*.

7. Know the nature and extent of abuse.

8. Be able to list the factors that are seen as causing child abuse.

9. Be familiar with the complex system of state intervention in abuse cases.

10. Discuss the association between child abuse and delinquent behavior.

Joey Williams entered the child welfare system at the age of nine, when it was discovered that he and his younger sister and brother were being sexually abused by their stepfather. The children had also been experiencing neglect due to a lack of sufficient resources in the family; they often went without food or proper clothing. Joey's mother struggled to provide structure for the children, but she was also facing many of her own personal problems. All three of the children were acting out and having difficulties in school. When Joey's stepfather was incarcerated, the child welfare system placed the children in separate foster homes and began to provide services for the family with the goal of returning the children to their mother's home. Joey had a difficult time adjusting to foster care and being separated from his family.

At the age of twelve, he was charged with sexual assault and labeled a "sexual offender." According to reports, Joey and another child about the same age, engaged in "consensual" sexual contact in the foster home. Joey was ordered to complete treatment for sexual offenders, was removed from the foster home, and entered a series of placements where he continued to have a very difficult time adjusting and maintaining positive behavior.

Joey spent many years in residential treatment centers and mental health hospitals, trying to get the help he needed. Professionals were concerned that he was a threat to the community, and therefore he could not be placed in a community setting. During this time, Joey completed all the required sexual offender treatment and never "re-offended," but he did continue to have significant behavior issues and to struggle with school. It was recommended by the court that Joey's mother participate in therapy and enter some programs that would assist the family, eventually facilitating Joey's return to his family. She did not comply with those recommendations however.

As Joey approached his seventeenth birthday, the professionals involved in his case began to prepare for him to exit the juvenile system. He had not committed any more law violations. His siblings had been able to return home to their mother, and it was also decided that Joey, with significant family supports and interventions, would also be able to return home. The family entered intensive therapy, which utilized a "wrap-around" approach that focused on family strengths and on the positive aspects of their situation. The wrap-around service model shifts the focus away from a family's pathologies and weaknesses and works with them to build on their assets, skills, and resources.

In Joey's family, there were many things going well. They needed some assistance getting a few items to meet the children's basic needs, but overall, they were doing much better in the areas of employment and housing. Joey received the correct combination of medications, appropriate therapy, and support to enable him to live at home again. Because he always had a passion for music, as part of his reintegration into the family home, the wrap-around funds were utilized to purchase guitar lessons for him, providing structure and a positive and creative outlet. Joey, his family, and the team of professionals involved with his case worked together very closely for a period of six months. The transition home was difficult at times, but ultimately successful. Joey studied for his GED and worked hard to accomplish his educational goals. The younger siblings also began to show signs of improvement and Joey became a role model in his family. Joey is doing well today, has a full-time job, and has not had any further problems with the law.

Many experts believe that family dysfunction is a key ingredient in the development of the emotional deficits that eventually lead to long-term social problems.[1] Interactions between parents and children, and between siblings, provide opportunities for children to acquire or inhibit antisocial behavior patterns.[2] Even kids who are predisposed toward delinquency, because of personality traits, such as low self-control and impulsive personality, may find their life circumstances improved and their involvement with antisocial behavior diminished if they are exposed to positive and effective parenting.[3]

Good parenting lowers the risk of delinquency for children living in high-crime areas. Research shows they are able to resist the temptation of the streets if they receive fair discipline and support from parents who provide them with positive role models.[4] However, children in affluent families who are being raised in a household characterized by abuse and conflict, or whose parents are absent or separated, will still be at risk for delinquency.[5] Nor is the relationship between family life and delinquency unique to U.S. culture; cross-national data support a significant association between family variables and delinquency.[6]

The assumed relationship between delinquency and family life is critical today, because the American family is changing. Extended families, once common, are now for the most part anachronisms. In their place is the **nuclear family**, described as a "dangerous hothouse of emotions," because of the close contact between parents and children; in these families, problems are unrelieved by contact with other kin living nearby.[7]

And now the nuclear family is showing signs of breakdown. About half of all marriages may one day end in divorce.[8] Much of the responsibility for child rearing is delegated to television and daycare providers. Despite these changes, some families are able to continue functioning as healthy units, producing well-adjusted children. Others have crumbled under the stress, severely damaging their children.[9] This is particularly true when child abuse and neglect become part of family life.

Because these issues are critical for understanding delinquency, this chapter is devoted to an analysis of the family's role in producing or inhibiting delinquency. We first cover the changing face of the American family. We will review the way family structure and function influences delinquent behavior. The relationship between child abuse, neglect, and delinquency is covered in some depth.

nuclear family
A family unit composed of parents and their children; this smaller family structure is subject to great stress due to the intense, close contact between parents and children.

A great deal of information on families and children can be found at the website of the **David and Lucile Packard Foundation** by going to www. thomsonedu.com/criminaljustice/siegel.

THE CHANGING AMERICAN FAMILY

The so-called traditional family—with a male breadwinner and a female who cares for the home—is a thing of the past. No longer can this family structure be considered the norm. Changing sex roles have created a family where women play a much greater role in the economic process; this has created a more egalitarian family structure. About three-quarters of all mothers of school-age children are employed, up from 50 percent in 1970 and 40 percent in 1960. The changing economic structure may be reflected in shifting sex roles. Fathers are now spending more time with their children on workdays than they did twenty years ago, and mothers are spending somewhat less time.[10]

Family Makeup

After a decades-long decline, about two-thirds of underage minors now live in two-parent families. However, significant racial differences in family makeup still exist: today about one-third of all African American children live in families that have two parents compared to about three-quarters of European American children.[11] And as many as 40 percent of European American children and 75 percent of African American children will experience parental separation or divorce before they reach age sixteen, and many of these children will experience multiple family disruptions over time.[12]

Though there has been a sharp decline in teen pregnancies over the past decade, more than 1.3 million children are still being born to unmarried women annually.[13]

Child Care

Charged with caring for children is a daycare system whose workers are often paid minimum wage. Of special concern are "family daycare homes," in which a single provider takes care of three to nine children. Several states neither license nor monitor these private providers. Even in states that mandate registration and inspection of daycare providers, it is estimated that 90 percent or more of the facilities operate "underground." It is not uncommon for one adult to care for eight infants, an impossible task regardless of training or feelings of concern.

Children from working poor families are most likely to suffer from inadequate child care; these children often spend time in makeshift arrangements that allow their parents to work, but lack the stimulating environment children need to thrive.[14] About 3.5 million children under age thirteen spend some time at home alone each week while their parents are at work.

Economic Stress

The family is also undergoing economic stress. Nearly 20 percent of all children live in poverty and about 8 percent live in extreme poverty—at least 50 percent below the poverty line. About 33 percent of all children live in families where no parent has full-time, year-round employment.[15] The majority of indigent families live in substandard housing without adequate health care, nutrition, or child care. Those whose incomes place them above the poverty line are deprived of government assistance. Recent political trends suggest that the social "safety net" is under attack and that poor families can expect less government aid in the coming years.

Will this economic pressure be reduced in the future? The number of senior citizens is on the rise. As people retire, there will be fewer workers to cover the costs of Social Security, medical care, and nursing home care. These costs will put greater economic stress on families. Voter sentiment has an impact on the allocation of public funds, and there is concern that an older generation, worried about health care costs, may be reluctant to spend tax dollars on at-risk kids.

THE FAMILY'S INFLUENCE ON DELINQUENCY

The effect of these family stressors can have a significant impact on children's behavior. The family is the primary unit in which children learn the values and attitudes that guide their actions throughout their lives. Family disruption or change can have a long-lasting impact on children. In contrast, effective parenting can help neutralize the effect of both individual (e.g., emotional problems) and social (e.g., delinquent peers) forces, which promote delinquent behaviors.[16]

Four categories of family dysfunction seem to promote delinquent behavior: families disrupted by spousal conflict or breakup, families involved in interpersonal conflict, ineffective parents who lack proper parenting skills, and families that contain deviant parents who may transmit their behavior to their children (see Figure 7.1).[17]

Figure 7.1   **Family Influences on Behavior**

Each of these four factors has been linked to antisocial behavior and delinquency. Interaction between these factors may escalate delinquent activity.

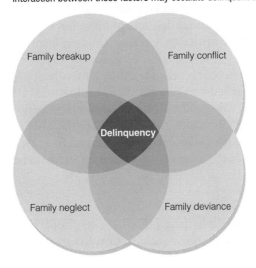

These factors may interact: drug-abusing parents may be more likely to experience family conflict, child neglect, and marital breakup. We now turn to the specific types of family problems that have been linked to delinquent behavior.

Family Breakup

One of the most enduring controversies in the study of delinquency is the relationship between a parent absent from the home and the onset of delinquent behavior. Research indicates that parents whose marriage is secure produce children who are secure and independent.[18] In contrast, research conducted both in the United and abroad, shows that children raised in homes with one or both parents absent may be prone to antisocial behavior.[19]

A number of experts contend that a **broken home** is a strong determinant of a child's law-violating behavior. The connection seems self-evident, because a child is first socialized at home. Any disjunction in an orderly family structure could be expected to have a negative impact on the child.

The suspected broken home–delinquency relationship is important, because, if current trends continue, less than half of all children born today will live continuously with their own mother and father throughout childhood. And because stepfamilies, or so-called **blended families**, are less stable than families consisting of two biological parents, an increasing number of children will experience family breakup two or even three times during childhood.[20]

Children who have experienced family breakup are more likely to demonstrate behavior problems and hyperactivity than children in intact families.[21] Family breakup is often associated with conflict, hostility, and aggression; children of divorce are suspected of having lax supervision, weakened attachment, and greater susceptibility to peer pressure.[22] One study of more than four thousand youths in Denver, Pittsburgh, and Rochester found, the more often children are forced to go through family transitions the more likely they are to engage in delinquent activity.[23]

The Effects of Divorce The relationship between broken homes and delinquency has been controversial, to say the least. It was established in early research, which suggested that a significant association existed between parental absence and youthful misconduct.[24] For many years the link was clear: children growing up in broken homes were much more likely to fall prey to delinquency than those who lived in two-parent households.[25]

Beginning in the late 1950s, some researchers began to question the link between broken homes and delinquency. Early studies, they claimed, used the records of police, courts, and correctional institutions.[26] This research may have been tainted by sampling bias: youths from broken homes may get arrested more often than youths from intact families, but this does not necessarily mean they engage in more frequent and serious delinquent behavior. Official statistics may reflect the fact that agents of the justice system treat children from disrupted households more severely, because they cannot call on parents for support. The *parens patriae* philosophy of the juvenile courts calls for official intervention when parental supervision is considered inadequate.[27] A number of subsequent studies, using self-report data, have failed to establish any clear-cut relationship between broken homes and delinquent behavior.[28] Boys and girls from intact families seem as likely to self-report delinquency as those whose parents are divorced or separated. Researchers concluded that the absence of parents has a greater effect on agents of the justice system than it does on the behavior of children.[29]

Divorce Reconsidered Although some researchers still question the divorce-delinquency link, there is growing sentiment that family breakup is traumatic and most likely has a direct influence on factors related to adolescent misbehavior.[30]

There is growing sentiment that family breakup is traumatic and most likely has a direct influence on factors related to adolescent misbehavior. Kids are more deeply affected by divorce, and for a longer period of time, than their parents.

In her study of the effects of parental absence on children, sociologist Sara McLanahan finds that children who grow up apart from their biological fathers typically do less well than children who grow up with both biological parents. They are less likely to finish high school and attend college, less likely to find and keep a steady job, and more likely to become teen mothers. Although most children who grow up with a single parent do quite well, differences between children in one- and two-parent families are significant, and there is fairly good evidence that father absence per se is responsible for some social problems.[31]

The McLanahan research has been supported by other studies showing that divorce is in fact related to delinquency and status offending, especially if a child had a close relationship with the parent who is forced to leave the home.[32] The effects of divorce seem gender-specific:

- Boys seem to be more affected by the post-divorce absence of the father. In post-divorce situations, fathers seem less likely to be around to solve problems, to discuss standards of conduct, or to enforce discipline. A divorced father who remains actively involved in his child's life reduces his son's chances of delinquency.

- Girls are more affected by both the quality of the mother's parenting and post-divorce parental conflict. It is possible that extreme levels of parental conflict may serve as a model to young girls coping with the aftermath of their parents' separation.[33]

- There are distinct racial and ethnic differences in the impact of divorce/separation on youth. Some groups (i.e., Hispanics, Asians) have been raised in cultures where divorce is rare and parents have less experience in developing child-rearing practices that buffer the effects of family break up on adolescent problem behavior.[34]

Divorce and Parental Deviance Divorce may influence children's misbehavior through its effect on parental misbehavior. As you may recall (Chapter 5) developmental/life course theorists, such as Robert Sampson and John Laub, believe that a good marriage helps men "knife off" from misbehavior. If marriage helps subdue antisocial behavior, then it stands to reason that divorce may encourage *parental deviance*. Parents who are in post-divorce turmoil may influence their children to misbehave.

When Sara Jaffee and her associates studied the quality of marriage they found that the less time fathers lived with their children, the more conduct problems their children had. However, when fathers engaged in high levels of antisocial behavior themselves, the more time they spent with their children, the more conduct problems their children had. Staying married, Jaffee concludes, may not be the answer to the problems faced by children living in single-parent families unless parents can refrain from deviant behaviors and become reliable sources of emotional and economic support.[35]

Family Conflict

Not all unhappy marriages end in divorce; some continue in an atmosphere of conflict. Intra-family conflict is a common experience in many American families.[36] The link between parental conflict and delinquency was established almost forty years ago when F. Ivan Nye found that a child's perception of his or her parents' marital happiness was a significant predictor of delinquency.[37] Contemporary studies also find that children who grow up in maladapted homes and witness discord or violence later exhibit emotional disturbance and behavior problems.[38] There seems to be little difference between the behavior of children who merely *witness* **intra-family violence** and those who are its *victims*.[39] In fact, some research efforts show that observing the abuse of a parent (mother) is a more significant determinant of delinquency than being the target of child abuse.[40]

intra-family violence
An environment of discord and conflict within the family; children who grow up in dysfunctional homes often exhibit delinquent behaviors, having learned at a young age that aggression pays off.

Research efforts have consistently supported the relationship between family conflict, hostility, and delinquency.[41] Adolescents who are incarcerated report growing up in dysfunctional homes.[42] Parents of beyond-control youngsters have been found to be inconsistent rule-setters, to be less likely to show interest in their children, and to display high levels of hostile detachment.[43]

Although damaged parent-child relationships are associated with delinquency, it is difficult to assess the relationship. It is often assumed that pre-existing family problems cause delinquency, but it may also be true that children who act out put enormous stress on a family. Kids who are conflict-prone may actually help to destabilize households. To avoid escalation of a child's aggression, these parents may give in to their children's demands. The children learn that aggression pays off.[44] Parents may feel overwhelmed and shut their child out of their lives. Adolescent misbehavior may be a precursor of family conflict; strife leads to more adolescent misconduct, producing an endless cycle of family stress and delinquency.[45]

Which is worse, growing up in a home marked by conflict or growing up in a broken home? Research shows that children in both broken homes and high-conflict intact homes were worse off than children in low-conflict, intact families.[46] However, even when parents are divorced, kids who maintain attachments to their parents are less likely to engage in delinquency than those who are alienated and detached.[47] See Exhibit 7.1 for other key findings on divorce.

Exhibit 7.1   **The Family Structure–Delinquency Link**

- Children growing up in families disrupted by parental death are better adjusted than children of divorce. Parental absence is not per se a cause of antisocial behavior.

- Remarriage does not lessen the effects of divorce on youth: children living with a stepparent exhibit (a) as many problems as youths in divorce situations and (b) considerably more problems than do children living with both biological parents.

- Continued contact with the non-custodial parent has little effect on a child's well-being.

- Evidence that the behavior of children of divorce improves over time is inconclusive.

- Post-divorce conflict between parents is related to child maladjustment.

- Parental divorce raises the likelihood of teenage marriage.

Sources: Nicholas Wolfinger, "Parental Divorce and Offspring Marriage: Early or Late? *Social Forces* 82:337–354 (2003); Paul Amato and Bruce Keith, "Parental Divorce and the Well-Being of Children: A Meta-Analysis," *Psychological Bulletin* 110:26–46 (1991).

The Chicken or the Egg?

Which comes first, bad parents or bad kids? Does poor parenting cause delinquency or do delinquents undermine their parents' supervisory abilities? In a recent survey, David Huh and colleagues surveyed almost five hundred adolescent girls from eight different schools to determine their perceived parental support and control and whether they engage in problem behaviors such as lying, stealing, running away, or substance abuse. Huh and his colleagues found little evidence that poor parenting is a direct cause of children's misbehavior problems or that it escalates misbehavior. Rather, their results suggested that children's problem behaviors undermine parenting effectiveness. *Increases* in adolescent behavior problems, such as substance abuse, resulted in *decreases* in parental control and support. Low parental control played a small role in escalating behavior problems. Huh suggests it is possible that the parents of adolescents who consistently misbehave may become more tolerant of their behavior and give up on attempts at control. As their kids behaviors become increasingly threatening, parents may detach and reject adolescents exhibiting problem behavior.

Huh is not alone. In her provocative book *The Nurture Assumption*, psychologist Judith Rich Harris questions the cherished belief that parents play an important role in a child's upbringing. Instead of family influence, Harris claims that genetics and environment determine, to a large extent, how a child turns out. Children's own temperament and peer relations shape their behavior and modify the characteristics they were born with; their interpersonal relations determine the kind of people they will be when they mature.

Harris reasons that parenting skills may be irrelevant to children's future success. Most parents don't have a single child-rearing style, and they may treat each child in the family independently. They are more permissive with their mild-mannered kids and more strict and punitive with those who are temperamental or defiant. Even if every child were treated the same in a family, this would not explain why siblings raised in the same family under relatively similar conditions turn out so differently.

Those sent to daycare are quite similar to those who remain at home; having working parents seems to have little long-term effect. Family structure also does not seem to matter: Adults who grew up in one-parent homes are as likely to be successful as those who were raised in two-parent households.

In addition to genetics, the child's total social environment is the other key influence that shapes behavior. Kids who act one way at home may be totally different at school or with their peers. Some who are mild mannered around the house are hell-raisers in the school yard, whereas others who bully their siblings are docile with friends. Children may conform to parental expectations at home, but leave those expectations behind in their own social environment. Children develop their own culture with unique traditions, words, rules, and activities, which often conflict with parental and adult values.

CRITICAL THINKING

1. Some studies now show that a given parenting style can have different effects on children with different temperaments. The result is that parenting can function to make children in the same family different rather than alike. From your own experiences, do parents treat all siblings in the family in a similar fashion, or are there clear inter-sibling differences? How might parenting style influence children's behavior within a family?

2. Can teen rebellion be linked to poor parenting? After all, what parents encourage their children to pierce their bodies or get tattoos?

INFOTRAC COLLEGE EDITION RESEARCH

To find out whether Harris's analysis of family functioning is correct, use "family" as a key word on InfoTrac College Edition.

Sources: David Huh, Jennifer Tristan, Emily Wade, and Eric Stice, "Does Problem Behavior Elicit Poor Parenting? A Prospective Study of Adolescent Girls," *Journal of Adolescent Research* 21:185–204 (2006); Judith Rich Harris, *The Nurture Assumption, Why Children Turn Out the Way They Do* (New York: Free Press, 1998).

---

parental efficacy
Families in which parents are able to integrate their children into the household unit while at the same time helping assert their individuality and regulate their own behavior.

Family Incompetence Children raised by parents who lack proper parenting skills are more at risk than those whose parents who are supportive and effectively control their children in a non-coercive fashion.[48] Delinquency will be reduced if parents provide the type of structure that integrates children into families, while giving them the ability to assert their individuality and regulate their own behavior, a phenomenon referred to as **parental efficacy**.[49] In some cultures emotional support from the mother is critical, whereas in others the father's support remains the key factor.[50]

A number of studies support the link between the quality of family life and delinquency. Children who feel inhibited with their parents and refuse to discuss important issues with them are more likely to engage in deviant activities. Kids who report having troubled home lives also exhibit lower levels of self-esteem and are more prone to antisocial behaviors.[51]

One reason for poor communication is parents who rely on authoritarian disciplinary practices. Holding a "my way or the highway" orientation and telling kids that "as long as you live in my house you will obey my rules" does little to improve communications and may instead produce kids who are rebellious and crime prone.[52] However, the

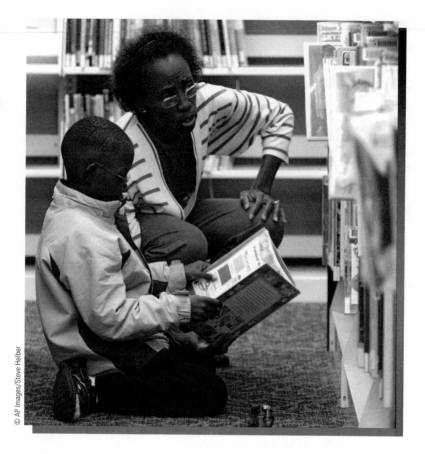

Although incompetent families produce delinquents, those that can provide strong guidance may compensate for deficiencies in other social institutions. Denise Armstrong helps her 8-year-old son, Timothy, pick out a book in a local library in Richmond, Virginia. Armstrong home schools her children, feeling she can do a better job instilling her values in her children than the public school system does.

© AP Images/Steve Helber

Focus on Delinquency feature on page 157, "The Chicken or the Egg?" shows not all experts agree on the association between poor parenting and juvenile misbehavior.

Poor child-parent communications have been related to dysfunctional activities such as running away, and in all too many instances these children enter the ranks of homeless street youths who get involved in theft and prostitution to survive.[53] In contrast, even children who appear to be at risk are better able to resist involvement in delinquent activity when they report a strong attachment to their parents.[54] Adolescents whose parents maintain close relationships with them report less delinquent behavior and substance use regardless of the type of family structure, that is, blended families, same-sex parents, and so on. This finding suggests that the quality of parent-adolescent relationships better predicts adolescent outcomes than *family* type.[55]

The importance of close relations with the family may diminish as children reach late adolescence and develop stronger peer-group relations, but most experts believe family influence remains considerable throughout life.[56]

Family Neglect

Studies show that the parents of delinquent youths tend to be neglectful and inconsistent in their discipline, either overly harsh or extremely lenient.[57] But what conclusions can we draw from this observation?

The link between discipline and deviant behavior is uncertain. Most Americans still support the use of corporal punishment in disciplining children. The use of physical punishment cuts across racial, ethnic, and religious groups.[58] However, despite this public support, there is growing evidence of a "violence begetting violence" cycle. Children who are subject to even minimal amounts of physical punishment may be more likely to use violence themselves; the effect seems greatest among Caucasian children and less among African American and Latino children.[59]

Sociologist Murray Straus reviewed the concept of discipline in a series of surveys and found a powerful relationship between exposure to physical punishment and later aggression.[60]

Nonviolent societies are also ones in which parents rarely punish their children physically; there is a link between corporal punishment, delinquency, spousal abuse, and adult crime.[61] Research conducted in ten European countries shows that the degree to which parents and teachers approve of corporal punishment is related to the homicide rate.[62]

Physical punishment weakens the bond between parents and children, lowers the children's self-esteem, and undermines their faith in justice. It is not surprising, then, that Straus finds a high correlation between physical discipline and street crime. It is possible that physical punishment encourages children to become more secretive and dishonest.[63] Overly strict discipline may have an even more insidious link to antisocial behaviors: abused children have a higher risk of neurological dysfunction than the non-abused, and brain abnormalities have been linked to violent crime.[64]

Inconsistent and Ineffective Supervision Evidence also exists that inconsistent supervision can promote delinquency. Early research by F. Ivan Nye found that mothers who threatened discipline, but failed to carry it out were more likely to have delinquent children than those who were consistent in their discipline.[65]

Nye's early efforts have been supported by research showing a strong association between ineffective or negligent supervision and a child's involvement in delinquency.[66] The data shows that youths who believe their parents care little about their activities are more likely to engage in criminal acts than those who believe their actions will be closely monitored.[67] Kids who are not closely supervised spend more time out in the community with their friends and are more likely to get into trouble. Poorly supervised kids may be more prone to acting impulsively and are therefore less able to employ self-control to restrain their activities.[68]

In contrast, children who are properly supervised, especially in disorganized areas, are less likely to succumb to the temptations of the streets. The ability of a family to provide parental supervision seems even more important for children growing up in poor neighborhoods with fewer social ties among adults. In these areas parents cannot call upon neighborhood resources to take up the burden of controlling children; there is, therefore, a greater burden placed on families to provide adequate supervision.[69]

Mother's Employment Parents who closely supervise their children, and have close ties with them, help reduce the likelihood of adolescent delinquent behavior.[70] When life circumstances prevent or interfere with adequate supervision delinquent opportunities may increase. Some critics have suggested that even in intact homes, a working mother who is unable to adequately supervise her children, provides the opportunity for delinquency. This phenomenon may be inflated by economic factors: In poor neighborhoods that lack collective efficacy, parents cannot call upon neighborhood resources to take up the burden of controlling children.[71]

While the suggestion that working mothers produce delinquent kids is troubling, the association is far from certain. There is also research that finds that a mother's employment may have little effect on youthful misbehavior.[72] So the true relationship between mother's employment and child misbehavior remains to be established.

Resource Dilution Parents may find it hard to control their children, because they have such large families that their resources, such as time, are spread too thin (**resource dilution**). It is also possible that the relationship is indirect, caused by the connection of family size to some external factor; resource dilution has been linked to educational underachievement, long considered a correlate of delinquency.[73] Middle children may suffer, because they are most likely to be home when large numbers of siblings are also at home and economic resources are most stretched.[74] Larger families are more likely to produce delinquents than smaller ones, and middle children are more likely to engage in delinquent acts than first- or last-born children.

Resource dilution may force some mothers into the workforce in order to support their young children. Critics have suggested that these working mothers are unable to

resource dilution
A condition that occurs when parents have such large families that their resources, such as time and money, are spread too thin, causing lack of familial support and control.

adequately supervise their children, leaving them prone to delinquency. However, recent research by Thomas Vander Ven and his associates found that having a mother who is employed has little if any effect on youthful misbehavior, especially if the children are adequately supervised.[75]

Family Deviance

A number of studies have found that parental deviance has a powerful influence on delinquent behavior.[76] The effects can be both devastating and long term: the children of deviant parents produce delinquent children themselves.[77]

Some of the most important data on the influence of parental deviance was gathered by British criminologist David P. Farrington whose research involves longitudinal data he and his colleagues have obtained from a number of ongoing projects including the Cambridge Youth Survey and the Cambridge Study in Delinquent Development (CSDD). Some of the most important results include:

- A significant number of delinquent youths have criminal fathers. About 8 percent of the sons of non-criminal fathers became chronic offenders, compared to 37 percent of youths with criminal fathers.[78]

- School yard bullying, may be both inter- and intra-generational. Bullies have children who bully others and these "second-generation bullies" grow up to become the fathers of children who are also bullies (see chapter 9 for more on bullying in the school yard).[79] Thus, one family may have a grandfather, father, and son who are or were school yard bullies.[80]

- Kids whose parents go to prison are much more likely to be at risk for delinquency than children of non-incarcerated parents. While it is possible that parental separation caused by incarceration is the key factor, kids who suffered parental separation due to illness, death, or divorce were less likely to become delinquents. Separation caused by parental imprisonment predicted antisocial behaviors up to age thirty-two signaling the long-term consequences of parental deviance.[81]

The cause of intergenerational deviance is uncertain. A number of factors may play a role:

- *Genetic Factors.* The link between parental deviance and child misbehavior may be genetic.[82] Parents of delinquent youth have been found to suffer neurological

There is a strong association between parental and children's deviance. In this photo from surveillance videotape in a Bedford, New Hampshire store, a woman with her daughter (behind the counter) and her son (at left) are shown in the process of stealing more than $2,000 worth of jewelry. The woman turned herself in after Bedford police made the video public.

© AP Images/Consignment Gallery release via Bedford, N.H. Police Dept.

conditions linked to antisocial behaviors and these conditions may be inherited genetically.[83]

■ *Substance Abuse.* Children of drug abusing parents are more likely to get involved in drug abuse and delinquency than the children on non-abusers.[84] This link might have a biological basis: parental substance abuse can produce children with neurological impairments that are related to delinquency.[85]

■ *Parenting.* The link between parental deviance and child's delinquency may be shaped by parenting ability: Deviant parents are the ones least likely to have close relationships with their offspring. They are more likely to use overly harsh and inconsistent discipline, a parenting style that has consistently been linked to the onset of delinquent behavior.[86] A recent study by Anne M. Dannerbeck of parents who have experienced incarceration found that once released they will exhibit lower levels of effective parenting and greater association with factors that can impede their parenting abilities (e.g., substance abuse and mental illness). As a result their children will be more likely to have experienced such negative effects of ineffective parenting as abuse and out of home placement, factors highly associated with delinquency.[87]

■ *Stigma.* The association between parental deviance and children's delinquency may be related to labeling and stigma. Social control agents may be quick to fix a delinquent label on the children of known law violators, increasing the likelihood that they will pick up an "official" delinquent label.[88] The resulting stigma increases the chances they may fall into a delinquent career.

Sibling Influences Some evidence also exists that siblings may influence behavior too; research shows that if one sibling is a delinquent there is a significant likelihood that his brother or sister will engage in delinquent behaviors.[89]

Not surprisingly, siblings who maintain a warm relationship and feel close to one another are also likely to behave in a similar fashion. If one of these siblings takes drugs and engages in delinquent behavior, so too will his brother or sister.[90] A number of interpretations of these data are possible:

■ Siblings who live in the same environment are influenced by similar social and economic factors; it is not surprising that their behavior is similar.

■ Deviance is genetically determined, and the traits that cause one sibling to engage in delinquency are shared by his or her brother or sister.

■ Deviant siblings grow closer because of shared interests. It is possible that the relationship is due to personal interactions: older siblings are imitated by younger siblings.

In summary, the research on delinquency and family relationships offers ample evidence that family life can be a potent force on a child's development. The delinquent child is likely to grow up in a large family with parents who may drink, participate in criminal acts, be harsh and inconsistent disciplinarians, be cold and unaffectionate, have marital conflicts, and be poor role models. Overall, the quality of a child's family life seems to be more important than its structure.

✔ Checkpoints

CHECKPOINTS

■ The family today is changing, and an increasing number of children will not live with their birth parents during their entire childhood.

■ Families are experiencing social and economic stresses.

■ A number of factors shape the family's influence on delinquency.

■ Most experts believe that children whose parents have divorced are at risk for delinquency.

■ Kids who grow up in conflict-ridden households are more likely to become delinquent.

■ Parent-child relations, including inconsistent discipline, have been linked to delinquency.

■ Parents who commit crimes and use drugs are likely to have children who also do so.

■ If one sibling is delinquent, so are her brothers and sisters.

CHILD ABUSE AND NEGLECT

Concern about the quality of family life has increased, because of reports that many children are physically abused or neglected by their parents and that this treatment has serious consequences for their behavior over the life course. Because of this topic's importance, the remainder of this chapter is devoted to the issue of child abuse and neglect and its relationship with delinquent behavior.

Historical Foundation

Parental abuse and neglect is not a modern phenomenon. Maltreatment of children has occurred throughout history. Some concern for the negative effects of such maltreatment was voiced in the eighteenth century in the United States, but concerted efforts to deal with the problem did not begin until 1874.

In that year, residents of a New York City apartment building reported to public health nurse Etta Wheeler that a child in one of the apartments was being abused by her stepmother. The nurse found a young child named Mary Ellen Wilson who had been repeatedly beaten and was malnourished from a diet of bread and water. Even though the child was seriously ill, the police agreed that the law entitled the parents to raise Mary Ellen as they saw fit. The New York City Department of Charities claimed it had no custody rights over Mary Ellen.

According to legend, Mary Ellen's removal from her parents had to be arranged through the Society for the Prevention of Cruelty to Animals (SPCA) on the ground that she was a member of the animal kingdom. The truth, however, is less sensational: Mary Ellen's case was heard by a judge. Because the child needed protection, she was placed in an orphanage.[91] The SPCA was actually founded the following year.[92]

Little research into the problems of maltreated children occurred before that of C. Henry Kempe of the University of Colorado. In 1962, Kempe reported the results of a survey of medical and law-enforcement agencies that indicated the child abuse rate was much higher than had been thought. He coined a term, ***battered child syndrome***, which he applied to cases of non-accidental injury of children by their parents or guardians.[93]

battered child syndrome
Non-accidental physical injury of children by their parents or guardians.

Defining Abuse and Neglect

Kempe's pioneering work has been expanded in a more generic expression of child abuse that includes neglect as well as physical abuse. Specifically, it describes any physical or emotional trauma to a child for which no reasonable explanation, such as

In 1874, Henry Bugh and Etta Angell Wheeler persuaded a New York court to take a child, Mary Ellen, away from her mother on the grounds of child abuse. This is the first recorded case in which a court was used to protect a child. Mary Ellen is shown at age nine when she appeared in court showing bruises from a whipping and several gashes from a pair of scissors. The second photograph shows her a year later.

American Humane Society

an accident, can be found. Child abuse is generally seen as a pattern of behavior rather than a single act. The effects of a pattern of behavior are cumulative. That is, the longer the abuse continues, the more severe the effect will be.[94]

Although the terms **child abuse** and neglect are sometimes used interchangeably, they represent different forms of maltreatment. **Neglect** refers to deprivations children suffer at the hands of their parents (lack of food, shelter, health care, love). *Abuse* is a more overt form of aggression against the child, one that often requires medical attention. The distinction between the terms is often unclear because, in many cases, both abuse and neglect occur simultaneously. What are the forms that abuse and neglect may take?

Physical abuse includes throwing, shooting, stabbing, burning, drowning, suffocating, biting, or deliberately disfiguring a child. Included within this category is shaken-baby syndrome (SBS), a form of child abuse affecting between 1,200 and 1,600 children every year. SBS is a collection of signs and symptoms resulting from violently shaking an infant or child.[95]

Physical neglect results from parents' failure to provide adequate food, shelter, or medical care for their children, as well as failure to protect them from physical danger.

Emotional abuse or neglect is manifested by constant criticism and rejection of the child.[96] Those who suffer emotional abuse have significantly lower self-esteem as adults.[97]

Emotional neglect includes inadequate nurturing, inattention to a child's emotional development, and lack of concern about maladaptive behavior. ***Abandonment*** refers to the situation in which parents leave their children with the intention of severing the parent-child relationship.[98]

Sexual abuse refers to the exploitation of children through rape, incest, and molestation by parents, family members, friends, or legal guardians. Sexual abuse can vary from rewarding children for sexual behavior that is inappropriate for their level of development to using force or the threat of force for the purposes of sex. It can involve children who are aware of the sexual content of their actions and others too young to have any idea what their actions mean.

The Effects of Abuse

Regardless of how it is defined, the effects of abuse can be devastating. Mental health and delinquency experts have found that abused kids experience mental and social problems across their lifespan, ranging from substance abuse to possession of a damaged personality.[99] Children who have experienced some form of maltreatment possess mental representations characterized by a devalued sense of self, mistrust of others, a tendency to perceive hostility in others in situations where the intentions of others are ambiguous, a tendency to generate antagonistic solutions to social conflicts. Victims of abuse are prone to suffer mental illness, such as dissociative identity disorder (DID), (sometimes known as multiple personality disorder [MPD]); research shows that child abuse is present in the histories of the vast majority of DID subjects.[100] Children who experience maltreatment are at increased risk for adverse health effects and behaviors across the life course, including smoking, alcoholism, drug abuse, eating disorders, severe obesity, depression, suicide, sexual promiscuity, and certain chronic diseases.[101] Maltreatment during infancy or early childhood can cause brain impairment, leading to physical, mental, and emotional problems such as sleep disturbances, panic disorder, and attention-deficit/hyperactivity disorder. Brain dysfunction is particularly common among victims of shaken baby syndrome: About 25 percent to 30 percent of infant

child abuse
Any physical, emotional, or sexual trauma to a child, including neglecting to give proper care and attention, for which no reasonable explanation can be found.

neglect
Passive neglect by a parent or guardian, depriving children of food, shelter, health care, and love.

abandonment
Parents physically leave their children with the intention of completely severing the parent-child relationship.

LOOKING BACK TO JOEY'S STORY

What should be done in situations where juveniles of similar ages engage in sexual contact? Should they be charged criminally or is there a better alternative?

victims with SBS die from their injuries; nonfatal consequences of SBS include varying degrees of visual impairment (e.g., blindness), motor impairment (e.g., cerebral palsy) and cognitive impairments.[102]

Psychologists suggest that maltreatment encourages children to use aggression as a means of solving problems and prevents them from feeling empathy for others. It diminishes their ability to cope with stress and makes them vulnerable to the violence in the culture. Abused children have fewer positive interactions with peers, are less well liked, and are more likely to have disturbed social interactions.[103]

Sexual Abuse Adolescent victims of sexual abuse are particularly at risk to stress and anxiety.[104] Kids who have undergone traumatic sexual experiences have been later found to suffer psychological deficits.[105] Many run away to escape their environment, which puts them at risk for juvenile arrest and involvement with the justice system.[106] Others suffer post-traumatic mental problems, including acute stress disorders, depression, eating disorders, nightmares, anxiety, suicidal ideation, and other psychological problems.[107] Stress however does not end in childhood. Children who are psychologically, sexually, or physically abused are more likely to suffer low self-esteem and be more suicidal as adults.[108] They are also placed at greater risk to be re-abused as adults than those who escaped childhood victimization.[109] The re-abused carry higher risks for psychological and physical problems, ranging from sexual promiscuity to increased HIV infection rates.[110] Abuse as a child may lead to despair, depression, and even homelessness as adults. One study of homeless women found that they were much more likely than other women to report childhood physical abuse, childhood sexual abuse, adult physical assault, previous sexual assault in adulthood, and a history of mental health problems.[111]

The Extent of Child Abuse

It is almost impossible to estimate the extent of child abuse. Many victims are so young that they have not learned to communicate. Some are too embarrassed or afraid to do so. Many incidents occur behind closed doors, and even when another adult witnesses inappropriate or criminal behavior, the adult may not want to get involved in a "family matter." Some indications of the severity of the problem came from a groundbreaking 1980 survey conducted by sociologists Richard Gelles and Murray Straus.[112] Gelles and Straus estimated that between 1.4 and 1.9 million children in the United States were subject to physical abuse from their parents. This abuse was rarely a onetime act. The average number of assaults per year was 10.5, and the median was 4.5. Gelles and Straus also found that 16 percent of the couples in their sample reported spousal abuse; 50 percent of the multi-child families reported attacks between siblings; 20 percent of the families reported incidents in which children attacked parents.[113]

The Gelles and Straus survey was a milestone in identifying child abuse as a national phenomenon. Subsequent surveys conducted in 1985 and 1992 indicated that the incidence of severe violence toward children had declined.[114] One reason was that parental approval of corporal punishment, which stood at 94 percent in 1968, decreased to 68 percent by 1994.[115] Recognition of the problem may have helped moderate cultural values and awakened parents to the dangers of physically disciplining children. Nonetheless, more than 1 million children were still being subjected to severe violence annually. If the definition of "severe abuse" used in the survey had included hitting with objects such as a stick or a belt, the number of child victims would have been closer to 7 million per year.

Monitoring Abuse Since the pioneering efforts by Gelles and Straus, the Department of Health and Human Services has been monitoring the extent of child maltreatment through its annual survey of Child Protective Services (CPS). The most recent survey indicates that CPS agencies investigated approximately 3.5 million allegations of child abuse in a single year and found evidence of abuse in about

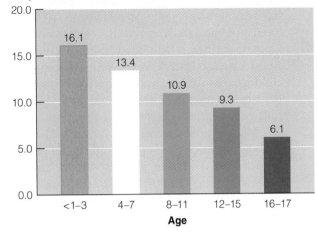

Figure 7.2 Victimization Rates by Age Group

Rate per 1,000 children

U.S. Department of Health and Human Services, Administration for Children and Families, Victimization Rates by Age Group, 2004. Available at: www.acf.hhs.gov/programs/cb/pubs/cm04/figure3_4.htm.

870,000 cases.[116] Although still a significant problem, the number and rate of abuse has been in decline. The rate of victimization has decreased more than 11 percent since 1990. The number of abuse cases has declined from 13.4 per 1,000 children in 1990 to 11.9 per 1,000 children today.

Who are the victims of abuse? As Figure 7.2 shows there is a direct association between age and abuse: victimization rates are higher for younger children than their older brothers and sisters. There are also racial differences in the abuse rate: African-American children, Pacific Islander children, and American Indian or Alaska Native children suffer child abuse rates (per 1,000 children) far higher than European American children, Hispanic children, and Asian children. An estimated 1,500 children die each year because of abuse, a rate of slightly more than 2 deaths per 100,000 children.

Sexual Abuse Attempts to determine the extent of sexual abuse indicate that perhaps one in ten boys and one in three girls have been the victims of some form of sexual exploitation. Richard J. Estes and Neil Alan Weiner, two researchers at the School of Social Welfare at the University of Pennsylvania, found that the problem of child sexual abuse is much more widespread than was previously believed or documented. Their research indicated that each year in the United States 325,000 children are subjected to some form of sexual exploitation, which includes sexual abuse, prostitution, use in pornography, and molestation by adults. Most are European American and middle-class. Equal numbers of boys and girls are involved, but the activities of boys generally receive less attention from authorities. Many of these kids are runaways (more than 120,000) whereas others have fled mental hospitals and foster homes. More than fifty thousand are thrown out of their home by a parent or guardian.[117]

Although sexual abuse is still quite prevalent, the number of reported cases has been in significant decline.[118] These data may either mean that the actual number of cases is truly in decline or that social service professionals are failing to recognize abuse cases because of overwork and understaffing.

Preventing child abuse before it occurs is the aim of **Prevent Child Abuse America**. Visit its website by going to www.thomsonedu.com/criminaljustice/siegel.

Causes of Child Abuse and Neglect

Maltreatment of children is a complex problem with neither a single cause nor a single solution. It cuts across racial, ethnic, religious, and socioeconomic lines. Abusive parents cannot be categorized by sex, age, or educational level.

Of all factors associated with child abuse, three are discussed most often: (1) parents who themselves suffered abuse tend to abuse their own children; (2) the presence of an unrelated adult increases the risk of abuse; and (3) isolated and alienated families tend to become abusive. A cyclical pattern of violence seems to be perpetuated from one generation to another. Evidence indicates that a large number of abused and neglected children grow into adulthood with a tendency to engage in violent behavior. The behavior of abusive parents can often be traced to negative experiences in their own childhood—physical abuse, emotional neglect, and incest. These parents become unable to separate their own childhood traumas from their relationships with their children. Abusive parents often have unrealistic perceptions of normal development. When their children are unable to act appropriately—when they cry or strike their parents—the parents may react in an abusive manner.[119] Parents may also become abusive if they are isolated from friends, neighbors, or relatives.

Many abusive parents describe themselves as alienated from their extended families, and they lack close relationships with persons who could provide help in stressful situations.[120] The relationship between alienation and abuse may be particularly acute in homes where there has been divorce or separation, or in which parents have never actually married; abusive punishment in single-parent homes has been found to be twice that of two-parent families.[121] Parents who are unable to cope with stressful events—divorce, financial stress, recurring mental illness, drug addiction—are most at risk.[122]

Substance Abuse and Child Abuse Abusive families suffer from severe stress, and it is therefore not surprising that they frequently harbor members who turn to drugs and alcohol. Studies have found a strong association between child abuse and parental alcoholism.[123] In addition, evidence exists of a significant relationship between cocaine and heroin abuse and neglect and abuse of children.

Stepparents and Abuse Research indicates that stepchildren share a greater risk for abuse than do biological offspring.[124] Stepparents may have less emotional attachment to the children of another. Often the biological parent has to choose between the new mate and the child, sometimes even becoming an accomplice in the abuse.[125]

Stepchildren are overrepresented in cases of **familicide**, mass murders in which a spouse and one or more children are slain. It is also more common for fathers who kill their biological children to commit suicide than those who kill stepchildren, an indication that the latter act is motivated by hostility and not despair.[126]

familicide
Mass murders in which a spouse and one or more children are slain.

Despite a decline in rate, child abuse and neglect remains an all too common national phenomenon. Jeffrey Caudill (left) pleaded guilty to child endangering charges in Franklin County Court of Commons Pleas in Columbus, Ohio on June 20, 2006 for torturing his two stepchildren by firing a BB gun at them and locking them in containers partially filled with water. He was sentenced to ten years in prison. His wife, Shelly Caudill, pleaded guilty to three counts of permitting child abuse.

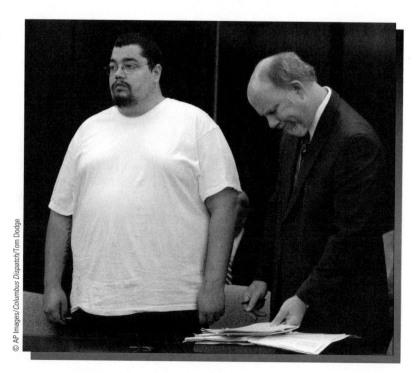

© AP Images/*Columbus Dispatch*/Tom Dodge

Social Class and Abuse Surveys indicate a high rate of reported abuse and neglect among people in lower economic classes. Children from families with a household income of less than fifteen thousand dollars per year experience more abuse than children living in more affluent homes. Child care workers indicate that most of their clients either live in poverty or face increased financial stress because of unemployment and economic recession. These findings suggest that parental maltreatment of children is predominantly a lower-class problem. Is this conclusion valid?

One view is that low-income families, especially those headed by a single parent, are often subject to greater environmental stress and have fewer resources to deal with such stress than families with higher incomes.[127] A relationship seems to exist between the burdens of raising a child without adequate resources and the use of excessive force. Self-report surveys do show that indigent parents are more likely than affluent parents to hold attitudes that condone physical chastisement of children.[128]

Higher rates of maltreatment in low-income families reflect the stress caused by the limited resources that lower-class parents have to help them raise their children; in contrast, middle-class parents devote a smaller percentage of their total resources to raising a family.[129]

This burden becomes especially onerous in families with emotionally and physically handicapped children. Stressed-out parents may consider special-needs children a drain on the families' finances with little potential for future success; research finds that children with disabilities are maltreated at a rate almost double that of other children.[130]

The Child Protection System: Philosophy and Practice

For most of our nation's history, courts have assumed that parents have the right to bring up their children as they see fit. In the 2000 case, *Troxel v. Granville*, the Supreme Court ruled that the due process clause of the Constitution protects against government interference with certain fundamental rights and liberty interests, including parents' fundamental right to make decisions concerning the care, custody, and control of their children.[131] If the care a child receives falls below reasonable standards, the state may take action to remove a child from the home and place her or him in a less threatening environment. In these extreme circumstances, the rights of both parents and children are constitutionally protected. In the cases of *Lassiter v. Department of Social Services* and *Santosky v. Kramer*, the U.S. Supreme Court recognized the child's right to be free from parental abuse and set down guidelines for a termination-of-custody hearing, including the right to legal representation.[132] States provide a guardian *ad litem* (a lawyer appointed by the court to look after the interests of those who do not have the capacity to assert their own rights). States also ensure confidentiality of reporting.[133]

Although child protection agencies have been dealing with abuse and neglect since the late nineteenth century, recent awareness of the problem has prompted judicial authorities to take increasingly bold steps to ensure the safety of children.[134] The assumption that the parent-child relationship is inviolate has been challenged. In 1974, Congress passed the Child Abuse Prevention and Treatment Act (CAPTA), which provides funds to states to bolster their services for maltreated children and their parents.[135] The act provides federal funding to states in support of prevention, investigation, and treatment. It also provides grants to public agencies and nonprofit organizations for demonstration programs.

The Child Abuse Prevention and Treatment Act has been the impetus for the states to improve the legal frameworks of their child protection systems. Abusive parents are subject to prosecution under statutes against assault, battery, and homicide.

Investigating and Reporting Abuse Maltreatment of children can easily be hidden from public view. Although state laws require doctors, teachers, and others who work with children to report suspected cases to child protection agencies, many maltreated children are out of the law's reach, because they are too young for school or because their parents do not take them to a doctor or a hospital. Parents abuse their children in private, and even when confronted, often accuse their children of lying or blame the children's medical problems on accidents. Social service agencies must find more effective ways to locate abused children and handle such cases once found.

All states have statutes requiring that persons suspected of abuse and neglect be reported. Many have made failure to report child abuse a criminal offense. Though such statutes are rarely enforced, teachers and nurses have been criminally charged for failing to report abuse or neglect cases.[136]

Once reported to a child protection agency, the case is screened by an intake worker and then turned over to an investigative caseworker. In some jurisdictions, if CPS substantiates a report, the case will likely be referred to a law enforcement agency that will have the responsibility of investigating the case, collecting evidence that can later be used in court proceedings. If the caseworker determines that the child is in imminent danger of severe harm, the caseworker may immediately remove the child from the home. A court hearing must be held shortly after to approve custody. Stories abound of children erroneously taken from their homes, but it is much more likely that these "gatekeepers" will consider cases unfounded and take no action. Among the most common reasons for screening out cases is that the reporting party is involved in a child custody case despite the research showing that the risk of abuse increases significantly in the aftermath of divorce.[137]

Even when there is compelling evidence of abuse, most social service agencies will try to involve the family in voluntary treatment. Case managers will do periodic follow-ups to determine if treatment plans are being followed. If parents are uncooperative, or if the danger to the children is so great that they must be removed from the home, a complaint will be filed in the criminal, family, or juvenile court system. To protect the child, the court could then issue temporary orders placing the child in shelter care during investigation, ordering services, or ordering suspected abusers to have no contact with the child.

The Process of State Intervention Although procedures vary from state to state, most follow a similar legal process once a social service agency files a court petition alleging abuse or neglect.[138] Figure 7.3 diagrams this process.

The Children's Bureau (CB), the oldest federal agency for children, is located in the U.S. Department of Health and Human Services' Administration for Children and Families, Administration on Children, Youth and Families. It is responsible for assisting states in the delivery of child welfare services, services designed to protect children and strengthen families. The website can be accessed by going to www.thomsonedu.com/criminaljustice/siegel.

Usually no more than ten out of every one hundred abuse cases actually reach the trial stage of the process. During this adversarial hearing, witnesses testify in order to prove the state's allegations. Here, Huron County Judge Timothy L. Cardwell listens to testimony from social worker Jo Johnson in Huron County Juvenile Court in Norwalk, Ohio, in a case involving abuse of adopted special needs children. Johnson testified that some of the eleven adoptive special needs children of Michael and Sharen Gravelle were found sleeping in cages.

© AP Images/Tony Dejak/Pool

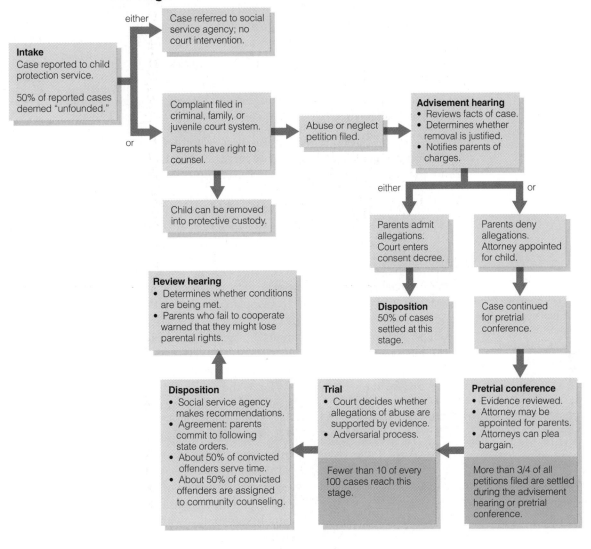

If the allegation of abuse is confirmed, the child may be placed in protective custody. Most state statutes require that the court be notified "promptly" or "immediately" if the child is removed; some states, including Arkansas, North Carolina, and Pennsylvania, have gone as far as requiring that no more than twelve hours elapse before official action is taken. If the child has not been removed from the home, state authorities are given more time to notify the court of suspected abuse. Some states set a limit of thirty days to take action, whereas others mandate that state action take no more than twenty days once the case has been investigated.

When an abuse or neglect petition is prosecuted, an **advisement hearing** (also called a *preliminary protective hearing* or *emergency custody hearing*) is held. The court will review the facts of the case, determine whether permanent removal of the child is justified, and notify the parents of the charges against them. Parents have the right to counsel in all cases of abuse and neglect, and many states require the court to appoint an attorney for the child as well. If the parents admit the allegations, the court enters a consent decree, and the case is continued for disposition. Approximately one-half of all cases are settled by admission at the advisement hearing. If the parents deny the petition, an attorney is appointed for the child and the case is continued for a **pretrial conference**.

At the pretrial conference, the attorney for the social service agency presents an overview of the case and the evidence. Such matters as admissibility of photos and

advisement hearing
A preliminary protective or temporary custody hearing in which the court will review the facts and determine whether removal of the child is justified and notify parents of the charges against them.

pretrial conference
The attorney for the social services agency presents an overview of the case, and a plea bargain or negotiated settlement can be agreed to in a consent decree.

written reports are settled. At this point the attorneys can negotiate a settlement of the case, in which the parents accept a treatment plan detailing:

- The types of services that the child and the child's family will receive, such as parenting classes, mental health or substance abuse treatment, and family counseling.

- Reunification goals, including visitation schedules and a target date for a child's return home.

- Concurrent plans for alternative permanent placement options should reunification goals not be met.

About three-fourths of the cases that go to pretrial conference are settled by a consent decree. About eighty-five out of every one hundred petitions filed are settled at either the advisement hearing or the pretrial conference.

Of the fifteen remaining cases, five are generally settled before trial. Usually no more than ten cases out of every one hundred actually reach the trial stage of the process. This is an adversarial hearing designed to prove the state's allegations.

Disposition

disposition hearing
The social service agency presents its case plan and recommendations for care of the child and treatment of the parents, including incarceration and counseling or other treatment.

The most crucial part of an abuse or neglect proceeding is the **disposition hearing**. The social service agency presents its case plan, which includes recommendations such as conditions for returning the child to the parents, or a visitation plan if the child is to be taken permanently from the parents. An agreement is reached by which the parents commit themselves to following the state orders. Between one-half and two-thirds of all convicted parents will be required to serve time in incarceration; almost half will be assigned to a form of treatment. As far as the children are concerned, some may be placed in temporary care; in other cases, parental rights are terminated and the child is placed in the custody of the child protective service. Legal custody can then be assigned to a relative or some other person.

LOOKING BACK TO JOEY'S STORY

What is the responsibility of a parent when his child is removed from their home? What should happen in situations where parents are not following the juvenile court-ordered recommendations?

In making their decisions, courts are guided by three interests: the role of the parents, protection for the child, and the responsibility of the state. Frequently, these interests conflict with each other. In fact, at times even the interests of the two parents are not in harmony. The state attempts to balance the parents' natural right to control their child's upbringing with the child's right to grow into adulthood free from harm. This is referred to as the **balancing-of-the-interests approach**.

balancing-of-the-interests approach
Efforts of the courts to balance the parents' natural right to raise a child with the child's right to grow into adulthood free from physical abuse or emotional harm.

review hearings
Periodic meetings to determine whether the conditions of the case plan for an abused child are being met by the parents or guardians of the child.

Periodically, **review hearings** are held to determine if the conditions of the case plan are being met. Parents who fail to cooperate are warned that they may lose their parental rights. Most abuse and neglect cases are concluded within a year. Either the parents lose their rights and the child is given a permanent placement, or the child is returned to the parents and the court's jurisdiction ends.

The Abused Child in Court

One of the most significant problems associated with abuse cases is the trauma a child must go through in a court hearing. Children get confused and frightened and may change their testimony. Much controversy has arisen over the accuracy of children's reports of physical and sexual abuse, resulting in hung juries. Prosecutors and experts have been accused of misleading children or eliciting incriminating testimony. In probably what is the most well-known case, the McMartin Day Care case in California, children told not only of being sexually abused but also of being forced to participate in bizarre satanic rituals during which the McMartin's mutilated animals and forced the children to touch corpses in hidden underground passageways. Prosecutors decided not to press forward after two trials ended in deadlock. Some jurors, when

The courts have granted leeway in the testimony of child abuse victims. Here, a social worker is shown using a doll to determine the sexual abuse of a young boy. Dolls such as this can be used during trial if they help victims tell their story.

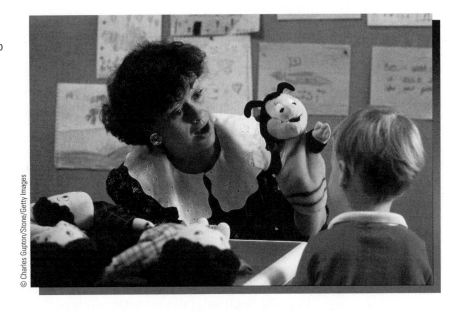

© Charles Gupton/Stone/Getty Images

interviewed after the verdict, said that while they believed that children had been abused the interviewing techniques used by prosecutors had been so suggestive that they had not been able to discern what really happened.[139]

State jurisdictions have instituted procedures to minimize the trauma to the child. Most have enacted legislation allowing videotaped statements, or interviews with child witnesses, taken at a preliminary hearing or at a formal deposition to be admissible in court. Videotaped testimony spares child witnesses the trauma of testifying in open court. States that allow videotaped testimony usually put some restrictions on its use: some prohibit the government from calling the child to testify at trial if the videotape is used; some states require a finding that the child is "medically unavailable," because of the trauma of the case before videotaping can be used; some require that the defendant be present during the videotaping; a few specify that the child not be able to see or hear the defendant.[140]

Most of the states now allow a child's testimony to be given on closed-circuit television (CCTV). The child is able to view the judge and attorneys, and the courtroom participants are able to observe the child. The standards for CCTV testimony vary widely. Some states, such as New Hampshire, assume that any child witness under age twelve would benefit from not having to appear in court. Others require an independent examination by a mental health professional to determine whether there is a "compelling need" for CCTV testimony.

In addition to innovative methods of testimony, children in sexual abuse cases have been allowed to use anatomically correct dolls to demonstrate happenings that they cannot describe verbally. The Victims of Child Abuse Act of 1990 allows children to use these dolls when testifying in federal courts; at least eight states have passed similar legislation.[141] Similarly, states have relaxed their laws of evidence to allow out-of-court statements by the child to a social worker, teacher, or police officer to be used as evidence (such statements would otherwise be considered **hearsay**). Typically, corroboration is required to support these statements if the child does not also testify.

The prevalence of sexual abuse cases has created new problems for the justice system. Often accusations are made in conjunction with marital disputes. The fear is growing that children may become pawns in custody battles; the mere suggestion of sexual abuse is enough to affect the outcome of a divorce action. The justice system must develop techniques that can get at the truth without creating a lifelong scar on the child's psyche.

Legal Issues A number of cases have been brought before the Supreme Court testing the right of children to present evidence at trial using nontraditional methods.

www The American Bar Association maintains a website with information on **legal rights of children in abuse cases**. The website can be accessed by going to www.thomsonedu.com/criminaljustice/siegel.

hearsay
Out-of-court statements made by one person and recounted in court by another; such statements are generally not allowed as evidence except in child abuse cases wherein a child's statements to social workers, teachers, or police may be admissible.

Two issues stand out. One is the ability of physicians and mental health professionals to testify about statements made to them by children, especially when the children are incapable of testifying. The second concerns the way children testify in court.

In a 1992 case, *White v. Illinois*, the Supreme Court ruled that the state's attorney is required neither to produce young victims at trial nor to demonstrate the reason why they were unavailable to serve as witnesses.[142] *White* involved statements given by the child to the child's babysitter and mother, a doctor, a nurse, and a police officer concerning the alleged assailant in a sexual assault case. The prosecutor twice tried to call the child to testify, but both times the four-year-old experienced emotional difficulty and could not appear in court. The outcome hinged solely on the testimony of the five witnesses.

By allowing others to testify as to what the child said, *White* removed the requirement that prosecutors produce child victims in court. This facilitates the prosecution of child abusers in cases where a court appearance by a victim would prove too disturbing or where the victim is too young to understand the court process.[143] The Court noted that statements made to doctors during medical examinations or those made when a victim is upset carry more weight than ones made after careful reflection. The Court ruled that such statements can be repeated during trial, because the circumstances in which they were made could not be duplicated simply by having the child testify to them in court.

In-Court Statements Children who are victims of sexual or physical abuse often make poor witnesses. Yet their testimony may be crucial. In a 1988 case, *Coy v. Iowa*, the Supreme Court placed limitations on efforts to protect child witnesses in court. During a sexual assault case, a "one-way" glass screen was set up so that the child victims would not be able to view the defendant (the defendant, however, could view the witnesses).[144] The Iowa statute that allowed the protective screen assumed that children would be traumatized by their courtroom experience. The court ruled that unless there is a finding that the child witness needs special protection, the Sixth Amendment of the Constitution grants defendants "face-to-face" confrontation with their accusers. In her dissenting opinion, Justice Sandra Day O'Connor suggested that if courts found it necessary, it would be appropriate to allow children to testify via CCTV or videotape.

Justice O'Connor's views became law in *Maryland v. Craig*.[145] In this case a daycare operator was convicted of sexually abusing a six-year-old child; one-way CCTV testimony was used during the trial. The decision was overturned in the Maryland Court of Appeals on the grounds that the procedures used were insufficient to show that the child could only testify in this manner, because a trial appearance would be too traumatic. On appeal, the court ruled that the Maryland statute that allows CCTV testimony is sufficient because it requires a determination that the child will suffer distress if forced to testify. The court noted that CCTV could serve as the equivalent of in-court testimony and would not interfere with the defendant's right to confront witnesses.

Disposition of Abuse and Neglect Cases

There is considerable controversy over what forms of intervention are helpful in abuse and neglect cases. Today, social service agents avoid removing children from the home whenever possible and instead try to employ techniques to control abusive relationships. In serious cases, the state may remove children from their parents and place them in shelter care or foster homes. Placement of children in foster care is intended to be temporary, but it is not uncommon for children to remain in foster care for three years or more.

Ultimately, the court has the power to terminate the rights of parents over their children, but because the effects of destroying the family unit are far reaching, the court does so only in the most severe cases. Judicial hesitancy is illustrated in a Virginia appellate case in which grandparents contested a father's being awarded custody of his children. Even though he had a history of alcohol abuse, had already been

CHECKPOINTS

■ Although the maltreatment of juveniles has occurred throughout history, the concept of child abuse is relatively recent.

■ C. Henry Kempe first recognized battered child syndrome.

■ We now recognize sexual, physical, and emotional abuse, as well as neglect.

■ More than 1 million confirmed cases of abuse occur each year.

■ The number of sexual abuse cases has declined.

■ There are a number of suspected causes of child abuse, including parental substance abuse, isolation, and a history of physical and emotional abuse.

■ A child protection system has been created to identify and try abuse cases.

■ The courts have made it easier for children to testify in abuse cases, by using CCTV, for example.

LOOKING BACK TO JOEY'S STORY

Do you agree or disagree with the way this case was handled from the beginning? What would you have done differently? Can you think of additional programs or services that could have been helpful in this situation?

found to be an unfit parent, and was awaiting appeal of his conviction for killing the children's mother, the trial court claimed that he had turned his life around and granted him custody.[146]

Despite such occurrences, efforts have been ongoing to improve the child protection system. Jurisdictions have expedited case processing, instituted procedures designed not to frighten child witnesses, coordinated investigations between social service and law enforcement agencies, and assigned an advocate or guardian *ad litem* to children in need of protection. ✔ Checkpoints

ABUSE, NEGLECT, AND DELINQUENCY

Experts fear that maltreated youth will later engage in violent and criminal acts. This assumed link between maltreatment and delinquency is supported by a number of criminological theories

- *Social control theory.* By disrupting normal relationships and impeding socialization, maltreatment reduces the social bond and frees individuals to become involved in deviance.
- *Social learning theory.* Maltreatment leads to delinquency, because it teaches children that aggression and violence are justifiable forms of behavior.
- *General strain theory.* Maltreatment creates the "negative affective states" that are related to strain, anger, and aggression.
- *Trait theory.* Maltreated youth will develop symptoms of psychological abnormality (e.g., depression, psychosis) that have been linked to antisocial behaviors.

A significant amount of literature suggests that being the target of abuse is associated with subsequent episodes of delinquency and violence.[147] The effects of abuse appear to be long term: Exposure to abuse in early life provides a foundation for violent and antisocial behavior in late adolescence and adulthood.[148] Delinquency researchers have used a number of techniques to gauge the association between abuse and antisocial behavior. A number of prominent forms are described below:

Clinical Histories Studies of juvenile offenders have confirmed that between 70 percent and 80 percent may have had abusive backgrounds. Many of these juveniles report serious injury, including bruises, lacerations, fractures, and being knocked unconscious by a parent or guardian.[149] Likewise, several studies reveal an association between homicide and maltreatment in early childhood.[150] Among children who kill or who attempt murder, the most common factor is a child's tendency to identify with aggressive parents and imitate their behavior.[151] One study of murder and murderous assault by juveniles indicated that in all cases "one or both parents had fostered and condoned murderous assault."[152]

Cohort Studies These findings do not necessarily prove that maltreatment causes delinquency. It is possible that child abuse is a reaction to misbehavior and not vice versa. In other words, it is possible that angry parents attack their delinquent and drug-abusing children and that child abuse is a *result* of delinquency, not its cause.

One way of solving this dilemma is to follow a cohort of youths who have been reported as victims of abuse and compare them with a similar cohort of non-abused youths. A classic study conducted by Jose Alfaro in New York found that about half of all children reported to area hospitals as abused children later acquired arrest records. Conversely, a significant number of boys (21 percent) and girls (29 percent) petitioned to juvenile court had prior histories as abuse cases. Children treated for abuse were disproportionately involved in violent offenses.[153]

Cathy Spatz Widom followed the offending careers of 908 youths reported as abused from 1967 to 1971 and compared them with a control group of 667 non-abused youths. Widom found that the abuse involved a variety of perpetrators, including parents, relatives, strangers, and even grandparents. Twenty-six percent of the abused sample had juvenile arrests, compared with 17 percent of the comparison group; 29 percent of those who were abused had adult criminal records, compared with 21 percent of the control group. Race, gender, and age also affected the probability that abuse would lead to delinquency. The highest risk group was composed of older African American males who had suffered abuse; about 67 percent of this group went on to become adult criminals. In contrast, only 4 percent of young, European American, non-abused females became adult offenders.[154] Her conclusion: being abused increases the likelihood of arrest both as a juvenile and as an adult.[155]

Widom also tested the hypothesis that victims of childhood violence resort to violence themselves as they mature. The children in her sample who suffered from physical abuse were the most likely to get arrested for violent crimes; their violent crime arrest rate was double that of the control group. More surprising was the discovery that neglected children maintained higher rates of violence than children in the comparison group. Clearly, family trauma of all kinds may influence violence.

Child Victims and Persistent Offending Widom also interviewed five hundred subjects twenty years after their childhood victimization. Preliminary analysis of this sample indicates that the long-term consequences of childhood victimization continue throughout life. Potential problems include mental health concerns, educational problems, health problems, and occupational difficulties. In a more recent analysis, Widom and Michael Maxfield found that by the time they reached age thirty-two, the abused children had a higher frequency of adult offending than the non-abused. People who began their offending careers as adults were also more likely to have been abused as children. Widom and Maxfield conclude that early intervention may be necessary to stop this cycle of violence.[156]

Sexual Abuse Cohort research shows that sexually abused youths are much more likely to suffer an arrest than non-abused children. The risk is greatest if the abuse took place when the child was less than seven years of age and if the offense was committed by a male.[157] Sexually abused girls share a significant risk of becoming violent over the life course. There is also evidence that sexual abuse victims are more likely to abuse others, especially if they were exposed to other forms of family violence.[158] Self-report studies also confirm that child maltreatment increases the likelihood of delinquency. The most severely abused youths are at the greatest risk for long-term serious delinquency.[159]

The Abuse-Delinquency Link

Many questions remain to be answered about the abuse-delinquency linkage, even though an association has found it does not necessarily mean that most abused children become delinquent. Many do not, and many delinquent youths come from what appear to be model homes. Though Widom found that more abused than non-abused children in her cohort became involved in delinquency, the majority of *both* groups did not engage in antisocial behavior.[160] And, although many studies have found an abuse-delinquency link, there are others that find the association is either non-significant or inconsistent (e.g., applying to girls and not to boys).[161]

Beyond the difficulty of showing a clear cut link between abuse and delinquency, it is also difficult to assess the temporal order of the linkage: Does early abuse lead to later delinquency? Or conversely, are antisocial kids subject to overly harsh parental discipline and abuse? It is also possible that a third explanation exists: Some external factor such as environmental deprivation causes both abuse and delinquency. That is, kids in lower class areas are the ones most likely to be abused and kids living in lower-class areas are also more likely to become delinquent. Hence, the observed association between abuse and delinquency may in fact be spurious.[162]

Research also shows that the timing and extent of abuse may shape its impact. Kids who are maltreated solely during early childhood may be less likely to engage in chronic delinquency than those whose abuse was lasting and persisted into later adolescence.[163] Timothy Ireland speculates that adolescents who have experienced persistent and long-term maltreatment are more likely to have families suffering an array of other social deficits, including poverty, parental mental illness, and domestic violence, which may make children more likely to engage in antisocial behavior. Persistent maltreatment also gives the victims little opportunity to cope or deal with their ongoing victimization.[164]

Finally, abuse may impact on some groups of adolescents more than it does others. When Kristi Holsinger and Alexander Holsinger surveyed incarcerated adolescent girls they found distinct racial differences in the way the girls reacted to abuse experiences.

For European American girls, they found a strong link between a history of abuse and indicators of poor mental health (e.g., suicide attempts and self-injurious behaviors); African American girls who suffered abuse are more likely to externalize their anger and violence. Holsinger and Holsinger speculate that because African American girls are socialized to be self-reliant and independent, they may be more likely to act in a stronger, more assertive manner. They have a higher self-esteem and fewer mental health issues. Conversely, because European American girls are raised to be dependent and accepting of feminine gender roles, when they experience abuse they tend to internalize their problems, a reaction that produces lower self-esteem and more mental health issues.[165]

LOOKING BACK TO JOEY'S STORY

Create a prevention program to assist abused children to avoid criminal behavior. What are the necessary elements? What services could be provided to impact these children's futures in a positive manner?

SUMMARY

- Poor family relationships have been linked to juvenile delinquency.
- Early theories viewed the broken home as a cause of youthful misconduct, but subsequent research found that divorce and separation play a smaller role than was previously believed.
- However, contemporary studies now show that parental absence may have a significant influence on delinquency, because it is more difficult for one parent to provide the same degree of discipline and support as two.
- The quality of family life also has a great influence on a child's behavior. Families in conflict produce more delinquents than those that function harmoniously.
- Families who neglect their children are at risk for delinquency. Inconsistent discipline and supervision have also been linked to juvenile crime.
- Parental and sibling misconduct is another factor that predicts delinquent behaviors.
- Concern over the relationship between family life and delinquency has been heightened by reports of widespread child abuse.
- Cases of abuse and neglect have been found in every social class and racial group.
- It has been estimated that there are 3 million reported cases of child abuse each year, of which almost nine hundred thousand are confirmed by child welfare investigators.
- Two factors are seen as causing child abuse. First, parents who themselves suffered abuse as children tend to abuse their own children. Second, isolated and alienated families tend to become abusive.
- Local, state, and federal governments have attempted to alleviate the problem of child abuse. All fifty states have statutes requiring that suspected cases of abuse be reported.
- There is a complex system of state intervention once allegations of child abuse are made. Thousands of youths are removed from their homes every year.
- A number of studies have linked abuse to delinquency. They show that a disproportionate number of court-adjudicated youths had been abused or neglected.
- Although the evidence is not conclusive, the data suggest that a strong relationship exists between child abuse and delinquent behavior.
- To make it easier to prosecute abusers, the Supreme Court has legalized the use of CCTV in some cases. Most states allow children to use anatomically correct dolls when testifying in court.

nuclear family, p. 152
broken home, p. 154
blended families, p. 154
intra-family violence, p. 156
parental efficacy, p. 157
resource dilution, p. 159

battered child syndrome, p. 162
child abuse, p. 163
neglect, p. 163
abandonment, p. 163
familicide, p. 166
advisement hearing, p. 169

pretrial conference, p. 169
disposition hearing, p. 170
balancing-of-the-interests approach, p. 170
review hearings, p. 170
hearsay, p. 171

QUESTIONS FOR DISCUSSION

1. What are the meanings of the terms *child abuse* and *child neglect*?

2. Discuss the association between child abuse and delinquency. Give two different explanations for the positive relationship between abuse and antisocial behavior.

3. What causes parents to abuse their children?

4. What is meant by the child protection system? Do courts act in the best interest of the child when they allow an abused child to remain with the family?

5. Should children be allowed to testify in court via CCTV? Does this approach prevent defendants in child abuse cases from confronting their accusers?

6. Is corporal punishment ever permissible as a disciplinary method?

APPLYING WHAT YOU HAVE LEARNED

You are an investigator with the county bureau of social services. A case has been referred to you by a middle school's head guidance counselor. It seems that a young girl, Emily M., has been showing up to school in a dazed and listless condition. She has had a hard time concentrating in class and seems withdrawn and uncommunicative. The thirteen-year-old has missed more than her normal share of school days and has often been late to class. Last week, she seemed so lethargic that her homeroom teacher sent her to the school nurse. A physical examination revealed that she was malnourished and in poor physical health. She also had evidence of bruising that could only come from a severe beating. Emily told the nurse that she had been punished by her parents for doing poorly at school and failing to do her chores at home.

When her parents were called to school to meet with the principal and guidance counselor, they claimed to be members of a religious order that believes children should be punished severely for their misdeeds. Emily had been placed on a restricted diet as well as beaten with a belt to correct her misbehavior. When the guidance counselor asked them if they would be willing to go into family therapy, they were furious

and told her to "mind her own business." It's a sad day, they said, when "God-fearing American citizens cannot bring up their children according to their religious beliefs." The girl is in no immediate danger because her punishment has not been life-threatening.

The case is then referred to your office. When you go to see the parents at home, they refuse to make any change in their behavior, claiming that they are in the right and you represent all that is wrong with society. The "lax" discipline you suggest leads to drugs, sex, and other teenage problems.

- Would you get a court order removing Emily from her house and requiring the parents to go into counseling?
- Would you report the case to the district attorney's office so it could take criminal action against her parents under the state's child protection act?
- Would you take no further action, reasoning that Emily's parents have the right to discipline their child as they see fit?
- Would you talk with Emily and see what she wants to happen?

DOING RESEARCH ON THE WEB

Before you answer these questions, use "child abuse" and "reporting child abuse" in key word searches on InfoTrac College Edition. To further help you answer these questions, go to **www.thomsonedu.com/criminaljustice/siegel**. You'll find information from Child USA and the National Clearinghouse on Child Abuse and Neglect Information to help you understand the issues surrounding child abuse.

CHAPTER 8

Peers and Delinquency: Juvenile Gangs and Groups

© Matt Cardy/Getty Images

CHAPTER OBJECTIVES

After reading this chapter you should:

1. Be familiar with the development of peer relations.
2. Know the various views of peer group cohesiveness.
3. Be able to define the concept of *the gang*.
4. Be familiar with the history of gangs.
5. Know the nature and extent of gang activity.
6. Recognize the various types of gangs.
7. Understand how gangs are structured.
8. Be familiar with the racial and ethnic makeup of gangs.
9. Discuss the various theories of gang development.
10. Know how police departments undertake gang prevention and suppression.

Luis was a sixteen-year-old Latino male who identified himself as involved in a gang. He was charged with substantial battery and resisting arrest, due to a fight at a party with a rival gang member. Luis already had a history of truancy and a police record for several thefts, vandalism, underage drinking, and curfew violations. He was smoking marijuana on a daily basis, not attending school, and had experienced little success in the educational environment outside of sports. Luis also exhibited significant anger management issues and was viewed as a threat to the community.

The family was supportive and very concerned about his behavior. Luis's mother was very involved in his life and was doing her best to raise her four children without any assistance or involvement from their father. Luis had felt like "the man of the family" from an early age. Within their family culture, Luis, being the oldest male, felt responsible for caring for his mother and younger siblings. He had joined a gang around the age of eleven in hopes that it would provide additional protection for his family. Despite the numerous concerns of his family and the juvenile court, Luis was allowed to return home until the next juvenile court proceeding. He was referred for electronic monitoring and an intensive home supervision program.

Luis arrived at his initial juvenile court plea hearing intoxicated and belligerent. There was great concern that Luis was using drugs and alcohol and that he needed treatment, but the prosecuting attorney did not agree and petitioned for him to be sent directly to a juvenile correctional facility. While the next court hearing was pending, Luis participated in an alcohol and drug assessment, and it was recommended that he enter a residential treatment facility for his drug and alcohol use, anger management issues, and gang involvement. During the wait between court proceedings, he was also involved in an intensive supervision program where he received individual counseling, group treatment, intensive monitoring of his whereabouts and school activities, family and individual crisis intervention, and significant redirection regarding his choices. He was also referred to an alternative school program where his chances for success would be better. Luis's mother was hopeful that the services would assist him and that Luis would start to turn his life around.

At the dispositional hearing, there was disagreement regarding the best plan for Luis, and a contested hearing took place. The prosecuting attorney wanted him sent directly to a juvenile correctional facility. The defense attorney argued that Luis needed alcohol and drug treatment, as well as other services, and that he should be sent to an inpatient treatment facility that had already agreed to take him. Luis's probation officer and his family all advocated for him to get

treatment. He had been doing better in the community setting with the additional services and supports. The judge listened to all of the testimony and expressed concerns regarding Luis's juvenile court involvement record and the safety of the community. At the same time, she wanted to give him a chance to be successful in drug treatment. In the end, the judge ordered Luis to the juvenile correctional facility, but "stayed" the order, permitting Luis to enter treatment. This "stay" meant that if Luis left the treatment facility, or if he was terminated from the program, he would automatically go to juvenile corrections. If he was successful in treatment, he would most likely return to the community with the needed supports and services. If at any time Luis decided not to cooperate with the community aftercare plans, or if he had any further law violations, he could also be immediately sent to juvenile corrections. Luis and his family seemed to understand the seriousness of the situation and Luis agreed to treatment.

Luis entered the voluntary ninety-day alcohol and drug treatment program and began to work on his sobriety, anger issues, gang involvement, and criminal thinking patterns. Although it was difficult to coordinate, given her work schedule and responsibility for the other children in the household, Luis's mother came to visit on a regular basis and participated in family sessions. The involved professionals assisted with coordinating child care and arranging transportation so she could be there for Luis, who struggled at first and was having a hard time adjusting to the rules of the facility. His mother and the team encouraged him to remain in treatment and try to focus on a positive future, and they reminded him of the "stayed" correctional order. Luis ultimately decided to engage in treatment and he completed the ninety-day program.

The team of professionals, along with Luis and his mother, created an aftercare plan that initially included ongoing drug counseling and support, individual counseling, intensive supervision and monitoring, group supports, and placement in an alternative educational setting. Through the alternative school, Luis got involved in a program that offers troubled youth the experience of building homes for underprivileged families. Luis was able to gain valuable work skills, as well as time to focus on positive activities. Although he still struggled with school, with his past gang involvement, and with making good choices, he was able to significantly decrease his police contacts and he had no further arrests as a juvenile. Luis remained at home with his mother and siblings and was eventually released from the juvenile court-order services. The "stayed" correctional order was in place until the juvenile court closed the case on Luis's eighteenth birthday.

Kids like Luis often find themselves trapped in a gang culture. Few issues in the study of delinquency are more important today than the problems presented by law-violating gangs and groups.[1] Although some gangs are made up of only a few loosely organized neighborhood youths, others have thousands of members who cooperate in complex illegal enterprises. A significant portion of all drug distribution in the nation's inner cities is believed to be gang-controlled; gang violence accounts for more than a thousand homicides each year. There has been an outcry from politicians to increase punishment for the "little monsters" and to save the "fallen angels," or the victimized youths who are innocent.[2] Nor is the gang problem unique to the United States. John Hagedorn, a noted gang expert finds that a global criminal economy, especially the illegal distribution of drugs, involves gangs as both major and bit players. Numerous gangs operate in distressed areas, such as the townships of South Africa, where they rule politically and control the underground economy. Chinese Triads operate all across the globe, but are especially active in South Asia and the United States. In Eastern Europe, the turmoil caused by the move to a market economy and the loss of social safety nets has strengthened gangs and drug organizations. In Albania, for example, one-quarter of all young males are involved in the drug economy.[3]

The problem of gang control is a difficult one. Many gangs flourish in inner-city areas that offer lower-class youths few conventional opportunities and members are resistant to offers of help that cannot deliver legitimate economic hope. Although gang members may be subject to arrest, prosecution, and incarceration, a new crop of young recruits is always ready to take the place of their fallen comrades. Those sent to prison find that, upon release, their former gangs are only too willing to have them return to action.

We begin this chapter with a discussion of peer relations, showing how they influence delinquent behavior. Then we explore the definition, nature, and structure of delinquent gangs. Finally, the chapter presents theories of gang formation, the extent of gang activity, and gang-control efforts.

ADOLESCENT PEER RELATIONS

Although parents are the primary source of influence and attention in children's early years, children between ages eight and fourteen seek out a stable peer group, and both the number and the variety of friendships increase as children go through adolescence. Friends soon begin to have a greater influence over decision making than parents.

As they go through adolescence, children form **cliques**, small groups of friends who share activities and confidences.[4] They also belong to **crowds**, loosely organized groups of children who share interests and activities, such as sports, religion, or hobbies. Intimate friends play an important role in social development, but adolescents are also deeply influenced by this wider circle of friends. Adolescent self-image is in part formed by perceptions of one's place in the social world.[5]

In later adolescence, acceptance by peers has a major impact on socialization. By their early teens, children report that their friends give them emotional support when they are feeling bad and that they can confide intimate feelings to peers without worrying about their confidences being betrayed.[6] Poor peer relations, such as negative interactions with best friends, has been found to be related to high social anxiety, whereas, in contrast, close affiliation with a high-status peer crowd seems to afford protection against depression and other negative adolescent psychological symptoms.[7]

Popular youths do well in school and are socially astute. In contrast, children who are rejected by their peers are more likely to display aggressive behavior and to disrupt group activities by bickering or behaving antisocially. Another group of kids—**controversial status youth**—are aggressive kids who are either highly liked or intensely disliked by their peers. These controversial youths are the ones most likely to become engaged in antisocial behavior. When they find themselves in leadership positions among their peers they get them involved in delinquent and problem behaviors.[8]

cliques
Small groups of friends who share intimate knowledge and confidences.

crowds
Loosely organized groups who share interests and activities.

For a general overview of **gangs in America** go to the website www.thomsonedu.com/criminaljustice/siegel.

controversial status youth
Aggressive kids who are either highly liked or intensely disliked by their peers and who are the ones most likely to become engaged in antisocial behavior.

Peer relations, in all cultures, have been linked to adolescent behavior choices, including substance abuse and delinquency.

© Janine Wiedel Photolibrary/Alamy

It is clear that peer status during childhood is an important contributor to a child's social and emotional development that follows the child across the life course. Girls who engage in aggressive behavior with childhood peers later have more conflict-ridden relationships with their romantic partners.[9] Boys who are highly aggressive and are therefore rejected by their peers in childhood are also more likely to engage in criminality and delinquency from adolescence into young adulthood.[10] Peer relations, then, are a significant aspect of maturation. Peer influence may be more important than parental nurturance in the development of long-term behavior.[11] Peers guide each other and help each other learn to share and cooperate, to cope with aggressive impulses, and to discuss feelings they would not dare bring up at home. Youths can compare their own experiences with peers and learn that others have similar concerns and problems.[12]

Peer Relations and Delinquency

Research shows that peer group relationships are closely tied to delinquent behaviors: delinquent acts tend to be committed in small groups rather than alone, a process referred to as *co-offending*.[13] Youths who report inadequate or strained peer relations are the ones most likely to become delinquent.[14] Adolescents who maintain delinquent friends are more likely to engage in antisocial behavior and drug abuse.[15]

Some kids are particularly susceptible to peer influence. A number of research efforts have found that boys who go through puberty at an early age were more likely to later engage in violence, property crimes, drug use, and precocious sexual behavior.[16] The boys who matured early were the most likely to develop strong attachments to delinquent friends and to be influenced by peer pressure.[17] The conclusion: the earlier youngsters develop relationships with delinquent peers and the closer those relationships get, the more likely they will become delinquent. It is not surprising that delinquent girls are significantly more likely than non-delinquent girls to identify males as their closest friends.[18] For girls, hanging out with males, who are at a higher risk for delinquency than female peers, may be a precursor to antisocial behavior choices.

Impact of Peer Relations

Does having antisocial peers cause delinquency, or are delinquents antisocial youths who seek out like-minded companions, because they can be useful in committing crimes? There are actually four independent viewpoints on this question.

1. According to the control theory approach articulated by Travis Hirschi (Chapter 4) delinquents are as detached from their peers as they are from other elements of society.[19] Although they appear to have close friends, delinquents actually lack the social skills to make their peer relations rewarding or fulfilling.[20] Antisocial adolescents seek out like-minded peers for criminal associations. If delinquency is committed in groups, it is because "birds of a feather flock together."

2. Delinquent friends cause law-abiding youth to "get in trouble." Kids who fall in with a "bad crowd" are at risk for delinquency. Youths who maintain friendships with antisocial peers are more likely to become delinquent regardless of their own personality or the type of supervision they receive at home.[21] Even previously law-abiding youths are more likely to get involved in delinquency if they become associated with friends who initiate them into delinquent careers.[22]

3. Antisocial youths join up with like-minded friends; deviant peers sustain and amplify delinquent careers.[23] As children move through the life course, antisocial friends help them maintain delinquent careers and obstruct the aging-out process.[24] In contrast, non-delinquent friends moderate delinquency.[25] If adulthood brings close and sustaining ties to conventional friends, and marriage and family, the level of deviant behavior will decline.[26]

4. Troubled kids choose delinquent peers out of necessity rather than desire. The social baggage they cart around prevents them from developing associations with conventional peers. Because they are impulsive, they may hook up with friends who are dangerous and get them into trouble.[27] Deviant peers do not cause straight kids to go bad, but they amplify the likelihood of a troubled kid getting further involved in antisocial behaviors.[28]

Although each of these scenarios has its advocates, the weight of the empirical evidence clearly indicates that delinquent peers have a significant influence on behavior: youths who are loyal to delinquent friends, belong to gangs, and have "bad companions" are the ones most likely to commit crimes and engage in violence.[29] Furthermore, the friendship patterns of delinquents may not be dissimilar from those of non-delinquents; delinquent youths report that their peer relations contain elements of caring and trust and that they can be open and intimate with their friends.[30] Warm intergroup associations contradict the control theory model, which holds that delinquents are loners, and support the cultural deviance view that delinquents form close-knit groups that sustain their behavior.

YOUTH GANGS

gang
Group of youths who collectively engage in delinquent behaviors.

As youths move through adolescence, they gravitate toward cliques that provide them with support, assurance, protection, and direction. In some instances, the peer group provides the social and emotional basis for antisocial activity. When this happens, the clique is transformed into a **gang**.

Today, such a powerful mystique has grown up around gangs that mere mention of the word evokes images of black-jacketed youths roaming the streets in groups bearing such names as the MS-13, Latin Kings, Crips, and Bloods. Films, television shows, novels, and even Broadway musicals, such as *West Side Story* or *Grease*, have popularized the youth gang.[31]

Considering the suspected role gangs play in violent crime and drug activity, it is not surprising that gangs have recently become the target of a great deal of research interest.[32] Important attempts have been made to gauge their size, location, makeup, and activities.

What Are Gangs?

Gangs are groups of youths who engage in delinquent behaviors. Yet gang delinquency differs from group delinquency. Whereas group delinquency consists of a short-lived alliance created to commit a particular crime or violent act, gang delinquency involves long-lived institutions that have a distinct structure and organization, including identifiable leadership, division of labor, rules, rituals, and possessions.

Delinquency experts are often at odds over the precise definition of a gang. The term is sometimes used broadly to describe any congregation of youths who have joined together to engage in delinquent acts. However, police departments often use it only to refer to cohesive groups that hold and defend territory, or turf.[33]

Academic experts have also created a variety of definitions. The core elements in the concept of the gang are that it is an **interstitial group**—one falling within the cracks and crevices of society—and that it maintains standard group processes, such as recruiting new members, setting goals, assigning roles, and developing status.[34]

Malcolm Klein argues that two factors stand out in all of these definitions:

1. Members have self-recognition of their gang status and use special vocabulary, clothing, signs, colors, graffiti, and names. Members set themselves apart from the community and are viewed as a separate entity by others. Once they get the label of gang, members eventually accept and take pride in their status.

2. There is a commitment to criminal activity, although even the most criminal gang members spend the bulk of their time in noncriminal activities.[35]

How Did Gangs Develop?

The youth gang is sometimes viewed as uniquely American, but gangs have also been reported in several other nations.[36] Nor are gangs a recent phenomenon. In the 1600s, London was terrorized by organized gangs that called themselves "Hectors," "Bugles," "Dead Boys," and other colorful names. In the seventeenth and eighteenth centuries, English gang members wore distinctive belts and pins marked with serpents, animals, stars, and the like.[37] The first mention of youth gangs in America occurred in the late 1780s, when prison reformers noted the presence of *gangs* of young people hanging out on Philadelphia's street corners. By the 1820s, New York's Bowery and Five Points districts, Boston's North End and Fort Hill, and the outlying Southwark and Moyamensing sections of Philadelphia were the locales of youth gangs with colorful names like the Roach Guards, Chichesters, the Plug Uglies, and the Dead Rabbits.[38]

In the 1920s, Frederick Thrasher initiated the study of the modern gang in his analysis of more than thirteen hundred youth groups in Chicago.[39] He found that the social, economic, and ecological processes that affect the structure of cities create cracks in the normal fabric of society—weak family controls, poverty, and social disorganization—and referred to this as an *interstitial area*. According to Thrasher, groups of youths develop to meet such needs as play, fun, and adventure, activities that sometimes lead to delinquent acts. Impoverished areas present many opportunities for conflict between groups of youths and adult authority. If this conflict continues, the groups become more solidified and their activities become primarily illegal, and the groups develop into gangs.

According to Thrasher, adult society does not meet the needs of lower-class youths, and the gang solves the problem by offering excitement, fun, and opportunity. The gang is not a haven for disturbed youths, but an alternative lifestyle for normal boys. Thrasher's work has had an important influence. Recent studies of delinquent gang behavior also view the gang as a means for lower-class boys to achieve advancement and opportunity as well as to defend themselves and to attack rivals. For example, the National Youth Gang Center defines gangs this way:

A youth gang is commonly thought of as a self-formed association of peers having the following characteristics: three or more members, generally ages twelve to twenty-four; a gang name and some sense of identity, generally indicated by such symbols as style of clothing, graffiti, and hand signs; some degree of permanence and organization; and an elevated level of involvement in delinquent or criminal activity.[40]

Gangs in the 1950s and 1960s In the 1950s and early 1960s, the threat of gangs and gang violence swept the public consciousness. Newspapers featured stories on the violent behavior of fighting gangs, such as the Egyptian Kings, the Vice Lords, and the Blackstone Rangers. Movies, such as *The Wild Ones* and *Blackboard Jungle*, were made about gangs, and the Broadway musical (and later movie) *West Side Story* romanticized violent gangs.

By the mid-1960s, the gang menace seemed to have disappeared. Some experts attribute the decline of gang activity to successful community-based programs.[41] Others believe gangs were eliminated, because police gang-control units infiltrated gangs, arrested leaders, and constantly harassed members.[42] Another explanation is the increase in political awareness that developed during the 1960s. Many gang leaders became involved in social or political activities. In addition, many gang members were drafted. Still another explanation is that many gang members became active users of heroin and other drugs, which curtailed their group-related criminal activity.[43]

Gangs Reemerge Interest in gang activity began anew in the early 1970s. Bearing such names as Savage Skulls and Black Assassins, gangs began to form in New York's South Bronx neighborhoods in the spring of 1971 and quickly spread to other parts of the city. By 1975, there were 275 police-verified gangs with eleven thousand members.[44]

Gang activity also re-emerged in other major cities, such as Chicago and Los Angeles. The Crips gang was created in Los Angeles, California in 1969 by teens Raymond Washington and Stanley "Tookie" Williams. Initially called the Baby Avenues they evolved to *Avenue Cribs*, and then *Cribs*. According to legend the gang name evolved into Crips because some of its members used canes to attack victims; it is also possible it was a simple spelling mistake in newspaper articles about the gang. As the Crips rose in power, other rival gangs formed an alliance that morphed into their most significant rival gang, the Bloods. Eventually both these gangs sent representatives to organize chapters in distant areas or to take over existing gangs.

Members of the New York youth gang the Savage Skulls fighting in the street in 1972. The trademark of the gang was a sleeveless denim jacket with a skull and crossbones design on the back. Based around Fox Street in the South Bronx, the gang fought battles with rival gangs, such as the Seven Immortals, and Savage Nomads. By 1975, there were 275 police-verified gangs with 11,000 members.

Why Did Gangs Reemerge?

One reason for the increase in gang activity may be involvement in the sale of illegal drugs.[45] Early gangs relied on group loyalty to encourage membership, but modern gang members are lured by the quest for drug profits. In some areas, gangs replaced organized crime families as the dominant suppliers of cocaine and crack. The traditional weapons of gangs—chains, knives, and homemade guns—were replaced by automatic weapons.

Gang formation was also the natural consequence of the economic and social dislocation that occurred when the economy shifted from a relatively high-paying manufacturing to low-wage service economy.[46] Some U.S. cities that required a large population base for their manufacturing plants now faced economic stress as these plants shut down. In this uneasy economic climate, gangs flourish, whereas the influence of successful adult role models and stable families declines. The presence of gangs in areas unaccustomed to delinquent group activity can have a devastating effect on community life.

While this social dislocation occurred, the media fell in love with gang images, which appeared in films and music videos. Gangsta rap became a national phenomenon. Because there has been a diffusion of the gang culture through the popular media, in which gang boys are made to appear as successful heroes, urban kids may find the lure of gangs and law-violating peer groups irresistible.

CONTEMPORARY GANGS

The gang cannot be viewed as a uniform or homogeneous social concept. Gangs vary by activity, makeup, location, leadership style, and age. The next sections describe some of the most salient features of contemporary gangs.

Extent

The federal government sponsors the National Youth Gang Survey (NYGS) to measure gang activity around the United States. The most recent survey found that a significant majority of urban areas report the presence of gangs, and that gangs exist in

Figure 8.1 **Estimated Total Gang Membership Percent Difference from the Nine-Year Average**

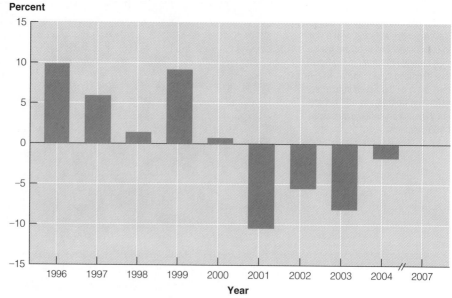

Source: National Youth Gang Survey Analysis. Available at: www.iir.com/NYGC/nygsa/measuring_the_extent_of_gang_problems.htm (accessed December 1, 2006).

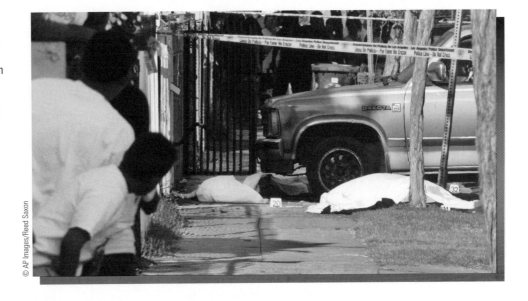

Onlookers peer past police barricades to see the covered bodies of three gang-related gunshot victims in South Los Angeles, June 30, 2006. Another juvenile injured at the scene was taken to the hospital in critical, but stable, condition. Gang activity is most common in larger metropolitan areas such as Los Angeles, Chicago, and Miami.

© AP Images/Reed Saxon

all levels of the social strata, from rural counties to metropolitan areas. However, as Figure 8.1 shows, gang activity has declined during the past decade.[47] Although the survey shows that there are fewer gang members today than in the past, at recent count an estimated 760,000 gang members and 24,000 gangs were active in more than 2,900 jurisdictions around the United States.

Location

Traditionally, gangs have operated in large urban areas experiencing rapid population change. In these transitional neighborhoods, diverse ethnic and racial groups find themselves in competition with one another.[48] Intergang conflict and homicide rates are high in these areas, which house the urban "underclass."[49] However, these communities eventually evolve into permanently **disorganized neighborhoods**, where population shifts slow down, permitting patterns of behavior and traditions to develop over a number of years. Most typical are the poverty-stricken areas of New York and Chicago and the Mexican American barrios of the southwestern states and California. These areas contain large, structured gang clusters that are resistant to change or control by law enforcement agencies.

Even though some people think of gangs as a purely urban phenomenon, an estimated fifteen thousand gangs with three hundred thousand members are located in small cities, suburban counties, and even rural areas. The growth of gangs in suburban and rural areas has been attributed to a restructuring of the population. There has been a massive movement of people out of the central city to outlying communities and suburbs. In some cities, once-fashionable neighborhoods have declined, whereas in others, downtown areas have undergone extensive renewal. Previously impoverished inner-city districts of major cities, such as New York and Chicago, are now quite fashionable and expensive, devoted to finance, retail stores, high-priced condos, and entertainment. Two aspects of this development inhibit urban gang formation: (1) there are few residential areas and thus few adolescent recruits, and (2) there is intensive police patrol.

Migration

Because of redevelopment, gangs in some areas have relocated or migrated; gang members have organized new chapters when they relocate to new areas. The most recent NYGS found many jurisdictions have experienced gang migration and in a few areas more than half of all gang members had come from other areas. Nonetheless, the survey shows that the majority of gang members are still home-grown.

disorganized neighborhood
Inner-city areas of extreme poverty where the critical social control mechanisms have broken down.

Why gang members migrate? Although the prevailing wisdom is that gang members move for criminal purposes, that is, to sell drugs to new customers at higher prices, the NYGS found that most did so for social reasons (e.g., members moving with families, pursuit of legitimate employment opportunities). Others sought new drug market opportunities or wanted to avoid law enforcement crackdowns in their hometowns. In all, less than 20 percent moved to a new location solely in order to participate in illegal ventures in a new area that may have less gang competition.[50]

Most migrators are African American or Hispanic males who maintain close ties with members of their original gangs "back home."[51] Some migrants join local gangs, shedding old ties and gaining new affiliations. Although some experts fear the outcome of migration, it appears the number of migrants is relatively small in proportion to the overall gang population, supporting the contention that most gangs actually are "homegrown."[52]

Gangs and Immigration Although migration of gang members from one locale to another has been a problem, it may be overshadowed by the immigration of gang members into and out of the United States, to and from other nation's. Immigration, particularly from Latin America and Asia, has brought people who have formed extremely violent gangs, such as Mara Salvatrucha (MS-13) and the 18th Street Gang, into the United States.[53] Both gangs were started in Los Angeles by immigrants from El Salvador fleeing a civil war. When they first arrived in Los Angeles, they were preyed upon by pre-existing Mexican gangs. The MS-13 gang was formed as a means of self-protection. The name refers to a *mara*, Spanish for "posse," or gang; *salvatruchas* is local slang for being alert and ready to take action; and the "13" is a reference to their beginnings on 13th Street in Los Angeles.

When law enforcement cracked down and deported members, the deportees quickly created outposts in El Salvador and throughout Central America. The Salvadoran government responded by criminalizing gang membership and arresting thousands.[54] Nonetheless, gang membership has continued to grow, and the Salvadoran gangs have actually returned to set up branches in the United States. Some experts believe that the ten-thousand–member MS-13 is now the nation's most dangerous gang, whereas others claim that the 18th Street Gang, with over twenty thousand members, is the largest. In either event, gang members are involved in burglaries, auto thefts, narcotic sales, home invasion robberies, weapons smuggling, carjacking, extortion, murder, rape, witness intimidation, illegal firearm sales, car theft, aggravated assaults, and drug trafficking. They also have been known to place a "tax" on prostitutes and non-gang member drug dealers who are working in MS-13 "turf." Failure to pay up will most likely result in violence.

Types

Gangs have been categorized by their dominant activity: some are devoted to violence and to protecting neighborhood boundaries, or turf; others are devoted to theft; some specialize in drug trafficking; others are concerned with recreation rather than crime.[55] Jeffrey Fagan found that most gangs fall into one of these four categories:

1. *Social gang.* Involved in few delinquent activities and little drug use other than alcohol and marijuana. Members are more interested in social activities.
2. *Party gang.* Concentrates on drug use and sales, but forgoes most delinquent behavior. Drug sales are designed to finance members' personal drug use.
3. *Serious delinquent gang.* Engages in serious delinquent behavior while avoiding drug dealing and usage. Drugs are used only on social occasions.
4. *Organized gang.* Heavily involved in criminality. Drug use and sales are related to other criminal acts. Gang violence is used to establish control over drug sale territories. This gang is on the verge of becoming a formal criminal organization.[56]

The format and structure of gangs may be changing. They are now commonly described as having a "hybrid gang culture," meaning they do not follow a single code of rules or method of operation. Today's gangs do have several common characteristics:

- a mixture of racial/ethnic groups,
- a mixture of symbols and graffiti associated with different gangs,
- wearing colors traditionally associated with a rival gang,
- less concern over turf or territory,
- members who sometimes switch from one gang to another.[57]

The following Focus on Delinquency presents research showing that not only are there different types of gangs, but there may also be different types of gang boys.

Cohesion

The standard definition of a gang implies that it is a cohesive group. However, some experts refer to gangs as **near-groups**, which have limited cohesion, impermanence, minimal consensus of norms, shifting membership, disturbed leadership, and limited definitions of membership expectations.[58] Gangs maintain a small core of committed members, who work constantly to keep the gang going, and a much larger group of affiliated youths, who participate in gang activity only when the mood suits them. James Diego Vigil found that boys in Latino **barrio** gangs (Hispanic neighborhood gangs) could be separated into regular members and those he describes as "peripheral," "temporary," and "situational."[59]

Current research indicates that, although some gangs remain near-groups, others become quite organized and stable. These gangs resemble traditional organized crime families more than temporary youth groups. Some, such as Chicago's Latin Kings and Gangster Disciples, have members who pay regular dues, are expected to attend gang meetings regularly, and carry out political activities to further gang ambitions.

Age

The ages of gang members range widely, perhaps from as young as eight to as old as fifty-five.[60] Traditionally, most members of offending groups were usually no more than a few years apart in age, with a leader who may be a few years older than most other members.[61] However, because members are staying in gangs longer than in the past the age spread between gang members has widened considerably.

Research indicates that youths first hear about gangs at around nine years of age, get involved in violence at ten or eleven, and join their first gang at twelve. By age thirteen, most members have (a) fired a pistol, (b) seen someone killed or seriously injured, (c) gotten a gang tattoo, and (d) been arrested.[62] Gang experts believe the average age of gang members has been increasing yearly, a phenomenon explained in part by the changing structure of the U.S. economy.[63]

Why Are Gang Members Aging? Gang members are getting older and the majority of them are now legal adults. As noted earlier, relatively high-paid, low-skilled factory jobs that would entice older gang members to leave the gang have been lost to overseas competition. A transformed U.S. economy now prioritizes information and services over heavy industry. This shift in emphasis undermines labor unions that might have attracted former gang boys. Equally damaging has been the embrace of social policies that stress security and the needs of the wealthy, whereas weakening the economic safety net for the poor, for example, reducing welfare eligibility. William Julius Wilson found that the inability of inner-city males to obtain adequate jobs means that they cannot afford to marry and raise families. Criminal records acquired at an early age quickly lock these

LOOKING BACK TO LUIS'S STORY

Unlike Luis, many kids are not helped and remain in gangs longer than ever before. Do you see a way, considering the global information economy, to wean kids out of gangs? Are there any alternatives? What about easing the entry requirements for the military?

Getting High and Getting By: Drug Dealing Gangs and Gang Boys in Southwest Texas

Avelardo Valdez and Stephen J. Sifaneck are two gang experts that have studied the role that Mexican American gangs and gang members play in drug markets, and the relationship between gang members' drug use and drug-selling behaviors. Using an innovative research design that involved identifying and observing gang members creating focus groups (essentially group interviews, relying on in-group interaction, designed to obtain perceptions on a defined area of interest), and life history interviews, they gained in-depth knowledge of the lives of 160 males in twenty-six different Hispanic gangs operating in Southwest Texas.

GANG CATEGORIES

Valdez and Sifaneck found that gangs could be divided into two separate categories according to their involvement in drug dealing criminal enterprise. One grouping, made up of nineteen of the twenty-six gangs they identified, shun drug dealing and are organized as traditional, territory-based gangs. They engage in gang rituals, such as identification with distinct colors, hand signs, and gang "placas" (symbols), and are involved in a variety of criminal acts, including auto theft, burglary, robbery, vandalism, criminal mischief, and petty crime; some members deal drugs on their own. Members of these types of gangs tend to act as individuals. Their violence is personal and random rather than collective and organized. Gang membership offers protection from rivals, other gang boys or people in the community who threaten them; protection is extended to those members who are involved in drug-selling and dealing activities.

The second group was made up of the remaining seven gangs that were organized into criminal drug-dealing enterprises. These have a more clearly defined leadership that takes a share of the profits generated from all gang members involved in the business. These gangs are not concerned with territorial issues or "turf violations," and do not engage in random acts of violence such as drive-by shootings. Violence among these gangs tends to be more organized and related to drug distribution (although some members may be involved in other criminal enterprises, such as auto theft and fencing stolen goods).

THE GANG MEMBER'S ROLE

The second dimension discovered by Valdez and Sifaneck was an individual gang member's role in selling and dealing drugs within the gang. The one extreme of this dimension is the user–seller who is primarily buying drugs for personal consumption, and selling a portion of the drugs to offset the costs associated with his own personal drug use. The other extreme of this dimension includes the dealers, gang members who deal drugs (marijuana, cocaine, and heroin) for their own profit. The cross-classification of drug style with gang type is illustrated in Figure 8.A.

Homeboys

Homeboys are gang members who belong to a street gang whose criminal behavior tends to be more individual, less organized, and less gang directed. Most of their violence is centered on interpersonal fights and random situational acts of violence often associated with male bravado. Most of these user–sellers usually buy just what they are going to use to get "high" and sell small remaining quantities to reduce the costs associated with their own consumption. These members usually "score" small amounts for themselves, friends, and other associates.

Hustlers: Drug Dealers in Non-Dealing Gangs

In this category gang members identified as hustlers are dealing drugs for profit within a street gang that is not characterized as a drug-dealing organization. However, it does provide protection to hustlers within the territory controlled by the gang. Protection is extended to those persons, because they are members of the organization rather than because of their

Figure 8.A **A Typology of Drug Dealers and User–Sellers in Street and Drug Gangs**

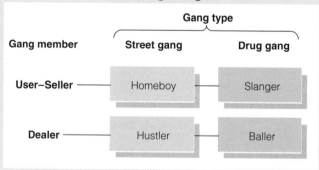

youths out of the job market so that remaining in a gang becomes an economic necessity.[64] In the wake of reduced opportunity for unskilled labor, gangs have become an important ghetto employer that offers low-level drug-dealing opportunities that are certainly not available in the non-gang world.[65]

Gender

Traditionally, gangs were considered a male-dominated enterprise. Of the more than a thousand groups included in Thrasher's original survey, only half a dozen were female gangs. Females were involved in gangs in three ways: as auxiliaries (or branches) of male gangs, as part of sexually mixed gangs, or as autonomous gangs.

drug selling activities. Profits generated by these hustlers are their own and are not used to support the collective activities of the street gang.

Slanger: Drug User/ Sellers in Drug Dealing Gangs

Gang members in this category are characterized as user–sellers in gangs that are organized as drug-dealing enterprises. Slangers are members who either choose not to participate in the higher levels of the gang's organized drug-dealing activities or who are excluded from those circles for various reasons. However, the slangers continue to use and sell drugs at an individual level mostly to help offset costs associated with their drug use and to support themselves economically. In the vernacular of the gangs, these members are dealing to "get high and get by." The slangers stand in contrast to the hard-core dealer members in the drug gang who are heavily involved in the gang's higher level organized drug distribution activities.

Ballers: Drug Dealers–Drug Dealing Gangs

Ballers are the individuals who control the drug distribution business in hard-core drug gangs. Ballers sit atop the gang's hierarchy and compose a leadership structure that provides protection to members against rival gangs and predatory adult criminals. Among these gang members, heroin use was generally discouraged, although as the gangs began to deal heroin, many ballers began shabanging (non-injection) and or picando (injecting), and some subsequently became addicted. One of the distinctions of ballers from seller–dealers, slangers, and homeboys is their generally lower visibility and the higher volume of drugs they deal. Furthermore, they avoid ostentatious aggressive behavior that attracts law enforcement like drive-by shootings. Violence among ballers is also more purposeful and revolved around business transactions.

GANGS IN CONTEXT

Valdez and Sifaneck found that gangs must be evaluated within the context of the community environment. Juvenile gang members' involvement in selling and dealing is influenced by the presence of adult criminals in the community. Many of these adult criminals were former juvenile gang members and later joined prison gangs. Their presence was a stabilizing force, giving the gang an intergenerational cohesiveness.

An important part of gang membership is protection it can give members in exchange for their commitment and obligation to the gang. Protection may often be misperceived by police as evidence that a gang is a drug-dealing enterprise when in reality, members may be operating independently from the gang as an organization. Often law enforcement personnel indiscriminately extend this perception to all Mexican American youth living in these neighborhoods resulting in continual harassment, shakedowns, and detainment of many innocent youth.

A serious consequence of this perception is that very often drug law enforcement indiscriminately arrests and prosecutes offenders without distinguishing the differences that constitute the four distinct types of gang members. Consequently, when "homeboys" are arrested for minor violations of drug laws, such as possession of small amounts of marijuana, they are often treated like "ballers" the big-time dealers. If gangs and gang members are to be dealt with in a realistic fashion, these distinctions must be recognized by law enforcement agents engaged in anti-gang activities.

CRITICAL THINKING

1. Of the four types of gang boys identified by Valdez and Sifaneck, which do you believe might be the easiest to wean away from the gang?
2. Is it realistic to believe that a government program could convince ballers to give up drug profits for some low-paying, albeit legitimate, job?

INFOTRAC COLLEGE EDITION RESEARCH

To read more about Hispanic gangs in the Southwest, go to the InfoTrac College Edition and read: L. Thomas Winfree Jr., Frances Bernat, and Finn-Aage Esbensen, "Hispanic and Anglo Gang Membership in Two Southwestern Cities," *The Social Science Journal* 38:105–118 (2001).

Source: Avelardo Valdez and Stephen J. Sifaneck, "Getting High and Getting By: Dimensions of Drug Selling Behaviors Among U.S. Mexican Gang Members in South Texas," *Journal of Research in Crime and Delinquency* 41:82–105 (2004).

Auxiliaries are a feminized version of the male gang name, such as the Lady Disciples rather than the Devil's Disciples.

Today the number of female gang members and female gangs is rapidly increasing and some jurisdictions report that 25 percent or more of all gang members are female.[66] However, national data indicate that (Figure 8.2) less than 10 percent of gang members are female; smaller cities and rural counties report a higher percentage of female gang membership compared to urban areas.[67]

Girls in the Gang Why do girls join gangs? There are a variety of reasons including, but not limited to financial opportunity, identity and status, peer pressure,

Figure 8.2 Percentage of Females in Gangs, by Area Type

Percent

Source: National Youth Gang Survey Analysis. Available at: www.iir.com/NYGC/nygsa/demographics.htm#anchorgender (accessed January 8, 2007).

family dysfunction, and protection.[68] Some admit that they join because they are bored and look to gangs for a social life; they are seeking fun and excitement and a means to find parties and meet boys. Still, others join simply because gangs are there in the neighborhood and are viewed as part of their way of life. And some are the children of gang members and are just following in their parents' footsteps.[69]

What benefits does gang membership offer to females? According to the "liberation" view, ganging can provide girls with a sense of "sisterhood," independence, and solidarity, as well as a chance to earn profit through illegal activities.

Mark Fleisher and Jessie Krienert's research in Illinois found that girls from tough inner-city neighborhoods drift into gangs to escape the turmoil of their home lives characterized by abuse, parental crime, and fatherless homes. Their affiliation begins when they hang around the street with gang boys, signaling their gang affiliation and symbolizing a lifestyle shift away from their home and school and into the street culture. The shift causes rifts with parents leading to more time on the street and closer gang ties.[70] These young girls, typically aged fourteen to fifteen are targets for sexual and criminal exploitation.

Although initial female gang participation may be forged by links to male gang members, once in gangs girls form close ties with other female members and engage in group criminal activity.[71] In contrast, the "social injury" view suggests that female members are still sexually exploited by male gang boys and are sometimes forced to exploit other females.

Girls who are members of male gang auxiliaries report that males control them by determining the arenas within which they can operate (i.e., the extent to which

The number and extent of girl gangs is increasing. In the Grape Street area of Los Angeles, a female gang member is about to kick another young woman. This is not a random or spontaneous attack, but part of the "court in" ceremony in which new members are initiated into the gang.

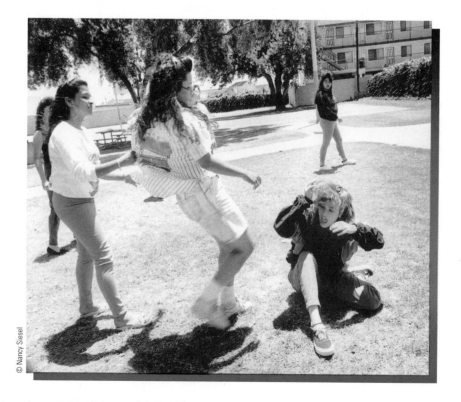

© Nancy Siesel

they may become involved in inter-gang violence). Males also play a divisive role in the girls' relationships with each other; this manipulation is absent for girls in independent gangs.[72] When criminologist Jody Miller studied female gangs in St. Louis, Missouri, and Columbus, Ohio, she found that girls in mixed gangs expressed little evidence of "sisterhood" and solidarity with other female gang members.[73] Rather, female gang members expressed hostility to other women in the gang, believing, for example, that those who suffered sexual assault by males in the same gang actually deserved what they got. Instead of trying to create a sense of sisterhood, female gang members tried to identify with males and view themselves as thereby becoming "one of the guys" in the gang.

Why then do girls join gangs if they are exploitive and provide little opportunities for "sisterhood?" Miller found that even though being a gang member is not a walk in the park, most girls join gangs in an effort to cope with their turbulent personal lives, which may provide them with an even harsher reality; they see the gang as an institution that can increase their status and improve their lifestyle. The gang provides them with an alternative to a tough urban lifestyle filled with the risk of violence and victimization. Many of the girl gang members had early exposure to neighborhood violence, had encounters with girl gangs while growing up, had experienced severe family problems (violence or abuse), and had close family members who were gang-involved.[74] Did they experience life benefits after they joined the gang? The evidence is mixed. Miller found that female gang members increased their delinquent activities and increased their risk of becoming a crime victim; they were more likely to suffer physical injury than girls who shunned gang membership. The risk of being sexually assaulted by male members of their own gang was also not insignificant. However, female gang membership did have some benefits: it protected female gang members from sexual assault by non-gang neighborhood men, which they viewed as a more dangerous and deadly risk.

Why do girls leave the gang? One not so surprising answer is that female gang members begin to drift away from gangs when they become young mothers. Fleisher and Krienert found that a majority of the Illinois gang girls they studied became inactive members soon after getting pregnant. Pregnancy leads to a disinterest in hanging around the streets and an interest in the safety of the fetus. Other girls became inactive after they decided to settle down and raise a family. But pregnancy seemed to be the primary motivating factor for leaving the gang life.[75]

Formation

Gang formation involves a sense of territoriality. Most gang members live in close proximity to one another, and their sense of belonging extends only to their small area of the city. At first, a gang may form when members of an ethnic minority join together for self-preservation. As the group gains domination over an area, it may view the area as its own territory, or turf, which needs to be defended from outsiders.

Once formed, gangs grow when youths who admire the older gang members "apply" and are accepted for membership. Sometimes the new members will be given a special identity that reflects their apprenticeship status. Joan Moore and her associates found that *klikas*, or youth cliques, in Hispanic gangs remain together as unique groups with separate names, identities, and experiences; they also have more intimate relationships among themselves than among the general gang membership.[76] She likens *klikas* to a particular class in a university, such as the class of 2006—a group of people gathered together as peers.

Moore also found that gangs can expand by including members' kin, even if they do not live in the neighborhood, and rival gang members who wish to join because they admire the gang's way of doing things. Adding outsiders gives the gang the ability to take over new territory. However, it also brings with it new problems, because it usually results in greater conflicts with rival gangs.

klikas
Subgroups of same-aged youths in Hispanic gangs that remain together and have separate names and a unique identity in the gang.

Leadership

Delinquent gangs tend to be small and transitory.[77] Youths often belong to more than a single group or clique and develop an extensive network of delinquent associates. Group roles can vary, and an adolescent who assumes a leadership role in one group may be a follower in another.

Those who assume leadership roles are described as "cool characters" who have earned their position by demonstrating fighting prowess, verbal quickness, or athletic distinction. They emphasize that leadership is held by one person and varies with particular activities, such as fighting, sex, and negotiations. In fact, in some gangs each age level has its own leaders. Older members are not necessarily considered leaders by younger members. In his analysis of Los Angeles gangs, Malcolm Klein observed that many gang leaders deny leadership. He overheard one gang boy claim, "We got no leaders, man. Everybody's a leader, and nobody can talk for nobody else."[78] The most plausible explanation of this ambivalence is the boy's fear that his decisions will conflict with those of other leaders.

There appear, then, to be diverse concepts of leadership, depending on the structure of the gang. Less-organized gangs are marked by diffuse and shifting leadership. More organized gangs have a clear chain of command and leaders who are supposed to plan activities and control members' behavior.[79]

Communications

Gangs seek recognition, both from their rivals and from the community. Image and reputation depend on the ability to communicate to the rest of the world.

One major source of communication is **graffiti** (see Figure 8.3). These wall writings are especially elaborate among Latino gangs, who call them *placasos* or *placa*, meaning *sign* or *plaque*. Latino graffiti usually contain the writer's street name and the name of the gang. Strength or power is asserted through the terms *rifa*, which means to rule, and *controllo*, indicating that the gang controls the area. Another common inscription is "p/v," for *por vida*; this refers to the fact that the gang expects to control the area "for life." The numeral 13 signifies that the gang is *loco*, or "wild." Crossed-out graffiti indicates that a territory is contested by a rival gang.

Gangs also communicate by means of a secret vocabulary. Members may refer to their *crew, posse, troop,* or *tribe.* Within larger gangs are "sets," who hang in particular neighborhoods, and "tips," small groups formed for particular purposes. Exhibit 8.1 contains other slang terms.

Flashing or tossing gang signs in the presence of rivals often escalates into a verbal or physical confrontation. Chicago gangs call this **representing**. Gang members will proclaim their affiliation and ask victims "Who do you ride?" or "What do you be about?"

graffiti
Inscriptions or drawings made on a wall or structure and used by delinquents for gang messages and turf definition.

To access a site that has a good selection of **West Coast gang graffiti**, go to www.thomsonedu.com/criminaljustice/siegel.

representing
Tossing or flashing gang signs in the presence of rivals, often escalating into a verbal or physical confrontation.

Figure 8.3 | Gang Symbols Used in Graffiti

National symbols of the Folk Nation gang

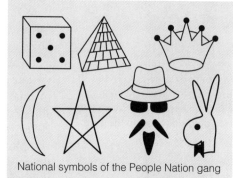

National symbols of the People Nation gang

Source: Polk County Florida Sheriff's Office, 2006. Available at: http://polksheriff.org/library/gangs/identifying.html (accessed January 8, 2007).

- **13 or XIII or X3 or TRECE**
  Thirteenth letter in the alphabet "M"; which symbolizes or identifies gang affiliation of Mexican heritage. Also may refer to allegiance to Southern California gangs.
- **14 or XIV or X4**
  Fourteenth letter of the alphabet "N"; refers to allegiance to Northern California or Norte Califas gangs.

- **8-BALL**
  A reference to a quantity of cocaine.
- **5-0**
  The police.
- **AK**
  Used to denote a semi-automatic assault rifle, such as AK47 or SKS rifles.
- **PV**
  Por vida—Spanish for "for life," "always."

An incorrect response will provoke an attack. False representing can be used to misinform witnesses and victims.

In some areas, gang members communicate their membership by wearing jackets with the name of their gang on the back. In Boston neighborhoods, certain articles of clothing (for example, sneakers) are worn to identify gang membership. In Los Angeles, the Crips are identified with the color blue and will wear some article of blue clothing to communicate their allegiance; their rivals, the Bloods, identify with the color red.

Ethnic and Racial Composition

According to the National Youth Gang Survey, African American and/or Hispanic/Latino youth predominate among documented gang members: About half are Latino, one-third African American, and about 10 percent European American with the rest being other races (e.g., Asian). This association applies to all types of environments except rural counties where African American gang members predominate. There is an association between gang membership size, gang-problem onset, and race/ethnicity characteristics: areas with smaller numbers of gang members or a relatively new emergence of gang problems are significantly more likely to report a greater percentage of

| Figure 8.4 | Racial Makeup of Gangs, by Area Type |

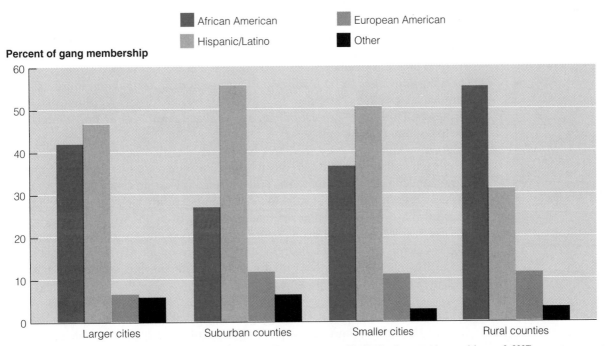

Source: National Youth Gang Survey Analysis. Available at: www.iir.com/NYGC/nygsa/demographics.htm#anchorregmat (accessed January 8, 2007).

European American gang members (Figure 8.4). Larger cities with newer gang problems are over twice as likely to report greater variation in racial/ethnic composition of gang members (that is, proportionally fewer African American and/or Hispanic/Latino gang members) than larger cities with long-standing gang problems.[80]

The ethnic distribution of gangs corresponds to their geographic location; the racial/ethnic composition of gangs is an extension of the characteristics of the larger community.[81] In Philadelphia and Detroit, the overwhelming number of gang members are African American. In New York and Los Angeles, Latino gangs predominate. Newly emerging immigrant groups are making their presence felt in gangs. Authorities in Buffalo, New York, estimate that 10 percent of their gang population is Jamaican. A significant portion of Honolulu's gangs are Filipinos.

African American Gangs

African American Gangs The first African American youth gangs were organized in the early 1920s.[82] Because they had few rival organizations, they were able to concentrate on criminal activity rather than defending their turf. By the 1930s, the expanding number of rival gangs spawned inner-city gang warfare.

In Los Angeles, the first African American youth gang formed in the 1920s was the Boozies. This gang virtually ran the inner city until the 1930s. In the next twenty years, a number of black gangs, including the Businessmen, Home Street, Slauson, and Neighborhood, emerged and met with varying degrees of criminal success. In the 1970s, the dominant Crips gang was formed. Other gangs merged into the Crips or affiliated with it by adding "Crips" to their name, so that the Main Street gang became the Main Street Crips. The dominance of the Crips has since been challenged by its arch rivals, the Bloods. Both of these groups, whose total membership exceeds twenty-five thousand youths, are heavily involved in drug trafficking.

In Chicago, the Blackstone Rangers dominated illicit activities for almost twenty-five years, beginning in the 1960s and lasting into the early 1990s, when its leader, Jeff Fort, and many of his associates were indicted and imprisoned.[83] The Rangers, who later evolved into the El Rukn gang, worked with "legitimate" businessmen to import and sell heroin. Earning millions in profits, they established businesses that helped them launder drug money. Though many of the convictions were later overturned, the power of El Rukn was ended.

One of the Rangers' chief rivals, the Black Gangster Disciples, morphed into the dominant gang in Chicago. They have a structure, activities, and relationships similar to traditional organized crime. Members are actively involved in politics through the formation of the "Growth and Development" movement. Gangster Disciples registered voters from the inner city and then "encouraged" the newly registered voters to vote for candidates loyal to their cause. While incarcerated, the Black Gangster Disciples united with allied gangs under the guise of the Brothers of Struggle (BOS). The gang continues to be involved in large-scale drug trafficking, murders, and white-collar crime.[84] They also have extensive ownership of "legitimate" private businesses. They offer "protection" against rival gangs and supply stolen merchandise to customers and employees.[85]

African American gang members have some unique characteristics. They frequently use nicknames. "Little 45" might be used by someone whose favorite weapon is a large handgun. Although TV shows portray gangs as wearing distinctive attire, members usually favor nondescript attire to reduce police scrutiny. However, gang members frequently have distinctive hairstyles, such as shaving or braids, which are designed to look like their leaders'. Tattooing is popular, and members often wear colored scarves or "rags" to identify their gang affiliation. It is also common for African American gang members to mark their territory with distinctive graffiti: drawings of guns, dollar signs, proclamations of individual power, and profanity.

Hispanic Gangs

Hispanic Gangs The popularity of gangs and gang culture is relatively high among youth of Hispanic background, explaining in part their disproportionate participation in gang membership.[86]

Hispanic and Asian American gang members beat up a teenage boy on the street as part of initiation into the gang. Mixed gangs are actually uncommon and most have a single ethnicity: Asian American, Hispanic, African American, or European American.

Hispanic gangs are made up of youths whose ethnic ancestry can be traced to one of several Spanish-speaking cultures. They are known for their fierce loyalty to their "home" gang. Admission to the gang usually involves an initiation ritual in which boys are required to prove their *machismo*. The most common test requires novices to fight several established members or to commit some crime, such as a robbery. The code of conduct associated with membership means never ratting on a brother, or even a rival.

In some areas, Hispanic gangs have a fixed leadership hierarchy. However, in Southern California, which has the largest concentration of Hispanic youth gangs, leadership is fluid. During times of crisis those with particular skills will assume command.[87] One boy will lead in combat, whereas another negotiates drug deals.

Hispanic gang members are known for their dress codes. Some wear dark-colored caps pulled down over the ears with a small roll at the bottom. Others wear a folded bandana over the forehead and tied in back. Another popular headpiece is the "stingy brim" fedora or a baseball cap with the wearer's nickname and gang affiliation written on the bill. Members favor tank-style T-shirts that give them quick access to weapons.

Members also mark off territory with colorful and intricate graffiti. Hispanic gang graffiti has very stylized lettering and frequently uses three-dimensional designs.

Hispanic gangs have a strong sense of turf, and a great deal of gang violence is directed at warding off any threat to their control. Slights by rivals, including put-downs, stare-downs ("mad-dogging"), defacing gang insignia, and territorial intrusions, can set off a violent confrontation, often with high-powered automatic weapons.

Asian Gangs Asian gangs are prominent in New York, Los Angeles, San Francisco, Seattle, and Houston. The earliest gangs, the Wah Ching, were formed in the nineteenth century by Chinese youths affiliated with adult crime groups (*tongs*). In the 1960s, two other gangs formed in San Francisco, the Joe Boys and Yu Li, and they now operate, along with the Wah Ching, in many major U.S. cities. National attention focused on the activities of these Chinese gangs in 1977 when a shootout in the Golden Dragon restaurant in San Francisco left five dead and eleven wounded.

In addition to Chinese gangs, Samoan gangs have operated on the West Coast, as have Vietnamese gangs. The formation of Vietnamese gangs can be tied to external factors, including racism and economic problems, and to internal problems, including family stress and failure to achieve the success enjoyed by other Asians. Vietnamese gangs are formed when youths feel they need their *ahns*, or brothers, for protection.[88]

Asian gang are unique and do not share many qualities with other ethnically centered groups. They tend to victimize members of their own ethnic group. They are more organized, have recognizable leaders, and are far more secretive than African American or Hispanic groups. They also tend to be far less territorial and less openly visible. Asian gangs are also known for the strict control gang elders have over younger members. Elders, some of whom may be in their thirties and forties are no longer engaged in street crime and violence, but may instead be involved in other forms of illegal activities such as running gambling parlors. They use the younger gang members to protect their business interests and to collect any unpaid gambling debts. In some jurisdictions, police can pressure the elders to control the violent tendencies of the younger members by threatening to crack down on their illegitimate business enterprises, (e.g., having patrol cars parked in front of suspected gambling locations).[89]

Anglo Gangs The first American youth gangs were made up of European American youths. During the 1950s, they competed with African American and Hispanic gangs in the nation's largest cities.

Today, Anglo gang activity is not uncommon, especially in smaller towns.[90] Many are derivatives of the English punk and **skinhead** movement of the 1970s. These youths, generally children of lower-class parents, sported wildly dyed hair often shaved into "mohawks," military clothes, and iron-cross earrings. Their creed was antiestablishment, and their anger was directed toward foreigners, who they believed were taking their jobs.

Today, European American gang members are often alienated middle-class youths rather than poor lower-class youths. They include "punkers" "stoners," "goths," and so on, who dress in heavy-metal fashions and engage in drug- and violence-related activities. Some espouse religious beliefs involving the occult and satanic worship. Some are obsessed with occult themes, suicide, ritual killings, and animal mutilations. They get involved in devil worship, tattoo themselves with occult symbols, and gouge their bodies to draw blood for satanic rituals.[91] Some skinhead groups are devoted to European American supremacist activities and are being actively recruited by adult hate groups.

A recent survey of almost six thousand youths found that about 25 percent of youths who claimed to be gang members were European American, a far higher number than that found in national surveys.[92]

Criminality and Violence

Regardless of their type, gang members typically commit more crimes than any other youths in the social environment.[93] Members self-report significantly more crime than nonmembers and the more enmeshed a youth is in a gang, the more likely he is to report criminal behavior, to have an official record, and to get sent to juvenile court; the gang membership–crime relationship begins as early as middle school.[94]

Although the association between gang membership and delinquency is unquestioned, there are actually three different explanations for the relationship.

- *Selection hypothesis*—kids with a history of crime and violence join gangs and maintain their persistent delinquency once they become members.
- *Facilitation hypothesis*—gang membership facilitates deviant behavior, because it provides the structure and group support for antisocial activities.
- *Enhancement hypothesis*—selection and facilitation work interactively increasing the likelihood of enhanced criminality.[95]

Gang criminality has numerous patterns.[96] Some gangs specialize in drug dealing. But not all gangs are major players in drug trafficking and those that are tend to distribute small amounts of drugs at the street level. The world of major dealing belongs to adults, not to gang youths.[97] Other gangs engage in a wide variety of criminal activity, ranging from felony assaults to drug dealing.[98] Gang members are most

skinhead
Member of European American supremacist gang, identified by a shaved skull and Nazi or Ku Klux Klan markings.

© Lyndsay Russell/Alamy

Although joining a gang does not turn otherwise law-abiding adolescents into chronic offenders, research does show that gang members increase the level and frequency of offending while involved in gang activities, and subsequently decrease their criminality once they leave the gang.

For an analysis of youth gang drug dealing, go to the website www. thomsonedu.com/criminaljustice/siegel.

commonly involved in such crimes as larceny/theft, aggravated assault, and burglary/breaking and entering; a significant portion are involved in street drug sales to generate profits for the gang.[99] Drug use is quite common. Geoffrey Hunt and his associates found that 82 percent of the female gang members they surveyed were multiple-drug users, using drugs such as cocaine, crack, LSD, PCP, methamphetamine, heroin, glue/inhalants, MDMA, and quaaludes.[100]

Do gang kids increase their involvement in criminal activity after they join gangs or do gangs recruit kids who are already high rate offenders? Data from the Rochester Youth Development Study (RYDS), a longitudinal cohort study of one thousand youths in upstate New York, supports the gang–crime association theory. Although only 30 percent of the youths in the sample report being gang members, they account for 65 percent of all reported delinquent acts. The RYDS data show that gang members account for 86 percent of all serious crimes, 63 percent of the alcohol use, and 61 percent of the drug abuse.[101] Gang members ratchet up their criminal activities. In the RYDS study, two-thirds (66 percent) of the chronic violent offenders were gang members.[102]

Gang Violence Not surprisingly, research shows that gang members are more violent than nonmembers. One reason is that kids who join gangs are also more likely to carry weapons than nonmembers.[103] Thornberry and his associates found that young gang members in Rochester, New York, were about ten times more likely to carry handguns than non-gang juvenile offenders, and gun-toting gang members committed about ten times more violent crimes than nonmembers.[104]

It is not surprising then that youth gangs are responsible for a disproportionate number of homicides. In two cities, Los Angeles and Chicago—considered the most gang-populated cities in the United States—over half of the annual homicides are attributed to gangs. Nationally, approximately one-fourth of all homicides are considered gang-related and the numbers are increasing.[105]

Research indicates that gang violence is impulsive and therefore comes in spurts. It usually involves defense of the gang and gang members' reputations.[106] Once the threat ends, the level of violence may recede, but it remains at a level higher than it was previously. Peaks in gang homicides tend to correspond to a series of escalating confrontations, usually over control of gang turf or a drug market.[107] The most dangerous areas are along disputed boundaries where a drug hot spot intersects with a turf hot spot. There are also "marauder" patterns in which members of rival gangs travel to their enemy's territory in search of victims.[108]

Violence is a core fact of gang formation and life.[109] Gang members feel threatened by other gangs and are wary of encroachments on their turf. It is not surprising that gangs try to recruit youths who are already gun owners; new members are likely to increase gun ownership and possession.[110] Gang members face a far greater chance of death at an early age than do nonmembers.[111]

Revenge, Honor, Courage, and Prestige When criminologist Scott Decker interviewed gang boys he found that violence is essential to the transformation of a peer group into a gang. When asked why he calls the group he belongs to a gang, one member replied: "There is more violence than a family. With a gang it's like fighting all the time, killing, shooting."[112]

When joining the gang, members may be forced to partake in violent rituals to prove their reliability. Gang members are ready to fight when others attack them or when they believe their territory or turf is being encroached upon. Violence may be directed against rival gang members accused of insults or against those involved in personal disputes. Gang members also expect to fight when they go to certain locations that are "off-limits" or attend events where violence is routine. Girl gang members may fight when they sense that a member of a rival gang is trying to hook up with their boyfriend. Gini Sykes spent two years hanging with girl gangs in New York City in order to develop an understanding of their lives and lifestyle. One girl, Tiny, told Gina how ferociousness made up for lack of stature:

> *Tiny fixed me with a cold stare that wiped away any earlier impression of childish cuteness. "See, we smaller girls, we go for your weak spot." Her gaze moved across my features. "Your face. Your throat. Your eyes, so we can blind you. I don't care if you have more weight on me. I'll still try to kill you because, you know, I have a bad temper—."*[113]

Tiny related the story of how she attacked a rival involved in a sexual encounter with her boyfriend:

> *"She was crying and begging, but she'd disrespected me in front of everybody. We started fighting and she pulled that blade out—." Tiny shrugged. "I just wasn't prepared. You can't tell when someone's got a razor in their mouth."*

After she was cut, Tiny went into a defensive rage, and

> *frantically felt for [her] wound, blood seeping between her fingers. Suddenly, in self-preservation, she grabbed [her rival's] neck, and blinded by her own blood, began smashing [the girl's] head into the concrete until [another gang member], hearing a siren, dragged her away. The girl had slashed Tiny's face eleven times.*

Gang members are sensitive to any rivals who question their honor. Once an insult is perceived, the gang's honor cannot be restored until the "debt" is repaid. Police efforts to cool down gang disputes only delay the revenge, which can be a beating or a drive-by shooting. Random acts of revenge have become so common that physicians now consider them a significant health problem—a major contributor to early morbidity and mortality among adolescents and children in major gang cities.[114]

Violence is used to maintain the gang's internal discipline. If subordinates disobey orders, perhaps by using rather than selling drugs, they may be subject to disciplinary action by other gang members.

Another common gang crime is extortion, called "turf tax," which involves forcing people to pay the gang to be protected from dangerous neighborhood youths. **Prestige crimes** occur when a gang member steals or assaults someone to gain prestige in the gang. These crimes may be part of an initiation rite or an effort to establish a special reputation, a position of responsibility, or a leadership role; to prevail in an internal power struggle; or to respond to a challenge from a rival.

✔ Checkpoints

WHY DO YOUTHS JOIN GANGS?

Although gangs flourish in inner-city areas, gang membership cannot be assumed to be solely a function of lower-class identity. Many lower-class youths do not join gangs, and middle-class youths are found in suburban skinhead groups. Let's look at some of the suspected causes of gang delinquency.

The Anthropological View

In the 1950s, Herbert Block and Arthur Niederhoffer suggested that gangs appeal to adolescents' longing for the tribal process that sustained their ancestors.[115] They found that gang processes do seem similar to the puberty rites of some tribal cultures; gang rituals help the child bridge the gap between childhood and adulthood. For example, tattoos and other identifying marks are an integral part of gang culture. Gang

---

prestige crimes
Stealing or assaulting someone to gain prestige in the neighborhood; often part of gang initiation rites.

CHECKPOINTS

■ Group relations are an essential part of childhood.

■ Most delinquent acts are committed in small groups.

■ Delinquent peers seem to sustain antisocial behaviors.

■ Sometimes antisocial cliques and friendship groups are transformed into organized gangs that have names, characteristic garb, signs, and permanence.

■ Gangs submerged during the 1960s, but have once again proliferated in urban areas.

■ Today, gangs are located in both urban and suburban areas.

■ Urban gangs have been involved in migration to other locales.

■ Most gangs are male-only, but the number of female gang members seems to be increasing.

■ Most gangs are racially and ethnically homogenous.

■ Most gangs are Hispanic or African American.

■ Although some gang boys have migrated, most gangs are homegrown.

■ Violence is a central part of the gang experience. Most gang kids carry and use weapons.

What Does This Mean to Me?

Hip Hop Nation

Gang expert John Hagedorn has noted that music is not often discussed in gang studies, although it has a strong influence on gangs in the United States and abroad. (John Hagedorn, "The Global Impact of Gangs," *Journal of Contemporary Criminal Justice* 21:153–169 (2005).

In Nigeria, he notes, gangs of Muslim youth enforce Sharia (Islamic Law) while wearing gold chains, using and selling drugs, and listening to rap music. Throughout Africa, Latin America, and Asia, rap music has captured the imagination of youth who find that embracing hip-hop helps them identify with African American youth in the United States who are rebelling against authority. Among the founders of hip-hop were former gang members, like Afrika Bambaata in the South Bronx, who consciously saw hip-hop as a way to pull youth away from gangs.

Do you believe that listening to rap and hip-hop encourages kids to join gangs and embrace the gang lifestyle and culture? What would you expect them to listen to, Bach and Beethoven?

initiation ceremonies are similar to the activities of young men in Pacific Island cultures. Many gangs put new members through a hazing to make sure they have "heart," a feature similar to tribal rites. In tribal societies, initiation into a cult is viewed as the death of childhood. By analogy, boys in lower-class urban areas yearn to join the gang and "really start to live." Membership in the gang "means the youth gives up his life as a child and assumes a new way of life."[116] Gang names are suggestive of "totemic ancestors," because they usually are symbolic (Cobras, Jaguars, and Kings, for example).

The Gang Prevention and Intervention Survey found that fully two-thirds of gang members reported having members in their gang whose parents are also active members. These data indicate that ganging is passed on as a rite of passage from one generation to the next.[117] James Diego Vigil has described the rituals of gang initiation, which include pummeling to show that the boy is ready to leave his matricentric (mother-dominated) household; this is reminiscent of tribal initiation rites.[118] These rituals become an important part of gang activities. Hand signs and graffiti have a tribal flavor. Gang members adopt nicknames that reflect personality or physical traits: the more volatile are called "Crazy," "Loco," or "Psycho," and those who wear glasses are dubbed "Professor."[119]

The Social Disorganization/Sociocultural View

Sociologists have commonly viewed the destructive sociocultural forces in poor inner-city areas as the major cause of gang formation. Thrasher introduced this concept, and it is found in the classic studies of Richard Cloward and Lloyd Ohlin and of Albert Cohen.[120] Irving Spergel's study *Racketville, Slumtown, and Haulburg* found that Slumtown—the area with the lowest income and the largest population—had the highest number of violent gangs.[121] According to Spergel, the gang gives lower-class youths a means of attaining status. Malcolm Klein's research of the late 1960s and 1970s also found that typical gang members came from dysfunctional and destitute families and lacked adequate role models.[122]

The social disorganization/sociocultural view retains its prominent position today. In *Barrio Gangs*,[123] Vigil shows that gang members are pushed into membership, because of poverty and minority status. Those who join gangs are the most marginal youths in their neighborhoods and families. Vigil finds that barrio dwellers experience psychological, economic, and social "stressors." Gang members usually have more than one of these problems, causing them to suffer from "multiple marginality." Barrio youths join gangs seeking a sense of belonging.[124]

Overall, the sociocultural view assumes that gangs are a natural response to lower-class life and a status-generating medium for boys whose aspirations cannot be realized by legitimate means. Youths who join gangs may hold conventional goals, but are either unwilling or unable to accomplish them through conventional means.[125] Gangs are not solely made up of youths who seek deviant peers to compensate for parental brutality or incompetence. They recruit youths from many different kinds of families. The gang thus is a coalition of troubled youths who are socialized mainly by the streets rather than by conventional institutions.[126]

Anomie/Alienation View

According to this view, conditions of anomie/alienation encourage gang formation on both a cultural and individual level. On a cultural level, youths are encouraged to join gangs during periods of social, economic, and cultural turmoil.[127] Immigration or emigration, rapidly expanding or contracting populations, and the incursion of different racial/ethnic groups, or even different segments or generations of the same racial/ethnic population, can create fragmented communities and gang problems.[128]

Historically, gangs formed during the Russian Revolution of 1917 and after the crumbling of the Soviet Union in the early 1990s. The rise of right-wing youth gangs in Germany is associated with the unification of East and West Germany. Skinhead groups have formed in Germany in response to immigration from Turkey and North Africa. In the United States, gangs have formed in areas where rapid change has unsettled communities. The gangs and militia groups in present day Iraq may have formed as a response to the upheaval in that society.

On an individual level, gang membership has appeal to adolescents who are alienated from both their families as well as the mainstream of society. It is not surprising that a) kids who have had problems with the law and suffer juvenile justice processing are more likely to join gangs than non-stigmatized kids, and b) joining gangs further involves them in criminal activities.[129]

The Psychological View

Some believe that gangs serve as an outlet for disturbed youths who suffer a multitude of personal problems and deficits. For example, Lewis Yablonsky found that violent gangs recruit their members from among the more sociopathic youths living in poverty-stricken communities.[130] Yablonsky views the sociopathic youth as one who "has not been trained to have human feelings or compassion or responsibility for another."[131]

Malcolm Klein's analysis of Los Angeles gang members also found that many suffer from a variety of personal deficits, including low self-concept, social deficits, poor impulse control, and limited life skills.[132] In their in-depth study of Rochester youth, Thornberry and his colleagues found that those who joined gangs suffered from a multitude of social problems, including early involvement in delinquency, violence, and drug abuse, dysfunctional family relations, educational deficits, and involvement with deviant peers.[133]

The Rational Choice View

Some youths may make a rational choice to join a gang. Members of the underclass turn to gangs as a method of obtaining desired goods and services, either directly, through theft and extortion, or indirectly, through drug dealing and weapons sales. In this case, joining a gang can be viewed as an "employment decision." Mercer Sullivan's study of Brooklyn gangs found that members call success at crime "getting paid." Gang boys also refer to the rewards of crime as "getting over," which refers to their pride at "beating the system" even though they are far from the economic mainstream.[134] According to this view, the gang boy has long been involved in criminal activity *prior* to his gang membership, and he joins the gang as a means of improving his illegal "productivity."[135]

Gang membership is *not* a necessary precondition for delinquency. Felix Padilla found this when he studied the Diamonds, a Latino gang in Chicago.[136] The decision to join the gang was made after an assessment of legitimate opportunities. The Diamonds made collective business decisions, and individuals who made their own deals were penalized. The gang maintained a distinct structure and carried out other functions similar to those of legitimate enterprises, including recruiting personnel and financing business ventures.

Drug use is a big part of the gang experience and drug users may join gangs to enhance availability of drugs and support for their usage.[137] Terence Thornberry and his colleagues at the Rochester Youth Development Study (RYDS) found that before youths join gangs, their substance abuse and delinquency rates are no higher than those of non-gang members. When they are in the gang, their crime and drug abuse rates increase, only to decrease when they leave the gang. Thornberry concludes that gangs facilitate criminality rather than provide a haven for youths who are disturbed or already highly delinquent. This research is important, because it lends support to the life course model: events that take place during the life cycle, such as joining a gang, have a significant impact on criminal behavior and drug abuse.[138]

Personal Safety According to Spergel, some adolescents choose to join gangs from a "rational calculation" to achieve safety.[139] Youths who are new to a community may believe they will be harassed or attacked if they remain "unaffiliated." Girls also join gangs for protection. Though they may be exploited by male gang members, they are protected from assaults by non-gang males in the neighborhood.[140]

Motivation may have its roots in inter-race or inter-ethnic rivalry; youths who reside in an area dominated by a different racial or ethnic group may be persuaded that gang membership is a means of protection. Ironically, gang members are more likely to be attacked than nonmembers.

Fun and Support Some youths join gangs simply to have fun.[141] They enjoy hanging out with others like themselves and want to get involved in exciting experiences. There is evidence that youths learn pro-gang attitudes from their peers and that these attitudes direct them to join gangs.[142]

Some experts suggest that youths join gangs in an effort to obtain a family-like atmosphere. Many gang members report that they have limited contact with their parents, many of whom are unemployed and have substance abuse problems.[143] Those members who have strained family relations are also the ones most likely to be involved in the most serious and frequent criminal activity.[144] Kids may join gangs then to compensate for the lack of a family life they have experienced at home. Concept Summary 8.1 summarizes these views. ✔ Checkpoints

CHECKPOINTS

■ There are different types of gangs—some are social, others criminal.

■ Gang membership seems to be aging; kids are staying longer in gangs.

■ Gangs communicate through wall writings (graffiti) and have their own slang terms and hand signs.

■ Many gangs are involved in drug dealing, whereas others specialize in violence.

■ There are a number of reasons why kids join gangs: anthropological, social, psychological, and rational choice views have been offered.

Concept Summary

Views of Gang Formation

View	Premise	Evidence
Anthropological	Gangs appeal to kids' tribal instincts.	Use of totems, signs, secret languages, and symbols.
Sociocultural	Gangs form because of destructive sociocultural forces in disorganized inner-city areas.	Concentration of gangs in inner-city areas.
Anomie/Alienation	Alienated kids join gangs. Anomic, social, and economic conditions encourage gang activity.	Upswing in gang activities after market forces create anomic situations. Gang activity increases with globalization.
Psychological	Kids with personality problems form gangs and become leaders.	Antisocial, destructive behavior patterns. Increase in violence.
Rational choice	Kids join gangs for protection, fun, and survival.	Presence of party gangs. Gang members protect one another.

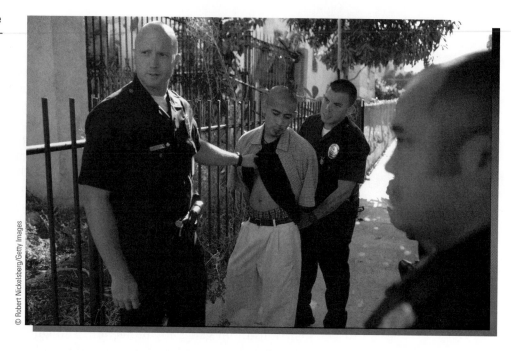

Over 25 Hispanic street gangs compete in the Rampart neighborhood of Los Angeles for the drug trade. Los Angeles' violent crime rates, traditionally one of the highest in California, have recently fallen as figures show a crime shift to outlying counties where real estate prices are more affordable. Police gang sweeps, such as the one shown here that occurred on August 6, 2006, may also convince members to relocate.

© Robert Nickelsberg/Getty Images

CONTROLLING GANG ACTIVITY

Two methods are used to control gang activity. One involves targeting by criminal justice agencies, and the other involves social service efforts. These methods will be discussed in the next sections.

Law Enforcement Efforts

In recent years gang control has often been left to local police departments. Gang control takes three basic forms:

1. *Youth services programs,* in which traditional police personnel, usually from the youth unit, are given responsibility for gang control

2. *Gang details,* in which one or more police officers, usually from youth or detective units, are assigned exclusively to gang-control work

3. *Gang units,* established solely to deal with gang problems, to which one or more officers are assigned exclusively to gang-control work.[145]

The most recent NYGS found that about one in four law enforcement agencies with a gang problem now operate a gang unit, including more than half of larger cities. Across all area types, agencies with long-standing gang problems and/or higher numbers of documented gang members are more likely to report operating a gang unit.[146] As Figure 8.5 shows the number of gang units in less populated areas is growing, whereas their counterparts in urban areas has declined.

The Chicago Police Department's gang crime section maintains intelligence on gang problems and trains its more than four hundred officers to deal with gang problems. Officers identify street gang members and enter their names in a computer bank that is programmed to alert the unit if the youths are picked up or arrested. Other police departments engage in "gang-breaking" activities. They attempt to arrest, prosecute, convict, and incarcerate gang leaders. For example, Los Angeles police conduct sweeps, in which more than a thousand officers are put on the street to round up gang members. Police say the sweeps let the gangs know "who the streets belong to" and show neighborhood residents that someone cares.[147]

Figure 8.5

Police Departments That Have Created Gang Units, by Area Type

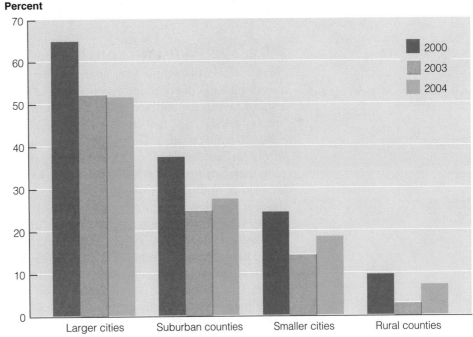

Percent

Source: National Youth Gang Survey Analysis, 2006. Available at: www.iir.com/NYGC/nygsa/gang_units.htm (accessed January 8, 2007).

Community Control Efforts

During the late nineteenth century, social workers of the YMCA worked with youths in Chicago gangs.[148] During the 1950s, the **detached street worker** program was developed in major centers of gang activity. Social workers went into the community to work with gangs on their own turf. They participated in gang activities and tried to get to know their members. The purpose was to act as advocates for the youths, to provide them with positive role models, and to treat individual problems.

Detached street worker programs are sometimes credited with curbing gang activities in the 1950s and 1960s, although some critics claimed that they turned delinquent groups into legitimate neighborhood organizations.[149] Others believe they helped maintain group solidarity, and as a result, new members were drawn to gangs.

Today, there are numerous community-level programs designed to limit gang activity. Some employ recreation areas open in the evening hours that provide supervised activities.[150] In some areas, citywide coordinating groups help orient gang-control efforts. In Los Angeles County, the Gang Alternative Prevention Program (GAPP) provides prevention services to juveniles before they become entrenched in gangs, including (1) individual and group counseling, (2) bicultural and bilingual services to adolescents and their parents, and (3) special programs, such as tutoring, parent training, job development, and recreational and educational experiences.[151] Some police departments also sponsor prevention programs such as school-based lectures, police-school liaisons, recreation programs, and street worker programs that offer counseling, assistance to parents, and other services.

Still another approach has been to involve schools in gang-control programs. Some invite law enforcement agents to lecture students on the dangers of gang involvement and teach them gang-resistance techniques. Others provide resources that can help parents prevent their children from joining gangs, or if they already are members, get them out.

detached street workers
Social workers who go out into the community and establish close relationships with juvenile gangs with the goal of modifying gang behavior to conform to conventional behaviors and help gang members get jobs and educational opportunities.

LOOKING BACK TO LUIS'S STORY

Luis was put in an aftercare plan that included ongoing drug counseling and support, individual counseling, intensive supervision and monitoring, group supports, and placement in an alternative educational setting. Can such measures turn kids living in high-risk neighborhoods around or was Luis's success a fluke?

Sociologist Irving Spergel, a leading expert on gangs, has developed a model for helping communities deal with gang-involved youth that has become the basis for gang-control efforts around the nation. His model includes the five distinct strategies contained in Exhibit 8.2.

Why Gang Control Is Difficult

Gang control can be difficult to attain. While aggressive police tactics can work, they also run the risk of becoming overzealous and alienating the community. Take for instance Los Angeles's anti-gang unit, the Community Resources Against Street Hoodlums (CRASH), which at its peak contained two hundred sworn officers. The unit conducted aggressive anti-gang actions, including Operation Hammer, which involved the unit moving through some of the city's toughest neighborhoods, arresting gang members for the slightest infractions, including wearing colors, flashing signs, jaywalking, and curfew violations. By making twenty-five thousand arrests per year, the unit significantly reduced gang activity. Problems began to emerge. Unit members developed a warlike mentality and CRASH officers began resisting supervision and flagrantly ignoring policies and procedures. This subculture eventually gave rise to the Rampart Corruption Scandal, in which Rampart CRASH unit officers in Los Angeles were found to be engaging in hard-core criminal activity. Officers admitted to attacking known gang members and falsely accusing them of crimes they had not committed. As a consequence, approximately ten years after it had been fully staffed and promoted as the ideal in anti-gang enforcement, LAPD's gang unit was shut down, because of corruption, the use of excessive force, and civil rights violations; the city had paid out about $70 million to settle lawsuits related to the scandal.[152] The Ramparts scandal serves as a cautionary tale for police departments attempting to control gang activity.

Social and economic solutions seem equally challenging. Experts suggest that to reduce the gang problem, hundreds of thousands of high-paying jobs are needed. Economic opportunities might prove to be particularly effective, because surveys reveal that many gang members might leave gangs if such opportunities existed.[153] This solution does not, however, seem practical. Many of the jobs for which undereducated gang boys can qualify are now being shipped overseas. Highly paid manufacturing jobs are particularly hard to obtain. It is unlikely that a boy who has five years as a Crip on his resume will be in demand for legitimate work opportunities. The more embedded youths become in criminal

LOOKING BACK TO LUIS'S STORY

How can probation officers and social workers best assist young people who may be gang affiliated? What can be done to prevent young people from joining gangs and/or help them get out of gang involvement?

For more on **gang prevention efforts**, go to the website www.thomsonedu.com/criminaljustice/siegel.

Exhibit 8.2	The Elements of Spergel's Community Gang Control Program

1. Community mobilization, including citizens, youth, community groups, and agencies.

2. Provision of academic, economic, and social opportunities. Special school training and job programs are especially critical for older gang members who are not in school, but may be ready to leave the gang or decrease participation in criminal gang activity for many reasons, including maturation and the need to provide for family.

3. Social intervention, using street outreach workers to engage gang-involved youth.

4. Gang suppression, including formal and informal social control procedures of the juvenile and criminal justice systems and community agencies and groups. Community-based agencies and local groups must collaborate with juvenile and criminal justice agencies in the surveillance and sharing of information under conditions that protect the community and the civil liberties of youths.

5. Organizational change and development—that is, the appropriate organization and integration of the preceding strategies and potential reallocation of resources.

Sources: Irving Spergel and Candice Kane, *Community-Based Youth Agency Model* (Washington, DC: Office of Juvenile Justice and Delinquency Prevention, 1990); Jim Burch and Candice Kane, *Implementing the OJJDP Comprehensive Gang Model* (Washington, DC: Office of Juvenile Justice and Delinquency Prevention, 1999).

enterprise, the less likely they are to find meaningful adult work. It is unlikely that gang members can suddenly be transformed into highly paid professionals.

Although social solutions to the gang problem seem elusive, the evidence shows that gang involvement is a socio-ecological phenomenon and must be treated as such. Youths who live in areas where their needs cannot be met by existing institutions join gangs when gang members are there to recruit them.[154] Social causes demand social solutions. Programs that enhance the lives of adolescents are the key to reducing gang delinquency. A more effective alternative would be to devote more resources to the most deteriorated urban areas, even if it requires pulling funds from other groups that receive government aid, such as the elderly.[155]

SUMMARY

- Peer relations are a critical element of maturation.
- Many experts believe that maintaining delinquent friends is a significant cause of antisocial behaviors.
- Some experts believe that criminal kids seek each other out.
- Gangs are law-violating youth groups that use special vocabulary, clothing, signs, colors, graffiti, and names, and whose members are committed to antisocial behavior.
- Gangs are a serious problem in many cities.
- Gangs have been around since the eighteenth century.
- The gang problem slowed down for a while in the 1960s, then re-emerged in the 1970s.
- There are now thousands of gangs containing more than 750,000 members.
- Most gang members are male, ages fourteen to twenty-one, and live in urban areas. Gangs can be classified by their structure, behavior, or status. Some are believed to be social groups, others are criminally oriented, and still others are violent.

- Hundreds of thousands of crimes are believed to be committed annually by gangs.
- Although some gangs specialize in drug dealing, gang kids engage in a wide variety of criminal offenses.
- Violence is an important part of being a gang member.
- Although most gang members are male, the number of females in gangs is growing at a faster pace. African American and Hispanic gangs predominate, but European American and Asian gangs are also quite common.
- We are still not sure what causes gangs. One view is that they serve as a bridge between adolescence and adulthood when adult control is lacking. Another view suggests that gangs serve as an alternative means of advancement for disadvantaged youths. Still another view is that some gangs are havens for disturbed youths.

KEY TERMS

cliques, p. 179
crowds, p. 179
controversial status youth, p. 179
gang, p. 181
interstitial group, p. 182

disorganized neighborhood, p. 185
near-groups, p. 187
barrio, p. 187
klikas, p. 191
graffiti, p. 192

representing, p. 192
skinhead, p. 196
prestige crimes, p. 198
detached street workers, p. 203

QUESTIONS FOR DISCUSSION

1. Do gangs serve a purpose? Differentiate between a gang and a fraternity.
2. Discuss the differences between violent, criminal, and drug-oriented gangs.
3. How do gangs in suburban areas differ from inner-city gangs?
4. Do delinquents have cold and distant relationships with their peers?
5. Can gangs be controlled without changing the economic opportunity structure of society? Are there any truly meaningful alternatives to gangs today for lower-class youths?

6. Can you think of other rituals in society that reflect an affinity or longing for more tribal times? (*Hint:* Have you ever pledged a fraternity or sorority, gone to a wedding, or attended a football game?) Do TV shows like "Survivor" show a longing for more tribal times? After all, they even use tribal names for the competing teams.

You are a professor at a local state university who teaches courses on delinquent behavior. One day you are approached by the director of the president's National Task Force on Gangs (NTFG). This group has been formed to pool resources from a variety of federal agencies, ranging from the FBI to Health and Human Services, in order to provide local jurisdictions with a comprehensive plan to fight gangs. The director claims that the gang problem is big and becoming bigger. Thousands of gangs are operating around the country, with hundreds of thousands of members. Government sources, he claims, indicate that there has been a significant growth in gang membership over the past twenty years. So far, the government has not been able to do anything at either a state or national level to stem this growing tide of organized criminal activity. The NTFG would like you to be part of the team that provides state and local jurisdictions with a gang control activity model, which, if implemented, would provide a cost-effective means of reducing both gang membership and gang activity.

- Would you recommend that police employ anti-gang units that use tactics developed in the fight against organized crime families?

- Would you recommend the redevelopment of deteriorated neighborhoods in which gangs flourish?

- Would you try to educate kids about the dangers of gang membership?

- Would you tell the director that gangs have always existed and there is probably not much the government can do to reduce their numbers?

DOING RESEARCH ON THE WEB

To read more about gang prevention efforts, go to InfoTrac College Edition and check out Lonnie Jackson, "Understanding and Responding to Youth Gangs: a Juvenile Corrections Approach," *Corrections Today 16*:62 (August 1999). To do more research on gangs, use "gangs" as a key word.

To read some comprehensive visions of gang prevention, go to the website **www.thomsonedu.com/criminaljustice/siegel**.

Schools and Delinquency

© David McNew/Getty Images

CHAPTER OBJECTIVES

After reading this chapter you should:

1. Understand the crisis that is facing the education system.
2. Be aware of the association between school failure and delinquency.
3. Be familiar with the factors that cause school failure.
4. Know what is meant by the term tracking.
5. Recognize the problem of truancy and what is being done to limit its occurrence.
6. Be familiar with the reasons why kids drop out of school.
7. Understand the nature of school crime and school shootings.
8. Know what school administrators are now doing to prevent delinquency on campus.
9. Be familiar with the various school-based delinquency prevention efforts.
10. Know the legal rights of students.

Ciara, age eleven, lives in the East Harlem borough of New York City with her mother and three siblings. Her father is not involved with the family, so they struggle to make ends meet and rely on Ciara's grandmother to provide for much of the children's care. From an early age, Ciara has had problems in school, both behaviorally and academically. Significantly behind her grade level in reading, regularly challenging her teachers and other adults, and being disruptive in class, Ciara was at great risk for dropping out of school and becoming involved in further delinquent behavior. And the group of older troubled teens whom she considered to be her only friends set poor examples for behavior, causing more problems for Ciara. The one area where she seemed confident and happy was on the basketball court, where Ciara exhibited talent and a love for the game.

When her school started a mandatory after-school program, Ciara began attending Drum Power, a youth leadership program that provides young people with an opportunity to learn the techniques and cultural/historical significance of West African Traditional, Afro-Cuban, and Afro-Brazilian drumming. The goal of the program is to build self-esteem and self-confidence through discovering the rewards of discipline, teamwork, creativity, responsibility, and self-respect. Interested in music, Ciara was drawn to both the power and rhythm of hand drumming. The process of learning traditional hand drumming requires discipline, commitment, and practice, and students learn that they can achieve their goals by employing their own positive energy and self-determination.

Ciara thrived in the program. Although she still posed many challenges to school staff and was at risk due to her living and community environment, she showed great interest, motivation, and success in the Drum Power program. She loved the drums and music, and was able to connect with her youth counselors running the program. Because Drum Power was based at the school, the program counselors could communicate on a daily basis with Ciara's teachers and the school staff regarding her progress and they were able to discuss any ongoing concerns. This provided immediate resolution when there were problems and ongoing accountability for Ciara. The program counselors also remained in close contact with her mother.

Participating in Drum Power for several years allowed Ciara to establish excellent relationships with her program counselors, who in turn provided great encouragement to Ciara, having a positive impact on her decisions and choices. Drumming was good for Ciara and her interest in music grew, but it was her relationships with the program counselors that made the most difference for her. She started to understand how her behavior and bad choices were affecting her life. Ciara learned the importance of self-control and setting priorities for herself daily. Seeing what a difference these things made for her, she could also begin to have a more positive vision for her life. Ciara's mother became more involved with school and also became involved with the Drum Power professionals. The support of the practitioners at school and at the Drum Power program was helpful to Ciara's mother, who had been struggling with her own set of issues, and now she was better able to encourage her daughter to be successful.

Ciara eventually graduated from the program. She continued with her education and hopes to attend college upon graduation from high school. She stayed out of the juvenile justice system and was able to make significant changes in her life with the support of the counselors at Drum Power.

School officials must make daily decisions on discipline and crime prevention, something they may not have thought much about when they decided on a career in education!

Because so much of an adolescent's time is spent in school, it would seem logical that some relationship exists between delinquent behavior and what is happening—or not happening—in classrooms.

academic achievement
Being successful in a school environment.

Numerous studies have confirmed that delinquency is related to **academic achievement** and experts have concluded that many of the underlying problems of delinquency, as well as their prevention and control, are intimately connected with the nature and quality of the school experience.[1] Although there are differences of opinion, most theorists agree that problems associated with the educational system bear some responsibility for the relatively high rate of juvenile crime.

In this chapter we first explore how educational achievement and delinquency are related and what factors in the school experience appear to contribute to delinquent behavior. Next, we turn to delinquency in the school setting—vandalism, theft, violence, and so on. Finally, we look at the attempts made by schools to prevent delinquency.

THE SCHOOL IN MODERN AMERICAN SOCIETY

The school plays a significant role in shaping the values of children.[2] In contrast to earlier periods, when formal education was a privilege of the upper classes, the U.S. system of compulsory public education has made schooling a legal obligation. Today, more than 90 percent of school-age children attend school, compared with only 7 percent in 1890.[3]

In contrast to the earlier, agrarian days of U.S. history, when most adolescents shared in the work of the family, today's young people spend most of their time in school. The school has become the primary instrument of socialization, the "basic conduit through which the community and adult influences enter into the lives of adolescents."[4]

Because young people spend a longer time in school, their adolescence is prolonged. As long as students are still dependent on their families and have not entered the work world, they are not considered adults. The responsibilities of adulthood come later to modern-day youths than to those in earlier generations, and some experts see this prolonged childhood as one factor contributing to the irresponsible and often irrational behavior of many juveniles who commit delinquent acts.

 The **U.S. Department of Education** seeks to ensure equal access to education and promote educational excellence for all Americans. View its website by going to www.thomsonedu.com/criminaljustice/siegel.

Socialization and Status

Another significant aspect of the educational experience is that children spend their school hours with their peers, and most of their activities after school take place with school friends. Young people rely increasingly on school friends and become less interested in adult role models. The norms of the peer culture are often at odds with those of adult society, and a pseudo-culture with a distinct social system develops. Law-abiding behavior may not be among the values promoted in such an atmosphere. Kids enmeshed in this youth culture may admire bravery, defiance, and having fun much more than adults do.

The school has become a primary determinant of economic and social status. In this technological age, education is the key to a job that will mark its holder as "successful." No longer can parents ensure the status of their children through social class alone. Educational achievement has become of equal, if not greater, importance as a determinant of economic success. This emphasis on the value of education is fostered by parents, the media, and the schools themselves. Regardless of their social or economic background, most children grow up believing education is the key to success. However, many youths do not meet acceptable standards of school achievement. Whether failure is measured by test scores, not being promoted, or dropping out, the incidence of school failure continues to be a major problem for U.S. society. A single school failure often leads to a pattern of chronic failure. The links between school failure and delinquency will be explored more fully in the next sections.

The school itself has become an engine of social change and improvement. School desegregation efforts has heralded a new age of improved race relations, which in the long run may help reduce crime rates. African American youth educated in states where a higher proportion of their classmates are European American experience significantly lower incarceration rates later as adults. The constructive effects of racial inclusiveness in the school setting have grown stronger over time highlighting the need for further educational integration.[5]

Education Trends

The role schools play in adolescent development is underscored by the problems faced by the U.S. education system. There has been some improvement in reading, math, and science achievement during the past decade, but in some cases improvements have been minimal. Figure 9.1 contains the latest data from The National Assessment of Educational Progress (NAEP), which has assessed performance in reading in grades 4 and 8 in public and private schools since 1992. The average reading score of fourth-graders today is not significantly different from that in 1992. The average score of eighth-graders rose slightly. In both grades, females outperformed males, and European American and Asian/Pacific Islander students had higher average scores than American Indian, African American, and Hispanic students. Income influenced reading scores: the level of poverty in the school, as measured by the percentage of students eligible for free or reduced-price lunch, was negatively associated with student achievement in both grades.

Cross-national surveys that compare academic achievement show that the United States trails in critical academic areas. As Table 9.1 shows, eighth-graders in the United States still lag behind students in some less-affluent nations (Hungary, Malaysia) in math achievement. High school students in the United States are consistently outperformed by those from Asian and some European countries on international assessments of mathematics and science, In contrast, fourth-graders score as well or better than most of their international peers. Does this mean that kids in the United States fall further behind as their education progresses?[6] One reason may be that many secondary school math and science teachers did not major in the subjects they teach. Another reason is that the United States, the richest country in the world, devotes less of its resources to education than do many other nations. Spending on elementary and secondary education (as a percentage of the U.S. gross domestic product) is less than that of other nations. And budget cutting has reduced educational resources in many communities and curtailed state support for local school systems.

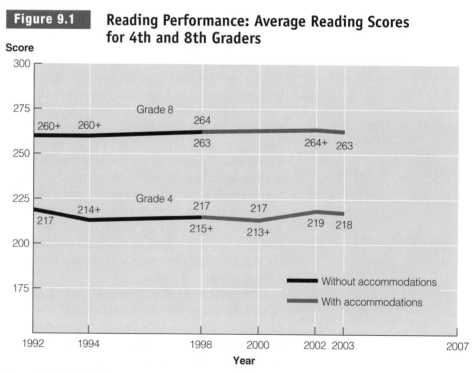

Figure 9.1   **Reading Performance: Average Reading Scores for 4th and 8th Graders**

Source: National Center for Education Statistics, *The Condition of Education 2005 in Brief.* Available at: http://nces.ed.gov/pubs2005/2005095.pdf, p. 7 (accessed January 9, 2007).

Table 9.1	Average Mathematics Scale Scores of Eighth-Grade Students By Country

Country	Average score
− International average	**466**
+ Singapore	605
+ Korea, Republic of	589
+ Hong Kong	586
+ Chinese Taipei	585
+ Japan	570
+ Belgium-Flemish	537
+ Netherlands	536
+ Estonia	531
+ Hungary	529
• Malaysia	508
• Latvia	508
• Russian Federation	508
• Slovak Republic	508
• Australia	505
• (United States)	**504**
• Lithuania	502
• Sweden	499
• Scotland	498

+ Average is higher than the U.S. average

• Average is not measurably different from the U.S. average

− Average is lower than the U.S. average

Sources: P. Gonzales, J.C Guzman, L. Partelow, E. Pahlke, L. Jocelyn, D Kastberg, and T. Williams, *Highlights From the Trends in International Mathematics and Science Study (TIMSS)* 2003. Available at: http://nces.ed.gov/programs/coe/2006/analysis/sa_table.asp?tableID=553 and http://nces.ed.gov/pubs2005/timss03/tables.asp (accessed November 29, 2006).

Educational Problems

These data highlight the fact that many children are at risk for educational problems, school failure, and delinquency. It is now estimated that one of every five children are unprepared when they first enter school at kindergarten. These disadvantaged children enter school lagging behind their more advantaged peers in terms of the knowledge and social competencies that are widely recognized as enabling children to perform at even the most basic level.[7] They face substantial gaps in measures of reading and mathematics proficiency, in prosocial behaviors and behavior problems, and in readiness to learn. About 18 percent of children overall are not familiar with basic rules of print or writing (e.g., knowing that English is read from left to right and top to bottom, or where a story ends), that fraction is 32 percent for children whose mothers have less than a high school education but only 8 percent for children whose mothers have a college degree or higher. Many children from disadvantaged backgrounds fail to meet grade-level expectations on core subjects. As a consequence they face higher rates of special education placement and grade repetition.[8] These disadvantages may increase their risk of leaving school early and becoming dropouts.

Dropping Out

Every day, hundreds of thousands of youth are absent from school; many are absent without an excuse and deemed **truant**. Some large cities report that unexcused absences can number in the thousands on certain days. Truancy can lead to school failure and dropping out.

When kids are alienated from school and persistent truants they may want to **drop out**, a step that may make them even more prone to antisocial behaviors. Though dropout rates are in decline (Figure 9.2) about 4 percent of both private and public high school students leave high school between the beginning of one school year and the beginning of the next without earning a high school diploma or its equivalent (e.g., a General Educational Development certificate, or GED).[9] Currently, about 10 percent of all students dropout before they finish high school.[10]

Dropping out is a serious issue, because once kids leave school they are more likely to engage in drug abuse and antisocial behavior and to persist in criminal behavior throughout adulthood.[11] The effects of dropping out may last a lifetime. Dropouts are much more likely to be unemployed than graduates, another factor that may increase their involvement in antisocial activities.

Why Do Kids Drop Out? When surveyed, most dropouts say they left either because they did not like school or because they wanted to get a job. Other risk factors include low academic achievement, poor problem-solving ability, low self-esteem, difficulty getting along with teachers, dissatisfaction with school, substance abuse, and being too old for grade level.[12] Some dropouts could not get along with teachers, had been expelled, or were under suspension. Almost half of all female dropouts left school, because they were pregnant or had already given birth.

Can technology help reduce truancy? Some school systems believe it can have an effect. Here Elliot Feldman, director of Alternative Education for the Boston school system, holds a new cell phone information device for truancy officers. The device helps keep track of kids found not in school and provides easy access to information regarding where the student is supposed to be. The bundle of paper is what truant officers used to have to refer to when looking up students' records.

truant
Being out of school without permission.

drop out
To leave school before completing the required program of education.

Poverty and family dysfunction increase the chances of dropping out among all racial and ethnic groups. Dropouts are more likely than graduates to have lived in single-parent families headed by parents who were educational underachievers themselves.

Some youths have no choice but to drop out. They are pushed out of school because they lack attention or have poor attendance records. Teachers label them troublemakers, and school administrators use suspensions, transfers, and other means to "convince" them that leaving school is their only option. Because minority students often come from circumstances that interfere with their attendance, they are more likely to be labeled *disobedient*.

Race-based disciplinary practices may help sustain high minority dropout rates. Although the African American dropout rate has declined faster than the European American dropout rate over the past three decades, minority students still drop out at a higher rate than European American students.

In his thoughtful book *Creating the Dropout*, Sherman Dorn shows that graduation rates slowly but steadily rose during the twentieth century, whereas regional, racial, and ethnic differences in graduation rates declined.[13] Nonetheless, Dorn argues that the relatively high dropout rate among minorities is the legacy of disciplinary policies instituted more than forty years ago when educational administrators

Figure 9.2 Status Dropout Rates of Youths Aged 16 to 24, by Race/Ethnicity

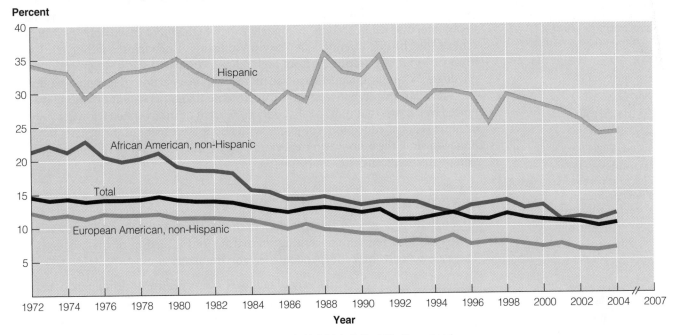

Source: National Center for Education Statistics, *The Condition of Education 2005 in Brief.* Available at: http://nces.ed.gov/pubs2005/2005095.pdf, p. 11 (accessed January 9, 2007).

opposed to school desegregation employed a policy of race-based suspension and expulsion directed at convincing minority students to leave previously all-European American high school districts. This legacy still affects contemporary school districts. Dorn believes that the dropout problem is a function of inequality of educational opportunity rather than the failure of individual students. The proportion of African Americans who fail to graduate from high school remains high compared with the proportion of European Americans who fail to graduate, because the educational system still fails to provide minority group members with the services and support they need.

LOOKING BACK TO CIARA'S STORY

Did the program Ciara attended shield her from the problems that she may have encountered in school? Can you think of other types of non-stigmatizing alternatives?

Though the drop out rate has declined, it remains a significant social problem with consequences that extend into adulthood and beyond. Estimates indicate that a high school dropout costs society $243,000 to $388,000 in present-value dollars over his or her lifetime, and if they turn to crime, costs society $1.3 to $1.5 million in present-value dollars.[14]

ACADEMIC PERFORMANCE AND DELINQUENCY

underachievers
Those who fail to meet expected levels of school achievement.

Whether they drop out or not, kids who do poorly in school are at risk for delinquent behavior; students who are chronic **underachievers** in school are among the most likely to be delinquent.[15] In fact, researchers find that school failure is a stronger predictor of delinquency than variables such as economic class membership, racial or ethnic background, or peer-group relations. Studies that compare the academic records of delinquents and non-delinquents—including their scores on standardized tests, failure rate, and other academic measures—have found that delinquents are often academically deficient, a condition that may lead to their leaving school and becoming involved in antisocial activities.[16] Children who report that they do not like school and do not do well in school are most likely to self-report delinquent acts.[17]

To learn more about math and science education, go to the Eisenhower National Clearinghouse for Mathematics and Science Education (ENC) by going to the website at www.thomsonedu.com/criminaljustice/siegel.

school failure
Failing to achieve success in school can result in frustration, anger, and reduced self-esteem, which may contribute to delinquent behavior.

In contrast, at-risk youths who do well in school are often able to avoid delinquent involvement.[18]

An association between academic failure and delinquency is commonly found among chronic offenders. Those leaving school without a diploma were more likely to become involved in chronic delinquency than high school graduates.[19] Only 9 percent of the chronic offenders in Marvin Wolfgang's Philadelphia *Delinquency in a Birth Cohort* study graduated from high school, compared with 74 percent of non-offenders.[20] Chronic offenders also had more disciplinary actions than non-offenders.[21]

The relationship between school achievement and persistent offending is supported by surveys that indicate that only 40 percent of incarcerated felons had twelve or more years of education, compared with about 80 percent of the general population.[22] In sum, the school experience can be a significant factor in shaping the direction of an adolescent's life course.

School Failure and Delinquency

Although there is general agreement that **school failure** and delinquency are related, some questions remain concerning the nature and direction of this relationship. There are actually three independent views on the association:

1. School failure is a direct cause of delinquent behavior. Children who fail at school soon feel frustrated and rejected. Believing they will never achieve success through conventional means, they seek out like-minded companions and together engage in antisocial behaviors. Educational failure evokes negative responses from important people in the child's life, including teachers, parents, and prospective employers. These reactions help solidify feelings of inadequacy, and in some cases, lead to a pattern of chronic delinquency.

2. School failure leads to emotional and psychological problems that are the actual cause of antisocial behavior. Academic failure reduces self-esteem and reduced self-esteem is an immediate cause of delinquency. Studies using a variety of measures of academic competence and self-esteem demonstrate that good students have a better attitude about themselves than poor students; low self-esteem has been found to contribute to delinquent behavior.[23] The association then runs from school failure to low self-concept to delinquency.

3. School failure and delinquency share a common cause. Both are caused by another condition so that although it appears that school failure precedes and causes delinquency the association is actually false and spurious. For example, prior substance abuse leads to both delinquency and school failure.

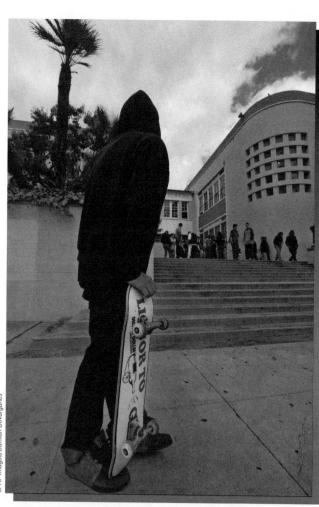

Andrew, a high school dropout, waits for his friends outside his old campus, Hollywood High School in Los Angeles. Some critics charge that California's high school dropout problem has been underestimated, with more accurate figures showing that only half of the African American, Hispanic, and American Indian students in the state are earning regular high school diplomas. Education experts are calling for greater accountability over the high number of dropouts instead of the current emphasis on test scores. What can be done to keep kids in school? Should high school dropouts be allowed to serve in the military?

Correlates of School Failure

Despite disagreement over the direction the relationship takes, there is little argument that delinquent behavior is influenced by educational experiences. A number of factors have been linked to school failure; the most prominent are discussed in the next sections.

Personal Problems Some kids have personal problems that they br̶̶̶̶
to school. Because of their deprived background and ragged socia̶̶̶
kids lack the verbal skills that are a prerequisite of educational success̶
in a dysfunctional family; a turbulent family life has been linked t̶
underachievement.

Still others suffer psychological abnormality. The adolescent who̶
at school and engages in delinquency may be experiencing depression a̶
mental deficits that are associated both with their school failure and involve̶
antisocial activities.[25] Personality structure may also be a key factor. Kids wh̶
low self-control are more likely to engage in delinquent behavior *and* fail in s̶
An impulsive personality can cause both school failure and delinquency.[26]

Social Class During the 1950s, research by Albert Cohen indicated that delinque̶
was a phenomenon of working-class students who were poorly equipped to functi̶
in middle-class schools. Cohen referred to this phenomenon as a failure to live up t̶
"middle-class measuring rods."[27] Jackson Toby reinforced this concept, contending
that the disadvantages lower-class children have in school (for example, lack of verbal
skills) are a result of their position in the social structure and that these disadvantages
foster delinquency.[28] These views have been supported by the higher-than-average
dropout rates among lower-class children.

One reason why lower-class children may do poorly in school is that economic
problems require them to take part-time jobs. Working while in school seems to
lower commitment to educational achievement and is associated with higher levels of
delinquent behavior.[29]

Not all experts agree with the social class–school failure–delinquency hypothesis.
There is evidence that boys who do poorly in school, regardless of their socioeconomic background, are more likely to be delinquent than those who perform well.[30]
Affluent students may be equally affected by school failure as lower-class youths, and
that middle-class youths who do poorly in school are more likely to become delinquent than their lower-class peers who also have academic performance problems.[31]
In fact, because expectations are so much higher for affluent youth, their failure to
achieve in school may have a more profound effect on their behavior and well-being
than it does on lower-class youth, who face so many other social problems. Not
surprisingly, middle-class kids who are involved in antisocial behaviors are more
likely to experience school failure than lower-class youth who experience similar social problems.[32]

tracking
Dividing students into groups according to their ability and achievement levels.

Tracking Most researchers have looked at academic **tracking**—dividing students
into groups according to ability and achievement level—as a contributor to school
failure. Placement in a non-college track means consignment to educational oblivion
without apparent purpose. Studies indicate that non–college-track students experience greater academic failure and progressive deterioration of achievement, participate less in extracurricular activities, have an increased tendency to drop out, and
commit more delinquent acts.

Some school officials begin tracking students in the lowest grade levels. Educators separate youths into groups that have innocuous names ("special enrichment
program"), but may carry the taint of academic incompetence. High school students may be tracked within individual subjects based on ability. Classes may be labeled in descending order: advanced placement, academically enriched, average,
basic, and remedial. It is common for students to have all their courses in only one
or two tracks.[33]

The effects of school labels accumulate over time. If students fail academically,
they are often destined to fail again. Repeated instances of failure can help produce
the career of the "misfit" or "dropout." Using a tracking system keeps certain students
from having any hope of achieving academic success, thereby causing lack of motivation, which may foster delinquent behavior.[34]

Some students may become alienated from school because they believe that educators have gone overboard in an attempt to maintain school discipline. Leonard Lopez and his son, Vincent, sit at home surrounded by folders of newspaper clippings and legal papers in Arlington, Texas. Vincent was removed from his junior high school and placed into an alternative school for five days after one of his drawings was considered as showing gang affiliation.

CHECKPOINTS

■ The school is one of the key institutions of socialization in contemporary society.

■ Despite its great wealth, the United States lags behind many nations in academic achievement.

■ Academic performance has been linked to delinquency.

■ School failure is linked to delinquency.

■ The causes of school failure include class conflict, alienation, and tracking.

■ Many kids drop out of school before they graduate and dropping out has been linked to delinquent behavior.

Alienation Student alienation has also been identified as a link between school failure and delinquency. Students who report they neither like school nor care about their teachers' opinions are more likely to exhibit delinquent behaviors.[35] Alienation may be a function of students' inability to see the relevance of what they are taught. The gap between their education and the real world leads some students to feel that the school experience is a waste of time.[36]

Many students, particularly those from low-income families, believe schooling has no payoff. Because this legitimate channel appears to be meaningless, delinquent acts become increasingly more attractive. This middle- and upper-class bias is evident in the preeminent role of the college preparatory curriculum in many school systems. Furthermore, both methods of instruction and curriculum materials reflect middle-class language and customs that have little meaning for the disadvantaged child.

In contrast, kids who form a bond to school also find that this commitment helps them resist delinquency-producing factors in the environment, for example, antisocial peers.[37] Youths who report liking school and being involved in school activities are also less likely to engage in delinquent behaviors.[38] Involvement is especially beneficial in schools where students are treated fairly and where rules are laid out clearly.[39] Schools might lower delinquency rates if they can develop programs that counteract student alienation. ✔ Checkpoints

DELINQUENCY IN SCHOOLS

In its pioneering study of school crime, *Violent Schools–Safe Schools* (1977),[40] the federal government found that although teenagers spend only 25 percent of their time in school, 40 percent of the robberies and 36 percent of the physical attacks involving this age group occur there. School crime has remained a national concern since the *Safe Schools* study was published.

The latest survey of school crime found that the more than 54 million students in pre-kindergarten through grade twelve were victims of about 1.9 million nonfatal crimes at school. As Figure 9.3 indicates, like the general crime rate school crime is also in a decline. Nonetheless, in a single year about 1.2 million thefts and 740,000 violent crimes—150,000 of which were serious violent crimes (rape, sexual assault, robbery, and aggravated assault)—occur on or near school grounds. These figures

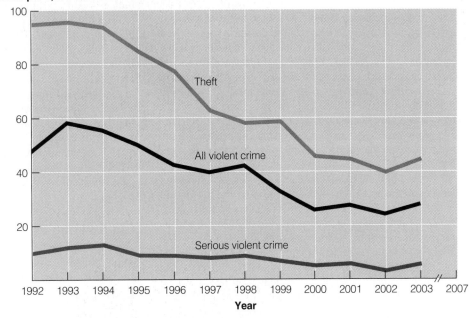

Figure 9.3 Rate of Student-Reported Nonfatal Crimes Against Students Aged 12 to 18 per 1,000 Students, by Type of Crime and Location

Source: National Center for Education Statistics, *The Condition of Education 2005 in Brief.* Available at: http://nces.ed.gov/pubs2005/2005095.pdf, p. 17 (accessed January 9, 2007).

represent victimization rates of forty-five thefts and twenty-eight violent crimes, including six serious violent crimes per one thousand students. About fifteen kids are killed in school each year and about eight commit suicide.[41]

Students are not alone in facing the threat of school crime. Teachers are the victims of approximately 183,000 total nonfatal crimes at school each year, including 119,000 thefts and 65,000 violent crimes. On average, these figures translate into an annual rate of thirty-nine crimes per one thousand teachers, including twenty-five thefts and fourteen violent crimes (including two serious violent crimes) per one thousand teachers. In addition, school bullying is a serious ongoing problem in our nation's schools. The following Focus on Delinquency feature analyzes this important topic.

School Shootings

Although incidents of school-based crime and violence are not uncommon, it is the highly publicized incidents of fatal school shootings that have helped focus attention on school crime. Upward of 10 percent of students report bringing weapons to school on a regular basis and knowing this, many of their peers report being afraid of school-based gun violence.[42]

Who brings guns to schools? Many of these kids have a history of being abused and bullied; many perceive a lack of support from peers, parents, and teachers.[43] Kids who have been the victims of crime themselves and who hang with peers who carry weapons are the ones most likely to bring guns to school.[44] A troubled kid who has little social support but carries deadly weapons makes for an explosive situation.

Nature and Extent of Shootings Social scientists are now conducting studies of these events in order to determine their trends and patterns. One recent study examined all 220 school-related shooting incidents over a five year period.[45] Of the 220 shooting incidents, 172 were homicides, 30 were suicides, 11 were homicide-suicides,

Bullying in School

Experts define bullying among children as repeated, negative acts committed by one or more children against another. These negative acts may be physical or verbal in nature—for example, hitting or kicking, teasing, or taunting—or they may involve indirect actions such as manipulating friendships or purposely excluding other children from activities. Implicit in this definition is an imbalance in real or perceived power between the bully and victim. It may come as no surprise that 30 percent to 50 percent of gay, lesbian, and bisexual young people, a group not known for its ability for violent retaliation, experience harassment in an educational setting.

Studies of bullying suggest that there are short- and long-term consequences for both the perpetrators and the victims of bullying. Students who are chronic victims of bullying experience more physical and psychological problems than their peers who are not harassed by other children, and they tend not to grow out of the role of victim. Young people mistreated by peers may not want to be in school and may thereby miss out on the benefits of school connectedness as well as educational advancement. Longitudinal studies have found that victims of bullying in early grades also reported being bullied several years later. Studies also suggest that chronically victimized students may, as adults, be at increased risk for depression, poor self-esteem, and other mental health problems, including schizophrenia.

It is not only victims who are at risk for short- and long-term problems; bullies too are at increased risk for negative outcomes.

One researcher found that those elementary students who were bullies attended school less frequently and were more likely to drop out than other students. Several studies suggest that bullying in early childhood may be a critical risk factor in the development of future problems with violence and delinquency. Bullies are more likely to carry weapons in and out of school and get involved with substance abuse. Research conducted in Scandinavia found that, in addition to threatening other children, bullies were several times more likely than their non-bullying peers to commit antisocial acts, including vandalism, fighting, theft, drunkenness, and truancy, and to have an arrest by young adulthood. Another study of more than five hundred children found that aggressive behavior at the age of eight was a powerful predictor of criminality and violent behavior at the age of thirty.

Can Bullying Be Prevented?

The first and best-known intervention to reduce bullying among school children was launched by Dan Olweus in Norway and Sweden in the early 1980s. Prompted by the suicides of several severely victimized children, Norway supported the development and implementation of a comprehensive program to address bullying among children in school. The program involved interventions at multiple levels:

- *School-wide interventions.* A survey of bullying problems at each school, increased supervision, school-wide assemblies, and teacher in-service training to raise the awareness of children and school staff regarding bullying

5 were legal intervention deaths, and 2 were unintentional firearm-related deaths. Although highly publicized in the media, this amounted to 0.068 per one hundred thousand students being affected by these shootings.

The research discovered that most shooting incidents occur around the start of the school day, the lunch period, or the end of the school day. In most of the shootings (55 percent), a note, threat, or other action indicating risk for violence occurred prior to the event. Shooters were also likely to have expressed some form of suicidal behavior prior to the event and to report having been bullied by their peers. These patterns may help school officials one day to identify potential risk factors and respond in a timely fashion.

Who Is the School Shooter? The United States Secret Service has developed a profile of school shootings and shooters after evaluating forty-one school shooters who participated in thirty-seven incidents.[46] They found that most attacks were neither spontaneous nor impulsive. Shooters typically developed a plan of attack well in advance; more than half had considered the attack for at least two weeks and had a plan for at least two days.

The attackers' mental anguish was well known, and these kids had come to the attention of someone (school officials, police, fellow students), because of their bizarre and disturbing behavior prior to the attack's taking place. One student told more than twenty friends beforehand about his plans, which included killing students and planting bombs. Threats were communicated in more than three-fourths of the cases, and in more than half the incidents the attacker told more than one person. Some people knew detailed information, whereas others knew "something spectacu-

- *Classroom-level interventions.* The establishment of classroom rules against bullying, regular class meetings to discuss bullying at school, and meetings with all parents
- *Individual-level interventions.* Discussions with students to identify bullies and victims

The program was found to be highly effective in reducing bullying and other antisocial behavior among students in primary and junior high schools. Within two years of implementation, both boys' and girls' self-reports indicated that bullying had decreased by half. These changes in behavior were more pronounced the longer the program was in effect. Moreover, students reported significant decreases in rates of truancy, vandalism, and theft, and indicated that their school's climate was significantly more positive as a result of the program. Not surprisingly, those schools that had implemented more of the program's components experienced the most marked changes in behavior. The core components of the Olweus anti-bullying program have been adapted for use in several other cultures, including Canada, England, and the United States and the results have been similar: schools that were more active in implementing the program observed the most marked changes in reported behaviors.

CRITICAL THINKING

Should schoolyard bullies be expelled from school? Would such a measure make a bad situation worse? For example, might expelled bullies shift their aggressive behavior from the schoolyard to the community?

INFOTRAC COLLEGE EDITION RESEARCH

To learn more about the cause and effect of school bullying, use the term in a key word search on InfoTrac College Edition.

Sources: Kate Gross, "Homophobic Bullying and Schools—Responding to the Challenge," *Youth Studies Australia* 25:60 (2006); T. Joscelyne and S. Holttum, "Children's Explanations of Aggressive Incidents at School Within an Attribution Framework," *Child and Adolescent Mental Health* 11:104–110 (2006); Dan Olweus, "A Useful Evaluation Design, and Effects of the Olweus Bullying Prevention Program," *Psychology, Crime & Law* 11:389–402 (2005); Jane Ireland and Rachel Monaghan, "Behaviors Indicative of Bullying among Young and Juvenile Male Offenders: A Study of Perpetrator and Victim Characteristics," *Aggressive Behavior* 32:172–180 (2006); Marla Eisenberg, Dianne Neumark-Sztainer, and Cheryl Perry, "Peer Harassment, School Connectedness, and Academic Achievement," *Journal of School Health* 73:311–316 (2003); Michael Reiff, "Bullying and Violence," *Journal of Developmental & Behavioral Pediatrics* 24:296–297 (2003); Susan Limber and Maury Nation, "Bullying Among Children and Youth," in June Arnette and Marjorie Walsleben, eds., *Combating Fear and Restoring Safety in Schools* (Washington, DC: Office of Juvenile Justice and Delinquency Prevention, 1998); Dan Olweus, "Victimization by Peers: Antecedents and Long-Term Outcomes," in K. H. Rubin and J. B. Asendorf, eds., *Social Withdrawal, Inhibitions, and Shyness* (Hillsdale, NJ: Erlbaum, 1993), pp. 315–341.

lar" was going to happen on a particular date. In less than one-fourth of the cases, the attacker make a direct threat to the target.

The Secret Service found that the shooters came from such a wide variety of backgrounds that no accurate or useful profile of at-risk kids could be developed. They ranged in age from eleven to twenty-one and came from a wide variety of ethnic and racial backgrounds; about 25 percent of the shooters were minority-group members. Some lived in intact families with strong ties to the community, whereas others were reared in foster homes with histories of neglect. Some were excellent students, whereas others were poor academic performers. Shooters could not be characterized as isolated and alienated; some had many friends and were considered popular. There was no evidence that shootings were a result of the onset of mental disorder. Drugs and alcohol seemed to have little involvement in school violence.

What the Secret Service did find, however, was that many of the shooters had a history of feeling extremely depressed or desperate, because they had been picked on or bullied. About three-fourths either threatened to kill themselves, made suicidal gestures, or tried to kill themselves before the attack; six of the students studied killed themselves during the incident. The most frequent motivation was revenge. More than three-fourths were known to hold a grievance, real or imagined, against the target or others. In most cases, this was the first violent act against the target. Two-thirds of the attackers described feeling persecuted, and in more than three-fourths of the incidents the attackers had difficulty coping with a major change in a significant relationship or a loss of status, such as a lost love or a humiliating failure. Not surprisingly, most shooters had experience with guns and weapons and had access to them at home.

What Does This Mean to Me?

"Bully for You!"

Research indicates that more than 80 percent of school kids say their behavior includes physical aggression, social ridicule, teasing, name calling, and issuing threats over the previous thirty days. Some kids seem proud of being bullies and think their behavior, no matter how destructive, is just having fun at another's expense. Many of us have been the targets of bullies, but felt unsure of how to cope with the problem. If you told the teacher or your parents you were a wimp; if you did nothing you remained a target.

1. Did you ever find yourself having to confront this dilemma, and if so what did you do to solve the problem?
2. Do you believe there is a link between being the victim of bullying and engaging in school violence? The Columbine shooters were believed to be targets of bullying. Could this have been the spark that caused them to snap?

The Causes of School Crime

What are the suspected causes of school violence? Research indicates that they may be found at the individual, school, and community level.

School Level Causes Schools with a high proportion of students behind grade level in reading, with many students from families on welfare, and located in a community with high unemployment, crime, and poverty rates, are also at risk for delinquency.[47] Research shows that the perpetrators and victims of school crime cannot be neatly divided into separate groups and that many offenders have been victims of delinquency themselves.[48] It is possible that school-based crimes have "survival value": striking back against a weaker victim is a method of regaining lost possessions or self-respect.[49]

Research also shows that school climate—the social and educational atmosphere of a school—is one of the most important predictors of campus crime and violence levels. In a landmark study, Rami Benbenishty and Ron Avi Astor compared violence rates in schools located in California with those in Israel. Although rates were different, the forms and patterns of school victimization—verbal-social, threats, and physical violence—were extremely similar across gender, ethnicity/culture, age, and within and between the U.S. and Israeli schools systems. What they did find was that victimization was dependent on the climate that exists within schools. School policy, teachers' relationships with students, and peer group support explained violence levels better than community or family influences.[50]

Individual Level Causes School crime may be a function of the number of students with emotional and psychological problems. Kids who feel isolated and alone with little parental attention may be the most prone to alienation and substance abuse.[51] As substance abuse increases among the student body, so too may school violence rates. The level of student drinking may increase violent crime rates.[52] Because heavy drinking reduces cognitive ability, information processing skills, and the ability to process and react to verbal and nonverbal behavior, a student argument may quickly turn into a full-scale battle.[53] Schools with high-achieving students, a drug-free environment, strong discipline, and involved parents have fewer behavioral problems in the student body.[54]

Community Level Causes Schools experiencing drug abuse and crime are most likely to be found in socially disorganized neighborhoods. A number of researchers have observed that school crime is a function of the community in which the school is located. Schools in high-crime areas experience more crime than schools in safer areas; there is less fear in schools in safer neighborhoods than in high-crime ones. Students who report being afraid in school are actually *more afraid* of being in city parks, streets, or subways.[55]

Other research efforts confirm the community influences on school crime. Communities with a high percentage of two-parent families experience fewer school problems; neighborhoods with high population density and transient populations also have problem-prone schools.[56] One study of violent crimes in the schools of Stockholm, Sweden, found that, although only one-fifth of schools were located in areas of social instability and disorganization, almost a third of all school crime happened in these schools.[57] This analysis suggests that it may be futile to attempt to eliminate school crime without considering the impact prevention efforts will have on the community.

Reducing School Crime

Schools around the country have mounted a campaign to reduce the incidence of delinquency on campus. Nearly all states have developed some sort of crime-free, weapon-free, or safe-school zone statute.[58] Most have defined these zones to include school transportation and school-sponsored functions. Schools are also cooperating with court officials and probation officers to share information and monitor students who have criminal records. School districts are formulating crisis prevention and intervention policies and are directing individual schools to develop safe-school plans.

Some schools have instituted strict controls over student activity—for example, making locker searches, preventing students from having lunch off campus, and using patrols to monitor drug use. According to one national survey, a majority of schools have adopted a **zero tolerance policy** that mandates predetermined punishments for specific offenses, most often possession of drugs, weapons, and tobacco, and also for engaging in violent behaviors.[59]

zero tolerance policy
Mandating specific consequences or punishments for delinquent acts and not allowing anyone to avoid these consequences.

School Security Efforts Almost every school attempts to restrict entry of dangerous persons by having visitors sign in before entering, and most close the campus for lunch. Schools have attempted to ensure the physical safety of students and staff by using mechanical security devices such as surveillance cameras, metal detectors, and electronic barriers to keep out intruders, and have also employed roving security guards.[60] Security measures include the following:

- *Access control.* About 75 percent of all schools control access to school buildings by locking or monitoring doors.
- *Control lighting.* Some administrators keep buildings dark at night, believing that brightly illuminated schools give the buildings too high a profile and attract vandals who might have not bothered with the facility, or even noticed it, if the premises were not illuminated.[61]
- *Gates.* About one-third of schools control access to school grounds with locked or monitored gates.

The local high school can be the single most dangerous area in the neighborhood. Brawls, fights, theft, and drug use are not uncommon. Schools have designed a number of security measures to crack down on crime. Here, students at Thomas Jefferson High School in Los Angeles are ordered to tuck in their shirts before entering school in the aftermath of two apparently racially motivated student brawls. A number of students suffered injuries while fleeing from a lunch period brawl involving about two hundred Hispanic and African American students. Stepped-up school police and Los Angeles police presence, strict regulation of clothing styles that could be associated with gangs, and a tightened school bell schedule that leaves little time to linger between classes are in effect to curb the violence.

© David McNew/Getty Images

- *Picture IDs.* One-quarter of schools require faculty or staff to wear picture IDs, 2 percent of primary schools, 6 percent of middle schools, and 13 percent of secondary schools require badges or picture IDs for students.
- *Control book bags.* About 6 percent of schools require clear book bags or ban book bags altogether.
- *Random checks.* About 15 percent of secondary schools use random metal detector checks, half use random dog sniffs, and one-quarter use random sweeps for contraband.
- *Security cameras.* About 14 percent of primary schools, 20 percent of middle schools, and 39 percent of secondary schools use one or more security cameras to monitor the school.[62]

Employing Law Enforcement Some districts have gone so far as to infiltrate undercover detectives on school grounds. These detectives attend classes, mingle with students, contact drug dealers, make buys, and arrest campus dealers.[63] New York City recently instituted a program that focuses on reducing crime in the city's twelve most dangerous schools. Though these schools constituted less than 1 percent of the city's enrollment, they account for 13 percent of all serious crimes and 11 percent of the total safety incidents. To reduce delinquency, the NYPD doubled the number of officers assigned to each school site and formed a 150-member task force of officers to focus on danger zones, such as hallways and cafeterias. The police also monitored the perimeters of the schools and organized truancy sweeps. Each school received frequent visits from school-safety teams made up of police officers, community workers, and educators. Evaluations showed that the schools receiving the extra enforcement averaged 3.02 criminal incidents per day down nearly 9 percent from 3.3 incidents per day before the program began.[64]

Improve School Climate Some critics complain that even when security methods are effective, they reduce staff and student morale. Tighter security may reduce acts of crime and violence in school, only to displace them to the community. Similarly, expelling or suspending troublemakers puts them on the street with nothing to do, so in the end, lowering the level of crime in schools may not reduce the total amount of crime committed by young people. A more realistic approach might involve early identification of at-risk students and teaching them pro-social skills rather than threatening them with consequence-based punishments.[65]

Another suggestion is that school-based crime may be reduced if the educational climate can be improved. Rather than install strict security, administrators might be better off improving the standards of the teaching staff, increasing the relevance of the curriculum, and providing law-related education classes. Schools that encourage order, organization, and student bonding have experienced a decline in disorder and crime.[66]

 The **National School Safety and Security Services** is a Cleveland (Ohio)-based consulting firm specializing in school security and crisis-preparedness training, security assessments, and related safety consulting for K–12 schools, law enforcement, and other youth safety providers. Their site contains a lot of information on school security. Visit it at www.thomsonedu.com/criminaljustice/siegel.

THE ROLE OF THE SCHOOL IN DELINQUENCY PREVENTION

Numerous organizations and groups have called for reforming the educational system to make it more responsive to the needs of students. Educational leaders now recognize that children undergo enormous pressures while in school that can lead to emotional and social problems. At one extreme are the pressures to succeed academically; at the other are the crime and substance abuse students face on school grounds. It is difficult to talk of achieving academic excellence in a deteriorated school dominated by gang members.

One way of improving schools and reducing delinquency is through sponsored educational reform. The cornerstone of the Bush administration's policy has been The No Child Left Behind Act of 2001 (NCLB) (Public Law 107-110). This act authorizes

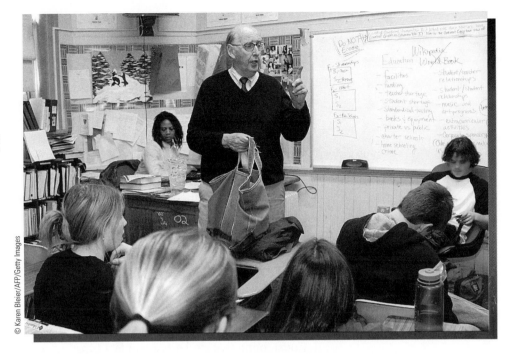

Schools have taken a leadership role in delinquency prevention efforts. Former journalist Colman McCarthy addresses students in his "Alternatives to Violence" class on April 5, 2006, at the School Without Walls in Washington, D.C. McCarthy has been teaching the class for more than 20 years with the theme that non-violent force is always stronger than violent force. McCarthy says students are thirsty to know alternatives to violence of all types—from armed violence and family violence to capital punishment.

© Karen Bleier/AFP/Getty Images

✔ **CHECKPOINTS**

■ A significant number of crimes occur in schools each year.

■ There has been a recent decline in school-based crime that reflects the general crime-rate decline.

■ Almost 2 million children were victimized between 1994 and 1998.

■ About 5 percent of students are bullied in school.

■ About three-quarters of all students report drugs in their school.

■ A number of efforts are being made to reduce school crime, including enforcing strict security measures through the use of armed guards.

■ Schools have been active in delinquency prevention.

■ After-school programs are becoming popular.

■ The programs that seem most effective focus on a range of social issues, including problem-solving skills, self-control, and stress management.

LOOKING BACK TO CIARA'S STORY

How did Ciara benefit from her treatment regime? Do you think kids benefit from special education programs or do they have hidden drawbacks?

federal programs aimed at improving America's primary and secondary schools by increasing the accountability for states, school districts, and schools and also providing parents more flexibility in choosing which schools their children will attend.[67] The NCLB increases focus on reading and relies on outcome-based education or the belief that high expectations and setting of goals will result in success for all students.[68] The NCLB has proven quite controversial because of funding issues.

School-Based Prevention Programs

Education officials have instituted numerous programs to make schools more effective instruments of delinquency prevention.[69] Some of the most prevalent strategies are as follows:

■ *Cognitive.* Increase students' awareness about the dangers of drug abuse and delinquency.

■ *Affective.* Improve students' psychological assets and self-image to give them the resources to resist antisocial behavior.

■ *Behavioral.* Train students in techniques to resist peer pressure.

■ *Environmental.* Establish school management and disciplinary programs that deter crime, such as locker searches.

■ *Therapeutic.* Treat youths who have already manifested problems.

More specific suggestions include creating special classes or schools with individualized programs that foster success for non-adjusting students. Efforts can be made to help students deal constructively with academic failure when it does occur.

Schools may not be able to reduce delinquency single-handedly, but a number of alternatives to their present operations could aid a community-wide effort to lessen juvenile crime. And reviews of some of the more successful programs show that the savings in terms of reduced delinquency, school costs, and so on far outweigh the amount of money spent on prevention. ✔ Checkpoints

The actions of education officials often run into opposition from the courts, which are concerned with maintaining the legal rights of minors. The U.S. Supreme Court has sought to balance the civil liberties of students with the school's mandate to provide a safe environment. Three of the main issues involved are privacy issues, free speech in school, and school discipline.

The Right to Personal Privacy

One major issue is the right of school officials to search students and their possessions on school grounds. Drug abuse, theft, assault and battery, and racial conflicts in schools have increased the need to take action against troublemakers. School administrators have questioned students about their illegal activities, conducted searches of students' persons and possessions, and reported suspicious behavior to the police.

In 1984, in *New Jersey v. T.L.O.*, the Supreme Court helped clarify a vexing problem: whether the Fourth Amendment's prohibition against unreasonable searches and seizures applies to school officials as well as to police officers.[70] In this case, the Court found that students are in fact constitutionally protected from illegal searches, but that school officials are not bound by the same restrictions as law enforcement agents. Police need "probable cause" before they can conduct a search, but educators can legally search students when there are reasonable grounds to believe the students have violated the law or broken school rules. In creating this distinction, the Court recognized the needs of school officials to preserve an environment conducive to education and to secure the safety of students.

One question left unanswered by *New Jersey v. T.L.O.* is whether teachers and other school officials can search lockers and desks. Here, the law has been controlled by state decisions, and each jurisdiction may create its own standards. Some allow teachers a free hand in opening lockers and desks.[71]

Drug Testing

Another critical issue involving privacy is the drug testing of students. In 1995, the Supreme Court extended schools' authority to search by legalizing a random drug-testing policy for student athletes. The Supreme Court's decision in *Vernonia School District 47J v. Acton* expanded the power of educators to ensure safe learning environments.[72] In this case, the Supreme Court extended one step further the schools' authority to search, despite court-imposed constitutional safeguards for children. Underlying this decision, like that of *New Jersey v. T.L.O.*, is recognition that the use of drugs is a serious threat to public safety and to the rights of children to receive a decent and safe education. In a subsequent case *Board of Education of Independent School District No. 92 of Pottawatomie County et al. v. Earls et al.* the court extended the right to test for drugs to all students. Because of its importance, *Earls* is discussed in the Juvenile Law in Review feature on page 226.

Academic Privacy

Students have the right to expect that their records will be kept private. Although state laws govern the disclosure of information from juvenile court records, a 1974 federal law—the Family Educational Rights and Privacy Act (FERPA)—restricts disclosure of information from a student's education records without parental consent.[73] The act defines an education record to include all records, files, and other materials, such as photographs, containing information related to a student that an education agency maintains. In 1994, Congress passed the Improving America's Schools Act, which allowed educational systems to disclose education records under these circumstances: (1) state law authorizes the disclosure, (2) the disclosure is to a juvenile justice agency, (3) the disclosure relates to the justice system's ability to provide pre-adjudication services to a student, and (4) state or local officials certify in writing that the institution or individual receiving the information has agreed not to disclose it to a third party other than another juvenile justice system agency.[74]

Free Speech

Freedom of speech is guaranteed in the First Amendment to the U.S. Constitution. This right has been divided into two categories as it affects children in schools. The first category involves **passive speech**, a form of expression not associated with actually speaking words; examples include wearing armbands or political protest buttons. The most important U.S. Supreme Court decision concerning a student's right to passive speech was in 1969 in the case of *Tinker v. Des Moines Independent Community School District*.[75] This case involved the right to wear black armbands to protest the war in Vietnam. Three high school students, ages fifteen, sixteen, and thirteen, were suspended for wearing the armbands in school. According to the Court, to justify prohibiting an expression of opinion, the school must be able to show that its action was caused by something more than a desire to avoid the unpleasantness that accompanies the expression of an unpopular view. Unless it can be shown that the forbidden conduct will interfere with the discipline required to operate the school, the prohibition cannot be sustained.[76]

The concept of free speech articulated in *Tinker* was used again in 1986 in *Bethel School District No. 403 v. Fraser*.[77] This case upheld a school system's right to discipline a student who uses obscene or profane language and gestures. The Court found that a school has the right to control offensive speech that undermines the educational mission. In a 1988 case, *Hazelwood School District v. Kuhlmeier*, the Court extended the right of school officials to censor **active speech** when it ruled that the principal could censor articles in a student publication.[78] In this case, students had written about their experiences with pregnancy and parental divorce. The majority ruled that censorship was justified, because school-sponsored publications were part of the curriculum and therefore designed to impart knowledge. Control over such activities could be differentiated from the action of the *Tinker* defendants' passive protests. In a dissent, Justice William J. Brennan accused school officials of favoring "thought control."

The Court may now be asked to address off-campus speech issues as well. Students have been suspended for posting messages school officials consider defamatory

passive speech
A form of expression protected by the First Amendment, but not associated with actually speaking words; examples include wearing symbols or protest messages on buttons or signs.

active speech
Expressing an opinion by speaking or writing; freedom of speech is a protected right under the First Amendment to the U.S. Constitution.

Students in Rochester, New York, are shown protesting a school ruling over the presence of metal detectors. The Supreme Court allows school officials to control student speech while on school premises if it interferes with the school's mission to implant "the shared values of a civilized social order." Student protest off-campus is still an open question. In the future, the courts may be asked to rule whether schools can control such forms of speech or whether students are shielded by the First Amendment.

© AP Images/Reed Hoffman/Democrat & Chronicle

Board of Education of Independent School District No. 92 of Pottawatomie County et al. v. Earls et al.

FACTS

The Tecumseh, Oklahoma, school district adopted a student activities drug-testing policy that requires all middle and high school students to consent to urinalysis testing for drugs to participate in any extracurricular activity. The policy was a response to increased perceptions of student drug use by faculty and administrators. Teachers saw students who appeared to be under the influence of drugs and heard students speaking openly about using drugs. A drug dog found marijuana near the school parking lot. Police found drugs or drug paraphernalia in a car driven by an extracurricular club member. And the school board president reported that people in the community were calling the board to discuss the "drug situation."

In practice, the policy was applied only to competitive extracurricular activities sanctioned by the Oklahoma Secondary Schools Activities Association (OSSAA). A group of students and their parents filed suit against the policy, arguing that it infringed on a student's right to personal privacy. The Tenth Circuit Court of Appeals agreed and held that before imposing a suspicionless drug-testing program, a school must demonstrate some identifiable drug abuse problem among a sufficient number of students such that testing that group will redress its drug problem. The federal court held that the school district had failed to demonstrate such a problem among Tecumseh students participating in competitive extracurricular activities. However, the Supreme Court reversed its decision and ruled that the policy is a reasonable means of furthering the school district's important interest in preventing and deterring drug use among its schoolchildren and does not violate the students' rights to privacy or their due process rights.

DECISION

The Court ruled that, so as not to violate due process, drug-testing policies had to be "reasonable." However, in contrast to searches for criminal evidence, students could be searched by school authorities (to determine whether they used drugs) without probable cause because the need for that level of evidence interferes with maintaining swift and informal disciplinary procedures that are needed to maintain order in a public school. Because the schools' responsibility for children cannot be disregarded, it would not be unreasonable to search students for drug usage even if no single student was suspected of abusing drugs.

The Court also ruled that within this context, students have a limited expectation of privacy. In their complaint, the students argued that children participating in non-athletic extracurricular activities have a stronger expectation of privacy than athletes who regularly undergo physicals as part of their participation in sports. However, the Court disagreed, maintaining that students who participate in competitive extracurricular activities voluntarily subject themselves to many of the same intrusions on their privacy as do athletes. Some of these clubs and activities require off-campus travel and communal undress, and all of

on websites.[79] In the future, the Court may be asked to rule on whether this speech is shielded by the First Amendment.

School Prayer

One of the most divisive issues involving free speech is school prayer. Although some religious-minded administrators, parents, and students want to have prayer sessions in schools or have religious convocations, others view the practice both as a violation of the principle of separation of church and state and as an infringement on the First Amendment right to freedom of religion. The 2000 case of *Santa Fe Independent School District, Petitioner v. Jane Doe* helps clarify the issue.[80]

Prior to 1995, the Santa Fe High School student who occupied the school's elective office of student council chaplain delivered a prayer over the public address system before each varsity football game for the entire season. After the practice was challenged in federal district court, the school district adopted a different policy that permitted, but did not require, prayer initiated and led by a student at each of the home games. The district court entered an order modifying that policy to permit only non-sectarian, non-proselytizing prayer. However, a federal appellate court held that, even as modified, the football prayer policy was invalid. This decision was upheld when the case was appealed to the United States Supreme Court. They ruled that prayers led by an "elected" student undermine the protection of minority viewpoints. Such a system encourages divisiveness along religious lines and threatens the imposition of coercion upon those students not desiring to parthem have their own rules and requirements that do not apply to the student body as a whole. Each of them must abide by OSSAA rules, and a faculty sponsor monitors students for compliance with the various rules dictated by the clubs and activities. Such regulation diminishes the student's expectation of privacy.

Finally, the Court concluded that the means used to enforce the Drug Policy was not overly invasive or an intrusion on the students' privacy. Under the policy, a faculty monitor would wait outside a closed restroom stall for the student to produce a sample and must listen for the normal sounds of urination to guard against tampered specimens and ensure an accurate chain of custody. This procedure is virtually identical to the "negligible" intrusion concept which was approved in an earlier case, *Vernonia v. Acton*, which applied to student athletes. The policy requires that test results be kept in confidential files separate from a student's other records and released to school personnel only on a "need to know" basis. Moreover, the test results are not turned over to any law enforcement authority. Nor do the test results lead to the imposition of discipline or have any academic consequences. Rather, the only consequence of a failed drug test is to limit the student's privilege of participating in extracurricular activities.

SIGNIFICANCE

In *Pottawatomie County*, the Court concluded that a drug-testing policy effectively serves a school district's interest in protecting its students' safety and health. It reasoned that preventing drug use by schoolchildren is an important governmental concern.

School districts need not show that kids participating in a particular activity have a drug problem in order to test them for usage. The need to prevent and deter the substantial harm of childhood drug use itself provides the necessary immediacy for a school testing policy. Given what it considers a "nationwide epidemic of drug use" it was entirely reasonable for the school district to enact a drug testing policy.

CRITICAL THINKING

Pottawatomie County extends the drug testing allowed in the *Vernonia* case from athletes to all students who participate in any form of school activity. Do you believe this is a reasonable exercise of state authority or a violation of due process? After all, the students being tested have not shown any evidence of drug abuse. Furthermore, non-athletic school activities do not provide the same degree of danger as an athletic activity during the course of which an impaired participant may suffer serious injury.

INFOTRAC COLLEGE EDITION RESEARCH

To read what former drug czar and values guru William Bennett has to say about the case, go to InfoTrac College Edition and read "Statement of Empower America Co-Director William J. Bennett on the Supreme Court's Decision in *Pottawatomie County v. Earls*," *US Newswire*, June 27, 2002.

Source: *Board of Education of Independent School District No. 92 of Pottawatomie County et al. v. Earls et al.*, 01.332 (2002).

ticipate in a religious exercise. The *Santa Fe* case severely limits school-sanctioned prayer at public events.

Despite the *Santa Fe* decision, the Court has not totally ruled out the role of religion in schools. In its ruling in *Good News Club v. Milford Central School* (2001), the Supreme Court required an upstate New York school district to provide space for an after-school Bible club for elementary students.[81] The Court ruled that it was a violation of the First Amendment's free speech clause to deny the club access to the school space on the ground that the club was religious in nature; the school routinely let secular groups use its space. The Court reasoned that because the club's meetings were to be held after school hours, were not sponsored by the school, and were open to any student who obtained parental consent, it could not be perceived that the school was endorsing the club, or that students might feel coerced to participate in its activities.

In its most recent statement on the separation of church and state, the Court refused to hear a case brought by a California father contesting the recital of the pledge of allegiance because it contains the phrase "under God."[82] Although the Court dismissed the case on a technical issue, some of the justices felt the issue should have been dealt with and dismissed for substantive reasons:

> To give the parent of such a child a sort of 'heckler's veto' over a patriotic ceremony willingly participated in by other students, simply because the Pledge of Allegiance contains the descriptive phrase 'under God,' is an unwarranted extension of the establishment clause, an extension which would have the unfortunate effect of prohibiting a commendable patriotic observance.[83]

School Discipline

in loco parentis
In the place of the parent; rights given to schools that allow them to assume parental duties in disciplining students.

Most states have statutes permitting teachers to use corporal punishment in public school systems. Under the concept of ***in loco parentis***, discipline is one of the parental duties given to the school system. In the 1977 case *Ingraham v. Wright*, the Court held that neither the Eighth nor the Fourteenth Amendment was violated by a teacher's use of corporal punishment to discipline students.[84] The Court established the standard that only reasonable discipline is allowed in school systems; today twenty-four states still allow physical punishment. With regard to suspension and expulsion, in 1976, in the case of *Goss v. Lopez*, the Supreme Court ruled that any time a student is to be suspended for up to ten days, he or she is entitled to a hearing.[85]

In summary, schools have the right to discipline students, but students are protected from unreasonable, excessive, and arbitrary discipline.

SUMMARY

- Youths spend much of their time in school because education has become increasingly important as a determinant of social and economic success.
- Educational institutions are among the primary instruments of socialization, and as such they are bound to influence the amount of delinquent behavior by school-age children.
- There is a strong association between school failure and delinquency.
- Those who claim a causal link between school failure and delinquency cite two major factors: (1) academic failure, which arises from lack of aptitude, labeling, or class conflict and results in tracking, and (2) alienation from the educational experience, which is the result of the impersonal nature of schools, the passive role assigned to students, and students' perception of their education as irrelevant to their future lives.

- Student misbehaviors, which may have their roots in the school experience, range from minor infractions of school rules (for example, smoking and loitering in the halls) to serious crimes, such as assault, arson, drug abuse, and vandalism.
- Truancy is a significant educational problem.
- Some dissatisfied students drop out of school, and research has shown a decline in delinquency among those who do drop out.
- The school has also been the setting for important delinquency prevention efforts. Among the measures taken are security squads, electronic surveillance, and teacher training.
- Students do not lose their legal rights at the schoolhouse door. Among the most important legal issues facing students are the right to privacy, free speech, fair discipline, and freedom of religion.

KEY TERMS

academic achievement, p. 208
truant, p. 212
drop out, p. 212
underachievers, p. 213

school failure, p. 214
tracking, p. 216
zero tolerance policy, p. 221
passive speech, p. 225

active speech, p. 225
in loco parentis, p. 228

QUESTIONS FOR DISCUSSION

1. Was there a delinquency problem in your high school? If so, how was it dealt with?

2. Should disobedient youths be suspended from school? Does this solution hurt or help?

3. What can be done to improve the delinquency prevention capabilities of schools?

4. Is school failure responsible for delinquency, or are delinquents simply school failures?

You are the principal of a suburban high school. It seems that one of your students, Steve Jones, has had a long-running feud with Mr. Metcalf, an English teacher whom he blames for giving him a low grade unfairly and for being too strict with other students. Steve set up a home-based website that posted insulting images of Metcalf and contained messages describing him in unflattering terms ("a slob who doesn't bathe often enough," for example). He posted a photo of the teacher with the caption "Public Enemy Number One." Word of the website has gotten out around school. Even though the students think it's funny and "cool," the faculty is outraged. You bring Steve into your office and ask him to take down the site, explaining that its existence has had a negative effect on school discipline and morale. He refuses, arguing that the site is home-based and you have no right to ask for its removal. Besides, he claims, it is just in fun and not really hurting anyone.

School administrators are asked to make these kinds of decisions every day, and the wrong choice can prove costly. You are aware that a case very similar to this one resulted in a thirty-thousand-dollar settlement in a damage claim against a school system when the principal did suspend a student for posting an insulting website and the student later sued for violating his right to free speech.

- Would you suspend Steve if he refuses your request to take down the site?

- Would you allow him to leave it posted and try to placate Mr. Metcalf?

- What would you do if Mr. Metcalf had posted a site ridiculing students and making fun of their academic abilities?

There are a number of important resources for educational law on the Internet. Check out the Education Law Association site, the Educational Resource Information Center, and Edlaw by going to **www.thomsonedu.com/criminaljustice/siegel** on the Web.

Drug Use and Delinquency

© Brent Stirton/Getty Images

CHAPTER OBJECTIVES

After reading this chapter you should:

1. Know which drugs are most frequently abused by American youth.

2. Understand the extent of the drug problem among American youth today.

3. Be able to discuss how teenage drug use in this country has changed in the past thirty years.

4. Know the main explanations for why youths take drugs.

5. Recognize the different behavior patterns of drug-involved youths.

6. Understand the relationship between drug use and delinquency.

7. Be familiar with the major drug-control strategies.

8. Be able to argue the pros and cons of government using different drug-control strategies.

Fernando Ellis was a fifteen-year-old young man of Latino heritage who was referred to the local health/substance abuse agency after he attempted to jump out of his father's moving vehicle during a verbal argument. Fernando had been using and was high on drugs at the time. Fernando was skipping school, using marijuana on a daily basis, and had numerous drug-related police contacts and charges. He was also on probation for selling drugs on school grounds.

Fernando's father worked long hours and drank to excess when he was at home. He introduced his son to alcohol and drugs at an early age, and offered little supervision or guidance. Fernando's mother was killed in an accident when Fernando was twelve years old, leaving his father to care for him and his three older siblings. In addition, Fernando was born with a birth defect that had often resulted in teasing by other children. At times, it was difficult to understand his speech and he walked with a significant limp. It appeared Fernando was trying to fit in, "be cool," and gain acceptance by engaging in criminal activity.

At the juvenile court hearing, Fernando was ordered to complete community service and individual counseling, and referred to the community mental health center for an alcohol and drug assessment, as well as a suicide risk assessment. He reluctantly cooperated with the order to avoid a more serious disposition.

Fernando's assessments indicated that although he did try to jump out of a moving car, he did not appear to be a suicide risk. He was under the influence at the time and in a very heated argument with his father. There was concern about his daily use of drugs and alcohol, and Fernando was referred to an outpatient drug treatment program at the center. In addition, Fernando met weekly with his counselor for individual counseling. They worked on his drug and alcohol issues, changing his behavior and habits, and on the grief and loss issues related to the sudden death of his mother. This loss was a significant turning point for Fernando. Up to that time, he had been a good student who was not involved with drugs. Everything changed when his mother was killed.

Over the course of his work with his counselor, Fernando began to process this significant loss, as well as make positive changes in his life. A team of professionals including his teachers, probation officer, drug and alcohol counselor, and a mentor provided by the school all worked with Fernando to help him realize his goals. He began to attend school on a more regular basis, worked to improve his relationships with his father and siblings, and to reduce his criminal activity and drug and alcohol use. Fernando continued to occasionally use alcohol, but eliminated his drug use. He also struggled with his home situation and sometimes ran away from home to stay with friends. Overall, Fernando significantly reduced his criminal activity, although he remained on probation for the duration of the court order.

substance abuse
Using drugs or alcohol in such a way as to cause physical harm to oneself.

The **Lindesmith Center** is one of the leading independent drug policy institutes in the United States. View its web-site by going to www.thomsonedu.com/criminaljustice/siegel.

There is little question that adolescent **substance abuse** and its association with delinquency is a vexing problem. Almost every town, village, and city in the United States has confronted some type of teenage substance abuse problem.

Self-report surveys indicate that just under half of high school seniors have tried drugs and almost three-quarters have used alcohol.[1] Adolescents at high risk for drug abuse often come from the most impoverished communities and experience a multitude of problems, including school failure and family conflict.[2] Equally troubling is the association between drug use and crime.[3] Research indicates that between 5 percent and 8 percent of all juvenile male arrestees in some cities test positive for cocaine.[4] Self-report surveys show that drug abusers are more likely to become delinquents than are non-abusers.[5] The pattern of drug use and crime makes teenage substance abuse a key national concern.

This chapter addresses some important issues involving teenage substance abuse, beginning with a review of the kinds of drugs children and adolescents are using and how often they are using them. Then we discuss who uses drugs and what causes substance abuse. After describing the association between drug abuse and delinquent behavior, the chapter concludes with a review of efforts to prevent and control the use of drugs in the United States.

FREQUENTLY ABUSED DRUGS

A wide variety of substances referred to as drugs are used by teenagers. Some are addicting, others not. Some create hallucinations, others cause a depressed stupor, and a few give an immediate uplift. In this section we will identify the most widely used substances and discuss their effects. All of these drugs can be abused, and because of the danger they present, many have been banned from private use. Others are available legally only with a physician's supervision, and a few are available to adults but prohibited for children.

Marijuana and Hashish

Commonly called "pot" or "grass," marijuana is produced from the leaves of *Cannabis sativa*. **Hashish** (hash) is a concentrated form of cannabis made from unadulterated resin from the female plant. The main active ingredient in both marijuana and hashish is tetrahydrocannabinol (THC), a mild hallucinogen. **Marijuana** is the drug most commonly used by teenagers.

Smoking large amounts of pot or hash can cause distortions in auditory and visual perception, even producing hallucinatory effects. Small doses produce an early excitement ("high") that gives way to drowsiness. Pot use is also related to decreased activity, overestimation of time and space, and increased food consumption. When the user is alone, marijuana produces a dreamy state. In a group, users become giddy and lose perspective.

Marijuana is not physically addicting, but its long-term effects have been the subject of much debate. During the 1970s, it was reported that smoking pot caused a variety of physical and mental problems, including brain damage and mental illness. Although the dangers of pot and hash may have been overstated, use of these drugs does present some health risks, including an increased risk of lung cancer, chronic bronchitis, and other diseases. Prospective parents should avoid smoking marijuana, because it lowers sperm counts in male users and females experience disrupted ovulation and a greater chance of miscarriage.[6]

Cocaine

Cocaine is an alkaloid derivative of the coca plant. When first isolated in 1860, it was considered a medicinal breakthrough that could relieve fatigue, depression, and other symptoms, and it quickly became a staple of patent medicines. When its addictive qualities and dangerous side effects became apparent, its use was controlled by the Pure Food and Drug Act of 1906.

Cocaine is the most powerful natural stimulant. Its use produces euphoria, restlessness, and excitement. Overdoses can cause delirium, violent manic behavior, and possible respiratory failure. The drug can be sniffed, or "snorted," into the nostrils, or it can be injected. The immediate feeling of euphoria, or "rush," is short-lived, and heavy users may snort coke as often as every ten minutes. Another dangerous practice is "speedballing"—injecting a mixture of cocaine and heroin.

Crack is processed street cocaine. Its manufacture involves using ammonia or baking soda (sodium bicarbonate) to remove the hydrochlorides and create a

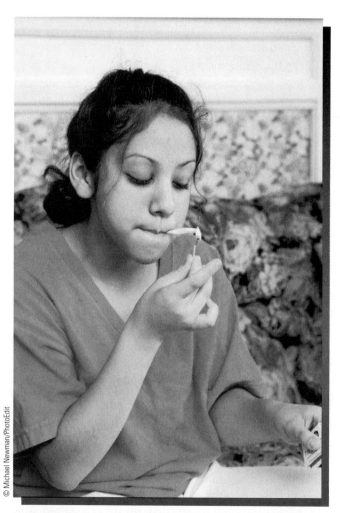

© Michael Newman/PhotoEdit

Marijuana is the drug most commonly used by teenagers. Surveys suggest that marijuana use among high school students is much lower today than it was during its peak in the mid-1990s.

cocaine
A powerful natural stimulant derived from the coca plant.

crack
A highly addictive crystalline form of cocaine containing remnants of hydrochloride and sodium bicarbonate; it makes a crackling sound when smoked.

crystalline form of cocaine that can be smoked. In fact, crack gets its name from the fact that the sodium bicarbonate often emits a crackling sound when the substance is smoked. Also referred to as "rock," "gravel," and "roxanne," crack gained popularity in the mid-1980s. It is relatively inexpensive, can provide a powerful high, and is highly addictive psychologically. Crack cocaine use has been in decline in recent years. Heavy criminal penalties, tight enforcement, and social disapproval have helped lower crack use.

Heroin

Narcotic drugs have the ability to produce insensibility to pain and to free the mind of anxiety and emotion. Users experience relief from fear and apprehension, release of tension, and elevation of spirits. This short period of euphoria is followed by a period of apathy, during which users become drowsy and may nod off. Heroin, the most commonly used narcotic in the United States, is produced from opium, a drug derived from the opium poppy flower. Dealers cut the drug with neutral substances (sugar or lactose), and street heroin is often only 1 percent to 4 percent pure.

heroin
A narcotic made from opium and then cut with sugar or some other neutral substance until it is only 1 percent to 4 percent pure.

addict
A person with an overpowering physical or psychological need to continue taking a particular substance or drug.

Heroin is probably the most dangerous commonly abused drug. Users rapidly build up a tolerance for it, fueling the need for increased doses to obtain the desired effect. At first heroin is usually sniffed or snorted; as tolerance builds, it is "skin popped" (shot into skin, but not into a vein); and finally it is injected into a vein, or "mainlined."[7] Through this progressive use, the user becomes an **addict**—a person with an overpowering physical and psychological need to continue taking a particular substance by any means possible. If addicts cannot get enough heroin to satisfy their habit, they will suffer withdrawal symptoms, which include irritability, depression, extreme nervousness, and nausea.

Alcohol

alcohol
Fermented or distilled liquids containing ethanol, an intoxicating substance.

Alcohol remains the drug of choice for most teenagers. Two-thirds of high school seniors reported using alcohol in the past year, and almost three-quarters (73 percent) say they have tried it at some time during their lifetime; by the twelfth grade 56 percent of American youth report that they have "been drunk."[8] More than 20 million Americans are estimated to be problem drinkers, and at least half of these are alcoholics.

Alcohol may be a factor in nearly half of all murders, suicides, and accidental deaths.[9] Alcohol-related deaths number one hundred thousand a year, far more than all other illegal drugs combined. Just over 1.4 million drivers are arrested each year for driving under the influence (including fourteen thousand teen drivers), and about 1.2 million more are arrested for other alcohol-related violations.[10] The economic cost is staggering. An estimated $185 billion is lost each year, including $36 billion from premature deaths, $88 billion in reduced work effort, and $19 billion arising from short- and long-term medical problems.[11]

Considering these problems, why do so many youths drink to excess? Youths who use alcohol report that it reduces tension, enhances pleasure, improves social skills, and transforms experiences for the better.[12] Although these reactions may follow the limited use of alcohol, alcohol in higher doses acts as a depressant. Long-term use has been linked with depression and physical ailments ranging from heart disease to cirrhosis of the liver. Many teens also think drinking stirs their romantic urges, but scientific evidence indicates that alcohol decreases sexual response.[13]

Other Drug Categories

Other drug categories include anesthetic drugs, inhalants, sedatives and barbiturates, tranquilizers, hallucinogens, stimulants, steroids, designer drugs, and cigarettes.

anesthetic drugs
Nervous system depressants.

Anesthetic Drugs **Anesthetic drugs** are central nervous system (CNS) depressants. Local anesthetics block nervous system transmissions; general anesthetics act on the brain to produce loss of sensation, stupor, or unconsciousness. The most widely abused anesthetic drug is *phencyclidine* (*PCP*), known as "angel dust." Angel dust can be sprayed on marijuana or other leaves and smoked, drunk, or injected. Originally developed as an animal tranquilizer, PCP creates hallucinations and a spaced-out feeling that causes heavy users to engage in violent acts. The effects of PCP can last up to two days, and the danger of overdose is high.

Inhalant Some youths inhale vapors from lighter fluid, shoe polish, paint thinner, cleaning fluid, or model airplane glue to reach a drowsy, dizzy state that is sometimes accompanied by hallucinations. **Inhalants** produce a short-term euphoria followed by a period of disorientation, slurred speech, and drowsiness. Amyl nitrite ("poppers") is a commonly used volatile liquid packaged in capsule form that is inhaled when the capsule is broken open.

Sedatives and Barbiturates **Sedatives,** the most commonly used drugs of the barbiturate family, depress the central nervous system into a sleeplike condition. On the illegal market sedatives are called "goofballs" or "downers" and are often known by the color of the capsules: "reds" (Seconal), "blue devils" (Amytal), and "rainbows" (Tuinal).

Sedatives can be prescribed by doctors as sleeping pills. Illegal users employ them to create relaxed, sociable feelings; overdoses can cause irritability, repellent behavior, and unconsciousness. Barbiturates are the major cause of drug-overdose deaths.

Tranquilizers **Tranquilizers** reduce anxiety and promote relaxation. Legally prescribed tranquilizers, such as Ampazine, Thorazine, Pacatal, and Sparine, were originally designed to control the behavior of people suffering from psychoses, aggressiveness, and agitation. Less powerful tranquilizers, such as Valium, Librium, Miltown, and Equanil, are used to combat anxiety, tension, fast heart rate, and headaches. The use of illegally obtained tranquilizers can lead to addiction, and withdrawal can be painful and hazardous.

Hallucinogens **Hallucinogens**, either natural or synthetic, produce vivid distortions of the senses without greatly disturbing the viewer's consciousness. Some produce hallucinations, and others cause psychotic behavior in otherwise normal people.

One common hallucinogen is mescaline, named after the Mescalero Apaches, who first discovered its potent effect. Mescaline occurs naturally in the peyote, a small cactus that grows in Mexico and the southwestern United States. After initial discomfort, mescaline produces vivid hallucinations and out-of-body sensations.

A second group of hallucinogens are synthetic alkaloid compounds, such as psilocybin. These can be transformed into lysergic acid diethylamide, commonly called LSD. This powerful substance stimulates cerebral sensory centers to produce visual hallucinations, intensify hearing, and increase sensitivity. Users often report a scrambling of sensations; they may "hear colors" and "smell music." Users also report feeling euphoric and mentally superior, although to an observer they appear disoriented. Anxiety and panic may occur, and overdoses can produce psychotic episodes, flashbacks, and even death.

Stimulants **Stimulants** ("uppers," "speed," "pep pills," "crystal") are synthetic drugs that stimulate action in the central nervous system. They increase blood pressure, breathing rate, and bodily activity, and elevate mood. Commonly used stimulants include Benzedrine ("bennies"), Dexedrine ("dex"), Dexamyl, Biphetamine ("whites"), and Methedrine ("meth," "speed," "crystal meth"). Methedrine is probably the most widely used and most dangerous amphetamine. Some people swallow it; heavy users inject it. Long-term heavy use can result in exhaustion, anxiety, prolonged depression, and hallucinations.

A more recent form of methamphetamine is a crystallized substance with the street name of "ice" or "crystal." Ice methamphetamine looks similar to shards of ice or chunks

inhalants
Volatile liquids that give off a vapor, which is inhaled, producing short-term excitement and euphoria followed by a period of disorientation.

sedatives
Drugs of the barbiturate family that depress the central nervous system into a sleeplike condition.

tranquilizers
Drugs that reduce anxiety and promote relaxation.

hallucinogens
Natural or synthetic substances that produce vivid distortions of the senses without greatly disturbing consciousness.

stimulants
Synthetic substances that produce an intense physical reaction by stimulating the central nervous system.

of rock salt and is highly pure and extremely addictive.[14] Smoking this ice or crystal causes weight loss, kidney damage, heart and respiratory problems, and paranoia.[15]

Methamphetamines in general, whether in its three main forms of powder, ice, or tablets, have become an increasingly important priority of United States law enforcement authorities. Although its use among secondary school students has shown a downward trend in the eight years it has been investigated (1999–2006),[16] authorities are concerned, because it has spread from its origins in the rural West to other parts of the country and into urban and suburban areas. According to the U.S. Department of Justice's National Drug Intelligence Center, methamphetamine availability is highest in the Pacific region, followed by the West, Southwest, Southeast, Midwest, and Northeast regions.[17] Other problems arise from the majority of it being produced domestically, either in "Mom and Pop" laboratories or super labs, which are mostly found in the Central Valley and southern areas of California; it can be made with many household products that are not feasible or are difficult to regulate; and its production presents many dangers to people and the environment.[18] A number of states like Oklahoma and Iowa have banned over-the-counter cold medicines like Sudafed that contain pseudoephedrine, an essential ingredient of methamphetamines, making them only available by prescription.[19]

Steroids Teenagers use highly dangerous **anabolic steroids** to gain muscle bulk and strength.[20] Black market sales of these drugs approach $1 billion annually. Although not physically addicting, steroids can become a kind of obsession among teens who desire athletic success. Long-term users may spend up to four hundred dollars a week on steroids and may support their habit by dealing the drug.

Steroids are dangerous because of the health problems associated with their long-term use: liver ailments, tumors, kidney problems, sexual dysfunction, hypertension, and mental problems such as depression. Steroid use runs in cycles, and other drugs—Clomid, Teslac, and Halotestin, for example—that carry their own dangerous side effects are often used to curb the need for high dosages of steroids. Finally, steroid users often share needles, which puts them at high risk for contracting HIV, the virus that causes AIDS.

Designer Drugs **Designer drugs** are lab-created synthetics that are designed at least temporarily to get around existing drug laws. The most widely used designer drug is Ecstasy, which is actually derived from speed and methamphetamine. After being swallowed, snorted, injected, or smoked, it acts simultaneously as a stimulant and a hallucinogen, producing mood swings, disturbing sleeping and eating habits, altering thinking processes, creating aggressive behavior, interfering with sexual function, and affecting sensitivity to pain. The drug can also increase blood pressure and heart rate. Teenage users taking Ecstasy at raves have died from heat stroke, because the drug can cause dehydration.

Cigarettes Many countries around the world have established laws to prohibit the sale of cigarettes to minors. The reality, however, is that in many countries children and adolescents have easy access to tobacco products.[21] In the United States, the Synar Amendment, enacted in 1992, requires states to enact and enforce laws restricting the sale of tobacco products to youths under

anabolic steroids
Drugs used by athletes and bodybuilders to gain muscle bulk and strength.

designer drugs
Lab-made drugs designed to avoid existing drug laws.

Faced with the increasing competitiveness of high school sports and the prospect of college athletic scholarships, some high school athletes turn to steroids. But any small gains on the playing field often come with a number of health and social problems. Here, Ryan O'Sullivan, a star athlete at Madison High School in Connecticut, arrives at Superior Court in New Haven to be arraigned on steroids charges.

the age of eighteen. States are required to reduce rates of illegal sales to minors to no more than 20 percent within several years. The FDA rules require age verification for anyone under the age of twenty-seven who is purchasing tobacco products. The FDA has also banned vending machines and self-service displays except in adult-only facilities. The signing of the Master Tobacco Settlement Agreement between 46 states and the tobacco industry in 1998, placed further restrictions on the advertising and marketing of cigarettes to young people and allocated substantial sums to antismoking campaigns.[22] Some efforts to enforce compliance with these restrictions and educate tobacco retailers about the new laws have produced promising results.[23] Despite all of these measures, almost one out of every two high school seniors in America (47 percent) report having smoked cigarettes over their lifetime. However, in recent years cigarette use by high school students has been on the decline.[24]

DRUG USE TODAY

Has America's long-standing war on drugs paid off? Has drug use declined, or is it on the upswing? A number of national surveys conduct annual reviews of teen drug use by interviewing samples of teens around the nation. What do national surveys tell us about the extent of drug use, and what have been the recent trends in teen usage?

The Monitoring the Future (MTF) Survey

One of the most important and influential surveys of teen substance abuse is the annual Monitoring the Future survey conducted by the Institute for Social Research at the University of Michigan. In all, about forty-five thousand students located in 433 secondary schools participate in the study.

The most recent MTF survey in 2006 indicates that, with few exceptions, drug use among American adolescents continued to decline from the peak levels reached in 1996 and 1997. Annual drug use was down by more than one-third (37 percent) for eighth graders during this time period, while reductions have been somewhat lower for those in the tenth (25 percent) and twelfth (14 percent) grades.[25] As Figure 10.1 shows, drug use peaked in the late 1970s and early 1980s and then began a decade-long decline until showing an uptick in the mid-1990s; usage for most drugs has been stable or in decline

Figure 10.1   **Trends in Annual Prevalence of Illicit Drug Use**

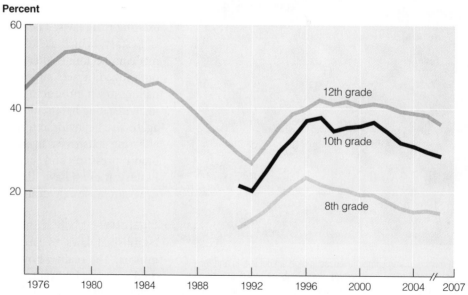

Source: Lloyd D. Johnston, Patrick M. O'Malley, Jerald G. Bachman, and John E. Schulenberg, *Teen Drug Use Continues Down in 2006, Particularly Among Older Teens; But Use of Prescription-Type Drugs Remains High* (Ann Arbor, MI: University of Michigan News and Information Services, December 21, 2006), Table 2.

since then. Especially encouraging has been a significant drop in the use of alcohol by the youngest kids in the survey—a 13 percent drop in annual rates in the last five years (from 38.7 percent in 2002 to 33.6 percent in 2006) and a 26 percent drop in the last 10 years (from 45.5 percent in 1997). There has also been a continuing decline in cigarette smoking, as well as the use of smokeless tobacco products. More troubling is the use of Ecstasy, which, because of its popularity at dance clubs and raves, rose among older teens (tenth- and twelfth-graders) for much of the late 1990s and up to 2001, but has since dropped sharply. In 2006, less than 3 percent (2.8 percent) of tenth-graders reported some use of Ecstasy during the previous twelve months (down from 4.9 percent in 2002); 4.1 percent of the twelfth-graders also reported some use (down from 7.4 percent in 2002). On the other hand, study authors drew particular attention to the relatively high usage rates of prescription-type drugs such as narcotics, tranquilizers, and sedatives. Annual use of OxyContin, a prescription painkiller narcotic, was down for the first time in the last five years among twelfth graders (from 5.5 percent in 2005 to 4.3 percent in 2006), but reached its highest level among younger students: 2.6 percent for eighth graders and 3.8 percent for tenth graders.[26] This may be part of a larger trend in the abuse of prescription drugs on the part of youths and young adults.[27]

The PRIDE Survey

A second source of information on teen drug and alcohol abuse is the National Parents' Resource Institute for Drug Education (PRIDE) survey, which is also conducted annually.[28] Typically, findings from the PRIDE survey correlate highly with the MTF drug survey. The most recent PRIDE survey (for the 2004–2005 school year) indicates little to no change in drug activity over the previous school year, but substantial decreases over the last ten years. For example, just over 22 percent of students in grades six to twelve claimed to have used drugs during the past year, down from about 30 percent in the 1995–1996 school year (Table 10.1). Cigarette smoking and alcohol use are also down from ten years ago. The fact that two surveys generate roughly the same pattern in drug abuse helps bolster their validity and give support to a decline in teenage substance abuse.

The National Survey on Drug Use and Health

Sponsored by the U.S. Department of Health and Human Services' Substance Abuse and Mental Health Services Administration, the National Survey on Drug Use and Health (NSDUH, formerly called the National Household Survey on Drug Abuse) interviews approximately seventy thousand people at home each year.[29] Like the MTF and PRIDE surveys, the latest NSDUH (2004) shows that drug and alcohol use, although still a problem, has stabilized or declined.

Although overall illicit drug use by youth aged twelve to seventeen has declined somewhat in recent years (a significant 8.6 percent reduction between 2002 and 2004),[30] it still remains a significant problem. For example, *heavy drinking* (defined as having five or more alcoholic drinks on the same occasion on at least five

Table 10.1 **Annual Drug Use, 1995–1996 Versus 2004–2005, Grades 6–12**

	1995–1996 (%)	*2004–2005 (%)*	*Rate of Decrease (%)*
Cigarettes	40.5	24.3	40.0
Any alcohol	58.8	47.2	19.7
Any illicit drug	29.5	22.3	24.4

Source: PRIDE Surveys, *PRIDE Questionnaire Report for Grades 6 thru 12: 2004–05 National Summary* (Bowling Green, KY: Author, August 17, 2006), Tables 2.9, 2.10.

different days in the past thirty days) was reported by about 7 percent of the population aged twelve and older, or just under 17 million people. Among youths aged twelve to seventeen, about 3 percent were heavy drinkers and 11 percent engaged in *binge drinking*, defined as having five or more alcoholic beverages on the same occasion at least once in the past thirty days.[31]

The latest NSDUH results also showed that—for the first time in the survey's decades-long history—overall illicit drug use in the past month by adolescent girls was identical to that of adolescent boys (10.6 percent for both). Girls continued to have a higher rate than boys in the misuse of prescription drugs when asked about lifetime (14.4 percent vs. 12.5 percent), past year (10.1 percent vs. 7.6 percent), and past month (4.1 percent vs. 3.2 percent) usage.[32] The survey also found that adolescent girls are closing the gap with their male counterparts in terms of usage of marijuana, alcohol, and cigarettes. In each of the last 3 years (2002–2004), more girls than boys started using marijuana, and in the latest survey more girls than boys started using alcohol (1.5 million compared to 1.3 million) and cigarettes (730,000 compared to 565,000). Some of this might be explained by teen girls having higher rates of depression and anxiety and greater concerns about weight and appearance and being more susceptible to pressure from friends when it comes to drinking.[33]

Are the Survey Results Accurate?

Student drug surveys must be interpreted with caution. First, it may be overly optimistic to expect that heavy users are going to cooperate with a drug-use survey, especially one conducted by a government agency. Even if they were willing, these students are likely to be absent from school during testing periods. Also, drug abusers are more likely to be forgetful and to give inaccurate accounts of their substance abuse.

Another problem is the likelihood that the most drug-dependent portion of the adolescent population is omitted from the sample. In some cities, almost half of all youths arrested dropped out of school before the twelfth grade, and more than half of these arrestees are drug users.[34] Juvenile detainees (those arrested and held in a lockup) test positively for cocaine at a rate many times higher than those reporting recent use in the MTF and PRIDE surveys.[35] The inclusion of eighth-graders in the MTF sample is one way of getting around the dropout problem. Nonetheless, high school surveys may be excluding some of the most drug-prone young people in the population.

There is evidence that the accuracy of reporting may be affected by social and personal traits: Girls are more willing than boys to admit taking drugs; kids from two-parent homes are less willing to admit taking drugs than kids growing up in single-parent homes. Julia Yun Soo Kim, Michael Fendrich, and Joseph Wislar speculate that it is culturally unacceptable for some subgroups in the population, such as Hispanic families, to use drugs, and therefore, in self-report surveys, they may under-represent their involvement.[36]

Although these problems are serious, they are consistent over time and therefore do not hinder the *measurement of change* or trends in drug usage. That is, prior surveys also omitted dropouts and other high-risk individuals. However, because these problems are built into every wave of the survey, any change recorded in the annual substance-abuse rate is probably genuine. So, although the *validity* of these surveys may be questioned, they are probably *reliable* indicators of trends in substance abuse. ✔ Checkpoints

CHECKPOINTS

■ Just under half of all high-school seniors have tried drugs.

■ Use of marijuana, alcohol, and cigarettes is on the decline.

■ Alcohol remains the drug of choice for most teens.

■ Prescription drugs and inhalants have become popular in recent years.

■ Teenage drug use is measured by three main national surveys: MTF, PRIDE Survey, and NSDUH.

■ Each of these surveys shows that overall illicit drug use has declined in recent years.

WHY DO YOUTHS TAKE DRUGS?

Why do youths engage in an activity that is sure to bring them overwhelming problems? It is hard to imagine that even the youngest drug users are unaware of the problems associated with substance abuse. Although it is easy to understand dealers' desires for quick profits, how can we explain users' disregard for long- and short-term consequences? Concept Summary 10.1 reviews some of the most likely reasons.

Key Reasons Why Youths Take Drugs

Social disorganization	Poverty, growing up in disorganized urban environment.
Peer pressure	Associating with youths who take drugs.
Family factors	Poor family life, including harsh punishment, neglect.
Genetic factors	Parents abuse drugs.
Emotional problems	Feelings of inadequacy; blame others for failures.
Problem behavior syndrome	Drug use is one of many problem behaviors.
Rational choice	Perceived benefits, including relaxation, greater creativity.

Social Disorganization

One explanation ties drug abuse to poverty, social disorganization, and hopelessness. Drug use by young minority group members has been tied to factors, such as racial prejudice, low self-esteem, poor socioeconomic status, and the stress of living in a harsh urban environment.[37] The association between drug use, race, and poverty has been linked to the high level of mistrust and defiance found in lower socioeconomic areas.[38]

Despite the long-documented association between social disorganization and drug use, the empirical data on the relationship between class and crime have been inconclusive. For example, the National Youth Survey (NYS), a longitudinal study of delinquent behavior conducted by Delbert Elliott and his associates, found little if any association between drug use and social class. The NYS found that drug use is higher among urban youths, but there was little evidence that minority youths or members of the lower class were more likely to abuse drugs than European American youths and the more affluent.[39] Research by the Rand Corporation indicates that many drug-dealing youths had legitimate jobs at the time they were arrested for drug trafficking.[40] Therefore, it would be difficult to describe drug abusers simply as unemployed dropouts.

Young people may take drugs for many reasons, including peer pressure, growing up in a rough neighborhood, poor family life, living with parents who abuse drugs, or to escape reality. This teen is one of a number who were interviewed and photographed for Jim Goldberg's book *Raised by Wolves*, a gritty and sobering account of life on the streets of Los Angeles and San Francisco.

© Jim Goldberg/Magnum Photos

Shared feelings and a sense of intimacy lead youths to become fully enmeshed in the "drug-use subculture." Drug users do in fact have intimate and warm relationships with substance-abusing peers, which helps support their habits and behaviors.

© Michelle D. Bridwell/PhotoEdit

Peer Pressure

Research shows that adolescent drug abuse is highly correlated with the behavior of best friends, especially when parental supervision is weak.[41] Youths in inner-city areas where feelings of alienation run high often come in contact with drug users who teach them that drugs provide an answer to their feelings of inadequacy and stress.[42] Perhaps they join with peers to learn the techniques of drug use; their friendships with other drug-dependent youths give them social support for their habit. Empirical research efforts show that a youth's association with friends who are substance abusers increases the probability of drug use.[43] The relationship is reciprocal: adolescent substance abusers seek out friends who engage in these behaviors, and associating with drug abusers leads to increased levels of drug abuse.

Peer networks may be the most significant influence on long-term substance abuse. Shared feelings and a sense of intimacy lead youths to become enmeshed in what has been described as the "drug-use subculture."[44] Research indicates that drug users do in fact have warm relationships with substance-abusing peers who help support their behaviors.[45] This lifestyle provides users with a clear role, activities they enjoy, and an opportunity for attaining status among their peers.[46] One reason it is so difficult to treat hard-core users is that quitting drugs means leaving the "fast life" of the streets.

Family Factors

Another explanation is that drug users have a poor family life. Studies have found that the majority of drug users have had an unhappy childhood, which included harsh punishment and parental neglect.[47] The drug abuse and family quality association may involve both racial and gender differences: females and European Americans who were abused as children are more likely to have alcohol and drug arrests as adults; abuse was less likely to affect drug use in males and African Americans.[48] It is also common to find substance abusers in large families and with parents who are divorced, separated, or absent.[49]

Social psychologists suggest that drug abuse patterns may also result from observation of parental drug use.[50] Youths who learn that drugs provide pleasurable sensations may be most likely to experiment with illegal substances; a habit may develop if the user experiences lower anxiety and fear.[51] Research shows, for example, that gang members raised in families with a history of drug use were more likely than other gang members to use cocaine and to use it seriously. And even among gang members parental drug abuse was a key factor in the onset of adolescent drug use.[52] Observing drug abuse may be a more important cause of drug abuse than other family-related problems.

Other family factors associated with teen drug abuse include parental conflict over child-rearing practices, failure to set rules, and unrealistic demands followed by harsh punishments. Low parental attachment, rejection, and excessive family conflict have all been linked to adolescent substance abuse.[53]

Genetic Factors

The association between parental drug abuse and adolescent behavior may have a genetic basis. Research has shown that biological children of alcoholics reared by non-alcoholic adoptive parents more often develop alcohol problems than the natural children of the adoptive parents.[54] A number of studies comparing alcoholism among identical and fraternal twins have found that the degree of concordance (that is, both siblings behaving identically) is twice as high among the identical twin groups.[55]

A genetic basis for drug abuse is also supported by evidence showing that future substance abuse problems can be predicted by behavior exhibited as early as six years of age. The traits predicting future abuse are independent from peer relations and environmental influences.[56]

Emotional Problems

As we have seen, not all drug-abusing youths reside in lower-class urban areas. To explain drug abuse across social classes, some experts have linked drug use to emotional problems that can strike youths in any economic class. Psychodynamic explanations of substance abuse suggest that drugs help youths control or express unconscious needs. Some psychoanalysts believe adolescents who internalize their problems may use drugs to reduce their feelings of inadequacy. Introverted people may use drugs as an escape from real or imagined feelings of inferiority.[57] Another view is that adolescents who externalize their problems and blame others for their perceived failures are likely to engage in antisocial behaviors, including substance abuse. Research exists to support each of these positions.[58]

addiction-prone personality
The view that the cause of substance abuse can be traced to a personality that has a compulsion for mood-altering drugs.

Drug abusers are also believed to exhibit psychopathic or sociopathic behavior characteristics, forming what is called an **addiction-prone personality**.[59] Drinking alcohol may reflect a teen's need to remain dependent on an overprotective mother or an effort to reduce the emotional turmoil of adolescence.[60]

Research on the psychological characteristics of narcotics abusers does, in fact, reveal the presence of a significant degree of pathology. Personality testing of users suggests that a significant percentage suffer from psychotic disorders. Studies have found that addicts suffer personality disorders characterized by a weak ego, low frustration tolerance, and fantasies of omnipotence. Up to half of all drug abusers may also be diagnosed with antisocial personality disorder (ASPD), which is defined as a pervasive pattern of disregard for the rights of others.[61]

To read more about the concept of addiction, go to the **Psychedelic Library** website by going to www.thomsonedu.com/criminaljustice/siegel.

Problem Behavior Syndrome

For some adolescents, substance abuse is one of many problem behaviors that begin early in life and remain throughout the life course.[62] Longitudinal studies show that youths who abuse drugs are maladjusted, emotionally distressed, and have many social problems.[63] Having a deviant lifestyle means associating with delinquent peers, living in a family in which parents and siblings abuse drugs, being alienated from the dominant values of society, and engaging in delinquent behaviors at an early age.[64] Youths who abuse drugs lack commitment to religious values, disdain education, and spend most of their time in peer activities.[65] Youths who take drugs do poorly in school, have high dropout rates, and maintain their drug use after they leave school.[66] (Chapter 5 provides an in-depth discussion of problem behavior syndrome.)

Rational Choice

Youths may choose to use drugs because they want to get high, relax, improve their creativity, escape reality, or increase their sexual responsiveness. Research indicates that adolescent alcohol abusers believe getting high will increase their sexual performance and facilitate their social behavior; they care little about negative consequences.[67] Substance abuse, then, may be a function of the rational, albeit mistaken, belief that substance abuse benefits the user.

For a Web-based antidrug education campaign, see **Freevibe** by going to www.thomsonedu.com/criminaljustice/siegel.

PATHWAYS TO DRUG ABUSE

gateway drug
A substance that leads to use of more serious drugs; alcohol use has long been thought to lead to more serious drug abuse.

Although there is not a single path to becoming a drug abuser, it is generally believed that most users start at a young age using alcohol as a **gateway drug** to harder substances. That is, drug involvement begins with drinking alcohol at an early age, which progresses to experimentation with marijuana, and finally to using cocaine and even heroin. Research on adolescent drug users in Miami found that youths who began their substance abuse careers early—by experimenting with alcohol at age seven, getting drunk at age eight, having alcohol with an adult present by age nine, and becoming regular drinkers by the time they were eleven years old—later became crack users.[68] Drinking with an adult present was a significant precursor of substance abuse and delinquency.[69]

Although the gateway concept is still being debated, there is little disagreement that serious drug users begin their involvement with alcohol.[70] Although most recreational users do not progress to "hard stuff," most addicts first experiment with recreational alcohol and recreational drugs before progressing to narcotics. By implication, if teen drinking could be reduced, the gateway to hard drugs would be narrowed.

Most experts believe that drug involvement begins with drinking alcohol at an early age, which progresses to experimentation with marijuana and finally to cocaine and then heroin. Although most recreational users do not progress to addictive drugs, few addicts begin their drug involvement with narcotics.

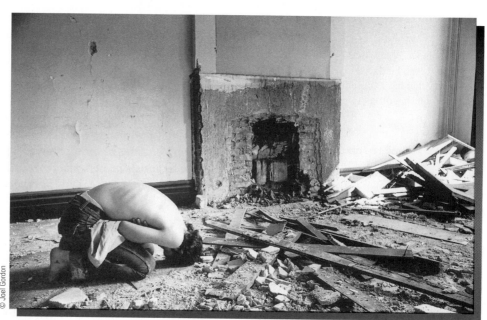

© Joel Gordon

What are the patterns of teenage drug use? Are all abusers similar, or are there different types of drug involvement? Research indicates that drug-involved youths do take on different roles, lifestyles, and behavior patterns, some of which are described in the next sections.[71]

Adolescents Who Distribute Small Amounts of Drugs

Many adolescents who use and distribute small amounts of drugs do not commit any other serious delinquent acts. They occasionally sell marijuana, crystal, and PCP to support their own drug use. Their customers include friends, relatives, and acquaintances. Deals are arranged over the phone, in school, or at public meeting places; however, the actual distribution occurs in more private arenas, such as at home or in cars. Petty dealers do not consider themselves seriously involved in drugs.

Adolescents Who Frequently Sell Drugs

A small number of adolescents are high-rate dealers who bridge the gap between adult drug distributors and the adolescent user. Though many are daily users, they take part in many normal activities, including going to school and socializing with friends.

Frequent dealers often have adults who "front" for them—that is, sell them drugs for cash. The teenagers then distribute the drugs to friends and acquaintances. They return most of the proceeds to the supplier, keeping a commission for themselves. They may also keep drugs for their personal use, and in fact, some consider their dealing as a way of "getting high for free." One young user, Winston, age seventeen, told investigators, "I sell the cracks for money and for cracks. The man, he give me this *much*. I sell most of it and I get the rest for me. I like this much. Every day I do this."[72] James Inciardi and his associates found that about 80 percent of the youths who dealt crack regularly were daily users.[73]

Frequent dealers are more likely to sell drugs in parks, schools, or other public places. Deals occur irregularly, so the chance of apprehension is not significant, nor is the payoff substantial. Robert MacCoun and Peter Reuter found that drug dealers make about thirty dollars per hour when they are working and clear on average about two thousand dollars per month. These amounts are greater than most dealers could hope to earn in legitimate jobs, but they are not enough to afford a steady stream of luxuries. Most smalltime dealers also hold conventional jobs.[74]

In a more recent analysis of the financial activities of a drug-selling street gang over a four-year period in which the gang was active, economists Steven Levitt and Sudhir Venkatesh found that the average hourly wage of drug dealers or "foot soldiers" was between $2.50 and $7.10 (see Table 10.2).[75] As an average wage per month, this comes to $140 to $470.[76] In a typical month, drug dealers worked just over fifty hours. As shown in Table 10.2, the hourly wage of drug dealers is substantially lower

Table 10.2 **Estimated Hourly Wages of Members in a Drug-Selling Gang**

	Drug Dealers	All Gang Members	Gang Leader
Year 1	$2.50	$5.90	$32.50
Year 2	$3.70	$7.40	$47.50
Year 3	$3.30	$7.10	$65.90
Year 4	$7.10	$11.10	$97.20

Notes: Estimated hourly wages include both official and unofficial income sources. All wages are in 1995 dollars.

Source: Adapted from Steven D. Levitt and Sudhir A. Venkatesh, "An Economic Analysis of a Drug-Selling Gang's Finances," *Quarterly Journal of Economics* 115:755–789 (2000), Table III.

than the average wage for all gang members and the gang leader. These more recent findings suggest that, at least for drug dealers, factors other than income may explain participation in this activity.

Teenage Drug Dealers Who Commit Other Delinquent Acts

A more serious type of drug-involved youth is the one who distributes multiple substances and commits both property and violent crimes. These youngsters make up about 2 percent of the teenage population, but they may commit up to 40 percent of the robberies and assaults and about 60 percent of all teenage felony thefts and drug sales. Few gender or racial differences exist among these youths: girls are as likely as boys to become persistent drug-involved offenders, European American youths as likely as African American youths, and middle-class adolescents raised outside cities as likely as lower-class city children.[77]

In cities, these youths frequently are hired by older dealers to act as street-level drug runners. Each member of a crew of three to twelve youths will handle small quantities of drugs; the supplier receives 50 percent to 70 percent of the drug's street value. The crew members also act as lookouts, recruiters, and guards. Although they may be recreational drug users themselves, crew members refrain from using addictive drugs such as heroin. Between drug sales, the young dealers commit robberies, burglaries, and other thefts.

Some experts question whether gangs are responsible for as much drug dealing as the media would have us believe. Some believe that the tightly organized "super" gangs are being replaced with loosely organized neighborhood groups. The turbulent environment of drug dealing is better handled by flexible organizations than by rigid, vertically organized gangs with a leader who is far removed from the action.[78]

Losers and Burnouts

Some drug-involved youths do not have the savvy to join gangs or groups and instead begin committing unplanned crimes that increase their chances of arrest. Their heavy drug use increases their risk of apprehension and decreases their value for organized drug distribution networks. Drug-involved "losers" can earn a living by steering customers to a seller in a "copping" area, touting drug availability for a dealer, or acting as a lookout. However, they are not considered trustworthy or deft enough to handle drugs or money. Although these offenders get involved in drugs at an early age, they receive little attention from the justice system until they have developed an extensive arrest record. By then they are approaching the end of their minority and will either desist or become so entrapped in the drug-crime subculture that little can be done to deter their illegal activities.

Persistent Offenders

About two-thirds of substance-abusing youths continue to use drugs in adulthood, but about half desist from other criminal activities. Those who persist in both substance abuse and crime maintain these characteristics:

- They come from poor families.
- Their family members include other criminals.
- They do poorly in school.
- They started using drugs and committing other delinquent acts at an early age.
- They use multiple types of drugs and commit crimes frequently.
- They have few opportunities in late adolescence to participate in legitimate and rewarding adult activities.[79]

Some evidence exists that these drug-using persisters have low nonverbal IQs and poor physical coordination. Nonetheless, there is little evidence to explain why some drug-abusing youths drop out of crime, whereas others remain active. ✔ Checkpoints

DRUG USE AND DELINQUENCY

An association between drug use and delinquency has been established, and this connection can take a number of forms. Crime may be an instrument of the drug trade: violence erupts when rival gangs use weapons to settle differences and establish territorial monopolies. In New York City, authorities report that crack gangs will burn down their rival's headquarters. It is estimated that between 35 percent and 40 percent of New York's homicides are drug-related.[80]

Drug users may also commit crimes to pay for their habits.[81] One study conducted in Miami found that 573 narcotics users *annually* committed more than two hundred thousand crimes to obtain cash. Similar research with a sample of 356 addicts accounted for 118,000 crimes annually.[82] If such proportions hold true, then the nation's estimated seven hundred thousand heroin addicts alone may be committing more than 100 million crimes each year.

Drug users may be more willing to take risks, because their inhibitions are lowered by substance abuse. Cities with high rates of cocaine abuse are also more likely to experience higher levels of armed robbery. It is possible that crack and cocaine users are more willing to engage in a risky armed robbery to get immediate cash than a burglary, which requires more planning and effort.[83]

The relationship between alcohol and drug abuse and delinquency has been substantiated by a number of studies. Some have found that youths who abuse alcohol are most likely to engage in violence; as adults, those with long histories of drinking are more likely to report violent offending patterns.[84]

The National Institute of Justice's Arrestee Drug Abuse Monitoring (ADAM) program tracked trends in drug use among arrestees in urban areas. Some, but not all, of its thirty-six sites collected data on juveniles. Due to lack of funding, the Department of Justice ended this program in 2004.[85] The most recent report (2002) found that, among juvenile detainees, almost 60 percent of juvenile males and 30 percent of juvenile females tested positive for marijuana, the most commonly used drug, and its prevalence was ten and six times higher than cocaine use for juvenile males and females, respectively. With the exception of methamphetamines, male detainees were more likely to test positive for the use of any drug than were female detainees.[86]

Similar results were found in the Northwestern Juvenile Project, a longitudinal study of 1,829 juvenile detainees in Chicago's Cook County Juvenile Temporary Detention Center. Two-thirds (67.4 percent) of juvenile males and 45 percent of juvenile females tested positive for marijuana, which was also the most commonly used drug, and its prevalence was fourteen and twelve times higher than cocaine use for juvenile males and females, respectively.[87] Although males and minority-group members have somewhat higher positive test rates than females and European Americans, drug use is prevalent among juvenile arrestees, reaffirming the close association between substance abuse and criminality.

There is evidence that incarcerated youths are much more likely to be involved in substance abuse than adolescents in the general population. For example, research by David Cantor on incarcerated youths in Washington, D.C., found their drug involvement more than double that of non-incarcerated area youths.[88]

Drugs and Chronic Offending

It is possible that most delinquents are not drug users, but that police are more likely to apprehend muddle-headed substance abusers than clear-thinking abstainers. A second, more plausible, interpretation of the existing data is that the drug abuse–crime connection is so powerful because many criminals are in fact substance abusers. Research by Bruce Johnson and his associates confirms this suspicion. Using data from a national self-report survey, these researchers found that less than 2 percent of the youths who responded to the survey (a) report using cocaine or heroin, and (b) commit two or more index crimes each year. However, these drug-abusing adolescents accounted for 40 percent to 60 percent of all the index crimes reported in the sample. Less than one-quarter of these delinquents committed crimes solely to support a drug habit. These data suggest that a small core of substance-abusing adolescents commit a significant proportion of all serious crimes. It is also evident that a behavior—drug abuse—that develops late in adolescence influences the extent of delinquent activity through the life course.[89]

Explaining Drug Use and Delinquency

The association between delinquency and drug use has been established in a variety of cultures.[90] It is far from certain, however, whether (a) drug use *causes* delinquency, (b) delinquency *leads* youths to engage in substance abuse, or (c) both drug abuse and delinquency are *functions* of some other factor.[91]

Some of the most sophisticated research on this topic has been conducted by Delbert Elliott and his associates at the Institute of Behavioral Science at the University of Colorado.[92] Using data from the National Youth Survey, the longitudinal study of self-reported delinquency and drug use mentioned earlier in this chapter, Elliott and his colleagues David Huizinga and Scott Menard found a strong association between delinquency and drug use.[93] However, the direction of the relationship is unclear. As a general rule, drug abuse appears to be a *type* of delinquent behavior and not a *cause* of delinquency.[94] Most youths become involved in delinquent acts *before* they are initiated into drugs; it is difficult therefore to conclude that drug use causes crime. In other research involving the National Youth Survey, Jason Ford found that there is a reciprocal and ongoing relationship between alcohol use and delinquency during adolescence, and that part of the reason for this reciprocal relationship is that both behaviors have the effect of weakening youths' bonds with society, thereby promoting continued alcohol use and delinquency.[95]

According to the Elliott research, both drug use and delinquency seem to reflect developmental problems; they are both part of a disturbed lifestyle. This research reveals some important associations between substance abuse and delinquency:

1. Alcohol abuse seems to be a cause of marijuana and other drug abuse, because most drug users started with alcohol, and youths who abstain from alcohol almost never take drugs.

2. Marijuana use is a cause of multiple drug use: about 95 percent of youths who use more serious drugs started on pot; only 5 percent of serious drug users never smoked pot.

3. Youths who commit felonies started off with minor delinquent acts. Few delinquents (1 percent) report committing only felonies.

DRUG CONTROL STRATEGIES

Billions of dollars are spent each year to reduce the importation of drugs, deter drug dealers, and treat users. Yet although the overall incidence of drug use has declined, drug use has concentrated in the nation's poorest neighborhoods, with a consequent association between substance abuse and crime.

A number of drug-control strategies have been tried. Some are designed to deter drug use by stopping the flow of drugs into the country, apprehending dealers, and cracking down on street-level drug deals. Another approach is to prevent drug use by educating would-be users and convincing them to "say no" to drugs. A third approach is to treat users so that they can terminate their addictions. Some of these efforts are discussed in the following sections.

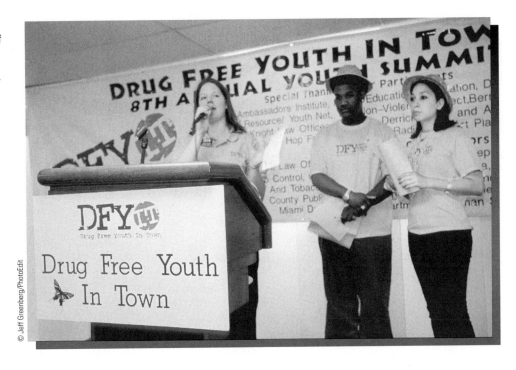

Strategies to control drugs and their use are wide-ranging, and the results of many of these strategies are disappointing. Here, teens participate in a youth anti-drug and anti-violence workshop in Miami, Florida, to learn more about what works and how teens can play a role in preventing drug use and violence.

Law Enforcement Efforts

Law enforcement strategies are aimed at reducing the supply of drugs and, at the same time, deterring would-be users from drug abuse.

Source Control One approach to drug control is to deter the sale of drugs through apprehension of large-volume drug dealers coupled with enforcement of drug laws that carry heavy penalties. This approach is designed to punish known dealers and users and to deter those who are considering entering the drug trade.

A great effort has been made to cut off supplies of drugs by destroying overseas crops and arresting members of drug cartels; this approach is known as *source control*. The federal government has been encouraging exporting nations to step up efforts to destroy drug crops and prosecute dealers. Other less aggressive source control approaches, such as crop substitution and alternative development programs for the largely poor farmers in other countries, have also been tried, and a recent review of international efforts suggests that, "some success can be achieved in reduction of narcotic crop production."[96] Three South American nations—Peru, Bolivia, and Colombia—have agreed to coordinate control efforts with the United States. However, translating words into deeds is a formidable task. Drug lords fight back through intimidation, violence, and corruption. The United States was forced to invade Panama with twenty thousand troops in 1989 to stop its leader, General Manuel Noriega, from trafficking in cocaine.

Even when efforts are successful in one area, they may result in a shift in production to another area or in the targeted crop being replaced by another. For example, between 1994 and 1999, enforcement efforts in Peru and Bolivia were so successful that they altered cocaine cultivation patterns. As a consequence, Colombia became the premier coca-cultivating country when the local drug cartels encouraged growers to cultivate coca plants. When the Colombian government mounted an effective eradication campaign in the traditional growing areas, the cartel linked up with rebel groups in remote parts of the country for their drug supply.[97] Leaders in neighboring countries expressed fear when, in August 2000, the United States announced $1.3 billion in military aid to fight Colombia's rural drug dealers/rebels, assuming that success would drive traffickers over the border.[98] Another unintended effect of this campaign has been a recent shift by drug cartels to exploit new crops, from a traditional

What Does This Mean to Me?

Reducing Drug Activity

There is no easy solution to reducing drug-related activities. Some experts argue that less serious drugs like marijuana should be de-criminalized, others call for the continued use of police stings and long sentences for drug violations, and some advocate for more education and treatment. Suppose in your community you have witnessed the harms associated with teenage drug use and drug selling, but have also seen the need for some users to get treatment rather than punishment.

1. What do you recommend be done to address the drug problem more effectively? Explain.
2. What are some things you could do in your community to help prevent children and youth from getting involved in drug-related activities?

emphasis on coca to opium poppy, the plant used to make heroin. It is estimated that Latin American countries, including Mexico, now supply upwards of 80 percent of the heroin consumed in the United States.[99] Perhaps not surprisingly, Afghanistan has since reclaimed its position as the world leader in opium production, accounting for 75 percent to 87 percent of the global market.[100] This has come about after the fall of the Taliban government in 2001, which had banned poppy growing. Now, almost all of the heroin sold in Russia and three-quarters of that sold in Europe comes from Afghanistan. This has occurred despite new laws against poppy growing, law enforcement efforts, and crop substitution efforts on the part of agricultural aid organizations. Breaking with religious beliefs, Taliban forces are now promoting the growing of poppy—in some areas distributing leaflets that order farmers to grow the crop—and providing protection to drug smugglers, all in an effort to finance their operations against the United States military and Coalition forces in the country.[101]

Border Control Law enforcement efforts have also been directed at interdicting drug supplies as they enter the country. Border patrols and military personnel have been involved in massive interdiction efforts, and many billion-dollar seizures have been made. It is estimated that between one-quarter and one-third of the annual cocaine supply shipped to the United States is seized by drug enforcement agencies. Yet U.S. borders are so vast and unprotected that meaningful interdiction is impossible. In 2001, U.S. law enforcement agencies seized 233,000 pounds of cocaine and almost 5,500 pounds of heroin.[102] Global rates of interception of cocaine indicate that only one-third of all imports are being seized by law enforcement.[103]

In recent years, another form of border control to interdict drugs entering the country has emerged: targeting Internet drug traffickers in foreign countries. With the increasing popularity of the Internet, some offenders are now turning to this source to obtain designer-type drugs. In Buffalo, New York, U.S. Customs discovered that a steady flow of packages containing the drug gamma-butyrolactone or GBL, an ingredient of GBH (gamma hydroxybutyrate), also known as the date-rape drug, were entering the country from Canada; the drug was disguised as a cleaning product. Operation Webslinger, a joint investigation of federal law enforcement agencies in the United States and Canada, was put in place to track down the suppliers. Within a year, Operation Webslinger had shut down four Internet drug rings operating in the United States and Canada, made 115 arrests in eighty-four cities, and seized the equivalent of twenty-five million doses of GBH and other, related drugs.[104] Shortly following this, another federal task force, known as Operation Gray Lord and involving the Food and Drug Administration (FDA) and the Drug Enforcement Administration (DEA), was set up to combat illegal sales of narcotics on the Internet.[105]

If all importation were ended, homegrown marijuana and lab-made drugs such as Ecstasy could become the drugs of choice. Even now, their easy availability and relatively low cost are increasing their popularity; they are a $10 billion business in the United States today. In 2003 (most recent data available), more than 10,100 illegal methamphetamine laboratories were seized by authorities across the United States, with the Midwest Region accounting for 30 percent (or 3,038 seizures).[106] Many of these labs were operated out of homes, putting children—3,300 children were found in 8,000 of these labs—at grave risk of being burned or injured, not to mention exposing them to illegal drugs.[107]

Targeting Dealers Law enforcement agencies have also made a concerted effort to focus on drug trafficking. Efforts have been made to bust large-scale drug rings. The long-term consequence has been to decentralize drug dealing and to encourage teenage gangs to become major suppliers. Ironically, it has proven easier for federal agents to infiltrate traditional organized crime groups than to take on drug-dealing gangs.

Police can also intimidate and arrest street-level dealers and users in an effort to make drug use so much of a hassle that consumption is cut back. Some street-level enforcement efforts have had success, but others are considered failures. "Drug sweeps" have clogged correctional facilities with petty offenders while draining police resources. These sweeps are also suspected of creating a displacement effect: stepped-up efforts to curb drug dealing in one area or city may encourage dealers to seek out friendlier territory.[108] People arrested on drug-related charges are among the fastest growing segments of both the juvenile and adult justice systems. National surveys have found that juvenile court judges are prone to use a get-tough approach on drug-involved offenders. They are more likely to be processed formally by the court than all other categories of delinquent offenders, including those who commit violent crimes, and to be detained between referral to court and disposition than property offenders.[109] Despite these efforts, juvenile drug use continues, indicating that a get-tough policy is not sufficient to deter drug use.

Go to the official site of **D.A.R.E.** via www.thomsonedu.com/ criminaljustice/spiegel.

Education Strategies

Another approach to reducing teenage substance abuse relies on educational programs. Drug education now begins in kindergarten and extends through the twelfth grade. An overwhelming majority of public school districts across the United States have implemented drug education programs with various components, including: teaching students about the causes and effects of alcohol, drug, and tobacco use; teaching students to resist peer pressure; and referring students for counseling and treatment.[110] Education programs, such as Project ALERT that now operates in all fifty states, have been shown to be successful in training middle-school youths to avoid recreational drugs and to resist peer pressure to use cigarettes and alcohol.[111] The most widely used drug prevention program, Drug Abuse Resistance Education (D.A.R.E.), is discussed in the accompanying Preventing and Treating Delinquency feature.

Two recent large-scale studies demonstrate the effectiveness of anti-drug messages targeted at youth. An evaluation of the National Youth Anti-Drug Media Campaign, which features ads showing the dangers of marijuana use, reported that 41 percent of students in grades seven to twelve "agree a lot" that the ads made them less likely to try or use drugs. Importantly, the study also reported that past-year marijuana use among the students was down 6 percent.[112] The second study, the National Survey on Drug Use and Health, which asked young people ages twelve to seventeen about anti-drug messages they had heard or seen outside of school hours, reported that past-month drug use by those exposed to the messages was 13 percent lower than those who had not been exposed to the messages.[113] These are encouraging findings given the limited effectiveness of D.A.R.E.

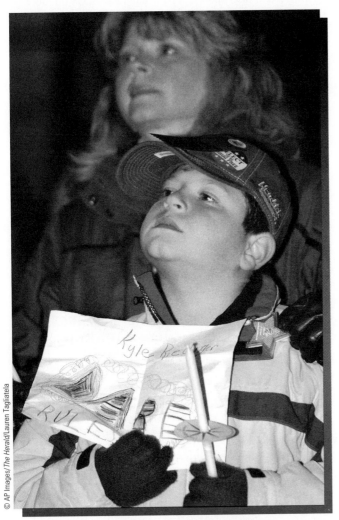

© AP Images/*The Herald*/Lauren Tagliatela

The Drug Abuse Resistance Education (D.A.R.E.) program employs uniformed police officers to give young students the skills for resisting peer pressure to experiment with tobacco, drugs, and alcohol. While reviews of its effectiveness have been mixed, the program remains popular among some constituents. Here, Kyle Riedinger, ten years old, holds a sign that says "D.A.R.E. Rules" as he and his mom Michele attend a drug-free rally.

Drug Abuse Resistance Education (D.A.R.E.)

The most widely known drug education program, Drug Abuse Resistance Education (D.A.R.E.), is an elementary school course designed to give students the skills they need to resist peer pressure to experiment with tobacco, drugs, and alcohol. It is unique because it employs uniformed police officers to carry the anti-drug message to the children before they enter junior high school. The program focuses on five major areas:

- Providing accurate information about tobacco, alcohol, and drugs
- Teaching students techniques to resist peer pressure
- Teaching students to respect the law and law enforcers
- Giving students ideas for alternatives to drug use
- Building the self-esteem of students

The D.A.R.E. program is based on the concept that the young students need specific analytical and social skills to resist peer pressure and "say no" to drugs. Instructors work with children to raise their self-esteem, provide them with decision-making tools, and help them identify positive alternatives to substance abuse.

The D.A.R.E. approach has been adopted widely since it was founded in 1983. D.A.R.E. America indicates that the program is now taught in almost 80 percent of school districts nationwide and in fifty-four other countries. It is also claimed that, in 2006, 26 million children in the United States and 10 million children in other countries participated in the program. More than 40 percent of all school districts incorporate assistance from local law enforcement agencies in their drug-prevention programming.

Does D.A.R.E. Work?

Although D.A.R.E. is popular with both schools and police agencies, a number of evaluations have not found it to have an impact on student drug usage. For example, in a highly sophisticated evaluation of the program, Donald Lynam and his colleagues found the program to be ineffective over both the short and long term. They followed a cohort of sixth-grade children who attended a total of thirty-one schools. Twenty-three of the schools were randomly assigned to receive D.A.R.E. in the sixth grade, whereas the other eight received whatever drug education was routinely provided in their classes. The research team assessed the participants yearly through the tenth grade and then recontacted them when they were twenty years old. They found that D.A.R.E. had no effect on students' drug use at any time through tenth grade. The ten-year follow-up failed to find any hidden or "sleeper" effects that were delayed in developing. At age twenty, there were no differences between those who went through D.A.R.E. and those who did not in their use of cigarettes, alcohol, marijuana, or other drugs; the only difference was that those who had participated in D.A.R.E. reported slightly lower levels of self-esteem at age twenty—an effect that proponents were not aiming for. In the most rigorous and comprehensive review so far on the effectiveness of D.A.R.E., the General Accountability Office (GAO, formerly the General Accounting Office), the research arm of Congress, found that the program neither prevents student drug use nor changes student attitudes toward drugs.

Changing the D.A.R.E. Curriculum

Although national evaluations and independent reviews have questioned the validity of D.A.R.E. and many communities have discontinued its use—due in part to the program not meeting U.S. Department of Education effectiveness standards—it is still widely employed in school districts around the country. To meet criticism head-on, D.A.R.E. began testing a new curriculum for middle and high school programs, known as "Take Charge of Your Life." The new program is aimed at older students and relies more on having them question their assumptions about drug use than on listening to lectures on the subject. The new program will work largely on changing social norms, teaching students to question whether they really have to use drugs to fit in with their peers. Emphasis will shift from fifth-grade students to those in the seventh grade and a booster program will be added in ninth grade, when kids are more likely to experiment with drugs. Police officers will now serve more as coaches than as lecturers, encouraging students to challenge the social norm of drug use in discussion groups. Students also will do more role-playing in an effort to learn decision-making skills. There will also be an emphasis on the role of media and advertising in shaping behavior. The new curricula is undergoing tests in a total of 83 high schools and 122 middle schools in six large cities—half the schools will continue using the curriculum they do now, and the other half will use the new D.A.R.E. program—so that the new curriculum may be scientifically evaluated. Early study results suggest that the new curriculum is being delivered as designed and is reaching the highest risk youth.

CRITICAL THINKING

1. Do you believe that an education program such as D.A.R.E. can turn kids away from drugs, or are the reasons for teenage drug use so complex that a single school-based program is doomed to fail?
2. If you ran D.A.R.E., what experiences would you give to the children? Do you think it would be effective to have current or ex-addicts address classes about how drugs influenced their lives?

INFOTRAC COLLEGE EDITION RESEARCH

For more information on the enhanced D.A.R.E. program, go to InfoTrac College Edition and read "Enhanced D.A.R.E. Program More Effective for Adolescent Boys," *Brown University Child and Adolescent Behavior Letter 19*:1 (April 2003).

Sources: Carnevale Associates, *A Longitudinal Evaluation of the New Curricula for the D.A.R.E. Middle (7th Grade) and High School (9th Grade) Programs: Take Charge of Your Life. Year Four Progress Report* (Washington, DC: Author, 2006); D.A.R.E. America (2006), www.dare.com; Carol Hirschon Weiss, Erin Murphy-Graham, and Sarah Birkeland, "An Alternative Route to Policy Influence: How Evaluations Affect D.A.R.E.," *American Journal of Evaluation 26*:12–30 (2005); Anthony Petrosino, "D.A.R.E. and Scientific Evidence: A 20 Year History," *Japanese Journal of Sociological Criminology 30*:72–88 (2005); Youth Illicit Drug Use Prevention: D.A.R.E. Long-Term Evaluations and Federal Efforts to Identify Effective Programs (Washington, DC: U.S. General Accountability Office, 2003), p. 2; Brian Vastag, "GAO: DARE Does Not Work," *Journal of the American Medical Association 289*:539 (2003); Donald R. Lynam, Rich Milich, Rick Zimmerman, Scott Novak, T. K. Logan, Catherine Martin, Carl Leukefeld, and Richard Clayton, "Project D.A.R.E.: No Effects at 10-Year Follow-Up," *Journal of Consulting and Clinical Psychology 67*:590–593 (1999).

Community Strategies

Community-based programs reach out to some of the highest risk youths, who are often missed by the well-known education programs that take place in schools.[114] Community programs try to get youths involved in after-school programs; offer counseling; deliver clothing, food, and medical care when needed; and encourage school achievement. Community programs also sponsor drug-free activities involving the arts, clubs, and athletics. In many respects, these evaluations of community programs have shown that they may encourage anti-drug attitudes and help insulate participating youths from an environment that encourages drugs.[115]

One of the most successful community-based programs to prevent substance abuse and delinquency is provided by the Boys and Girls Clubs (BGCs) of America. One study examined the effectiveness of BGCs for high-risk youths in public housing developments at five sites across the country. The usual services of BGCs, which include reading classes, sports, and homework assistance, were offered, as well as a program to prevent substance abuse, known as SMART Moves (Skills Mastery and Resistance Training). This program targets the specific pressures that young people face to try drugs and alcohol and provides education to parents and the community at large to assist youth in learning about the dangers of substance abuse and strategies for resisting the pressures to use drugs and alcohol.[116] Evaluation results showed that housing developments with BGCs, with and without SMART Moves, produced a reduction in substance abuse, drug trafficking, and other drug-related delinquency activity.[117]

Treatment Strategies

Each year more than 150,000 youths ages twelve to seventeen are admitted to treatment facilities in the United States, with just over half (52 percent) being referred through the juvenile justice system. Almost two-thirds (64 percent) of all admissions involved marijuana as the primary drug of abuse.[118]

Several approaches are available to treat these users. Some efforts stem from the perspective that users have low self-esteem and employ various techniques to build up their sense of self. Some use psychological counseling, and others, such as the **multisystemic treatment (MST)** technique developed by Scott Henggeler, direct attention to family, peer, and psychological problems by focusing on problem solving and communication skills.[119] In a long-term evaluation of MST, Henggeler found that adolescent substance abusers who went through the program were significantly less likely to recidivate than youths who received traditional counseling services. However, mixed treatment effects were reported for future substance abuse by those who received MST compared with those who did not.[120]

multisystemic treatment (MST)
Addresses a variety of family, peer, and psychological problems.

LOOKING BACK TO FERNANDO'S STORY

If you were going to use a multisystemic treatment approach with Fernando, who would you involve and what issues would you plan to address? Do you think this approach could be successful in the case? Why or why not?

Another approach is to involve users in outdoor activities, wilderness training, and after-school community programs.[121] More intensive efforts use group therapy, in which leaders try to give users the skills and support to help them reject social pressure to use drugs. These programs are based on the Alcoholics Anonymous philosophy that users must find the strength to stay clean and that support from those who understand their experiences can be a successful way to achieve a drug-free life.

Residential programs are used with more heavily involved drug abusers. Some are detoxification units that use medical procedures to wean patients from the more addicting drugs. Others are therapeutic communities that attempt to deal with the psychological causes of drug use. Hypnosis, aversion therapy (getting users to associate drugs with unpleasant sensations, such as nausea), counseling, biofeedback, and other techniques are often used.

There is little evidence that these residential programs can efficiently terminate teenage substance abuse.[122] Many are restricted to families whose health insurance will pay for short-term residential care; when the coverage ends, the children are released. Adolescents do not often enter these programs voluntarily, and most have little motivation to change.[123] A stay can stigmatize residents as "addicts" even though they never used hard drugs; while in treatment, they may be introduced to hard-core users with whom they will associate upon release. One residential program that holds promise for reducing teenage substance abuse is UCLA's Comprehensive Residential Education, Arts, and Substance Abuse Treatment (CREASAT) program, which integrates "enhanced substance abuse services" (group therapy, education, vocational skills) and visual and performing arts programming.[124]

Harm Reduction

A **harm reduction** approach involves lessening the harms caused to youths by drug use and by some of the more punitive responses to drug use. Harm reduction encapsulates some of the efforts advanced under the community and treatment strategies noted above, but maintains as its primary focus efforts to minimize the harmful effects of drug use. This approach includes the following components:

- The availability of drug treatment facilities so that all addicts who wish to do so can overcome their habits and lead drug-free lives.

- The use of health professionals to administer drugs to addicts as part of a treatment and detoxification program.

- Needle exchange programs that will slow the transmission of HIV and educate drug users about how HIV is contracted and spread.

- Special drug courts or pretrial diversion programs that compel drug treatment.[125] (Juvenile drug courts are discussed in chapter 11.)

To learn more about the harm reduction approach to teenage drug use, check out the **Harm Reduction Coalition** by going to the website at www.thomsonedu.com/criminaljustice/siegel.

Needle exchange programs—providing drug users with clean needles in exchange for used ones—have been shown to maintain the low prevalence of HIV transmission among drug users and lower rates of hepatitis C. Methadone maintenance clinics in which heroin users receive doctor-prescribed methadone (a nonaddictive substance that satisfies the cravings caused by heroin) have been shown to reduce illegal heroin use and criminal activity.[126]

Critics of the harm reduction approach warn that it condones or promotes drug use, "encouraging people either to continue using drugs or to start using drugs, without recognizing the dangers of their addiction."[127] Advocates, on the other hand, refer to harm reduction as a valuable interim measure in dealing with drug use: "There are safer ways of using drugs and harm reduction for patients is a valuable interim measure to help them make informed choices and improve their overall health."[128] Advocates also call for this approach to replace the "War on Drugs," and claim that this change in drug policy will go a long way toward solving two key problems caused by punitive response. First, it will reduce the number of offenders, both juvenile and adult, being sent to already overcrowded institutionalized settings for what amounts to less serious offenses. Second, it will discourage police crackdowns in minority neighborhoods that result in racial minorities being arrested and formally processed at much higher rates for drug offenses.[129]

The War on Drugs has been a major source of the racial discrimination that occurs in the juvenile justice system. (For more on racial discrimination in the juvenile justice system, see chapters 12, 13, and 14.) The latest data (2002) show that African Americans make up 16 percent of the juvenile population, but account for 21 percent (40,570) of all drug law violations referred to juvenile court. This is down from 44 percent in 1990 and 33 percent in 1995. African American juveniles involved in drug offense cases are also more likely to be detained (held in a detention facility or in shelter care to await court appearances) than European American juveniles.[130] ✔ **Checkpoints**

WHAT DOES THE FUTURE HOLD?

legalization of drugs
Decriminalizing drug use to reduce the association between drug use and crime.

To find out more about the **federal government's drug control strategies**, go to the website at www. thomsonedu.com/criminaljustice/siegel.

The United States appears willing to go to great lengths to fight the drug war.[131] Law enforcement efforts, along with prevention programs and treatment projects, have been stepped up. Yet all drug-control strategies are doomed to fail as long as youths want to take drugs and dealers find that their sale is a lucrative source of income. Prevention, deterrence, and treatment strategies ignore the core reasons for the drug problem: poverty, alienation, and family disruption. As the gap between rich and poor widens and the opportunities for legitimate advancement decrease, it should come as no surprise that adolescent drug use continues.

Some commentators have called for the **legalization of drugs**. This approach can have the short-term effect of reducing the association between drug use and crime (because, presumably, the cost of drugs would decrease), but it may have grave consequences. Drug use would most certainly increase, creating an overflow of unproductive people who must be cared for by the rest of society. The problems of teenage alcoholism should serve as a warning of what can happen when controlled substances are made readily available. However, the implications of decriminalization should be further studied: What effect would a policy of partial decriminalization (for example, legalizing small amounts of marijuana) have on drug use rates? Does a get-tough policy on drugs "widen the net"? Are there alternatives to the criminalization of drugs that could help reduce their use?[132] The Rand Corporation study of drug dealing in Washington, D.C., suggests that law enforcement efforts may have little influence on drug-abuse rates as long as dealers can earn more than the minimal salaries they might earn in the legitimate business world. Only by giving youths legitimate future alternatives can hard-core users be made to forgo drug use willingly.[133]

SUMMARY

- Alcohol is the drug most frequently abused by American teens. Other popular drugs include marijuana; cocaine and its derivative, crack; and designer drugs such as Ecstasy.
- Self-report surveys indicate that just under half of all high school seniors have tried drugs. Surveys of arrestees indicate that a significant proportion of teenagers are drug users and many are high school dropouts. The number of drug users may be even higher than surveys suggest, because these surveys may be missing the most delinquent youths.
- Although the national survey conducted by PRIDE shows that teenage drug use increased slightly in the past year, both it and the Monitoring the Future survey, also national, report that drug and alcohol use are much lower today than five and ten years ago.
- There are many explanations for why youths take drugs, including growing up in disorganized areas in which there is a high degree of hopelessness, poverty, and despair; peer pressure; parental substance abuse; emotional problems; and suffering from general problem behavior syndrome.
- A variety of youths use drugs. Some are occasional users who sell to friends. Others are seriously involved in both

drug abuse and delinquency; many of these are gang members. There are also "losers," who filter in and out of the justice system. A small percentage of teenage users remain involved with drugs into adulthood.
- It is not certain whether drug abuse causes delinquency. Some experts believe there is a common cause for both delinquency and drug abuse—perhaps alienation and rage.
- Many attempts have been made to control the drug trade. Some try to inhibit the importation of drugs, others to close down major drug rings, and a few to stop street-level dealing. There are also attempts to treat users through rehabilitation programs, to reduce juvenile use by educational efforts, and implement harm reduction measures. Some communities have mounted grassroots drives. These efforts have not been totally successful, although overall use of drugs may have declined somewhat.
- It is difficult to eradicate drug abuse because there is so much profit to be made from the sale of drugs. One suggestion: legalize drugs. But critics warn that such a step may produce greater numbers of substance abusers.

QUESTIONS FOR DISCUSSION

1. Discuss the differences between the various categories and types of substances of abuse. Is the term *drugs* too broad to have real meaning?

2. Why do you think youths take drugs? Do you know anyone with an addiction-prone personality?

3. What policy do you think might be the best strategy to reduce teenage drug use? Source control? Reliance on treatment? National education efforts? Community-level enforcement? Harm reduction measures?

4. Do you consider alcohol a drug? Should greater controls be placed on the sale of alcohol?

5. Do TV shows and films glorify drug usage and encourage youths to enter the drug trade? Should all images of drinking and smoking be banned from TV? What about advertisements that try to convince youths how much fun it is to drink beer or smoke cigarettes?

APPLYING WHAT YOU HAVE LEARNED

The president has appointed you the new "drug czar." You have $10 billion under your control with which to wage your campaign. You know that drug use is unacceptably high, especially among poor, inner-city kids, and that a great deal of criminal behavior is drug-related, and that drug-dealing gangs are expanding around the United States.

At an open hearing, drug control experts express their policy strategies. One group favors putting the money into hiring new law enforcement agents who will patrol borders, target large dealers, and make drug raids here and abroad. They also call for such get-tough measures as the creation of strict drug laws, the mandatory waiver of young drug dealers to the adult court system, and the death penalty for drug-related gang killings.

A second group believes the best way to deal with drugs is to spend the money on community treatment programs, expanding the number of beds in drug detoxification units, and funding research on how to reduce drug dependency clinically.

A third group argues that neither punishment nor treatment can restrict teenage drug use and that the best course is to educate at-risk kids about the dangers of substance abuse and then legalize all drugs, but control their distribution. This course of action will help reduce crime and violence among drug users and also balance the national debt, because drugs could be heavily taxed.

- Do you believe drugs should be legalized? If so, what might be the negative consequences of legalization?
- Can any law enforcement strategies reduce drug consumption?
- Is treatment an effective drug-control technique?

DOING RESEARCH ON THE WEB

To research this topic, use "youth and drugs" as a key term on InfoTrac College Edition. The Open Society Institute, Centers for Disease Control and Prevention Health Programs, National Institute on Drug Abuse, National Center on Addiction and Substance Abuse at Columbia University, Partnership for a Drug-Free America, and the U.S. Bureau of Customs and Border Protection provide more information on different approaches to reducing teenage drug use. Before you answer the questions here, check out their websites by going to **www.thomsonedu.com/criminaljustice/siegel**.

Secondary Prevention Efforts: Family and Community

Primary prevention interventions typically take place early in childhood and are based on different views of theories of the onset of delinquency. They aim to stop antisocial activities before they occur. In contrast, secondary prevention efforts take place later, after children have shown signs that they are involved in antisocial activities. Most are based on the assumption that children's relationship with their environment, their school, neighborhood, family, and peers can either increase their risk of delinquent involvement or help shield them from inducements to commit crime. Therefore, these prevention programs usually target such issues as adjusting to a disrupted home environment, coping with school-related problems, helping kids plan for their future, and providing alternatives to antisocial peers. The following sections review a few prominent examples of secondary delinquency prevention programs.

MENTORING

Mentoring programs usually involve nonprofessional volunteers spending time with young people who are at risk for delinquency, dropping out of school, school failure, and other social problems. They mentor in a supportive, nonjudgmental manner while also acting as role models.[1] In recent years there has been a large increase in the number of mentoring programs, many of them aimed at preventing delinquency.[2]

One of the mentoring programs most successful in preventing juvenile delinquency is the Quantum Opportunities Program (QOP). QOP was implemented in five sites: Milwaukee; Oklahoma City; Philadelphia; Saginaw, Michigan; and San Antonio. The program ran for four years, or up to grade twelve, and was designed around the provision of three "quantum opportunities":

- Educational activities (peer tutoring, computer-based instruction, homework assistance)
- Service activities (volunteering with community projects)
- Development activities (curricula focused on life and family skills, and college and career planning)

Incentives in the form of cash and college scholarships were also offered to students for work carried out in these three areas. These incentives served to provide short-run motivation for school completion and future academic and social achievement. In addition, staff received cash incentives and bonuses for keeping youths involved in the program.[3]

An evaluation of the program six months after it ended found that youths who participated were less likely to be arrested compared to the control group (17 percent vs. 58 percent). A number of other significant effects were observed. For example, compared with the control group, QOP group members were

- More likely to have graduated from high school (63 percent vs. 42 percent)
- More likely to be enrolled in some form of postsecondary education (42 percent vs. 16 percent)
- Less likely to have dropped out of high school (23 percent vs. 50 percent)[4]

Another mentoring program that has also had some success in preventing delinquency and related behavior problems is offered by Big Brothers Big Sisters (BBBS) of America, a national youth-mentoring organization, founded in 1904 and committed to improving the life chances of at-risk children and teens. The BBBS program brings together unrelated pairs of adult volunteers and youths, ages ten to sixteen. Rather than trying to address particular problems facing a youth, the program focuses on providing a youth with an adult friend. The premise behind this is that "[t]he friendship forged with a youth by the Big Brother or Big Sister creates the framework through which the mentor can support and aid the youth.[5] The program also stresses that this friendship needs to be long lasting. To this end, mentors meet with youths on average three or four times a month (for three to four hours each time) for at least one year. An evaluation of the program took place at eight sites across the country and involved randomly assigning more than 1,100 youths to a program group that received mentoring or to a control group that did not. Eighteen months after the start of the program, it was found that those youths who received the program, compared to their control counterparts, were significantly less likely to have hit someone (32 percent), initiated illegal drug use (46 percent less), or been truant from school (30 percent less). The program group members were also more likely than the controls to do better in school and have better relationships with their parents and peers.[6]

Despite these findings, the overall evidence of the impact of mentoring on delinquency remains mixed.[7] So, why do some mentoring programs work and not others? The biggest issue has to do with what the mentors actually do and how they do it. In each of the profiled programs, mentors are a source of support and guidance to help young people deal with a broad range of issues that have to do with their family, school, and future career. They work one-on-one with young people, in many cases forming strong bonds. Care is taken in matching the mentor and young person. For future mentoring programs to be successful they should follow the approaches adopted by these programs.

AFTER-SCHOOL PROGRAMS

More than two-thirds of all married couples with school-age children (ages six to seventeen) have both parents working outside the home, and the proportion of single parents with school-age children working outside the home is even higher.[8] This leaves many unsupervised young people in communities during the after-school hours (2:00 P.M. to 6:00 P.M.), which is believed to be the main reason for the elevated rates of delinquency during this period of time.[9] After-school programs have become a popular response to this problem in recent years. After-school options include child-care centers, tutoring programs at school, dance groups, basketball leagues, and drop-in clubs. State and federal budgets for education, public safety, delinquency prevention, and child care provide some funding for after-school programs.

Some of the most successful after-school programs are provided by the Boys and Girls Clubs of America. Founded in 1902, the Boys and Girls Clubs of America is a nonprofit organization with a membership today of more than 1.3 million boys and girls nationwide. Boys and Girls Clubs (BGC) provide programs in six main areas: cultural enrichment, health and physical education, social recreation, personal and educational development, citizenship and leadership development, and environmental education.[10]

Evaluations of the Boys and Girls Club programs show that they are mostly successful and produce reductions in substance abuse, drug trafficking, and other drug-related delinquency activity.[11]

In a large-scale study of after-school programs in the state of Maryland, Denise Gottfredson and her colleagues found that participation in the programs reduced delinquent behavior among children in middle school, but not elementary school. The researchers found that increasing intentions not to use drugs as well as positive peer associations were the key reasons for the favorable effects on delinquency among the older children. Interestingly, decreasing the time spent unsupervised or increasing the involvement in constructive activities was found to play no significant role.[12]

Although the evidence shows that after-school programs can be successful, there is a need for further evaluation.[13] The fact that some (but not all) types of delinquency are elevated during the after-school hours underscores the importance of high-quality after-school programs.[14]

JOB TRAINING

As you may recall, the effects of having an after-school job can be problematic. Some research indicates that it may be associated with delinquency and substance abuse. However, helping kids to prepare for the adult workforce is an important aspect of delinquency prevention. Job training programs play an important role in improving the chances of young people obtaining jobs in the legal economy and thereby may reduce delinquency.[15]

The most well known and largest job training program in the United States is the Job Corps, established in 1964 as a federal training program for disadvantaged, unemployed youths. The Department of Labor, which was the designer of the national program, was hopeful that spinoff benefits in the form of reduced dependence on social assistance and a reduction in delinquency would occur as a result of empowering at-risk youth to achieve stable, long-term employment opportunities. The program is still active today, operating out of 119 centers across the nation, and each year it provides services to more than sixty thousand new young people at a cost of over $1 billion.[16]

The main goal of the Job Corps is to improve the employability of participants by offering a comprehensive set of services that largely includes vocational skills training, basic education (the ability to obtain graduate equivalent degrees [GEDs]), and health care. Job Corps is provided to young people between the ages of sixteen and twenty-four. Most of those enrolled in the program are at high risk for substance abuse, delinquency, and social assistance dependency. Two out of five come from families on social assistance, four out of five have dropped out of school, and the average family income is six thousand dollars per year.[17] Almost all Job Corps centers require the participants to live in the centers while taking the program.

A large-scale evaluation of Job Corps involving almost twelve thousand young people found that the program was successful in reducing delinquency. Arrest rates were 16 percent lower for those who received the program than a comparison group. Program group members were less likely to be convicted and serve jail time upon conviction. Also, there were higher employment rates and greater earnings for those who received the program.[18] An earlier evaluation of Job Corps found it to be a worthwhile investment of public resources: for each dollar that was spent on the program, $1.45 was saved to government or taxpayers, crime victims, and program participants.[19] A more recent analysis of the program's costs and benefits also found it to be a worthwhile investment of public resources, saving society at large two dollars for each dollar spent on the program.[20]

Job training is an important component of an overall strategy to reduce delinquency. The developmental stage of transition to work is difficult for many young people. Coming from a disadvantaged background, having poor grades in school or perhaps dropping out of school, and having some involvement in delinquency can all pose difficulties in securing a steady, well-paying job in early adulthood.

COMPREHENSIVE COMMUNITY-BASED PROGRAMS

Comprehensive community-based delinquency prevention programs combine many interventions targeted at an array of risk factors for delinquency, and are typically implemented in neighborhoods with high delinquency and crime rates. Experimentation with this type of delinquency prevention program began as early as the 1930s, with Shaw and McKay's Chicago Area Project.[21] The Mobilization for Youth program of the 1960s is another example of a comprehensive community-based initiative to prevent juvenile delinquency. Neither of these programs was found to be overly successful in reducing delinquency. Few of these types of programs have been evaluated.

One contemporary example of a comprehensive community-based delinquency prevention program that has been evaluated is the Children At Risk (CAR) program, which is now undergoing further experimentation and is known as CASASTART or the Center on Addiction and Substance Abuse's Striving Together to Achieve Rewarding Tomorrows.[22] CAR was set up to help improve the lives of young people at high risk for delinquency, gang involvement, substance abuse, and other problem behaviors. It was delivered to a large number of young people in poor and high-crime neighborhoods in five cities across the country. It involved a wide range of preventive measures, including case management and family

counseling, family skills training, tutoring, mentoring, after-school activities, and community policing. The program was different in each neighborhood. A study of all five cities showed that one year after the program ended, the young people who received the program, compared with a control group, were less likely to have committed violent delinquent acts and used or sold drugs. Some of the other beneficial results for those in the program included less association with delinquent peers, less peer pressure to engage in delinquency, and more positive peer support.[23]

Comprehensive community-based delinquency prevention programs are made up of a range of different types of interventions, and typically involve an equally diverse group of community and government agencies that are concerned with the problem of juvenile delinquency, such as the YMCA/YWCA, Boys and Girls Clubs of America, social services, and health. For example, the Communities That Care (CTC) program emphasizes the reduction of risk factors for delinquency and the enhancement of protective factors against delinquency for different developmental stages from birth through adolescence.[24] CTC follows a rigorous, multilevel planning process that includes drawing upon interventions that have previously demonstrated success and tailoring them to the needs of the community.[25] Two recent case studies of CTC demonstrate its ability to help mobilize communities to plan and implement delinquency prevention programs based on the highest quality research evidence on what works best.[26]

The CTC and other comprehensive programs rely on a systematic planning model to develop preventive interventions. This includes analysis of the delinquency problem, identification of available resources in the community, development of priority delinquency problems, and identification of successful programs in other communities and tailoring them to local conditions and needs.[27] Not all comprehensive community-based prevention programs follow this model, but there is evidence to suggest that this approach will produce the greatest reductions in juvenile delinquency.[28] One of the main drawbacks to this approach is the difficulty in sustaining the level of resources and the cooperation between agencies that are necessary to lower the rates of juvenile delinquency across a large geographical area such as a city.[29]

FUTURE OF DELINQUENCY PREVENTION

Despite the success of many different types of secondary prevention programs, from mentoring to job training, these programs receive a small fraction of what is spent on the juvenile justice system to deal with young people once they have broken the law.[30] To many juvenile justice officials, policy makers, and politicians, prevention is tantamount to being soft on crime, and delinquency prevention programs are often referred to as "pork barrel," or wasteful, spending.[31] There is also concern about the labeling and stigmatization associated with programs that target high-risk populations: children and families receiving support may be called hurtful names or looked down upon by fellow community members.[32]

Notwithstanding these important issues, the future of secondary delinquency prevention is likely to be very bright. With many local efforts, state initiatives, and a growing list of national programs showing positive results, the prevention of delinquency is proving its worth.

The History and Development of Juvenile Justice

© Jeff Greenberg/Alamy

CHAPTER OBJECTIVES

After reading this chapter you should:

1. Understand the major social changes leading to creation of the first modern juvenile court in Chicago in 1899.

2. Be familiar with some of the landmark Supreme Court decisions that have influenced present-day juvenile justice procedures.

3. Be able to comment on the nature of delinquency cases being processed in juvenile court.

4. Know how children are processed by the juvenile justice system, beginning with investigation and arrest and concluding with reentry into society.

5. Understand the conflicting values in contemporary juvenile justice.

6. Recognize key similarities and differences between the adult and juvenile justice systems.

7. Be able to argue the pros and cons of the juvenile justice system's goal to treat rather than punish and assess if this goal is being met today.

8. Understand the need for and be aware of the key elements of a comprehensive juvenile justice strategy to deal with juvenile delinquency.

9. See the difference between prevention and intervention efforts to reduce juvenile delinquency.

10. Be able to identify and comment on pressing issues in the future of juvenile justice.

Jennifer, a bright young European American female, lived in a fast-paced urban community with her parents and two younger brothers. At sixteen years old, she was in trouble. Jennifer went to a party one night and found out that her boyfriend, Sam, whom she had dated for several months and with whom she felt she had a serious relationship, had been cheating on her with a classmate. She was irate. Although Sam was not at the party, the other girl was there. She and Jennifer had words and threw a few punches at each other. Both were asked to leave, but Jennifer refused and the police were called to the party. Jennifer received a ticket for disorderly conduct.

At Jennifer's initial hearing on the matter, she was told about Youth Court. If she would agree to plead guilty to the charge and attend and cooperate with Youth Court recommendations, her record would be cleared. The Youth Court is set up as a first offenders diversion program and gives young people a chance to get back on track.

In Youth Court, one jury member serves as spokesperson to explain the process of court. Jury members introduce themselves, answer any questions the defendant may have regarding the process, listen carefully to the teen's explanation for their behavior, and have an equal say in the recommendation outcome. The jury requests information regarding the teen's school activities, employment, extracurricular activities, and any consequences the teen may have received from her parents or school for her actions. They ask follow-up questions for clarification, and they take their duties seriously. The teens involved on the Youth Court juries are committed to confidentiality and fairness, and members recuse themselves from cases if they feel they know the defendant too well, or are related in any way. The program director is responsible for reviewing and approving the jury's recommendations and also serves as a consultant to the jury participants.

Jennifer agreed to the Youth Court diversion program and the referral was made. Facing a jury of her peers, she explained what happened the night she received the ticket. The Youth Court encourages family involvement, so Jennifer's mother accompanied her for support. Jennifer explained that she had recently lost a close relative and that she had been under a lot of stress when the fight occurred. She was sorry for her behavior and wanted things to be better.

The jury "sentenced" Jennifer to attend counseling and a drug and alcohol pre-assessment, as well as to write a paper on how to better handle her anger. Defendants in the court are also required to serve on two future juries themselves and given ninety days to comply or the case is returned to juvenile court for disposition. Jennifer cooperated with the requirements and her record was cleared. She completed her jury duty and has chosen to continue as a regular volunteer. According to the program director, Jennifer is an "excellent volunteer with great leadership potential." She avoided any further delinquent behavior, graduated from high school, and is now pursuing a degree in computer science.

JUVENILE JUSTICE IN THE NINETEENTH CENTURY

At the beginning of the nineteenth century, delinquent, neglected, and runaway children in the United States were treated in the same way as adult criminal offenders.[1] Like children in England, when convicted of crimes they received harsh sentences similar to those imposed on adults. The adult criminal code applied to children, and no juvenile court existed.

During the early nineteenth century, various pieces of legislation were introduced to humanize criminal procedures for children. The concept of probation, introduced in Massachusetts in 1841, was geared toward helping young people avoid imprisonment. Many books and reports written during this time heightened public interest in juvenile care.

Despite this interest, no special facilities existed for the care of youths in trouble with the law, nor were there separate laws or courts to control their behavior. Youths who committed petty crimes, such as stealing or vandalism, were viewed as wayward children or victims of neglect and were placed in community asylums or homes. Youths who were involved in more serious crimes were subject to the same punishments as adults—imprisonment, whipping, or death.

Several events led to reforms and nourished the eventual development of the juvenile justice system: urbanization, the child-saving movement and growing interest in the concept of *parens patriae,* and development of institutions for the care of delinquent and neglected children.

Urbanization

Especially during the first half of the nineteenth century, the United States experienced rapid population growth, primarily due to an increased birthrate and expanding immigration. The rural poor and immigrant groups were attracted to urban commercial centers that promised jobs in manufacturing. In 1790, 5 percent of the population lived in cities. By 1850, the share of the urban population had increased to 15 percent; it jumped to 40 percent in 1900, and 51 percent in 1920.[2] New York more than quadrupled its population in the thirty-year stretch between 1825 and 1855—from 166,000 in 1825 to 630,000 in 1855.[3]

Urbanization gave rise to increased numbers of young people at risk, who overwhelmed the existing system of work and training. To accommodate destitute youths, local jurisdictions developed poorhouses (almshouses) and workhouses. The poor, the insane, the diseased, and vagrant and destitute children were all housed there in crowded and unhealthy conditions.

By the late eighteenth century, many began to question the family's ability to exert control over children. Villages developed into urban commercial centers and work began to center around factories, not the home. Children of destitute families left home or were cast loose to make out as best they could; wealthy families could no longer absorb vagrant youth as apprentices or servants.[4] Chronic poverty became an American dilemma. The affluent began to voice concern over the increase in the number of people in what they considered the "dangerous classes"—the poor, single, criminal, mentally ill, and unemployed.

Urbanization and industrialization also generated the belief that certain segments of the population (youths in urban areas, immigrants) were susceptible to the influences of their decaying environment. The children of these classes were considered a group that might be "saved" by a combination of state and community intervention.[5] Intervention in the lives of these so-called dangerous classes became acceptable for wealthy, civic-minded citizens. Such efforts included *settlement houses,* a term used around the turn of the twentieth century to describe shelters, and nonsecure residential facilities for vagrant children.

The Child-Saving Movement

The problems generated by urban growth sparked interest in the welfare of the "new" Americans, whose arrival fueled this expansion. In 1817, prominent New Yorkers formed the Society for the Prevention of Pauperism. Although they concerned themselves with attacking taverns, brothels, and gambling parlors, they also were concerned that the moral training of children of the dangerous classes was inadequate. Soon other groups concerned with the plight of poor children began to form. Their focus was on extending government control over youthful activities (drinking, vagrancy, and delinquency) that had previously been left to private or family control.

These activists became known as *child savers.* Prominent among them were penologist Enoch Wines; Judge Richard Tuthill; Lucy Flowers, of the Chicago Women's Association; Sara Cooper, of the National Conference of Charities and Corrections; and Sophia Minton, of the New York Committee on Children.[6] Poor children could become a financial burden, and the child savers believed these children presented a threat to the moral fabric of society. Child-saving organizations influenced state legislatures to enact laws giving courts the power to commit children who were runaways or criminal offenders to specialized institutions.

To learn more about this era, go to the **Library of Congress** website devoted to American history via www.thomsonedu.com/criminaljustice/siegel.

Here, young boys are shown working in the machine shop of the Indiana Youth Reformatory, circa 1910.

© American Correctional Association

House of Refuge
A care facility developed by the child savers to protect potential criminal youths by taking them off the street and providing a family-like environment.

www To read more about the **child savers**, go to the website www.thomsonedu.com/criminaljustice/siegel.

The most prominent of the care facilities developed by child savers was the **House of Refuge**, which opened in New York in 1825.[7] It was founded on the concept of protecting potential criminal youths by taking them off the streets and reforming them in a family-like environment. When the House of Refuge opened, the majority of children admitted were status offenders placed there because of vagrancy or neglect. Children were placed in the institution by court order, sometimes over their parents' objections. Their length of stay depended on need, age, and skill. Once there, youths were required to do piecework provided by local manufacturers or to work part of the day in the community. The institution was run like a prison, with strict discipline and absolute separation of the sexes. Such a harsh program drove many children to run away, and the House of Refuge was forced to take a more lenient approach.

Despite criticism, the concept enjoyed expanding popularity. In 1826, the Boston City Council founded the House of Reformation for juvenile offenders. Similar institutions were opened elsewhere in Massachusetts and in New York in 1847.[8] The courts committed children found guilty of criminal violations, or found to be beyond the control of their parents, to these schools. Because the child savers considered parents of delinquent children to be as guilty as convicted offenders, they sought to have the reform schools establish control over the children. Refuge managers believed they were preventing poverty and crime by separating destitute and delinquent children from their parents and placing them in an institution.[9]

The philosophy of *parens patriae*—that is, the duty of the state to act on behalf of the child and provide care and protection equivalent to that of a parent—was extended to refuge programs, which were given parental control over a committed child. Scholar Robert Mennel summarizes this attitude: "The doctrine of *parens patriae* gave refuge managers the best of two worlds, familial and legal: it separated delinquent children from their natural parents and it circumvented the rigor of criminal law by allowing courts to commit children, under loosely worded statutes, to specially created schools instead of jails."[10]

Were They Really Child Savers?

Debate continues over the true objectives of the early child savers. Some historians conclude that they were what they seemed—concerned citizens motivated by humanitarian ideals.[11] Modern scholars, however, have reappraised the child-saving movement. In *The Child Savers*, Anthony Platt paints a picture of representatives of the ruling class who were galvanized by immigrants and the urban poor to take action to preserve their own way of life.[12]

Other critical thinkers followed Platt in finding that child saving was motivated more by self-interest than by benevolence. For example, Randall Shelden and Lynn Osborne traced the child-saving movement in Memphis, Tennessee, and found that its leaders were a small group of upper-class citizens who desired to control the behavior and lifestyles of lower-class youth. The outcome was ominous. Most cases petitioned to the juvenile court (which opened in 1910) were for petty crimes and status offenses, yet 25 percent of the youths were committed to some form of incarceration; more than 96 percent of the actions with which females were charged were status offenses.[13]

In summary, these scholars believe that the reformers applied the concept of *parens patriae* for their own purposes, including the continuance of middle- and upper-class values and the furtherance of a child labor system consisting of marginal and lower-class skilled workers.

In the course of "saving children" by turning them over to houses of refuge, the basic legal rights of children were violated: children were simply not granted the same constitutional protections as adults.

Development of Juvenile Institutions

State intervention in the lives of children continued well into the twentieth century. The child savers influenced state and local governments to create institutions, called *reform schools,* devoted to the care of vagrant and delinquent youths. State institutions opened in Westboro, Massachusetts, in 1848, and in Rochester, New York, in 1849.[14] Institutional programs began in Ohio in 1850, and in Maine, Rhode Island, and Michigan in 1906. Children spent their days working in the institution, learning a trade where possible, and receiving some basic education. They were racially and sexually segregated, discipline was harsh, and their physical care was poor. Beverly Smith found that girls admitted to the Western House of Refuge in Rochester, during the 1880s were often labeled criminals, but were in reality abused and neglected. They too were subject to harsh working conditions, strict discipline, and intensive labor.[15] Most of these institutions received state support, unlike the privately funded houses of refuge and settlement houses.

Although some viewed reform schools as humanitarian answers to poorhouses and prisons, many were opposed to such programs. As an alternative, New York philanthropist Charles Loring Brace helped develop the **Children's Aid Society** in 1853.[16] Brace's formula for dealing with delinquent youths was to rescue them from the harsh environment of the city and provide them with temporary shelter.

Deciding there were simply too many needy children to care for in New York City, and believing the urban environment was injurious to children, Brace devised what he called his *placing-out plan* to send these children to western farms where they could be cared for and find a home. They were placed on what became known as **orphan trains**, which made pre-announced stops in western farming communities. Families wishing to take in children would meet the train, be briefly introduced to the passengers, and leave with one of the children. Brace's plan was activated in 1854 and very soon copied by other child-care organizations. Though the majority of the children benefited from the plan and did find a new life, others were less successful and some were exploited

Children's Aid Society
Child-saving organization that took children from the streets of large cities and placed them with farm families on the prairie.

orphan train
A practice of the Children's Aid Society in which urban youths were sent west for adoption with local farm couples.

To read more about the life of Charles Loring Brace, go to the website www.thomsonedu.com/criminaljustice/siegel.

This engraving depicts the work of the Children's Aid Society, founded in 1853.

Stock Montage

and harmed by the experience. By 1930, political opposition to Brace's plan, coupled with the negative effects of the Great Depression, spelled the end of the orphan trains, but not before 150,000 children were placed in rural homesteads. Concept Summary 11.1 describes those first juvenile institutions and organizations.

Society for the Prevention of Cruelty to Children (SPCC)

Society for the Prevention of Cruelty to Children (SPCC)
First established in 1874, these organizations protected children subjected to cruelty and neglect at home or at school.

In 1874, the first **Society for the Prevention of Cruelty to Children (SPCC)** was established in New York; by 1900 there were three hundred such societies in the United States.[17] Leaders of the SPCCs were concerned that abused boys would

The First Juvenile Institutions and Organizations

Reform schools	Devoted to the care of vagrant and delinquent youths.
Children's Aid Society	Designed to protect delinquent youths from the city's dangers through the provision of temporary shelter.
Orphan trains	The practice of using trains to place delinquent urban youths with families in western farming communities.
Society for the Prevention of Cruelty to Children	Designed to protect abused and neglected children by placing them with other families and advocating for criminal penalties for negligent parents.

CHECKPOINTS

■ The movement to treat children in trouble with the law as a separate category began in the nineteenth century.

■ Urbanization created a growing number of at-risk youth in the nation's cities.

■ The child savers sought to control children of the lower classes.

■ The House of Refuge was developed to care for unwanted or abandoned youth.

■ Some critics now believe the child savers were motivated by self-interest and not benevolence.

■ Charles Loring Brace created the Children's Aid Society to place urban kids with farm families.

become lower-class criminals and that mistreated young girls might become sexually promiscuous women. A growing crime rate and concern about a rapidly changing population served to swell SPCC membership. In addition, these organizations protected children who had been subjected to cruelty and neglect at home and at school.

SPCC groups influenced state legislatures to pass statutes protecting children from parents who did not provide them with adequate food and clothing or made them beg or work in places where liquor was sold.[18] Criminal penalties were created for negligent parents, and provisions were established for removing children from the home. In some states, agents of the SPCC could actually arrest abusive parents; in others, they would inform the police about suspected abuse cases and accompany officers when they made an arrest.[19] ✔ Checkpoints

A CENTURY OF JUVENILE JUSTICE

Although reform groups continued to lobby for government control over children, the committing of children under the doctrine of *parens patriae* without due process of law began to be questioned. Could the state incarcerate children who had not violated the criminal law? Should children be held in facilities that housed adults? Serious problems challenged the effectiveness of the existing system; institutional deficiencies, the absence of due process for poor, ignorant, and noncriminal delinquents, and the treatment of these children by inadequate private organizations all spurred the argument that a juvenile court should be established.

Increasing delinquency rates also hastened the development of a juvenile court. Theodore Ferdinand's analysis of the Boston juvenile court found that in the 1820s and 1830s very few juveniles were charged with serious offenses. By 1850, juvenile delinquency was the fastest growing component of the local crime problem.[20] Ferdinand concluded that the flow of juvenile cases strengthened the argument that juveniles needed their own court.

The Illinois Juvenile Court Act and Its Legacy

The child-saving movement culminated in passage of the Illinois Juvenile Court Act of 1899. The principles motivating the Illinois reformers were these:

1. Children should not be held as accountable as adult transgressors.

2. The objective of the juvenile justice system is to treat and rehabilitate rather than punish.

3. Disposition should be predicated on analysis of the youth's special circumstances and needs.

4. The system should avoid the trappings of the adult criminal process with all its confusing rules and procedures.

The Illinois Juvenile Court Act was a major event in the juvenile justice movement. Just what were the ramifications of passage of this act? The traditional interpretation is that the reformers were genuinely motivated to pass legislation that would serve the best interests of the child. U.S. Supreme Court Justice Abe Fortas took this position in the landmark 1967 *in re Gault* case:

> *The early reformers were appalled by adult procedures and penalties and by the fact that children could be given long prison sentences and mixed in jails with hardened criminals. They were profoundly convinced that society's duty to the child could not be confined by the concept of justice alone. . . . The child—essentially good, as they saw it—was to be made to feel that he was the object of the state's care and solicitude, not that he was under arrest or on trial. . . . The idea of crime and punishment was to be abandoned. The child was to be treated and rehabilitated, and the procedures from apprehension through institutionalization were to be clinical rather than punitive.[21]*

The child savers believed that children were influenced by their environments. Society was to be concerned with what their problems were and how these problems could be handled in the interests of the children and the state.

Interpretations of its intentions differ, but unquestionably the Illinois Juvenile Court Act established juvenile delinquency as a legal concept. For the first time the distinction was made between children who were neglected and those who were delinquent. Delinquent children were those under the age of sixteen who violated the law. Most important, the act established a court and a probation program specifically for children. In addition, the legislation allowed children to be committed to institutions and reform programs under the control of the state. The key provisions of the act were these:

- A separate court was established for delinquent and neglected children.
- Special procedures were developed to govern the adjudication of juvenile matters.
- Children were to be separated from adults in courts and in institutional programs.
- Probation programs were to be developed to assist the court in making decisions in the best interests of the state and the child.

Following passage of the Illinois Juvenile Court Act, similar legislation was enacted throughout the nation; by 1917, juvenile courts had been established in all but three states. The special courts these laws created maintained jurisdiction over pre-delinquent (neglected and dependent) and delinquent children. Juvenile court jurisdiction was based primarily on a child's noncriminal actions and status, not strictly on a violation of criminal law. The *parens patriae* philosophy predominated, ushering in a form of personalized justice that still did not provide juvenile offenders with the full array of constitutional protections available to adult criminal offenders. The court's process was paternalistic rather than adversarial. Attorneys were not required, and hearsay evidence, inadmissible in criminal trials, was admissible in the adjudication of juvenile offenders. Verdicts were based on a *preponderance of the evidence* instead of the stricter standard used by criminal courts, *beyond a reasonable doubt*, and children were often not granted any right to appeal their convictions.

The major functions of the juvenile justice system were to prevent juvenile crime and to rehabilitate juvenile offenders. The roles of the judge and the probation staff were to diagnose the child's condition and prescribe programs to alleviate it. Until 1967, judgments about children's actions and consideration for their constitutional rights were secondary.

By the 1920s, noncriminal behavior, in the form of incorrigibility and truancy from school, was added to the jurisdiction of many juvenile court systems. Of particular interest was the sexual behavior of young girls, and the juvenile court enforced a strict moral code on working-class girls, not hesitating to incarcerate those who were sexually active.[22] Programs of all kinds, including individualized counseling and institutional care, were used to *cure* juvenile criminality.

By 1925, juvenile courts existed in virtually every jurisdiction in every state. Although the juvenile court concept expanded rapidly, it cannot be said that each state implemented it thoroughly. Some jurisdictions established elaborate juvenile court systems, whereas others passed legislation but provided no services. Some courts had trained juvenile court judges; others had non-lawyers sitting in juvenile cases. Some courts had extensive probation departments; others had untrained probation personnel.

Great diversity also marked juvenile institutions. Some maintained a lenient orientation, but others relied on harsh punishments, including beatings, straitjacket restraints, immersion in cold water, and solitary confinement with a diet of bread and water.

These conditions were exacerbated by the rapid growth in the juvenile institutional population. Between 1890 and 1920, the number of institutionalized youths jumped 112 percent, a rise that far exceeded the increase in the total number of adolescents in the United States.[23] Although social workers and court personnel deplored the increased institutionalization of youth, the growth was due in part to the successful efforts by reformers to close poorhouses, thereby creating a need for institutions to house their displaced populations. In addition, the lack of a coherent national policy on needy children allowed private entrepreneurs to fill the void.[24] Although the increase in institutionalization seemed contrary to the goal of rehabilitation, such an approach was preferable to the poorhouse and the streets.

Reforming the System

Reform of this system was slow in coming. In 1912, the U.S. Children's Bureau was formed as the first federal child welfare agency. By the 1930s, the bureau began to investigate the state of juvenile institutions and tried to expose some of their more repressive aspects.[25] After World War II, critics, such as Paul Tappan and Francis Allen, began to identify problems in the juvenile justice system, among which were the neglect of procedural rights and the warehousing of youth in ineffective institutions. Status offenders commonly were housed with delinquents and given sentences that were more punitive than those given to delinquents.[26]

From its origin, the juvenile court system denied children procedural rights normally available to adult offenders. Due process rights, such as representation by counsel, a jury trial, freedom from self-incrimination, and freedom from unreasonable search and seizure, were not considered essential for the juvenile court system, because its primary purpose was not punishment but rehabilitation. However, the dream of trying to rehabilitate children was not achieved. Individual treatment approaches failed, and delinquency rates soared.

Reform efforts, begun in earnest in the 1960s, changed the face of the juvenile justice system. In 1962, New York passed legislation creating a family court system.[27] The new court assumed responsibility for all matters involving family life, with emphasis on delinquent and neglected children. In addition, the legislation established the PINS classification (person in need of supervision). This category included individuals involved in such actions as truancy and incorrigibility. By using labels like PINS and CHINS (children in need of supervision) to establish jurisdiction over children, juvenile courts expanded their role as social agencies. Because noncriminal children were now involved in the juvenile court system to a greater degree, many juvenile courts had to improve their social services. Efforts were made to personalize the system of justice for children. These reforms were soon followed by a due process revolution, which ushered in an era of procedural rights for court-adjudicated youth. The next section discusses some key cases that transformed the practice of juvenile justice.

In the 1960s and 1970s, the U.S. Supreme Court radically altered the juvenile justice system when it issued a series of decisions that established the right of juveniles to receive due process of law.[28] The Court established that juveniles had the same rights as adults in important areas of trial process, including the right to confront witnesses, notice of charges, and the right to counsel.

Federal Commissions In addition to the legal revolution brought about by the Supreme Court, a series of national commissions sponsored by the federal government helped change the shape of juvenile justice. In 1967, the *President's Commission on Law Enforcement and the Administration of Justice*, organized by President Lyndon Johnson, suggested that the juvenile justice system must provide underprivileged youths with opportunities for success, including jobs and education. The commission also recognized the need to develop effective law enforcement procedures to control hard-core offenders while also granting them due process. The commission's report acted as a catalyst for passage of the federal *Juvenile Delinquency Prevention and Control (JDP) Act of 1968*. This law created a Youth Development and Delinquency Prevention Administration, which concentrated on helping states develop new juvenile justice programs, particularly programs involving diversion of youth, decriminalization, and decarceration. In 1968, Congress also passed the *Omnibus Safe Streets and Crime Control Act*.[29] Title I of this law established the **Law Enforcement Assistance Administration (LEAA)** to provide federal funds for improving the adult and juvenile justice systems. In 1972, Congress amended the JDP to allow the LEAA to focus its funding on juvenile justice and delinquency-prevention programs. State and local governments were required to develop and adopt comprehensive plans to obtain federal assistance.

Because crime continued to receive much publicity, a second effort called the *National Advisory Commission on Criminal Justice Standards and Goals* was established in 1973 by the Nixon administration.[30] Its report identified such strategies as preventing delinquent behavior, developing diversion activities, establishing dispositional alternatives, providing due process for all juveniles, and controlling violent and chronic delinquents. This commission's recommendations formed the basis for the *Juvenile Justice and Delinquency Prevention Act of 1974*.[31] This act eliminated the Youth Development and Delinquency Prevention Administration and replaced it with the **Office of Juvenile Justice and Delinquency Prevention (OJJDP)** within the LEAA. In 1980, the LEAA was phased out, and the OJJDP became an independent agency in the Department of Justice. Throughout the 1970s, its two most important goals were removing juveniles from detention in adult jails, and eliminating the incarceration together of delinquents and status offenders. During this period, the OJJDP stressed the creation of formal diversion and restitution programs.

The latest effort has been the *Violent Crime Control and Law Enforcement Act of 1994*.[32] The largest piece of crime legislation in the history of the United States, it provided for a hundred thousand new police officers and billions of dollars for prisons and prevention programs for both adult and juvenile offenders. A revitalized juvenile justice system would need both a comprehensive strategy to prevent and control delinquency and a consistent program of federal funding.[33] ✔ Checkpoints

JUVENILE JUSTICE TODAY

Today the juvenile justice system exercises jurisdiction over two distinct categories of offenders—delinquents and status offenders.[34] *Delinquent children* are those who fall under a jurisdictional age limit, which varies from state to state, and who commit an act in violation of the penal code. *Status offenders* are commonly characterized in state statutes as persons or children in need of supervision (PINS or CHINS). Most states distinguish such behavior from delinquent conduct to lessen the effect of any stigma on children as a result of their involvement with the juvenile court. In addition, juvenile courts generally have jurisdiction over situations involving conduct directed at (rather than committed by) juveniles, such as parental neglect, deprivation, abandonment, and abuse.

Law Enforcement Assistance Administration (LEAA)
Unit in the U.S. Department of Justice established by the Omnibus Crime Control and Safe Streets Act of 1968 to administer grants and provide guidance for crime prevention policy and programs.

Office of Juvenile Justice and Delinquency Prevention (OJJDP)
Branch of the U.S. Justice Department charged with shaping national juvenile justice policy through disbursement of federal aid and research funds.

 To read about the **Juvenile Justice and Delinquency Prevention Act of 1974**, click on Web Links under the Chapter Resources at www.thomsonedu.com/criminaljustice/siegel.

CHECKPOINTS

■ The juvenile court movement spread rapidly around the nation.

■ Separate courts and correctional systems were created for youth. However, children were not given the same legal rights as adults.

■ Reformers helped bring due process rights to minors and create specialized family courts.

■ Federal commissions focused attention on juvenile justice and helped revise the system.

Table 11.1 Oldest Age for Juvenile Court Jurisdiction in Delinquency Cases

Age	State (Total Number)
15	Connecticut, New York, North Carolina (3)
16	Georgia, Illinois, Louisiana, Massachusetts, Michigan, Missouri, New Hampshire, South Carolina, Texas, Wisconsin (10)
17	Alabama, Alaska, Arizona, Arkansas, California, Colorado, Delaware, Florida, Hawaii, Idaho, Indiana, Iowa, Kansas, Kentucky, Maine, Maryland, Minnesota, Mississippi, Montana, Nebraska, Nevada, New Jersey, New Mexico, North Dakota, Ohio, Oklahoma, Oregon, Pennsylvania, Rhode Island, South Dakota, Tennessee, Utah, Vermont, Virginia, Washington, West Virginia, Wyoming (37 and the District of Columbia)

Source: Howard N. Snyder and Melissa Sickmund, *Juvenile Offenders and Victims: 2006 National Report* (Pittsburgh, PA: National Center for Juvenile Justice, 2006), p. 103.

The states have also set different maximum ages below which children fall under the jurisdiction of the juvenile court. Most states (and the District of Columbia) include all children under eighteen, others set the upper limit at seventeen, and still others include children under sixteen (Table 11.1).

Today's juvenile justice system exists in all states by statute. Each jurisdiction has a juvenile code and a special court structure to accommodate children in trouble. Nationwide, the juvenile justice system consists of thousands of public and private agencies, with a total budget amounting to billions of dollars. Most of the nation's police agencies have juvenile components, and there are more than three thousand juvenile courts and about an equal number of juvenile correctional facilities.

Figure 11.1 depicts the numbers of juvenile offenders removed at various stages of the juvenile justice process. These figures do not take into account the large number of children who are referred to community diversion and mental health programs. There are thousands of these programs throughout the nation. This multitude of agencies and people dealing with juvenile delinquency has led to the development of what professionals view as an incredibly expansive and complex system.

The Juvenile Justice Process

How are children processed by the juvenile justice system?[35] Most children come into the justice system as a result of contact with a police officer. When a juvenile commits a serious crime, the police are empowered to make an arrest. Less serious offenses may also require police action, but in these instances, instead of being arrested, the child may be warned or a referral may be made to a social service program. A little more than 70 percent of all children arrested are referred to the juvenile court.[36] Figure 11.2 on page 271 outlines the **juvenile justice process**, and a detailed analysis of this process is presented in the next sections.

Police Investigation When youths commit a crime, police have the authority to investigate the incident and decide whether to release the youths or commit them to the juvenile court. This is often a discretionary decision, based not only on the nature of the offense, but also on conditions existing at the time of the arrest. Such factors as the seriousness of the offense, the child's past contacts with the police, and whether the child denies committing the crime determine whether a petition is filed. As you may recall, juveniles in custody today have constitutional rights similar to those of adult offenders. They are protected against unreasonable search and seizure under the Fourth and Fourteenth Amendments of the Constitution. The Fifth Amendment places limitations on police interrogation procedures.

juvenile justice process
Under the *parens patriae* philosophy, juvenile justice procedures are informal and nonadversarial, invoked for juvenile offenders rather than against them; a petition instead of a complaint is filed; courts make findings of involvement or adjudication of delinquency instead of convictions; and juvenile offenders receive dispositions instead of sentences.

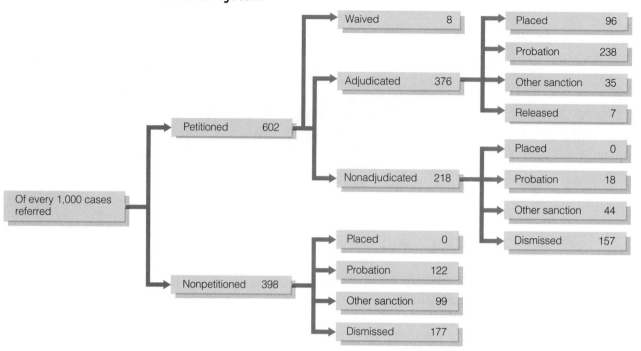

Note: Cases are categorized by their most severe or restrictive sanction. Detail may not add to totals because of rounding.

Source: Howard N. Snyder and Melissa Sickmund, *Juvenile Ofenders and Victims: 2006 National Report* (Pittsburgh, PA: National Center for Juvenile Justice, 2006), p. 178.

detention hearing
A hearing by a judicial officer of a juvenile court to determine whether a juvenile is to be detained or released while proceedings are pending in the case.

adjudicatory hearing
The fact-finding process wherein the juvenile court determines whether there is sufficient evidence to sustain the allegations in a petition.

Detention If the police decide to file a petition, the child is referred to juvenile court. The primary decision at this point is whether the child should remain in the community or be placed in a detention facility or in shelter care (temporary foster homes, detention boarding homes, programs of neighborhood supervision). In the past, children were routinely held in detention facilities to await court appearances. Normally, a **detention hearing** is held to determine whether to remand the child to a shelter. At this point, the child has a right to counsel and other procedural safeguards. A child who is not detained is usually released to a parent or guardian. Most state juvenile court acts provide for a child to return home to await further court action, except when it is necessary to protect the child, when the child presents a serious danger to the public, or when it is not certain that the child will return to court. In many cases the police will refer the child to a community service program instead of filing a formal charge.

Pretrial Procedures In most jurisdictions, the adjudication process begins with some sort of hearing. At this hearing, juvenile court rules normally require that juveniles be informed of their right to a trial, that the plea or admission be voluntary, and that they understand the charges and consequences of the plea. The case will often not be further adjudicated if a child admits to the crime at the initial hearing.

In some cases, youths may be detained at this stage pending a trial. Juveniles who are detained are eligible for bail in a handful of jurisdictions. Plea bargaining may also occur at any stage of the proceedings. A plea bargain is an agreement between the prosecution and the defense by which the juvenile agrees to plead guilty for certain considerations, such as a lenient sentence. This issue is explored more thoroughly in chapter 13, which discusses pretrial procedures.

If the child denies the allegation of delinquency, an **adjudicatory hearing** or trial is scheduled. Under extraordinary circumstances, a juvenile who commits a serious

Figure 11.2 **Case Flow Through the Juvenile Justice Process**

Source: This figure can be accessed online through the Office of Juvenile Justice and Delinquency Prevention at http://ojjdp.ncjrs. org/ojstatbb/structure_process/case.html.

crime may be waived to adult court. Today, most jurisdictions have laws providing for such transfers. Whether such a transfer occurs depends on the type of offense, the youth's prior record, the availability of treatment services, and the likelihood that the youth will be rehabilitated in the juvenile court system.

Adjudication Adjudication is the trial stage of the juvenile court process. If the child does not admit guilt at the initial hearing and is not waived to an adult court, the adjudication hearing is held to determine the facts of the case. The court hears evidence on the allegations in the delinquency petition. This is a trial on the merits (dealing with issues of law and facts), and rules of evidence similar to those of criminal proceedings generally apply. At this stage, the juvenile offender is entitled to many of the procedural guarantees given adult offenders. These include the right to counsel, freedom from self-incrimination, the right to confront and cross-examine witnesses, and in certain instances, the right to a jury trial. In addition, many states have their own procedures concerning rules of evidence, competence of witnesses, pleadings, and pretrial motions. At the end of the adjudicatory hearing, the court enters a judgment against the juvenile.

Disposition If the adjudication process finds the child delinquent guilty, the court must decide what should be done to treat the child. Most juvenile court acts require a dispositional hearing separate from the adjudication. This two-stage decision is often referred to as a **bifurcated process**. The dispositional hearing is less formal than adjudication. Here, the judge imposes a **disposition** on the offender in light of the offense, the youth's prior record, and his or her family background. The judge can prescribe a wide range of dispositions, ranging from a reprimand to probation to institutional commitment. In theory, the judge's decision serves the best interests of the child, the family, and the community.

Treatment After disposition in juvenile court, delinquent offenders may be placed in some form of correctional treatment. Probation is the most commonly used formal sentence for juvenile offenders, and many states require that a youth fail on probation before being sent to an institution (unless the criminal act is extremely serious). Probation involves placing the child under the supervision of the juvenile probation department for the purpose of community treatment. The most severe of

bifurcated process
The procedure of separating adjudicatory and dispositionary hearings so different levels of evidence can be heard at each.

disposition
For juvenile offenders, the equivalent of sentencing for adult offenders; juvenile dispositions should be more rehabilitative than retributive.

the statutory dispositions available to the juvenile court involves commitment of the child to an institution. The committed child may be sent to a state training school or a private residential treatment facility. These are usually minimum-security facilities with small populations and an emphasis on treatment and education. Some states, however, maintain facilities with populations of over a thousand youths. Currently there are more than one hundred thousand youths in some form of correctional institution in the United States.

Some jurisdictions allow for a program of juvenile aftercare or parole. A youth can be paroled from an institution and placed under the supervision of a parole officer. This means that he or she will complete the period of confinement in the community and receive assistance from the parole officer in the form of counseling, school referral, and vocational training.

Juveniles who are committed to treatment programs or control programs have a legal right to treatment. States are required to provide suitable rehabilitation programs that include counseling, education, and vocational services. Appellate courts have ruled that, if such minimum treatment is not provided, individuals must be released from confinement.

Conflicting Values in Juvenile Justice This overview of the juvenile justice process hints at the often-conflicting values at the heart of the system. Efforts to ensure that juveniles are given appropriate treatment are consistent with the doctrine of *parens patriae* that predominated in the first half of the twentieth century (see Table 11.2 for a timeline of ideologies of juvenile justice). Over the past century, the juvenile court has struggled to provide treatment for juvenile offenders while guaranteeing them constitutional due process. But the system has been so overwhelmed by the increase in violent juvenile crime and family breakdown that some judges and politicians have suggested abolishing the juvenile system. Even those experts who want to retain an independent juvenile court have called for its restructuring. Crime-control advocates want to reduce the court's jurisdiction over juveniles charged with serious crimes and liberalize the prosecutor's ability to try them in adult courts. In contrast, child advocates suggest that the court scale back its judicial role and transfer its functions to community groups and social service agencies.[37] ✔ Checkpoints

LOOKING BACK TO JENNIFER'S STORY

Some might argue that Jennifer's referral to Youth Court was too lenient. Do you think this was an appropriate treatment consistent with parens patriae? *Explain.*

petition
Document filed in juvenile court alleging that a juvenile is a delinquent, a status offender, or a dependent and asking that the court assume jurisdiction over the juvenile.

Criminal Justice Versus Juvenile Justice

The components of the adult and juvenile criminal processes are similar. However, the juvenile system has a separate organizational structure. In many communities, juvenile justice is administered by people who bring special skills to the task. Also, more kinds of facilities and services are available to juveniles than to adults.

One concern of the juvenile court reform movement was to make certain that the stigma attached to a convicted offender would not be affixed to young people in juvenile proceedings. Thus, even the language used in the juvenile court differs from that used in the adult criminal court (Exhibit 11.1). Juveniles are not indicted for a crime; they have a **petition** filed against them. Secure pretrial holding facilities are called *detention centers* rather than jails. Similarly, the criminal trial is called a *hearing* in the juvenile justice system. The Focus on Delinquency feature on page 275 compares the two systems.

A COMPREHENSIVE JUVENILE JUSTICE STRATEGY

At a time when much attention is focused on serious juvenile offenders, a comprehensive strategy has been called for to deal with all aspects of juvenile crime. This strategy focuses on crime prevention and expanding options for handling juvenile

Table 11.2 Timeline of Juvenile Justice Ideology

Timeline	Activity
Prior to 1899	Juveniles treated similarly to adult offenders. No distinction by age or capacity to commit criminal acts.
1899 to 1950s	Children treated differently, beginning with the Illinois Juvenile Court Act of 1899. By 1925 juvenile court acts are established in virtually every state.
1950s to 1970s	Recognition by experts that the rehabilitation model and the protective nature of *parens patriae* have failed to prevent delinquency.
1960s to 1970s	Constitutional due process is introduced into the juvenile justice system. The concept of punishing children or protecting them under *parens patriae* is under attack by the courts.
1970s to 1980s	Failure of rehabilitation and due process protections to control delinquency leads to a shift to a crime-control and punishment philosophy similar to that of the adult criminal justice system.
Early 1990s	Mixed constitutional protections with some treatment. Uncertain goals and programs; the juvenile justice system relies on punishment and deterrence.
Mid-1990s to present	Attention given to strategy that focuses on reducing the threat of juvenile crime and expanding options for handling juvenile offenders. Emphasis is placed on "what works" and implementing the best intervention and control programs. Effort is made to utilize the restorative justice model, which involves balancing the needs of the victim, the community, and the juvenile.

Exhibit 11.1 Comparison of Terms Used in Juvenile and Adult Justice Systems

	Juvenile Terms	Adult Terms
The person and the act	Delinquent child	Criminal
	Delinquent act	Crime
Pre-adjudicatory stage	Take into custody	Arrest
	Petition	Indictment
	Agree to a finding	Plead guilty
	Deny the petition	Plead not guilty
	Adjustment	Plea bargain
	Detention facility; child care shelter	Jail
Adjudicatory stage	Substitution	Reduction of charges
	Adjudication or fact-finding hearing	Trial
	Adjudication	Conviction
Post-adjudicatory stage	Dispositional hearing	Sentencing hearing
	Disposition	Sentence
	Commitment	Incarceration
	Youth development center; treatment; training school	Prison
	Residential child care facility	Halfway house
	Aftercare	Parole

offenders. It addresses the links between crime and poverty, child abuse, drugs, weapons, and school behavior. Programs are based on a continuum of care that begins in early childhood and progresses through late adolescence. The components of this strategy include prevention in early childhood; intervention for at-risk teenage youths; graduated sanctions to hold juvenile offenders accountable for crimes; proper utilization of detention and confinement; and placement of serious juvenile offenders in adult courts.[38] There are many expected benefits from the use of this comprehensive strategy (Exhibit 11.2). Proponents of this strategy have called for an expanded framework that focuses on youth facing a wider range of problem behaviors, including mental health, school, and drug use problems, and a greater integration of services across juvenile justice, child welfare, and other youth-serving agencies.[39]

Prevention

Research has identified an array of early risk factors that may suggest future delinquency. For young children, some of the most important risk factors include low intelligence and attainment, impulsiveness, poor parental supervision, parental conflict, and living in crime-ridden and deprived neighborhoods.[40] A number of early childhood programs have been shown to be effective in tackling these risk factors and preventing delinquency and later criminal offending, including preschool intellectual enrichment, child skills training, parent management training, and parent education programs such as home visiting.[41] Some of these programs can pay back program costs and produce substantial monetary benefits for the government and taxpayers.[42] There is a number of promising federal early childhood programs. Head Start provides children in poverty with, among other things, an enriched educational environment to develop learning and cognitive skills to be better prepared for the early school years. One study found that children who attended Head Start, at ages three to five, were significantly less likely to report being arrested or referred to court for a crime by ages eighteen to thirty compared to their siblings who did not attend the program.[43] Smart Start is designed to make certain children are healthy before starting school. State-funded home-visiting programs like those in Hawaii and Colorado are especially concerned with reducing child abuse and neglect and bettering the lives of at-risk families and their children.[44]

Intervention

Intervention programs are focused on teenage youths considered to be at higher risk for engaging in petty delinquent acts, using drugs or alcohol, or associating with antisocial peers.[45] Interventions at this stage are designed to ward off involvement in more serious delinquency. Many jurisdictions are developing intervention programs for teenage youths. An example is the Big Brothers/Big Sisters program, which matches a volunteer adult with a youngster. Similarly, in the Office of Juvenile Justice and Delinquency Prevention's Juvenile Mentoring Program (JUMP), responsible and caring adults volunteer their time as mentors to youths at risk for delinquency and dropping out of school. The mentors work one-on-one with the children, offering support and guidance.[46] Job training, through the likes of Job Corps and YouthBuild U.S.A., is another important intervention that receives government funding. These programs improve the chances of young people obtaining jobs in the legal economy and thereby may reduce delinquency. Efforts are also being made to deter them from

Similarities and Differences Between Juvenile and Adult Justice Systems

Since its creation, the juvenile justice system has sought to maintain its independence from the adult justice system. Yet there are a number of similarities that characterize the institutions, processes, and law of the two systems.

Similarities

- Police officers, judges, and correctional personnel use discretion in decision making in both the adult and the juvenile systems.
- The right to receive *Miranda* warnings applies to juveniles as well as to adults.
- Juveniles and adults are protected from prejudicial lineups or other identification procedures.
- Similar procedural safeguards protect juveniles and adults when they make an admission of guilt.
- Prosecutors and defense attorneys play equally critical roles in juvenile and adult advocacy.
- Juveniles and adults have the right to counsel at most key stages of the court process.
- Pretrial motions are available in juvenile and criminal court proceedings.
- Negotiations and plea bargaining exist for juvenile and adult offenders.
- Juveniles and adults have a right to a hearing and an appeal.
- The standard of evidence in juvenile delinquency adjudications, as in adult criminal trials, is proof beyond a reasonable doubt.
- Juveniles and adults can be placed on probation by the court.
- Both juveniles and adults can be placed in pretrial detention facilities.
- Juveniles and adults can be kept in detention without bail if they are considered dangerous.
- After trial, both can be placed in community treatment programs.
- Juveniles and adults can be required to undergo drug testing.

Differences

- The primary purpose of juvenile procedures is protection and treatment. With adults, the aim is to punish the guilty.
- Age determines the jurisdiction of the juvenile court. The nature of the offense determines jurisdiction in the adult

system. Juveniles can be ordered to the criminal court for trial as adults.
- Juveniles can be apprehended for acts that would not be criminal if they were committed by an adult (status offenses).
- Juvenile proceedings are not considered criminal; adult proceedings are.
- Juvenile court procedures are generally informal and private.
- Those of adult courts are more formal and are open to the public.
- Courts cannot release identifying information about a juvenile to the press, but they must release information about an adult.
- Parents are highly involved in the juvenile process but not in the adult process.
- The standard of arrest is more stringent for adults than for juveniles.
- Juveniles are released into parental custody. Adults are generally given the opportunity for bail.
- Juveniles have no constitutional right to a jury trial. Adults have this right. Some state statutes provide juveniles with a jury trial.
- Juveniles can be searched in school without probable cause or a warrant.
- A juvenile's record is generally sealed when the age of majority is reached. The record of an adult is permanent.
- A juvenile court cannot sentence juveniles to county jails or state prisons; these are reserved for adults.

CRITICAL THINKING

1. What are some of the key principles of the juvenile justice system that distinguish it from the adult justice system and that have come under increased scrutiny of late?
2. What can be done to ensure that these key principles are protected so that the juvenile justice system remains distinct from the adult system?

INFOTRAC COLLEGE EDITION RESEARCH

For more information on how the juvenile justice system is becoming increasingly like the adult justice system, go to InfoTrac College Edition and read L. Mara Dodge, "Our Juvenile Court Has Become More Like a Criminal Court: A Century of Reform at the Cook County (Chicago) Juvenile Court," *Michigan Historical Review* 26(2):51 (2000); Joseph V. Penn, "Justice for Youth? A History of the Juvenile and Family Court," *Brown University Child and Adolescent Behavior Letter* 17(9):1 (September 2001).

becoming involved with gangs, because gang members ordinarily have higher rates of serious violent behavior.

Graduated Sanctions

Graduated sanction programs for juveniles are another solution being explored by states across the country. Types of graduated sanctions include immediate sanctions for nonviolent offenders (these consist of community-based diversion and day

Mentoring is one of many types of interventions that have been used with teens considered to be at high risk for engaging in delinquency. These two teens, juniors at North High School in Evansville, Indiana, are part of a mentor program to help incoming freshman.

teen courts
Courts that make use of peer juries to decide nonserious delinquency cases.

treatment); intermediate sanctions, such as probation and electronic monitoring, which target repeat minor offenders and first-time serious offenders; and secure institutional care, which is reserved for repeat serious offenders and violent offenders. The philosophy behind this approach is to limit the most restrictive sanctions to the most dangerous offenders, whereas increasing restrictions and intensity of treatment services as offenders move from minor to serious offenses.[47]

Institutional Programs

Another key to a comprehensive strategy is improving institutional programs. Many experts believe that juvenile incarceration is overused, particularly for nonviolent offenders. That is why the concept of *deinstitutionalization*—removing as many youths from secure confinement as possible—was established by the Juvenile Justice and Delinquency Act of 1974. Considerable research supports the fact that warehousing juveniles without proper treatment does little to deter criminal behavior. The most effective secure corrections programs are those that provide individual services for a small number of participants.[48]

Alternative Courts

drug courts
Courts whose focus is providing treatment for youths accused of drug-related acts.

systematic review
A type of review that uses rigorous methods for locating, appraising, and synthesizing evidence from prior evaluation studies.

meta-analysis
A statistical technique that synthesizes results from prior evaluation studies.

New venues of juvenile justice that provide special services to youth while helping to alleviate the case flow problems that plague overcrowded juvenile courts are being implemented across the United States. For example, as of 2006 there were 411 juvenile **drug courts** (another 127 are in the planning process) operating in forty-seven states and the District of Columbia, Guam, Northern Mariana Islands, and Puerto Rico.[49] These special courts have jurisdiction over the burgeoning number of cases involving substance abuse and trafficking. Although juvenile drug courts operate under a number of different frameworks the aim is to place nonviolent first offenders into intensive treatment programs rather than in a custodial institution.[50]

In a **systematic review** and **meta-analysis** of the effects of drug courts, David Wilson and his colleagues found that drug courts are an effective alternative crime control measure to reducing recidivism rates among drug-involved offenders. Of the

CHECKPOINTS

■ There are conflicting values in juvenile justice. Some experts want to get tough with young criminals, whereas others want to focus on rehabilitation.

■ There are distinct differences between the juvenile and adult justice system.

■ The terminology used in juvenile justice is designed to shield kids from stigma.

■ Some state jurisdictions are creating comprehensive juvenile care mechanisms using a variety of treatment programs.

■ Some states are experimenting with peer-run teen courts.

thirty-eight studies included in the review, only three were of juvenile drug courts. This is explained, in part, by the relatively recent interest of juvenile justice agencies in experimenting with drug courts. The findings of the three juvenile drug courts were mixed. On the one hand, their overall effectiveness was significantly greater than the adult drug courts for all offenses measured. On the other hand, they were no more effective in reducing drug offenses than traditional juvenile court processing or adult drug courts.[51]

Similar findings were found in a recent three-year evaluation of a juvenile drug court in Maricopa County, Arizona. (This study was not included in the above review; it was published after the review was completed.) Drug-involved juvenile offenders assigned to drug court, compared to similar youths who received a disposition of probation, were less likely to commit further criminal offenses, but there was no difference in marijuana use between the two groups and cocaine use was higher among drug court youths. The authors found that family stability, school attendance, and legal indicators were important to the effectiveness of the drug court in reducing recidivism.[52]

Teen courts, also called youth courts, are another alternative to traditional forms of juvenile court that have received increased attention of late in an effort to relieve overcrowding and provide a more effective response to reducing recidivism. The Preventing and Treating Delinquency feature on page 280 discusses this alternative. ✔ Checkpoints

LOOKING BACK TO JENNIFER'S STORY

What types of juvenile delinquent behavior/charges would not be appropriate for a teen court? What are the most appropriate types of cases for this intervention and why?

FUTURE OF JUVENILE JUSTICE

The future of the juvenile court is subject to wide-ranging and sometimes contentious debate. Some experts, including Barry Feld, believe that over the years the juvenile justice system has taken on more of the characteristics of the adult courts, which he refers to as the "criminalizing" of the juvenile court,[53] or in a more stern admonition has said: "Despite juvenile courts' persisting rehabilitative rhetoric, the reality of *treating* juveniles closely resembles *punishing* adult criminals."[54] Robert Dawson suggests that because the legal differences between the juvenile and criminal systems are narrower than they ever have been, it may be time to abolish the juvenile court.[55] Other experts, such as Peter Greenwood, contends that, despite these and other limitations, the treatment programs that the "modern" juvenile court currently provides play a central role in society's response to the most serious delinquents.[56] He argues that this comes with a number of specific responsibilities that juvenile courts must take on so as to ensure that these programs are indeed effective, including: awareness of the most up-to-date scientific evidence on the effectiveness of court-based programs; diversion of cases that can be handled informally outside of the system; disposition of cases to appropriate programs; and quality control.[57]

These concerns reflect the changes that have been ongoing in the juvenile justice system. During the 1990s, there was a nationwide effort to modify the system in response to the public's perceived fear of predatory juvenile offenders and the reaction to high-profile cases such as the Columbine tragedy. As a result, states began to institute policies that critics believed undermined the true purpose of the juvenile court movement.[58] Between 1992 and 1995, forty states and the District of Columbia changed their transfer statutes to make it easier to waive juveniles to adult courts, and since 1992, only one state—Nebraska—has not changed its transfer statutes for this purpose.[59] By the end of 2004 legislative session (the most recent data available), there were twenty-three states and the District of Columbia where no minimum age is specified to transfer a juvenile to adult court (Table 11.3).

Table 11.3 Minimum Age Specified in Statute for Transferring Juveniles to Adult Court

Age	State (Total Number)
None	Alaska, Arizona, Delaware, Florida, Georgia, Hawaii, Idaho, Indiana, Maine, Maryland, Montana, Nebraska, Nevada, Oklahoma, Oregon, Pennsylvania, Rhode Island, South Carolina, South Dakota, Tennessee, Washington, West Virginia, Wisconsin (23 and the District of Columbia)
10	Kansas, Vermont (2)
12	Colorado, Missouri (2)
13	Illinois, Mississippi, New Hampshire, New York, North Carolina, Wyoming (6)
14	Alabama, Arkansas, California, Connecticut, Iowa, Kentucky, Louisiana, Massachusetts, Michigan, Minnesota, Nevada, New Jersey, North Dakota, Ohio, Texas, Utah, Virginia (16)
15	New Mexico (1)

Sources: Patrick Griffin, "Montana Transfer Provisions," in *State Juvenile Justice Profiles* (Pittsburgh, PA: National Center for Juvenile Justice, 2005); Howard N. Snyder and Melissa Sickmund, *Juvenile Offenders and Victims: 2006 National Report* (Pittsburgh, PA: National Center for Juvenile Justice, 2006), p. 114.

Getting tough on juvenile crime is the primary motivation for moving cases to the adult criminal justice system.[60] Some commentators argue that waiving juveniles is a statement that juvenile crime is taken seriously by society; others believe the fear of being waived serves as a deterrent.[61] Some states, such as Arizona, have initiated legislation that significantly restricts eligibility for juvenile justice processing and criminalizing acts that heretofore would have fallen under the jurisdiction of the juvenile court. For example, the Arizona legislation provides for the statutory exclusion for fifteen-, sixteen-, and seventeen-year-olds charged with violent crimes or if they had two prior felony adjudications and were charged with any third felony. It also added the provision, "once an adult, always an adult," where, if a juvenile was previously tried and convicted in criminal court, any future offenses involving that juvenile will be tried in adult court.[62] Thirty-two other states and the District of Columbia also have the once an adult, always an adult provision.[63] Although there is no mistaking the intention of this provision—to get tough on juvenile crime—some experts point out that inconsistencies that it created between the two justice systems may have inadvertently also produced a number of legal loopholes.[64]

These changes concern juvenile justice advocates such as Hunter Hurst, director of the National Center for Juvenile Justice, who warns:

> *How could the wholesale criminalization of children possibly be a wise thing? If their vulnerability to predation in jails and prisons does not destroy them, won't the so-called taint of criminality that they carry with them for the rest of their lives be an impossible social burden for them and us? . . . Have our standards of decency devolved to the point where protection of children is no longer a compelling state interest? In many ways the answer is yes.*[65]

The National Research Council and Institute of Medicine's Panel on Juvenile Crime also expressed alarm over an increasingly punitive juvenile justice system and called for a number of changes to uphold the importance of treatment for juveniles. One of their recommendations is particularly noteworthy:

> *The federal government should assist the states through federal funding and incentives to reduce the use of secure detention and secure confinement, by developing community-based alternatives. The effectiveness of such programs both for the protection of the community and the benefit of the youth in their charge should be monitored.*[66]

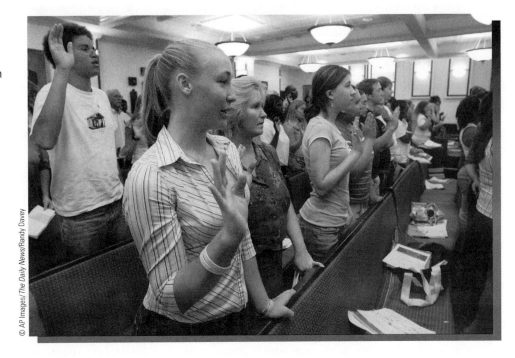

In teen courts, which are increasingly being used across the country as alternatives to traditional forms of juvenile courts, young people rather than adults determine the disposition in a case. Shown here is the swearing-in ceremony for participants at Onslow County's Teen Court annual training session in Jacksonville, North Carolina.

Although calling for reforms to the juvenile justice system was a key element of this national panel's final report, panel members were equally, and perhaps more concerned with the need to prevent delinquency before it occurs and intervene with at-risk children and adolescents. Importantly, there is growing public support for prevention and intervention programs designed to reduce delinquency.[67] The panel also called attention to the need for more rigorous experimentation with prevention and intervention programs with demonstrated success in reducing risk factors associated with delinquency.[68] Some states, like Washington, have begun to incorporate a research-based approach to guide juvenile justice programming and policy.[69]

It should be noted that there is some, albeit limited, evidence that points to a slowdown of sorts in recent years in this get-tough approach toward juvenile offenders. In an analysis of state juvenile transfer laws, Howard Snyder and Melissa Sickmund report that there has been a considerable reduction in the number of states that have expanded their transfer provisions. From 2003 through 2004, only two states enacted further provisions to make it easier to waive juveniles to adult courts.[70] However, it is important to note that very few if any states have reversed their restrictive transfer laws.

Those who support the juvenile justice concept believe that it is too soon to write off the rehabilitative ideal that has always underpinned the separate treatment of juvenile offenders. They note that fears of a juvenile crime wave are misplaced and that the actions of a few violent children should not mask the needs of millions who can benefit from solicitous treatment rather than harsh punishments. Authors Alida Merlo, Peter Benekos, and William Cook note that a child is more likely to be hit by lightning than shot in a school.[71] And although a get-tough approach may be able to reduce the incidence of some crimes, economic analysis indicates that the costs incurred by placing children in more punitive secure facilities outweigh the benefits accrued in crime reduction.[72]

To read more about **juvenile drug courts**, go to the website www.thomsonedu.com/criminaljustice/siegel.

LOOKING BACK TO JENNIFER'S STORY

If you were the program director of a teen court, what would you do if the jury was being too punitive with a peer? It is important to respect the jury's decisions, but there are times when an adult may need to step in. What would be the best process for this?

Teen Courts

To relieve overcrowding and provide an alternative to traditional forms of juvenile courts, jurisdictions across the country are now experimenting with teen courts, also called youth courts. These differ from other juvenile justice programs, because young people rather than adults determine the disposition in a case. Cases handled in these courts typically involve young juveniles (ages ten to fifteen) with no prior arrest records who are being charged with minor law violations, such as shoplifting, vandalism, and disorderly conduct. Usually, young offenders are asked to volunteer to have their case heard in a teen court instead of the more formal court of the traditional juvenile justice system.

As in a regular juvenile court, teen court defendants may go through an intake process, a preliminary review of charges, a court hearing, and disposition. In a teen court, however, other young people are responsible for much of the process. Charges may be presented to the court by a fifteen-year-old "prosecutor." Defendants may be represented by a sixteen-year-old "defense attorney." Other youths may serve as jurors, court clerks, and bailiffs. In some teen courts, a youth "judge" (or panel of youth judges) may choose the best disposition or sanction for each case. In a few teen courts, teens even determine whether the facts in a case have been proven by the prosecutor (similar to a finding of guilt). Offenders are often ordered to pay restitution or perform community service. Some teen courts require offenders to write formal apologies to their victims; others require offenders to serve on a subsequent teen court jury. Many courts use other innovative dispositions, such as requiring offenders to attend classes designed to improve their decision-making skills, enhance their awareness of victims, and deter them from future theft.

Although decisions are made by juveniles, adults are also involved in teen courts. They often administer the programs, and they are usually responsible for essential functions such as budgeting, planning, and personnel. In many programs, adults supervise the courtroom activities, and they often coordinate the community service placements where the young offenders work to fulfill the terms of their dispositions. In some programs, adults act as the judges and teens serve as attorneys and jurors.

Proponents of teen court argue that the process takes advantage of one of the most powerful forces in the life of an adolescent—the desire for peer approval and the reaction to peer pressure. According to this argument, youth respond better to pro-social peers than to adult authority figures. Thus, teen courts are seen as a potentially effective alternative to traditional juvenile courts that are staffed with paid professionals such as lawyers, judges, and probation officers. Teen court advocates also point out that the benefits extend beyond defendants. Teen courts may benefit the volunteer youth attorneys and judges, who probably learn more about the legal system than they ever could in a classroom. The presence of a teen court may also encourage the entire community to take a more active role in responding to juvenile crime. In sum, teen courts offer at least four potential benefits:

- *Accountability.* Teen courts may help ensure that young offenders are held accountable for their illegal behavior, even when their offenses are relatively minor and would not likely result in sanctions from the traditional juvenile justice system.
- *Timeliness.* An effective teen court can move young offenders from arrest to sanctions within a matter of days rather than the months that may pass with traditional juvenile courts. This rapid response may increase the positive impact of court sanctions, regardless of their severity.
- *Cost savings.* Teen courts usually depend heavily on youth and adult volunteers. If managed properly, they may

SUMMARY

- Urbanization created a growing number of at-risk youth in the nation's cities. The juvenile justice system was established at the turn of the twentieth century after decades of efforts by child-saving groups. These reformers sought to create an independent category of delinquent offender and keep their treatment separate from adults.
- Over the past four decades, the U.S. Supreme Court and lower courts have granted procedural safeguards and the protection of due process in juvenile courts. Major court decisions have laid down the constitutional requirements for juvenile court proceedings. In years past, the protections currently afforded to both adults and children were not available to children.

- For both violent and property offenses, more than half of all formally processed delinquency cases in 2002 resulted in the youth being adjudicated delinquent.
- The juvenile justice process consists of a series of steps: the police investigation, the intake procedure in the juvenile court, the pretrial procedures used for juvenile offenders, and the adjudication, disposition, and post-dispositional procedures.
- There are conflicting values in juvenile justice. Some experts want to get tough with young criminals, whereas others want to focus on rehabilitation.
- The adult and juvenile justice systems have a number of key similarities and differences. One of the similarities is the right to receive *Miranda* warnings; this applies to

handle a substantial number of offenders at relatively little cost to the community.

- *Community cohesion.* A well-structured and expansive teen court program may affect the entire community by increasing public appreciation of the legal system, enhancing community-court relationships, encouraging greater respect for the law among youth, and promoting volunteerism among both adults and youths.

The teen court movement is one of the fastest-growing delinquency intervention programs in the country, with more than one thousand of these courts in operation in forty-eight states and the District of Columbia, serving an estimated 110,000 to 125,000 young offenders each year; another 100,000 youth benefit from their participation as volunteers. Some recent evaluations (but not all) of teen courts have found that they did not "widen the net" of justice by handling cases that in the absence of the teen court would have been subject to a lesser level of processing. Also, in the OJJDP Evaluation of Teen Courts Project, which covered four states—Alaska, Arizona, Maryland, and Missouri—and compared five hundred first-time offending youths referred to teen court with five hundred similar youths handled by the regular juvenile justice system, it was found that six-month recidivism rates were lower for those who went through the teen court program in three of the four jurisdictions. Importantly, in these three teen courts, the six-month recidivism rates were under 10 percent. Similar findings were reported in a rigorous evaluation of a teen court in Florida, and in one for repeat offenders in Washington State. However, other recent evaluations of teen courts in Kentucky, New Mexico, and Delaware indicate that short-term recidivism rates range from 25 percent to 30 percent. The conclusions from the OJJDP teen court evaluation may be the best guide for future experimentation with teen courts:

Teen courts and youth courts may be preferable to the normal juvenile justice process in jurisdictions that do not, or cannot, *provide meaningful sanctions for all young, first-time juvenile offenders. In jurisdictions that do not provide meaningful sanctions and services for these offenders, youth court may still perform just as well as a more traditional, adult-run program.*

CRITICAL THINKING

1. Could teen courts be used to try serious criminal acts, such as burglary and robbery?
2. Is a conflict of interest created when teens judge the behavior of other teens? Does the fact that they themselves may one day become defendants in a teen court influence their decision making?

Sources: Jeffrey A. Butts and Janeen Buck, "Teen Courts: A Focus on Research," *Juvenile Justice Bulletin October 2000* (Washington, DC: Office of Juvenile Justice and Delinquency Prevention, 2000); Jeffrey A. Butts, "Encouraging Findings from the OJJDP Evaluation," *In Session: Newsletter of the National Youth Court Center 2*(3):1, 7 (Summer 2002); Kevin Minor, James Wells, Irinia Soderstrom, Rachel Bingham, and Deborah Williamson, "Sentence Completion and Recidivism Among Juveniles Referred to Teen Courts," *Crime & Delinquency 45*:467–480 (1999); Paige Harrison, James R. Maupin, and G. Larry Mays, "Teen Court: An Examination of Processes and Outcomes," *Crime & Delinquency 47*:243–264 (2001); Arthur H. Garrison, "An Evaluation of a Delaware Teen Court," *Juvenile and Family Court Journal 52*:11–21 (2001); Anthony P. Logalbo and Charlene M. Callahan, "An Evaluation of a Teen Court as a Juvenile Crime Diversion Program," *Juvenile and Family Court Journal 52*:1–11 (2001); Andrew Rasmussen, "Teen Court Referral, Sentencing, and Subsequent Recidivism: Two Proportional Hazards Models and a Little Speculation," *Crime & Delinquency 50*:615–635 (2004); Deborah Kirby Forgays and Lisa DeMilio, "Is Teen Court Effective for Repeat Offenders?: A Test of the Restorative Justice Approach," *International Journal of Offender Therapy and Comparative Criminology 49*:107–118 (2005); Sarah S. Pearson and Sonia Jurich, *Youth Court: A Community Solution for Embracing At-Risk Youth: A National Update* (Washington, DC: American Youth Policy Forum, 2005).

juveniles as well as adults. One of the differences is that juvenile proceedings are not considered criminal, whereas adult proceedings are.

- There has been a movement to toughen the juvenile justice system, and because of this many view the importance of treatment as having been greatly diminished. Proponents of treatment argue that it is best suited to the developmental needs of juveniles. Critics contend that treatment simply serves to mollycoddle juveniles and reduces the deterrent value of the juvenile court.
- A comprehensive juvenile justice strategy has been developed to preserve the need for treatment services for juveniles while also using appropriate sanctions to hold them accountable for their actions. Elements of this strategy include delinquency prevention, intervention programs, graduated sanctions, improvement of institutional programs, and treating juveniles like adults. New courts, such as drug courts and teen courts, are now in place.

- Prevention efforts are targeted at children and teens in an effort to prevent the onset of delinquency. Intervention efforts are targeted at children and teens considered at higher risk for delinquency and are designed to ward off involvement in more serious delinquent behavior.
- The future of the juvenile justice system continues to be debated. A number of state jurisdictions, although fewer today than in the 1990s, are revising their juvenile codes to restrict eligibility in the juvenile justice system, and to remove the most serious offenders. At the same time there are some promising signs, such as juvenile crime rates being lower than in decades past, public support for prevention and intervention programs, and some states beginning to incorporate research-based initiatives to guide juvenile justice programming and policy.

QUESTIONS FOR DISCUSSION

1. What factors precipitated the development of the Illinois Juvenile Court Act of 1899?

2. One of the most significant reforms in dealing with the juvenile offender was the opening of the New York House of Refuge in 1825. What were the social and judicial consequences of this reform on the juvenile justice system?

3. The child savers have been accused of wanting to control the lives of poor and immigrant children for their own benefit. Are there any parallels to the child-saving movement in modern-day America?

4. Should there be a juvenile justice system, or should juveniles who commit serious crimes be treated as adults, while the less serious crimes are handled by social welfare agencies?

5. The Supreme Court has made a number of major decisions in the area of juvenile justice. What are these decisions? What is their impact on the juvenile justice system?

6. What is the meaning of the term *procedural due process of law*? Explain why and how procedural due process has had an impact on juvenile justice.

7. The formal components of the criminal justice system are often considered to be the police, the court, and the correctional agency. How do these components relate to the major areas of the juvenile justice system? Is the operation of justice similar in the juvenile and adult systems?

8. What role has the federal government played in the juvenile justice system over the last twenty-five years?

APPLYING WHAT YOU HAVE LEARNED

Fourteen-year-old Daphne A., a product of the city's best private schools, lives with her wealthy family in a fashionable neighborhood. Her father is an executive at a local financial services conglomerate and earns close to a million dollars per year. Daphne, however, is always in trouble at school, and teachers report she is impulsive and has poor self-control. At times she can be kind and warm, but on other occasions she is obnoxious, unpredictable, insecure, and demanding of attention. She is overly self-conscious about her body and has a drinking problem.

Despite repeated promises to get her life together, Daphne likes to hang out at night in a local park, drinking with neighborhood kids. On more than one occasion she has gone to the park with her friend Chris G., a quiet boy with his own personal problems. His parents have separated and he is prone to severe anxiety attacks. He has been suspended from school, and diagnosed with depression, for which he takes two drugs—an antidepressant and a sedative.

One night, the two met up with Michael M., a forty-four-year-old man with a long history of alcoholism. After a night of drinking, a fight broke out and Michael was stabbed, his throat cut, and his body dumped in a pond.

Soon after the attack, Daphne called 911, telling police that a friend "jumped in the lake and didn't come out." Police searched the area and found the slashed and stabbed body in the water; the body had been disemboweled in an attempt to sink it. When the authorities traced the call, Daphne was arrested, and she confessed to police that she had helped Chris murder the victim.

During an interview with court psychiatrists, Daphne admits she participated in the killing, but cannot articulate what caused her to get involved. She had been drinking and remembers little of the events. She said she was flirting with Michael and Chris stabbed him in a jealous rage. She speaks in a flat, hollow voice and shows little remorse for her actions. It was a spur-of-the-moment thing, she claims, and after all it was Chris who had the knife and not she. Later, Chris claims that Daphne instigated the fight, egged him on, taunting him that he was too scared to kill someone. Chris says that Daphne, while drunk, often talked of killing an adult because she hates older people, especially her parents.

If Daphne is tried as a juvenile, she can be kept in institutions until she is seventeen; the sentence could be expanded to age twenty-one, but only if she is a behavior problem in custody and demonstrates conclusive need for further secure treatment.

- Should the case of Daphne A. be dealt with in the juvenile court, even though the maximum possible sentence she can receive is two to six years? If not, over what kind of cases should the juvenile court have jurisdiction?
- How does the concept of *parens patriae* apply in cases such as that of Daphne A.?

- If you believe that the juvenile court is not equipped to handle cases of extremely violent youth, then should it be abolished?
- What reforms must be made in the juvenile justice system to rehabilitate adolescents like Daphne? Or should it even try?

DOING RESEARCH ON THE WEB

Before you answer these questions, you may want to learn more about this topic by checking out the websites of the American Youth Policy Forum, Office of Juvenile Justice and Delinquency Prevention, National Center for Juvenile Justice, National Crime Prevention Council, Fight Crime: Invest in Kids, and Office of the Surgeon General by going to **www.thomsonedu.com/criminaljustice/siegel**.

To research the debate on the most effective strategies to address serious and violent juvenile offending, use "juvenile and violence" in a key word search on InfoTrac College Edition.

Police Work with Juveniles

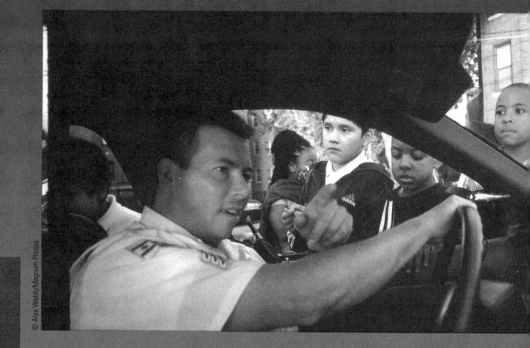

© Alex Webb/Magnum Photos

CHAPTER OBJECTIVES

After reading this chapter you should:

1. Be able to identify key historical events that have shaped juvenile policing in America today.
2. Understand key roles and responsibilities of the police in responding to juvenile offenders.
3. Be able to comment on the organization and management of police services for juveniles.
4. Be aware of major court cases that have influenced police practices.
5. Understand key legal aspects of police work, including search and seizure and custodial interrogation, and how they apply to juveniles.
6. Be able to describe police use of discretion and factors that influence discretion.
7. Understand the importance of police use of discretion with juveniles and some of the associated problems.
8. Be aware of the major policing strategies to prevent delinquency.
9. See the pros and cons of police using different delinquency prevention strategies.

Rico grew up in Harlem, one of twelve children raised primarily by their mother, a strong and determined African American woman who struggled daily to provide for the basic needs and safety of her family. Rico's father, a man of Puerto Rican descent, was heavily involved in criminal activity and drifted in and out of their lives for brief periods of time.

Rico attended a large New York public high school with approximately eight thousand students. Violence and gang activity were common in both his community and in the school setting; sexual assaults took place in school stairwells, fights occurred on a daily basis, young drug dealers did business in the hallways, and there had been some murders in school. Rico found it difficult to focus on academics with such chaos and fear all around him. The school, like many in the area, enlisted the assistance of the New York City Police Department in an effort to create a safer learning environment. Eight full-time uniformed and armed police officers patrolled the school daily. They had the ability and discretion to arrest on site and to intervene as needed, and they worked in collaboration with the educators and administrators to reduce violence and crime on school grounds. In the lunchroom, halls, and school auditorium, police officers were dressed in full uniform and acted clearly as authority figures. The officers also worked hard to be approachable and friendly to the students. They made efforts to have relationships with the students so that they could be a resource during challenging times.

Rico was a brilliant and gifted young man who, despite being in some trouble during his younger years, aspired to go to college and make a better life for himself. Several of his teachers encouraged him in his studies and although he was thriving academically, he needed a safer environment where he could focus on his education.

During his freshman year, Rico and some other students were playing cards in front of the school during a lunch break when another student threw a glass bottle at Rico's head and threatened his life. Rico went after the young man and a fight ensued. The police at the school intervened to stop the fight and address the young men's behavior. Although both teens could have been arrested for disorderly conduct or battery, Rico explained to them that he was defending himself, and the officers agreed. Knowing he was an excellent student who did not typically engage in this type of conduct, the officers chose to talk with Rico and try to encourage him in a more positive direction, rather than arresting him.

After graduating from high school, Rico attended the University of Cincinnati on a full athletic scholarship for football and track, and he also became a member of the U.S. Boxing Team. Upon completing his undergraduate degree, Rico attended medical school. Today he is Dr. Richard Larkin, assistant professor at a community college in Illinois. He is currently teaching and working on his Ph.D. in biochemistry. In addition to crediting the New York Police Department and his teachers for their efforts, he credits his mother's hard work, strict discipline, and tremendous drive for his success.

HISTORY OF JUVENILE POLICING

pledge system
Early English system in which neighbors protected each other from thieves and warring groups.

watch system
Replaced the pledge system in England; watchmen patrolled urban areas at night to provide protection from harm.

Providing specialized police services for juveniles is a relatively recent phenomenon. At one time citizens were responsible for protecting themselves and maintaining order.

The origin of police agencies can be traced to early English society.[1] Before the Norman Conquest, the **pledge system** assumed that neighbors would protect each other from thieves and warring groups. Individuals were entrusted with policing themselves and resolving minor problems. By the thirteenth century, however, the **watch system** was created to police larger communities. Men were organized in church parishes to patrol areas at night and guard against disturbances and breaches of the peace. This was followed by establishment of the constable, who was responsible for dealing with more serious crimes. By the seventeenth century, the constable, the justice of the peace, and the night watchman formed the nucleus of the police system in England.

When the Industrial Revolution brought thousands of people from the countryside to work in factories, the need for police protection increased. As a result, the first organized police force was established in London in 1829. The British "bobbies" (so called after their founder, Sir Robert Peel) were not successful at stopping crime

Modern policing began in England. This nineteenth-century photo shows Tom Smith, a well-known "peeler." English policemen became known as peelers in reference to Home Secretary Sir Robert Peel, who organized the police force in 1829. They were also referred to as "bobbies" after their creator—a name that has stuck to the present day.

 For a comprehensive history of the **London Metropolitan Police** from 1829 to 2003, go to the website www. thomsonedu.com/criminaljustice/siegel.

and were influenced by the wealthy for personal and political gain.[2]

In the American colonies, the local sheriff became the most important police official. By the mid-1800s, city police departments had formed in Boston, New York, and Philadelphia. Officers patrolled on foot, and conflicts often arose between untrained officers and the public.

When children violated the law they were often treated the same as adult offenders. But even at this stage a belief existed that the enforcement of criminal law should be applied differently to children. (See chapter 1 for more on the development of the concept of a separate status of childhood in America.)

During the late nineteenth century and into the first half of the twentieth, the problems of how to deal with growing numbers of unemployed and homeless youths increased. Groups, such as the Wickersham Commission of 1931 and the International Association of Chiefs of Police, became the leading voices for police reform.[3] Their efforts resulted in the creation of specialized police units, known as *delinquency control squads.*

The most famous police reformer of the 1930s was August Vollmer. As the police chief in Berkeley, California, Vollmer instituted numerous reforms, including university training, modern management techniques, and prevention programs, as well as juvenile aid bureaus.[4] These bureaus were the first organized police services for juvenile offenders.

In the 1960s, policing entered a turbulent period.[5] The U.S. Supreme Court handed down decisions designed to restrict police operations and discretion. Civil unrest produced growing tensions between police and the public. Urban police departments were unable to handle the growing crime rate. Federal funding from the Law Enforcement Assistance Administration (LEAA), an agency set up to fund justice-related programs, was a catalyst for developing hundreds of new police programs and enhancing police services for children. By the 1980s, most urban police departments recognized that the problem of juvenile delinquency required special attention.

Today, the role of the juvenile police officer—an officer assigned to juvenile work—has taken on added importance. Most of the nation's urban law enforcement agencies now have specialized juvenile police programs. Typically, such programs involve prevention (police athletic leagues, Project D.A.R.E., community outreach), and law enforcement work (juvenile court, school policing, gang control). Other concerns of the programs include child abuse, domestic violence, and missing children.

POLICE AND JUVENILE OFFENDERS

In the minds of most citizens, the primary responsibility of the police is to protect the public. Based on films, books, and TV shows that depict the derring-do of police officers, the public has obtained an image of crime fighters who always get their man. Since the 1960s, however, the public has become increasingly aware that the reality of police work is substantially different from its fictional glorification. When police departments failed to bring the crime rate down despite massive government subsidies, when citizens complained of civil rights violations, and when tales of police corruption became widespread, it was evident that a crisis was imminent in American policing.

Recently, a new view of policing has emerged among the police themselves. Rather than seeing themselves as crime fighters who track down serious criminals or stop armed robberies in progress, many police departments have adopted the concept that the police role should be to maintain order and be a visible and accessible component of the community. The argument is that police efforts can be successful only when conducted in partnership with concerned citizens. This movement is referred to as **community policing**.[6]

Interest in community policing does not mean that the crime-control model of law enforcement is history. An ongoing effort is being made to improve the crime-fighting capability of police agencies and there are some indications that the effort is paying off.[7] Some research suggests that police innovation in crime-fighting techniques contributed to the substantial reduction in crime rates during the 1990s, whereas other research suggests that the reduction simply had more to do with cities hiring more police.[8]

Working with juvenile offenders may be especially challenging for police officers, because the desire to help young people and to steer them away from crime seems to conflict with the traditional police duties of crime prevention and maintenance of order. In addition, the police are faced with a nationwide adolescent drug problem and renewed gang activity. Although the need to help troubled youths may conflict with traditional police roles, it fits nicely with the newly emerging community policing models. Improving these relationships is critical, because many juveniles do not have a high regard for the police; minority teens are especially critical of police performance.[9]

One large-scale study carried out to investigate juveniles' attitudes toward police confirmed this long-held finding. Although African American teens rated the police less favorably than all other racial groups for all questions asked (for example, "Are police friendly? Are police courteous?"), the most striking racial differences pertained to the question about police honesty: only 15 percent of African American youths said the police were honest. In contrast, 57 percent of European Americans, 51 percent of Asians, 31 percent of Hispanics, and 30 percent of Native Americans said they were.[10] Another study focusing solely on the attitudes of female juveniles toward the police found similar results. Of the more than 400 female high school students interviewed, African Americans compared to their European American counterparts were significantly more likely to report having an overall negative attitude toward police. When asked about police honesty ("In general, I trust the police"), the difference was even greater: only 22 percent of African American female juveniles either agreed or strongly agreed with the statement compared to 56 percent of European American female juveniles.[11] In addition to the importance these results hold for improving police relations with juveniles, especially minorities, to prevent crime, the results may also hold special significance for the reporting of crimes to the police to address juvenile victimization. Research shows that juvenile crime victims are much less likely than adult victims to contact the police. This disparity in reporting crimes to the police holds true even after taking account of a number of important factors, such as crime severity, school victimization, and reporting crimes to officials other than police.[12]

Police Roles

Juvenile officers operate either as specialists in a police department or as part of the juvenile unit of a police department. Their role is similar to that of officers working with adult offenders: to intervene if the actions of a citizen produce public danger or disorder. Most juvenile officers are appointed after having had some general patrol experience. A desire to work with juveniles, as well as an aptitude for the work, are considered essential for the job. Officers must also have a thorough knowledge of the law, especially the constitutional protections available to juveniles. Some officers undergo special training in the handling of aggressive or potentially aggressive juveniles.[13]

community policing
Police strategy that emphasizes fear reduction, community organization, and order maintenance rather than crime fighting.

juvenile officers
Police officers who specialize in dealing with juvenile offenders; they may operate alone or as part of a juvenile police unit in the department.

One of the main functions of police is to deter juvenile crime. In recent decades, policing has taken on many new functions, including being a visible and accessible component of the community and working with residents to address delinquency problems. This is known as community policing.

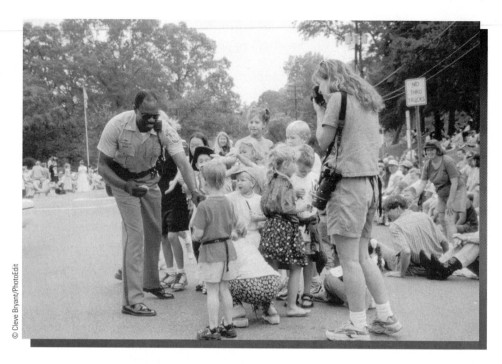

© Cleve Bryant/PhotoEdit

Most officers regard the violations of juveniles as nonserious unless they are committed by chronic troublemakers or involve significant damage to persons or property. Police encounters with juveniles are generally the result of reports made by citizens, and the bulk of such encounters pertain to matters of minor legal consequence.[14]

Of course, police must also deal with serious juvenile offenders whose criminal acts are similar to those of adults, but these are a small minority of the offender population. Thus, police who deal with delinquency must concentrate on being peacekeepers and crime preventers.[15]

Handling juvenile offenders can produce major **role conflicts** for police. They may experience a tension between their desire to perform what they consider their primary duty, law enforcement, and the need to aid in the rehabilitation of youthful offenders. Police officers' actions in cases involving adults are usually controlled by the law and their own judgment or discretion. (The concept of *discretion* is discussed later in this chapter.) In contrast, a case involving a juvenile often demands that the officer consider the "best interests of the child" and how the officer's actions will influence the child's future well-being. However, in recent years police have become more likely to refer juvenile offenders to courts. It is estimated that 70 percent of all juvenile arrests are referred to juvenile court, whereas just over 20 percent of all juvenile arrests are handled informally within the police department or are referred to a community-service agency (Figure 12.1). These informal dispositions are the result of the police officer's discretionary authority.

Police intervention in situations involving juveniles can be difficult and emotional. The officer often encounters hostile behavior from the juvenile offender, as well as agitated witnesses. Overreaction by the officer can result in a violent incident. Even if the officer succeeds in quieting or dispersing the witnesses, they will probably reappear the next day, often in the same place.[16]

Role conflicts are common, because most encounters between police and juveniles are brought about by loitering and rowdiness rather than by serious law violations. Public concern has risen about out-of-control youth. Yet, because of legal constraints and family interference, the police are often limited in the ways in which they can respond to such offenders.[17]

Another role conflict arises in the use of juveniles as police **informants**. Informants are individuals who have access to criminal networks and who, under conditions of anonymity, provide information to authorities in exchange for money or

role conflicts
Conflicts police officers face that revolve around the requirement to perform their primary duty of law enforcement and a desire to aid in rehabilitating youthful offenders.

informant
A person who has access to criminal networks and shares information with authorities in exchange for money or special treatment under conditions of anonymity.

Figure 12.1   Police Response to Juvenile Crime

To understand how police deal with juvenile crime, picture a funnel, with the result shown here. For every five hundred juveniles taken into custody, 70 percent are sent to juvenile court, and just over 20 percent are released.

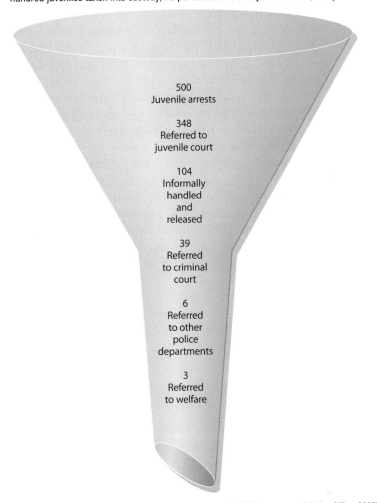

500
Juvenile arrests

348
Referred to
juvenile court

104
Informally
handled
and
released

39
Referred
to criminal
court

6
Referred
to other
police
departments

3
Referred
to welfare

Source: FBI, *Crime in the United States, 2004* (Washington, DC: U.S. Government Printing Office, 2005), Table 68.

special treatment.[18] Police rely on informants, both adult and juvenile, to obtain evidence to make arrests in serious cases that the police may otherwise not be able to solve, such as gun and drug trafficking. Juvenile informants are also used in less serious cases where age is important to the crime; for example, when retailers sell cigarettes or alcohol to minors. Police must balance the need to obtain evidence and the vulnerabilities of and extra safeguards that are needed for juveniles in these cases. As criminologist Mary Dodge notes, there is a need for a higher degree of scrutiny in the use of juvenile police informants and this practice should not be warranted in all circumstances.[19]

What role should the police play in mediating problems with youths: law enforcer or delinquency prevention worker? The answer may lie somewhere between the two. Most police departments operate juvenile programs that combine law enforcement and delinquency prevention, and the police work with the juvenile court to determine a role most suitable for their community.[20] Police officers may even act as prosecutors in some rural courts when attorneys are not available. Thus, the police role with juveniles extends from the on-the-street encounter to the station house to the courtroom. For juvenile matters involving minor criminal conduct or incorrigible behavior, the police ordinarily select the least restrictive alternative, which includes such measures as temporary assistance or referral to community agencies. In contrast, violent juvenile crime requires that the police arrest youths while providing constitutional safeguards similar to those available for adult offenders.

Police and Violent Juvenile Crime

Violent juvenile offenders are defined as those adjudicated delinquent for crimes of homicide, rape, robbery, aggravated assault, and kidnapping. Juveniles account for nearly 16 percent of all violent crime arrests.[21] Since the mid-1990s, the juvenile violence rate has declined rather substantially, leveling off in more recent years. Many experts predicted a surge of violence as children of baby boomers entered their "prime crime" years, whereas others predicted that juvenile arrests for violent crime would double by the year 2010.[22] (See chapter 2 for more on juvenile crime rates.)

As a result of these predictions, police and other justice agencies are experimenting with different methods of controlling violent youth. Some of these methods, such as placing more officers on the beat, have existed for decades; others rely on state-of-the-art technology to pinpoint the locations of violent crimes and develop immediate countermeasures. Research shows that there are a number of effective policing practices, including increased directed patrols in street-corner hot spots of crime, proactive arrests of serious repeat offenders, and **problem-oriented policing**.[23] These strategies address problems of community disorganization and can be effective deterrents when combined with other laws and policies, such as targeting illegal gun carrying.[24] Although many of these policing strategies are not new, implementing them as one element of an overall police plan may have an impact on preventing juvenile violence.

Finally, one key component of any innovative police program dealing with violent juvenile crime is improved communications between the police and the community. Community policing is discussed in more detail at the conclusion of this chapter.

✔ Checkpoints

POLICE AND THE RULE OF LAW

When police are involved with the criminal activity of juvenile offenders, their actions are controlled by statute, constitutional case law, and judicial review. Police methods of investigation and control include the arrest procedure, search and seizure, and custodial interrogation.

The Arrest Procedure

When a juvenile is apprehended, the police must decide whether to release him or her or make a referral to the juvenile court. Cases involving serious crimes against property or persons are often referred to court. Less serious cases, such as disputes between juveniles, petty shoplifting, runaways, and assaults of minors, are often diverted from court action.

Most states require that the law of **arrest** be the same for both adults and juveniles. To make a legal arrest, an officer must have probable cause to believe that an offense took place and that the suspect is the guilty party. **Probable cause** is usually defined as falling somewhere between a mere suspicion and absolute certainty. In misdemeanor cases the police officer must personally observe the crime to place a suspect in custody. For a felony, the police officer may make the arrest without having observed the crime if the officer has probable cause to believe the crime occurred and the person being arrested committed it. A felony is a serious offense; a misdemeanor is a minor or petty crime. Crimes such as murder, rape, and robbery are felonies; crimes such as petty larceny and disturbing the peace are misdemeanors.

The main difference between arrests of adult and juvenile offenders is the broader latitude police have to control youthful behavior. Most juvenile codes, for instance, provide broad authority for the police to take juveniles into custody.[25] Such statutes are designed to give the police the authority to act *in loco parentis* (Latin for "in place of the parent"). Accordingly, the broad power granted to police is consistent with the notion that a juvenile is not arrested, but rather taken into custody—which implies a protective rather than a punitive form of detention.[26] Once a juvenile is

problem-oriented policing
Law enforcement that focuses on addressing the problems underlying incidents of juvenile delinquency rather than the incidents alone.

arrest
Taking a person into the custody of the law to restrain the accused until he or she can be held accountable for the offense in court proceedings.

probable cause
Reasonable ground to believe the existence of facts that an offense was committed and that the accused committed that offense.

Navajo Nation police officers search students for weapons at the high school near Ganado, Arizona, on September 6, 2006. A student reported seeing weapons at the school. The Supreme Court allows police officers and security agents greater latitude in searching students on school premises than they would have with other citizens, on the grounds that campuses must be safe and crime-free environments.

© AP Images/Donovan Quintero

arrested, however, the constitutional safeguards of the Fourth and Fifth Amendments available to adults are applicable to the juvenile as well.

As you may recall, there is currently a trend toward treating juvenile offenders more like adults. Related to this trend are efforts by the police to provide a more legalistic and less informal approach to the arrest process, and a more balanced approach to case disposition.[27]

Search and Seizure

search and seizure
The U.S. Constitution protects citizens from any search and seizure by police without a lawfully obtained search warrant; such warrants are issued when there is probable cause to believe that an offense has been committed.

Do juveniles have the same right to be free from unreasonable **search and seizure** as adults? In general, a citizen's privacy is protected by the Fourth Amendment of the Constitution, which states:

> *The right of the people to be secure in their persons, houses, papers, and effects, against unreasonable searches and seizures, shall not be violated, and no warrants shall issue, but upon probable cause, supported by oaths or affirmation, and particularly describing the place to be searched, and the persons or things to be seized.*[28]

Most courts have held that the Fourth Amendment ban against unreasonable search and seizure applies to juveniles and that illegally seized evidence is inadmissible in a juvenile trial. To exclude incriminating evidence, a juvenile's attorney makes a pretrial motion to suppress the evidence, the same procedure used in the adult criminal process.

A full discussion of search and seizure is beyond the scope of this text, but it is important to note that the Supreme Court has ruled that police may stop a suspect and search for evidence without a warrant under certain circumstances. A person may be searched after a legal arrest, but then only in the immediate area of the suspect's control. For example, after an arrest for possession of drugs, the pockets of a suspect's jacket may be searched;[29] an automobile may be searched if there is probable cause to believe a crime has taken place;[30] a suspect's outer garments may be frisked if police are suspicious of his or her activities;[31] and a search may be conducted if a person volunteers for the search.[32] These rules are usually applied to juveniles as well as to adults. Concept Summary 12.1 reviews when warrantless searches are allowed.

Warrantless Searches

Action	Scope of Search
Stop-and-frisk	Pat-down of a suspect's outer garments.
Search incident to arrest	Full body search after a legal arrest.
Automobile search	If probable cause exists, full search of car, including driver, passengers, and closed containers found in trunk. Search must be reasonable.
Consent search	Warrantless search of person or place is justified if suspect knowingly and voluntarily consents to search.
Plain view	Suspicious objects seen in plain view can be seized without a warrant.
Electronic surveillance	Material can be seized electronically without a warrant if suspect has no expectation of privacy.

Custodial Interrogation

In years past, police often questioned juveniles without their parents or even an attorney present. Any incriminating statements arising from such **custodial interrogation** could be used at trial. However, in the 1966 *Miranda* case, the Supreme Court placed constitutional limitations on police interrogation procedures with adult offenders. *Miranda* held that persons in police custody must be told the following:

- They have the right to remain silent.
- Any statements they make can be used against them.
- They have the right to counsel.
- If they cannot afford counsel, it will be furnished at public expense.[33]

The **Miranda warning** has been made applicable to children taken into custody. The Supreme Court case of *in re Gault* stated that constitutional privileges against self-incrimination are applicable in juvenile cases too. Because *in re Gault* implies that *Miranda* applies to custodial interrogation in criminal procedure, state court jurisdictions apply the requirements of *Miranda* to juvenile proceedings as well. Since the *Gault* decision in 1967, virtually all courts that have ruled on the question of the *Miranda* warning have concluded that the warning does apply to the juvenile process.

One problem associated with custodial interrogation of juveniles has to do with waiver of *Miranda* rights: Under what circumstances can juveniles knowingly and willingly waive the rights given them by *Miranda v. Arizona*? Does a youngster, acting alone, have sufficient maturity to appreciate the right to remain silent?

Most courts have concluded that parents or attorneys need not be present for children effectively to waive their rights.[34] In a frequently cited California case, *People v. Lara*, the court said that the question of a child's waiver is to be determined by the *totality of the circumstances doctrine*.[35] This means that the validity of the waiver rests not only on the age of the child, but also on a combination of other factors, including the child's education, the child's knowledge of the charge, whether the child was allowed to consult with family or friends, and the method of interrogation.[36]

The waiver of *Miranda* rights by a juvenile is one of the most controversial legal issues addressed in the state courts. It has also been the subject of federal constitutional review. In two cases, *Fare v. Michael C.* and *California v. Prysock*, the Supreme Court has attempted to clarify children's rights when they are interrogated by the police. In *Fare v. Michael C.*, the Court ruled that a child's asking to speak to his probation officer was not the equivalent of asking for an attorney; consequently, statements he made to the police absent legal counsel were admissible in court.[37] In *California v. Prysock*, the Court was asked to rule on the adequacy of a *Miranda* warning given Randall Prysock, a young murder suspect.[38] After reviewing the taped exchange between the police interrogator and the boy, the Court upheld Prysock's conviction

custodial interrogation
Questions posed by the police to a suspect held in custody in the prejudicial stage of the juvenile justice process; juveniles have the same rights as adults against self-incrimination when being questioned.

Miranda warning
Supreme Court decisions require police officers to inform individuals under arrest of their constitutional rights; warnings must also be given when suspicion begins to focus on an individual in the accusatory stage.

 To read more about the *Miranda* decision, go to www.thomsonedu.com/criminaljustice/siegel.

when it ruled that even though the *Miranda* warning was given in slightly different language and out of exact context, its meaning was easily understandable, even to a juvenile.

Taken together, *Fare* and *Prysock* make it seem indisputable that juveniles are at least entitled to receive the same *Miranda* rights as adults. *Miranda v. Arizona* is a historic decision that continues to protect the rights of all suspects placed in custody.[39]

DISCRETIONARY JUSTICE

Today, juvenile offenders receive nearly as much procedural protection as adult offenders. However, the police have broader authority in dealing with juveniles than with adults. Granting such **discretion** to juvenile officers raises some important questions: Under what circumstances should an officer arrest status offenders? Should a summons be used in lieu of arrest? Under what conditions should a juvenile be taken into protective custody?

When police confront a case involving a juvenile offender, they rely on their discretion to choose an appropriate course of action. *Police discretion* is selective enforcement of the law by authorized police agents. Discretion gives officers a choice among possible courses of action within the limits of their power.[40] It is a prime example of low-visibility decision making, or decisions by public officials that the public is not in a position to regulate or criticize.[41]

Much discretion is exercised in juvenile work because of the informality that has been built into the system in an attempt to individualize justice.[42] Furthermore, officials in the juvenile justice system make decisions about children that often are without oversight or review. The daily procedures of juvenile personnel are rarely subject to judicial review, except when they clearly violate a youth's constitutional rights. As a result, discretion sometimes deteriorates into discrimination and other abuses on the part of the police. The real danger in discretion is that it allows the law to discriminate against precisely those elements in the population—the poor, the ignorant, the unpopular—who are least able to draw attention to their plight.[43]

LOOKING BACK TO RICO'S STORY

In Rico's case, he did not receive any serious consequences for his actions. Do you agree with what the officers did and why? Why do you think he wasn't charged?

The problem of discretion in juvenile justice is one of extremes. Too little discretion provides insufficient flexibility to treat juvenile offenders as individuals. Too much discretion can lead to injustice. Guidelines and controls are needed to structure the use of discretion.

Generally, the first contact a youth has with the juvenile justice system is with the police. Research indicates that most police decisions arising from this initial contact involve discretion.[44] These studies show that many juvenile offenders are never referred to juvenile court.

In a classic 1963 study, Nathan Goldman examined the arrest records of more than a thousand juveniles from four communities in Pennsylvania.[45] He concluded that more than 64 percent of police contacts with juveniles were handled informally. Subsequent research offered additional evidence of informal disposition of juvenile cases.[46] For example, in the 1970s, Paul Strasburg found that about 50 percent of all children who come in contact with the police do not get past the initial stage of the juvenile justice process.[47]

To read about **trends in juvenile arrests**, go to the website www.thomsonedu.com/criminaljustice/siegel.

A recent study analyzed juvenile data collected as part of the Project on Policing Neighborhoods—a comprehensive study of police patrols in Indianapolis, Indiana, and St. Petersburg, Florida. This study indicated that police still use discretion.[48] It found that 13 percent of police encounters with juveniles resulted in arrest.[49] As shown in Table 12.1, the most likely disposition of police encounters with juveniles is a command or threat to arrest (38 percent), and the second most likely is search or interrogation of the suspects (24 percent).

After arrest, the most current data show an increase in the number of cases referred to the juvenile court. The FBI estimates that 70 percent of all juvenile arrests are referred

Table 12.1 Disposition of Police Encounters with Juveniles

Disposition	Juveniles (%)
Release	14
Advise	11
Search/interrogate	24
Command/threaten	38
Arrest	13

Source: Robert E. Worden and Stephanie M. Myers, *Police Encounters with Juvenile Suspects* (Albany: Hindelang Criminal Justice Research Center and School of Criminal Justice, State University of New York, 2001), Table 3.

to juvenile court.[50] Despite the variations between the estimates, these studies indicate that the police use significant discretion in their decisions regarding juvenile offenders. Research shows that differential decision making goes on without clear guidance.

If all police officers acted in a fair and just manner, the seriousness of the crime, the situation in which it occurred, and the legal record of the juvenile would be the factors that affected their decision making. Research does show that police are much more likely to take formal action if the crime is serious and has been reported by a victim who is a respected member of the community, and if the offender is well known to them.[51] However, there are other factors that are believed to shape police discretion; they are discussed next.

Environmental Factors

How does a police officer decide what to do with a juvenile offender? The norms of the community affect the decision. Some officers work in communities that tolerate a fair amount of personal freedom. In liberal environments, the police may be inclined to release juveniles rather than arrest them. Other officers work in conservative communities that expect a no-nonsense approach to police enforcement. Here, police may be more inclined to arrest a juvenile.

Police officers may be influenced by their perception of community alternatives to police intervention. Some officers may make an arrest because they believe nothing else can be done.[52] Others may favor referring juveniles to social service agencies, particularly if they believe the community has a variety of good resources. These referrals save time and effort, records do not have to be filled out, and court appearances can be avoided. The availability of such options allows for greater latitude in police decision making.[53]

Police Policy

The policies and customs of the local police department also influence decisions. Juvenile officers may be pressured to make more arrests or to refrain from making arrests under certain circumstances. Directives instruct officers to be alert to certain types of juvenile violations. The chief of police might initiate policies governing the arrest practices of the juvenile department. For example, if local merchants complain that youths congregating in a shopping center parking lot are inhibiting business, police may be called on to make arrests. Under other circumstances, an informal warning might be given. Similarly, a rash of deaths caused by teenage drunk driving may galvanize the local media to demand police action. The mayor and the police chief, sensitive to possible voter dissatisfaction, may then demand that formal police action be taken in cases of drunk driving.

Another source of influence is pressure from supervisors. Some supervising officers may believe it is important to curtail disorderly conduct or drug use. In addition, officers may be influenced by the discretionary decisions made by their peers.

Justice in Policing A growing body of research shows that by police exercising a greater degree of fairness or **procedural justice** in making arrests and handling offenders after arrest they can better gain offender's cooperation as well as deter them from further involvement in criminal activity.[54] One of the first studies to assess the effect of police fairness on criminal offending was carried out by criminologist Ray Paternoster and his colleagues. As part of the Milwaukee domestic assault experiment, they found that men who were arrested for assaulting their female spouses were much less likely—by almost 40 percent—to commit another act of assault against their spouses if they were handled by police in a fair and just manner compared to a similar group of men who were not handled in a fair way.[55] Although it is difficult to know if this research is leading police departments to implement policies on procedural fairness and train their officers appropriately, police scholars have called for more research on the subject to better understand the mechanisms that result in crime control effectiveness.[56]

Situational Factors

In addition to the environment, a variety of situational factors affect a police officer's decisions. Situational factors are those attached to a particular crime, such as specific traits of offenders. Traditionally, it was believed that police officers relied heavily on the demeanor and appearance of the juvenile in making decisions. Some research shows that the decision to arrest is often based on factors, such as dress, attitude, speech, and level of hostility toward the police.[57] Kids who displayed "attitude" were believed to be the ones more likely to be arrested than those who were respectful and contrite.[58] However, more recent research has challenged the influence of demeanor on police decision making, suggesting that it is delinquent behavior and actions that occur during police detention that influence the police decision to take formal action.[59] For example, a person who struggles or touches police during a confrontation is a likely candidate for arrest, but those who merely sport a bad attitude or negative demeanor are as likely to suffer an arrest as the polite and contrite.[60] It is possible that the earlier research reflected a time when police officers demanded absolute respect and were quick to take action when their authority was challenged. The more recent research may indicate that police, through training or experience, are now less sensitive to slights and confrontational behavior and view them as just part of the job. Most studies conclude that the following variables are important in the police discretionary process:

- The attitude of the complainant
- The type and seriousness of the offense
- The race, sex, and age of the offender
- The attitude of the offender
- The offender's prior contacts with the police
- The perceived willingness of the parents to assist in solving the problem (in the case of a child)
- The setting or location in which the incident occurs
- Whether the offender denies the actions or insists on a court hearing (in the case of a child)
- The likelihood that a child can be served by an agency in the community[61]

Bias and Police Discretion

Do police allow bias to affect their decisions on whether to arrest youths? Do they routinely use "racial profiling" when they decide to make an arrest? A great deal of debate has been generated over this issue. Some experts believe that police decision making is deeply influenced by the offender's personal characteristics, whereas others maintain that crime-related variables are more significant.

When a juvenile commits a crime, police have the authority to investigate the incident and decide whether to release the child or place him under arrest. This is often a discretionary decision based not only on the nature of the offense and the behavior of the juvenile during his interaction with the police, but also on such factors as the seriousness of the crime, the child's past record, and whether the victim wishes to press charges.

© Michael A. Dwyer/Stock, Boston

Racial Bias It has long been charged that police are more likely to act formally with African American suspects and use their discretion to benefit European Americans.[62] In the context of traffic stops by police, the phrase "Driving While Black" has been coined to refer to the repeated findings of many studies that African American drivers are disproportionately stopped by police and that race is the primary reason for this practice.[63] African American youth are arrested at a rate disproportionate to their representation in the population (compare Table 12.2 to the data on page 34). Research on this issue has yielded mixed conclusions. One view is that, although discrimination may have existed in the past, there is no longer a need to worry about racial discrimination, because minorities now possess sufficient political status to protect them within the justice system.[64] As Harvard University law professor Randall Kennedy forcefully argues, even if a law enforcement policy exists that dispropor-

---

Table 12.2   **African American Representation in Arrest Statistics**

Most Serious Offense	African American Juvenile Arrests in 2004 (%)
Murder	47
Forcible rape	32
Robbery	53
Aggravated assault	33
Burglary	27
Larceny/theft	28
Motor vehicle theft	34
Weapons	35
Drug abuse violations	33
Curfew and loitering	32
Runaways	21

Note: Percentage is of all juvenile arrests.

Source: FBI, *Crime in the United States, 2004* (Washington, DC: U.S. Government Printing Office, 2005), Table 43.

tionately affects African American suspects, it might be justified as a "public good" because law-abiding African Americans are statistically more often victims of crimes committed by other African Americans.[65]

In contrast to these views, several research efforts do show evidence of police discrimination against African American youths.[66] Donna Bishop and Charles Frazier found that race can have a direct effect on decisions made at several junctures of the juvenile justice process.[67] According to Bishop and Frazier, African Americans are more likely than European Americans to be recommended for formal processing, referred to court, adjudicated delinquent, and given harsher dispositions for comparable offenses. In the arrest category, specifically, being African American increases the probability of formal police action.[68] (For more on racial bias, see chapter 2.)

Gender Bias Is there a difference between police treatment of male and female offenders? Some experts favor the *chivalry hypothesis*, which holds that police are likely to act paternally toward young girls and not arrest them. Others believe that police may be more likely to arrest female offenders, because their actions violate officers' stereotypes of the female.

There is some research support for various forms of gender bias. The nature of this bias may vary according to the seriousness of the offense and the age of the offender. Studies offer a variety of conclusions, but there seems to be general agreement that police are less likely to process females for delinquent acts and that they discriminate against them by arresting them for status offenses. Examples of the conclusions reached by some of these studies follow:

- Police tend to be more lenient toward females than males with regard to acts of delinquency. Merry Morash found that boys who engage in "typical male" delinquent activities are much more likely to develop police records than females.[69]

- Females who have committed minor or status offenses seem to be referred to juvenile court more often than males. Meda Chesney-Lind has found that adolescent female status offenders are arrested for less serious offenses than boys.[70]

- Recent evidence has confirmed earlier studies showing that the police, and most likely the courts, apply a double standard in dealing with male and female juvenile offenders. Bishop and Frazier found that both female status offenders and male delinquents are differently disadvantaged in the juvenile justice system in that, for status offenses, females are more likely to be arrested, and for other offenses, males are more likely to be arrested.[71] Chesney-Lind and Shelden report that in many other countries female teens are also more likely than male teens to be arrested for status offenses and referred to juvenile court for status offenses.[72] (Gender bias is discussed in more detail in chapter 6.)

Organizational Bias The policies of some police departments may result in biased practices. Research has found that police departments can be characterized by their professionalism (skills and knowledge) and bureaucratization.[73] Departments that are highly bureaucratized (with a high emphasis on rules and regulations) and at the same time unprofessional are most likely to be insulated from the communities they serve. Organizational policy may be influenced by the perceptions of police decision makers. A number of experts have found that law enforcement administrators have a stereotyped view of the urban poor as troublemakers who must be kept under control.[74] Consequently, lower-class neighborhoods experience much greater police scrutiny than middle-class areas, and their residents face a proportionately greater chance of arrest. For example, there is a significant body of literature that shows that police are more likely to "hassle" or arrest African American males in poor neighborhoods.[75] It is therefore not surprising, as Harvard criminologist Robert Sampson has found, that teenage residents of neighborhoods with low socioeconomic status have a significantly greater chance of acquiring police records than youths living in higher socioeconomic areas, regardless of the actual crime rates in these areas.[76]

To read about what is being done to **reduce racial profiling**, click on Web Links under the Chapter Resources at the website www.thomsonedu.com/criminaljustice/siegel.

CHECKPOINTS

- Most states require that the law of arrest be the same for both adults and juveniles.

- The main difference between arrests of adult and juvenile offenders is the broader latitude police have to control youthful behavior.

- Most courts have held that the Fourth Amendment ban against unreasonable search and seizure applies to juveniles.

- Most courts have concluded that parents or attorneys need not be present for children effectively to waive their right to remain silent.

- The police have broader authority in dealing with juveniles than in dealing with adults.

- A great deal of discretion is exercised in juvenile work, because of the informality that has been built into the system.

- It has long been charged that police are more likely to act formally with African American youth and use their discretion to benefit European American adolescents.

- Police tend to be more lenient toward females than males with regard to acts of delinquency, but more restrictive with status offenses.

Sampson's research indicates that, although police officers may not discriminate on an individual level, departmental policy that focuses on lower-class areas may result in class and racial bias in the police processing of delinquent youth. ✔ Checkpoints

POLICE WORK AND DELINQUENCY PREVENTION

Police have taken the lead in delinquency prevention. They have used a number of strategies: some rely on their deterrent powers; others rely on their relationship with schools, the community, and other juvenile justice agencies; and others rely on a problem-solving model. Concept Summary 12.2 lists the main police strategies to prevent delinquency.

Aggressive Law Enforcement

One method of contemporary delinquency prevention relies on aggressive patrolling targeted at specific patterns of delinquency. Police departments in Chicago and Los Angeles have at one time used *saturation patrol,* targeting gang areas and arresting members for any law violations. These tactics have not proven to be effective against gangs. For example, the Dallas Police Department initiated a successful gang-control effort that employed such tactics as saturating known gang areas with antigang units as well as making aggressive enforcement of curfew and truancy laws. Targeting truancy and curfew laws led to a significant reduction in gang activity, but the saturation patrols proved ineffective.[77]

Police in Schools

One of the most important institutions playing a role in delinquency prevention is the school (see chapter 9). In schools across the country, there are more than fourteen thousand full-time police working as school resource officers. In addition to helping to make the school environment safe for students and teachers, school resource officers work closely with staff and administrators in developing delinquency prevention programs.[78] For example, these officers and liaison officers from schools and police departments have played a leadership role in developing recreational programs for juveniles. In some instances, police have actually operated such programs. In others, they have encouraged community support for recreational activities, including Little League baseball, athletic clubs, camping outings, and police athletic and scouting programs.

LOOKING BACK TO RICO'S STORY

Do you agree that police officers should have the right to use their discretion in school settings? What are the benefits of this approach?

The Gang Resistance Education and Training (G.R.E.A.T.) program is one example of a police and school partnership to prevent delinquency. Modeled after D.A.R.E. (Drug Abuse Resistance Education; see chapter 10), G.R.E.A.T. was developed among a num-

Concept Summary **Police Strategies to Prevent Delinquency**

Strategy	Scope
Aggressive law enforcement	High visibility; make arrests for minor and serious infractions.
Police in schools	Collaborate with school staff to create a safer school environment and develop programs.
Community policing	Engage citizens and community-based organizations.
Problem-oriented policing	Focus on problems underlying criminal incidents; often engage community and other juvenile justice agencies.

Increased youth gang and violence problems have given rise to many innovative police-led delinquency prevention programs. One of these is the Gang Resistance Education and Training (G.R.E.A.T.) program, which aims to reduce gang activity. Partnering with schools across the country, trained police officers instruct middle-school students on conflict resolution, social responsibility, and the dangers of gang life.

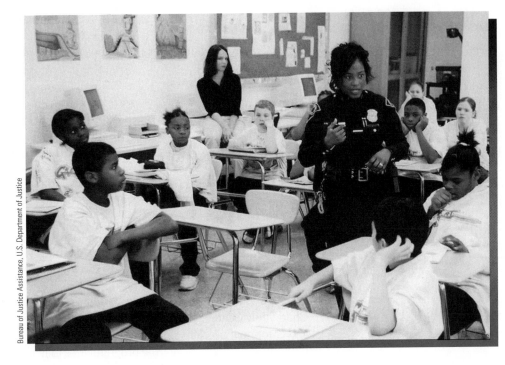

Bureau of Justice Assistance, U.S. Department of Justice

You can visit G.R.E.A.T.'s website by going to www.thomsonedu.com/criminaljustice/siegel.

ber of Arizona police departments in an effort to reduce adolescent involvement in criminal behavior. Today the program is in school curricula in all fifty states and the District of Columbia.[79] The program's primary objective is the prevention of delinquency and gang involvement. Trained police officers administer the program in school classrooms about once a week. The program consists of four components: a thirteen-week middle school curriculum (see Exhibit 12.1 for its thirteen lessons), a six-week elementary school curriculum, a summer program, and family training.

Evaluations of G.R.E.A.T. when it was just an eight-week program for middle-school students showed mixed results in reducing delinquency and gang involvement.

Exhibit 12.1   **Lessons of the Middle School G.R.E.A.T. Program**

- *Welcome to G.R.E.A.T.* Students get acquainted with the program.
- *What's the Real Deal?* Students learn about facts and myths about gangs and violence.
- *It's About Us.* Students learn about their roles and responsibilities to their community and what they can do about gangs.
- *Where Do We Go From Here?* Students are taught how to set realistic and achievable goals.
- *Decisions, Decisions, Decisions.* Students learn the impact of decisions on goals.
- *Do You Hear What I Am Saying?* Students are taught effective communication skills.
- *Walk in Someone Else's Shoes.* Students learn about expressing empathy for others.

- *Say It Like You Mean It.* Students learn about self-expression.
- *Getting Along Without Going Along.* Students become acquainted with negative influences and peer pressure and how to resist them.
- *Keeping Your Cool.* Students are taught techniques to control anger.
- *Keeping It Together.* Students are taught techniques to recognize anger in others and how to diffuse that anger.
- *Working It Out.* Students learn about resolving interpersonal conflict and where to go for help.
- *Looking Back.* Students review what they have learned and think about how to make their school safe.

Source: Bureau of Justice Assistance, Gang Resistance Education and Training (Washington, DC: Office of Justice Programs, Bureau of Justice Assistance, 2006. Available at: www.great-online.org (accessed December 5, 2006).

The Debate Over Police in Schools

Police have long played a role in working with schools to improve their safety and prevent delinquency in the community through the organization of various programs. But some view police in schools as an infringement on students' personal freedom. Others call for greater use of police in schools, especially in those that have experienced violent incidents by students against other students and teachers.

- Do you feel all high schools should have a police presence? What about elementary and middle schools?
- In looking back on your high school, can you recall an event when a school resource officer made a difference in your life or a friend's life?

One evaluation found that students who completed the curriculum developed more pro-social attitudes and have lower rates of gang membership and delinquency than those in a comparison group who were not exposed to G.R.E.A.T.[80] Another evaluation of the program, four years after students completed the curriculum, did not find any significant differences for gang membership or delinquency compared to a control group. The evaluation did find that those who took the program held more pro-social attitudes than those who were not in the program.[81] These evaluations contributed to the new and more comprehensive program, which was implemented on a national scale in 2003. Future evaluations will tell if these changes improve G.R.E.A.T.'s impact on delinquency, youth violence, and gang involvement.

Another example of police working in close collaboration with schools is the Community Outreach Through Police in Schools Program. This program brings together Yale University's Child Study Center and the New Haven Police Department to address the mental health and emotional needs of middle-school students who have been exposed to violence in the community. Specifically, the program aims to help these students:

- Better understand the way their feelings affect their behavior.
- Develop constructive means of responding to violence and trauma.
- Change their attitudes toward police and how to seek help in their community.[82]

An evaluation of the program found that students benefited from it in a number of ways, including improved emotional and psychological functioning (for example, feeling less nervous, having fewer thoughts of death), as well as improved attitudes toward and relationships with the police.[83] The accompanying What Does This Mean to Me? feature offers another perspective on police in schools.

Community Policing

One of the most important changes in U.S. law enforcement is the emergence of the community policing model of delinquency prevention. This concept is based on the premise that the police can carry out their duties more effectively if they gain the trust and assistance of concerned citizens. Under this model, the main police role should be to increase feelings of community safety and encourage area residents to cooperate with their local police agencies.[84]

The community policing model has been translated into a number of policy initiatives. It has encouraged police departments to get officers out of patrol cars, where they were insulated from the community, and onto the streets via foot or bicycle patrol.[85] The official survey of policing in the United States—the Law Enforcement Management and Administrative Statistics (LEMAS) survey—reports that 58 percent of local police departments, employing 82 percent of all officers, had full-time community policing officers. Across the country, local police departments employ about 55,000 community policing officers.[86] However, the use of community policing officers has decreased in recent years. Between 2000 and 2003 (the most recent data available), the percentage of local police departments using community policing officers was lower, sometimes substantially, in all sizes of cities, from rural to large urban.[87] The main reason for this has been a reduction in federal funding.

One community policing program, the Youth Firearms Violence Initiative (YFVI) of the federal Office of Community Oriented Policing Services (COPS), which is running in ten cities across the United States, aims to reduce juvenile gun violence. Each city was provided with up to $1 million to pay for interventions that incorporated community policing strategies. The strategies include these:

- Working in partnership with other city agencies to promote education, prevention, and intervention programs related to handguns and their safety.
- Developing community-based programs focused on youth handgun violence.
- Developing programs involving and assisting families in addressing youth handgun problems.[88]

The YFVI programs also include some traditional law enforcement measures, such as the setup of new enforcement units within the police department and standard surveillance and intelligence-gathering techniques. An evaluation of the YFVI was conducted in all ten cities, but in only five cities (Baltimore; Cleveland; Inglewood, California; Salinas, California; and San Antonio) was program effectiveness in reducing gun violence measured. Police-reported gun crimes were reduced in each of the five cities and in every target area of the cities with the exception of one area in Baltimore. The evaluation also examined the percentage change of gun crimes involving young people in the before and after periods. The results were not as encouraging. Only San Antonio demonstrated a significant reduction in the percentage of gun crimes involving youths, from 57 percent to 55 percent.[89]

The Office of Community Oriented Policing Services is also involved in other initiatives to reduce gun violence by serious juvenile offenders.[90] One of these initiatives is Project Safe Neighborhoods, which brings together federal, state, and local law enforcement, prosecutors, and community leaders to deter and punish gun crime.[91]

Efforts are being made by police departments to involve citizens in delinquency control. Community policing is a philosophy that promotes community, government, and police partnerships that address juvenile crime, as well as adult crime.[92] Although there is not a great deal of evidence that these efforts can lower crime rates,[93] they do seem to be effective methods of improving perceptions of community safety and the quality of community life,[94] and involving citizens in the juvenile justice network. Under the community policing philosophy, prevention programs may become more effective crime control measures. Programs that combine the reintegration of youths into the community after institutionalization with police surveillance and increased communication are vital for improving police effectiveness with juveniles.[95]

To learn about other **community policing programs**, go to the website www.thomsonedu.com/criminaljustice/siegel.

Problem-Oriented Policing

Also referred to as *problem-solving policing*, problem-oriented policing involves a systematic analysis and response to the problems or conditions underlying criminal incidents rather than the incidents themselves.[96] The theory is that by attending to the underlying problems that cause criminal incidents, the police will have a greater chance of preventing the crimes from recurring—the main problem with reactive or "incident-driving policing."[97] However, as noted by Harvard criminologist Mark Moore, "This is not the same as seeking out the root causes of the crime problem in general. It is a much shallower, more situational approach."[98]

The systematic nature of problem-oriented policing is characterized by its adherence to a four-step model, often referred to as S.A.R.A., which stands for *Scanning, Analysis, Response,* and *Assessment*. Descriptions of the four steps are as follows:

1. *Scanning* involves identifying a specific crime problem through various data sources (for example, victim surveys, 911 calls).
2. *Analysis* involves carrying out an in-depth analysis of the crime problem and its underlying causes.
3. *Response* brings together the police and other partners to develop and implement a response to the problem based on the results produced in the analysis stage.
4. *Assessment* is the stage in which the response to the problem is evaluated.[99]

Like community policing, problem-oriented policing is viewed as a proactive delinquency prevention strategy. Unlike community policing, however, the engagement of

Boston's Operation Ceasefire

One of the most successful examples of problem-oriented policing focused on reducing juvenile crime and violence is the program known as Operation Ceasefire. Implemented in Boston, this program aims to reduce youth homicide victimization and youth gun violence. Although it is a police-led program, Operation Ceasefire involves many other juvenile and criminal justice and social agencies, including probation and parole, the Bureau of Alcohol, Tobacco and Firearms (ATF), gang outreach and prevention street workers, and the Drug Enforcement Administration (DEA). This group of agencies has become known as the Ceasefire Working Group. The program has two main elements:

1. A direct law enforcement focus on illicit gun traffickers who supply youth with guns
2. An attempt to generate a strong deterrent to gang violence

A wide range of measures have been used to reduce the flow of guns to youth, including pooling the resources of local, state, and federal justice authorities to track and seize illegal guns and targeting traffickers of the types of guns most used by gang members. The response to gang violence has been to pull every deterrence "lever" available, including shutting down drug markets, serving warrants, enforcing probation restrictions, and making disorder arrests. The Ceasefire Working Group delivered its message clearly to gang members: "We're ready, we're watching, we're waiting: Who wants to be next?"

An evaluation from before the program started to the time it ended showed a 63 percent reduction in the mean monthly number of youth homicide victims across the city. The program was also associated with significant decreases in the mean monthly number of gun assaults and overall gang violence across the city. In a comparison with other New England cities and large cities across the United States, most of which also experienced a reduction in youth homicides over the same period, it was found that the significant reduction in youth homicides in Boston was due to Operation Ceasefire.

Maintaining the level of intensity of this program, and the cooperation of the many agencies involved, which are essential ingredients of its success, has not been easy. In recent years, there have been cutbacks in local policing, fewer federal criminal justice resources made available to the program, and a perception that the deterrence strategy is no longer focused on the most dangerous suspects. Recent research suggests that in order for the program to maintain its success it will also have to adapt to changes in the nature of gang and youth violence across the city.

Although the city of Boston works to improve its program, similar problem-oriented policing programs have been established in cities across the country, including Oakland, California, and Atlanta. An evaluation of Operation Ceasefire in the Hollenbeck area of Los Angeles, which suffers from exceptionally high rates of gang-related gun violence, showed promising results.

CRITICAL THINKING

1. What is the importance of having a multidisciplinary team as part of the program?
2. With comprehensive programs it is often difficult to assess the independent effects of the different program elements. In your opinion, what is the most important element of this program? Why?

INFOTRAC COLLEGE EDITION RESEARCH

For more information on problem-oriented policing and juvenile delinquency, go to InfoTrac College Edition and read Terry Eisenberg and Bruce Glasscock, "Looking Inward with Problem-Oriented Policing," *FBI Law Enforcement Bulletin 70*:1 (July 2001).

Sources: Anthony A. Braga, David M. Kennedy, Elin J. Waring, and Anne Morrison Piehl, "Problem-Oriented Policing, Deterrence, and Youth Violence: An Evaluation of Boston's Operation Ceasefire," *Journal of Research in Crime and Delinquency 38*:195–225 (2001); Fox Butterfield, "Killing of Girl, 10, and Increase in Homicides Challenge Boston's Crime-Fighting Model," *New York Times*, 14 July 2002; Arthur L. Kellerman, Dawna Fuqua-Whitley, and Constance S. Parramore, *Reducing Gun Violence: Community Problem Solving in Atlanta* (Washington, DC: National Institute of Justice, 2006); David M. Kennedy, Anthony A. Braga, and Anne Morrison Piehl, "Developing and Implementing Operation Ceasefire," in *Reducing Gun Violence: The Boston Gun Project's Operation Ceasefire*. Research report (Washington, DC: National Institute of Justice, 2001); David M. Kennedy, "Pulling Levers: Chronic Offenders, High-Crime Settings, and a Theory of Prevention," *Valparaiso University Law Review 31*:449–484 (1997); David M. Kennedy, "Pulling Levers: Getting Deterrence Right," *National Institute of Justice Journal*, July 1998, pp. 2–8; Jack McDevitt, Anthony A. Braga, Dana Nurge, and Michael Buerger, "Boston's Youth Violence Prevention Program: A Comprehensive Community-Wide Approach," in Scott H. Decker, ed., *Policing Gangs and Youth Violence* (Belmont, CA: Wadsworth, 2003); Jesse McKinley, "Oakland Fights Crime with Talk," *New York Times*, 22 August 2006; George E. Tita, K. Jack Riley, Greg Ridgeway, and Peter W. Greenwood, *Reducing Gun Violence: Operation Ceasefire in Los Angeles* (Washington, DC: National Institute of Justice, 2005).

the community in problem-oriented policing is not imperative, but more often than not these operations involve close collaborations with the community. Collaborations with other juvenile justice agencies are also common in problem-oriented policing operations.

As you may recall, problem-oriented policing has been shown to be effective in reducing juvenile delinquency in some circumstances. One of the most successful applications of this policing strategy is Boston's Operation Ceasefire, which is the subject of this chapter's Preventing and Treating Delinquency feature.

Following on the success of the Boston program, the Office of Juvenile Justice and Delinquency Prevention (OJJDP) launched a comprehensive initiative to reduce juvenile gun violence in four other cities (Baton Rouge and Shreveport, Louisiana;

To learn about other **problem-oriented policing programs**, go to the website www.thomsonedu.com/criminaljustice/siegel.

■ Police departments have used aggressive saturation patrol, targeting gang areas and arresting members for any law violations.

■ Prevention programs between the police and the schools have been implemented in many communities.

■ Police are now identifying the needs of youth in the community and helping the community meet those needs.

■ Problem-oriented or problem-solving policing, which very often involves community groups and other juvenile justice agencies, is an innovative and successful approach to preventing delinquency.

■ Many experts consider police-based delinquency prevention efforts to be crucial to the development of a comprehensive approach to youth crime.

Oakland, California; and Syracuse, New York). Called the Partnerships to Reduce Juvenile Gun Violence Program, problem-oriented policing strategies are at the center of the program, but other intervention strategies are also important. These include specific delinquency prevention strategies (job training and mentoring), juvenile justice sanctions, and a public information campaign designed to communicate the dangers and consequences of gun violence to juveniles, families, and community residents.[100] An evaluation of the implementation of the program found that three of the four cities were successful in developing comprehensive strategies.[101] With successful implementation and inclusion of many of the components of the Boston program, this program offers promise.

Around the same time in the late 1990s, the federal COPS office initiated a national Problem-Solving Partnerships (PSP) program with the objective of assisting police agencies to "solve recurrent crime and disorder problems by helping them form community partnerships and engage in problem-solving activities."[102] Various case studies to emerge out of a national evaluation of this program by the Police Executive Research Forum identify a wide range of successful efforts to reduce delinquency.[103] Closely related, the COPS office also initiated a series of guides to aid police in addressing specific crime problems, with one focusing on underage drinking.[104]

Today, many experts consider delinquency prevention efforts to be crucial to the development of a comprehensive approach to youth crime. Although such efforts cut across the entire juvenile justice system, police programs have become increasingly popular. ✔ Checkpoints

SUMMARY

■ Modern policing developed in England at the beginning of the nineteenth century. The Industrial Revolution, recognition of the need to treat children as a distinguishable group, and growing numbers of unemployed and homeless youths were among some of the key events that helped shape juvenile policing in America.

■ The role of juvenile officers is similar to that of officers working with adult offenders: to intervene if the actions of a citizen produce public danger or disorder. Juvenile officers must also have a thorough knowledge of the law, especially the constitutional protections available to juveniles.

■ Juvenile officers operate either as specialists in a police department or as part of the juvenile unit of a police department.

■ Through the *Miranda v. Arizona* decision, the U.S. Supreme Court established a clearly defined procedure for custodial interrogation.

■ Most courts have held that the Fourth Amendment ban against unreasonable search and seizure applies to juveniles and that illegally seized evidence is inadmissible in a juvenile trial. Most courts have concluded that parents or attorneys need not be present for children effectively to waive their right to remain silent.

■ Discretion is a low-visibility decision made in the administration of adult and juvenile justice. Discretionary decisions are made without guidelines from the police administrator. Numerous factors influence the decisions police make about juvenile offenders, including the seriousness of the offense, the harm inflicted on the victim, and the likelihood that the juvenile will break the law again.

■ Discretion is essential in providing individualized justice, but problems such as discrimination, unfairness, and bias toward particular groups of juveniles must be controlled.

■ Police have taken the lead in delinquency prevention. Major policing strategies to prevent delinquency include aggressive law enforcement, police in schools, community policing, and problem-oriented policing.

■ The ever-changing nature of juvenile delinquency calls for further experimentation and innovation in policing strategies to prevent delinquency. Tailoring policing activities to local conditions and engaging the community and other stakeholders are important first steps.

KEY TERMS

1. The term *discretion* is often defined as selective decision making by police and others in the juvenile justice system who are faced with alternative modes of action. Discuss some of the factors affecting the discretion of the police when dealing with juvenile offenders.

2. What role should police organizations play in delinquency prevention and control? Is it feasible to expect police departments to provide social services to children and families? How could police departments be better organized to provide for the control of juvenile delinquency?

3. What qualities should a juvenile police officer have? Should a college education be a requirement?

4. In light of the traditional and protective roles assumed by law enforcement personnel in juvenile justice, is there any reason to require a *Miranda* warning for youths taken into custody?

5. Can the police and community be truly effective in forming a partnership to reduce juvenile delinquency? Discuss the role of the juvenile police officer in preventing and investigating juvenile crime.

6. The experience of Boston's successful Operation Ceasefire program suggests that it may be difficult to sustain the needed intensity and problem-solving partnerships to keep violent juvenile crime under control over the long term. What other innovative problem-oriented policing measures could be employed to achieve this?

APPLYING WHAT YOU HAVE LEARNED

You are a newly appointed police officer assigned to a juvenile unit of a medium-size urban police department. Wayne G. is an eighteen-year-old European American male who was caught shoplifting with two male friends of the same age. Wayne attempted to leave a large department store with a twenty-five-dollar shirt and was apprehended by a police officer in front of the store.

Wayne seemed quite remorseful about the offense. He said several times that he didn't know why he did it and that he had not planned to do it. He seemed upset and scared, and although admitting the offense, did not want to go to court. Wayne had three previous contacts with the police as a juvenile: one for malicious mischief when he destroyed some property, another involving a minor assault on a boy, and a third involving another shoplifting charge. In all three cases, Wayne promised to refrain from ever committing such acts again, and as a result was not required to go to court. The other shoplifting incident involved a baseball worth only three dollars.

Wayne appeared at the police department with his mother. His parents are divorced. The mother did not seem overly concerned about the case and felt that her son was not really to blame. She argued that he was always getting in trouble and she was not sure how to control him. She blamed most of his troubles with the law on his being in the wrong crowd. Besides, a twenty-five-dollar shirt was "no big deal" and she offered to pay back the store. The store had left matters in the hands of the police and would support any decision you make.

Deciding what to do in a case like Wayne's is a routine activity for most police officers. When dealing with juveniles, they must consider not only the nature of the offense but also the needs of the juvenile. Police officers realize that actions they take can have a long-term effect on an adolescent's future.

- Would you submit Wayne's case for prosecution, release him with a warning, or use some other tactic?
- Should police officers be forced to act as counselors for troubled youth?

DOING RESEARCH ON THE WEB

Before you answer, you may want to learn more about this topic by checking out the websites of the International Association of Chiefs of Police, the Police Foundation, COPS on Community Policing, and the Police Executive Research Forum. Just go to **www.thomsonedu.com/criminaljustice/siegel** to access these sites.

To research police handling of juveniles suspected of committing crimes, use "police and discretion" in a key word search on InfoTrac College Edition.

Juvenile Court Process: Pretrial, Trial, and Sentencing

© Larry Kolvoord/The Image Works

CHAPTER OBJECTIVES

After reading this chapter you should:

1. Understand the roles and responsibilities of the main players in the juvenile court.

2. Be able to discuss key issues of the pre-adjudicatory stage of juvenile justice, including detention, intake, diversion, pretrial release, plea bargaining, and waiver.

3. Be able to argue the pros and cons of waiving youths to adult court.

4. Understand key issues of the trial stage of juvenile justice, including constitutional rights of youths and disposition.

5. Be familiar with major U.S. Supreme Court decisions that have influenced the handling of juveniles at the pre-adjudicatory and trial stages.

6. Know the most common dispositions for juvenile offenders.

7. Be able to argue the pros and cons of confidentiality in juvenile proceedings and privacy of juvenile records.

Cliff is a sixteen-year-old European American being raised by his grandparents in a small rural community. He and his younger sisters were removed from their parental home when Cliff was seven due to domestic violence and parental drug abuse. Although Cliff was well cared for by his grandparents, he engaged in several delinquent behaviors. He was charged with disorderly conduct for breaking windows in the family home and for threatening to physically assault his grandfather. Doing poorly in school, his grades dropped dramatically and several times concerned family members called the police worried that Cliff was using drugs.

Cliff began dating a girl he met at school, but her parents did not approve and they refused to allow her to go out with him. Upset about the situation, Cliff reacted by taking his anger out on his family and by threatening suicide. He was hospitalized for an evaluation and diagnosed with bipolar disorder. He was at risk for being removed from the family home and placed in detention. Fortunately for Cliff, he received juvenile probation and was ordered by the court to receive a mental health assessment and treatment. Cliff also received medications and a referral for a Functional Family Therapy (FFT) intervention.

The FFT program has three phases that target juvenile delinquents and their families. During FFT intervention, other services to the family are stopped in order for the family to focus on the FFT process and plan. During the first phase of the program, attempts are made to engage and motivate all family members to participate in the process. Also during this initial phase, the family therapists focus on redefining the problem (Cliff's problematic behavior and mental health concerns) as a family issue, and encouraging family members to view the issues in a new light. Everyone has a part in the problem and thus in the solution. They create real and obtainable goals and provide assistance to increase the family's problem-solving skills. This again takes the focus off the adolescent and distributes the responsibility among all family members. In the last phase, the therapists worked with Cliff's family to generalize their new skills to many different situations.

The FFT therapists worked with Cliff's family for four months, and then did a follow-up call at six and twelve months. They saw a reduction in Cliff's problematic behavior and criminal activity, as well as fewer calls to the police over the course of the intervention.

THE JUVENILE COURT AND ITS JURISDICTION

Today's juvenile delinquency cases are sometimes handled as part of a criminal trial court jurisdiction, or even within the probate court. Also called surrogate court in some states, probate court is a court of special jurisdiction that handles wills, administration of estates, and guardianship of minors and incompetents. However, in most jurisdictions they are treated in the structure of a family court or an independent juvenile court (fourteen states use more than one method to process juvenile cases).[1] The independent juvenile court is a specialized court for children, designed to promote rehabilitation of youth in a framework of procedural due process. It is concerned with acting both in the best interest of the child and in the best interest of public protection, two often incompatible goals. Family courts, in contrast, have broad jurisdiction over a wide range of personal and household problems, including delinquency, paternity, child support, and custody issues. The major advantages of such a system are that it can serve sparsely populated areas, permits judicial personnel and others to deal exclusively with children's matters, and can obtain legislative funding more readily than other court systems.

Court Case Flow

In 2002 (the latest data available), a little more than 1.6 million delinquency cases were referred to juvenile court. This represents an 11 percent decrease in court case flow from the peak year in 1997. This recent decline (between 1997 and 2002) has been characterized as a downward trend, and comes after a steady increase or upward trend in court case flow that began in the mid-1980s.[2]

There were distinct gender- and race-based differences in the juvenile court population. In 2002, 74 percent of delinquency cases involved a male and 26 percent involved a female. However, the number of females processed by juvenile courts has increased in the last decade, when about 20 percent of the cases involved females. Similarly, 29 percent of the juvenile court population was made up of African American youth, although African Americans make up only 16 percent of the general population.[3]

The Actors in the Juvenile Courtroom

The key players in the juvenile court are the defense attorneys, prosecutors, and judges.

The Defense Attorney As the result of a series of Supreme Court decisions, the right of a delinquent youth to have counsel at state trials has become a fundamental part of the juvenile justice system.[4] Today, courts must provide counsel to indigent defendants who face the possibility of incarceration. Over the past three decades, the rules of juvenile justice administration have become extremely complex. Preparation of a case for juvenile court often involves detailed investigation of a crime, knowledge of court procedures, use of rules of evidence, and skills in trial advocacy. The right to counsel is essential if children are to have a fair chance of presenting their cases in court.[5]

In many respects, the role of the **juvenile defense attorney** is similar to that in the criminal and civil areas. Defense attorneys representing children in the juvenile court play an active and important part in virtually all stages of the proceedings. For example, the defense attorney helps to clarify jurisdictional problems and to decide whether there is sufficient evidence to warrant filing a formal petition. The defense attorney helps outline the child's position regarding detention hearings and bail, and explores the opportunities for informal adjustment of the case. If no adjustment or diversion occurs, the defense attorney represents the child at adjudication, presenting evidence and cross-examining witnesses to see that the child's position is made clear to the court. Defense attorneys also play a critical role in the disposition hearing. They present evidence bearing on the treatment decision and help the court formulate alternative plans for the child's care. Finally, defense attorneys pursue any appeals

juvenile defense attorneys Represent children in juvenile court and play an active role at all stages of the proceedings.

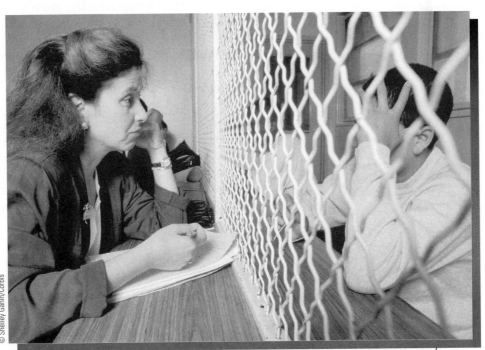

Juvenile defense attorneys play an active and important part in virtually all stages of the juvenile court proceedings, ranging from representing youths in police custody to filing their final appeals.

© Shelley Ganin/Corbis

from the trial, represent the child in probation revocation proceedings, and generally protect the child's right to treatment.

Important to these roles is the attorney-juvenile relationship and the competence of the attorney. Some studies report that many juvenile offenders do not trust their attorney,[6] but juvenile offenders represented by private attorneys are more trusting in their attorney than those represented by court-appointed attorneys.[7] One possible reason for this difference may be the belief among juveniles that because court-appointed attorneys work for the "system" they might share information with the judge, police, or others.[8] Another important dimension of the attorney-juvenile relationship is effective participation of the juvenile as a defendant, which "requires a personally relevant understanding of the lawyer's advocacy role and the confidential nature of the attorney-client relationship."[9] A recent study investigating effective participation among juvenile and adult defendants concluded that juveniles are in need of extra procedural safeguards, such as training for lawyers on how to be more effective counselors.[10] There may also be a need to improve the competency of juvenile defense attorneys, as well as to overcome some of the time constraints they face in case preparation. In a study of legal representation of juveniles charged with felonies in three juvenile courts in Missouri, it was found that they were more likely to receive an out-of-home placement disposition (instead of a less punitive disposition) if they had an attorney, even after controlling for other legal and individual factors.[11] Another study found that youth not represented by an attorney were more likely to have the charges dismissed than similar youth represented by an attorney, with the effect being more pronounced for minorities.[12] (See the following section for other problems specific to public defenders.)

In some cases, a **guardian *ad litem*** may be appointed by the court.[13] The guardian *ad litem*—ordinarily seen in abuse, neglect, and dependency cases—may be appointed in delinquency cases when there is a question of a need for a particular treatment (for example, placement in a mental health center) and offenders and their attorneys resist placement. The guardian *ad litem* may advocate for the commitment on the ground that it is in the child's best interests. The guardian *ad litem* fulfills many roles, ranging from legal advocate to concerned individual who works with parents and human service professionals in developing a proper treatment plan that best serves the interests of the minor child.[14]

Court-Appointed Special Advocates (CASA)

Court-Appointed Special Advocates (CASA) are volunteers who advise the juvenile court about child placement. The CASA programs (*casa* is Spanish for "home") have demonstrated that volunteers can investigate the needs of children and provide a vital link among the judge, the attorneys, and the child in protecting the juvenile's right to a safe placement.[15]

Public Defender Services for Children

To satisfy the requirement that indigent children be provided with counsel, the federal government and the states have expanded **public defender** services. Three alternatives exist for providing children with legal counsel: (1) an all-public defender program; (2) an appointed private-counsel system; and (3) a combination system of public defenders and appointed private attorneys.

The public defender program is a statewide program established by legislation and funded by the state government to provide counsel to children at public expense. This program allows access to the expertise of lawyers who spend a considerable amount of time representing juvenile offenders every day. Defender programs generally provide separate office space for juvenile court personnel, as well as support staff and training programs for new lawyers.

In many rural areas where individual public defender programs are not available, defense services are offered through appointed private counsel. Private lawyers are assigned to individual juvenile court cases and receive compensation for the time and services they provide. When private attorneys are used in large urban areas, they are

guardian *ad litem*
A court-appointed attorney who protects the interests of the child in cases involving the child's welfare.

public defender
An attorney who works in a public agency or under private contractual agreement as defense counsel to indigent defendants.

generally selected from a list established by the court, and they often operate in conjunction with a public defender program. The weaknesses of a system of assigned private counsel include assignment to cases for which the lawyers are unqualified, inadequate compensation, and lack of support or supervisory services.

Although efforts have been made to supply juveniles with adequate legal representation, many juveniles still go to court unrepresented, or with an overworked lawyer who provides inadequate representation. Many juvenile court defense lawyers work on more than five hundred cases per year, and more than half leave their jobs in under two years.[16] Other problems facing juvenile public defenders include lack of resources for independent evaluations, expert witnesses, and investigatory support; lack of computers, telephones, files, and adequate office space; inexperience, lack of training, low morale, and salaries lower than those of their counterparts who defend adults or serve as prosecutors; and inability to keep up with rapidly changing juvenile codes.[17] In a six-state study of access to counsel and quality of legal representation for indigent juveniles, the American Bar Association found these and many other problems,[18] as shown in Exhibit 13.1. With juvenile offenders facing the prospect of much longer sentences, mandatory minimum sentences, and time in adult prisons, the need for quality defense attorneys for juveniles has never been greater.

juvenile prosecutor
Government attorney responsible for representing the interests of the state and bringing the case against the accused juvenile.

The Prosecutor The **juvenile prosecutor** is the attorney responsible for bringing the state's case against the accused juvenile. Depending on the level of government and the jurisdiction, the prosecutor can be called a *district attorney*, *county attorney*, *state*

Exhibit 13.1 **Selected Problems in Public Defender Services for Indigent Juveniles in Six States**

Maine
- Juvenile defenders are paid $50 per hour, with a cap of $315; therefore, defenders are expected to spend only a little over six hours on each case.
- In 2002, only two hours of juvenile-justice-related training were available to defenders.

Maryland
- In one jurisdiction, juvenile public defenders handle about 360 cases each year; this is almost double the ABA standard's recommended maximum of 200.
- In ten of the jurisdictions studied, more than a third of juveniles waived their right to counsel.

Montana
- Nearly all the interviewed youth revealed that their attorneys had done no investigation into their cases.
- There are no minimum requirements for attorneys seeking appointment to defend children and youth in the justice system.

North Carolina
- Some 44 percent of juvenile defense attorneys surveyed reported that they rarely or never see the police report or other investigative material prior to their first meeting with a client.
- Some 44 percent also said they had no or inadequate access to investigators.

Pennsylvania
- About 94 percent of juvenile defense attorneys do not have access to independent investigators or social workers.
- Of the forty public defender offices that confirmed representing youth at dispositional reviews, only 9 percent usually interview the youth before hearings.

Washington
- In some counties, up to 30 percent of children appear without counsel.
- Juvenile defenders working full-time reported that they are assigned an average of close to four hundred cases annually.

Sources: *Statistics: Juvenile Indigent Defense Reports by the Numbers* (Chicago: Juvenile Justice Center, 2003); *Montana: An Assessment of Access to Counsel and Quality of Representation in Delinquency Proceedings* (Chicago: American Bar Association, 2003), p. 5.

attorney, or *United States attorney*. Prosecutors are members of the bar selected for their positions by political appointment or popular election.

For the first sixty years of its existence, the juvenile court did not include a prosecutor, because the concept of an adversary process was seen as inconsistent with the philosophy of treatment. The court followed a social-service helping model, and informal proceedings were believed to be in the best interests of the child. Today, in a more legalistic juvenile court, almost all jurisdictions require by law that a prosecutor be present in the juvenile court.

A number of states have passed legislation giving prosecutors control over intake and waiver decisions. Some have passed concurrent-jurisdiction laws that allow prosecutors to decide in which court to bring serious juvenile cases. In some jurisdictions, it is the prosecutor and not the juvenile court judge who is entrusted with the decision of whether to waive a case to adult court.

The prosecutor has the power either to initiate or to discontinue delinquency or status-offense allegations. Like police officers, prosecutors have broad discretion in the exercise of their duties. Because due process rights have been extended to juveniles, the prosecutor's role in the juvenile court has in some ways become similar to the prosecutor's role in the adult court.

Because children are committing more serious crimes today and because the courts have granted juveniles constitutional safeguards, the prosecutor is likely to play an increasingly significant role in the juvenile court system. According to authors James Shine and Dwight Price, the prosecutor's involvement will promote a due process model that should result in a fairer, more just system for all parties. But they also point out that, to meet current and future challenges, prosecutors need more information on such issues as how to identify repeat offenders, how to determine which programs are most effective, how early-childhood experiences relate to delinquency, and what measures can be used in place of secure placements without reducing public safety.[19]

Today, prosecutors are addressing the problems associated with juvenile crime. A balanced approach has been recommended—one that emphasizes enforcement, prosecution, and detention of serious offenders, and the use of proven prevention and intervention programs.[20]

The Juvenile Court Judge Even with the elevation of the prosecutor's role, the **juvenile court judge** is still the central character in a court of juvenile or family law. The responsibilities of this judge have become far more extensive and complex in recent years. Juvenile or family court judges perform the functions listed in Exhibit 13.2.

In addition, judges often have extensive influence over other agencies of the court: probation, the court clerk, the law enforcement officer, and the office of the

juvenile court judge
A judge elected or appointed to preside over juvenile cases whose decisions can only be reviewed by a judge of a higher court.

| Exhibit 13.2 | **Duties of the Juvenile Court Judge** |

- Rule on pretrial motions involving such legal issues as arrest, search and seizure, interrogation, and lineup identification.
- Make decisions about the continued detention of children prior to trial.
- Make decisions about plea-bargaining agreements and the informal adjustment of juvenile cases.
- Handle trials, rule on the appropriateness of conduct, settle questions of evidence

- and procedure, and guide the questioning of witnesses.
- Assume responsibility for holding disposition hearings and deciding on the treatment accorded the child.
- Handle waiver proceedings.
- Handle appeals where allowed by statute.

✔ CHECKPOINTS

■ In most jurisdictions, kids are adjudicated within the structure of either a family court or an independent juvenile court.

■ More than 1.6 million delinquency cases are adjudicated annually.

■ All juveniles must be provided with legal counsel if they face the possibility of incarceration.

■ A guardian *ad litem* is an attorney who represents the child during special legal proceedings, including abuse, neglect, and dependency cases.

■ Court-Appointed Special Advocates (CASA) are volunteers who advise the juvenile court about child placement.

■ The juvenile prosecutor is the attorney responsible for bringing the state's case against the accused juvenile.

■ The juvenile judge must ensure that the children and families who come before the court can receive the proper care and help.

juvenile prosecutor. Juvenile court judges exercise considerable leadership in developing solutions to juvenile justice problems. In this role, they must respond to the pressures the community places on juvenile court resources. According to the *parens patriae* philosophy, the juvenile judge must ensure that the necessary community resources are available so that the children and families who come before the court can receive the proper care and help.[21] This may be the most untraditional role for the juvenile court judge, but it may also be the most important.

In some jurisdictions, juvenile court judges handle family-related cases exclusively. In others they preside over criminal and civil cases as well. Traditionally, juvenile court judges have been relegated to a lower status than other judges. The National Council of Juvenile and Family Court Judges, as part of a larger effort to improve juvenile courts, recently took up this issue by recommending that, "Juvenile delinquency court judges should have the same status as the highest level of trial court in the state and should have multiple year or permanent assignments."[22] Furthermore, judges assigned to juvenile courts have not ordinarily been chosen from the highest levels of the legal profession. Such groups as the American Judicature Society have noted that the field of juvenile justice has often been shortchanged by the appointment of unqualified judges. In some jurisdictions, particularly major urban areas, juvenile court judges may be of the highest caliber, but many courts continue to function with mediocre judges.

Inducing the best-trained individuals to accept juvenile court judgeships is a very important goal. Where the juvenile court is part of the highest general court of trial jurisdiction, the problem of securing qualified personnel is not as great. However, if the juvenile court is of limited or specialized jurisdiction and has the authority to try only minor cases, it may attract only poorly trained personnel. Lawyers and judges who practice in juvenile court receive little respect. The juvenile court has a negative image, because even though what it does is of great importance to parents, children, and society in general, it has been placed at the lowest level of the judicial hierarchy.

✔ Checkpoints

JUVENILE COURT PROCESS

Now that we have briefly described the setting of the juvenile court and the major players who control its operations, we turn to a discussion of the procedures that shape the contours of juvenile justice: the pretrial process and the juvenile trial and disposition. Many critical decisions are made at this stage of the juvenile justice system: whether to detain or release the youth to the community; whether to waive youths to the adult court or retain them in the juvenile justice system; whether to treat them in the community or send them to a secure treatment center. Each of these can have a profound influence on the child, with effects lasting throughout the life course. What are these critical stages, and how are decisions made within them?

Release or Detain?

After a child has been taken into custody and a decision is made to treat the case formally (that is, with a juvenile court hearing), a decision must be made either to release the child into the custody of parents or to detain the child in the temporary care of the state, in physically restrictive facilities pending court disposition or transfer to another agency.[23] Nationally, about 70 percent of all states have detention centers administered at the county level, about 34 percent have state-level facilities, 16 percent have court-administered facilities, and 11 percent contracted with private vendors to operate facilities.[24]

Detention can be a traumatic experience, because many facilities are prison-like, with locked doors and barred windows. Consequently, most experts in juvenile justice advocate that detention be limited to alleged offenders who require secure custody

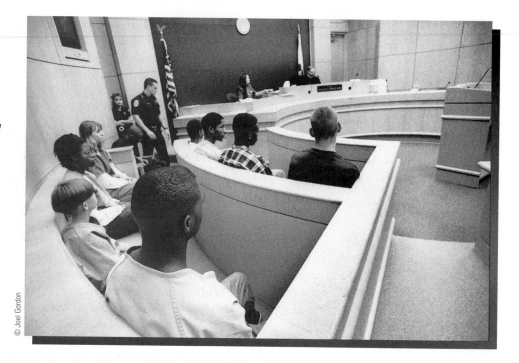

These teens wait during the intake process in a juvenile court in Orlando, Florida. Many critical decisions are made before the juvenile trial begins: whether to detain youths or release them to the community; whether to waive them to the adult court or retain them in the juvenile justice system; whether to treat them in the community or send them to a secure treatment center.

© Joel Gordon

for the protection of themselves and others. However, children who are neglected and dependent, runaways, or homeless may under some circumstances be placed in secure detention facilities along with violent and dangerous youth until more suitable placements can be found.[25] Others have had a trial, but have not been sentenced, or are awaiting the imposition of their sentence. Some may have violated probation and are awaiting a hearing while being kept alongside a severely mentally ill adolescent for whom no appropriate placement can be found. Another group are adjudicated delinquents awaiting admittance to a correctional training school.[26] Consequently, it is possible for nonviolent status offenders to be housed in the same facility with delinquents who have committed felony-type offenses. A recent study of child detention centers in New Jersey found that one out of every four youths in the centers (about twenty-five hundred out of ten thousand) were placed there inappropriately and should have instead been placed in hospitals, foster care homes, or other non-custodial settings. Because of the inappropriate placement in detention facilities, many of these youths were preyed upon by violent youth, did not receive much needed medical or mental care, or resorted to self-harm or suicide attempts as a way to cope or escape from the dangerous and chaotic setting.[27]

To remedy these situations, an ongoing effort has been made to remove status offenders, neglected or abused children, and foster care youths from detention facilities that also house juvenile delinquents, as well as develop alternatives to detention centers, such as temporary foster homes, detention boarding homes, and programs of neighborhood supervision. These alternatives, referred to as **shelter care**, enable youths to live in a more homelike setting while the courts dispose of their cases.

Project Confirm in New York City is one example of an effort to reduce the detention of foster care youths who have been arrested. Very often these youths who otherwise would have been released are placed in detention facilities because their guardians fail to appear in court, a result of a breakdown in communication between (and within) the child welfare and juvenile justice systems. The project involves two main strategies to overcome this problem: notifying project staff upon a youth's arrest to allow for a search of child welfare databases, and court conferencing among child

LOOKING BACK TO CLIFF'S STORY

How do you think this case may have ended if Cliff was initially placed in detention?

shelter care
A place for temporary care of children in physically unrestricting facilities.

welfare and juvenile justice authorities. An evaluation of the project found that disparity in detention experienced by foster care youths compared to a similar group of non-foster care youths was reduced among those charged with minor offenses and with no prior detentions, but increased among those charged with more serious offenses and prior police contact. The authors speculate that the improved quality of information provided by the project to the court, especially prior detentions, coupled with court officials' preconceived notions of the likelihood of these youths to commit another crime or fail to appear in court, resulted in more serious cases being detained.[28]

National Detention Trends Despite an ongoing effort to limit detention, juveniles are still being detained in one out of every five delinquency cases (20 percent), with some variation across the major offense categories: violent (25 percent), property (17 percent), drugs (20 percent), and public order (21 percent). Although the detention rate for delinquency cases is down from 1990, in which the percent of cases detained was highest (23 percent), between 1990 and 2002, the total number of juveniles held in short-term detention facilities increased 9 percent, from 302,800 to 329,800.[29]

The typical delinquent detainee is male, over sixteen years of age, and charged with a violent crime, whereas the typical status offense detainee is female, under sixteen years of age, and a runaway.[30] Racial minorities are heavily overrepresented in detention, especially those who are indigent and whose families may be receiving public assistance. Minority overrepresentation is particularly vexing, considering that detention may increase the risk of a youth's being adjudicated and eventually confined.[31]

In a study of the extent of racial discrimination and disparity among male juvenile property offenders in six Missouri counties at four stages of juvenile justice (decision to file a petition, pretrial detention, adjudication, and disposition), it was found that African American youth were more likely than European American youth to be detained prior to adjudication (40 percent compared to 22 percent).[32] The study also found that African American youth were more likely to be formally referred and European American youth were more likely to be adjudicated. The authors speculate that a "correction of biases" may be one of the reasons for European American youth being more likely than African American youth to be adjudicated; that is, "judges may dismiss black youths because they feel that a detained youth has been punished enough already."[33]

The Decision to Detain Most children taken into custody by the police are released to their parents or guardians. Some are held overnight until their parents can be notified. Police officers normally take a child to a place of detention only after other alternatives have been exhausted. Many juvenile courts in urban areas have staff members, such as intake probation officers, on duty twenty-four hours a day to screen detention admissions.

Ordinarily, delinquent children are detained if the police believe they are inclined to run away while awaiting trial, or if they are likely to commit an offense dangerous to the parent. There is evidence that some decision makers are more likely to detain minority youth, especially if they dwell in dangerous lower-class areas.[34]

Generally, children should not be held in a detention facility or shelter-care unit for more than twenty-four hours without a formal petition (a written request to the court) being filed to extend the detention period. To detain a juvenile, there must be clear evidence of probable cause that the child has committed the offense and will flee if not detained. Although the requirements for detention hearings vary, most jurisdictions require that they occur almost immediately after the child's admission to a detention facility and provide the youth with notice and counsel.

New Approaches to Detention Efforts have been ongoing to improve the process and conditions of detention. Experts maintain that detention facilities should provide youth with education, visitation, private communications, counseling, continuous supervision, medical and health care, nutrition, recreation, and reading. Detention should also include, or provide, a system for clinical observation and diagnosis that complements the wide range of helpful services.[35]

The consensus today is that juvenile detention centers should be reserved for youths who present a clear threat to the community. In some states, nonsecure facilities are being used to service juveniles for a limited period. Alternatives to secure detention include in-home monitoring, home detention, day-center electronic monitoring, high-intensity community supervision, and comprehensive case management programs. The successful Detention Diversion Advocacy Program (DDAP) relies on a case management strategy. Because this is an important development, it is covered in more detail in the accompanying Preventing and Treating Delinquency feature.

Undoubtedly, juveniles pose special detention problems, but some efforts are being made to improve programs and to reduce pretrial detention use, especially in secure settings. Of all the problems associated with detention, however, none is as critical as the issue of placing youths in adult jails.

To find out more about the needs of detention, go to the *Juvenile Detention Training Needs Assessment Research Report,* by David W. Roush. You can find it by going to the website www.thomsonedu.com/criminaljustice/siegel.

Restricting Detention in Adult Jails A significant problem in juvenile justice is placing youths in adult jails. This is usually done in rural areas where no other facility exists. Almost all experts agree that placing children under the age of eighteen in any type of jail facility should be prohibited, because youngsters can easily be victimized by other inmates and staff, be forced to live in squalid conditions, and be subject to physical and sexual abuse.

Until a few years ago, placing juveniles in adult facilities was common, but efforts have been made to change this situation. In 1989, the Juvenile Justice and Delinquency Prevention Act (JJDPA) of 1974 was amended to require that states remove all juveniles from adult jails and lockups. According to federal guidelines, all juveniles in state custody must be separated from adult offenders or the state could lose federal juvenile justice funds. The Office of Juvenile Justice and Delinquency Prevention (OJJDP) defines separation as the condition in which juvenile detainees have either totally independent facilities or shared facilities that are designed so that juveniles and adults neither have contact nor share programs or staff.[36]

Much debate has arisen over whether the initiative to remove juveniles from adult jails has succeeded. Most indications are that the number of youths being held in adult facilities has declined significantly from the almost five hundred thousand a year recorded in 1979.[37]

Removing Status Offenders Along with removing all juveniles from adult jails, the OJJDP has made deinstitutionalization of status offenders a cornerstone of its policy. The Juvenile Justice and Delinquency Prevention Act of 1974 prohibits the placement of status offenders in secure detention facilities.

Bail for Children One critical detention issue is whether juveniles can be released on **bail.** Adults retain the right, via the Eighth Amendment to the Constitution, to reasonable bail in non-capital cases. Most states, however, refuse juveniles the right to bail. They argue that juvenile proceedings are civil, not criminal, and that detention is rehabilitative, not punitive. In addition, they argue that juveniles do not need a constitutional right to bail, because statutory provisions allow children to be released into parental custody.

State juvenile bail statutes fall into three categories: those guaranteeing the right to bail, those that grant the court discretion to give bail, and those that deny a juvenile the right to bail.[38] This disparity may be a function of the lack of legal guidance on the matter. The U.S. Supreme Court has never decided the issue of juvenile bail. Some courts have stated that bail provisions do not apply to juveniles. Others rely on the Eighth Amendment against cruel and unusual punishment, or on state constitutional provisions or statutes, and conclude that juveniles do have a right to bail.

bail
Amount of money that must be paid as a condition of pretrial release to ensure that the accused will return for subsequent proceedings; bail is normally set by the judge at the initial appearance, and if unable to make bail the accused is detained in jail.

The Detention Diversion Advocacy Program

The Detention Diversion Advocacy Program (DDAP) employs the efforts of a staff of laypersons or nonlegal experts to advocate for youthful offenders at disposition hearings. It relies on a case-management strategy coordinating human services, opportunities, or benefits. Case-management efforts are designed to integrate services across a cluster of organizations, to ensure continuity of care, and to facilitate development of client skills (for example, job interviewing, or reading and writing skills) by involving a variety of social networks and service providers (social agencies that provide specific services to youth, like drug counseling and crisis intervention).

Detention advocacy involves identifying youths likely to be detained pending their adjudication. DDAP clients are identified primarily through referrals from the public defender's office, the probation department, community agencies, and parents. Admission to DDAP is restricted to youth currently held, or likely to be held, in secure detention. Once a potential client is identified, DDAP case managers present a release plan to the judge that includes a list of appropriate community services (tutoring, drug counseling, family counseling) that will be made available on the youth's behalf. The plan also includes specified objectives (improved grades, victim restitution, drug-free status) as a means of evaluating the youth's progress in the program. Emphasis is placed on allowing the youth to live at home while going through the program. If this is not a viable option, program staff will identify and secure a suitable alternative. If the judge deems the release plan acceptable, the youth is released to DDAP supervision.

The DDAP case-management model provides frequent and consistent support and supervision to the children and their families. Case managers link youths to community-based services and closely monitor their progress. The DDAP program requires the case manager to have daily contact with the youth, the family, and significant others, including a minimum of three in-person meetings with the youth each week. The youth's family members, particularly parents and guardians, are provided with additional services that usually include assistance in securing employment, day care, drug treatment services, and income support (for example, food stamps).

Evaluations of the DDAP program indicated that it is very successful:

- The overall recidivism rate of the DDAP group was 34 percent, compared with 60 percent for the comparison group.
- Only 14 percent of the DDAP group had two or more subsequent referrals, compared with 50 percent of the comparison group.
- Only 9 percent of the DDAP group returned to court on a violent crime charge, compared with 25 percent of the comparison group.
- Only 5 percent of the DDAP group had two or more subsequent petitions, compared with 22 percent of the comparison group.

CRITICAL THINKING

1. Should adolescents be detained for nonviolent offenses, such as substance abuse or theft?
2. Do you believe that the decision to detain children should be based on an evaluation of their behavior or their parents' behavior and ability to provide care and supervision? If the latter, is that a violation of due process? In other words, why should children be punished for their parents' shortcomings?

INFOTRAC COLLEGE EDITION RESEARCH

To learn more about the concept of "juvenile detention," use the term as a subject guide on InfoTrac College Edition.

Source: Randall G. Shelden, "Detention Diversion Advocacy: An Evaluation," *Juvenile Justice Bulletin* (Washington, DC: Office of Juvenile Justice and Delinquency Prevention, 1999).

preventive detention
Keeping the accused in custody prior to trial, because the accused is suspected of being a danger to the community.

intake
Process during which a juvenile referral is received and a decision made to file a petition in juvenile court to release the juvenile, to place the juvenile under supervision, or to refer the juvenile elsewhere.

Preventive Detention Although the U.S. Supreme Court has not yet decided whether juveniles have a right to traditional money bail, it has concluded that the state has a right to detain dangerous youth until their trial, a practice called **preventive detention**. On June 4, 1984, the U.S. Supreme Court dealt with this issue in *Schall v. Martin,* when it upheld the state of New York's preventive detention statute.[39] Because this is a key case in juvenile justice, it is the subject of the Juvenile Law in Review feature on page 318. Today, most states allow "dangerous" youths to be held indefinitely before trial. Because preventive detention may attach a stigma of guilt to a child presumed innocent, the practice remains a highly controversial one, and the efficacy of such laws remains unknown.[40]

The Intake Process

The term *intake* refers to the screening of cases by the juvenile court system. The child and the child's family are screened by intake officers to determine whether the services of the juvenile court are needed. Intake officers may send the youth home

The intake process refers to the screening of cases by the juvenile court system. Intake officers, who are often probation staff members, determine whether the services of the juvenile court are needed. Here, juvenile offenders beginning the intake process are searched by a correctional officer at the Department of Youth Services Detention Center in Rathbone, Ohio.

© AP Images/Will Shiling

with no further action, divert the youth to a social agency, petition the youth to the juvenile court, or file a petition and hold the youth in detention. The intake process reduces demands on court resources, screens out cases that are not in the court's jurisdiction, and enables assistance to be obtained from community agencies without court intervention. Juvenile court intake is provided for by statute in almost all the states.

Sixteen percent (263,400) of all delinquency cases in 2002 were dismissed at intake, often because they were not legally sufficient. Another 26 percent (417,200) were processed informally, with the juvenile voluntarily agreeing to the recommended disposition (for example, voluntary treatment).[41] Intake screening allows juvenile courts to enter into consent decrees with juveniles without filing petitions and without formal adjudication. The *consent decree* is a court order authorizing disposition of the case without a formal label of delinquency. It is based on an agreement between the intake department of the court and the juvenile who is the subject of the complaint.

But intake also suffers from some problems. Although almost all state juvenile court systems provide intake and diversion programs, there are few formal criteria for selecting children for such alternatives. There are also legal problems associated with the intake process. Among them are whether the child has a right to counsel, whether the child is protected against self-incrimination, and to what degree the child needs to consent to nonjudicial disposition as recommended by the intake officer. Finally, intake dispositions are often determined by the prior record rather than by the seriousness of the offense or the social background of the child. This practice departs from the philosophy of *parens patriae*.[42]

Diversion

diversion
Officially halting or suspending a formal criminal or juvenile justice proceeding at any legally prescribed processing point after a recorded justice system entry, and referral of that person to a treatment or care program or a recommendation that the person be released.

One of the most important alternatives chosen at intake is *nonjudicial disposition*, or as it is variously called, *nonjudicial adjustment, handling or processing, informal disposition, adjustment,* or (most commonly) **diversion**. Juvenile diversion is the process of placing youths suspected of law-violating behavior into treatment programs prior to formal trial and disposition to minimize their penetration into the justice system and thereby avoid stigma and labeling.

Diversion implies more than simply screening out cases for which no additional treatment is needed. Screening involves abandoning efforts to apply coercive measures

Who Gets Diversion?

Factors Considered	Criteria for Eligibility
Past criminal record	It is the juvenile's first offense.
Type of offense	It is a nonviolent or status offense.
Other circumstances	The juvenile abuses drugs or alcohol.

to a defendant. In contrast, diversion encourages an individual to participate in some specific program or activity to avoid further prosecution.

Most court-based diversion programs employ a particular formula for choosing youths. Criteria, such as being a first offender, a nonviolent offender, or a status offender, or being drug- or alcohol-dependent, are used to select clients. In some programs, youths will be asked to partake of services voluntarily in lieu of a court appearance. In other programs, prosecutors will agree to defer, and then dismiss, a case once a youth has completed a treatment program. Finally, some programs can be initiated by the juvenile court judge after an initial hearing. Concept Summary 13.1 lists the factors considered in diversion decisions.

In sum, diversion programs have been created to remove non-serious offenders from the justice system, provide them with non-punitive treatment services, and help them avoid the stigma of a delinquent label.

LOOKING BACK TO CLIFF'S STORY

How should the juvenile justice system handle cases where adolescents are suffering from significant mental health issues and committing crimes? How might a teen's mental health issues affect his behavior and his ability to understand the consequences of his behavior? Should mental health treatment be court ordered? Should juvenile probation officers be required to have a solid understanding of mental health issues?

widening the net

Phenomenon that occurs when programs created to divert youths from the justice system actually involve them more deeply in the official process.

Issues in Diversion: Widening the Net Diversion has been viewed as a promising alternative to official procedures, but over the years its basic premises have been questioned.[43] The most damaging criticism has been that diversion programs are involving those children in the juvenile justice system who previously would have been released without official notice. This is referred to as **widening the net**. Various studies indicate that police and court personnel are likely to use diversion programs for youths who ordinarily would have been turned loose at the intake or arrest stage.[44] Why does this "net widening" occur? One explanation is that police and prosecutors find diversion a more attractive alternative than either official processing or outright release—diversion helps them resolve the conflict between doing too much and doing too little.

Diversion has also been criticized as ineffective; that is, youths being diverted make no better adjustment in the community than those who go through official channels. However, not all experts are critical of diversion. Some challenge the net-widening concept as naive: How do we know that diverted youths would have had less interface with the justice system if diversion didn't exist?[45] Even if juveniles escaped official labels for their current offense, might they not eventually fall into the hands of the police? The rehabilitative potential of diversion should not be overlooked.[46] There is some evidence that diversion with a treatment component for juveniles suffering from mental health problems can delay or prevent further delinquent activity.[47]

Some experts even argue that diversion has been the centerpiece or at least a core element of the juvenile justice system's success in limiting the growth of juvenile incarceration rates over the last three decades, which were dwarfed by the dramatic increase in incarceration rates among young adult offenders (ages eighteen to twenty-four) over the same period of time.[48] In the words of Franklin Zimring,

> *the angry assaults on juvenile courts throughout the 1990s are a tribute to the efficacy of juvenile justice in protecting delinquents from the incarcerative explosion that had happened everywhere else.*[49]

Schall v. Martin

Facts

Gregory Martin was arrested in New York City on December 13, 1977, on charges of robbery, assault, and criminal possession of a weapon. Because he was arrested at 11:30 P.M. and lied about his residence, Martin was kept overnight in detention and brought to juvenile court the next day for an "initial appearance," accompanied by his grandmother. The family court judge, citing possession of a loaded weapon, the false address given to police, and the fact that Martin was left unsupervised late in the evening, ordered him detained before trial under section 320.5(3)(6) of the New York State code, which authorizes pretrial detention of an accused juvenile delinquent if "there is a substantial probability that he will not appear in court on the return date or there is a serious risk that he may before the return date commit an act which if committed by an adult would constitute a crime." Later, at trial, Martin was found to be a delinquent and sentenced to two years' probation.

During the time he was in pretrial detention, Martin's attorneys filed a class action on behalf of all youths subject to preventive detention in New York, charging that this form of detention was a denial of due process rights under the Fifth and Fourteenth Amendments. The New York appellate courts upheld Martin's claim on the ground that because, at adjudication, most delinquents are released or placed on probation, it was unfair to incarcerate them before trial. The prosecution brought the case to the U.S. Supreme Court for final judgment.

Decision

The U.S. Supreme Court upheld the state's right to place juveniles in preventive detention, holding that the practice serves the legitimate objective of protecting both the juvenile and society from pretrial crime. Pretrial detention need not be considered punishment merely because the juvenile is eventually released or put on probation. In addition, there are procedural safeguards, such as notice and a hearing, and a statement of facts that must be given to juveniles before they are placed in detention. The Court also found that detention based on prediction of future behavior was not a violation of due process. Many decisions are made in the justice system, such as the decision to sentence or grant parole, that are based in part on a prediction of future behavior, and these have all been accepted by the courts as legitimate exercises of state power.

Significance of the Case

Schall v. Martin established the right of juvenile court judges to deny youths pretrial release if they perceive them to be dangerous. However, the case also established a due process standard for detention hearings that includes notice and a statement of substantial reasons for the detention. Despite these measures, opponents hold that preventive detention deprives offenders of their freedom because guilt has not been proven. It is also unfair, they claim, to punish people for what judicial authorities believe they may do in the future, because it is impossible to predict who will be a danger to the community. Moreover, because judges are able to use discretion in their detention decisions, an offender could unfairly be deprived of freedom without legal recourse.

CRITICAL THINKING

1. Is the use of pretrial detention warranted for all juveniles charged with violent crimes? Explain.
2. Should judicial discretion be limited in decisions on pretrial release or detention?

INFOTRAC COLLEGE EDITION RESEARCH

To learn about innovations in pretrial detention for juveniles, read Amanda Paulson, "Chicago's Alternative to Locking Up Youth," *Christian Science Monitor,* January 21, 2004, p. 1.

Source: *Schall v. Martin,* 104 S.Ct. 2403 (1984).

The Petition

complaint
Report made by the police or some other agency to the court that initiates the intake process.

A **complaint** is the report made by the police or some other agency to the court to initiate the intake process. Once the agency makes a decision that judicial disposition is required, a petition is filed. The petition is the formal complaint that initiates judicial action against a juvenile charged with delinquency or a status offense. The petition includes basic information, such as the name, age, and residence of the child; the parents' names; and the facts alleging the child's delinquency. The police officer, a family member, or a social service agency can file a petition.

If after being given the right to counsel, the child admits the allegation in the petition, an initial hearing is scheduled for the child to make the admission before the court and information is gathered to develop a treatment plan. If the child does not admit to any of the facts in the petition, a date is set for a hearing on the petition. This hearing, whose purpose is to determine the merits of the petition, is similar to the adult trial. Once a hearing date has been set, the probation department is normally asked to prepare a social study report. This predisposition report contains relevant information about the child, along with recommendations for treatment and service.

plea bargaining
The exchange of prosecutorial and judicial concessions for a guilty plea by the accused; plea bargaining usually results in a reduced charge or a more lenient sentence.

CHECKPOINTS

■ Detention is the temporary care of children by the state in physically restrictive facilities pending court disposition or transfer to another agency.

■ The federal government has encouraged the removal of status offenders from detention facilities that also house juvenile delinquents; it has encouraged the removal of delinquents from adult jails.

■ Racial minorities are over-represented in detention.

■ Experts maintain that detention facilities should provide youth with treatment, such as education, counseling, and health care.

■ Intake refers to the screening of cases by the juvenile court system to determine whether the services of the juvenile court are needed.

■ One of the most important alternatives chosen at intake is nonjudicial disposition, or as it is most commonly called, diversion.

■ The petition is the formal complaint that initiates judicial action against a juvenile charged with delinquency or a status offense.

When a date has been set for the hearing on the petition, parents or guardians and other persons associated with the petition (witnesses, the arresting police officer, and victims) are notified. On occasion, the court may issue a summons—a court order requiring the juvenile or others involved in the case to appear for the hearing. The statutes in a given jurisdiction govern the contents of the petition. Some jurisdictions, for instance, allow for a petition to be filed based on the information of the complainant alone. Others require that the petition be filed under oath or that an affidavit accompany the petition. Some jurisdictions authorize only one official, such as a probation officer or prosecutor, to file the petition. Others allow numerous officials, including family and social service agencies, to set forth facts in the petition. ✔ Checkpoints

The Plea and Plea Bargaining

In the adult criminal justice system, the defendant normally enters a plea of guilty or not guilty. More than 90 percent of all adult defendants plead guilty. A large proportion of those pleas involve **plea bargaining**, the exchange of prosecutorial and judicial concessions for guilty pleas.[50] Plea bargaining permits a defendant to plead guilty to a less-serious charge, in exchange for an agreement by the prosecutor to recommend a reduced sentence to the court. It involves a discussion between the child's attorney and the prosecutor by which the child agrees to plead guilty to obtain a reduced charge or a lenient sentence.

Few juvenile codes require a guilty or not-guilty plea when a petition is filed against a child. In most jurisdictions an initial hearing is held at which the child either submits to a finding of the facts or denies the petition.[51] If the child admits to the facts, the court determines an appropriate disposition. If the child denies the allegations, the case normally proceeds to trial. When a child enters no plea, the court ordinarily imposes a denial of the charges. This may occur when a juvenile doesn't understand the nature of the complaint or isn't represented by an attorney.

A high percentage of juvenile offenders enter guilty pleas—that is, they admit to the facts of the petition. How many of these pleas involve plea bargaining is unknown. In the past it was believed that plea bargaining was unnecessary in the juvenile justice system, because there was little incentive to bargain in a system that does not have jury trials or long sentences. In addition, because the court must dispose of cases in the best interests of the child, plea negotiation seemed unnecessary. Consequently, there has long been a debate over the appropriateness of plea bargaining in juvenile justice. The arguments in favor of plea bargaining include lower court costs and efficiency. Counterarguments hold that plea bargaining with juveniles is an unregulated and unethical process. When used, experts believe the process requires the highest standards of good faith by the prosecutor.[52]

Plea bargaining negotiations generally involve one or more of the following: reduction of a charge, change in the proceedings from that of delinquency to a status offense, elimination of possible waiver to the criminal court, and agreements regarding dispositional programs for the child. In states where youths are subject to long mandatory sentences, reduction of the charges may have a significant impact on the outcome of the case. In states where youths

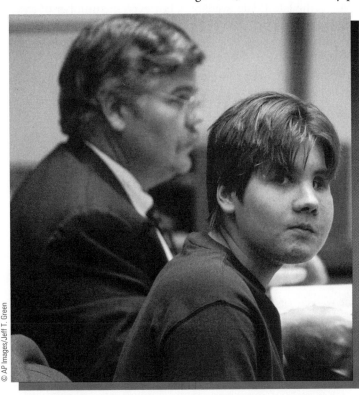

Plea bargaining involves the exchange of prosecutorial and judicial concessions for a guilty plea that usually results in a reduced charge or more lenient disposition. Here, Sean Fitzpatrick and his defense attorney await the teen's disposition in the Spokane County Juvenile Justice Center in Washington, following a plea agreement to spare him time in a juvenile facility in exchange for the youth talking to other teens about the need to seek help for depression. Fitzpatrick brought a gun to school in the hope that police would kill him. His misshapen face is the result of a police bullet that tore through his left eye socket and palate.

© AP Images/Jeff T. Green

may be waived to the adult court for committing certain serious crimes, a plea reduction may result in the juvenile court's maintaining jurisdiction.

There is little clear evidence on how much plea bargaining occurs in the juvenile justice system, but it is apparent that such negotiations do take place and seem to be increasing. Joseph Sanborn found that about 20 percent of the cases processed in Philadelphia resulted in a negotiated plea. Most were for reduced sentences, typically probation in lieu of incarceration. Sanborn found that plea bargaining was a complex process, depending in large measure on the philosophy of the judge and the court staff. In general, he found it to have greater benefit for the defendants than for the court.[53]

In summary, the majority of juvenile cases that are not adjudicated seem to be the result of admissions to the facts rather than actual plea bargaining. Plea bargaining is less common in juvenile courts than in adult courts, because incentives, such as dropping multiple charges or substituting a misdemeanor for a felony, are unlikely. Nonetheless, plea bargaining is firmly entrenched in the juvenile process. Any plea bargain, however, must be entered into voluntarily and knowingly; otherwise, the conviction may be overturned on appeal.

TRANSFER TO THE ADULT COURT

transfer process
Transferring a juvenile offender from the jurisdiction of juvenile court to adult criminal court.

One of the most significant actions that can occur in the early court processing of a juvenile offender is the **transfer process**. Otherwise known as *waiver*, *bind over*, or *removal*, this process involves transferring a juvenile from the juvenile court to the criminal court. Virtually all state statutes allow for this kind of transfer.

The number of delinquency cases judicially waived to criminal court peaked in 1994 at 13,200 cases, an increase of 83 percent over the number of cases waived in 1985 (7,200). From 1994 to 2002 (the latest data available), however, the number of cases waived to criminal court has actually declined 46 percent to 7,100 cases, representing less than 1 percent of the formally processed delinquency caseload. Between 1985 and 2002, person offense cases were the most likely to be waived to criminal court.[54] Figure 13.1 shows numbers of delinquency cases waived to criminal court from 1985 to 2002.

Waiver Procedures

Today, all states allow juveniles to be tried as adults in criminal courts in one of three ways:

1. *Concurrent jurisdiction.* In fifteen states and the District of Columbia, the prosecutor has the discretion of filing charges for certain offenses in either juvenile or criminal court.

2. *Statutory exclusion policies.* In twenty-nine states, certain offenses are automatically excluded from juvenile court. These offenses can be minor, such as traffic violations, or serious, such as murder or rape. Statutory exclusion accounts for the largest number of juveniles tried as adults.

3. *Judicial waiver.* In the waiver (or bind over or removal) of juvenile cases to criminal court, a hearing is held before a juvenile court judge, who then decides whether jurisdiction should be waived and the case transferred to criminal court. Forty-five states and the District of Columbia (not Massachusetts, Montana, Nebraska, New Mexico, and New York) offer provisions for juvenile waivers.[55]

Due Process in Transfer Proceedings

The standards for transfer procedures are set by state statute. Some jurisdictions allow for transfer between the ages of fourteen and seventeen. Others restrict waiver proceedings to mature juveniles and specify particular offenses. In a few jurisdictions, any child can be transferred to the criminal court system, regardless of age.

Figure 13.1

Delinquency Cases Waived to Criminal Court

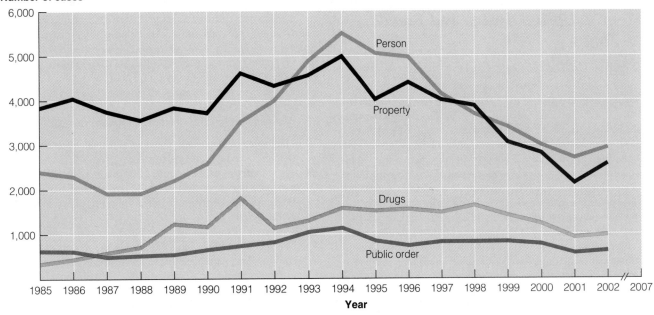

Number of cases

Source: Howard N. Snyder and Melissa Sickmund, *Juvenile Offenders and Victims: 2006 National Report* (Pittsburgh, PA: National Center for Juvenile Justice, 2006), p. 186. Available at: www.ojjdp.ncjrs.org/ojstatbb/nr2006/downloads/chapter6.pdf (accessed January 10, 2007).

Those states that have amended their waiver policies with statutory exclusion policies now exclude certain serious offenses from juvenile court jurisdiction. For example, Indiana excludes cases involving sixteen- and seventeen-year-olds charged with murder, drug and weapons offenses, and certain felonies and other person offenses. In Illinois, youths ages thirteen and older who are charged with murder and youths ages fifteen and older who are charged with drug and weapons offenses and certain felonies and other person offenses are automatically sent to criminal court; in Nevada and Pennsylvania, any child accused of murder, regardless of age, is tried before the criminal court.[56] Other jurisdictions use exclusion to remove traffic offenses and public-ordinance violations.

The trend toward excluding serious violent offenses from juvenile court jurisdictions grew in response to the demand to get tough on crime. In addition, large numbers of youth under age eighteen are tried as adults in states where the upper age of juvenile court jurisdiction is fifteen or sixteen.

In a small number of states, statutes allow prosecutors to file particularly serious cases in either the juvenile court or the adult court.[57] Prosecutor discretion may occasionally be a more effective transfer mechanism than the waiver process, because the prosecutor can file a petition in criminal or juvenile court without judicial approval.

Since 1966, the U.S. Supreme Court and other federal and state courts have attempted to ensure fairness in the waiver process by handing down decisions that spell out the need for due process. Two Supreme Court decisions, *Kent v. United States* (1966) and *Breed v. Jones* (1975), are relevant.[58] The *Kent* case declared a District of Columbia transfer statute unconstitutional and attacked the subsequent conviction of the child by granting him the specific due process rights of having an attorney present at the hearing and access to the evidence that would be used in the case. In *Breed v. Jones*, the U.S. Supreme Court declared that the child was to be granted the protection of the double-jeopardy clause of the Fifth Amendment after he was tried as a delinquent in the juvenile court: once found to be a delinquent, the youth could

Kent v. United States and Breed v. Jones

Kent v. United States: Facts

Morris Kent was arrested at age sixteen in connection with charges of housebreaking, robbery, and rape. As a juvenile, he was subject to the exclusive jurisdiction of the District of Columbia Juvenile Court. The District of Columbia statute declared that the court could transfer the petitioner "after full investigation" and remit him to trial in the U.S. District Court. Kent admitted his involvement in the offenses and was placed in a receiving home for children. Subsequently, his mother obtained counsel, and they discussed with the social service director the possibility that the juvenile court might waive its jurisdiction.

Kent was detained at the receiving home for almost a week. There was no arraignment, no hearing, and no hearing for petitioner's apprehension. Kent's counsel arranged for a psychiatric examination, and a motion requesting a hearing on the waiver was filed. The juvenile court judge did not rule on the motion and entered an order that stated: "After full investigation, the court waives its jurisdiction and directs that a trial be held under the regular proceedings of the criminal court." The judge made no finding and gave no reasons for his waiver decision. It appeared that the judge denied motions for a hearing, recommendations for hospitalization for psychiatric observation, requests for access to the social service file, and offers to prove that the petitioner was a fit subject for rehabilitation under the juvenile court.

After the juvenile court waived its jurisdiction, Kent was indicted by the grand jury and was subsequently found guilty of housebreaking and robbery and not guilty by reason of insanity on the charge of rape. Kent was sentenced to serve a period of thirty to ninety years on his conviction.

Decision

The petitioner's lawyer appealed the decision on the basis of the infirmity of the proceedings by which the juvenile court waived its jurisdiction. He further attacked the waiver on statutory and constitutional grounds, stating: "(1) no hearing occurred, (2) no findings were made, (3) no reasons were stated before the waiver, and (4) counsel was denied access to the social service file." The U.S. Supreme Court found that the juvenile court order waiving jurisdiction and remitting the child to trial in the district court was invalid.

Its arguments were based on the following criteria:

- The theory of the juvenile court act is rooted in social welfare procedures and treatments.
- The philosophy of the juvenile court, namely *parens patriae,* is not supposed to allow procedural unfairness.
- Waiver proceedings are critically important actions in the juvenile court.
- The juvenile court act requiring full investigation in the District of Columbia should be read in the context of constitutional principles relating to due process of law. These principles require at a minimum that the petitioner be entitled to a hearing, access to counsel, access by counsel to social service records, and a statement of the reason for the juvenile court decision.

Significance of the Case

This case examined for the first time the substantial degree of discretion associated with a transfer proceeding in the District of Columbia. Thus, the Supreme Court significantly limited its holding to the statute involved but justified its reference to constitutional principles relating to due process and the assistance of counsel. In addition, it said that the juvenile court waiver hearings need to measure up to the essentials of due process and fair treatment. Furthermore, in an appendix to its opinion, the Court set up criteria concerning waiver of the jurisdictions. These are:

- The seriousness of the alleged offense to the community
- Whether the alleged offense was committed in an aggressive, violent, or willful manner

---

no longer be tried as an adult. The accompanying Juvenile Law in Review feature discusses these two important cases in more detail.

Today, as a result of *Kent* and *Breed*, states that have transfer hearings provide a legitimate transfer hearing, sufficient notice to the child's family and defense attorney, the right to counsel, and a statement of the reason for the court order regarding transfer. These procedures recognize that the transfer process is critical in determining the statutory rights of the juvenile offender.

Should Youths Be Transferred to Adult Court?

Most juvenile justice experts oppose waiver, because it clashes with the rehabilitative ideal. Basing waiver decisions on type and seriousness of offense rather than on the rehabilitative needs of the child has advanced the *criminalization* of the juvenile court and interfered with its traditional mission of treatment and rehabilitation.[59] And despite this sacrifice, there is little evidence that strict waiver policies can lower crime rates.[60] For example, in a 22-state analysis of the deterrent effects of statutory exclusion laws

- Whether the alleged offense was committed against persons or against property
- The prosecutive merit of the complaint
- The sophistication and maturity of the juvenile
- The record and previous history of the juvenile
- Prospects for adequate protection of the public and the likelihood of reasonable rehabilitation

Breed v. Jones: Facts

In 1971, a petition in the juvenile court of California was filed against Jones, who was then seventeen, alleging that he had committed an offense that, if committed by an adult, would constitute robbery. The petitioner was detained pending a hearing. At the hearing the juvenile court took testimony, found that the allegations were true, and sustained the petition. The proceedings were continued for a disposition hearing, at which point Jones was found unfit for treatment in the juvenile court. It was ordered that he be prosecuted as an adult offender. At a subsequent preliminary hearing, the petitioner was held for criminal trial, an information or charge was filed against him for robbery, and he was tried and found guilty. He was committed to the California Youth Authority over objections that he was being subjected to double jeopardy.

Petitioner Jones sought an appeal in the federal district court on the basis of the double-jeopardy argument that jeopardy attaches at the juvenile delinquency proceedings. The writ of habeas corpus was denied.

Decision

The U.S. Supreme Court held that the prosecution of Jones as an adult in the California Superior Court, after an adjudicatory finding in the juvenile court that he had violated a criminal statute and a subsequent finding that he was unfit for treatment as a juvenile, violated the double-jeopardy clause of the Fifth Amendment to the U.S. Constitution as applied to the states through the Fourteenth Amendment. Thus, Jones's trial in the California Superior Court for the same offense as that for which he was tried in the juvenile court violated the policy of the double-jeopardy clause, even if he never faced the risk of more than one punishment. *Double jeopardy* refers to the risk or potential risk of trial and conviction, not punishment.

Significance of the Case

The *Breed* case provided answers on several important transfer issues: (1) it prohibits trying a child in an adult court when there has been a prior adjudicatory juvenile proceeding; (2) probable cause may exist at a transfer hearing, and this does not violate subsequent jeopardy if the child is transferred to the adult court; (3) because the same evidence is often used in both the transfer hearing and subsequent trial in either the juvenile or adult court, a different judge is often required for each hearing.

CRITICAL THINKING

Do you believe that some cases should be automatically waived to the adult system, or should all juvenile offenders be evaluated for the possibility of treatment in the juvenile court before a waiver decision is made?

INFOTRAC COLLEGE EDITION RESEARCH

Use "juvenile waiver" as a subject guide on InfoTrac College Edition to find out more about this issue.

Sources: *Kent v. United States*, 383 U.S. 541, 86 S.Ct. 1045, 16 L.Ed.2d 84 (1966); *Breed v. Jones*, 421 U.S. 519, 95 S.Ct. 1779 (1975).

enacted since 1979, criminologists Benjamin Steiner, Craig Hemmens, and Valerie Bell found no reduction in arrest rates for violent juvenile crime in twenty-one of the twenty-two states.[61]

Some experts also question whether juveniles waived to adult court, particularly younger ones, are competent to be tried as adults. Adjudicative competency pertains to the mental capacity or cognitive skills of the youth to understand the nature and object of the proceedings against him or her.[62] Two recent studies found that the mental competency of youths under the age of 16 to stand trial is far below that of similarly charged adults, with one study comparing the competency of young juvenile offenders to that of severely mentally impaired adults.[63]

Waiver can also create long-term harm. Waived children may be stigmatized by a conviction in the criminal court. Labeling children as adult offenders early in life may seriously impair their future educational, employment, and other opportunities. Youthful offenders convicted in adult courts are more likely to be incarcerated and to receive longer sentences than if they remained in the juvenile court. In one study in Pennsylvania, the average sentence length for juvenile offenders sentenced in adult court was found to be significantly longer than for a similar group of young adult offenders (eighteen months compared to six months).[64] And these children may be incarcerated under conditions so extreme and in institutions where they may be physically and sexually exploited, that they will become permanently damaged.[65] In a small-scale study of female youths transferred to criminal court and subsequently placed in a prison for adult women, it was found that the prison was severely limited in its ability to care for and provide needed treatment services for these youths compared with the adults.[66]

Waivers don't always support the goal of increased public protection. Because juveniles may only serve a fraction of the prison sentence imposed by the criminal court, the actual treatment of delinquents in adult court is similar to what they might have received had they remained in the custody of juvenile authorities.[67] Also, transferred juveniles convicted of felonies are not more likely to be sentenced to prison than similarly charged felons who are under the age of eighteen, but considered adults by the state.[68] Once they are released, waived juveniles have a higher recidivism rate than those kept in juvenile court.[69] This has prompted some critics to ask: Why bother transferring these children?

Sometimes waiver can add an undue burden to youthful offenders. Studies have found that, although transfer to criminal court was intended for the most serious juvenile offenders, many transferred juveniles were not violent offenders, but repeat property offenders.[70] Cases involving waiver take significantly longer than comparable juvenile court cases, during which time the waived youth is more likely to be held in a detention center.

Transfer decisions are not always carried out fairly or equitably and there is evidence that minorities are waived at a rate that is greater than their representation in the population.[71] Just over one-third (35 percent) of all waived youth are African Americans, even though they represent 29 percent of the juvenile court population.[72] A federal study of juveniles waived to criminal court in the nation's forty largest counties found that 62 percent of waived youth were African American.[73] However, between the peak year of 1994 and 2002, the number of judicially waived cases involving African American youth decreased 57 percent (from 5,724 to 2,468 cases) compared with a 36 percent decrease for European American youth (from 6,942 to 4,432 cases).[74]

In Support of Waiver Not all experts challenge the waiver concept. Waiver is attractive to conservatives, because it jibes with the get-tough policy that is currently popular. Some have argued that the increased use of waiver can help get violent offenders off the streets and should be mandatory for juveniles committing serious violent crimes.[75] Others point to studies that show that, for the most part, transfer is reserved for the most serious cases and the most serious juvenile offenders. Kids are most likely to be transferred to criminal court if they have injured someone with a weapon or if they have a long juvenile court record.[76] The most recent federal study of waiver found that 27 percent of juveniles tried in criminal court were sent to prison. This outcome might be expected because those waived to criminal court were more likely (64 percent) than adults (24 percent) to be charged with a violent felony. These juvenile defendants were generally regarded as serious offenders, because 52 percent did not receive pretrial release, 63 percent were convicted of a felony, and 43 percent of those convicted received a prison sentence.[77] In an analysis of a Virginia statute that grants prosecutors the authority to certify a juvenile offender to criminal court at intake, it was found that serious offenders were more likely to be waived to criminal court.[78] Clearly, many waived juveniles might be considered serious offenders.

Author Franklin Zimring argues that, despite its faults, waiver is superior to alternative methods for handling the most serious juvenile offenders.[79] Some cases involving serious offenses, he argues, require a minimum criminal penalty greater than that available to the juvenile court. It is also possible that some juveniles take advantage of decisions to transfer them to the adult court. Although the charge against a child may be considered serious in the juvenile court, the adult criminal court will not find it so; consequently, a child may have a better chance for dismissal of the charges, or acquittal, after a jury trial.

In sum, though the use of waiver has declined in recent years, it is still being used today as an important strategy for attacking serious youth crime.[80] Its continued use can be attributed to the ongoing get-tough attitude toward the serious juvenile offender.

JUVENILE COURT TRIAL

If the case cannot be decided during the pretrial stage, it will be brought for trial in the juvenile court. An adjudication hearing is held to determine the merits of the petition claiming that a child is either a delinquent youth or in need of court supervision. The judge is required to make a finding based on the evidence and arrive at a judgment. The adjudication hearing is comparable to an adult trial. Rules of evidence in adult criminal proceedings are generally applicable in juvenile court, and the standard of proof used—*beyond a reasonable doubt*—is similar to that used in adult trials.

State juvenile codes vary with regard to the basic requirements of due process and fairness. Most juvenile courts have bifurcated hearings—that is, separate hearings for adjudication and disposition (sentencing). At disposition hearings, evidence can be submitted that reflects nonlegal factors, such as the child's home life.

Most state juvenile codes provide specific rules of procedure. These rules require that a written petition be submitted to the court, ensure the right of a child to have an attorney, provide that the adjudication proceedings be recorded, allow the petition to be amended, and provide that a child's plea be accepted. Where the child admits to the facts of the petition, the court generally seeks assurance that the plea is voluntary. If plea bargaining is used, prosecutors, defense counsel, and trial judges take steps to ensure the fairness of such negotiations.

At the end of the adjudication hearing, most juvenile court statutes require the judge to make a factual finding on the legal issues and evidence. In the criminal court, this finding is normally a prelude to reaching a verdict. In the juvenile court, however, the finding itself is the verdict—the case is resolved in one of three ways:

1. The juvenile court judge makes a finding of fact that the child or juvenile is not delinquent or in need of supervision.

2. The juvenile court judge makes a finding of fact that the juvenile is delinquent or in need of supervision.

3. The juvenile court judge dismisses the case because of insufficient or faulty evidence.

In some jurisdictions, informal alternatives are used, such as filing the case with no further consequences or continuing the case without a finding for a period of time (for example, six months). If the juvenile does not get into further difficulty during that time, the case is dismissed. These alternatives involve no determination of delinquency or noncriminal behavior. Because of the philosophy of the juvenile court that emphasizes rehabilitation over punishment, a delinquency finding is not the same thing as a criminal conviction. The disabilities associated with conviction, such as disqualifications for employment or being barred from military service, do not apply in an adjudication of delinquency.

There are other differences between adult and juvenile proceedings. For instance, whereas adults are entitled to public trials by a jury of their peers, these rights are not extended to juveniles.[81] Because juvenile courts are treating some defendants in a similar way as adult criminals, an argument can be made that the courts should extend to these youths the Sixth Amendment right to a public jury trial.[82] For the most part, however, state juvenile courts operate without recognizing a juvenile's constitutional right to a jury trial.

To get **information on juvenile courts**, go to the website of the National Center for State Courts via www.thomsonedu.com/criminaljustice/siegel.

Constitutional Rights at Trial

due process

Basic constitutional principle based on the concept of the primacy of the individual and the complementary concept of limitation on governmental power; safeguards the individual from unfair state procedures in judicial or administrative proceedings; due process rights have been extended to juvenile trials.

In addition to mandating state juvenile code requirements, the U.S. Supreme Court has mandated the application of constitutional due process standards to the juvenile trial. **Due process** is addressed in the Fifth and Fourteenth Amendments to the U.S. Constitution. It refers to the need for rules and procedures that protect individual rights, such as the right to due process. Due process means that no person can be deprived of life, liberty, or property without protections, such as legal counsel, an open and fair hearing, and an opportunity to confront those making accusations against him or her.

For many years, children were deprived of their due process rights, because the *parens patriae* philosophy governed their relationship to the juvenile justice system. Such rights as having counsel and confronting one's accusers were deemed unnecessary. After all, why should children need protection from the state when the state was seen as acting in their interest? As we have seen, this view changed in the 1960s, when the U.S. Supreme Court began to grant due process rights and procedures to minors. The key case was that of Gerald Gault; it articulated the basic requirements of due process that must be satisfied in juvenile court proceedings. Because *Gault* remains the key constitutional case in the juvenile justice system, it is discussed in depth in the Juvenile Law in Review feature on page 329.

The *Gault* decision reshaped the constitutional and philosophical nature of the juvenile court system, and with the addition of legal representation, made it more similar to the adult system.[83] Following the *Gault* case, the U.S. Supreme Court decided in *in re Winship* that the amount of proof required in juvenile delinquency adjudications is "beyond a reasonable doubt," a level equal to the requirements in the adult system.[84]

Although the ways in which the juvenile court operates were altered by *Gault* and *Winship,* the trend toward increased rights for juveniles was somewhat curtailed by the U.S. Supreme Court's decision in *McKeiver v. Pennsylvania* (1971), which held that trial by jury in a juvenile court's adjudicative stage is not a constitutional

For a review of **due process issues in juvenile justice**, visit the website www.thomsonedu.com/criminaljustice/siegel.

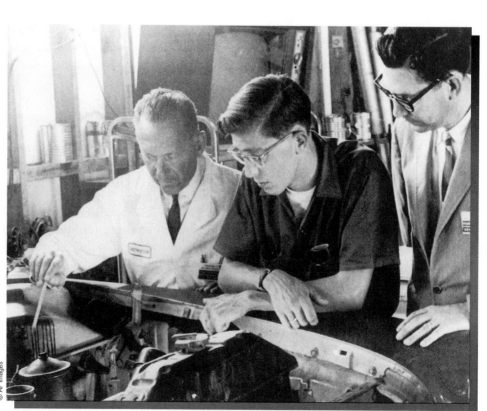

© AP Images

The appeal of Gerald Gault (center) heralded in the due process revolution in juvenile justice. The *Gault* case redefined the relationship between juveniles, their parents, and the state. It remains the single most significant constitutional case in the area of juvenile justice.

To read more about *Gault* or to get the actual case transcript, go to the website www.thomsonedu.com/criminaljustice/siegel.

requirement.[85] This decision does not prevent states from giving the juvenile a trial by jury, but in most states a child has no such right.

Once an adjudicatory hearing has been completed, the court is normally required to enter a judgment or finding against the child. This may take the form of declaring the child delinquent, adjudging the child to be a ward of the court, or possibly even suspending judgment so as to avoid the stigma of a juvenile record. After a judgment has been entered, the court can begin its determination of possible dispositions.

Disposition

The sentencing step of the juvenile justice process is called *disposition*. At this point the court orders treatment for the juvenile.[86] According to prevailing juvenile justice philosophy, dispositions should be in the *best interest of the child*, which in this context means providing the help necessary to resolve or meet the adolescent's personal needs while also meeting society's needs for protection.

As already noted, in most jurisdictions, adjudication and disposition hearings are bifurcated, so that evidence that could not be entered during the juvenile trial can be considered at the dispositional hearing. At the hearing, the defense counsel represents the child, helps the parents understand the court's decision, and influences the direction of the disposition. Others involved at the dispositional stage include representatives of social service agencies, psychologists, social workers, and probation personnel.

The Predisposition Report After the child has admitted to the allegations, or the allegations have been proved in a trial, the judge normally orders the probation department to complete a predisposition report. The predisposition report, which is similar to the presentence report of the adult justice system, has a number of purposes:

- It helps the judge decide which disposition is best for the child.
- It aids the juvenile probation officer in developing treatment programs where the child is in need of counseling or community supervision.
- It helps the court develop a body of knowledge about the child that can aid others in treating the child.[87]

Some state statutes make the predisposition report mandatory. Other jurisdictions require the report only when there is a probability that the child will be institutionalized. Some appellate courts have reversed orders institutionalizing children where the juvenile court did not use a predisposition report in reaching its decision. Access to predisposition reports is an important legal issue.

In the final section of the predisposition report, the probation department recommends a disposition to the presiding judge. This is a critical aspect of the report, because it has been estimated that the court follows more than 90 percent of all probation-department recommendations.

Juvenile Court Dispositions Historically, the juvenile court has had broad discretionary power to make dispositional decisions. The major categories of dispositional choices are community release, out-of-home placement, fines or restitution, community service, and institutionalization. A more detailed list of the dispositions open to the juvenile court judge appears in Exhibit 13.3.[88]

Most state statutes allow the juvenile court judge to select whatever disposition seems best suited to the child's needs, including institutionalization. In some states the court determines commitment to a specific institution; in other states the youth corrections

LOOKING BACK TO CLIFF'S STORY

The Functional Family Therapy (FFT) approach takes the focus of the intervention off the adolescent and places responsibility on the entire family to create solutions. Why do you think it works for many juveniles involved in the justice system? What are your concerns about this approach? Do you think there are some situations where this type of intervention may not be appropriate or successful and why?

Exhibit 13.3 **Common Juvenile Dispositions**

Disposition	Action Taken
Informal consent decree	In minor or first offenses, an informal hearing is held, and the judge will ask the youth and his or her guardian to agree to a treatment program, such as counseling. No formal trial or disposition hearing is held.
Probation	A youth is placed under the control of the county probation department and required to obey a set of probation rules and participate in a treatment program.
Home detention	A child is restricted to his or her home in lieu of a secure placement. Rules include regular school attendance, curfew observance, avoidance of alcohol and drugs, and notification of parents and the youth worker of the child's whereabouts.
Court-ordered school attendance	If truancy was the problem that brought the youth to court, a judge may order mandatory school attendance. Some courts have established court-operated day school and court-based tutorial programs staffed by community volunteers.
Financial restitution	A judge can order the juvenile offender to make financial restitution to the victim. In most jurisdictions, restitution is part of probation (see chapter 14), but in a few states, such as Maryland, restitution can be a sole order.
Fines	Some states allow fines to be levied against juveniles age sixteen and older.
Community service	Courts in many jurisdictions require juveniles to spend time in the community working off their debt to society. Community service orders are usually reserved for victimless crimes, such as vandalism of school property. Community service orders are usually carried out in schools, hospitals, or nursing homes.
Outpatient psychotherapy	Youths who are diagnosed with psychological disorders may be required to undergo therapy at a local mental health clinic.
Drug and alcohol treatment	Youths with drug- or alcohol-related problems may be allowed to remain in the community if they agree to undergo drug or alcohol therapy.
Commitment to secure treatment	In the most serious cases a judge may order an offender admitted to a long-term treatment center, such as a training school, camp, ranch, or group home. These may be either state-run or privately run institutions, and are usually located in remote regions. Training schools provide educational, vocational, and rehabilitation programs in a secure environment (see chapter 14).
Commitment to a residential community program	Youths who commit crimes of a less serious nature, but who still need to be removed from their homes can be placed in community-based group homes or halfway houses. They attend school or work during the day and live in a controlled, therapeutic environment at night.
Foster home placement	Foster homes are usually sought for dependent or neglected children and status offenders. Today judges are placing delinquents with insurmountable problems at home in state-licensed foster care homes.

agency determines where the child will be placed. In addition to the dispositions shown in Exhibit 13.3, some states grant the court the power to order parents into treatment or suspend a youth's driver's license.

Today it is common for juvenile court judges to employ a graduated sanction program for juveniles: immediate sanctions for nonviolent offenders, which consist of community-based diversion and day treatment imposed on first-time nonviolent offenders; intermediate sanctions, which target repeat minor offenders and first-time serious offenders; and secure care, which is reserved for repeat serious offenders and violent offenders.[89]

In 2002, juveniles were adjudicated delinquent in two-thirds (67 percent) of the 934,900 cases brought before a judge. Once adjudicated, the majority of these juveniles (62 percent or 385,400 cases) were placed on formal probation, just under one quarter (23 percent or 144,000 cases) were placed in a residential facility, and

In re Gault

Facts

Gerald Gault, fifteen years of age, was taken into custody by the sheriff of Gila County, Arizona, because a woman complained that he and another boy had made an obscene telephone call to her. At the time, Gault was under a six-month probation disposition after being found delinquent for stealing a wallet. As a result of the woman's complaint, the boy was taken to a children's home. His parents were not informed that he was being taken into custody. His mother appeared in the evening and was told by the superintendent of detention that a hearing would be held in the juvenile court the following day. On the day in question, the police officer who had taken him into custody filed a petition alleging his delinquency. Gault, his mother, and the police officer appeared before the judge in his chambers. Mrs. Cook, the complainant, was not at the hearing. The boy was questioned about the telephone calls and sent back to the detention home and subsequently released a few days later.

On the day of his release, Mrs. Gault received a letter indicating that a hearing would be held on his delinquency a few days later. A hearing was held, and the complainant again was not present. There was no transcript or recording of the proceedings, and the juvenile officer stated that Gault had admitted making the lewd telephone calls. Neither the boy nor his parents were advised of any right to remain silent, right to be represented by counsel, or any other constitutional rights. At the conclusion of the hearing, the juvenile court committed Gault as a juvenile delinquent to the state industrial school for the period of his minority.

This meant that, at age fifteen, Gerald Gault was sentenced to remain in the state school until he reached the age of twenty-one, unless he was discharged sooner. An adult charged with the same crime would have received a maximum punishment of no more than a $50 fine or two months in prison.

Decision

Gault's attorneys filed a writ of habeas corpus, which was denied by the Superior Court of the State of Arizona. That decision was subsequently affirmed by the Arizona Supreme Court. On appeal to the U.S. Supreme Court, Gault's counsel argued that the juvenile code of Arizona under which the boy was found delinquent was invalid, because it was contrary to the due process clause of the Fourteenth Amendment. In addition, Gault was denied the following basic due process rights: (1) notice of the charges with respect to their timeliness and specificity, (2) right to counsel, (3) right to confrontation and cross-examination, (4) privilege against self-incrimination, (5) right to a transcript of the trial record, and (6) right to appellate review. In deciding the case, the U.S. Supreme Court had to determine whether procedural due process of law in the context of fundamental fairness under the Fourteenth Amendment applied to juvenile delinquency proceedings in which a child is committed to a state industrial school.

The Court, in a far-reaching opinion, agreed that Gerald Gault's constitutional rights had been violated. Notice of charges was an essential ingredient of due process of law, as was the right to counsel, the right to cross-examine and to confront witnesses, and the privilege against self-incrimination. The questions of appellate review and a right to a transcript were not answered by the Court in this case.

Significance of the Case

The *Gault* case established that a child has the due process constitutional rights listed here in delinquency adjudication proceedings, where the consequences were that the child could be committed to a state institution. It was confined to rulings at the adjudication stage of the juvenile process.

This decision was significant not only because of the procedural reforms it initiated, but also because of its far-reaching impact throughout the entire juvenile justice system. *Gault* instilled in juvenile proceedings the development of due process standards at the pretrial, trial, and posttrial stages of the juvenile process. Although recognizing the history and development of the juvenile court, it sought to accommodate the motives of rehabilitation and treatment with children's rights. It recognized the principle of fundamental fairness of the law for children as well as for adults. Judged in the context of today's juvenile justice system, *Gault* redefined the relationships among juveniles, their parents, and the state. It remains the single most significant constitutional case in the area of juvenile justice.

CRITICAL THINKING

The *Gault* case is hailed as a milestone for giving juveniles due process rights. Does the provision of those rights actually harm juveniles? In other words, would it have been advisable to keep attorneys and legal process out of the juvenile court? Is it too late to transform the system so that it reflects its original ideals?

INFOTRAC COLLEGE EDITION RESEARCH

How has the *Gault* case shaped the philosophy of the juvenile court? To find out, read Lise A. Young, "Suffer the Children: The Basic Principle of Juvenile Justice Is to Treat the Child, Not Punish the Offense," *America* 185(12):19 (October 22, 2001).

Source: *In re Gault,* 387 U.S. 1; 87 S.Ct. 1248 (1967).

14 percent (or 85,000 cases) were given another disposition, such as referral to an outside agency, community service, or restitution.[90]

Although the juvenile court has been under pressure to get tough on youth crime, these figures show that probation is the disposition of choice, even in the most serious cases,[91] and its use has grown in recent years. Between 1985 and 2002, the number of cases in which the court ordered an adjudicated delinquent to be placed on formal probation increased 85 percent (from 189,600 to 385,400), whereas the number of cases involving placement in a residential facility increased 44 percent (from 100,400 to 144,000).[92]

Juvenile Sentencing Structures

least detrimental alternative
Choosing a program that will best foster a child's growth and development.

For most of the juvenile court's history, disposition was based on the presumed needs of the child. Although critics have challenged the motivations of early reformers in championing rehabilitation, there is little question that the rhetoric of the juvenile court has promoted that ideal.[93] For example, in their classic work *Beyond the Best Interest of the Child*, Joseph Goldstein, Anna Freud, and Albert Solnit said that placement of children should be based on the **least detrimental alternative** available in order to foster the child's development.[94] Most states have adopted this ideal in their sentencing efforts, and state courts usually insist that the purpose of disposition must be rehabilitation and not punishment.[95] Consequently, it is common for state courts to require judges to justify their sentencing decisions if it means that juveniles are to be incarcerated in a residential treatment center: they must set forth in writing the reasons for the placement, address the danger the child poses to society, and explain why a less restrictive alternative has not been used.[96]

indeterminate sentence
Does not specify the length of time the juvenile must be held; rather, correctional authorities decide when the juvenile is ready to return to society.

Traditionally, states have used the **indeterminate sentence** in juvenile court. In about half the states, this means having the judge place the offender with the state department of juvenile corrections until correctional authorities consider the youth ready to return to society or until the youth reaches legal majority. A preponderance of states consider eighteen to be the age of release; others peg the termination age at nineteen; a few can retain minority status until the twenty-first birthday. In practice, few youths remain in custody for the entire statutory period, but juveniles are usually released if their rehabilitation has been judged to have progressed satisfactorily. This practice is referred to as the individualized treatment model.

determinate sentence
Specifies a fixed term of detention that must be served.

mandatory sentences
Sentences are defined by a statutory requirement that states the penalty to be set for all cases of a specific offense.

Another form of the indeterminate sentence allows judges to specify a maximum term. Under this form of sentencing, youths may be released if the corrections department considers them to be rehabilitated or they reach the automatic age of termination (usually eighteen or twenty-one). In states that stipulate a maximum sentence, the court may extend the sentence, depending on the youth's progress in the institutional facility.

A number of states have changed from an indeterminate to a **determinate sentence**. This means sentencing juvenile offenders to a fixed term of incarceration that must be served in its entirety. Other states have passed laws creating **mandatory sentences** for serious juvenile offenders. Juveniles receiving mandatory sentences are usually institutionalized for the full sentence and are not eligible for early parole. The difference between mandatory and determinate sentences is that the mandatory sentence carries a statutory requirement that a certain penalty be set in all cases on conviction for a specified offense.

When making disposition decisions, juvenile court judges have a wide range of options, including referral to programs that will enhance life skills and help youths form a positive bond to society. Here, 16-year-old Warren Messner fights back tears after being sentenced to 22.8 years in prison by Circuit Judge Joseph Will in Daytona Beach, Florida, on April 24, 2006. Messner, along with three other teens, pleaded guilty to the beating murder of Michael Roberts, a homeless man.

© AP Photo/*Daytona Beach News-Journal*/David Tucker

Sentencing Reform

During the past decade there have been a number of attempts to create rational sentencing in juvenile justice. In some instances the goal has been to reduce judicial discretion, in others to toughen sentencing practices and create mandatory periods of incarceration for juveniles who commit serious crimes. However, not all statutory changes have had the desired effect. For instance, New York State has implemented a juvenile offender law requiring that juveniles accused of violent offenses be tried in criminal court as a get-tough-on-crime measure; evaluations found that many youths ended up receiving lighter sentences than they would have in the family court.[97]

Probably the best-known effort to reform sentencing in the juvenile court is the state of Washington's Juvenile Justice Reform Act of 1977. This act created a mandatory sentencing policy requiring juveniles ages eight to seventeen who are adjudicated delinquent to be confined to an institution for a minimum time.[98] The intent of the act was to make juveniles accountable for criminal behavior and to provide for punishment commensurate with the age, crime, and prior history of the offender. Washington's approach is based on the principle of *proportionality*. How much time a youth must spend in confinement is established by the Juvenile Dispositions Standards Commission, based on the three stated criteria. The introduction of such mandatory sentencing procedures reduces disparity in the length of sentences, according to advocates of a get-tough juvenile justice system.

Blended Sentences State sentencing trends indicate that punishment and accountability, in addition to rehabilitation, have become equally important in juvenile justice policy. As a result, many states have created blended sentencing structures for cases involving serious offenders. Blended sentencing allows the imposition of juvenile and adult sanctions for juvenile offenders adjudicated in juvenile court or convicted in criminal court. In other words, this expanded sentencing authority allows criminal and juvenile courts to impose either a juvenile or an adult sentence, or both, in cases involving juvenile offenders. When both sentences are imposed simultaneously, the court suspends the adult sanction. If the youth follows the conditions of the juvenile sentence and commits no further violation, the adult sentence is revoked. Blended sentences of one type or another exist in twenty-six states.[99]

The Death Penalty for Juveniles

On March 1, 2005, the U.S. Supreme Court, in the case of *Roper v. Simmons*, put an end to the practice of the death penalty for juveniles in the United States. At issue was the minimum age that juveniles who were under the age of eighteen when they committed their crimes could be eligible for the death penalty.[100] At the time, sixteen- and seventeen-year-olds were eligible for the death penalty, and twenty-one states permitted the death penalty for juveniles,[101] with a total of seventy-two juvenile offenders on death row.[102] In a 5-4 decision, the Court ruled that the juvenile death penalty was in violation of the Eighth Amendment's ban on cruel and unusual punishment.[103]

The execution of minor children has not been uncommon in our nation's history; at least 366 juvenile offenders have been executed since 1642.[104] This represented about 2 percent of the total of more than eighteen thousand executions carried out since colonial times. Between the reinstatement of the death penalty in 1976 and the last execution of a juvenile in 2003, twenty-two juvenile offenders had been executed in seven states. Texas accounted for thirteen of these twenty-two executions. All twenty-two of the executed juvenile offenders were male, twenty-one committed their crimes at age seventeen, and just over half (thirteen of them) were minorities.[105]

Past Legal Issues In *Thompson v. Oklahoma* (1988), the U.S. Supreme Court prohibited the execution of persons *under age sixteen*, but left open the age at which execution would be legally appropriate.[106] They then answered this question in two 1989 cases, *Wilkins v. Missouri* and *Stanford v. Kentucky*, in which they ruled that states were free to impose the death penalty for murderers who committed their crimes after they reached age sixteen or seventeen.[107] According to the majority opinion, society at that time had not formed a consensus that the execution of such minors constitutes cruel and unusual punishment.

Those who oppose the death penalty for children find that it has little deterrent effect on youngsters who are impulsive and do not have a realistic view of the

final order
Order that ends litigation between two parties by determining all their rights and disposing of all the issues.

appellate process
Allows the juvenile an opportunity to have the case brought before a reviewing court after it has been heard in juvenile or family court.

writ of habeas corpus
Judicial order requesting that a person detaining another produce the body of the prisoner and give reasons for his or her capture and detention.

destructiveness of their misdeeds or their consequences. Victor Streib, the leading critic of the death penalty for children, argues that such a practice is cruel and unusual punishment for four primary reasons: the condemnation of children makes no measurable contribution to the legitimate goals of punishment; condemning any minor to death violates contemporary standards of decency; the capacity of the young for change, growth, and rehabilitation makes the death penalty particularly harsh and inappropriate; and both legislative attitudes and public opinion reject juvenile executions.[108] Those who oppose the death penalty for children also refer to a growing body of research that shows that the brain continues to develop through the late teen years, in addition to important mental functions, such as planning, judgment, and emotional control.[109] Opposition to the juvenile death penalty is also backed-up by declining public support in the United States (at least for the execution of juveniles) and world opinion.[110] Supporters of the death penalty hold that, regardless of their age, people can form criminal intent and therefore should be responsible for their actions. If the death penalty is legal for adults, they assert, then it can also be used for children who commit serious crimes. ✔ Checkpoints

The Child's Right to Appeal

Regardless of the sentence imposed, juveniles may want to appeal the decision made by the juvenile court judge. Juvenile court statutes normally restrict appeals to cases where the juvenile seeks review of a **final order**, one that ends the litigation between two parties by determining all their rights and disposing of all the issues.[111] The **appellate process** gives the juvenile the opportunity to have the case brought before a reviewing court after it has been heard in the juvenile or family court. Today, the law does not recognize a federal constitutional right of appeal. In other words, the U.S. Constitution does not require any state to furnish an appeal to a juvenile charged and found to be delinquent in a juvenile or family court. Consequently, appellate review of a juvenile case is a matter of statutory right in each jurisdiction. However, the majority of states do provide juveniles with some method of statutory appeal.

The appeal process was not always part of the juvenile law system. In 1965, few states extended the right of appeal to juveniles.[112] Even in the *Gault* case in 1967, the U.S. Supreme Court refused to review the Arizona juvenile code, which provided no appellate review in juvenile matters. It further rejected the right of a juvenile to a transcript of the original trial record.[113] Today, however, most jurisdictions that provide a child with some form of appeal also provide for counsel and for securing a record and transcript, which are crucial to the success of any appeal.

Because juvenile appellate review is defined by individual statutes, each jurisdiction determines for itself what method of review will be used. There are two basic methods of appeal: the direct appeal and the collateral attack.

The *direct appeal* normally involves an appellate court review to determine whether, based on the evidence presented at the trial, the rulings of law and the judgment of the court were correct. The second major area of review involves the collateral attack of a case. The term *collateral* implies a secondary or indirect method of attacking a final judgment. Instead of appealing the juvenile trial because of errors, prejudice, or lack of evidence, *collateral review* uses extraordinary legal writs to challenge the lower-court position. One such procedural device is the writ of habeas corpus. Known as the *Great Writ*, the **writ of habeas corpus** refers to a procedure for determining the validity of a person's custody. In the context of the juvenile court, it is used to challenge the custody of a child in detention or in an institution. This writ is often the method by which the Supreme Court exercises its discretionary authority to hear cases involving constitutional issues. Even though there is no constitutional right to appeal a juvenile case and each jurisdiction provides for appeals differently, juveniles have a far greater opportunity for appellate review today than in years past.

Confidentiality in Juvenile Proceedings

confidentiality
Restricting information in juvenile court proceedings in the interest of protecting the privacy of the juvenile.

Along with the rights of juveniles at adjudication and disposition, the issue of **confidentiality** in juvenile proceedings has also received attention in recent years. The debate on confidentiality in the juvenile court deals with two areas: open versus closed hearings, and privacy of juvenile records. Confidentiality has become moot in some respects, because many legislatures have broadened access to juvenile records.

Open Versus Closed Hearings Generally, juvenile trials are closed to the public and the press, and the names of the offenders are kept secret. The U.S. Supreme Court has ruled on the issue of privacy in three important decisions. In *Davis v. Alaska*, the Court concluded that any injury resulting from the disclosure of a juvenile's record is outweighed by the right to completely cross-examine an adverse witness.[114] The *Davis* case involved an effort to obtain testimony from a juvenile probationer who was a witness in a criminal trial. After the prosecutor was granted a court order preventing the defense from making any reference to the juvenile's record, the Supreme Court reversed the state court, claiming that a juvenile's interest in confidentiality was secondary to the constitutional right to confront adverse witnesses.

The decisions in two subsequent cases, *Oklahoma Publishing Co. v. District Court* and *Smith v. Daily Mail Publishing Co.*, sought to balance juvenile privacy with freedom of the press. In the *Oklahoma* case, the Supreme Court ruled that a state court was not allowed to prohibit the publication of information obtained in an open juvenile proceeding.[115] The case involved an eleven-year-old boy suspected of homicide, who appeared at a detention hearing where photographs were taken and published in local newspapers. When the local district court prohibited further disclosure, the publishing company claimed that the court order was a restraint in violation of the First Amendment, and the Supreme Court agreed.

The *Smith* case involved the discovery and publication of the identity of a juvenile suspect in violation of a state statute prohibiting publication. The Supreme Court, however, declared the statute unconstitutional, because it believed the state's interest in protecting the child's identity was not of such a magnitude as to justify the use of such a statute.[116] Therefore, if newspapers lawfully obtain pictures or names of juveniles, they may publish them. Based on these decisions, it appears that the Supreme Court favors the constitutional rights of the press over the right to privacy of the juvenile offender.

Privacy of Juvenile Records For most of the twentieth century, juvenile records were kept confidential.[117] Today, however, the record itself, or information contained in it, can be opened by court order in many jurisdictions on the basis of statutory exception. The following groups can ordinarily gain access to juvenile records: law enforcement personnel, the child's attorney, parents or guardians, military personnel, and public agencies such as schools, court-related organizations, and correctional institutions.

Today, most states recognize the importance of juvenile records in sentencing. Many first-time adult offenders committed numerous crimes as juveniles, and evidence of these crimes may not be available to sentencing for the adult offenses unless states pass statutes allowing access. Knowledge of a defendant's juvenile record may help prosecutors and judges determine appropriate sentencing for offenders ages eighteen to twenty-four, the age group most likely to be involved in violent crime.

According to experts such as Ira Schwartz, the need for confidentiality to protect juveniles is far less than the need to open up the courts to public scrutiny.[118] The problem of maintaining confidentiality of juvenile records will become more acute in the future as electronic information storage makes these records both more durable and more accessible.

In conclusion, virtually every state provides prosecutors and judges with access to the juvenile records of adult offenders. There is great diversity, however, regarding provisions for the collection and retention of juvenile records.[119]

SUMMARY

- Prosecutors, judges, and defense attorneys are the key players in the juvenile court. The juvenile prosecutor is the attorney responsible for bringing the state's case against the accused juvenile. The juvenile judge must ensure that the children and families who come before the court receive the proper help. Defense attorneys representing children in the juvenile court play an active part in virtually all stages of the proceedings.

- Many decisions about what happens to a child may occur prior to adjudication. Key issues include detention, intake, diversion, pretrial release, plea bargaining, and waiver. Because the juvenile justice system is not able to try every child accused of a crime or a status offense due to personnel limitations, diversion programs seem to hold greater hope for the control of delinquency. As a result, such subsystems as statutory intake proceedings, plea bargaining, and other informal adjustments are essential ingredients in the administration of the juvenile justice system.

- Each year, thousands of youths are transferred to adult courts because of the seriousness of their crimes. This process, known as *waiver*, is an effort to remove serious offenders from the juvenile process and into the more punitive adult system. Most juvenile experts oppose waiver because it clashes with the rehabilitative ideal. Supporters argue that its increased use can help get violent juvenile offenders off the street, and they point to studies that show that, for the most part, transfer is reserved for the most serious cases and the most serious juvenile offenders.

- Most jurisdictions have a bifurcated juvenile code system that separates the adjudication hearing from the dispositional hearing. Juveniles alleged to be delinquent have virtually all the rights given a criminal defendant at trial—except possibly the right to a trial by jury. In addition, juvenile proceedings are generally closed to the public.

- *In re Gault* is the key legal case that set out the basic requirements of due process that must be satisfied in juvenile court proceedings. In *Roper v. Simmons*, the U.S. Supreme Court ruled that the death penalty for juveniles is prohibited, because it constitutes cruel and unusual punishment.

- The major categories of dispositional choice in juvenile cases are community release, out-of-home placements, fines or restitution, community service, and institutionalization. Although the traditional notion of rehabilitation and treatment as the proper goals for disposition is being questioned, many juvenile codes do require that the court consider the *least restrictive alternative*.

- Many state statutes require that juvenile hearings be closed and that the privacy of juvenile records be maintained to protect the child from public scrutiny and to provide a greater opportunity for rehabilitation. This approach may be inconsistent with the public's interest in taking a closer look at the juvenile justice system.

KEY TERMS

juvenile defense attorney, p. 307
guardian *ad litem*, p. 308
public defender, p. 308
juvenile prosecutor, p. 309
juvenile court judge, p. 310
shelter care, p. 312
bail, p. 314
preventive detention, p. 315

intake, p. 315
diversion, p. 316
widening the net, p. 317
complaint, p. 318
plea bargaining, p. 318
transfer process, p. 320
due process, p. 326
least detrimental alternative, p. 330

indeterminate sentence, p. 330
determinate sentence, p. 330
mandatory sentences, p. 330
final order, p. 332
appellate process, p. 332
writ of habeas corpus, p. 332
confidentiality, p. 333

QUESTIONS FOR DISCUSSION

1. Discuss and identify the major participants in the juvenile adjudication process. What are each person's role and responsibilities in the course of a juvenile trial?

2. The criminal justice system in the United States is based on the adversarial process. Does the same principle apply in the juvenile justice system?

3. Children have certain constitutional rights at adjudication, such as the right to an attorney and the right to confront and cross-examine witnesses. But they do not have the right to a trial by jury. Should juvenile offenders have a constitutional right to a jury trial? Should each state make that determination? Discuss the legal decision that addresses this issue.

4. What is the point of obtaining a predisposition report in the juvenile court? Is it of any value in cases where the child is released to the community? Does it have a significant value in serious juvenile crime cases?

5. The standard of proof in juvenile adjudication is to show that the child is guilty beyond a reasonable doubt. Explain the meaning of this standard of proof in the U.S. judicial system.

6. Should states adopt get-tough sentences in juvenile justice or adhere to the individualized treatment model?

7. What are blended sentences?

8. Do you agree with the Supreme Court's 2005 ruling that prohibits the death penalty for juvenile offenders?

APPLYING WHAT YOU HAVE LEARNED

As an experienced family court judge, you are often faced with difficult decisions, but few are more difficult than the case of John M., arrested at age fourteen for robbery and rape. His victim, a young neighborhood girl, was badly injured in the attack and needed extensive hospitalization; she is now in counseling. Even though the charges are serious, because of his age, John can still be subject to the jurisdiction of the juvenile division of the state family court. However, the prosecutor has filed a petition to waive jurisdiction to the adult court. Under existing state law, a hearing must be held to determine whether there is sufficient evidence that John cannot be successfully treated in the juvenile justice system and therefore warrants transfer to the adult system; the final decision on the matter is yours alone.

At the waiver hearing, you discover that John is the oldest of three siblings living in a single-parent home. He has had no contact with his father for more than ten years. His psychological evaluation showed hostility, anger toward females, and great feelings of frustration. His intelligence is below average, and his behavioral and academic records are poor. In addition, he seems to be involved with a local youth gang, although he denies any formal association with them. This is his first formal involvement with the juvenile court. Previous contact was limited to an informal complaint for disorderly conduct at age thirteen, which was dismissed by the court's intake department. During the hearing, John verbalizes what you interpret to be superficial remorse for his offenses.

To the prosecutor, John seems to be a youth with poor controls who is likely to commit future crimes. The defense attorney argues that there are effective treatment opportunities within the juvenile justice system that can meet John's needs. Her views are supported by an evaluation of the case conducted by the court's probation staff, which concludes that the case can be dealt with in the confines of juvenile corrections.

If the case remains in the juvenile court, John can be kept in custody in a juvenile facility until age eighteen; if transferred to felony court, he could be sentenced to up to twenty years in a maximum-security prison. As judge, you recognize the seriousness of the crimes committed by John and realize that it is very difficult to predict or assess his future behavior and potential dangerousness.

- Would you authorize a waiver to adult court or keep the case in the juvenile justice system?
- Can fourteen-year-olds truly understand the seriousness of their behavior?
- Should a juvenile court judge consider the victim in making a disposition decision?

DOING RESEARCH ON THE WEB

Before you answer these questions, research waivers to adult court by using "juveniles and waivers" in a key word search on InfoTrac College Edition. To get further information on this topic, go to www.thomsonedu.com/criminaljustice/siegel on the Web to access the sites of the American Bar Association Juvenile Justice Center; OJJDP Statistical Briefing Book; American Youth Policy Forum on Juvenile Justice; the Juvenile Justice Division of the Child Welfare League of America; and the National Council on Crime and Delinquency and Children's Research Center.

Juvenile Corrections: Probation, Community Treatment, and Institutionalization

© Joel Gordon

CHAPTER OBJECTIVES

After reading this chapter you should:

1. Be able to distinguish between community treatment and institutional treatment for juvenile offenders.

2. Be familiar with the disposition of probation, including how it is administered and by whom and recent trends in its use compared with other dispositions.

3. Be aware of new approaches for providing probation services to juvenile offenders and comment on their effectiveness in reducing recidivism.

4. Understand key historical developments of secure juvenile corrections in this country, including the principle of *least restrictive alternative*.

5. Be familiar with recent trends in the use of juvenile institutions for juvenile offenders and how their use differs across states.

6. Understand key issues facing the institutionalized juvenile offender.

7. Be able to identify the various juvenile correctional treatment approaches that are in use today and comment on their effectiveness in reducing recidivism.

8. Know the nature of aftercare for juvenile offenders and comment on recent innovations in juvenile aftercare and reentry programs.

Karen Gilligan, age sixteen, was the oldest of four children living with their parents in a small rural community. Her mother worked two jobs, her father was unemployed, and both parents drank heavily. Karen's high school attendance was sporadic. She started to experiment with alcohol and vandalized local businesses. After being arrested in a stolen car on several occasions, Karen was referred to juvenile court and was put on community supervision and probation. An initial assessment was provided by her probation officer, and formal dispositional recommendations were made to the court. She would remain at home on house arrest for sixty days, attend school regularly and maintain at least a C average, follow an alcohol and drug assessment program, and participate in weekly family therapy with her parents. Karen was also ordered to cooperate with the juvenile restitution program, pay her restitution in full within six months, and participate in the Community Adolescent Intensive Supervision Program, as arranged by her probation officer.

Not used to being accountable to anyone, Karen struggled initially with all the new rules and expectations. She missed some of her initial appointments and skipped some classes at school. Karen's probation officer began making unannounced visits to her at school, trying to help her understand the consequences of her behavior. Through the intensive supervision program, Karen was required to meet everyday after school at a local community center where she received tutoring, group counseling with other offenders, and the guidance of many counselors. The group sessions focused on changing negative thinking, alternatives to aggression, and avoiding criminal behavior, gang involvement, and drugs and alcohol.

It was clear to her probation officer that Karen possessed many strengths and positive attributes. She enjoyed dancing and singing, and even liked school at times. The team of professionals encouraged her to focus on these qualities. With help, Karen began to understand her destructive behavior and seek alternatives for turning her life around. She spoke with her probation officer about creating life goals and making plans for achieving them.

In addition to Karen's individual counseling, her family participated in weekly family therapy to talk about their issues and to address how to best support the children. Initially, the sessions were very challenging and stressful for the entire family. They blamed each other for their difficulties, and Karen seemed to be the target of much of the anger expressed by her parents. The therapist worked with them to reduce the conflict and help them establish goals for their therapy that could improve their family life.

During the many months of intensive supervision, treatment, and family therapy, Karen was able to stop her delinquent behavior, pay her restitution, attend school regularly, and improve her communication with her parents. Through therapy, Karen's mother also acknowledged that she needed some assistance with her drinking and entered treatment. Karen's probation officer provided the court with regular monthly progress reports showing significant improvement in her behavior and lifestyle choices. Karen has proven her success and remains living with her parents and siblings. She plans to attend a local college after graduation to prepare for a career in the medical field.

community treatment
Using nonsecure and non-institutional residences, counseling services, victim restitution programs, and other community services to treat juveniles in their own communities.

There are many choices of correctional treatments available for juveniles, all of which can be subdivided into two major categories: community treatment and institutional treatment. **Community treatment** refers to efforts to provide care, protection, and treatment for juveniles in need. These efforts include probation; treatment services (such as individual and group counseling); restitution; and other programs. The term *community treatment* also refers to the use of privately maintained residences, such as foster homes, small-group homes, and boarding schools, which are located in the community. Nonresidential programs, where youths remain in their own homes, but are required to receive counseling, vocational training, and other services, also fall under the rubric of community treatment.

Institutional treatment facilities are correctional centers operated by federal, state, and county governments; these facilities restrict the movement of residents through staff monitoring, locked exits, and interior fence controls. There are several types of institutional facilities in juvenile corrections, including reception centers that screen juveniles and assign them to an appropriate facility; specialized facilities that provide specific types of care, such as drug treatment; training schools or reformatories for youths needing a long-term secure setting; ranch or forestry camps that provide long-term residential care; and boot camps, which seek to rehabilitate youth through the application of rigorous physical training.

Choosing the proper mode of juvenile corrections can be difficult. Some experts believe that any hope for rehabilitating juvenile offenders and resolving the problems of juvenile crime lies in community treatment programs. Such programs are smaller than secure facilities for juveniles, operate in a community setting, and offer creative approaches to treating the offender. In contrast, institutionalizing young offenders may do more harm than good. It exposes them to prison-like conditions and to more experienced delinquents without giving them the benefit of constructive treatment programs.

Those who favor secure treatment are concerned about the threat that violent young offenders present to the community and believe that a stay in a juvenile institution may have a long-term deterrent effect. They point to the findings of Charles Murray and Louis B. Cox, who uncovered what they call a **suppression effect**, a reduction in the number of arrests per year following release from a secure facility, which is not achieved when juveniles are placed in less punitive programs.[1] Murray and Cox concluded that the justice system must choose the outcome it wants to achieve: prevention of delinquency, or the care and protection of needy youths. If the former is a proper goal, institutionalization or the threat of institutionalization is desirable. Not surprisingly, secure treatment is still being used extensively, and the populations of these facilities continue to grow as state legislators pass more stringent and punitive sentencing packages aimed at repeat juvenile offenders.

suppression effect
A reduction of the number of arrests per year for youths who have been incarcerated or otherwise punished.

JUVENILE PROBATION

probation
Nonpunitive, legal disposition of juveniles emphasizing community treatment in which the juvenile is closely supervised by an officer of the court and must adhere to a strict set of rules to avoid incarceration.

Probation and other forms of community treatment generally refer to nonpunitive legal dispositions for delinquent youths, emphasizing treatment without incarceration. Probation is the primary form of community treatment used by the juvenile justice system. A juvenile who is on probation is maintained in the community under the supervision of an officer of the court. Probation also encompasses a set of rules and conditions that must be met for the offender to remain in the community. Juveniles on probation may be placed in a wide variety of community-based treatment programs that provide services ranging from group counseling to drug treatment.

Community treatment is based on the idea that the juvenile offender is not a danger to the community and has a better chance of being rehabilitated in the community. It provides offenders with the opportunity to be supervised by trained personnel who can help them reestablish forms of acceptable behavior in a community setting. When applied correctly, community treatment maximizes the liberty of the individual and at the same time vindicates the authority of the law and protects the public; promotes rehabilitation by maintaining normal community contacts; avoids the negative effects of confinement, which often severely complicate the reintegration of the offender into the community; and greatly reduces the financial cost to the public.[2]

Historical Development

Although the major developments in community treatment have occurred in the twentieth century, its roots go back much further. In England, specialized procedures for dealing with youthful offenders were recorded as early as 1820, when the magistrates of the Warwickshire quarter sessions (periodic court hearings held in a county, or shire, of England) adopted the practice of sentencing youthful criminals to prison terms of one day, then releasing them conditionally under the supervision of their parents or masters.[3]

In the United States, juvenile probation developed as part of the wave of social reform characterizing the latter half of the nineteenth century. Massachusetts took the first step. Under an act passed in 1869, an agent of the state board of charities was authorized to appear in criminal trials involving juveniles, to find them suitable homes, and to visit them periodically. These services were soon broadened, so that by 1890, probation had become a mandatory part of the court structure.[4]

Probation was a cornerstone in the development of the juvenile court system. In fact, in some states, supporters of the juvenile court movement viewed probation as the first step toward achieving the benefits that the new court was intended to provide. The rapid spread of juvenile courts during the first decades of the twentieth century encouraged the further development of probation. The two were closely related, and to a large degree, both sprang from the conviction that the young could be rehabilitated and that the public was responsible for protecting them.

Expanding Community Treatment

By the mid-1960s, juvenile probation had become a complex institution that touched the lives of an enormous number of children. To many experts, institutionalization of even the most serious delinquent youths was a mistake. Reformers believed that confinement in a high-security institution could not solve the problems that brought a youth into a delinquent way of life, and that the experience could actually help amplify delinquency once the youth returned to the community.[5] Surveys indicating that 30 percent to 40 percent of adult prison inmates had prior experience with the juvenile court, and that many had been institutionalized as youths, gave little support to the argument that an institutional experience can be beneficial or reduce recidivism.[6]

Contemporary Juvenile Probation

Traditional probation is still the backbone of community-based corrections. As Figure 14.1 shows, almost 385,400 juveniles were placed on formal probation in 2002, which amounts to 62 percent of all juvenile dispositions. The use of probation has increased

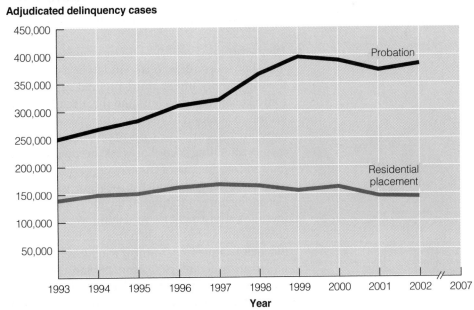

Figure 14.1   **Probation and Correctional Population Trends**

Note: There was a substantial increase in the number of cases in which adjudicated juveniles were placed on probation between 1993 and 2002.

Source: Howard N. Snyder and Melissa Sickmund, *Juvenile Offenders and Victims: 2006 National Report* (Pittsburgh, PA: National Center for Juvenile Justice, 2006), pp. 174–175. Available at: www.ojjdp.ncjrs.org/ojstatbb/nr2006/downloads/chapter6.pdf (accessed January 10, 2007).

Probation is the most widely used legal disposition for juvenile offenders. It emphasizes community treatment without incarceration and requires juveniles to be closely supervised and adhere to a number of conditions. Here, Amy Lee Bowman, 17, appears at her arraignment in New Bedford District Court in Massachusetts, on a charge of conspiracy to commit murder at her high school. Bowman pleaded not guilty and was released on the condition that she have daily contact with a probation officer.

significantly since 1993, when 224,500 adjudicated youths were placed on probation.[7] These figures show that, regardless of public sentiment, probation continues to be a popular dispositional alternative for judges. Here are the arguments in favor of probation:

1. For youths who can be supervised in the community, probation represents an appropriate disposition.

2. Probation allows the court to tailor a program to each juvenile offender, including those involved in interpersonal offenses. Recent research, however, raises questions about the adequacy of the present system to attend to the specific needs of female youths on probation.[8]

3. The justice system continues to have confidence in rehabilitation while accommodating demands for legal controls and public protection, even when caseloads may include many more serious offenders than in the past.

4. Probation is often the disposition of choice, particularly for status offenders.[9]

The Nature of Probation In most jurisdictions, probation is a direct judicial order that allows a youth who is found to be a delinquent or status offender to remain in the community under court-ordered supervision. A probation sentence implies a contract between the court and the juvenile. The court promises to hold a period of institutionalization in abeyance; the juvenile promises to adhere to a set of rules mandated by the court. The rules of probation vary, but they typically involve conditions such as attending school or work, keeping regular hours, remaining in the jurisdiction, and staying out of trouble.

In the juvenile court, probation is often ordered for an indefinite period. Depending on the statutes of the jurisdiction, the seriousness of the offense, and the juvenile's adjustment on probation, youths can remain under supervision until the court no longer has jurisdiction over them (that is, when they reach the age of majority). State statutes determine if a judge can specify how long a juvenile may be placed under an order of probation. In most jurisdictions, the status of probation is reviewed regularly to ensure that a juvenile is not kept on probation needlessly. Generally, discretion lies with the probation officer to discharge youths who are adjusting to the treatment plan.

Conditions of Probation Probation conditions are rules mandating that a juvenile on probation behave in a particular way. They can include restitution or reparation, intensive supervision, intensive counseling, participation in a therapeutic program, or participation in an educational or vocational training program. In addition to these specific conditions, state statutes generally allow courts to insist that probationers lead law-abiding lives, maintain a residence in a family setting, refrain from associating with certain types of people, and remain in a particular area unless they have permission to leave.

Although probation conditions vary, they are never supposed to be capricious, cruel, or beyond the capacity of the juvenile to satisfy. Furthermore, conditions of probation should relate to the crime that was committed and to the conduct of the child.

Courts have invalidated probation conditions that were harmful or that violated the juvenile's due process rights. Restricting a child's movement, insisting on a mandatory program of treatment, ordering indefinite terms of probation, and demanding financial reparation where this is impossible are all grounds for appellate court review. For example, it would not be appropriate for a probation order to bar a youth from visiting his girlfriend (unless he had threatened or harmed her) merely because her parents objected to the relationship.[10] However, courts have ruled that it is permissible to bar juveniles from such sources of danger as a "known gang area" in order to protect them from harm.[11]

If a youth violates the conditions of probation—and especially if the juvenile commits another offense—the court can revoke probation. In this case, the contract is terminated and the original commitment order may be enforced. The juvenile court ordinarily handles a decision to revoke probation upon recommendation of the probation officer. Today, as a result of Supreme Court decisions dealing with the rights of adult probationers, a juvenile is normally entitled to legal representation and a hearing when a violation of probation occurs.[12]

LOOKING BACK TO KAREN'S STORY

Do you agree/disagree with the probation officer's recommendations to the court? What would you have done differently? Can you think of additional programs/services that would have been helpful in this situation?

juvenile probation officer
Officer of the court involved in all four stages of the court process—intake, predisposition, postadjudication, and postdisposition—who assists the court and supervises juveniles placed on probation.

social investigation report (also known as predisposition report)
Developed by the juvenile probation officer, this report includes clinical diagnosis of the juvenile and the need for court assistance, relevant environmental and personality factors, and other information to assist the court in developing a treatment plan.

✔ CHECKPOINTS

■ Community treatment refers to efforts to provide care, protection, and treatment for juveniles in need.

■ Institutional treatment facilities restrict the movement of residents through staff monitoring, locked exits, and interior fence controls.

■ Probation is the primary form of community treatment used by the juvenile justice system.

■ First developed in Massachusetts, probation had become a cornerstone of the court structure by 1890.

■ Massachusetts has closed most of its secure juvenile facilities and relies almost entirely on community treatment.

■ Probation is a direct judicial order that allows a youth to remain in the community under court-ordered supervision.

■ Probation conditions are rules mandating that a juvenile on probation behave in a particular way.

■ The juvenile probation officer plays an important role in the justice process, beginning with intake and continuing throughout the period in which a juvenile is under court supervision.

Duties of Juvenile Probation Officers

The **juvenile probation officer** plays an important role in the justice process, beginning with intake and continuing throughout the period in which a juvenile is under court supervision. Probation officers are involved at four stages of the court process. At *intake*, they screen complaints by deciding to adjust the matter, refer the child to an agency for service, or refer the case to the court for judicial action. During the *predisposition* stage, they participate in release or detention decisions. At the *postadjudication* stage, they assist the court in reaching its dispositional decision. During *postdisposition*, they supervise juveniles placed on probation.

At intake, the probation staff has preliminary discussions with the child and the family to determine whether court intervention is necessary or whether the matter can be better resolved by some form of social service. If the child is placed in a detention facility, the probation officer helps the court decide whether the child should continue to be held or be released pending the adjudication and disposition of the case.

The probation officer exercises tremendous influence over the child and the family by developing a **social investigation** or **predisposition report** and submitting it to the court. This report is a clinical diagnosis of the child's problems and the need for court assistance based on an evaluation of social functioning, personality, and environmental issues. The report includes an analysis of the child's feelings about the violations and the child's capacity for change. It also examines the influence of family members, peers, and other environmental influences in producing and possibly resolving the problems. All of this information is brought together in a complex, but meaningful picture of the offender's personality, problems, and environment.

So important is the influence of juvenile probation officers that it has, especially at the disposition phase, prompted some to ask if there may be a disparity in the handling of cases. In one study conducted in a juvenile probation department in a southwestern state, William Reese and his colleagues found some evidence of dispositional disparity

Exhibit 14.1   Duties of the Juvenile Probation Officer

- Provide direct counseling and casework services.
- Interview and collect social service data.
- Make diagnostic recommendations.
- Maintain working relationships with law enforcement agencies.
- Use community resources and services.
- Direct volunteer case aides.

- Write predisposition or social investigation reports.
- Work with families of children under supervision.
- Provide specialized services, such as group therapy.
- Supervise specialized caseloads involving children with special problems.
- Make decisions about revocation of probation and its termination.

LOOKING BACK TO KAREN'S STORY

Initially, Karen struggled with rules and expectations. Her probation officer worked with her to help her accomplish the goals. What types of things could you say to a juvenile who is in this situation? How would you try to motivate a teen in trouble with the law?

conditions of probation
Rules and regulations mandating that a juvenile on probation behave in a particular way.

among juvenile probation officers and that this was best explained by the officer's background characteristics, organizational situations, and attitudes toward delinquency.[13]

Juvenile probation officers also provide the child with supervision and treatment in the community. Treatment plans vary in approach and structure. Some juveniles simply report to the probation officer and follow the **conditions of probation**. In other cases, the probation officer may need to provide extensive counseling to the child and family, or more often, refer them to other social service agencies, such as a drug treatment center. Exhibit 14.1 summarizes the probation officer's role. Performance of such a broad range of functions requires good training. Today, juvenile probation officers have legal or social work backgrounds or special counseling skills. ✔ Checkpoints

PROBATION INNOVATIONS

Community corrections have traditionally emphasized offender rehabilitation. The probation officer has been viewed as a caseworker or counselor whose primary job is to help the offender adjust to society. Offender surveillance and control have seemed more appropriate for law enforcement, jails, and prisons than for community corrections.[14] Since 1980, a more conservative justice system has reoriented toward social control. Although the rehabilitative ideals of probation have not been abandoned, new programs have been developed that add a control dimension to community corrections. In some cases this has involved the use of police officers, working in collaboration with probation officers, to enhance the supervision of juvenile probationers.[15] These programs can be viewed as "probation plus," because they add restrictive penalties and conditions to community-service orders. More punitive than probation, this kind of intermediate sanction can be politically attractive to conservatives while still appealing to liberals as alternatives to incarceration. What are some of these new alternative sanctions? (See Concept Summary 14.1.)

Intensive Supervision

juvenile intensive probation supervision (JIPS)
A true alternative to incarceration that involves almost daily supervision of the juvenile by the probation officer assigned to the case.

Juvenile intensive probation supervision (JIPS) involves treating offenders who would normally have been sent to a secure treatment facility as part of a very small probation caseload that receives almost daily scrutiny.[16] The primary goal of JIPS is *decarceration*; without intensive supervision, youngsters would normally be sent to secure juvenile facilities that are already overcrowded. The second goal is control; high-risk juvenile offenders can be maintained in the community under much closer security than traditional probation efforts can provide. A third goal is maintaining

Community-Based Corrections

Although correctional treatment in the community generally refers to non-punitive legal dispositions, in most cases there are still restrictions designed to protect the public and hold juvenile offenders accountable for their actions.

Type	Main Restrictions
Probation	Regular supervision by a probation officer; youth must adhere to conditions such as attend school or work, stay out of trouble.
Intensive supervision	Almost daily supervision by a probation officer; adhere to similar conditions as regular probation.
House arrest	Remain at home during specified periods; often there is monitoring through random phone calls, visits, or electronic devices.
Restorative justice	Restrictions may be prescribed by community members to help repair harm done to victim.
Balanced probation	Restrictions are tailored to the risk the juvenile offender presents to the community.
Restitution	None.
Residential programs	Placement in a residential, nonsecure facility, such as group home or foster home; adhere to conditions; close monitoring.

community ties and reintegration; offenders can remain in the community and complete their education while avoiding the pains of imprisonment.

Intensive probation programs get mixed reviews. Some jurisdictions find that they are more successful than traditional probation supervision and come at a much cheaper cost than incarceration.[17] However, some studies indicate that the failure rate is high and that younger offenders who commit petty crimes are the

A number of probation innovations have been experimented with to keep juvenile offenders from being sent to secure juvenile facilities. One of these is juvenile intensive supervision, which, in addition to having to follow strict conditions, requires the juvenile to report to a probation officer as often as every day.

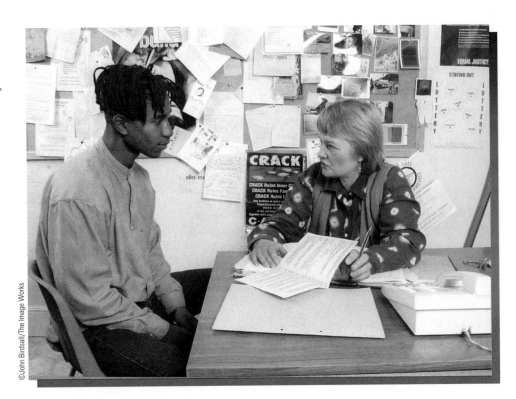

©John Birdsall/The Image Works

most likely to fail when placed in intensive supervision programs.[18] It is not surprising that intensive probation clients fail more often, because, after all, they are more serious offenders who might otherwise have been incarcerated and are now being watched and supervised more closely than probationers. In one experimental study of intensive probation supervision plus a coordinated team approach for high risk juveniles, known as the Los Angeles County Repeat Offender Prevention Program (ROPP), mixed results were found for those who received the program compared to a similar group of youths who received regular probation only: recidivism was reduced in the short-term, but not over the long-term, school performance was increased, and there was no difference in probation technical violations.[19] In another recent California experiment of juvenile intensive probation supervision, no significant differences were observed in recidivism rates among those youths who received intensive probation compared to a similar group of youths who received regular probation.[20]

An innovative experiment in three Mississippi counties examined the differential effects on juvenile justice costs for intensive supervision and monitoring, regular probation, and cognitive behavioral treatment, which involved sessions on problem solving, social skills, negotiation skills, the management of emotion, and values enhancement, to improve the thinking and reasoning ability of juvenile offenders. After one year of the program, the intensive supervision treatment was found to be less cost-effective than the other two treatments, with the cognitive behavioral treatment imposing the fewest costs on the juvenile justice system.[21]

Electronic Monitoring

Another program, which has been used with adult offenders and is finding its way into the juvenile justice system, is **house arrest**, which is often coupled with **electronic monitoring**. This program allows offenders sentenced to probation to remain in the community on condition that they stay at home during specific periods (for example, after school or work, on weekends, and in the evenings). Offenders may be monitored through random phone calls, visits, or in some jurisdictions, electronic devices.

Most systems employ radio transmitters that receive a signal from a device worn by the offender and relay it back to the computer via telephone lines. Probationers are fitted with an unremovable monitoring device that alerts the probation department's computers if they leave their place of confinement.[22]

There is widespread belief that electronic monitoring is effective, with some evaluations showing that recidivism rates are no higher than in traditional programs, costs are lower, and institutional overcrowding is reduced. Some studies also reveal that electronic monitoring seems to work better with some individuals than others: serious felony offenders, substance abusers, repeat offenders, and people serving the longest sentences are the most likely to fail.[23] However, in a recent evidence-based review on the effects of electronic monitoring on recidivism, criminologists Marc Renzema and Evan Mayo-Wilson find that the results do not support the claim that it works at the present time. This conclusion was largely based on there being too few high-quality studies available and a difficulty in isolating the independent effects of programs that combine electronic monitoring with other interventions. The researchers do not call for an end to the use of electronic monitoring, but call for new and better experiments.[24]

house arrest
Offender is required to stay home during specific periods of time; monitoring is done by random phone calls and visits or by electronic devices.

electronic monitoring
Active monitoring systems consist of a radio transmitter worn by the offender that sends a continuous signal to the probation department computer; passive systems employ computer-generated random phone calls that must be answered in a certain period of time from a particular phone.

LOOKING BACK TO KAREN'S STORY

While electronic monitoring was not used, do you think it was a good idea to put Karen on house arrest in her parental home? What problems could have come of this? If Karen had continued to break the law, should she have been removed? When should a juvenile delinquent be removed from her parents' home due to her criminal behavior? What crimes do you think would justify an automatic removal and what would need to be accomplished for the child to return?

Restorative Justice

Restorative justice is a non-punitive strategy for delinquency control that attempts to address the issues that produce conflict between two parties (offender and victim) and, hence, reconcile the parties. Restoration rather than retribution or punishment is at the heart of the restorative justice approach. Seven core values characterize restorative justice:

- Crime is an offense against human relationships.
- Victims and the community are central to justice processes.
- The first priority of justice processes is to assist victims.
- The second priority of justice processes is to restore the community, to the degree possible.
- The offender has a personal responsibility to victims and to the community for crimes committed.
- The offender will develop improved competency and understanding as a result of the restorative justice experience.
- Stakeholders share responsibilities for restorative justice through partnerships for action.[25]

Criminologists Heather Strang and Lawrence Sherman carried out a systematic review and meta-analysis of the effects of restorative justice on juvenile re-offending and victim satisfaction. The review involved two studies from Australia and one from the United States that evaluated the restorative justice practice of face-to-face conferences. (The main reason for the small number of studies is that the authors used only those studies that employed the highest quality evaluation design—randomized controlled experiments—to assess program effects.) The conferences proceeded as follows:

> *Any victims (or their representatives) present have the opportunity to describe the full extent of the harm a crime has caused, offenders are required to listen to the victims and to understand the consequences of their own actions, and all participants are invited to deliberate about what actions the offender could take to repair them. The precondition of such a conference is that the offender does not dispute the fact that he is responsible for the harm caused, and the conference cannot and will not become a trial to determine what happened.[26]*

The review found evidence that this form of restorative justice can be an effective strategy in reducing repeat offending by juveniles who have committed violent crimes. The type of violence includes minor offenses of battery to middle-level offenses of assault and aggravated assault. The review also found that face-to-face conferences can be effective in preventing victims from committing crimes of retaliation against their perpetrators. Perhaps not surprisingly, across all studies, victim satisfaction levels strongly favored restorative justice compared to traditional juvenile justice proceedings.[27] Successful results have also been demonstrated in other restorative justice programs for juvenile offenders.[28]

Balanced Probation

balanced probation
Programs that integrate community protection, accountability of the juvenile offender, competency, and individualized attention to the juvenile offender; based on the principle that juvenile offenders must accept responsibility for their behavior.

Some jurisdictions have also turned to a **balanced probation** approach in an effort to enhance the success of probation.[29] Balanced probation systems integrate community protection, the accountability of the juvenile offender, and individualized attention to the offender. These programs are based on the view that juveniles are responsible for their actions and have an obligation to society whenever they commit an offense. The probation officer establishes a program tailored to the offender while helping the offender accept responsibility for his or her actions. The balanced approach is promising, because it specifies a distinctive role for the juvenile probation system.[30]

One promising program that adheres to a balanced probation approach is the California 8% Solution, which is run by the Orange County Probation Department. The "8 percent" refers to the percentage of juvenile offenders who are responsible for the majority of crime: in the case of Orange County, 8 percent of first-time offenders were responsible for 55 percent of repeat cases over a three-year period. This 8 percent problem has become the 8 percent solution thanks to the probation department initiating a comprehensive, multiagency program targeting this group of offenders.[31]

Once the probation officer identifies an offender for the program—the 8% Early Intervention Program—the youth is referred to the Youth and Family Resource Center. Here the youth's needs are assessed and an appropriate treatment plan is developed. Some of the services provided to youths include these:

- An outside school for students in junior and senior high school
- Transportation to and from home
- Counseling for drug and alcohol abuse
- Employment preparation and job placement services
- At-home, intensive family counseling for families[32]

Restitution

Victim restitution is another widely used method of community treatment. In most jurisdictions, restitution is part of a probationary sentence and is administered by the county probation staff. In many jurisdictions, independent restitution programs have been set up by local governments; in others, restitution is administered by a private nonprofit organization.[33]

Restitution can take several forms. A juvenile can reimburse the victim of the crime or donate money to a charity or public cause; this is referred to as **monetary restitution**. In other instances, a juvenile may be required to provide some service directly to the victim (**victim service restitution**) or to assist a community organization (**community service restitution**).

Requiring youths to reimburse the victims of their crimes is the most widely used method of restitution in the United States. Less widely used, but more common in Europe, is restitution to a charity. In the past few years numerous programs have been set up to enable juvenile offenders to provide a service to the victim or participate in community programs—for example, working in schools for mentally challenged children. In some cases, juveniles are required to contribute both money and community service. Other programs emphasize employment.[34]

Restitution programs can be employed at various stages of the juvenile justice process. They can be part of a diversion program prior to conviction, a method of informal adjustment at intake, or a condition of probation. Restitution has a number of advantages: it provides alternative sentencing options; it offers monetary compensation or service to crime victims; it allows the juvenile the opportunity to compensate the victim and take a step toward becoming a productive member of society; it helps relieve overcrowded juvenile courts, probation caseloads, and detention facilities. Finally, like other alternatives to incarceration, restitution has the potential for allowing vast savings in the operation of the juvenile justice system. Monetary restitution programs in particular may improve the public's attitude toward juvenile justice by offering equity to the victims of crime and ensuring that offenders take responsibility for their actions.

The use of restitution is increasing. In 1977, there were fewer than fifteen formal restitution programs around the United States. By 1985, formal programs existed in four hundred jurisdictions, and thirty-five states had statutory provisions that gave courts the authority to order juvenile restitution.[35] Today, all fifty states, as well as the District of Columbia, have statutory restitution programs.

monetary restitution
Offenders compensate crime victims for out-of-pocket losses caused by the crime, including property damage, lost wages, and medical expenses.

victim service restitution
Offenders provide some service directly to the crime victim.

community service restitution
Offenders assist some worthwhile community organization for a period of time.

Does Restitution Work? How successful is restitution as a treatment alternative? Most evaluations have shown that it is reasonably effective, and should be expanded.[36] In an analysis of restitution programs across the country, Peter Schneider and Matthew Finkelstein found that between 73 percent and 74 percent of youths who received restitution as a condition of probation successfully completed their orders. The researchers also found that juvenile restitution programs that reported a reduction in recidivism rates were the ones that had high successful completion rates.[37]

Anne Schneider conducted a thorough analysis of restitution programs in four different states and found that participants had lower recidivism rates than youths in control groups (regular probation caseloads).[38] Although Schneider's data indicate that restitution may reduce recidivism, the number of youths who had subsequent involvement in the justice system still seemed high. In short, there is evidence that most restitution orders are successfully completed and that youths who make restitution are less likely to become recidivists; however, the number of repeat offenses committed by juveniles who made restitution suggests that, by itself, restitution is not the answer to the delinquency problem.

Another criticism of restitution programs is that they foster involuntary servitude. Indigent clients may be unfairly punished when they are unable to make restitution payments or face probation violations. To avoid such bias, probation officers should first determine why payment has stopped and then suggest appropriate action, rather than simply treating nonpayment as a matter of law enforcement.

Residential Community Treatment

Many experts believe that institutionalization of even the most serious delinquent youths is a mistake. Confinement in a high-security institution usually cannot solve the problems that brought a youth into a delinquent way of life, and the experience may actually amplify delinquency once the youth returns to the community. Many agree that warehousing juveniles without attention to their treatment needs does little to prevent their return to criminal behavior. Research has shown that the most effective secure-corrections programs provide individualized services for a small number of participants. Large training schools have not proved to be effective.[39] This realization has produced a wide variety of residential community-treatment programs to service youths who need a more secure environment than can be provided by probation services, but who do not require a placement in a state-run juvenile correctional facility.

How are community corrections implemented? In some cases, youths are placed under probation supervision, and the probation department maintains a residential treatment facility. Placement can also be made to the department of social services or juvenile corrections with the direction that the youth be placed in a residential facility. **Residential programs** are generally divided into four major categories: group homes, including boarding schools and apartment-type settings; foster homes; family group homes; and rural programs.

Group homes are nonsecure residences that provide counseling, education, job training, and family living. They are staffed by a small number of qualified persons, and generally house twelve to fifteen youngsters. The institutional quality of the environment is minimized, and the kids are given the opportunity to build a close relationship with the staff. They reside in the home, attend public schools, and participate in community activities.

Foster care programs involve one or two juveniles who live with a family—usually a husband and wife who serve as surrogate parents. The juveniles enter into a close relationship with the foster parents and receive the attention and care they did not receive in their own homes. The quality of the foster home experience depends on the foster parents. Foster care for adjudicated juvenile offenders has not been extensive in the United States. Welfare departments generally handle foster placements, and

residential programs
Residential, nonsecure facilities, such as a group home, foster home, family group home, or rural home where the juvenile can be closely monitored and develop close relationships with staff members.

group homes
Nonsecured, structured residences that provide counseling, education, job training, and family living.

foster care programs
Placement with families who provide attention, guidance, and care.

funding of this treatment option has been a problem for the juvenile justice system. However, foster home services have expanded as a community treatment approach.

One example of a successful foster care program is the multidimensional treatment foster care (MTFC) program, developed by social scientists at the Oregon Social Learning Center. Designed for the most serious and chronic male young offenders, this program combines individual therapy, such as skill building in problem solving for the youths and family therapy for the biological or adoptive parents. The foster care families receive training by program staff, so that they can provide the young people with close supervision, fair and consistent limits and consequences, and a supportive relationship with an adult.[40] Foster care families also receive close supervision and are consulted regularly on the progress of the youth by program staff. An experiment of MTFC found that one year after the completion of the program, participating youths were significantly less likely to be arrested than a control group.[41]

Family group homes combine elements of foster care and group home placements. Juveniles are placed in a group home that is run by a family rather than by a professional staff. Troubled youths have an opportunity to learn to get along in a family-like situation, and at the same time the state avoids the start-up costs and neighborhood opposition often associated with establishing a public institution.

Rural programs include forestry camps, ranches, and farms that provide recreational activities or work for juveniles. Programs usually handle from thirty to fifty youths. Such programs have the disadvantage of isolating juveniles from the community, but reintegration can be achieved if a youth's stay is short and if family and friends are allowed to visit.

Most residential programs use group counseling as the main treatment tool. Although group facilities have been used less often than institutional placements, there is a trend toward developing community-based residential facilities; see the What Does This Mean to Me? feature on page 350.

As jurisdictions continue to face ever-increasing costs for juvenile justice services, community-based programs will play an important role in providing rehabilitation of juvenile offenders and ensuring public safety. ✔ **Checkpoints**

CHECKPOINTS

- There are new programs being developed that are "probation plus," because they add restrictive penalties and conditions to community service orders.

- Juvenile intensive probation supervision (JIPS) involves treatment as part of a very small probation caseload that receives almost daily scrutiny.

- Electronic monitoring combined with house arrest is being implemented in juvenile correction policy.

- Balanced probation systems integrate community protection, accountability of the juvenile offender, and individualized attention to the offender.

- Monetary restitution allows a juvenile to reimburse the victim of the crime or donate money to a charity or public cause.

- Community service restitution allows juveniles to engage in public works as part of their disposition.

- Residential community programs are usually divided into four major categories: group homes, foster homes, family group homes, and rural programs.

SECURE CORRECTIONS

When the court determines that community treatment can't meet the special needs of a delinquent youth, a judge may refer the juvenile to a secure treatment program. Today, correctional institutions operated by federal, state, and county governments are generally classified as secure or open facilities. *Secure facilities* restrict the movement of residents through staff monitoring, locked exits, and interior fence controls. *Open institutions* generally do not restrict the movement of the residents and allow much greater freedom of access to the facility.[42] In the following sections, we analyze the state of secure juvenile corrections, beginning with some historical background. This is followed by a discussion of life in institutions, the juvenile client, treatment issues, legal rights, and aftercare and reentry programs.

family group homes
A combination of foster care and group home; they are run by a single family rather than by professional staff.

rural programs
Specific recreational and work opportunities provided for juveniles in a rural setting, such as a forestry camp, a farm, or a ranch.

reform schools
Institutions in which educational and psychological services are used in an effort to improve the conduct of juveniles who are forcibly detained.

History of Juvenile Institutions

Until the early 1800s, juvenile offenders, as well as neglected and dependent children, were confined in adult prisons. The inhumane conditions in these institutions were among the factors that led social reformers to create a separate children's court system in 1899.[43] Early juvenile institutions were industrial schools modeled after adult prisons, but designed to protect children from the evil influences in adult facilities. The first was the New York House of Refuge, established in 1825. Not long after, states began to establish **reform schools** for juveniles. Massachusetts was the first, opening the Lyman School for Boys in Westborough in 1846. New York opened the State Agricultural and Industrial School in 1849, and Maine opened the Maine Boys' Training

Young boys watched by their master are shown working in the Carpentry and Joinery Department of the New York State Industrial School in Rochester, New York, 1886. The boys were required to work six and a half hours a day.

From the Collection of the Rochester Public Library/Local History Division

cottage system
Housing in a compound of small cottages, each of which accommodates twenty to forty children.

School in 1853. By 1900, thirty-six states had reform schools.[44] Although it is difficult to determine the exact population of these institutions, by 1880 there were approximately eleven thousand youths in correctional facilities, a number that more than quadrupled by 1980.[45] Early reform schools were generally punitive in nature and were based on the concept of rehabilitation (or reform) through hard work and discipline.

In the second half of the nineteenth century, emphasis shifted to the **cottage system**. Juvenile offenders were housed in compounds of cottages, each of which could accommodate twenty to forty children. A set of "parents" ran each cottage, creating a homelike atmosphere. This setup was believed to be more conducive to rehabilitation.

The first cottage system was established in Massachusetts in 1855, the second in Ohio in 1858.[46] The system was held to be a great improvement over reform schools. The belief was that, by moving away from punishment and toward rehabilitation, not only could offenders be rehabilitated but also crime among unruly children could be prevented.[47]

Twentieth-Century Developments The early twentieth century witnessed important changes in juvenile corrections. Because of the influence of World War I, reform schools began to adopt a militaristic style. Living units became barracks, cottage groups became companies, house fathers became captains, and superintendents became majors or colonels. Military-style uniforms were standard wear.

In addition, the establishment of the first juvenile court in 1899 reflected the expanded use of confinement for delinquent children. As the number of juvenile offenders increased, the forms of juvenile institutions varied to include forestry camps, ranches, and vocational schools. Beginning in the 1930s, camps modeled after the camps run by the Civilian Conservation Corps became a part of the juvenile correctional system. These camps centered on conservation activities and work as a means of rehabilitation.

Los Angeles County was the first to use camps during this period.[48] Southern California was experiencing problems with transient youths who came to California with no money and then got into trouble with the law. Rather than filling up the jails, the county placed these offenders in conservation camps, paid them low wages, and released them when they had earned enough money to return home. The camps proved more rehabilitative than training schools, and by 1935 California had

Community Treatment for Juvenile Offenders: Not in My Backyard

How would you react to the announcement that a community treatment center for juvenile offenders is to open in your neighborhood? You are aware of studies that show that juvenile offenders can be treated in the community as effectively as in an institution. Yet the public sometimes has a negative impression of community treatment, especially when it is offered to juvenile offenders who pose a threat to society, and it is not uncommon for neighborhood groups to oppose the location of corrections programs in their community.

- Is this concern warranted? Explain.
- What arguments might you make to allay the public's concerns and win support for community-based programs?

established a network of forestry camps for delinquent boys. The idea soon spread to other states.[49]

Also during the 1930s, the U.S. Children's Bureau sought to reform juvenile corrections. The bureau conducted studies to determine the effectiveness of the training school concept. Little was learned from these programs, because of limited funding and bureaucratic ineptitude, and the Children's Bureau failed to achieve any significant change. But such efforts recognized the important role of positive institutional care.[50]

Another innovation came in the 1940s with passage of the American Law Institute's Model Youth Correction Authority Act. This act emphasized reception/classification centers. California was the first to try out this idea, opening the Northern Reception Center and Clinic in Sacramento in 1947. Today, there are many such centers scattered around the United States.

Since the 1970s, a major change in institutionalization has been the effort to remove status offenders from institutions housing juvenile delinquents. This includes removing status offenders from detention centers and removing all juveniles from contact with adults in jails. This *decarceration* policy mandates that courts use the **least restrictive alternative** in providing services for status offenders. A noncriminal youth should not be put in a secure facility if a community-based program is available. In addition, the federal government prohibits states from placing status offenders in separate facilities that are similar in form and function to those used for delinquent offenders. This is to prevent states from merely shifting their institutionalized population around so that one training school houses all delinquents, and another houses all status offenders, but actual conditions remain the same.

Throughout the 1980s and into the 1990s, admissions to juvenile correctional facilities grew substantially.[51] Capacities of juvenile facilities also increased, but not enough to avoid overcrowding. Training schools became seriously overcrowded in some states, causing private facilities to play an increased role in juvenile corrections. Reliance on incarceration became costly to states: inflation-controlled juvenile corrections expenditures for public facilities grew to more than $2 billion in 1995, an increase of 20 percent from 1982.[52] A 1994 report issued by the Office of Juvenile Justice and Delinquency Prevention (OJJDP) said that crowding, inadequate health care, lack of security, and poor control of suicidal behavior was widespread in juvenile corrections facilities. Despite new construction, crowding persisted in more than half the states.[53]

least restrictive alternative
A program with the least restrictive or secure setting that will benefit the child.

JUVENILE INSTITUTIONS TODAY: PUBLIC AND PRIVATE

Most juveniles are housed in public institutions that are administered by state agencies: child and youth services, health and social services, corrections, or child welfare.[54] In some states these institutions fall under a centralized system that covers adults as well as juveniles. Recently, a number of states have removed juvenile corrections from an existing adult corrections department or mental health agency. However, the majority of states still place responsibility for the administration of juvenile corrections within social service departments.

Supplementing publicly funded institutions are private facilities that are maintained and operated by private agencies funded or chartered by state authorities. Most of today's private institutions are relatively small facilities holding fewer than thirty youths. Many have a specific mission or focus (for example, treating females who display serious emotional problems). Although about 80 percent of public institutions can be characterized as secure, only 20 percent of private institutions are high-security facilities.

Population Trends

Whereas most delinquents are held in public facilities, most status offenders are held in private facilities. At last count (2003), there were slightly less than 97,000 juvenile offenders being held in public (69 percent) and private (31 percent) facilities in the United States. Between 1991 and 1999, the number of juveniles held in custody increased 41 percent, followed by a 10 percent drop from 1999 to 2003. Over this full period of time (1991 to 2003), the number of juveniles held in custody increased 27 percent.[55] The juvenile custody rate varies widely among states: Wyoming makes the greatest use of custodial treatment, incarcerating 606 delinquents in juvenile facilities per 100,000 juveniles in the population, whereas Vermont and Hawaii have the lowest juvenile custody rates (72 and 97, respectively). Although not a state, the District of Columbia actually has the highest juvenile custody rate in the nation, at 625 per 100,000 juveniles. This is more than twice the national average (see Table 14.1).[56] Some states rely heavily on privately run facilities, whereas others place many youths in out-of-state facilities.

Table 14.1 — State Comparison of Numbers and Rates of Juvenile Offenders in Custody, 2003

State of offense	Number	Rate	State of offense	Number	Rate
U.S. total	96,655	307	Rhode Island	342	295
			South Dakota	522	564
Upper age 17			Tennessee	1,434	226
Alabama	1,794	351	Utah	954	307
Alaska	336	370	Vermont	51	72
Arizona	1,890	284	Virginia	2,376	289
Arkansas	675	217	Washington	1,656	236
California	16,782	392	West Virginia	498	269
Colorado	1,776	344	Wyoming	357	606
Delaware	333	364			
Dist. of Columbia	285	625	**Upper age 16**		
Florida	8,208	452	Georgia	2,451	273
Hawaii	129	97	Illinois	2,715	212
Idaho	489	287	Louisiana	1,821	387
Indiana	3,045	415	Massachusetts	1,302	216
Iowa	975	299	Michigan	2,706	257
Kansas	1,071	336	Missouri	1,413	246
Kentucky	837	185	New Hampshire	198	150
Maine	222	153	South Carolina	1,443	346
Maryland	1,167	181	Texas	7,662	318
Minnesota	1,527	259	Wisconsin	1,524	274
Mississippi	528	152			
Montana	261	245	**Upper age 15**		
Nebraska	672	331	Connecticut	627	210
Nevada	921	362	New York	4,308	272
New Jersey	1,941	199	North Carolina	1,203	169
New Mexico	606	258			
North Dakota	246	347			
Ohio	4,176	318			
Oklahoma	1,059	265			
Oregon	1,275	323			
Pennsylvania	4,341	317			

Note: The rate is the number of juvenile offenders in residential placement in 2003 per 100,000 juveniles ages ten through the upper age of original juvenile court jurisdiction in each state. The U.S. totals include 1,398 juvenile offenders in private facilities for whom state of offense was not reported and 124 juvenile offenders in tribal facilities.

Source: Howard H. Snyder and Melissa Sickmund, *Juvenile Offenders and Victims: 2006 National Report* (Pittsburgh, PA: National Center for Juvenile Justice, 2006), p. 201.

Although the number of institutionalized youths appears to have stabilized in the last few years, the data may reveal only the tip of the iceberg. The data do not include many minors who are incarcerated after they are waived to adult courts or who have been tried as adults because of exclusion statutes. Most states place underage juveniles convicted of adult charges in youth centers until they reach the age of majority, whereupon they are transferred to an adult facility. In addition, there may be a hidden, or subterranean, correctional system that places wayward youths in private mental hospitals and substance-abuse clinics for behaviors that might otherwise land them in a correctional facility or community-based program.[57] These data suggest that the number of institutionalized children may be far greater than reported in the official statistics.[58] Studies also show that large numbers of youths are improperly incarcerated because of a lack of appropriate facilities. A nationwide survey carried out by congressional investigators as part of the House Committee on Government Reform found that fifteen thousand children with psychiatric disorders who were awaiting mental health services were improperly incarcerated in secure juvenile detention facilities in 2003.[59] In New Jersey, investigations into the state's child welfare system found that large numbers of teenage foster children were being held in secure juvenile detention facilities. Other states resort to similar practices, citing a lack of appropriate non-correctional facilities.[60]

Physical Conditions

The physical plans of juvenile institutions vary in size and quality. Many of the older training schools still place all offenders in a single building, regardless of the offense. More acceptable structures include a reception unit with an infirmary, a security unit, and dormitory units or cottages. Planners have concluded that the most effective design for training schools is to have facilities located around a community square. The facilities generally include a dining hall and kitchen area, a storage warehouse, academic and vocational training rooms, a library, an auditorium, a gymnasium, an administration building, and other basic facilities.

The individual living areas also vary, depending on the type of facility and the progressiveness of its administration. Most traditional training school conditions were appalling. Today, however, most institutions provide toilet and bath facilities, beds, desks, lamps, and tables. New facilities usually try to provide a single room for each individual. However, the Juvenile Residential Facility Census, which collects information about the facilities in which juvenile offenders are held, found that 36 percent of the 2,964 facilities that reported information were overcrowded—that is, they had more residents than available standard beds.[61] Some states, like Massachusetts and Rhode Island, report that upwards of 70 percent of all of their facilities for juvenile offenders are overcrowded.[62]

The physical conditions of secure facilities for juveniles have come a long way from the training schools of the turn of the twentieth century. However, many administrators realize that more modernization is necessary to comply with national standards for juvenile institutions.[63] Although some improvements have been made, there are still enormous problems to overcome.

THE INSTITUTIONALIZED JUVENILE

The typical resident of a juvenile facility is a seventeen-year-old European American male incarcerated for an average stay of 3.5 months in a public facility or 4 months in a private facility. Private facilities tend to house younger youths, whereas public institutions provide custodial care for older ones, including a small percentage between eighteen and twenty-one years of age. Most incarcerated youths are person, property, or drug offenders.[64]

Mental health needs are particularly acute among institutionalized juveniles. Research suggests that as much as 65 percent of youths in the juvenile justice system suffer from mental health problems, and a large proportion of these youths enter the system without previously having been diagnosed or receiving treatment.[65] Incarcerated youths suffering from mental health problems may find it harder to adjust to their new environment, which may in turn lead to acting out behaviors, disciplinary problems, and problems in participating in treatment programs. All of these problems increase the risk of recidivism upon release to the community.[66] Even with a diagnosis treatment services can be scarce in the juvenile justice system. One study found that only one out of four (23 percent) juvenile offenders diagnosed with a mental disorder received any treatment.[67] Contributing to the problem is that there is little information on what treatment works best for these juveniles.[68] Columbia University's Center for the Promotion of Mental Health in Juvenile Justice is leading a national effort to improve this state of affairs, as well as the need for improved mental health assessments at intake.

www To learn more about Columbia University's Center for the Promotion of Mental Health in Juvenile Justice, go on the Internet and check out www. thomsonedu.com/criminaljustice/siegel.

Minority youths are incarcerated at a rate two to four times that of European American youths. The difference is greatest for African American youths, with a custody rate of 754 per 100,000 juveniles; for European American youths the rate is 190.[69] In a number of states, such as New Jersey, South Dakota, and Wisconsin, the difference in custody rates between African American and European American youths is considerably greater (Table 14.2). Research has found that this overrepresentation is not a result of differentials in arrest rates, but often stems from disparity at early stages of case processing.[70] Of equal importance, minorities are more likely to be confined in secure public facilities rather than in open, private facilities that might provide more costly and effective treatment,[71] and among minority groups African American youths are more likely to receive more punitive treatment—throughout the juvenile justice system—compared with others.[72]

Minority youths accused of delinquent acts are less likely than European American youths to be diverted from the court system into informal sanctions and are more likely to receive sentences involving incarceration. Today, more than six in ten juveniles in custody belong to racial or ethnic minorities, and seven in ten youths held in custody for a violent crime are minorities.[73] Racial disparity in juvenile disposition is an ongoing problem that demands immediate public scrutiny.[74] In response, many jurisdictions have initiated studies of racial disproportion in their juvenile justice systems, along with federal requirements to reduce disproportionate minority confinement (DMC), as contained in the Juvenile Justice and Delinquency Prevention Act of 2002.[75] The most recent federal government report on state compliance to reduce DMC demonstrates that some progress has been made but that many challenges remain, including the basic need to identify factors that contribute to DMC (at least eighteen states have yet to initiate this process), incomplete and inconsistent data systems, and the need for ongoing evaluation of focused interventions and system-wide efforts to reduce DMC.[76]

For more than two decades, shocking exposés, sometimes resulting from investigations by the U.S. Department of Justice's civil rights division, continue to focus public attention on the problems of juvenile corrections.[77] Today, more so than in years past, some critics believe public scrutiny has improved conditions in training schools. There is greater professionalism among the staff, and staff brutality seems to have diminished. Status offenders and delinquents are, for the most part, held in separate facilities. Confinement length is shorter, and rehabilitative programming has increased. However, there are significant differences in the experiences of male and female delinquents in institutions.

Male Inmates

Males make up the great bulk of institutionalized youth, accounting for six out of every seven juvenile offenders in residential placement,[78] and most programs are directed toward their needs. In many ways their experiences mirror those of adult

Table 14.2 State Comparison of Custody Rates Between European American and African American Juvenile Offenders, 2003

State of offense	European American	African American	State of offense	European American	African American
U.S. Average	**190**	**754**	New Hampshire	144	579
Alabama	235	586	New Jersey	51	795
Alaska	177	339	New Mexico	153	823
Arizona	223	579	New York	138	712
Arkansas	142	468	North Carolina	106	332
California	217	1,246	North Dakota	235	1,384
Colorado	268	1,150	Ohio	207	916
Connecticut	105	669	Oklahoma	196	673
Delaware	128	1,029	Oregon	291	1,075
Dist. of Columbia	347	683	Pennsylvania	139	1,207
Florida	355	973	Rhode Island	192	1,425
Georgia	142	500	South Carolina	201	567
Hawaii	62	199	South Dakota	310	3,199
Idaho	250	725	Tennessee	143	507
Illinois	120	589	Texas	194	771
Indiana	316	1,188	Utah	258	951
Iowa	242	1,337	Vermont	71	0
Kansas	213	1,320	Virginia	143	715
Kentucky	133	653	Washington	200	770
Louisiana	202	663	West Virginia	229	953
Maine	149	182	Wisconsin	143	1,389
Maryland	98	319	Wyoming	507	3,035
Massachusetts	111	811			
Michigan	169	602			
Minnesota	156	1,149			
Mississippi	75	246			
Missouri	159	690			
Montana	188	418			
Nebraska	214	1,529			
Nevada	289	958			

Note: The custody rate is the number of juvenile offenders in residential placement on October 22, 2003, per 100,000 juveniles age ten through the upper age of original juvenile court jurisdiction in each state. The U.S. total includes 1,398 juvenile offenders in private facilities for whom state of offense was not reported and 124 juvenile offenders in tribal facilities.

Source: Howard N. Snyder and Melissa Sickmund, *Juvenile Offenders and Victims: 2006 National Report* (Pittsburgh, PA: National Center for Juvenile Justice, 2006), p. 213.

offenders. In an important paper, Clement Bartollas and his associates identified an inmate value system that they believed was common in juvenile institutions:

"Exploit whomever you can."
"Don't play up to staff."
"Don't rat on your peers."
"Don't give in to others."[79]

In addition to these general rules, the researchers found that there were separate norms for African American inmates ("exploit Whites"; "no forcing sex on Blacks"; "defend your brother") and for European American ("don't trust anyone"; "everybody for himself").

Other research efforts confirm the notion that residents do in fact form cohesive groups and adhere to an informal inmate culture.[80] The more serious the youth's

www To read about life in a secure Canadian facility, go to the website maintained by the **Prince George Youth Custody Center** in British Columbia, which provides a range of programs to allow youths to make maximal constructive use of their time while in custody. Go to www.thomsonedu.com/criminaljustice/siegel.

record and the more secure the institution, the greater the adherence to the inmate social code. Male delinquents are more likely to form allegiances with members of their own racial group and attempt to exploit those outside the group. They also scheme to manipulate staff and take advantage of weaker peers. However, in institutions that are treatment-oriented, and where staff-inmate relationships are more intimate, residents are less likely to adhere to a negativistic inmate code.

Female Inmates

Between 1991 and 2003, the number of female juvenile offenders in custody increased by more than half (52 percent), from 9,600 to 14,590. Over this same period of time, the proportion of female juvenile offenders of the total number of offenders in custody increased 15 percent, from 13 percent in 1991 to 15 percent in 2003.[81]

The growing involvement of female youths in criminal behavior and the influence of the feminist movement have drawn more attention to the female juvenile offender. This attention has revealed a double standard of justice. For example, girls are more likely than boys to be incarcerated for status offenses. Institutions for girls are generally more restrictive than those for boys, and they have fewer educational and vocational programs and fewer services. Institutions for girls also do a less-than-adequate job of rehabilitation. It has been suggested that this double standard operates, because of a male-dominated justice system that seeks to "protect" young girls from their own sexuality.[82]

Over the years, the number of females held in public institutions has declined, albeit less so in the past few years. This represents the continuation of a long-term trend to remove girls, many of whom are nonserious offenders, from closed institutions and place them in private or community-based facilities. In 2003, 36 percent of all female youths in residential placement were held in private facilities; for male youths it was 31 percent.[83]

The same double standard that brings a girl into an institution continues to exist once she is in custody. Females tend to be incarcerated for longer terms than males. In addition, institutional programs for girls tend to be oriented toward reinforcing traditional roles for women. Most of these programs also fail to take account of the different needs of African American and European American females, as in the case of coping with past abuse.[84] How well these programs rehabilitate girls is questionable.

Many of the characteristics of juvenile female offenders are similar to those of their male counterparts, including poor social skills and low self-esteem. Other problems are

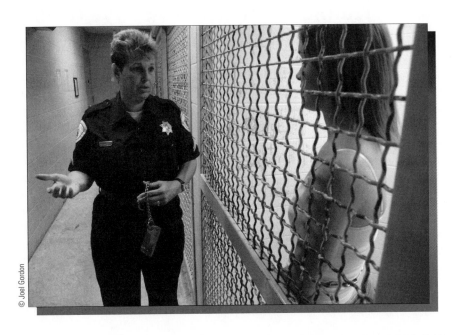

A female juvenile inmate speaks with a correction officer in a juvenile facility in Florida. Although the trend has been to remove female juvenile inmates from closed institutions and place them in private or community-based facilities, female inmates continue to face numerous obstacles, including being placed in institutions far from family members and receiving inadequate educational and recreational services.

© Joel Gordon

more specific to the female juvenile offender (sexual abuse issues, victimization histories, lack of placement options).[85] In addition, there have been numerous allegations of emotional and sexual abuse by correctional workers, who either exploit vulnerable young women or callously disregard their emotional needs. An interview survey conducted by the National Council on Crime and Delinquency uncovered numerous incidents of abuse, and bitter resentment by the young women over the brutality of their custodial treatment.[86]

Although there are more coed institutions for juveniles than in the past, most girls remain incarcerated in single-sex institutions that are isolated in rural areas and rarely offer adequate rehabilitative services. Several factors account for the different treatment of girls. One is sexual stereotyping by administrators, who believe that teaching girls "appropriate" sex roles will help them function effectively in society. These beliefs are often held by the staff as well, many of whom have highly sexist ideas of what is appropriate behavior for adolescent girls. Another factor that accounts for the different treatment of girls is that staff members often are not adequately trained to understand and address the unique needs of this population.[87] Girls' institutions tend to be smaller than boys' institutions and lack the money to offer as many programs and services as the larger male institutions.[88]

It appears that although society is more concerned about protecting girls who act out, it is less concerned about rehabilitating them because the crimes they commit are not serious. These attitudes translate into fewer staff, older facilities, and poorer educational and recreational programs than those found in boys' institutions.[89] To help address these and other problems facing female juveniles in institutions, the American Bar Association and the National Bar Association recommend a number of important changes, including these:

- Identify, promote, and support effective gender-specific, developmentally sound, culturally sensitive practices with girls.
- Promote an integrated system of care for at-risk and delinquent girls and their families based on their competencies and needs.
- Assess the adequacy of services to meet the needs of at-risk or delinquent girls and address gaps in service.
- Collect and review state and local practices to assess the gender impact of decision making and system structure.[90] ✔ Checkpoints

✔ CHECKPOINTS

■ Massachusetts opened the first juvenile correctional facility, the Lyman School for Boys in Westborough, in 1846.

■ Since the 1970s, a major change in institutionalization has been the effort to remove status offenders from institutions housing juvenile delinquents.

■ Throughout the 1980s and into the 1990s, admissions to juvenile correctional facilities grew substantially.

■ Today, there are slightly less than ninety-seven thousand juveniles being held in public and private facilities.

■ There may be a hidden juvenile correctional system that places wayward youths in private mental hospitals and substance abuse clinics.

■ The typical resident of a juvenile facility is a seventeen-year-old European American male incarcerated for an average stay of 3.5 months in a public facility or four months in a private facility.

■ Minority youths are incarcerated at a rate two to four times that of European Americans.

■ Males make up the bulk of institutionalized youth, and most programs are directed toward their needs.

■ Female inmates are believed to be the target of sexual abuse and are denied the same treatment options as males.

CORRECTIONAL TREATMENT FOR JUVENILES

Nearly all juvenile institutions implement some form of treatment program: counseling, vocational and educational training, recreational programs, and religious counseling. In addition, most institutions provide medical programs as well as occasional legal service programs. Generally, the larger the institution, the greater the number of programs and services offered.

The purpose of these programs is to rehabilitate youths to become well-adjusted individuals and send them back into the community to be productive citizens. Despite good intentions, however, the goal of rehabilitation is sometimes not attained due in large part to poor implementation of the programs.[91] A significant number of juvenile offenders commit more crimes after release[92] and some experts believe that correctional treatment has little effect on recidivism.[93] However, a large scale empirical review of institutional treatment programs found that serious juvenile offenders who receive treatment have recidivism rates about 10 percent lower than similar untreated juveniles, and that the best programs reduced recidivism by as much as 40 percent.[94] The most successful of these institutional treatment programs provide training to improve interpersonal skills and family-style teaching to improve behavioral skills (see Exhibit 14.2).

Exhibit 14.2 — Effectiveness of Institutional Treatment Programs for Serious Juvenile Offenders

Positive Effects, Consistent Evidence

- Interpersonal skills
- Family style group home

Positive Effects, Less Consistent Evidence

- Behavioral programs
- Community residential
- Multiple services

Mixed but Generally Positive Effects, Inconsistent Evidence

- Individual counseling
- Guided group
- Group counseling

Weak or No Effects, Inconsistent Evidence

- Employment related
- Drug abstinence
- Wilderness/challenge

Weak or No Effects, Consistent Evidence

- Milieu therapy

Source: Mark W. Lipsey and David B. Wilson, "Effective Intervention for Serious Juvenile Offenders: A Synthesis of Research," in Rolf Loeber and David P. Farrington, eds., *Serious and Violent Juvenile Offenders: Risk Factors and Successful Interventions* (Thousand Oaks, CA: Sage, 1998), p. 332, Table 13.8.

What are the drawbacks to correctional rehabilitation? One of the most common problems is the lack of well-trained staff members. Budgetary limitations are a primary concern. It costs a substantial amount of money per year to keep a child in an institution, which explains why institutions generally do not employ large professional staffs.

However, some correctional programs are highly cost-efficient, producing monetary benefits that outweigh the costs of running the program.[95] In a recent study with the provocative title, "Are Violent Delinquents Worth Treating?," researchers Michael Caldwell, Michael Vitacco, and Gregory Van Rybroek found that an institutional treatment program for violent juvenile offenders that was effective in reducing recidivism rates produced cost savings to taxpayers that were seven times greater than what it cost to run the program. These findings can be particularly influential on policy makers and government funding agencies.[96]

The most glaring problem with treatment programs is that they are not administered as intended. Although the official goals of many may be treatment and rehabilitation, the actual programs may center around security and punishment. The next sections describe some treatment approaches that aim to rehabilitate offenders.

Individual Treatment Techniques: Past and Present

In general, effective individual treatment programs are built around combinations of psychotherapy, reality therapy, and behavior modification. **Individual counseling** is one of the most common treatment approaches, and virtually all juvenile institutions use it to some extent. This is not surprising, because psychological problems such as depression are prevalent in juvenile institutions.[97] Individual counseling does not attempt to change a youth's personality. Rather, it attempts to help individuals understand and solve their current adjustment problems. Some institutions employ counselors who are not professionally qualified, which subjects offenders to a superficial form of counseling.

Professional counseling may be based on **psychotherapy**. Psychotherapy requires extensive analysis of the individual's childhood experiences. A skilled therapist attempts to help the individual make a more positive adjustment to society by altering

individual counseling
Counselors help juveniles understand and solve their current adjustment problems.

psychotherapy
Highly structured counseling in which a therapist helps a juvenile solve conflicts and make a more positive adjustment to society.

reality therapy
A form of counseling that emphasizes current behavior and requires
the individual to accept responsibility for all of his or her actions.

behavior modification
A technique for shaping desired
behaviors through a system of
rewards and punishments.

To learn more about reality therapy,
go to **William Glasser's** website
by going to www.thomsonedu.com/
criminaljustice/siegel on the Web.

group therapy
Counseling several individuals
together in a group session.

If you want to learn more about
**improving the conditions of
children in custody**, go to www.
thomsonedu.com/criminaljustice/
siegel on the Web.

guided group interaction (GGI)
Through group interactions a
delinquent can acknowledge and
solve personal problems with support from other group members.

positive peer culture (PPC)
Counseling program in which peer
leaders encourage other group
members to modify their behavior
and peers help reinforce acceptable
behaviors.

milieu therapy
All aspects of the environment are
part of the treatment, and meaningful change, increased growth,
and satisfactory adjustment are
encouraged.

negative behavior patterns learned in childhood. Another frequently used treatment is **reality therapy**.[98] This approach, developed by William Glasser during the 1970s, emphasizes current, rather than past, behavior by stressing that offenders are com-pletely responsible for their own actions. The object of reality therapy is to make individuals more responsible people. This is accomplished by giving them confidence through developing their ability to follow a set of expectations as closely as possible. The success of reality therapy depends greatly on the warmth and concern of the counselor.

Behavior modification is used in many institutions.[99] It is based on the theory that all behavior is learned and that current behavior can be shaped through rewards and punishments. This type of program is easily used in an institutional setting that offers privileges as rewards for behaviors, such as work, study, or the development of skills. It is reasonably effective, especially when a contract is formed with the youth to modify certain behaviors. When youths are aware of what is expected of them, they plan their actions to meet these expectations and then experience the anticipated consequences. In this way, youths can be motivated to change.

Group Treatment Techniques

Group therapy is more economical than individual therapy, because one therapist can counsel more than one individual at a time. Also, the support of the group is often valuable to individuals in the group, and individuals derive hope from other members of the group who have survived similar experiences. Another advantage of group therapy is that a group can often solve a problem more effectively than an individual.

One disadvantage of group therapy is that it provides little individual attention. Everyone is different, and some group members may need more individualized treat-ment. Also, there is the concern that by providing therapy in a group format, those who are more chronically involved in delinquency may negatively affect those who are marginally involved.[100]

Guided group interaction (GGI) is a fairly common method of group treatment. It is based on the theory that, through group interactions a delinquent can acknowl-edge and solve personal problems. A leader facilitates interaction, and a group culture develops. Individual members can be mutually supportive and reinforce acceptable behavior. In the 1980s, a version of GGI called **positive peer culture (PPC)** became popular. These programs used groups in which peer leaders encourage other youths to conform to conventional behaviors. The rationale is that if negative peer influence can encourage youths to engage in delinquent behavior, then positive peer influence can help them conform.[101] Though research results are inconclusive, there is evidence that PPC may facilitate communication ability for incarcerated youth.[102]

Another common group treatment approach, **milieu therapy**, seeks to make all aspects of the inmates' environment part of their treatment and to minimize differences between custodial staff and treatment personnel. Milieu therapy, based on psychoana-lytic theory, was developed during the late 1940s and early 1950s by Bruno Bettel-heim.[103] This therapy attempted to create a conscience, or superego, in delinquent youths by getting them to depend on their therapists to a great extent and then threat-ening them with loss of the caring relationship if they failed to control their behavior. Today, milieu therapy more often makes use of peer interactions and attempts to create an environment that encourages meaningful change, growth, and satisfactory adjust-ment. This is often accomplished through peer pressure to conform to group norms.

Educational, Vocational, and Recreational Programs

Because educational programs are an important part of social development and have therapeutic as well as instructional value, they are an essential part of most treatment programs. What takes place through education is related to all other

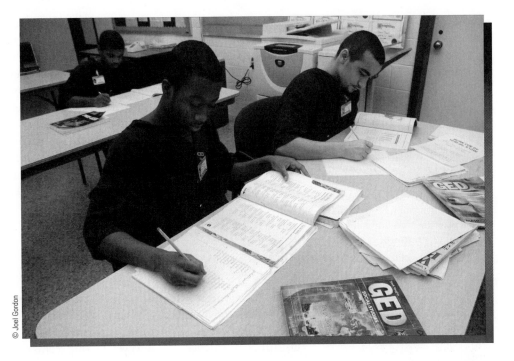

Most juvenile facilities have ongoing vocational and educational programs. Here, juvenile inmates complete assignments as part of a GED program at a juvenile facility.

aspects of the institutional program—work activities, cottage life, recreation, and clinical services.

Educational programs are probably the best-staffed programs in training schools, but even at their best, most of them are inadequate. Educational programs contend with myriad problems. Many of the youths coming into these institutions are mentally challenged, have learning disabilities, and are far behind their grade levels in basic academics. Most have become frustrated with the educational experience, dislike school, and become bored with any type of educational program. Their sense of frustration often leads to disciplinary problems.

Ideally, institutions should allow the inmates to attend a school in the community or offer programs that lead to a high school diploma or GED certificate. Unfortunately, not all institutions offer these types of programs. Secure institutions, because of their large size, are more likely than group homes or day treatment centers to offer programs, such as remedial reading, physical education, and tutoring. Some offer computer-based learning and programmed learning modules.

Vocational training has long been used as a treatment technique for juveniles. Early institutions were even referred to as "industrial schools." Today, vocational programs in institutions include auto repair, printing, woodworking, computer training, food service, cosmetology, secretarial training, and data processing. A common drawback of vocational training programs is sex-typing. The recent trend has been to allow equal access to all programs offered in institutions that house girls and boys. Sex-typing is more difficult to avoid in single-sex institutions, because funds aren't usually available for all types of training.

To see how **positive peer culture** can be used effectively, go to www.thomsonedu.com/criminaljustice/siegel on the Web.

Wilderness Programs

wilderness probation
Programs involving outdoor expeditions that provide opportunities for juveniles to confront the difficulties of their lives while achieving positive personal satisfaction.

Wilderness probation programs involve troubled youths in outdoor activities as a mechanism to improve their social skills, self-concept, and self-control. Typically, wilderness programs maintain exposure to a wholesome environment; where the concepts of education and the work ethic are taught and embodied in adult role models, troubled youth can regain a measure of self-worth.

A number of wilderness programs for juvenile offenders have been evaluated for their effects on recidivism. In a detailed review of the effects of wilderness programs—those emphasizing physical activity over more therapeutic goals—on recidivism, Doris

MacKenzie concludes that these programs do not work.[104] Although some of the programs show success, such as the Spectrum Wilderness Program in Illinois,[105] others had negative effects; that is, the group that received the program had higher arrest rates than the comparison group that did not. Taken together, the programs suffered from poor implementation, weak evaluation designs or problems with too few subjects or large dropout rates, and failure to adhere to principles of successful rehabilitation, such as targeting high-risk youths and lasting for a moderate period of time.[106] However, wilderness programs that include a therapeutic component have been shown to be effective in reducing juvenile offending. Sandra Wilson and Mark Lipsey found that, on average, these programs produced a 20 percent reduction in recidivism rates, with the most successful ones offering more intensive physical activity or therapeutic services.[107]

Juvenile Boot Camps

Correctional **boot camps** were designed with the idea of combining the get-tough elements of adult programs with education, substance abuse treatment, and social skills training. In theory, a successful boot camp program should rehabilitate juvenile offenders, reduce the number of beds needed in secure institutional programs, and thus reduce the overall cost of care. The Alabama boot camp program for youthful offenders estimated savings of $1 million annually when compared with traditional institutional sentences.[108] However, no one seems convinced that participants in these programs have lower recidivism rates than those who serve normal sentences. Ronald Corbett and Joan Petersilia do note, however, that boot camp participants seem to be less antisocial upon returning to society.[109]

However, the bottom line for juvenile boot camps, like other correctional sanctions, is whether or not they reduce recidivism. A recent **meta-analysis** of the effects of juvenile boot camps on recidivism found this to be an ineffective correctional approach to reducing it; from the seventeen different program samples, the control groups had, on average, lower recidivism rates than the treatment groups (boot camps).[110] Interestingly, when compared with the effects of twenty-six program samples of boot camps for adults, the juvenile boot camps had a higher average recidivism rate, although the difference was not significant.[111]

Why do boot camps for juveniles fail to reduce future offending? The main reason is that they provide little in the way of therapy or treatment to correct offending behavior.[112] Experts have also suggested that part of the reason for not finding differences in recidivism between boot camps and other correctional alternatives (the control groups) may be due to juveniles in the control groups receiving enhanced treatment, whereas juveniles in the boot camps are spending more time on physical activities.[113]

The ineffectiveness of boot camps to reduce reoffending in the community by juvenile offenders (and adult offenders) appears to have resulted in this approach falling into disfavor with some correctional administrators. At the height of its popularity in the mid-1990s, more than seventy-five state-run boot camps were in operation in more than thirty states across the country; today, fifty-one remain.[114] Despite this, boot camps appear to still have a place among the array of sentencing options, if for no other reason than to appease the public with the promise of tougher sentences and lower costs.[115] If boot camps are to become a viable alternative for juvenile corrections, they must be seen not as a panacea that provides an easy solution to the problems of delinquency, but merely part of a comprehensive approach to juvenile care that is appropriate to a select group of adolescents.[116] ✔ Checkpoints

THE LEGAL RIGHT TO TREATMENT

The primary goal of placing juveniles in institutions is to help them re-enter the community successfully. Therefore, lawyers claim that children in state-run institutions have a legal right to treatment.

boot camps
Programs that combine get-tough elements with education, substance abuse treatment, and social skills training.

meta-analysis
An analysis technique that synthesizes results across many programs over time.

 To read more about **boot camps**, go to www.thomsonedu.com/criminaljustice/siegel on the Web.

✔ CHECKPOINTS

■ Nearly all juvenile institutions implement some form of treatment program.

■ Reality therapy, a commonly used individual approach, emphasizes current, rather than past, behavior by stressing that offenders are completely responsible for their own actions.

■ Group therapy is more commonly used with kids than individual therapy.

■ Guided group interaction and positive peer culture are popular group treatment techniques.

■ Many but not all institutions either allow juveniles to attend a school in the community or offer programs that lead to a high school diploma or GED certificate.

■ Wilderness programs involve troubled youth using outdoor activities as a mechanism to improve their social skills, self-concepts, and self-control.

■ Correctional boot camps emphasize the get-tough elements of adult programs.

To learn more about the right to treatment, read **"Meeting the Needs of the Mentally Ill—A Case Study of the 'Right to Treatment' as Legal Rights Discourse in the USA,"** by Michael McCubbin and David N. Weisstub at www.thomsonedu.com/criminaljustice/siegel on the Web.

The concept of a **right to treatment** was introduced to the mental health field in 1960 by Morton Birnbaum, who argued that individuals who are deprived of their liberty because of a mental illness are entitled to treatment to correct that condition.[117] The right to treatment has expanded to include the juvenile justice system, an expansion bolstered by court rulings that mandate that rehabilitation and not punishment or retribution be the basis of juvenile court dispositions.[118] It stands to reason then that, if incarcerated, juveniles are entitled to the appropriate social services that will promote their rehabilitation.

One of the first cases to highlight this issue was *Inmates of the Boys' Training School v. Affleck* in 1972.[119] In its decision, a federal court argued that rehabilitation is the true purpose of the juvenile court and that, without that goal, due process guarantees are violated. It condemned such devices as solitary confinement, strip cells, and lack of educational opportunities, and held that juveniles have a statutory right to treatment. The court also established the following minimum standards for all juveniles confined in training schools:

- A room equipped with lighting sufficient for an inmate to read until 10 P.M.
- Sufficient clothing to meet seasonal needs
- Bedding, including blankets, sheets, pillows, and pillowcases, to be changed once a week
- Personal hygiene supplies, including soap, toothpaste, towels, toilet paper, and toothbrush
- A change of undergarments and socks every day
- Minimum writing materials: pen, pencil, paper, and envelopes
- Prescription eyeglasses, if needed
- Equal access to all books, periodicals, and other reading materials located in the training school
- Daily showers
- Daily access to medical facilities, including provision of a twenty-four-hour nursing service
- General correspondence privileges[120]

In 1974, in the case of *Nelson v. Heyne*, the First Federal Appellate Court affirmed that juveniles have a right to treatment and condemned the use of corporal punishment in juvenile institutions.[121] In *Morales v. Turman*, the court held that all juveniles confined in training schools in Texas have a right to treatment, including development of education skills, delivery of vocational education, medical and psychiatric treatment, and adequate living conditions.[122] In a more recent case, *Pena v. New York State Division for Youth*, the court held that the use of isolation, hand restraints, and tranquilizing drugs at Goshen Annex Center violated the Fourteenth Amendment right to due process and the Eighth Amendment right to protection against cruel and unusual punishment.[123]

The right to treatment has also been limited. For example, in *Ralston v. Robinson*, the Supreme Court rejected a youth's claim that he should continue to be given treatment after he was sentenced to a consecutive term in an adult prison for crimes committed while in a juvenile institution.[124] In the *Ralston* case, the offender's proven dangerousness outweighed the possible effects of rehabilitation. Similarly, in *Santana v. Callazo*, the U.S. First Circuit Court of Appeals rejected a suit brought by residents at the Maricao Juvenile Camp in Puerto Rico on the ground that the administration had failed to provide them with an individualized rehabilitation plan or adequate treatment. The circuit court concluded that it was a legitimate exercise of state authority to incarcerate juveniles solely to protect society if they are dangerous.

The Struggle for Basic Civil Rights

Several court cases have led federal, state, and private groups—for example, the American Bar Association, the American Correctional Association, and the National Council on Crime and Delinquency—to develop standards for the juvenile justice system. These standards provide guidelines for conditions and practices in juvenile institutions and call on administrators to maintain a safe and healthy environment for incarcerated youths.

For the most part, state-sponsored brutality has been outlawed, although the use of restraints, solitary confinement, and even medication for unruly residents has not been eliminated. The courts have ruled that corporal punishment in any form violates standards of decency and human dignity.

There are a number of mechanisms for enforcing these standards. For example, the federal government's Civil Rights of Institutionalized Persons Act (CRIPA) gives the Civil Rights Division of the U.S. Department of Justice (DOJ) the power to bring actions against state or local governments for violating the civil rights of persons institutionalized in publicly operated facilities.[125] CRIPA does not create any new substantive rights; it simply confers power on the U.S. Attorney General to bring action to enforce previously established constitutional or statutory rights of institutionalized persons; about 25 percent of cases involve juvenile detention and correctional facilities.

What provisions does the juvenile justice system make to help institutionalized offenders return to society? The remainder of this chapter is devoted to this topic.

JUVENILE AFTERCARE AND REENTRY

aftercare
Transitional assistance to juveniles equivalent to adult parole to help youths adjust to community life.

Aftercare in the juvenile justice system is the equivalent of parole in the adult criminal justice system. When juveniles are released from an institution, they may be placed in an aftercare program of some kind, so that those who have been institutionalized are not simply returned to the community without some transitional assistance. Whether individuals who are in aftercare as part of an indeterminate sentence remain in the community or return to the institution for further rehabilitation

Aftercare—the equivalent of parole in the adult criminal justice system—includes a range of services designed to help juveniles adjust to community life upon release from an institution. Here, Tristan Cassidy, 17 (top) and Scott Epperley, 15, work on a project for their geography class at the Northwest Regional Learning Center (NRLC) in Everett, Washington. The NRLC is a detention school for juveniles on probation or in aftercare that serves as a last chance for some to earn their high school diploma if their former schools will not accept them back.

© AP Images/Chris Goodenow

depends on their actions during the aftercare period. Aftercare is an extremely important stage in the juvenile justice process, because few juveniles age out of custody.[126]

Reentry involves aftercare services, but includes preparation for release from confinement, also called prerelease planning.[127] Reentry is further distinguished from aftercare in that reentry is seen as the whole process and experience of the transition of juveniles from "juvenile and adult correctional settings back into schools, families, communities, and society at large.[128] The concept of reentry, which is also the term given to it in the adult criminal justice system, is by no means new.[129] Recently, however, it has come to characterize the larger numbers of juvenile and adult offenders returning to communities each year and the increased needs these offenders exhibit with respect to employment, education, and mental health and substance abuse problems.[130] For juvenile offenders, reentry goes beyond the all-too-common practice of juveniles being placed in aftercare programs that are the same as adult parole programs, which "fail to take account of their unique needs and the challenges they face."[131] (See Exhibit 14.3 for a profile of juvenile offenders returning to the community.) Through the Serious and Violent Offender Reentry Initiative (SVORI), the federal government has invested $150 million on reentry programs for adult and juvenile offenders in all 50 states, the District of Columbia, and the Virgin Islands.[132]

Supervision

One purpose of aftercare and reentry is to provide support during the readjustment period following release. First, individuals whose activities have been regimented for some time may not find it easy to make independent decisions. Second, offenders may perceive themselves as scapegoats, cast out by society. Finally, the community may view the returning minor with a good deal of prejudice; adjustment problems may reinforce a pre-existing need to engage in deviant behavior.

Juveniles in aftercare programs are supervised by parole caseworkers or counselors whose job is to maintain contact with the juvenile, make sure that a corrections plan is followed, and show interest and caring. The counselor also keeps the youth informed of services that may assist in reintegration and counsels the youth and his or her family. Unfortunately, aftercare caseworkers, like probation officers, often carry such large caseloads that their jobs are next to impossible to do adequately.

The Intensive Aftercare Program (IAP) Model New models of aftercare have been aimed at the chronic or violent offender. The **Intensive Aftercare Program (IAP)** model developed by David Altschuler and Troy Armstrong offers a continuum

---

reentry
The process and experience of returning to society upon release from a custody facility post-adjudication.

For more information on **SVORI** programs for juvenile offenders, go to www.thomsonedu.com/criminaljustice/siegel on the Web.

Intensive Aftercare Program (IAP)
A balanced, highly structured, comprehensive continuum of intervention for serious and violent juvenile offenders returning to the community.

| Exhibit 14.3 | A Profile of Juvenile Reentry |

The latest data indicate that about one hundred thousand juvenile offenders each year are released from custody facilities following adjudication (or conviction in the adult system) and return to the communities from which they came. A profile of these juveniles shows that:

- 86 percent are male.
- 12 percent are age 14 or younger and 44 percent are age 17 or older.

- 40 percent are white, 38 percent are black, and 18 percent are Hispanic.
- 34 percent are committed for a violent offense, 32 percent for a property offense, 10 percent for a drug offense, 10 percent for public order offense, 10 percent for a technical violation of probation or parole, and 5 percent for a status offense.

Reentry services play an important role in their successful reintegration to society.

Source: Howard N. Snyder and Melissa Sickmund, *Juvenile Offenders and Victims: 2006 National Report* (Pittsburgh, PA: National Center for Juvenile Justice, 2006), p. 232.

of intervention for serious juvenile offenders returning to the community following placement.[133] The IAP model begins by drawing attention to five basic principles, which collectively establish a set of fundamental operational goals:

1. Preparing youth for progressively increased responsibility and freedom in the community

2. Facilitating youth-community interaction and involvement

3. Working with both the offender and targeted community support systems (families, peers, schools, employers) on qualities needed for constructive interaction and the youths' successful community adjustment

4. Developing new resources and supports where needed

5. Monitoring and testing the youths and the community on their ability to deal with each other productively. These basic goals are then translated into practice, which incorporates individual case planning with a family and community perspective.

The program stresses a mix of intensive surveillance and services and a balance of incentives and graduated consequences coupled with the imposition of realistic, enforceable conditions. There is also "service brokerage," in which community resources are used and linkage with social networks established.[134]

The IAP initiative was designed to help correctional agencies implement effective aftercare programs for chronic and serious juvenile offenders. After more than twelve years of testing, the program is now being aimed at determining how juveniles are prepared for reentry into their communities, how the transition is handled, and how the aftercare in the community is provided.[135] The Preventing and Treating Delinquency feature "Using the Intensive Aftercare Program (IAP) Model" illustrates how it is being used in three state jurisdictions and reports on the latest evaluation results.

Aftercare Revocation Procedures

Juvenile parolees are required to meet set standards of behavior, which generally include but are not limited to the following:

- Adhere to a reasonable curfew set by youth worker or parent.
- Refrain from associating with persons whose influence would be detrimental.
- Attend school in accordance with the law.
- Abstain from drugs and alcohol.
- Report to the youth worker when required.
- Refrain from acts that would be crimes if committed by an adult.
- Refrain from operating an automobile without permission of the youth worker or parent.
- Refrain from being habitually disobedient and beyond the lawful control of parent or other legal authority.
- Refrain from running away from the lawful custody of parent or other lawful authority.

If these rules are violated, the juvenile may have his parole revoked and be returned to the institution. Most states have extended the same legal rights enjoyed by adults at parole revocation hearings to juveniles who are in danger of losing their aftercare privileges, as follows:

Using the Intensive Aftercare Program (IAP) Model

How has the IAP model been used around the nation and has it proven effective?

Colorado

Although adolescents are still institutionalized, community-based providers begin weekly services (including multifamily counseling and life-skills services) that continue during aftercare. Sixty days prior to release, IAP youths begin a series of step-down measures, including supervised trips to the community, and thirty days before release, there are overnight or weekend home passes. Upon release to parole, most program youths go through several months of day treatment that, in addition to services, provides a high level of structure during the day. As a youth's progress warrants, the frequency of supervision decreases.

Nevada

Once the parole plan is finalized, all IAP youth begin a thirty-day prerelease phase, during which IAP staff provide a series of services that continue through the early months of parole. These consist primarily of two structured curricula on life skills and substance abuse. The initial thirty days of release are considered an institutional furlough (that is, the kids are still on the institutional rolls) that involves intensive supervision and service. During furlough, they are involved in day programming and are subject to frequent drug testing and evening and weekend surveillance. Upon successful completion of the furlough, the IAP transition continues through the use of phased levels of supervision. During the first three months, three contacts per week with the case manager or field agent are required. This level of supervision is reduced to two contacts per week for the next two months, and then to once a week during the last month of parole.

Virginia

Virginia's transition differs from the other two sites in that its central feature is the use of group home placements as a bridge between the institution and the community. Immediately after release from the institution, youths enter one of two group homes for a thirty- to sixty-day period. The programs and services in which they will be involved in the community are initiated shortly after placement in the home. Virginia uses a formal step-down system to ease the intensity of parole supervision gradually. In the two months following the youth's release from the group home, staff are required to contact him or her five to seven times per week. This is reduced to three to five times per week during the next two months, and again to three times per week during the final thirty days.

Does the IAP Model Work?

In each state one site was chosen to assess the effectiveness of the IAP model: Denver, Colorado; Las Vegas, Nevada; and Norfolk, Virginia. An experimental evaluation that randomly assigned juveniles to the program or a control group was used to assess the model's effectiveness on recidivism. As shown in the table, the program produced some benefits in Norfolk, but in Denver program youths were more likely than their control counterparts to recidivate and to be sentenced to a period of incarceration. The researchers call for caution in interpreting these results. In the case of Denver, control group youths received services similar to those in the IAP. They also note that this was the first test of a "very complex intervention." Suggestions for improvement to the IAP include: maximizing parental involvement, emphasizing education and employment skills, and strengthening community support networks.

CRITICAL THINKING

1. What is the importance of reducing the number of supervision contacts with the juvenile offender toward the end of the aftercare program?
2. Should juvenile offenders who have committed less serious offenses also have to go through intensive aftercare programs?

Sources: Richard G. Wiebush, Dennis Wagner, Betsie McNulty, Yanqing Wang, and Thao N. Le, *Implementation and Outcome Evaluation of the Intensive Aftercare Program* (Washington, DC: OJJDP, 2005); Steve V. Gies, *Aftercare Services* (Washington, DC: OJJDP Juvenile Justice Bulletin, 2003); Richard G. Wiebush, Betsie McNulty, and Thao N. Le, *Implementation of the Intensive Community-Based Aftercare Program* (Washington, DC: OJJDP Juvenile Justice Bulletin, 2000).

Table 14.A The IAP Model's Effects on Recidivism

	Denver		Las Vegas		Norfolk	
	IAP	Control	IAP	Control	IAP	Control
Arrested (%)	69	65	77	77	60	67
Convicted (%)	42	33	59	60	44	59
Incarcerated (%)	41	26	45	41	56	58

- Juveniles must be informed of the conditions of parole and receive notice of any obligations.
- Juveniles have the right to legal counsel at state expense if necessary.
- They maintain the right to confront and cross-examine witnesses against them.
- They have the right to introduce documentary evidence and witnesses.
- They have the right to a hearing before an officer who shall be an attorney but not an employee of the revoking agency.[136]

SUMMARY

- Community treatment encompasses efforts to keep offenders in the community and spare them the stigma of incarceration. The primary purpose is to provide a nonrestrictive or home setting, employing educational, vocational, counseling, and employment services. Institutional treatment encompasses provision of these services but in more restrictive and sometimes secure facilities.
- The most widely used community treatment method is probation. Behavior is monitored by probation officers. If rules are violated, youths may have their probation revoked.
- It is now common to enhance probation with more restrictive forms of treatment, such as intensive supervision and house arrest with electronic monitoring. Restitution programs involve having juvenile offenders either reimburse their victims or do community service.
- Residential community treatment programs allow youths to live at home while receiving treatment. There are also residential programs that require that youths reside in group homes while receiving treatment.
- The secure juvenile institution was developed in the mid-nineteenth century as an alternative to placing youths in adult prisons. Youth institutions evolved from large, closed institutions to cottage-based education and rehabilitation-oriented institutions.
- The juvenile institutional population has decreased in recent years, but a large number of youths continue to be "hidden" in private medical centers and drug treatment clinics.
- A disproportionate number of minorities are incarcerated in more secure, state-run youth facilities.
- Most juvenile institutions maintain intensive treatment programs featuring individual or group therapy. Little evidence has been found that any single method is effective in reducing recidivism, yet rehabilitation remains an important goal of juvenile practitioners.
- The right to treatment is an important issue in juvenile justice. Legal decisions have mandated that a juvenile cannot simply be warehoused in a correctional center, but must receive proper care and treatment to aid rehabilitation. What constitutes proper care is still being debated, however.
- Juveniles released from institutions are often placed on parole, or aftercare. There is little evidence that community supervision is more beneficial than simply releasing youths. Many jurisdictions are experiencing success with halfway houses and reintegration centers and other reentry programs.

KEY TERMS

community treatment, p. 337
suppression effect, p. 338
probation, p. 338
juvenile probation officer, p. 341
social investigation report, predisposition report, p. 341
conditions of probation, p. 342
juvenile intensive probation supervision (JIPS), p. 342
house arrest, p. 344
electronic monitoring, p. 344
balanced probation, p. 345
monetary restitution, p. 346

victim service restitution, p. 346
community service restitution, p. 346
residential programs, p. 347
group homes, p. 347
foster care programs, p. 347
family group homes, p. 348
rural programs, p. 348
reform schools, p. 348
cottage system, p. 349
least restrictive alternative, p. 350
individual counseling, p. 357
psychotherapy, p. 357
reality therapy, p. 358

behavior modification, p. 358
group therapy, p. 358
guided group interaction (GGI), p. 358
positive peer culture (PPC), p. 358
milieu therapy, p. 358
wilderness probation, p. 359
boot camps, p. 360
meta-analysis, p. 360
right to treatment, p. 361
aftercare, p. 362
reentry, p. 363
Intensive Aftercare Program (IAP), p. 363

1. Would you want a community treatment program in your neighborhood? Why or why not?

2. Is widening the net a real danger, or are treatment-oriented programs simply a method of helping troubled youths?

3. If youths violate the rules of probation, should they be placed in a secure institution?

4. Is juvenile restitution fair? Should a poor child have to pay back a wealthy victim, such as a store owner?

5. What are the most important advantages to community treatment for juvenile offenders?

6. What is the purpose of juvenile probation? Identify some conditions of probation and discuss the responsibilities of the juvenile probation officer.

7. Has community treatment generally proven successful?

8. Why have juvenile boot camps not been effective in reducing recidivism?

APPLYING WHAT YOU HAVE LEARNED

As a local juvenile court judge you have been assigned the case of Jim Butler, a thirteen-year-old so short he can barely see over the bench. On trial for armed robbery, the boy has been accused of threatening a woman with a knife and stealing her purse. Barely a teenager, he has already had a long history of involvement with the law. At age eleven he was arrested for drug possession and placed on probation; soon after, he stole a car. At age twelve he was arrested for shoplifting. Jim is accompanied by his legal guardian, his maternal grandmother. His parents are unavailable, because his father abandoned the family years ago and his mother is currently undergoing inpatient treatment at a local drug clinic. After talking with his attorney, Jim decides to admit to the armed robbery. At a dispositional hearing, his court-appointed attorney tells you of the tough life Jim has been forced to endure. His grandmother states that, although she loves the boy, her advanced age makes it impossible for her to provide the care he needs to stay out of trouble. She says that Jim is a good boy who has developed a set of bad companions; his current scrape was precipitated by his friends. A representative of the school system testifies that Jim has above-average intelligence and is actually respectful of teachers. He has potential, but his life

circumstances have short-circuited his academic success. Jim himself shows remorse and appears to be a sensitive youngster who is easily led astray by older youths.

You must now make a decision. You can place Jim on probation and allow him to live with his grandmother while being monitored by county probation staff. You can place him in a secure incarceration facility for up to three years. You can also put him into an intermediate program such as a community-based facility, which would allow him to attend school during the day while residing in a halfway house and receiving group treatment in the evenings. Although Jim appears salvageable, his crime was serious and involved the use of a weapon. If he remains in the community he may offend again; if he is sent to a correctional facility, he will interact with older, tougher kids. What mode of correctional treatment would you choose?

- Would you place Jim on probation and allow him to live with his grandmother while being monitored?
- Would you send him to a secure incarceration facility for up to three years?
- Would you put him into an intermediate program such as a community-based facility?

DOING RESEARCH ON THE WEB

Before you answer these questions, you may want to research the effectiveness of different types of correctional treatment for juvenile offenders. Use "juvenile correctional treatment" in a key word search on InfoTrac College Edition. To learn more about juvenile treatment options, access **www.thomsonedu.com/criminaljustice/siegel** on the Web to go to the California Department of the Youth Authority, Center for the Study and Prevention of Violence, Washington State Institute for Public Policy on Juvenile Justice, the National Council on Crime and Delinquency and Children's Research Center, and the Urban Institute.

Tertiary Prevention Efforts: The Role of the Juvenile Justice System

Juvenile justice measures designed to prevent delinquency can include the police making an arrest as part of an operation to crack down on gang problems or a juvenile court sanction to a secure correctional facility. Although these measures have as an objective the prevention of future delinquent activities (or repeat offending, or recidivism), they can also be referred to as measures of delinquency control or delinquency repression. This is because, unlike with the other strategies to prevent delinquency—the primary prevention and secondary prevention efforts discussed in the two earlier preventing delinquency essays—juvenile justice measures also have as an objective the protection of the public. For this to happen there also needs to be some type of formal control exercised over offenders.

From a public health perspective, juvenile justice measures are a form of tertiary-level delinquency prevention. Tertiary prevention focuses on intervening with offenders once a delinquent activity or crime has been committed. This form of delinquency prevention is considered reactive—there is a response only after (for the most part) a crime has taken place. It can also be considered the measure of last resort.

Many experts argue that there is an overreliance on police, courts, and corrections to prevent juvenile crime.[1] Many are also of the opinion that this approach has become increasingly harsh or punitive in recent years. Juvenile courts have delivered harsher sentences, there has been a greater reliance on the use of confinement than rehabilitation, and a growing number of juvenile offenders are serving time in prison.[2] This increased punitiveness has led many scholars to argue that the treatment and protection aims of the juvenile system have become more a matter of the abstract than of reality. According to University of Minnesota law professor Barry Feld:

> Evaluations of juvenile court sentencing practices, treatment effectiveness, and conditions of confinement reveal increasingly punitive juvenile court and corrections systems. These various indicators strongly suggest that despite juvenile courts' persisting rehabilitative rhetoric, the reality of treating juveniles closely resembles punishing adult criminals.[3]

For some, this increased punitiveness in dealing with juvenile offenders makes the juvenile justice system seem less appealing as a vehicle for preventing delinquency. It may be that more checks and balances are needed for tertiary prevention measures, such as in the case of the juvenile court.[4] It may also be that a greater balance needs to be struck among this approach and primary and secondary delinquency prevention strategies. But the juvenile system plays an integral role in addressing juvenile delinquency, and there are many promising delinquency prevention programs operated by the police, courts, and corrections.

POLICE

The police are the first contact that juvenile offenders have with the juvenile justice system. Working with juvenile offenders presents special challenges for police, such as role conflicts arising from traditional policing practices and wanting to steer youths away from crime, the use of discretion, and the low regard held by youths toward police. But police have taken the lead in delinquency prevention. They have used a number of strategies: some rely on their deterrent powers whereas others rely on their relationship with schools, the community, and other juvenile justice agencies, or another on a problem-solving model.

These policing innovations have produced results.[5] Boston's Operation Ceasefire, which brought together the police, juvenile probation, social services, and other key local, state, and federal agencies, more than halved the number of juvenile homicide victims and greatly reduced gang activity across the city.[6] Another promising example of police taking the lead in preventing delinquency is the Partnerships to Reduce Juvenile Gun Violence Program. This involves problem-oriented policing strategies and other interventions, including a public information campaign to communicate the dangers and consequences of gun violence to juveniles, families, and community residents.[7] These policing innovations, notably Operation Ceasefire or similar versions of it, have been replicated in cities across the country, with many producing promising results in reducing serious and violent juvenile offending.[8]

COURTS

Many critical decisions are made at this stage of the juvenile justice system that have implications for preventing delinquency in the short or long term. Some of these are whether to detain a youth or release the youth to the community, whether to waive youths to the adult court or retain them in the juvenile system, or whether to treat them in the community or send them to a secure treatment center.

In recent years, the juvenile court has introduced a number of innovations to foster more effective delinquency prevention for specific types of juvenile offenders. One of these is the juvenile drug court. Although these courts operate under a number of different frameworks, the aim is to place nonviolent first offenders into intensive treatment programs rather than into a custodial institution. Teen or youth court is another alternative to the traditional juvenile court in which young people rather than adults determine the disposition in a case. Cases handled in these courts typically involve young juveniles with no prior arrest records who have been charged with minor law violations. A recent evaluation of teen courts in four states found promising results in reducing recidivism.[9]

CORRECTIONS

At this stage of the juvenile system, measures to prevent delinquency can be organized into two main categories: community treatment and institutional treatment. Community treatment covers a wide range of modalities, including probation, treatment services (such as individual and group counseling), and restitution. There are also a wide variety of institutional treatments for juvenile offenders, ranging from training schools or reformatories to boot camps.

There exists much debate about the effectiveness of community versus institutional treatment. Considerable research shows that warehousing juveniles without proper treatment does little to prevent future delinquent activities. The most effective secure corrections programs are those that provide individual services for a small number of participants.[10] Evaluations of community treatment provide evidence of a number of successful ways to prevent delinquency without jeopardizing the safety of community residents.[11]

There is also a long-standing debate about the effectiveness of correctional treatments compared with other delinquency prevention measures. In their assessment of the full range of interventions to prevent serious and violent juvenile offending, Rolf Loeber and David Farrington found that it is never too early and never too late to make a difference.[12]

Notes

Chapter 1. Childhood and Delinquency

[1] *Current Population Reports*, *Series P-20* (Washington, DC: U.S. Department of Commerce, Bureau of the Census, 2006).

[2] *America's Children: Key National Indicators of Well-Being* (Washington, DC: Interagency Forum on Child and Family Statistics, 2003).

[3] Nanette Davis, *Youth Crisis: Growing Up in the High-Risk Society* (New York: Praeger/Greenwood, 1998).

[4] Steven Martino, Rebecca Collins, Marc Elliott, Amy Strachman, David Kanouse, and Sandra Berry, "Exposure to Degrading Versus Nondegrading Music Lyrics and Sexual Behavior Among Youth," *Pediatrics* 118:430–441 (2006).

[5] Erik Erikson, *Childhood and Society* (New York: Norton, 1963).

[6] Roger Gould, "Adult Life Stages: Growth Toward Self-Tolerance," *Psychology Today* 8:74–78 (1975).

[7] Anthony Jackson and Gayle Davis, *Turning Points 2000: Educating Adolescents in the 21st Century* (New York: Carnegie Council on Adolescent Development, Task Force on Education of Young Adolescents, 2000), p. 27.

[8] Rima Shore, *KIDS COUNT Indicator Brief: Reducing the Teen Death Rate* (Baltimore: Annie E. Casey Foundation, 2005).

[9] Greg Duncan, W. Jean Yeung, Jeanne Brooks-Gunn, and Judith Smith, "How Much Does Childhood Poverty Affect the Life Chances of Children?" *American Sociological Review* 63:406–423 (1998).

[10] Children's Defense Fund, *The State of America's Children, 2005* (Washington, DC: Children's Defense Fund, 2006): p. ii. Available at: http://cdf.convio.net/site/DocServer/Greenbook_2005.pdf?docID= 1741 (accessed November 15, 2006).

[11] Ibid. pp. 31–33.

[12] Jeanne Brooks-Gunn and Greg J. Duncan, "The Effects of Poverty on Children," *Future of Children* 7:34–39 (1997).

[13] *The State of America's Children, 2005*, p. 31.

[14] Ibid.

[15] National Center for Health Statistics, *Cohabitation, Marriage, Divorce, and Remarriage in the United States*, Series Report 23 (2002).

[16] *The State of America's Children, 2005*, p. 118.

[17] David Eggebeen and Daniel Lichter, "Race, Family Structure, and Changing Poverty Among American Children," *American Sociological Review* 56:801–817 (1991).

[18] Tami Videon, "The Effects of Parent-Adolescent Relationships and Parental Separation on Adolescent Well-Being," *Journal of Marriage & the Family* 64:489–504 (2002).

[19] Gary Evans, Nancy Wells, and Annie Moch, "Housing and Mental Health: A Review of the Evidence and a Methodological and Conceptual Critique," *Journal of Social Issues* 59:475–501 (2003).

[20] *The State of America's Children, 2005*, pp. 10–11.

[21] National Center for Education Statistics, Digest of Education Statistics, 2005. Available at: http://nces.ed.gov/pubsearch/pubsinfo.asp? pubid=2006030 (accessed November 15, 2006).

[22] Lloyd Johnston, Patrick O'Malley, Jerald Bachman, and John Schulenberg, "Teen Drug Use Down but Progress Halts Among Youngest Teens," University of Michigan News Service press release, Ann Arbor (December 19, 2005).

[23] Federal Bureau of Investigation, *Crime in the United States, 2002* (Washington, DC: U.S. Government Printing Office, 2003), p. 244.

[24] Patrick Nickoletti and Heather Taussig, "Outcome Expectancies and Risk Behaviors in Maltreated Adolescents," *Journal of Research on Adolescence* 16:217–228 (2006); Nanette Davis, *Youth Crisis: Growing Up in the High-Risk Society*.

[25] John Whitehead and Steven Lab, "A Meta-Analysis of Juvenile Correctional Treatment," *Journal of Research in Crime and Delinquency* 26:276–295 (1989).

[26] Francis Cullen, Sandra Evans Skovron, Joseph Scott, and Velmer Burton, "Public Support for Correctional Treatment: The Tenacity of Rehabilitative Ideology," *Criminal Justice and Behavior* 17:6–18 (1990).

[27] Rhena Izzo and Robert Ross, "Meta-Analysis of Rehabilitation Programs for Juvenile Delinquents," *Criminal Justice and Behavior* 17:134–142 (1990).

[28] Gordon Bazemore and Lynette Feder, "Judges in the Punitive Juvenile Court: Organizational, Career, and Ideological Influences on Sanctioning Orientation," *Justice Quarterly* 14:87–114 (1997).

[29] *Roper v. Simmons* 543 U.S. 551 (2005).

[30] See Lawrence Stone, *The Family, Sex, and Marriage in England: 1500–1800* (New York: Harper & Row, 1977).

[31] This section relies on Jackson Spielvogel, *Western Civilization* (St. Paul, MN: West, 1991), pp. 279–286.

[32] Ibid.

[33] Philippe Aries, *Centuries of Childhood: A Social History of Family Life* (New York: Vintage Books, 1962).

[34] Nicholas Orme, *Medieval Children* (New Haven: Yale University Press, 2003).

[35] See Aries, *Centuries of Childhood*.

[36] See Douglas R. Rendleman, "*Parens Patriae*: From Chancery to the Juvenile Court," *South Carolina Law Review* 23:205 (1971).

[37] See Stone, *The Family, Sex, and Marriage in England*; and Lawrence Stone, ed., *Schooling and Society: Studies in the History of Education* (Baltimore: Johns Hopkins University Press, 1970).

[38] Ibid.

[39] See Wiley B. Sanders, *Some Early Beginnings of the Children's Court Movement in England*, National Probation Association Yearbook (New York: National Council on Crime and Delinquency, 1945).

[40] Rendleman, "*Parens Patriae*," p. 205.

[41] Douglas Besharov, *Juvenile Justice Advocacy—Practice in a Unique Court* (New York: Practicing Law Institute, 1974), p. 2.

[42] *Wellesley v. Wellesley*, 4 Eng. Rep. 1078 (1827).

[43] Rendleman, "*Parens Patriae*," p. 209.

[44] Anthony Platt, "The Rise of the Child Saving Movement: A Study in Social Policy and Correctional Reform," *Annals of the American Academy of Political and Social Science* 381:21–38 (1969).

[45] Robert Bremner, ed., and John Barnard, Hareven Tamara, and Robert Mennel, asst. eds., *Children and Youth in America* (Cambridge, MA: Harvard University Press, 1970), p. 64.

[46] Elizabeth Pleck, "Criminal Approaches to Family Violence: 1640–1980," in Lloyd Ohlin and Michael Tonry, eds., *Family Violence* (Chicago: University of Chicago Press, 1989), pp. 19–58.

[47] Ibid.

[48] John R. Sutton, *Stubborn Children: Controlling Delinquency in the United States, 1640–1981* (Berkeley: University of California Press, 1988).

[49] Pleck, "Criminal Approaches to Family Violence," p. 29.

[50] John Demos, *Past, Present, and Personal* (New York: Oxford University Press, 1986), pp. 80–88.

[51] Elizabeth Pleck, *Domestic Tyranny: The Making of Social Policy Against Family Violence from Colonial Times to the Present* (New York: Oxford University Press, 1987), pp. 28–30.

[52] Graeme Newman, *The Punishment Response* (Philadelphia: Lippincott, 1978), pp. 53–79; Aries, *Centuries of Childhood*. The history of childhood juvenile justice is discussed in detail in chapter 12.

[53] Stephen J. Morse, "Immaturity and Irresponsibility," *Journal of Criminal Law and Criminology* 88:15–67 (1997).

[54] Shay Bilchik, "Sentencing Juveniles to Adult Facilities Fails Youths and Society," *Corrections Today* 65:21 (2003).

[55] Ibid.

[56] Hunter Hurst, "Status Offenders: Where Have They Gone and Who Cares?" (Pittsburgh: National Center for Juvenile Justice, 2003).

[57] See, generally, David Rothman, *The Discovery of the Asylum* (Boston: Little, Brown, 1971).

[58] Reports of the Chicago Bar Association Committee, 1899, cited in Anthony Platt, *The Child Savers: The Invention of Delinquency* (Chicago: University of Chicago Press, 1969), p. 119.

[59] Susan Datesman and Mikel Aickin, "Offense Specialization and Escalation Among Status Offenders," *Journal of Criminal Law and Criminology* 75:1246–1275 (1985).

[60] Ibid.

[61] *Juvenile Justice and Delinquency Prevention Act (JJDPA)* of 1974, as amended (42 U.S.C. 5601 *et seq.*).

[62] Runaway and Homeless Youth Act (RHYA) of 1974 (42 U.S.C. § 5701 *et seq.*).

[63] 42 U.S.C.A. 5601B5751 (1983 and Supp. 1987).

[64] Office of Juvenile Justice and Delinquency Prevention, *State Compliance Based on 1998 Reports: Deinstitutionalization of Status Offenders* (Washington, DC: Office of Juvenile Justice and Delinquency Prevention, 2000).

[65] National Council on Crime and Delinquency, "Juvenile Curfews— A Policy Statement," *Crime and Delinquency* 18:132–133 (1972).

[66] National Advisory Commission on Criminal Justice Standards and Goals, *Juvenile Justice and Delinquency Prevention* (Washington, DC: U.S. Government Printing Office, 1977), p. 311.

[67] Gail Robinson and Tim Arnold, "Changes in Laws Impacting Juveniles—An Overview," *The Advocate* 22:14–15 (2000).

[68] Barry Feld, "Criminalizing the American Juvenile Court," in Michael Tonry, ed., *Crime and Justice: A Review of Research* (Chicago: University of Chicago Press, 1993), p. 232.

[69] Sean Kidd, "Factors Precipitating Suicidality Among Homeless Youth: A Quantitative Follow-up," *Youth & Society* 37:393–422 (2006); Kimberly Tyler, Les Whitbeck, Dan Hoyt, and Kurt Johnson, "Self-Mutilation and Homeless Youth: The Role of Family Abuse, Street Experiences, and Mental Disorders," *Journal of Research on Adolescence* 13:457–474 (2003).

[70] Carolyn Smith, "Factors Associated with Early Sexual Activity Among Urban Adolescents," *Social Work* 42:334–346 (1997).

Chapter 2. The Nature and Extent of Delinquency

[1] The data used here is from FBI, *Crime in the United States, 2005*. Available at: www.fbi.gov/ucr/05cius/ (accessed November 15, 2006).

[2] Thomas Bernard, "Juvenile Crime and the Transformation of Juvenile Justice: Is There a Juvenile Crime Wave?" *Justice Quarterly* 16:336–356 (1999).

[3] James A. Fox, *Trends in Juvenile Violence: A Report to the United States Attorney General on Current and Future Rates of Juvenile Offending* (Boston: Northeastern University, 1996).

[4] Steven Levitt, "The Limited Role of Changing Age Structure in Explaining Aggregate Crime Rates," *Criminology* 37:581–599 (1999).

[5] Steven Levitt, "Understanding Why Crime Fell in the 1990s: Four Factors That Explain the Decline and Six That Do Not," *Journal of Economic Perspectives* 18:163–190 (2004).

[6] Julie Phillips, "The Relationship Between Age Structure and Homicide Rates in the United States, 1970 to 1999," *Journal of Research in Crime and Delinquency* 43:230–260 (2006).

[7] Adam Watkins, "Examining the Disparity Between Juvenile and Adult Victims in Notifying the Police: A Study of Mediating Variables," *Journal of Research in Crime and Delinquency* 42:333–353 (2005).

[8] Fox Butterfield, "Possible Manipulation of Crime Data Worries Top Police," *New York Times,* 3 August 1998, p. 1.

[9] A pioneering effort of self-report research is A. L. Porterfield's *Youth in Trouble* (Fort Worth, TX: Leo Potishman Foundation, 1946); for a review, see Robert Hardt and George Bodine, *Development of Self-Report Instruments in Delinquency Research: A Conference Report* (Syracuse, NY: Syracuse University Youth Development Center, 1965); see also Fred Murphy, Mary Shirley, and Helen Witmer, "The Incidence of Hidden Delinquency," *American Journal of Orthopsychiatry* 16:686–696 (1946).

[10] David Kirk, "Examining the Divergence Across Self-report and Official Data Sources on Inferences About the Adolescent Life-course of Crime," *Journal of Quantitative Criminology* 22:107–129 (2006).

[11] Jennifer Roberts, Edward Mulvey, Julie Horney, John Lewis, and Michael Arter, "A Test of Two Methods of Recall for Violent Events," *Journal of Quantitative Criminology* 21:175–193 (2005).

[12] Lila Kazemian and David Farrington, "Comparing the Validity of Prospective, Retrospective, and Official Onset for Different Offending Categories," *Journal of Quantitative Criminology* 21:127–147 (2005).

[13] Vincent Webb, Charles Katz, and Scott Decker, "Assessing the Validity of Self-Reports by Gang Members: Results From the Arrestee Drug Abuse Monitoring Program" *Crime & Delinquency* 52:232–252 (2006).

[14] For example, the following studies have noted the great discrepancy between official statistics and self-report studies: Maynard Erickson and LaMar Empey, "Court Records, Undetected Delinquency, and Decision Making," *Journal of Criminal Law, Criminology, and Police Science* 54:456–469 (1963); Martin Gold, "Undetected Delinquent Behavior," *Journal of Research in Crime and Delinquency* 3:27–46 (1966); James Short and F. Ivan Nye, "Extent of Unrecorded Delinquency, Tentative Conclusions," *Journal of Criminal Law, Criminology, and Police Science* 49:296–302 (1958).

[15] Jerald Bachman, Lloyd Johnston, and Patrick O'Malley, *Monitoring the Future: Questionnaire Responses from the Nation's High School Seniors, 2002* (Ann Arbor, MI: Institute for Social Research, 2003).

[16] Julia Yun Soo Kim, Michael Fendrich, and Joseph S. Wislar, "The Validity of Juvenile Arrestees' Drug Use Reporting: A Gender Comparison," *Journal of Research in Crime and Delinquency* 37:419–432 (2000).

[17] Barbara Warner and Brandi Wilson Coomer, "Neighborhood Drug Arrest Rates: Are They a Meaningful Indicator of Drug Activity? A Research Note," *Journal of Research in Crime and Delinquency* 40:123–139 (2003).

[18] Alfred Blumstein, Jacqueline Cohen, and Richard Rosenfeld, "Trend and Deviation in Crime Rates: A Comparison of UCR and NCVS Data for Burglary and Robbery," *Criminology* 29:237–248 (2001). See also Michael Hindelang, Travis Hirschi, and Joseph Weis, *Measuring Delinquency* (Beverly Hills, CA: Sage, 1981).

[19] Brad Bushman, Morgan Wang, and Craig Anderson, "Is the Curve Relating Temperature to Aggression Linear or Curvilinear? Assaults and Temperature in Minneapolis Reexamined," *Journal of Personality & Social Psychology* 89:62–66 (2005).

[20] Paul Bell, "Reanalysis and Perspective in the Heat-Aggression Debate," *Journal of Personality & Social Psychology* 89:71–73 (2005); Ellen Cohn, "The Prediction of Police Calls for Service: The Influence of Weather and Temporal Variables on Rape and Domestic Violence," *Journal of Environmental Psychology* 13:71–83 (1993).

[21] Michael Hindelang, Travis Hirschi, and Joseph Weis, *Measuring Delinquency* (Beverly Hills, CA: Sage, 1981); Gary Jensen and Raymond Eve, "Sex Differences in Delinquency: An Examination of Popular Sociological Explanation," *Criminology* 13:427–448 (1976); Michael Hindelang, "Age, Sex, and the Versatility of Delinquent Involvements," *Social Problems* 18:522–535 (1979); James Short and F. Ivan Nye, "Extent of Unrecorded Juvenile Delinquency, Tentative Conclusions," *Journal of Criminal Law, Criminology, and Police Science* 49:296–302 (1958).

[22] Darrell Steffensmeier, Jennifer Schwartz, Hua Zhong, and Jeff Ackerman, "An Assessment of Recent Trends in Girls' Violence Using Diverse Longitudinal Sources: Is the Gender Gap Closing," *Criminology* 43:355–406 (2005).

[23] Leroy Gould, "Who Defines Delinquency? A Comparison of Self-Report and Officially Reported Indices of Delinquency for Three Racial Groups," *Social Problems* 16:325–336 (1969); Harwin Voss, "Ethnic Differentials in Delinquency in Honolulu," *Journal of Criminal Law, Criminology, and Police Science* 54:322–327 (1963); Ronald Akers, Marvin Krohn, Marcia Radosevich, and Lonn Lanza-Kaduce, "Social Characteristics and Self-Reported Delinquency," in Gary Jensen, ed., *Sociology of Delinquency* (Beverly Hills, CA: Sage, 1981), pp. 48–62.

24 David Huizinga and Delbert Elliott, "Juvenile Offenders: Prevalence, Offender Incidence, and Arrest Rates by Race," *Crime and Delinquency* 33:206–223 (1987); see also Dale Dannefer and Russell Schutt, "Race and Juvenile Justice Processing in Court and Police Agencies," *American Journal of Sociology* 87:1113–1132 (1982).

25 Paul Tracy, "Race and Class Differences in Official and Self-Reported Delinquency," in Marvin Wolfgang, Terrence Thornberry, and Robert Figlio, eds., *From Boy to Man, from Delinquency to Crime* (Chicago: University of Chicago Press, 1987), p. 120.

26 Bachman, Johnston, and O'Malley, *Monitoring the Future*, pp. 102–104.

27 Samuel Walker, Cassia Spohn, and Miriam DeLone, *The Color of Justice: Race, Ethnicity, and Crime in America* (Belmont, CA: Brooks/Cole, 1992), pp. 46–47.

28 Miriam Sealock and Sally Simpson, "Unraveling Bias in Arrest Decisions: The Role of Juvenile Offender Typescripts," *Justice Quarterly* 15:427–457 (1998).

29 Hurbert Blalock, Jr., *Toward a Theory of Minority-Group Relations* (New York: Capricorn Books, 1967).

30 Rodney Engen, Sara Steen, and George Bridges, "Racial Disparities in the Punishment of Youth: A Theoretical and Empirical Assessment of the Literature," *Social Problems* 49:194–221 (2002).

31 Karen Parker, Briam Stults, and Stephen Rice, "Racial Threat, Concentrated Disadvantage and Social Control: Considering the Macro-Level Sources of Variation in Arrests," *Criminology* 43:1111–1134 (2005); Lisa Stolzenberg, J. Stewart D'Alessio, and David Eitle, "A Multilevel Test of Racial Threat Theory," *Criminology* 42:673–698 (2004).

32 Michael Leiber and Kristan Fox, "Race and the Impact of Detention on Juvenile Justice Decision Making," *Crime and Delinquency* 51:470–497 (2005); Traci Schlesinger, "Racial and Ethnic Disparity in Pretrial Criminal Processing," *Justice Quarterly* 22:170–192 (2005).

33 Christina DeJong and Kenneth Jackson, "Putting Race into Context: Race, Juvenile Justice Processing, and Urbanization," *Justice Quarterly* 15:487–504 (1998).

34 Engen, Steen, and Bridges, "Racial Disparities in the Punishment of Youth."

35 David Eitle, Stewart D'Alessio, and Lisa Stolzenberg, "Racial Threat and Social Control: A Test of the Political, Economic, and Threat of Black Crime Hypotheses," *Social Forces* 81:557–576 (2002); Michael Leiber and Jayne Stairs, "Race, Contexts, and the Use of Intake Diversion," *Journal of Research in Crime and Delinquency* 36:56–86 (1999); Darrell Steffensmeier, Jeffery Ulmer, and John Kramer, "The Interaction of Race, Gender, and Age in Criminal Sentencing: The Punishment Cost of Being Young, Black, and Male," *Criminology* 36:763–98 (1998).

36 For a general review, see William Wilbanks, *The Myth of a Racist Criminal Justice System* (Pacific Grove, CA: Brooks/Cole, 1987).

37 Walker, Spohn, and DeLone, *The Color of Justice*, pp. 47–48.

38 Mallie Paschall, Robert Flewelling, and Susan Ennett, "Racial Differences in Violent Behavior Among Young Adults: Moderating and Confounding Effects," *Journal of Research in Crime and Delinquency* 35:148–165 (1998).

39 Gary LaFree and Richard Arum, "The Impact of Racially Inclusive Schooling on Adult Incarceration Rates Among U.S. Cohorts of African Americans and Whites Since 1930," *Criminology* 44:73–103 (2006).

40 Julie Phillips, "Variation in African-American Homicide Rates: An Assessment of Potential Explanations," *Criminology* 35:527–559 (1997).

41 Melvin Thomas, "Race, Class, and Personal Income: An Empirical Test of the Declining Significance of Race Thesis, 1968–1988," *Social Problems* 40:328–339 (1993).

42 Thomas McNulty and Paul Bellair, "Explaining Racial and Ethnic Differences in Adolescent Violence: Structural Disadvantage, Family Well-Being, and Social Capital," *Justice Quarterly* 20:1–32 (2003); Julie Phillips, "White, Black, and Latino Homicide Rates: Why the Difference?" *Social Problems* 49:349–374 (2002).

43 Phillips, "White, Black, and Latino Homicide Rates: Why the Difference?"

44 Carl Pope and William Feyerherm, "Minority Status and Juvenile Processing: An Assessment of the Research Literature." Paper presented at the American Society of Criminology Meeting, Reno, Nevada, November 1989.

45 Robert Agnew, "A General Strain Theory of Community Differences in Crime Rates," *Journal of Research in Crime and Delinquency* 36:123–155 (1999).

46 Bonita Veysey and Steven Messner, "Further Testing of Social Disorganization Theory: An Elaboration of Sampson and Groves's 'Community Structure and Crime,'" *Journal of Research in Crime and Delinquency* 36:156–174 (1999).

47 James Short and Ivan Nye, "Reported Behavior as a Criterion of Deviant Behavior," *Social Problems* 5:207–213 (1958).

48 Classic studies include Ivan Nye, James Short, and Virgil Olsen, "Socio-economic Status and Delinquent Behavior," *American Journal of Sociology* 63:381–389 (1958); Robert Dentler and Lawrence Monroe, "Social Correlates of Early Adolescent Theft," *American Sociological Review* 26:733–743 (1961); Charles Tittle, Wayne Villemez, and Douglas Smith, "The Myth of Social Class and Criminality: An Empirical Assessment of the Empirical Evidence," *American Sociological Review* 43:643–656 (1978).

49 R. Gregory Dunaway, Francis Cullen, Velmer Burton, and T. David Evans, "The Myth of Social Class and Crime Revisited: An Examination of Class and Adult Criminality," *Criminology* 38:589–632 (2000).

50 Margaret Farnworth, Terence Thornberry, Marvin Krohn, and Alan Lizotte, *Measurement in the Study of Class and Delinquency: Integrating Theory and Research.* Working paper no. 4, rev (Albany, NY: Rochester Youth Development Survey, 1992), p. 19.

51 G. Roger Jarjoura and Ruth Triplett, "Delinquency and Class: A Test of the Proximity Principle," *Justice Quarterly* 14:765–792 (1997).

52 See, generally, David Farrington, "Age and Crime," in Michael Tonry and Norval Morris, eds., *Crime and Justice: An Annual Review*, vol. 7 (Chicago: University of Chicago Press, 1986), pp. 189–250.

53 Travis Hirschi and Michael Gottfredson, "Age and the Explanation of Crime," *American Journal of Sociology* 89:552–584 (1983).

54 Michael Gottfredson and Travis Hirschi, "The True Value of Lambda Would Appear to Be Zero: An Essay on Career Criminals, Criminal Careers, Selective Incapacitation, Cohort Studies, and Related Topics," *Criminology* 24:213–234 (1986); further support for their position can be found in Lawrence Cohen and Kenneth Land, "Age Structure and Crime," *American Sociological Review* 52:170–183 (1987).

55 Lila Kazemian and David Farrington, "Exploring Residual Career Length and Residual Number of Offenses for Two Generations of Repeat Offenders," *Journal of Research in Crime and Delinquency* 43:89–113 (2006).

56 David Greenberg, "Age, Crime, and Social Explanation," *American Journal of Sociology* 91:1–21 (1985).

57 Robert Sampson and John Laub, *Crime in the Making: Pathways and Turning Points Through Life* (Cambridge, MA: Harvard University Press, 1993).

58 Marvin Wolfgang, Robert Figlio, and Thorsten Sellin, *Delinquency in a Birth Cohort* (Chicago: University of Chicago Press, 1972); Lyle Shannon, *Assessing the Relationship of Adult Criminal Careers to Juvenile Careers: A Summary* (Washington, DC: U.S. Department of Justice, 1982); D. J. West and David P. Farrington, *The Delinquent Way of Life* (London: Heinemann, 1977); Donna Hamparian, Richard Schuster, Simon Dinitz, and John Conrad, *The Violent Few* (Lexington, MA: Lexington Books, 1978).

59 Rolf Loeber and Howard Snyder, "Rate of Offending in Juvenile Careers: Findings of Constancy and Change in Lambda," *Criminology* 28:97–109 (1990).

60 Margo Wilson and Martin Daly, "Life Expectancy, Economic Inequality, Homicide, and Reproductive Timing in Chicago Neighbourhoods," *British Journal of Medicine* 31:1271–1274 (1997).

61 Edward Mulvey and John LaRosa, "Delinquency Cessation and Adolescent Development: Preliminary Data," *American Journal of Orthopsychiatry* 56:212–224 (1986).

62 Timothy Brezina, "Delinquent Problem-Solving: An Interpretive Framework for Criminological Theory and Research," *Journal of Research in Crime and Delinquency* 37:3–30 (2000).

63 Gordon Trasler, "Cautions for a Biological Approach to Crime," in Sarnoff Mednick, Terrie Moffitt, and Susan Stack, eds., *The Causes of Crime, New Biological Approaches* (Cambridge: Cambridge University Press, 1987), pp. 7–25.

64 Alicia Rand, "Transitional Life Events and Desistance from Delinquency and Crime," in Wolfgang, Thornberry, and Figlio, eds., *From Boy to Man*, pp. 134–163.

65 Marc LeBlanc, "Late Adolescence Deceleration of Criminal Activity and Development of Self- and Social-Control," *Studies on Crime and Crime Prevention* 2:51–68 (1993).

[66] Barry Glassner, Margaret Ksander, Bruce Berg, and Bruce Johnson, "Note on the Deterrent Effect of Juvenile Versus Adult Jurisdiction," *Social Problems* 31:219–221 (1983).

[67] Neal Shover and Carol Thompson, "Age, Differential Expectations, and Crime Desistance," *Criminology* 30:89–104 (1992).

[68] D. Wayne Osgood, "The Covariation Among Adolescent Problem Behaviors." Paper presented at the American Society of Criminology Meeting, Baltimore, November 1990.

[69] Stephen Tibbetts, "Low Birth Weight, Disadvantaged Environment, and Early Onset: A Test of Moffitt's Interactional Hypothesis." Paper presented at the American Society of Criminology Meeting, Boston, November 1995.

[70] Arnold Barnett, Alfred Blumstein, and David Farrington, "A Prospective Test of a Criminal Career Model," *Criminology* 27:373–388 (1989).

[71] Wolfgang, Figlio, and Sellin, *Delinquency in a Birth Cohort*.

[72] Paul Tracy, Marvin Wolfgang, and Robert Figlio, *Delinquency in Two Birth Cohorts, Executive Summary* (Washington, DC: U.S. Department of Justice, 1985).

[73] Shannon, *Assessing the Relationship of Adult Criminal Careers to Juvenile Careers;* Howard Snyder, *Court Careers of Juvenile Offenders* (Washington, DC: Office of Juvenile Justice and Delinquency Prevention, 1988); Donald J. West and David P. Farrington, *The Delinquent Way of Life* (London: Heinemann, 1977); Donna Hamparian, Richard Schuster, Simon Dinitz, and John Conrad, *The Violent Few* (Lexington, MA: Lexington Books, 1978).

[74] See, generally, Wolfgang, Thornberry, and Figlio, *From Boy to Man*.

[75] Paul Tracy and Kimberly Kempf-Leonard, *Continuity and Discontinuity in Criminal Careers* (New York: Plenum, 1996).

[76] R. Tremblay, R. Loeber, C. Gagnon, P. Charlebois, S. Larivee, and M. LeBlanc, "Disruptive Boys with Stable and Unstable High Fighting Behavior Patterns During Junior Elementary School," *Journal of Abnormal Child Psychology* 19:285–300 (1991).

[77] Peter Jones, Philip Harris, James Fader, and Lori Grubstein, "Identifying Chronic Juvenile Offenders," *Justice Quarterly* 18:478–507 (2001).

[78] Jennifer White, Terrie Moffitt, Felton Earls, Lee Robins, and Phil Silva, "How Early Can We Tell? Predictors of Childhood Conduct Disorder and Adolescent Delinquency," *Criminology* 28:507–535 (1990).

[79] Kimberly Kempf-Leonard, Paul Tracy, and James Howell, "Serious, Violent, and Chronic Juvenile Offenders: The Relationship of Delinquency Career Types to Adult Criminality," *Justice Quarterly* 18:449–478 (2001).

[80] Kimberly Kempf, "Crime Severity and Criminal Career Progression," *Journal of Criminal Law and Criminology* 79:524–540 (1988).

[81] Jeffrey Fagan, "Social and Legal Policy Dimensions of Violent Juvenile Crime," *Criminal Justice and Behavior* 17:93–133 (1990).

[82] Peter Greenwood, *Selective Incapacitation* (Santa Monica, CA: Rand, 1982).

[83] Terence Thornberry, David Huizinga, and Rolf Loeber, "The Prevention of Serious Delinquency and Violence," in James Howell, Barry Krisberg, J. David Hawkins, and John Wilson, eds., *Sourcebook on Serious, Violent, and Chronic Juvenile Offenders* (Thousand Oaks, CA: Sage, 1995).

[84] Data here comes from Shannan Catalano, *Criminal Victimization, 2005* (Washington, DC: Bureau of Justice Statistics, 2006).

[85] Ted Miller, Mark Cohen, and Brian Wiersema, *The Extent and Costs of Crime Victimization: A New Look* (Washington, DC: National Institute of Justice, 1995).

[86] Craig A. Perkins, *Age Patterns of Victims of Serious Violent Crime* (Washington, DC: Bureau of Justice Statistics, 1997).

Chapter 3. Choice and Trait Theories

[1] U.S. Census Bureau, *Income, Poverty and Health Insurance in the United States: 2005* (P60-231). Available at: www.census.gov/prod/2006pubs/p60-231.pdf (accessed November 21, 2006).

[2] Marvin Wolfgang, Robert Figlio, and Thorsten Sellin, *Delinquency in a Birth Cohort* (Chicago: University of Chicago Press, 1972).

[3] Alan Lizotte, Terence Thornberry, Marvin Krohn, Deborah Chard-Wierschem, and David McDowall, "Neighborhood Context and Delinquency: A Longitudinal Analysis," in H. J. Kerner and E. Weitekamp, eds., *Cross-National Longitudinal Research on Human Development and Criminal Behavior* (Dordrecht, The Netherlands: Kluwer Academic Publishers, 1993), pp. 11–15.

[4] Jeremy Bentham, in Wilfrid Harrison, ed., *A Fragment on Government and an Introduction to the Principles of Morals and Legislation* (Oxford, England: Basil Blackwell, 1948).

[5] See, generally, Ernest Van den Haag, *Punishing Criminals* (New York: Basic Books, 1975).

[6] Timothy Brezina, "Delinquent Problem-Solving: An Interpretive Framework for Criminological Theory and Research," *Journal of Research in Crime and Delinquency* 37:3–30 (2000).

[7] Bruce Jacobs and Jody Miller, "Crack Dealing, Gender, and Arrest Avoidance," *Social Problems* 45:550–566 (1998).

[8] Pierre Tremblay and Carlo Morselli, "Patterns in Criminal Achievement: Wilson and Abrahamsen Revisited," *Criminology* 38:633–660 (2000).

[9] John Petraitis, Brian Flay, and Todd Miller, "Reviewing Theories of Adolescent Substance Use: Organizing Pieces in the Puzzle," *Psychological Bulletin* 117:67–86 (1995).

[10] Travis Hirschi, "Rational Choice and Social Control Theories of Crime," in D. Cornish and R. Clarke, eds., *The Reasoning Criminal* (New York: Springer-Verlag, 1986), p. 114.

[11] Melanie Wellsmith and Amy Burrell, "The Influence of Purchase Price and Ownership Levels on Theft Targets: The Example of Domestic Burglary," *British Journal of Criminology* 45:741–764 (2005).

[12] William Smith, Sharon Glave Frazee, and Elizabeth Davison, "Furthering the Integration of Routine Activity and Social Disorganization Theories: Small Units of Analysis and the Study of Street Robbery as a Diffusion Process," *Criminology* 38:489–521 (2000).

[13] Wim Bernasco and Paul Nieuwbeerta, "How Do Residential Burglars Select Target Areas? A New Approach to the Analysis of Criminal Location Choice," *British Journal of Criminology* 45:296–315 (2005).

[14] Christopher Uggen and Melissa Thompson, "The Socioeconomic Determinants of Ill-Gotten Gains: Within-Person Changes in Drug Use and Illegal Earnings," *American Journal of Sociology* 109:146–185 (2003).

[15] Timothy Brezina, "Delinquent Problem Solving: An Interpretive Framework for Criminological Theory and Research," *Journal of Research in Crime and Delinquency* 37:3–30 (2000); Andy Hochstetler, "Opportunities and Decisions: Interactional Dynamics in Robbery and Burglary Groups," *Criminology* 39:737–763 (2001).

[16] Pierre Tremblay and Carlo Morselli, "Patterns in Criminal Achievement: Wilson and Abrahmsen Revisited," *Criminology* 38:633–660 (2000).

[17] Steven Levitt and Sudhir Alladi Venkatesh, "An Economic Analysis of a Drug-Selling Gang's Finances," NBER Working Papers 6592 (Cambridge, MA: National Bureau of Economic Research, Inc., 1998).

[18] Bill McCarthy, "New Economics of Sociological Criminology," *Annual Review of Sociology* 28:417–442 (2002).

[19] D. Wayne Osgood, Janet Wilson, Patrick O'Malley, Jerald Bachman, and Lloyd Johnston, "Routine Activities and Individual Deviant Behavior," *American Sociological Review* 61:635–655 (1996).

[20] Brenda Sims Blackwell, "Perceived Sanction Threats, Gender, and Crime: A Test and Elaboration of Power-Control Theory," *Criminology* 38:439–488 (2000).

[21] Dana Haynie, "Contexts of Risk? Explaining the Link Between Girls' Pubertal Development and Their Delinquency Involvement," *Social Forces* 82:355–397 (2003).

[22] Raymond Paternoster, Shawn Bushway, Robert Brame, and Robert Apel, "The Effect of Teenage Employment on Delinquency and Problem Behaviors," *Social Forces* 82:297–336 (2003).

[23] Matthew Ploeger, "Youth Employment and Delinquency: Reconsidering a Problematic Relationship," *Criminology* 35:659–675 (1997).

[24] Jeremy Staff and Christopher Uggen, "The Fruits of Good Work: Early Work Experiences and Adolescent Deviance," *Journal of Research in Crime and Delinquency* 40:263–290 (2003).

[25] Michael Hindelang, Michael Gottfredson, and James Garofalo, *Victims of Personal Crime: An Empirical Foundation for a Theory of Personal Victimization* (Cambridge, MA: Ballinger, 1978).

[26] Lawrence Cohen and Marcus Felson, "Social Change and Crime Rate Trends: A Routine Activities Approach," *American Sociological Review* 44:588–608 (1979).

[27] David Maume, "Inequality and Metropolitan Rape Rates: A Routine Activity Approach," *Justice Quarterly* 6:513–527 (1989).

[28] Gordon Knowles, "Deception, Detection, and Evasion: A Trade Craft Analysis of Honolulu, Hawaii's Street Crack Cocaine Traffickers," *Journal of Criminal Justice* 27:443–455 (1999).

29 Paul Bellair, "Informal Surveillance and Street Crime: A Complex Relationship," *Criminology* 38:137–167 (2000).

30 Denise Osborn, Alan Trickett, and Rob Elder, "Area Characteristics and Regional Variates as Determinants of Area Property Crime Levels," *Journal of Quantitative Criminology* 8:265–282 (1992).

31 Matthew Robinson, "Lifestyles, Routine Activities, and Residential Burglary Victimization," *Journal of Criminal Justice* 22:37–52 (1999).

32 Melanie Wellsmith and Amy Burrell, "The Influence of Purchase Price and Ownership Levels on Theft Targets: The Example of Domestic Burglary," *British Journal of Criminology* 45:741–764 (2005).

33 Brandon Welsh and David Farrington, "Surveillance for Crime Prevention in Public Space: Results and Policy Choices in Britain and America," *Criminology and Public Policy* 3:701–730 (2004).

34 Robert O'Brien, "Relative Cohort Sex and Age-Specific Crime Rates: An Age-Period-Relative-Cohort-Size Model," *Criminology* 27:57–78 (1989).

35 Rolf Becker and Guido Mehlkop, "Social Class and Delinquency: An Empirical Utilization of Rational Choice Theory with Cross-Sectional Data of the 1990 and 2000 German General Population Surveys (Allbus)," *Rationality & Society* 18:193–235 (2006).

36 Daniel Nagin and Greg Pogarsky, "Integrating Celerity, Impulsivity, and Extralegal Sanction Threats into a Model of General Deterrence: Theory and Evidence," *Criminology* 39:865–892 (2001).

37 Ibid.

38 Cesare Beccaria, *On Crimes and Punishments and Other Writings*, Richard Bellamy, ed., Richard Davies, trans. (London: Cambridge University Press, 1995)

39 Daniel Nagin and Greg Pogarsky, "An Experimental Investigation of Deterrence: Cheating, Self-Serving Bias, and Impulsivity," *Criminology* 41:167–195 (2003).

40 Tomislav V. Kovandzic and John J. Sloan, "Police Levels and Crime Rates Revisited: A County-Level Analysis from Florida (1980–1998)," *Journal of Criminal Justice* 30:65–76 (2002).

41 Richard Timothy Coupe and Laurence Blake, "The Effects of Patrol Workloads and Response Strength on Arrests at Burglary Emergencies," *Journal of Criminal Justice* 33:239–255 (2005).

42 Gordon Bazemore and Mark Umbreit, "Rethinking the Sanctioning Function in Juvenile Court: Retributive or Restorative Responses to Youth Crime," *Crime and Delinquency* 41:296–316 (1995).

43 Michael White, James Fyfe, Suzanne Campbell, and John Goldkamp, "The Police Role in Preventing Homicide: Considering the Impact of Problem-Oriented Policing on the Prevalence of Murder," *Journal of Research in Crime and Delinquency* 40:194–226 (2003).

44 Eric Fritsch, Tory Caeti, and Robert Taylor, "Gang Suppression Through Saturation Patrol, Aggressive Curfew, and Truancy Enforcement: A Quasi-Experimental Test of the Dallas Anti-Gang Initiative," *Crime and Delinquency* 45:122–139 (1999).

45 Bruce Jacobs, "Anticipatory Undercover Targeting in High Schools," *Journal of Criminal Justice* 22:445–457 (1994).

46 Eric Jensen and Linda Metsger, "A Test of the Deterrent Effect of Legislative Waiver on Violent Juvenile Crime," *Crime and Delinquency* 40:96–104 (1994).

47 Wanda Foglia, "Perceptual Deterrence and the Mediating Effect of Internalized Norms Among Inner-City Teenagers," *Journal of Research in Crime and Delinquency* 34:414–442 (1997); Donald Green, "Measures of Illegal Behavior in Individual-Level Deterrence Research," *Journal of Research in Crime and Delinquency* 26:253–275 (1989); Charles Tittle, *Sanctions and Social Deviance: The Question of Deterrence* (New York: Praeger, 1980).

48 Greg Pogarsky, KiDeuk Kim, Ray Paternoster, "Perceptual Change in the National Youth Survey: Lessons for Deterrence Theory and Offender Decision-Making," *Justice Quarterly* 22:1–29 (2005).

49 Bureau of Justice Statistics, *Prisoners and Drugs* (Washington, DC: U.S. Government Printing Office, 1983); idem, *Prisoners and Alcohol* (Washington, DC: U.S. Government Printing Office, 1983).

50 Maynard Erickson and Jack Gibbs, "Punishment, Deterrence, and Juvenile Justice," in D. Shichor and D. Kelly, eds., *Critical Issues in Juvenile Justice* (Lexington, MA: Lexington Books, 1980), pp. 183–202.

51 Doris Layton MacKenzie and Spencer De Li, "The Impact of Formal and Informal Social Controls on the Criminal Activities of Probationers," *Journal of Research in Crime and Delinquency* 39:243–276 (2002).

52 Christina Dejong, "Survival Analysis and Specific Deterrence: Integrating Theoretical and Empirical Models of Recidivism," *Criminology* 35:561–576 (1997).

53 Paul Tracy and Kimberly Kempf-Leonard, *Continuity and Discontinuity in Criminal Careers* (New York: Plenum, 1996).

54 Pamela Lattimore, Christy Visher, and Richard Linster, "Predicting Rearrest for Violence Among Serious Youthful Offenders," *Journal of Research in Crime and Delinquency* 32:54–83 (1995).

55 Greg Pogarsky and Alex R. Piquero, "Can Punishment Encourage Offending? Investigating the 'Resetting' Effect," *Journal of Research in Crime and Delinquency* 40:92–117 (2003).

56 David Altschuler, "Juveniles and Violence: Is There an Epidemic and What Can Be Done?" Paper presented at the American Society of Criminology Meeting, Boston, November 1995; Charles Murray and Louis B. Cox, *Beyond Probation* (Beverly Hills, CA: Sage, 1979).

57 Patricia Brantingham, Paul Brantingham, and Wendy Taylor, "Situational Crime Prevention as a Key Component in Embedded Crime Prevention," *Canadian Journal of Criminology & Criminal Justice* 47:271–292 (2005).

58 Marcus Felson, "Routine Activities and Crime Prevention," in National Council for Crime Prevention, Studies on Crime and Crime Prevention, Annual Review, vol. 1 (Stockholm: Scandinavian University Press, 1992), pp. 30–34.

59 Andrew Fulkerson, "Blow and Go: The Breath-Analyzed Ignition Interlock Device as a Technological Response to DWI," *American Journal of Drug and Alcohol Abuse* 29:219–235 (2003).

60 Barry Webb, "Steering Column Locks and Motor Vehicle Theft: Evaluations for Three Countries," in Ronald Clarke, ed., *Crime Prevention Studies* (Monsey, NY: Criminal Justice Press, 1994), pp. 71–89.

61 David Farrington and Brandon Welsh, "Improved Street Lighting and Crime Prevention," *Justice Quarterly* 19:313–343 (2002).

62 Brandon Welsh and David Farrington, "Effects of Closed-Circuit Television on Crime," *Annals of the American Academy of Political and Social Science* 587:110–136 (2003).

63 Kenneth Novak, Jennifer Hartman, Alexander Holsinger, and Michael Turner, "The Effects of Aggressive Policing of Disorder on Serious Crime," *Policing* 22:171–190 (1999).

64 Lawrence Sherman, "Police Crackdowns: Initial and Residual Deterrence," in Michael Tonry and Norval Morris, eds., *Crime and Justice: A Review of Research*, vol. 12 (Chicago: University of Chicago Press, 1990), pp. 1–48.

65 Anthony Braga, David Weisburd, Elin Waring, Lorraine Green Mazerolle, William Spelman, and Francis Gajewski, "Problem-Oriented Policing in Violent Crime Places: A Randomized Controlled Experiment," *Criminology* 39:541–580 (1999).

66 Eric Fritsch, Tory Caeti, and Robert Taylor, "Gang Suppression Through Saturation Patrol, Aggressive Curfew, and Truancy Enforcement: A Quasi-Experimental Test of the Dallas Anti-Gang Initiative," *Crime and Delinquency* 45:122–139 (1999).

67 For an excellent review of Lombroso's work, as well as that of other well-known theorists, see Randy Martin, Robert Mutchnick, and W. Timothy Austin, *Criminological Thought: Pioneers Past and Present* (New York: Macmillan, 1990).

68 Marvin Wolfgang, "Cesare Lombroso," in Herman Mannheim, ed., *Pioneers in Criminology* (Montclair, NJ: Patterson Smith, 1970), pp. 232–271.

69 Gina Lombroso-Ferrero, *Criminal Man According to the Classification of Cesare Lombroso* (1911; reprint, Montclair, NJ: Patterson Smith, 1972), p. 7.

70 Edwin Driver, "Charles Buckman Goring," in Herman Mannheim, ed., *Pioneers in Criminology* (Montclair, NJ: Patterson Smith, 1970), pp. 429–442.

71 See, generally, Thorsten Sellin, "Enrico Ferri," in Herman Mannheim, ed., *Pioneers in Criminology* (Montclair, NJ: Patterson Smith, 1970), pp. 361–384.

72 Driver, "Charles Buckman Goring," pp. 434–435.

73 Ibid., p. 440.

74 Nicole Hahn Rafter, "Criminal Anthropology in the United States," *Criminology* 30:525–547 (1992).

75 B. R. McCandless, W. S. Persons, and A. Roberts, "Perceived Opportunity, Delinquency, Race, and Body Build Among Delinquent Youth," *Journal of Consulting and Clinical Psychology* 38:281–383 (1972).

76 Edmond O. Wilson, *Sociobiology: The New Synthesis* (Cambridge, MA: Harvard University Press, 1975).

77 For a general review, see John Archer, "Human Sociobiology: Basic Concepts and Limitations," *Journal of Social Issues* 47:11–26 (1991).

[78] Arthur Caplan, *The Sociobiology Debate: Readings on Ethical and Scientific Issues* (New York: Harper & Row, 1978).

[79] Dalton Conley and Neil Bennett, "Is Biology Destiny? Birth Weight and Life Chances," *American Sociological Review* 654:458–467 (2000).

[80] Diana Fishbein, "Selected Studies on the Biology of Crime," in John Conklin, ed., *New Perspectives in Criminology* (Needham Heights, MA: Allyn & Bacon, 1996), pp. 26–38.

[81] See, generally, Adrian Raine, *The Psychopathology of Crime* (San Diego: Academic Press, 1993); see also Leonard Hippchen, *The Ecologic-Biochemical Approaches to Treatment of Delinquents and Criminals* (New York: Van Nostrand Reinhold, 1978).

[82] "Diet and the Unborn Child: The Omega Point," *The Economist*, January 19, 2006.

[83] Amy Schonfeld, Sarah Mattson, and Edward Riley, "Moral Maturity and Delinquency after Prenatal Alcohol Exposure," *Journal of Studies on Alcohol* 66:545–554 (2005).

[84] Emily Oken, Robert O. Wright, Ken P. Kleinman, David Bellinger, Chitra J. Amarasiriwardena, Howard Hu, Janet W. Rich-Edwards, and Matthew W. Gillman, "Maternal Fish Consumption, Hair Mercury, and Infant Cognition in a U.S. Cohort," *Environmental Health Perspectives* 113:1376–1380 (2005).

[85] Mark Opler, Alan Brown, Joseph Graziano, Manisha Desai, Wei Zheng, Catherine Schaefer, Pamela Factor-Litvak, and Ezra S. Susser, "Prenatal Lead Exposure, Δ-Aminolevulinic Acid, and Schizophrenia," *Environmental Health Perspectives* 112:548–553 (2004); Jeff Evans, "Asymptomatic, High Lead Levels Tied to Delinquency," *Pediatric News* 37:13 (2003); Herbert Needleman, Christine McFarland, Roberta Ness, Stephen Fienberg, and Michael Tobin, "Bone Lead Levels in Adjudicated Delinquents: A Case Control Study," *Neurotoxicology and Teratology* 24:711–717 (2002); Jeff Evans, "Asymptomatic, High Lead Levels Tied to Delinquency," *Pediatric News* 37:13 (2003).

[86] K. Murata, P. Weihe, E. Budtz-Jorgensen, P. J. Jorgensen, and P. Grandjean, "Delayed Brainstem Auditory Evoked Potential Latencies in 14-Year-Old Children Exposed to Methylmercury," *Journal of Pediatrics* 144:177–183 (2004); Eric Konofal, Samuele Cortese, Michel Lecendreux, Isabelle Arnulf, and Marie Christine Mouren, "Effectiveness of Iron Supplementation in a Young Child with Attention-Deficit/Hyperactivity Disorder," *Pediatrics* 116:732–734 (2005).

[87] Eric Konofal, Michel Lecendreux, Isabelle Arnulf, and Marie-Christine Mouren, "Iron Deficiency in Children with Attention-Deficit/Hyperactivity Disorder," *Archives of Pediatric and Adolescent Medicine* 158:1113–1115 (2004).

[88] Alexandra Richardson and Paul Montgomery, "The Oxford-Durham Study: A Randomized Controlled Trial of Dietary Supplementation with Fatty Acids in Children with Developmental Coordination Disorder," *Pediatrics* 115:1360–1366 (2005).

[89] Courtney Van de Weyer, "Changing Diets, Changing Minds: How Food Affects Mental Well-Being and Behaviour," Sustain: The Alliance for Better Food and Farming, Available at: www.sustainweb.org/pdf/MHRep_LowRes.pdf (accessed March 26, 2006).

[90] Stephen Schoenthaler and Ian Bier, "The Effect of Vitamin–Mineral Supplementation on Juvenile Delinquency Among American Schoolchildren: A Randomized Double-Blind Placebo-Controlled Trial," *Journal of Alternative and Complementary Medicine: Research on Paradigm, Practice, and Policy* 6:7–18 (2000).

[91] Christy Miller Buchanan, Jacquelynne Eccles, and Jill Becker, "Are Adolescents the Victims of Raging Hormones? Evidence for Activational Effects of Hormones on Moods and Behavior at Adolescence," *Psychological Bulletin* 111:62–107 (1992).

[92] Diana Fishbein, "Selected Studies on the Biology of Crime."

[93] Anthony Walsh, "Genetic and Cytogenetic Intersex Anomalies: Can They Help Us to Understand Gender Differences in Deviant Behavior?" *International Journal of Offender Therapy and Comparative Criminology* 39:151–166 (1995).

[94] Celina Cohen-Bendahan, Jan Buitelaar, Stephanie van Goozen, Jacob Orlebeke, and Peggy Cohen-Kettenis, "Is There an Effect of Prenatal Testosterone on Aggression and Other Behavioral Traits? A Study Comparing Same-Sex and Opposite-Sex Twin Girls," *Hormones and Behavior* 47:230–237 (2005).

[95] Laurence Tancredi, *Hardwired Behavior: What Neuroscience Reveals about Morality* (London: Cambridge University Press, 2005).

[96] "McLean Researchers Document Brain Damage Linked to Child Abuse and Neglect." Information provided by newsletter of McLean's Hospital, Belmont, MA, December 14, 2000.

[97] Yaling Yang, Adrian Raine, Todd Lencz, Susan Bihrle, Lori Lacasse, and Patrick Colletti, "Prefrontal White Matter in Pathological Liars," *British Journal of Psychiatry* 187:320–325 (2005).

[98] Adrian Raine, Patricia Brennan, Brigitte Mednick, and Sarnoff Mednick, "High Rates of Violence, Crime, Academic Problems, and Behavioral Problems in Males with Both Early Neuromotor Deficits and Unstable Family Environments," *Archives of General Psychiatry* 53:544–549 (1966).

[99] Peer Briken, Niels Habermann, Wolfgang Berner, and Andreas Hill, "The Influence of Brain Abnormalities on Psychosocial Development, Criminal History and Paraphilias in Sexual Murderers," *Journal of Forensic Sciences* 50:1–5 (2005).

[100] Adrian Raine, P. Brennan, and S. Mednick, "Interaction Between Birth Complications and Early Maternal Rejection in Predisposing to Adult Violence: Specificity to Serious, Early Onset Violence," *American Journal of Psychiatry* 154:1265–1271 (1997).

[101] Joel Zimmerman, William Rich, Ingo Keilitz, and Paul Broder, "Some Observations on the Link Between Learning Disabilities and Juvenile Delinquency," *Journal of Criminal Justice* 9:9–17 (1981); J. W. Podboy and W. A. Mallory, "The Diagnosis of Specific Learning Disabilities in a Juvenile Delinquent Population," *Juvenile and Family Court Journal* 30:11–13 (1978).

[102] Charles Murray, "The Link Between Learning Disabilities and Juvenile Delinquency: Current Theory and Knowledge" (Washington, DC: U.S. Government Printing Office, 1976).

[103] Terrie Moffitt, "The Neuropsychology of Conduct Disorder." Mimeo (Madison: University of Wisconsin, 1992).

[104] Ibid.

[105] National Center for Addiction and Substance Abuse (CASA) at Columbia University, Substance Abuse and Learning Disabilities: Peas in a Pod or Apples and Oranges? (New York: CASA, 2000).

[106] Jack Katz, *Seduction of Crime: Moral and Sensual Attractions of Doing Evil* (New York: Basic Books, 1988), pp. 12–15.

[107] Lee Ellis, "Arousal Theory and the Religiosity-Criminality Relationship," in Peter Cordella and Larry Siegel, eds., *Contemporary Criminological Theory* (Boston: Northeastern University, 1996), pp. 65–84.

[108] Adrian Raine, Peter Venables, and Sarnoff Mednick, "Low Resting Heart Rate at Age 3 Years Predisposes to Aggression at Age 11 Years: Evidence from the Mauritius Child Health Project," *Journal of the American Academy of Adolescent Psychiatry* 36:1457–1464 (1997).

[109] For a review, see Lisabeth Fisher DiLalla and Irving Gottesman, "Biological and Genetic Contributors to Violence—Widom's Untold Tale," *Psychological Bulletin* 109:125–129 (1991).

[110] Anita Thapar, Kate Langley, Tom Fowler, Frances Rice, Darko Turic, Naureen Whittinger, John Aggleton, Marianne Van den Bree, Michael Owen, and Michael O'Donovan, "Catechol O-methyltransferase Gene Variant and Birth Weight Predict Early-Onset Antisocial Behavior in Children with Attention-Deficit/Hyperactivity Disorder," *Archives of General Psychiatry* 62:1275–1278 (2005).

[111] For an early review, see Barbara Wooton, *Social Science and Social Pathology* (London: Allen and Unwin, 1959); John Laub and Robert Sampson, "Unraveling Families and Delinquency: A Re-analysis of the Gluecks' Data," *Criminology* 26:355–380 (1988).

[112] Donald J. West and David P. Farrington, "Who Becomes Delinquent?" in Donald J. West and David P. Farrington, eds., *The Delinquent Way of Life* (London: Heinemann, 1977), pp. 1–28; D. J. West, *Delinquency: Its Roots, Careers, and Prospects* (Cambridge, MA: Harvard University Press, 1982).

[113] West, Delinquency, p. 114.

[114] David Farrington, "Understanding and Preventing Bullying," in Michael Tonry, ed., *Crime and Justice*, vol. 17 (Chicago: University of Chicago Press, 1993), pp. 381–457.

[115] Terence Thornberry, Adrienne Freeman-Gallant, Alan Lizotte, Marvin Krohn, and Carolyn Smith, "Linked Lives: The Intergenerational Transmission of Antisocial Behavior," *Journal of Abnormal Child Psychology* 31:171–185 (2003).

[116] David Rowe and David Farrington, "The Familial Transmission of Criminal Convictions," *Criminology* 35:177–201 (1997).

[117] Edwin J. C. G. van den Oord, Frank Verhulst, and Dorret Boomsma, "A Genetic Study of Maternal and Paternal Ratings of Problem Behaviors in 3-Year-Old Twins," *Journal of Abnormal Psychology* 105:349–357 (1996).

[118] Ibid., p. 95.

[119] Ping Qin, "The Relationship of Suicide Risk to Family History of Suicide and Psychiatric Disorders," *Psychiatric Times* 20:13 (2003).

[120] Jane Scourfield, Marianne Van den Bree, Neilson Martin, and Peter McGuffin, "Conduct Problems in Children and Adolescents: A Twin Study," *Archives of General Psychiatry* 61:489–496 (2004); Jeanette Taylor, Bryan Loney, Leonardo Bobadilla, William Iacono, and Matt McGue, "Genetic and Environmental Influences on Psychopathy Trait Dimensions in a Community Sample of Male Twins," *Journal of Abnormal Child Psychology* 31:633–645 (2003).

[121] Ginette Dionne, Richard Tremblay, Michel Boivin, David Laplante, and Daniel Perusse, "Physical Aggression and Expressive Vocabulary in 19-Month-Old Twins," *Developmental Psychology* 39:261–273 (2003).

[122] Sara R. Jaffee, Avshalom Caspi, Terrie Moffitt, Kenneth Dodge, Michael Rutter, Alan Taylor, and Lucy Tully, "Nature x Nurture: Genetic Vulnerabilities Interact with Physical Maltreatment to Promote Conduct Problems," *Development and Psychopathology* 17:67–84 (2005).

[123] Thomas Bouchard, "Genetic and Environmental Influences on Intelligence and Special Mental Abilities," *American Journal of Human Biology* 70:253–275 (1998).

[124] Remi Cadoret, Colleen Cain, and Raymond Crowe, "Evidence for a Gene-Environment Interaction in the Development of Adolescent Antisocial Behavior," *Behavior Genetics* 13:301–310 (1983).

[125] David Rowe, *The Limits of Family Influence: Genes, Experiences, and Behavior* (New York: Guilford Press, 1995); Cadoret, Cain, and Crowe, "Evidence for a Gene-Environment Interaction."

[126] Bernard Hutchings and Sarnoff Mednick, "Criminality in Adoptees and Their Adoptive and Biological Parents: A Pilot Study," in Sarnoff A. Mednick and Karl O. Christiansen, eds., *Biosocial Bases of Criminal Behavior* (New York: Gardner, 1977).

[127] For similar findings, see William Gabrielli and Sarnoff Mednick, "Urban Environment, Genetics, and Crime," *Criminology* 22:645–653 (1984).

[128] For a thorough review of this issue, see David Brandt and S. Jack Zlotnick, *The Psychology and Treatment of the Youthful Offender* (Springfield, IL: Charles C. Thomas, 1988).

[129] Spencer Rathus, *Psychology* (New York: Holt, Rinehart & Winston, 1996), pp. 11–21.

[130] See, generally, Sigmund Freud, *An Outline of Psychoanalysis*, James Strachey, trans. (New York: Norton, 1963).

[131] Seymour Halleck, *Psychiatry and the Dilemmas of Crime* (Berkeley: University of California Press, 1971).

[132] Robert Krueger, Avshalom Caspi, Phil Silva, and Rob McGee, "Personality Traits Are Differentially Linked to Mental Disorders: A Multitrait-Multidiagnosis Study of an Adolescent Birth Cohort," *Journal of Abnormal Psychology* 105:299–312 (1996).

[133] See, generally, Erik Erikson, *Identity, Youth, and Crisis* (New York: Norton, 1968).

[134] David Abrahamsen, *Crime and the Human Mind* (New York: Columbia University Press, 1944), p. 137.

[135] Michael Pullmann, Jodi Kerbs, Nancy Koroloff, Ernie Veach-White, Rita Gaylor, and DeDe Sieler, "Juvenile Offenders with Mental Health Needs: Reducing Recidivism Using Wraparound," *Crime and Delinquency* 52:375–397 (2006).

[136] James Sorrells, "Kids Who Kill," *Crime and Delinquency* 23:312–320 (1977).

[137] Beyers and Loeber, "Untangling Developmental Relations."

[138] See, generally, Fritz Redl and Hans Toch, "The Psychoanalytic Perspective," in Hans Toch, ed., *Psychology of Crime and Criminal Justice* (New York: Holt, Rinehart & Winston, 1979), pp. 193–195.

[139] August Aichorn, *Wayward Youth* (New York: Viking Press, 1935).

[140] Dorothy Espelage, Elizabeth Cauffman, Lisa Broidy, Alex Piquero, Paul Mazerolle, and Hans Steiner, "A Cluster-Analytic Investigation of MMPI Profiles of Serious Male and Female Juvenile Offenders," *Journal of the American Academy of Child & Adolescent Psychiatry* 42:770–777 (2003).

[141] Paige Crosby Ouimette, "Psychopathology and Sexual Aggression in Nonincarcerated Men," *Violence and Victimization* 12:389–397 (1997).

[142] Ellen Kjelsberg, "Gender and Disorder Specific Criminal Career Profiles in Former Adolescent Psychiatric In-Patients," *Journal of Youth & Adolescence* 33:261–270 (2004).

[143] Richard Rowe, Julie Messer, Robert Goodman, Robert Meltzer, and Howard Meltzer, "Conduct Disorder and Oppositional Defiant Disorder in a National Sample: Developmental Epidemiology," *Journal of Child Psychology & Psychiatry & Allied Disciplines* 45:609–621 (2004).

[144] Minna Ritakallio, Riittakerttu Kaltiala-Heino, Janne Kivivuori, Tiina Luukkaala, and Matti Rimpel, "Delinquency and the Profile of Offences Among Depressed and Non-Depressed Adolescents," *Criminal Behaviour & Mental Health* 16:100–110 (2006).

[145] Grégoire Zimmermann, "Delinquency in Male Adolescents: The Role of Alexithymia and Family Structure," *Journal of Adolescence* 29:321–332 (2006).

[146] Ching-hua Ho, J. B Kingree, and Martie Thompson, "Associations Between Juvenile Delinquency and Weight-Related Variables: Analyses from a National Sample of High School Students," *International Journal of Eating Disorders* 39:477–483 (2006).

[147] Jennifer Beyers and Rolf Loeber, "Untangling Developmental Relations Between Depressed Mood and Delinquency in Male Adolescents," *Journal of Abnormal Child Psychology* 31:247–267 (2003).

[148] Brandt and Zlotnick, *The Psychology and Treatment of the Youthful Offender*, pp. 72–73.

[149] Eric Silver, "Mental Disorder and Violent Victimization: The Mediating Role of Involvement in Conflicted Social Relationships," *Criminology* 40:191–212 (2002).

[150] Ibid.

[151] Stacy De Coster and Karen Heimer, "The Relationship Between Law Violation and Depression: An Interactionist Analysis," *Criminology* 39:799–836 (2001).

[152] B. Lögdberg, L-L. Nilsson, M. T. Levander, and S. Levander, "Schizophrenia, Neighbourhood, and Crime," *Acta Psychiatrica Scandinavica* 110:92–97 (2004); Stacy DeCoster and Karen Heimer, "The Relationship Between Law Violation and Depression: An Interactionist Analysis," *Criminology* 39:799–837 (2001).

[153] Courtenay Sellers, Christopher Sullivan, Bonita Veysey, and Jon Shane, "Responding to Persons with Mental Illnesses: Police Perspectives on Specialized and Traditional Practices," *Behavioral Sciences & the Law* 23:647–657 (2005).

[154] Paul Hirschfield, Tina Maschi, Helene Raskin White, Leah Goldman Traub, and Rolf Loeber, "Mental Health and Juvenile Arrests: Criminality, Criminalization, or Compassion?" *Criminology* 44:593–630 (2006).

[155] Walter Mischel, Yuichi Shoda, and Philip Peake, "The Nature of Adolescent Competencies Predicted by Preschool Delay of Gratification," *Journal of Personality and Social Psychology* 54:687–696 (1988); Albert Bandura and Richard Walters, *Social Learning and Personality Development* (New York: Holt, Rinehart & Winston, 1963).

[156] David Perry, Louise Perry, and Paul Rasmussen, "Cognitive Social Learning Mediators of Aggression," *Child Development* 57:700–711 (1986).

[157] Bonnie Carlson, "Children's Beliefs About Punishment," *American Journal of Orthopsychiatry* 56:308–312 (1986).

[158] See, generally, Jean Piaget, *The Moral Judgment of the Child* (London: Kegan Paul, 1932).

[159] Lawrence Kohlberg, *Stages in the Development of Moral Thought and Action* (New York: Holt, Rinehart & Winston, 1969).

[160] L. Kohlberg, K. Kauffman, P. Scharf, and J. Hickey, *The Just Community Approach in Corrections: A Manual* (Niantic: Connecticut Department of Corrections, 1973).

[161] Quinten Raaijmakers, Rutger Engels, and Anne Van Hoof, "Delinquency and Moral Reasoning in Adolescence and Young Adulthood," *International Journal of Behavioral Development* 29:247–258 (2005); Scott Henggeler, *Delinquency in Adolescence* (Newbury Park, CA: Sage, 1989), p. 26.

[162] K. A. Dodge, "A Social Information Processing Model of Social Competence in Children," in M. Perlmutter, ed., *Minnesota Symposium in Child Psychology*, vol. 18 (Hillsdale, NJ: Erlbaum, 1986), pp. 77–125.

[163] Elizabeth Cauffman, Laurence Steinberg, and Alex Piquero, "Psychological, Neuropsychological, and Physiological Correlates of Serious Antisocial Behavior in Adolescence: The Role of Self-Control," *Criminology* 43:133–176 (2005).

164 Donald Lynam and Joshua Miller, "Personality Pathways to Impulsive Behavior and Their Relations to Deviance: Results from Three Samples," *Journal of Quantitative Criminology* 20:319–341 (2004).

165 Adrian Raine, Peter Venables, and Mark Williams, "Better Autonomic Conditioning and Faster Electrodermal Half-Recovery Time at Age 15 Years as Possible Protective Factors against Crime at Age 29 Years," *Developmental Psychology* 32:624–630 (1996).

166 Jean Marie McGloin and Travis Pratt, "Cognitive Ability and Delinquent Behavior Among Inner-City Youth: A Life-Course Analysis of Main, Mediating, and Interaction Effects," *International Journal of Offender Therapy & Comparative Criminology* 47:253–271 (2003).

167 Tony Ward and Claire Stewart, "The Relationship Between Human Needs and Criminogenic Needs," *Psychology, Crime & Law* 9:219–225 (2003).

168 David Ward, Mark Stafford, and Louis Gray, "Rational Choice, Deterrence, and Theoretical Integration," *Journal of Applied Social Psychology* 36:571–585 (2006).

169 Coralijn Nas, Bram Orobio de Castro, and Willem Koops, "Social Information Processing in Delinquent Adolescents," *Psychology, Crime & Law* 11:363–375 (2005).

170 Elizabeth Kubik and Jeffrey Hecker, "Cognitive Distortions About Sex and Sexual Offending: A Comparison of Sex Offending Girls, Delinquent Girls, and Girls from the Community," *Journal of Child Sexual Abuse* 14:43–69 (2005).

171 L. Huesmann and L. Eron, "Individual Differences and the Trait of Aggression," *European Journal of Personality* 3:95–106 (1989).

172 Judith Baer and Tina Maschi, "Random Acts of Delinquency: Trauma and Self-Destructiveness in Juvenile Offenders," *Child & Adolescent Social Work Journal* 20:85–99 (2003).

173 Rolf Loeber and Dale Hay, "Key Issues in the Development of Aggression and Violence from Childhood to Early Adulthood," *Annual Review of Psychology* 48:371–410 (1997).

174 Kathleen Cirillo, B. E. Pruitt, Brian Colwell, Paul M. Kingery, Robert S. Hurley, and Danny Ballard, "School Violence: Prevalence and Intervention Strategies for At-Risk Adolescents," *Adolescence* 33:319–331 (1998).

175 Leilani Greening, "Adolescent Stealers' and Nonstealers' Social Problem-Solving Skills," *Adolescence* 32:51–56 (1997).

176 Graeme Newman, *Understanding Violence* (New York: Lippincott, 1979), pp. 145–146.

177 Kathleen Cirillo, B. E. Pruitt, Brian Colwell, Paul Kingery, Robert Hurley, and Danny Ballard, "School Violence: Prevalence and Intervention Strategies for At-Risk Adolescents," *Adolescence* 33:319–331 (1998).

178 See, generally, Walter Mischel, *Introduction to Personality,* 4th ed. (New York: Holt, Rinehart & Winston, 1986).

179 Sheldon Glueck and Eleanor Glueck, *Unraveling Juvenile Delinquency* (Cambridge, MA: Harvard University Press, 1950).

180 Essi Viding, James Blair, Terrie Moffitt, and Robert Plomin, "Evidence for Substantial Genetic Risk for Psychopathy in 7-Year-Olds," *Journal of Child Psychology and Psychiatry* 46:592–597 (2005).

181 Edelyn Verona and Joyce Carbonell, "Female Violence and Personality," *Criminal Justice and Behavior* 27:176–195 (2000); David Farrington, "Psychobiological Factors in the Explanation and Reduction of Delinquency," *Today's Delinquent* 7:37–51 (1988).

182 See, generally, Hans Eysenck, *Personality and Crime* (London: Routledge and Kegan Paul, 1977).

183 Hans Eysenck and M.W. Eysenck, *Personality and Individual Differences* (New York: Plenum, 1985).

184 Catrien Bijleveld and Jan Hendriks, "Juvenile Sex Offenders: Differences Between Group and Solo Offenders," *Psychology, Crime & Law* 9:237–246 (2003).

185 Linda Mealey, "The Sociobiology of Sociopathy: An Integrated Evolutionary Model," *Behavioral and Brain Sciences* 18:523–540 (1995).

186 Peter Johansson and Margaret Kerr, "Psychopathy and Intelligence: A Second Look," *Journal of Personality Disorders* 19:357–369 (2005).

187 Sue Kellett and Harriet Gross, "Addicted to Joyriding? An Exploration of Young Offenders' Accounts of Their Car Crime," *Psychology, Crime & Law* 12:39–59 (2006).

188 Lewis Yablonsky, *The Violent Gang* (New York: Penguin Books, 1971), pp. 195–205.

189 Helene Raskin White, Erich Labouvie, and Marsha Bates, "The Relationship Between Sensation Seeking and Delinquency: A Longitudinal Analysis," *Journal of Research in Crime and Delinquency* 2:197–211 (1985).

190 Rathus, *Psychology*, p. 452.

191 Kent Kiehl, Andra Smith, Robert Hare, Adrianna Mendrek, Bruce Forster, Johann Brink, and Peter F. Liddle, "Limbic Abnormalities in Affective Processing by Criminal Psychopaths as Revealed by Functional Magnetic Resonance Imaging," *Biological Psychiatry* 5:677–684 (2001).

192 David Lykken, "Psychopathy, Sociopathy, and Crime," *Society* 34:30–38 (1996).

193 L. M. Terman, "Research on the Diagnosis of Predelinquent Tendencies," *Journal of Delinquency* 9:124–130 (1925); L. M. Terman, *Measurement of Intelligence* (Boston: Houghton Mifflin, 1916); for example, see M. G. Caldwell, "The Intelligence of Delinquent Boys Committed to Wisconsin Industrial School," *Journal of Criminal Law and Criminology* 20:421–428 (1929); and C. Murcheson, *Criminal Intelligence* (Worcester, MA: Clark University, 1926), pp. 41–44.

194 Henry Goddard, *Efficiency and Levels of Intelligence* (Princeton, NJ: Princeton University Press, 1920).

195 William Healy and Augusta Bronner, *Delinquency and Criminals: Their Making and Unmaking* (New York: Macmillan, 1926).

196 Joseph Lee Rogers, H. Harrington Cleveland, Edwin van den Oord, and David Rowe, "Resolving the Debate Over Birth Order, Family Size, and Intelligence," *American Psychologist* 55:599–612 (2000).

197 Kenneth Eels, *Intelligence and Cultural Differences* (Chicago: University of Chicago Press, 1951), p. 181.

198 Sorel Cahahn and Nora Cohen, "Age Versus Schooling Effects on Intelligence Development," *Child Development* 60:1239–1249 (1989).

199 Robert McCall and Michael Carriger, "A Meta-Analysis of Infant Habituation and Recognition Memory Performance as Predictors of Later IQ," *Child Development* 64:57–79 (1993).

200 Edwin Sutherland, "Mental Deficiency and Crime," in Kimball Young, ed., *Social Attitudes* (New York: Henry Holt, 1973), ch. 15.

201 H. D. Day, J. M. Franklin, and D. D. Marshall, "Predictors of Aggression in Hospitalized Adolescents," *Journal of Psychology* 132:427–435 (1998); Scott Menard and Barbara Morse, "A Structuralist Critique of the IQ-Delinquency Hypothesis: Theory and Evidence," *American Journal of Sociology* 89:1347–1378 (1984).

202 Travis Hirschi and Michael Hindelang, "Intelligence and Delinquency: A Revisionist Review," *American Sociological Review* 42:471–586 (1977).

203 Terrie Moffitt and Phil Silva, "IQ and Delinquency: A Direct Test of the Differential Detection Hypothesis," *Journal of Abnormal Psychology* 97:1–4 (1988); E. Kandel, S. Mednick, L. Sorenson-Kirkegaard, B. Hutchings, J. Knop, R. Rosenberg, and F. Schulsinger, "IQ as a Protective Factor for Subjects at a High Risk for Antisocial Behavior," *Journal of Consulting and Clinical Psychology* 56:224–226 (1988); Christine Ward and Richard McFall, "Further Validation of the Problem Inventory for Adolescent Girls: Comparing Caucasian and Black Delinquents and Nondelinquents," *Journal of Consulting and Clinical Psychology* 54:732–733 (1986).

204 Terri Moffitt, William Gabrielli, Sarnoff Mednick, and Fini Schulsinger, "Socioeconomic Status, IQ, and Delinquency," *Journal of Abnormal Psychology* 90:152–156 (1981); for a similar finding, see L. Hubble and M. Groff, "Magnitude and Direction of WISC-R Verbal Performance IQ Discrepancies Among Adjudicated Male Delinquents," *Journal of Youth and Adolescence* 10:179–183 (1981).

205 Jennifer White, Terrie Moffitt, and Phil Silva, "A Prospective Replication of the Protective Effects of IQ in Subjects at High Risk for Juvenile Delinquency," *Journal of Consulting and Clinical Psychology* 37:719–724 (1989).

206 Donald Lynam, Terrie Moffitt, and Magda Stouthamer-Loeber, "Explaining the Relations Between IQ and Delinquency: Class, Race, Test Motivation, School Failure, or Self-Control," *Journal of Abnormal Psychology* 102:187–196 (1993).

207 David Farrington, "Juvenile Delinquency," in John C. Coleman, ed., *The School Years* (London: Routledge, 1992), p. 137.

208 Glenn Walters and Thomas White, "Heredity and Crime: Bad Genes or Bad Research," *Justice Quarterly* 27:455–485 (1989), p. 478.

209 Lee Ellis, "Genetics and Criminal Behavior," *Criminology* 10:58 (1982).

210 Sheryl Ellis, "It Does Take a Village: A Youth Violence Program in Kincheloe, Michigan, Galvanizes the Community," *Corrections Today* 60:100–103 (1998).

211 Joan McCord and William McCord, "A Follow-Up Report on the Cambridge-Somerville Youth Study," *Annals* 322:89–98 (1959).

212 Edwin Schur, *Radical Nonintervention: Rethinking the Delinquency Problem* (Englewood Cliffs, NJ: Prentice-Hall, 1973).

Chapter 4. Sociological Views of Delinquency

[1] Edwin Lemert, *Human Deviance, Social Problems, and Social Control* (Englewood Cliffs, NJ: Prentice-Hall, 1967).

[2] See, generally, Stephen Cernkovich and Peggy Giordano, "Family Relationships and Delinquency," *Criminology* 25:295–321 (1987); Paul Howes and Howard Markman, "Marital Quality and Child Functioning: A Longitudinal Investigation," *Child Development* 60:1044–1051 (1989).

[3] Lance Hannon, "Extremely Poor Neighborhoods and Homicide," *Social Science Quarterly* 86:1418–1434 (2005); Geetanjali Dabral Datta, S.V S.V Subramanian, Graham Colditz, Ichiro Kawachi, Julie Palmer, and Lynn Rosenberg, "Individual, Neighborhood, and State-Level Predictors of Smoking Among U.S. Black Women: A Multilevel Analysis," *Social Science & Medicine* 63:1034–1044 (2006).

[4] Stacey Nofziger and Don Kurtz, "Violent Lives: A Lifestyle Model Linking Exposure to Violence to Juvenile Violent Offending," *Journal of Research in Crime and Delinquency* 42:3–26 (2006); Joanne Kaufman, "Explaining the Race/Ethnicity–Violence Relationship: Neighborhood Context and Social Psychological Processes," *Justice Quarterly* 22:224–251 (2005).

[5] Justin Patchin, Beth Huebner, John McCluskey, Sean Varano, and Timothy Bynum, "Exposure to Community Violence and Childhood Delinquency," *Crime and Delinquency* 52:307–332 (2006).

[6] Gary LaFree, *Losing Legitimacy: Street Crime and the Decline of Social Institutions in America* (Boulder, CO: Westview, 1998).

[7] Sam Roberts, *Who We Are Now: The Changing Face of America in the Twenty-First Century* (New York: Times Books, Henry Holt, 2004).

[8] Emilie Andersen Allan and Darrell Steffensmeier, "Youth, Underemployment, and Property Crime: Differential Effects of Job Availability and Job Quality on Juvenile and Young Adult Arrest Rates," *American Sociological Review* 54:107–123 (1989).

[9] *U.S. Department of Census Data, Race and Income* (Washington, DC: Census Bureau, 2003).

[10] Ronald Mincy, ed., *Black Males Left Behind* (Washington, DC: Urban Institute, 2006); Erik Eckholm, "Plight Deepens for Black Men, Studies Warn," *New York Times*, March 20, 2006.

[11] Oscar Lewis, "The Culture of Poverty," *Scientific American* 215:19–25 (1966).

[12] Laura G. De Haan and Shelley MacDermid, "The Relationship of Individual and Family Factors to the Psychological Well-Being of Junior High School Students Living in Urban Poverty," *Adolescence* 33:73–90 (1998).

[13] Julian Chow and Claudia Coulton, "Was There a Social Transformation of Urban Neighborhoods in the 1980s?" *Urban Studies* 35:135–175 (1998).

[14] Rodrick Wallace, "Expanding Coupled Shock Fronts of Urban Decay and Criminal Behavior: How U.S. Cities Are Becoming 'Hollowed Out,'" *Journal of Quantitative Criminology* 7:333–355 (1991).

[15] Ken Auletta, *The Under Class* (New York: Random House, 1982).

[16] William Julius Wilson, *The Truly Disadvantaged* (Chicago: University of Chicago Press, 1987).

[17] Jeanne Brooks-Gunn and Greg J. Duncan, "The Effects of Poverty on Children," *The Future of Children* 7:34–39 (1997).

[18] Brooks-Gunn and Duncan, "The Effects of Poverty on Children."

[19] G. R. Patterson, L. Crosby, and S. Vuchnich, "Predicting Risk for Early Police Arrest," *Journal of Quantitative Criminology* 8:335–353 (1992).

[20] Clifford R. Shaw and Henry D. McKay, *Juvenile Delinquency and Urban Areas*, rev. ed. (Chicago: University of Chicago Press, 1972).

[21] Ibid.

[22] Robert Bursik and Harold Grasmick, "The Multiple Layers of Social Disorganization." Paper presented at the annual meeting of the American Society of Criminology, New Orleans, November 1992; Robert Bursik and Harold Grasmick, "Longitudinal Neighborhood Profiles in Delinquency: The Decomposition of Change," *Journal of Quantitative Criminology* 8:247–256 (1992).

[23] Delber Elliott, William Julius Wilson, David Huizinga, Robert Sampson, Amanda Elliott, and Bruce Rankin, "The Effects of Neighborhood Disadvantage on Adolescent Development," *Journal of Research in Crime and Delinquency* 33:414 (1996).

[24] Robert Bursik and Harold Grasmick, "Economic Deprivation and Neighborhood Crime Rates, 1960–1980," *Law and Society Review* 27:263–278 (1993).

[25] For a classic look, see Frederick Thrasher, *The Gang* (Chicago: University of Chicago Press, 1927).

[26] Dana Haynie, Eric Silver, and Brent Teasdale, "Neighborhood Characteristics, Peer Networks, and Adolescent Violence," *Journal of Quantitative Criminology* 22:147–169 (2006).

[27] National Survey on Drug Use and Health (NSDUH), *Youth Violence and Illicit Drug Use*, 2006. Available at: www.oas.samhsa.gov/2k6/youthViolence/youthViolence.htm (accessed February 8, 2006).

[28] Ruth Peterson, Lauren Krivo, and Mark Harris, "Disadvantage and Neighborhood Violent Crime: Do Local Institutions Matter?" *Journal of Research in Crime and Delinquency* 37:31–63 (2000).

[29] D. Wayne Osgood and Jeff Chambers, "Social Disorganization Outside the Metropolis: An Analysis of Rural Youth Violence," *Criminology* 38:81–117 (2000).

[30] Beverly Stiles, Xiaoru Liu, and Howard Kaplan, "Relative Deprivation and Deviant Adaptations: The Mediating Effects of Negative Self-Feelings," *Journal of Research in Crime and Delinquency* 37:64–90 (2000).

[31] Karen Parker and Scott Maggard, "Structural Theories and Race-Specific Drug Arrests: What Structural Factors Account for the Rise in Race-Specific Drug Arrests Over Time," *Crime and Delinquency* 51:521–547 (2005).

[32] Ellen Kurtz, Barbara Koons, and Ralph Taylor, "Land Use, Physical Deterioration, Resident-Based Control, and Calls for Service on Urban Street Blocks," *Justice Quarterly* 15:121–149 (1998).

[33] Gregory Squires and Charis Kubrin, "Privileged Places: Race, Uneven Development and the Geography of Opportunity in Urban America," *Urban Studies* 42:47–68 (2005); Matthew Lee, Michael Maume, and Graham Ousey, "Social Isolation and Lethal Violence across the Metro/Nonmetro Divide: The Effects of Socioeconomic Disadvantage and Poverty Concentration on Homicide," *Rural Sociology* 68:107–131 (2003).

[34] Lee, Maume, and Ousey, "Social Isolation and Lethal Violence across the Metro/Nonmetro Divide"; Charis E. Kubrin, "Structural Covariates of Homicide Rates: Does Type of Homicide Matter?" *Journal of Research in Crime and Delinquency* 40:139–170 (2003); Darrell Steffensmeier and Dana Haynie, "Gender, Structural Disadvantage, and Urban Crime: Do Macrosocial Variables Also Explain Female Offending Rates?" *Criminology* 38:403–438 (2000).

[35] Micere Keels, Greg Duncan, Stefanie Deluca, Ruby Mendenhall, and James Rosenbaum, "Fifteen Years Later: Can Residental Mobility Programs Provide a Long-Term Escape from Neighborhood Segregation, Crime, and Poverty?" *Demography* 42:51–72 (2005).

[36] Allen Liska and Paul Bellair, "Violent-Crime Rates and Racial Composition: Convergence Over Time," *American Journal of Sociology* 101:578–610 (1995).

[37] Patricia McCall and Karen Parker, "A Dynamic Model of Racial Competition, Racial Inequality, and Interracial Violence," *Sociological Inquiry* 75:273–294 (2005).

[38] Steven Barkan and Steven Cohn, "Why Whites Favor Spending More Money to Fight Crime: The Role of Racial Prejudice," *Social Problems* 52:300–314 (2005).

[39] Pamela Wilcox, Neil Quisenberry, and Shayne Jones, "The Built Environment and Community Crime Risk Interpretation," *Journal of Research in Crime and Delinquency* 40:322–345 (2003).

[40] Yili Xu, Mora Fiedler, and Karl Flaming, "Discovering the Impact of Community Policing: The Broken Windows Thesis, Collective Efficacy, and Citizens' Judgment," *Journal of Research in Crime and Delinquency* 42:147–186 (2005).

[41] Pamela Wilcox Rountree and Kenneth Land, "Burglary Victimization, Perceptions of Crime Risk, and Routine Activities: A Multilevel Analysis Across Seattle Neighborhoods and Census Tracts," *Journal of Research in Crime and Delinquency* 33:147–180 (1996).

[42] See, generally, Wesley Skogan, "Fear of Crime and Neighborhood Change," in Albert Reiss and Michael Tonry, eds., *Communities and Crime* (Chicago: University of Chicago Press, 1986), pp. 191–232.

[43] Jeffery Will and John McGrath, "Crime, Neighborhood Perceptions, and the Underclass: The Relationship Between Fear of Crime and Class Position," *Journal of Criminal Justice* 23:163–176 (1995).

[44] John Hagan, Carla Shedd, and Monique Payne, "Race, Ethnicity, and Youth Perceptions of Criminal Injustice," *American Sociological Review* 70:381–407 (2005).

[45] Margo Wilson and Martin Daly, "Life Expectancy, Economic Inequality, Homicide, and Reproductive Timing in Chicago Neighborhoods," *British Medical Journal* 314:1271–1275 (1997).

46 Randy LaGrange, Kenneth Ferraro, and Michael Supancic, "Perceived Risk and Fear of Crime: Role of Social and Physical Incivilities," *Journal of Research in Crime and Delinquency* 29:311–334 (1992).

47 Karen Parker, Brian Stults, and Stephen Rice, "Racial Threat, Concentrated Disadvantage, and Social Control: Considering the Macro-Level Sources of Variation in Arrests," *Criminology* 43:1111–1134 (2005).

48 Michael Reisig and Jeffrey Michael Cancino, "Incivilities in Nonmetropolitan Communities: The Effects of Structural Constraints, Social Conditions, and Crime," *Journal of Criminal Justice* 32:15–29 (2004).

49 Robert Sampson, Jeffrey Morenoff, and Felton Earls, "Beyond Social Capital: Spatial Dynamics of Collective Efficacy for Children," *American Sociological Review* 64:633–660 (1999).

50 Fred Markowitz, Paul Bellair, Allen Liska, and Jianhong Liu, "Extending Social Disorganization Theory: Modeling the Relationships Between Cohesion, Disorder, and Fear," *Criminology* 39:293–320 (2001).

51 Robert J. Sampson and Stephen W. Raudenbush, *Disorder in Urban Neighborhoods: Does It Lead to Crime?* (Washington, DC: National Institute of Justice, 2001).

52 Bridget Freisthler, Elizabeth Lascala, Paul Gruenewald, and Andrew Treno, "An Examination of Drug Activity: Effects of Neighborhood Social Organization on the Development of Drug Distribution Systems," *Substance Use & Misuse* 40:671–686 (2005).

53 Chris Gibson, Jihong Zhao, Nicholas Lovrich, and Michael Gaffney, "Social Integration, Individual Perceptions of Collective Efficacy, and Fear of Crime in Three Cities," *Justice Quarterly* 19:537–564 (2002); Felton Earls, *Linking Community Factors and Individual Development* (Washington, DC: National Institute of Justice, 1998).

54 Bursik and Grasmick, "The Multiple Layers of Social Disorganization." Paper presented at the annual meeting of the American Society of Criminology, New Orleans, November 1992.

55 George Capowich, "The Conditioning Effects of Neighborhood Ecology on Burglary Victimization," *Criminal Justice and Behavior* 30:39–62 (2003); Ruth Peterson, Lauren Krivo, and Mark Harris, "Disadvantage and Neighborhood Violent Crime: Do Local Institutions Matter?" *Journal of Research in Crime and Delinquency* 37:31–63 (2000).

56 Andrea Altschuler, Carol Somkin, and Nancy Adler, "Local Services and Amenities, Neighborhood Social Capital, and Health," *Social Science and Medicine* 59:1219–1230 (2004).

57 Jennifer Beyers, John Bates, Gregory Pettit, and Kenneth Dodge, "Neighborhood Structure, Parenting Processes, and the Development of Youths' Externalizing Behaviors: A Multilevel Analysis," *American Journal of Community Psychology* 31:35–53 (2003).

58 Ronald Simons, Leslie Gordon Simons, Callie Harbin Burt, Gene Brody, and Carolyn Cutrona, "Collective Efficacy, Authoritative Parenting and Delinquency: A Longitudinal Test of a Model Integrating Community and Family-Level Processes," *Criminology* 43:989–1029 (2005).

59 See, for example, Robert Merton, *Social Theory and Social Structure* (Glencoe, IL: Free Press, 1957).

60 Robert Agnew, "Foundation for a General Strain Theory of Crime and Delinquency," *Criminology* 30:47–87 (1992).

61 Ibid., p. 57.

62 Tami Videon, "The Effects of Parent-Adolescent Relationships and Parental Separation on Adolescent Well-Being," *Journal of Marriage & the Family* 64:489–504 (2002).

63 Cesar Rebellon, "Reconsidering the Broken Homes/Delinquency Relationship and Exploring Its Mediating Mechanism(s)," *Criminology* 40:103–135 (2002).

64 Timothy Brezina, "Adolescent Maltreatment and Delinquency: The Question of Intervening Processes," *Journal of Research in Crime and Delinquency* 35:71–99 (1998).

65 Robert Agnew, Timothy Brezina, John Paul Wright, and Francis T. Cullen, "Strain, Personality Traits, and Delinquency: Extending General Strain Theory," *Criminology* 40:43–71 (2002).

66 Lee Ann Slocum, Sally Simpson, and Douglas Smith, "Strained Lives and Crime: Examining Intra-Individual Variation in Strain and Offending in a Sample of Incarcerated Women," *Criminology* 43:1067–1110 (2005).

67 Paul Mazerolle, Velmer Burton, Francis Cullen, T. David Evans, and Gary Payne, "Strain, Anger, and Delinquent Adaptations Specifying General Strain Theory," *Journal of Criminal Justice* 28:89–101 (2000).

68 Stephen Cernkovich, Peggy Giordano, and Jennifer Rudolph, "Race, Crime, and the American Dream," *Journal of Research in Crime and Delinquency* 37:131–170 (2000).

69 Paul Mazerolle, Velmer Burton, Francis Cullen, T. David Evans, and Gary Payne, "Strain, Anger, and Delinquent Adaptations: Specifying General Strain Theory," *Journal of Criminal Justice* 28:89–101 (2000); Paul Mazerolle and Alex Piquero, "Violent Responses to Strain: An Examination of Conditioning Influences," *Violence and Victimization* 12:323–345 (1997).

70 George E. Capowich, Paul Mazerolle, and Alex Piquero, "General Strain Theory, Situational Anger, and Social Networks: An Assessment of Conditioning Influences," *Journal of Criminal Justice* 29:445–461 (2001).

71 Robert Agnew, "Experienced, Vicarious, and Anticipated Strain: An Exploratory Study on Physical Victimization and Delinquency," *Justice Quarterly* 19:603–633 (2002).

72 Albert Cohen, *Delinquent Boys* (New York: Free Press, 1955).

73 Richard Cloward and Lloyd Ohlin, *Delinquency and Opportunity* (New York: Free Press, 1960).

74 See, for example, Irving Spergel, *Racketville, Slumtown, and Haulburg* (Chicago: University of Chicago Press, 1964).

75 James Short, "Gangs, Neighborhoods, and Youth Crime," *Criminal Justice Research Bulletin* 5:1–11 (1990).

76 Michael Leiber, Mahesh Nalla, and Margaret Farnworth, "Explaining Juveniles' Attitudes Toward the Police," *Justice Quarterly* 15:151–173 (1998).

77 A. Leigh Ingram, "Type of Place, Urbanism, and Delinquency: Further Testing of the Determinist Theory," *Journal of Research in Crime and Delinquency* 30:192–212 (1993).

78 Alan Lizotte, Terence Thornberry, Marvin Krohn, Deborah Chard-Wierschem, and David McDowall, "Neighborhood Context and Delinquency: A Longitudinal Analysis," in H. J. Kerner and E. Weitekamp, eds., *Cross-National Longitudinal Research on Human Development and Criminal Behavior* (Dordrecht, The Netherlands: Kluwer Academic Publishers, 1993), pp. 1–11.

79 Eric Stewart, Ronald Simons, and Rand Conger, "Assessing Neighborhood and Social Psychological Influences on Childhood Violence in an African-American Sample," *Criminology* 40:801–830 (2002).

80 Ronald Simons, Chyi-In Wu, Kuei-Hsiu Lin, Leslie Gordon, and Rand Conger, "A Cross-Cultural Examination of the Link Between Corporal Punishment and Adolescent Antisocial Behavior," *Criminology* 38:47–79 (2000).

81 Kristi Holsinger and Alexander Holsinger, "Differential Pathways to Violence and Self-Injurious Behavior: African American and White Girls in the Juvenile Justice System," *Journal of Research in Crime and Delinquency* 42:211–242 (2005); Carolyn Smith and Terence Thornberry, "The Relationship Between Childhood Maltreatment and Adolescent Involvement in Delinquency," *Criminology* 33:451–479 (1995).

82 John Paul Wright and Francis Cullen, "Parental Efficacy and Delinquent Behavior: Do Control and Support Matter?" *Criminology* 39:677–706 (2001).

83 Karol Kumpfer and Rose Alvarado, "Strengthening Approaches for the Prevention of Youth Problem Behaviors," *American Psychologist* 58:457–465 (2003); Carter Hay, "Parenting, Self-Control, and Delinquency: A Test of Self-Control Theory," *Criminology* 39:707–736 (2001).

84 Alexander Vazsonyi and Lloyd Pickering, "The Importance of Family and School Domains in Adolescent Deviance: African-American and Caucasian Youth," *Journal of Youth and Adolescence* 32:115–129 (2003).

85 Christopher B. Swanson, *Who Graduates? Who Doesn't? A Statistical Portrait of Public High School Graduation, Class of 2001* (Washington, DC: Urban Institute, 2004).

86 Dana Haynie, Eric Silver, and Brent Teasdale, "Neighborhood Characteristics, Peer Networks, and Adolescent Violence," *Journal of Quantitative Criminology* 22:147–169 (2006).

87 Paul Friday, Xin Ren, Elmar Weitekamp, Hans-Jürgen Kerner, and Terrance Taylor, "A Chinese Birth Cohort: Theoretical Implications," *Journal of Research in Crime and Delinquency* 42:123–146 (2005).

88 Daneen Deptula and Robert Cohen, "Aggressive, Rejected, and Delinquent Children and Adolescents: A Comparison of Their Friendships," *Aggression & Violent Behavior* 9:75–104 (2004); Stephen W. Baron "Self-Control, Social Consequences, and Criminal Behavior: Street Youth and the General Theory of Crime," *Journal of Research in Crime and Delinquency* 40:403–425 (2003).

[89] Sylvie Mrug, Betsy Hoza, and William Bukowski, "Choosing or Being Chosen by Aggressive-Disruptive Peers: Do They Contribute to Children's Externalizing and Internalizing Problems?" *Journal of Abnormal Child Psychology* 32:53–66 (2004).

[90] John Paul Wright and Francis Cullen, "Employment, Peers, and Life-Course Transitions," *Justice Quarterly* 21:183–205 (2004).

[91] Robert Apel, Raymond Paternoster, Shawn Bushway, and Robert Brame, "A Job Isn't Just a Job: The Differential Impact of Formal Versus Informal Work on Adolescent Problem Behavior," *Crime and Delinquency* 52:333–369 (2006).

[92] Jeremy Staff and Christopher Uggen, "The Fruits of Good Work: Early Work Experiences and Adolescent Deviance," *Journal of Research in Crime and Delinquency* 40:263–290 (2003).

[93] Edwin Sutherland, *Principles of Criminology* (Philadelphia: Lippincott, 1939).

[94] Paul Vowell and Jieming Chen, "Predicting Academic Misconduct: A Comparative Test of Four Sociological Explanations," *Sociological Inquiry* 74:226–249 (2004).

[95] Carlo Morselli, Pierre Tremblay, and Bill McCarthy, "Mentors and Criminal Achievement," *Criminology* 44:17–43 (2006).

[96] Travis Hirschi, *Causes of Delinquency* (Berkeley: University of California Press, 1969).

[97] Bobbi Jo Anderson, Malcolm Holmes, and Erik Ostresh, "Male and Female Delinquents' Attachments and Effects of Attachments on Severity of Self-Reported Delinquency," *Criminal Justice and Behavior* 26:425–452 (1999).

[98] Patricia Jenkins, "School Delinquency and the School Social Bond," *Journal of Research in Crime and Delinquency* 34:337–367 (1997).

[99] Thomas Vander Ven, Francis Cullen, Mark Carrozza, and John Paul Wright, "Home Alone: The Impact of Maternal Employment on Delinquency," *Social Problems* 48:236–257 (2001).

[100] Jennifer Kerpelman and Sondra Smith-Adcock, "Female Adolescents' Delinquent Activity: The Intersection of Bonds to Parents and Reputation Enhancement," *Youth & Society* 37:176–200 (2005); Helen Garnier and Judith Stein, "An 18-Year Model of Family and Peer Effects on Adolescent Drug Use and Delinquency," *Journal of Youth and Adolescence* 31:45–56 (2002).

[101] Sonia Cota-Robles and Wendy Gamble, "Parent-Adolescent Processes and Reduced Risk for Delinquency: The Effect of Gender for Mexican American adolescents," *Youth & Society* 37:375–392 (2006).

[102] Jonathan Zaff, Kristin Moore, Angela Romano Papillo, and Stephanie Williams, "Implications of Extracurricular Activity Participation During Adolescence on Positive Outcomes," *Journal of Adolescent Research* 18:599–631 (2003); Robert Agnew and David Peterson, "Leisure and Delinquency," *Social Problems* 36:332–348 (1989).

[103] Cernkovich, Giordano, and Rudolph, "Race, Crime, and the American Dream."

[104] Peggy Giordano, Stephen Cernkovich, and M. D. Pugh, "Friendships and Delinquency," *American Journal of Sociology* 91:1170–1202 (1986).

[105] Denise Kandel and Mark Davies, "Friendship Networks, Intimacy, and Illicit Drug Use in Young Adulthood: A Comparison of Two Competing Theories," *Criminology* 29:441–467 (1991).

[106] For a review of this position, see Anne R. Mahoney, "The Effect of Labeling Upon Youths in the Juvenile Justice System: A Review of the Evidence," *Law and Society Review* 8:583–614 (1974); see also David Matza, *Becoming Deviant* (Englewood Cliffs, NJ: Prentice-Hall, 1974).

[107] Bernburg, Marvin Krohn, and Craig Rivera, "Official Labeling, Criminal Embeddedness, and Subsequent Delinquency: A Longitudinal Test of Labeling Theory," *Journal of Research in Crime and Delinquency* 43:67–88 (2006).

[108] The self-labeling concept originated in Edwin Lemert, *Social Pathology* (New York: McGraw-Hill, 1951); see also Frank Tannenbaum, *Crime and the Community* (Boston: Ginn, 1936).

[109] Harold Garfinkel, "Conditions of Successful Degradation Ceremonies," in Jerome Manis and Bernard Meltzer, eds., *Symbolic Interactionism* (New York: Allyn & Bacon, 1972), pp. 201–208.

[110] M. A. Bortner, *Inside a Juvenile Court: The Tarnished Ideal of Individualized Justice* (New York: NYU Press, 1982).

[111] Edwin Lemert, *Human Deviance, Social Problems, and Social Control* (Englewood Cliffs, NJ: Prentice-Hall, 1967), p. 15.

[112] Lening Zhang, "Official Offense Status and Self-Esteem Among Chinese Youths," *Journal of Criminal Justice*, 31:99–105 (2003).

[113] Mike Adams, Craig Robertson, Phyllis Gray-Ray, and Melvin Ray, "Labeling and Delinquency," *Adolescence* 38:171–186 (2003).

[114] Charles H. Cooley, *Human Nature and the Social Order* (New York: Scribner's, 1902).

[115] Ross Matsueda, "Reflected Appraisals, Parental Labeling, and Delinquency: Specifying a Symbolic Interactionist Theory," *American Journal of Sociology* 97:1577–1611 (1992).

[116] Raymond Paternoster and Leeann Iovanni, "The Labeling Perspective and Delinquency: An Elaboration of the Theory and an Assessment of the Evidence," *Justice Quarterly* 6:358–394 (1989).

[117] Gregg Barak, "Revisionist History, Visionary Criminology, and Needs-Based Justice," *Contemporary Justice Review* 6:217–225 (2003).

[118] Kitty Kelley Epstein, "The Whitening of the American Teaching Force: A Problem of Recruitment or a Problem of Racism?" *Social Justice* 32:89–102 (2005).

[119] Robert Meier, "The New Criminology: Continuity in Criminological Theory," *Journal of Criminal Law and Criminology* 67:463 (1977).

[120] Malcolm Holmes, "Minority Threat and Police Brutality: Determinants of Civil Rights Criminal Complaints in U.S. Municipalities," *Criminology* 38:343–368 (2000).

[121] Ibid.

[122] Robert Gordon, "Capitalism, Class, and Crime in America," *Crime and Delinquency* 19:174 (1973).

[123] Richard Quinney, *Class, State, and Crime* (New York: Longman, 1977), p. 52.

[124] Anthony Platt, "The Triumph of Benevolence: The Origins of the Juvenile Justice System in the United States," in Richard Quinney, ed., *Criminal Justice in America: A Critical Understanding* (Boston: Little, Brown, 1974), p. 367; see also Anthony Platt, *The Child Savers: The Invention of Delinquency* (Chicago: University of Chicago Press, 1969).

[125] Barry Krisberg and James Austin, *Children of Ishmael* (Palo Alto, CA: Mayfield, 1978), p. 2.

[126] Herman Schwendinger and Julia Schwendinger, "Delinquency and Social Reform: A Radical Perspective," in Lamar Empey, ed., *Juvenile Justice* (Charlottesville: University of Virginia Press, 1979), p. 250.

[127] Operation Weed and Seed Executive Offices, U.S. Department of Justice, Washington, DC, 1998; *Weed and Seed In-sites*, vol. I, no. 5, August–September 1998.

[128] Shadd Maruna, Thomas Lebel, Nick Mitchell, and Michelle Maples, "Pygmalion in the Reintegration Process: Desistance From Crime Through the Looking Glass," *Psychology, Crime & Law* 10:271–281 (2004).

[129] Terence Thornberry, David Huizinga, and Rolf Loeber, "The Prevention of Serious Delinquency and Violence," in James Howell, Barry Krisberg, J. David Hawkins, and John Wilson, eds., *Sourcebook on Serious, Violent, and Chronic Juvenile Offenders* (Thousand Oaks, CA: Sage, 1995).

[130] Malcolm Klein, "Deinstitutionalization and Diversion of Juvenile Offenders: A Litany of Impediments," in Norval Morris and Michael Tonry, eds., *Crime and Justice*, vol. 1 (Chicago: University of Chicago Press, 1979).

[131] Kathleen Daly and Russ Immarigeon, "The Past, Present, and Future of Restorative Justice: Some Critical Reflections," *Contemporary Justice Review* 1:21–45 (1998).

[132] Kay Pranis, "Peacemaking Circles: Restorative Justice in Practice Allows Victims and Offenders to Begin Repairing the Harm," *Corrections Today* 59:72–76 (1997).

[133] Carol LaPrairie, "The 'New' Justice: Some Implications for Aboriginal Communities," *Canadian Journal of Criminology* 40:61–79 (1998).

[134] Gene Stephens, "The Future of Policing: From a War Model to a Peace Model," in Brendan Maguire and Polly Radosh, eds., *The Past, Present, and Future of American Criminal Justice* (Dix Hills, NY: General Hall, 1996), pp. 77–93.

[135] This section is based on Gordon Bazemore and Mara Schiff, "Paradigm Muddle or Paradigm Paralysis? The Wide and Narrow Roads to Restorative Justice Reform (or, a Little Confusion May Be a Good Thing)," *Contemporary Justice Review* 7:37–57 (2004).

[136] Jay Zaslaw and George Ballance, "The Socio-Legal Response: A New Approach to Juvenile Justice in the '90s," *Corrections Today* 58:72–75 (1996).

[137] Gordon Bazemore, "Restorative Justice and Earned Redemption: Communities, Victims, and Offender Reintegration," *American Behavioral Scientist* 41:768–814 (1998).

Chapter 5. Developmental Views of Delinquency

[1] Marvin Krohn, Alan Lizotte, and Cynthia Perez, "The Interrelationship Between Substance Use and Precocious Transitions to Adult Sexuality," *Journal of Health and Social Behavior* 38:88 (1997).

[2] Peggy Giordano, Stephen Cernkovich, and Jennifer Rudolph, "Gender, Crime, and Desistance: Toward a Theory of Cognitive Transformation?" *American Journal of Sociology* 107:990–1064 (2002).

[3] John Hagan and Holly Foster, "S/He's a Rebel: Toward a Sequential Stress Theory of Delinquency and Gendered Pathways to Disadvantage in Emerging Adulthood," *Social Forces* 82:53–86 (2003).

[4] See, generally, Sheldon Glueck and Eleanor Glueck, *500 Delinquent Careers* (New York: Knopf, 1930); Sheldon Glueck and Eleanor Glueck, *One Thousand Juvenile Delinquents* (Cambridge, MA: Harvard University Press, 1934); Sheldon Glueck and Eleanor Glueck, *Predicting Delinquency* (Cambridge, MA: Harvard University Press, 1967), pp. 82–83.

[5] Sheldon Glueck and Eleanor Glueck, *Unraveling Juvenile Delinquency* (Cambridge, MA: Harvard University Press, 1950).

[6] Ibid., p. 48.

[7] Rolf Loeber and Marc LeBlanc, "Toward a Developmental Criminology," in Norval Morris and Michael Tonry, eds., *Delinquency and Justice*, vol. 12 (Chicago: University of Chicago Press, 1990), pp. 375–473; Rolf Loeber and Marc LeBlanc, "Developmental Criminology Updated," in Michael Tonry, ed., *Delinquency and Justice,* vol. 23 (Chicago: University of Chicago Press, 1998), pp. 115–198.

[8] Alex R. Piquero and He Len Chung, "On the Relationships Between Gender, Early Onset, and the Seriousness of Offending," *Journal of Delinquent Justice* 29:189–206 (2001).

[9] Rolf Loeber and David Farrington, "Young Children Who Commit Delinquency: Epidemiology, Developmental Origins, Risk Factors, Early Interventions, and Policy Implications," *Development and Psychopathology* 12:737–762 (2000).

[10] W. Alex Mason, Rick Kosterman, J. David Hawkins, Todd Herrenkohl, Liliana Lengua, and Elizabeth McCauley, "Predicting Depression, Social Phobia, and Violence in Early Adulthood From Childhood Behavior Problems," *Journal of the American Academy of Child & Adolescent Psychiatry* 43:307–315 (2004); Rolf Loeber and David Farrington, "Young Children Who Commit Crime: Epidemiology, Developmental Origins, Risk Factors, Early Interventions, and Policy Implications," *Development and Psychopathology* 12:737–762 (2000); Patrick Lussier, Jean Proulx, and Marc Leblanc, "Criminal Propensity, Deviant Sexual Interests and Criminal Activity of Sexual Aggressors Against Women: A Comparison of Explanatory Models," *Criminology* 43:249–281 (2005).

[11] Hanno Petras, Nicholas Alongo, Sharon Lambert, Sandra Barrueco, Cindy Schaeffer, Howard Chilcoat, and Sheppard Kellam, "The Utility of Elementary School TOCA-R Scores in Identifying Later Criminal Court Violence Among Adolescent Females," *Journal of the American Academy of Child & Adolescent Psychiatry* 44:790–797 (2005); Hanno Petras, Howard Chilcoat, Philip Leaf, Nicholas Ialongo, and Sheppard Kellam, "Utility of TOCA-R Scores During the Elementary School Years in Identifying Later Violence Among Adolescent Males," *Journal of the American Academy of Child and Adolescent Psychiatry* 43:88–96 (2004).

[12] Ronald Prinz and Suzanne Kerns, "Early Substance Use by Juvenile Offenders," *Child Psychiatry & Human Development* 33:263–268 (2003).

[13] David Gadd and Stephen Farrall, "Criminal Careers, Desistance and Subjectivity: Interpreting Men's Narratives of Change," *Theoretical Criminology* 8:123–156 (2004).

[14] Ick-Joong Chung, Karl G Hill, J. David Hawkins, Lewayne Gilchrist, and Daniel Nagin, "Childhood Predictors of Offense Trajectories," *Journal of Research in Crime and Delinquency* 39:60–91 (2002).

[15] Elaine Eggleston and John Laub, "The Onset of Adult Offending: A Neglected Dimension of the Criminal Career," *Journal of Criminal Justice* 30:603–622 (2002).

[16] Terrie Moffitt, "Natural Histories of Delinquency," in Elmar Weitekamp and Hans-Jurgen Kerner, eds., *Cross-National Longitudinal Research on Human Development and Delinquent Behavior* (Dordrecht, Netherlands: Kluwer, 1994), pp. 3–65.

[17] Alex Piquero and Timothy Brezina, "Testing Moffitt's Account of Adolescent-Limited Delinquency," *Criminology* 39:353–370 (2001).

[18] Amy D'Unger, Kenneth Land, Patricia McCall, and Daniel Nagin, "How Many Latent Classes of Delinquent/Criminal Careers Result from Mixed Poisson Regression Analyses?" *American Journal of Sociology* 103:1593–1630 (1998).

[19] Adrian Raine, Rolf Loeber, Magda Touthamer-Loeber, Terrie Moffitt, Avshalom Caspi, and Don Lynam, "Neurocognitive Impairments in Boys on the Life-Course Persistent Antisocial Path," *Journal of Abnormal Psychology* 114:38–49 (2005).

[20] Michael Newcomb, "Pseudomaturity Among Adolescents: Construct Validation, Sex Differences, and Associations in Adulthood," *Journal of Drug Issues* 26:477–504 (1996).

[21] Per-Olof Wikstrom and Rolf Loeber, "Do Disadvantaged Neighborhoods Cause Well-Adjusted Children to Become Adolescent Delinquents? A Study of Male Juvenile Serious Offending, Individual Risk and Protective Factors, and Neighborhood Context," *Criminology* 38:1109–1142 (2000).

[22] Eila Sailas, Benjamin Feodoroff, Nina Lindberg, Matti Virkkunen, Reijo Sund, and Kristian Wahlbeck, "The Mortality of Young Offenders Sentenced to Prison and its Association with Psychiatric Disorders: A Register Study," *European Journal of Public Health* 16:193–197 (2006).

[23] Magda Stouthamer-Loeber and Evelyn Wei, "The Precursors of Young Fatherhood and Its Effect on Delinquency of Teenage Males," *Journal of Adolescent Health* 22:56–65 (1998); Richard Jessor, John Donovan, and Francis Costa, *Beyond Adolescence: Problem Behavior and Young Adult Development* (New York: Cambridge University Press, 1991).

[24] Marvin Krohn, Alan Lizotte, and Cynthia Perez, "The Interrelationship Between Substance Use and Precocious Transitions to Adult Sexuality," *Journal of Health and Social Behavior* 38:88 (1997); Richard Jessor, "Risk Behavior in Adolescence: A Psychosocial Framework for Understanding and Action," in D. E. Rogers and E. Ginzburg, eds., *Adolescents at Risk: Medical and Social Perspectives* (Boulder, CO: Westview, 1992).

[25] Ick-Joong Chung, J. David Hawkins, Lewayne Gilchrist, Karl Hill, and Daniel Nagin, "Identifying and Predicting Offending Trajectories Among Poor Children," *Social Service Review* 76:663–687 (2002).

[26] Vladislav Ruchkin, Mary Schwab-Stone, Roman Koposov, Robert Vermeiren, and Robert King, "Suicidal Ideations and Attempts in Juvenile Delinquents," *Child Psychology & Psychiatry & Allied Disciplines* 44:1058–1067 (2003).

[27] J. Rayner, T. Kelly, and F. Graham, "Mental Health, Personality and Cognitive Problems in Persistent Adolescent Offenders Require Long-Term Solutions: A Pilot Study," *Journal of Forensic Psychiatry & Psychology* 16:248–262 (2005).

[28] Marvin Krohn, Alan Lizotte, and Cynthia Perez, "The Interrelationship Between Substance Use and Precocious Transitions to Adult Sexuality," *Journal of Health and Social Behavior* 38:88 (1997); Jessor, "Risk Behavior in Adolescence."

[29] Deborah Capaldi and Gerald Patterson, "Can Violent Offenders Be Distinguished from Frequent Offenders? Prediction from Childhood to Adolescence," *Journal of Research in Crime and Delinquency* 33:206–231 (1996).

[30] Margit Wiesner and Deborah Capaldi, "Relations of Childhood and Adolescent Factors to Offending Trajectories of Young Men," *Journal of Research in Crime and Delinquency* 40:231–262 (2003).

[31] Rolf Loeber, Phen Wung, Kate Keenan, Bruce Giroux, Magda Stouthamer-Loeber, Wemoet Van Kammen, and Barbara Maughan, "Developmental Pathways in Disruptive Behavior," *Development and Psychopathology* 11:12–48 (1993).

[32] Mark Lipsey and James Derzon, "Predictors of Violent or Serious Delinquency in Adolescence). Margit Wiesner and Michael Windle, "Young Adult Substance Use and Depression as a Consequence of Delinquency Trajectories During Middle Adolescence," *Journal of Research on Adolescence* 16:239–264 (2006).

[33] Glenn Clingempeel and Scott Henggeler, "Aggressive Juvenile Offenders Transitioning into Emerging Adulthood: Factors Discriminating Persistors and Desistors," *American Journal of Orthopsychiatry* 73:310–323 (2003).

[34] Marshall Jones and Donald Jones, "The Contagious Nature of Antisocial Behavior," *Criminology* 38:25–46 (2000).

[35] Terrie Moffitt, Avshalom Caspi, Michael Rutter, and Phil Silva, *Sex Differences in Antisocial Behavior: Conduct Disorder, Delinquency, and Violence in the Dunedin Longitudinal Study* (London: Cambridge University Press, 2001).

[36] See, for example, the *Rochester Youth Development Study* (Albany, NY: Hindelang Delinquent Justice Research Center, 2003).

[37] David Farrington, "The Development of Offending and Antisocial Behavior from Childhood to Adulthood." Paper presented at the Congress on Rethinking Delinquency, University of Minho, Braga, Portugal, July 1992.

[38] Robert Sampson and John Laub, *Crime in the Making: Pathways and Turning Points Through Life* (Cambridge, MA: Harvard University Press, 1993); John Laub and Robert Sampson, "Turning Points in the Life Course: Why Change Matters to the Study of Crime." Paper presented at the annual meeting of the American Society of Criminology, New Orleans, November 1992.

[39] Terri Orbuch, James House, Richard Mero, and Pamela Webster, "Marital Quality Over the Life Course," *Social Psychology Quarterly* 59:162–171 (1996); Lee Lillard and Linda Waite, " 'Til Death Do Us Part: Marital Disruption and Mortality," *American Journal of Sociology* 100:1131–1156 (1995).

[40] Mark Warr, "Life-Course Transitions and Desistance from Crime," *Criminology* 36:183–216 (1998).

[41] Nan Lin, *Social Capital: A Theory of Social Structure and Action* (Cambridge, UK: Cambridge University Press, 2002).

[42] Sampson and Laub, *Crime in the Making*, p. 249.

[43] Ross Macmillan, Barbara J. McMorris, and Candace Kruttschnitt, "Linked Lives: Stability and Change in Maternal Circumstances and Trajectories of Antisocial Behavior in Children," *Child Development* 75:205–220 (2004).

[44] John Hagan, Ross MacMillan, and Blair Wheaton, "New Kid in Town: Social Capital and the Life Course Effects of Family Migration on Children," *American Sociological Review* 61:368–385 (1996).

[45] Robert Sampson and John Laub, "A Life-Course Theory of Cumulative Disadvantage and the Stability of Delinquency," in Terence Thornberry, ed., *Developmental Theories of Crime and Delinquency* (Somerset, NJ: Transaction Publishing, 1997), pp. 138–162.

[46] Raymond Paternoster and Robert Brame, "Multiple Routes to Delinquency? A Test of Developmental and General Theories of Crime," *Criminology* 35:49–84 (1997).

[47] Pamela Webster, Terri Orbuch, and James House, "Effects of Childhood Family Background on Adult Marital Quality and Perceived Stability," *American Journal of Sociology* 101:404–432 (1995).

[48] Robert Hoge, D. A. Andrews, and Alan Leschied, "An Investigation of Risk and Protective Factors in a Sample of Youthful Offenders," *Journal of Child Psychology and Psychiatry* 37:419–424 (1996).

[49] Avshalom Caspi, Terrie Moffitt, Bradley Entner Wright, and Phil Silva, "Early Failure in the Labor Market: Childhood and Adolescent Predictors of Unemployment in the Transition to Adulthood," *American Sociological Review* 63:424–451 (1998).

[50] John Paul Wright, David E. Carter, and Francis T. Cullen, "A Life-Course Analysis of Military Service in Vietnam," *Journal of Research in Crime and Delinquency* 42:55–83 (2005).

[51] Robert Sampson and John Laub, "Socioeconomic Achievement in the Life Course of Disadvantaged Men: Military Service as a Turning Point, circa 1940–1965," *American Sociological Review* 61:347–367 (1996).

[52] Daniel Nagin and Raymond Paternoster, "Personal Capital and Social Control: The Deterrence Implications of a Theory of Offending," *Criminology* 32:581–606 (1994).

[53] James Q. Wilson and Richard Herrnstein, *Crime and Human Nature* (New York: Simon & Schuster, 1985).

[54] David Rowe, D. Wayne Osgood, and W. Alan Nicewander, "A Latent Trait Approach to Unifying Criminal Careers," *Criminology* 28:237–270 (1990).

[55] Lee Ellis, "Neurohormonal Bases of Varying Tendencies to Learn Delinquent and Criminal Behavior," in E. Morris and C. Braukmann, eds., *Behavioral Approaches to Crime and Delinquency* (New York: Plenum, 1988), pp. 499–518.

[56] David Rowe, Alexander Vazsonyi, and Daniel Flannery, "Sex Differences in Crime: Do Means and Within-Sex Variation Have Similar Causes?" *Journal of Research in Crime and Delinquency* 32:84–100 (1995).

[57] Michael Gottfredson and Travis Hirschi, *A General Theory of Crime* (Stanford, CA: Stanford University Press, 1990).

[58] Ibid., p. 27.

[59] Kevin Beaver and John Paul Wright, "Evaluating the Effects of Birth Complications on Low Self-Control in a Sample of Twins," *International Journal of Offender Therapy & Comparative Criminology* 49:450–472 (2005).

[60] Robert Agnew, "The Contribution of Social-Psychological Strain Theory to the Explanation of Crime and Delinquency," *Advances in Criminological Theory* 6:211–213 (1994).

[61] Ibid., p. 90.

[62] Ibid., p. 89.

[63] Alex Piquero and Stephen Tibbetts, "Specifying the Direct and Indirect Effects of Low Self-Control and Situational Factors in Offenders' Decision Making: Toward a More Complete Model of Rational Offending," *Justice Quarterly* 13:481–508 (1996).

[64] David Forde and Leslie Kennedy, "Risky Lifestyles, Routine Activities, and the General Theory of Crime," *Justice Quarterly* 14:265–294 (1997).

[65] Marianne Junger and Richard Tremblay, "Self-Control, Accidents, and Delinquency," *Criminal Justice and Behavior* 26:485–501 (1999).

[66] Gottfredson and Hirschi, *A General Theory of Crime*, p. 112.

[67] Ibid.

[68] Dennis Giever, "An Empirical Assessment of the Core Elements of Gottfredson and Hirschi's General Theory of Crime." Paper presented at the annual meeting of the American Society of Criminology, Boston, November 1995.

[69] David Farrington, Darrick Jolliffe, Rolf Loeber, Magda Stouthamer-Loeber, and Larry Kalb, "The Concentration of Offenders in Families, and Family Criminality in the Prediction of Boy's Delinquency," *Journal of Adolescence* 24:579–596 (2001).

[70] Daniel Nagin and Greg Pogarsky, "Time and Punishment: Delayed Consequences and Criminal Behavior," *Journal of Quantitative Criminology* 20:295–317 (2004); Peter Muris and Cor Meesters, "The Validity of Attention Deficit Hyperactivity and Hyperkinetic Disorder Symptom Domains in Nonclinical Dutch Children," *Journal of Clinical Child & Adolescent Psychology* 32:460–466 (2003); David Brownfield and Ann-Marie Sorenson, "Self-Control and Juvenile Delinquency: Theoretical Issues and an Empirical Assessment of Selected Elements of a General Theory of Crime," *Deviant Behavior* 14:243–264 (1993); Harold Grasmick, Charles Tittle, Robert Bursik, and Bruce Arneklev, "Testing the Core Empirical Implications of Gottfredson and Hirschi's General Theory of Crime," *Journal of Research in Crime and Delinquency* 30:5–29 (1993).

[71] Alexander Vazsonyi, Janice Clifford Wittekind, Lara Belliston, and Timothy Van Loh, "Extending the General Theory of Crime to 'The East': Low Self-Control in Japanese Late Adolescents," *Journal of Quantitative Criminology* 20:189–216 (2004); Alexander Vazsonyi, Lloyd Pickering, Marianne Junger, and Dick Hessing, "An Empirical Test of a General Theory of Crime: A Four-Nation Comparative Study of Self-Control and the Prediction of Deviance," *Journal of Research in Crime and Delinquency* 38:91–131 (2001).

[72] Christopher Sullivan, Jean Marie McGloin, Travis Pratt, and Alex Piquero, "Rethinking the 'Norm' of Offender Generality: Investigating Specialization in the Short-Term," *Criminology* 44:199–233 (2006).

[73] Annemaree Carroll, Francene Hemingway, Julie Bower, Adrian Ashman, Stephen Houghton, and Kevin Durkin, "Impulsivity in Juvenile Delinquency: Differences Among Early-Onset, Late-Onset, and Non-Offenders," *Journal of Youth & Adolescence* 35:517–527 (2006).

[74] Christopher Schreck, "Criminal Victimization and Low Self-Control: An Extension and Test of a General Theory of Crime," *Justice Quarterly* 16:633–654 (1999).

[75] Ronald Akers, "Self-Control as a General Theory of Crime," *Journal of Quantitative Criminology* 7:201–211 (1991).

[76] Richard Wiebe, "Reconciling Psychopathy and Low Self-Control," *Justice Quarterly* 20:297–336 (2003).

[77] Alan Feingold, "Gender Differences in Personality: A Meta-Analysis," *Psychological Bulletin* 116:429–456 (1994).

[78] Charles Tittle, David Ward, and Harold Grasmick, "Gender, Age, and Crime/Deviance: A Challenge to Self-Control Theory," *Journal of Research in Crime and Delinquency* 40:426–453 (2003).

[79] Dana Haynie, Peggy Giordano, Wendy Manning, and Monica Longmore, "Adolescent Romantic Relationships and Delinquency Involvement," *Criminology* 43:177–210.

[80] Brent Benda, "Gender Differences in Life-Course Theory of Recidivism: A Survival Analysis," *International Journal of Offender Therapy & Comparative Criminology* 49:325–342 (2005).

[81] Gottfredson and Hirschi, *A General Theory of Crime*, p. 153.

[82] Scott Menard, Delbert Elliott, and Sharon Wofford, "Social Control Theories in Developmental Perspective," *Studies on Crime and Delinquency Prevention* 2:69–87 (1993).

83 Dustin Pardini, Jelena Obradovic, and Rolf Loeber, "Interpersonal Callousness, Hyperactivity/Impulsivity, Inattention, and Conduct Problems as Precursors to Delinquency Persistence in Boys: A Comparison of Three Grade-Based Cohorts," *Journal of Clinical Child & Adolescent Psychology* 35:46–59 (2006).

84 Ojmarrh Mitchell and Doris Layton MacKenzie, "The Stability and Resiliency of Self-Control in a Sample of Incarcerated Offenders" *Crime and Delinquency* 52:432–449 (2006).

85 Charles R. Tittle and Harold G. Grasmick, "Delinquent Behavior and Age: A Test of Three Provocative Hypotheses," *Journal of Criminal Law and Criminology* 88:309–342 (1997).

86 L. Thomas Winfree, Jr., Terrance Taylor, Ni He, and Finn-Aage Esbensen, "Self-Control and Variability Over Time: Multivariate Results Using a 5-Year, Multisite Panel of Youths," *Crime and Delinquency* 52:253–286 (2006).

87 Alex Piquero, John MacDonald, Adam Dobrin, Leah Daigle, and Francis Cullen, "Self-Control, Violent Offending, and Homicide Victimization: Assessing the General Theory of Crime," *Journal of Quantitative Criminology* 21:55–71 (2005).

88 Ibid.

89 Ibid.

90 Douglas Longshore, Eunice Chang, and Nena Messina, "Self-Control and Social Bonds: A Combined Control Perspective on Juvenile Offending," *Journal of Quantitative Criminology* 21:419–437 (2005).

91 Callie Harbin Burt, Ronald Simons, and Leslie Simons, "A Longitudinal Test of the Effects of Parenting and the Stability of Self-Control: Negative Evidence for the General Theory of Crime," *Criminology* 44:353–396 (2006).

92 Travis Pratt and Frank Cullen, "The Empirical Status of Gottfredson and Hirschi's General Theory of Crime: A Meta-Analysis," *Criminology* 38:938–964 (2000); Douglas Longshore, "Self-Control and Delinquent Opportunity: A Prospective Test of the General Theory of Delinquency," *Social Problems* 45:102–114 (1998).

93 Otwin Marenin and Michael Resig, "A General Theory of Crime and Patterns of Crime in Nigeria: An Exploration of Methodological Assumptions," *Journal of Crime and Justice* 23:501–518 (1995).

94 Bruce Arneklev, Harold Grasmick, Charles Tittle, and Robert Bursik, "Low Self-Control and Imprudent Behavior," *Journal of Quantitative Criminology* 9:225–246 (1993).

95 Kevin Thompson, "Sexual Harassment and Low Self-Control: An Application of Gottfredson and Hirschi's General Theory of Crime." Paper presented at the annual meeting of the American Society of Criminology, Phoenix, November 1993.

96 Bradley Entner Wright, Avshalom Caspi, Terrie Moffitt, and Phil Silva, "Low Self-Control, Social Bonds, and Delinquency: Social Causation, Social Selection, or Both?" *Criminology* 37:479–514 (1999).

97 Ibid., p. 504.

98 Stephen Cernkovich and Peggy Giordano, "Stability and Change in Antisocial Behavior: The Transition from Adolescence to Early Adulthood," *Criminology* 39:371–410 (2001).

99 Heather Lonczk, Robert Abbott, J. David Hawkins, Rick Kosterman, and Richard Catalano, "Effects of the Seattle Social Development Project on Sexual Behavior, Pregnancy, Birth, and Sexually Transmitted Disease Outcomes by Age 21 Years," *Archive of Pediatrics and Adolescent Medicine* 156:438–447 (2002).

100 Kathleen Bodisch Lynch, Susan Rose Geller, and Melinda G. Schmidt, "Multi-Year Evaluation of the Effectiveness of a Resilience-Based Prevention Program for Young Children," *Journal of Primary Prevention* 24:335–353 (2004).

101 This section leans on Thomas Tatchell, Phillip Waite, Renny Tatchell, Lynne Durrant, and Dale Bond, "Substance Abuse Prevention in Sixth Grade: The Effect of a Prevention Program on Adolescents' Risk and Protective Factors," *American Journal of Health Studies* 19:54–61 (2004).

102 Nancy Tobler and Howard Stratton, "Effectiveness of School Based Drug Prevention Programs: A Meta-Analysis of the Research," *Journal of Primary Prevention* 18:71–128 (1997).

New Directions in Preventing Delinquency: Primary Prevention Efforts: Early Childhood

1 Nancy Tobler and Howard Stratton, "Effectiveness of School Based Drug Prevention Programs: A Meta-Analysis of the Research," *Journal of Primary Prevention* 18:71–128 (1997).

2 Chemung County Health Department, Community Health Assessment 2005–2010. Available at: www.chemungcountyhealth.org/usr/PDFs/Chemung%20County%20Community%20Health%20Assessment%202005–201027.pdf (accessed October 10, 2006); David L. Olds, Charles R. Henderson, Robert Chamberlin, and Robert Tatelbaum, "Preventing Child Abuse and Neglect: A Randomized Trial of Nurse Home Visitation," *Pediatrics* 78:65–78 (1986).

3 David L. Olds, Charles R. Henderson, Charles Phelps, Harriet Kitzman, and Carole Hanks, "Effects of Prenatal and Infancy Nurse Home Visitation on Government Spending," *Medical Care* 31:158 (1993).

4 Peter Greenwood, Lynn Karoly, Susan Everingham, Jill Houbé, M. Rebecca Kilburn, C. Peter Rydell, Matthew Sanders, and James Chiesa, "Estimating the Costs and Benefits of Early Childhood Interventions: Nurse Home Visits and the Perry Preschool," In *Costs and Benefits of Preventing Crime*, Brandon C. Welsh, David P. Farrington, and Lawrence W. Sherman, eds. (Boulder, CO: Westview Press, 2001); Steve Aos, Roxanne Lieb, Jim Mayfield, Marna Miller, and Annie Pennucci, *Benefits and Costs of Prevention and Early Intervention Programs for Youth* (Olympia, WA: Washington State Institute for Public Policy, 2004).

5 Ned Calonge, "Community Interventions to Prevent Violence: Translation into Public Health Practice," *American Journal of Preventive Medicine* 28:4–5 (2005).

6 David P. Farrington and Brandon C. Welsh, "Delinquency Prevention Using Family-Based Interventions," *Children and Society* 13:287–303 (1999); David P. Farrington and Brandon C. Welsh, "Family-Based Crime Prevention," in Lawrence W. Sherman, David P. Farrington, Brandon C. Welsh, and Doris Layton MacKenzie, eds., *Evidence-Based Crime Prevention* (London, England: Routledge, 2002).

7 Gerald R. Patterson, Patricia Chamberlain, and John B. Reid, "A Comparative Evaluation of a Parent-Training Program," *Behavior Therapy* 13:638–650 (1982); Gerald R. Patterson, John B. Reid, and Thomas J. Dishion, *Antisocial Boys* (Eugene, OR: Castalia, 1992).

8 Peter W. Greenwood, Karyn E. Model, C. Peter Rydell, and James Chiesa, *Diverting Children from a Life of Crime: Measuring Costs and Benefits* (Santa Monica, CA: Rand, 1996).

9 Alex Mason, Rick Kosterman, J. David Hawkins, Kevin P. Haggerty, and Richard L. Spoth. "Reducing Adolescents' Growth in Substance Use and Delinquency: Randomized Trial Effects of a Parent-Training Prevention Intervention," *Prevention Science* 4:203–212 (2003).

10 Adrian Raine, Kjetil Mellingen, Jianghong Liu, Peter Venables, and Sarnoff Mednick, "Effects of Environmental Enrichment at Age Three to Five Years on Schizotypal Personality and Antisocial Behavior at Ages Seventeen and Twenty-Three Years," *American Journal of Psychiatry* 160:1–9 (2003).

11 David P. Farrington, "Early Developmental Prevention of Juvenile Delinquency," *Criminal Behavior and Mental Health* 4:216–217 (2000).

12 Lawrence J. Schweinhart, Helen V. Barnes, and David P. Weikart, *Significant Benefits: The High/Scope Perry Preschool Study Through Age 27* (Ypsilanti, MI: High/Scope Press, 1993), p. 3.

13 Lawrence Schweinhart, Jeanne Montie, Xiang Zongping, W. Steven Barnett, Clive R. Belfield, and Milagros Nores, *Lifetime Effects: The High/Scope Perry Preschool Study Through Age 40* (Ypsilanti, MI: High/Scope Press, 2005)

14 Office of Juvenile Justice and Delinquency Prevention, Model Program Guide. Available at: www.dsgonline.com/mpg2.5//TitleV_MPG_Table_Ind_Rec.asp?id=326 (accessed September 26, 2006).

15 Richard E. Tremblay and Wendy M. Craig, "Developmental Crime Prevention," in Michael Tonry and David P. Farrington, eds., *Building a Safer Society: Strategic Approaches to Crime Prevention. Crime and Justice: A Review of Research*, vol. 19 (Chicago: University of Chicago Press, 1995), pp. 151–236.

Chapter 6. Gender and Delinquency

1 Cesare Lombroso, *The Female Offender* (New York: Appleton, 1920); W. I. Thomas, *The Unadjusted Girl* (New York: Harper & Row, 1923).

2 Cesare Lombroso and William Ferrero, *The Female Offender* (New York: Philosophical Library, 1895).

3 Kerry Carrington, "Does Feminism Spoil Girls? Explanations for Official Rises in Female Delinquency," *Australian and New Zealand Journal of Criminology* 39:34–53 (2006).

[4] Cheryl Maxson and Monica Whitlock, "Joining the Gang: Gender Differences in Risk Factors for Gang Membership," in C. Ronald Huff, ed., *Gangs in America III* (Thousand Oaks, CA: Sage, 2002), pp. 19–35.

[5] David Finkelhor and Richard Ormrod, "Prostitution of Juveniles: Patterns From NIBRS," *Juvenile Justice Bulletin*, June 2004 (Washington, DC: The Office of Juvenile Justice and Delinquency Prevention, 2004). Available at: www.ncjrs.org/html/ojjdp/203946/contents.html (accessed November 21, 2006).

[6] This section relies on Spencer Rathus, *Psychology in the New Millennium* (Fort Worth, TX: Harcourt Brace, 1996); see also Darcy Miller, Catherine Trapani, Kathy Fejes-Mendoza, Carolyn Eggleston, and Donna Dwiggins, "Adolescent Female Offenders: Unique Considerations," *Adolescence* 30:429–435 (1995).

[7] Rolf Loeber and Dale Hay, "Key Issues in the Development of Aggression and Violence from Childhood to Early Adulthood," *Annual Review of Psychology* 48:371–410 (1997).

[8] Allison Morris, *Women, Crime, and Criminal Justice* (Oxford, England: Basil Blackwell, 1987).

[9] Dennis Giever, "An Empirical Assessment of the Core Elements of Gottfredson and Hirschi's General Theory of Crime." Paper presented to the American Society of Criminology meeting, Boston, November 1995.

[10] Loeber and Hay, "Key Issues in the Development of Aggression and Violence," p. 378.

[11] John Mirowsky and Catherine Ross, "Sex Differences in Distress: Real or Artifact?" *American Sociological Review* 60:449–468 (1995).

[12] Philip Cook and Susan Sorenson, "The Gender Gap Among Teen Survey Respondents: Why Are Boys More Likely to Report a Gun in the Home Than Girls?" *Journal of Quantitative Criminology* 22:61–76 (2006).

[13] Ibid., pp. 460–465.

[14] For a review of this issue, see Anne Campbell, *Men, Women, and Aggression* (New York: Basic Books, 1993).

[15] Thomas Parsons, Albert Rizzo, Cheryl Van Der Zaag, Jocelyn McGee, and J. Galen Buckwalter, "Gender Differences and Cognition Among Older Adults," *Aging, Neuropsychology & Cognition* 12:78–88 (2005).

[16] Diane Halpern and Mary LaMay, "The Smarter Sex: A Critical Review of Sex Differences in Intelligence," *Educational Psychology Review* 12:229–246 (2000).

[17] Parsons, Rizzo, Van Der Zaag, McGee, and Buckwalter, "Gender Differences and Cognition Among Older Adults."

[18] James Messerschmidt, *Masculinities and Crime: Critique and Reconceptualization of Theory* (Lanham, MD: Rowman and Littlefield, 1993).

[19] Debra Kaysen, Miranda Morris, Shireen Rizvi, and Patricia Resick, "Peritraumatic Responses and Their Relationship to Perceptions of Threat in Female Crime Victims," *Violence Against Women* 11:1515–1535 (2005).

[20] D. J. Pepler and W. M. Craig, "A Peek Behind the Fence: Naturalistic Observations of Aggressive Children with Remote Audiovisual Recording," *Developmental Psychology* 31:548–553 (1995).

[21] Daniel Mears, Matthew Ploeger, and Mark Warr, "Explaining the Gender Gap in Delinquency: Peer Influence and Moral Evaluations of Behavior," *Journal of Research in Crime and Delinquency* 35:251–266 (1998).

[22] John Gibbs, Dennis Giever, and Jamie Martin, "Parental Management and Self-Control: An Empirical Test of Gottfredson and Hirschi's General Theory," *Journal of Research in Crime and Delinquency* 35:40–70 (1998); Velmer Burton, Francis Cullen, T. David Evans, Leanne Fiftal Alarid, and R. Gregory Dunaway, "Gender, Self-Control, and Crime," *Journal of Research in Crime and Delinquency* 35:123–147 (1998).

[23] Camilla Benbow, David Lubinski, Daniel Shea, and Hossain Eftekhari-Sanjani, "Sex Differences in Mathematical Reasoning Ability at Age 13: Their Status 20 Years Later," *Psychological Science* 11:474–480 (2000).

[24] Ann Beutel and Margaret Mooney Marini, "Gender and Values," *American Sociological Review* 60:436–448 (1995).

[25] American Association of University Women, *Shortchanging Girls, Shortchanging America: Executive Summary* (Washington, DC: American Association of University Women, 1991).

[26] Spencer Rathus, *Voyages in Childhood* (Belmont, CA: Wadsworth, 2004).

[27] Carol Gilligan, *In a Different Voice* (Cambridge, MA: Harvard University Press, 1982).

[28] David Roalf, Natasha Lowery, and Bruce Turetsky, "Behavioral and Physiological Findings of Gender Differences in Global-Local Visual Processing," *Brain & Cognition* 60:32–42 (2006).

[29] David Rowe, Alexander Vazsonyi, and Daniel Flannery, "Sex Differences in Crime: Do Means and Within-Sex Variation Have Similar Causes?" *Journal of Research in Crime and Delinquency* 32:84–100 (1995).

[30] Sandra Bem, *The Lenses of Gender* (New Haven: Yale University Press, 1993).

[31] Walter DeKeseredy and Martin Schwartz, "Male Peer Support and Woman Abuse," *Sociological Spectrum* 13:393–413 (1993).

[32] Johannes Landsheer and C. van Dijkum, "Male and Female Delinquency Trajectories from Pre- Through Middle Adolescence and Their Continuation in Late Adolescence," *Adolescence* 40:729–748 (2005).

[33] Eleanor Maccoby, "Gender and Group Process: A Developmental Perspective," *Current Directions in Psychological Science* 11:54–58 (2002).

[34] Jean Bottcher, "Social Practices of Gender: How Gender Relates to Delinquency in the Everyday Lives of High-Risk Youths," *Criminology* 39:893–932 (2001).

[35] Audrey Zakriski, Jack Wright, and Marion Underwood, "Gender Similarities and Differences in Children's Social Behavior: Finding Personality in Contextualized Patterns of Adaptation," *Journal of Personality & Social Psychology* 88:844–855 (2005).

[36] *Monitoring the Future, 2005* (Ann Arbor, MI: Institute for Social Research, 2006).

[37] Lombroso and Ferrero, *The Female Offender.*

[38] Ibid., p. 122.

[39] Ibid., pp. 51–52.

[40] For a review, see Anne Campbell, *Girl Delinquents* (Oxford, England: Basil Blackwell, 1981), pp. 41–48.

[41] Cyril Burt, *The Young Delinquent* (New York: Appleton, 1925); see also Warren Middleton, "Is There a Relation Between Kleptomania and Female Periodicity in Neurotic Individuals?" *Psychology Clinic* (December 1933), pp. 232–247.

[42] William Healy and Augusta Bronner, *Delinquents and Criminals: Their Making and Unmaking* (New York: Macmillan, 1926).

[43] Ibid., p. 10.

[44] Miriam Sealock and Sally Simpson, "Unraveling Bias in Arrest Decisions: The Role of Juvenile Offender Typescripts," *Justice Quarterly* 15:427–457 (1998); Christina Polsenberg and Kenneth Jackson, "Putting Race into Context: Race, Juvenile Justice Processing, and Urbanization." Paper presented at the American Society of Criminology meeting, Boston, November 1995 (rev. version, January 1996); for a general review, see Carl Pope and William Feyerherm, "Minority Status and Juvenile Justice Processing (Part I)," *Criminal Justice Abstracts* 22:327–335 (1990); see also Douglas Smith and Jody Klein, "Police Control of Interpersonal Disputes," *Social Problems* 31:468–481 (1984).

[45] Sigmund Freud, *An Outline of Psychoanalysis,* trans. James Strachey (New York: Norton, 1949), p. 278.

[46] Dorie Klein, "The Etiology of Female Crime: A Review of the Literature," in Freda Adler and Rita Simon, eds., *The Criminology of Deviant Women* (Boston: Houghton Mifflin, 1979), pp. 69–71.

[47] Peter Blos, "Pre-Oedipal Factors in the Etiology of Female Delinquency," *Psychoanalytic Studies of the Child* 12:229–242 (1957).

[48] Sheldon Glueck and Eleanor Glueck, *Five Hundred Delinquent Women* (New York: Knopf, 1934).

[49] J. Cowie, V. Cowie, and E. Slater, *Delinquency in Girls* (London: Heinemann, 1968).

[50] Anne Campbell, "On the Invisibility of the Female Delinquent Peer Group," *Women and Criminal Justice* 2:41–62 (1990).

[51] Carolyn Smith, "Factors Associated with Early Sexual Activity Among Urban Adolescents," *Social Work* 42:334–346 (1997).

[52] For a review, see Christy Miller Buchanan, Jacquelynne Eccles, and Jill Becker, "Are Adolescents the Victims of Raging Hormones? Evidence for Activational Effects of Hormones on Moods and Behavior at Adolescence," *Psychological Bulletin* 111:63–107 (1992).

[53] L. Kris Gowen, S. Shirley Feldman, Rafael Diaz, and Donnovan Somera Yisrael, "A Comparison of the Sexual Behaviors and Attitudes of Adolescent Girls with Older Versus Similar-Aged Boyfriends," *Journal of Youth and Adolescence* 33:167–176 (2004).

[54] Dana Haynie, "Contexts of Risk? Explaining the Link Between Girls' Pubertal Development and Their Delinquency Involvement," *Social Forces* 82:355–397 (2003).

[55] Avshalom Caspi, Donald Lyman, Terrie Moffitt, and Phil Silva, "Unraveling Girls' Delinquency: Biological, Dispositional, and Contextual Contributions to Adolescent Misbehavior," *Developmental Psychology* 29:283–289 (1993).

56 Eleanor Maccoby and Carol Jacklin, *The Psychology of Sex Differences* (Stanford, CA: Stanford University Press, 1974).

57 Kathleen Pajer, William Gardner, Robert Rubin, James Perel, and Stephen Neal, "Decreased Cortisol Levels in Adolescent Girls with Conduct Disorder," *Archives of General Psychiatry* 58:297–302 (2001).

58 Alan Booth and D. Wayne Osgood, "The Influence of Testosterone on Deviance in Adulthood: Assessing and Explaining the Relationship," *Criminology* 31:93–118 (1993).

59 D. H. Baucom, P. K. Besch, and S. Callahan, "Relationship Between Testosterone Concentration, Sex Role Identity, and Personality Among Females," *Journal of Personality and Social Psychology* 48:1218–1226 (1985).

60 Lee Ellis, "Evidence of Neuroandrogenic Etiology of Sex Roles from a Combined Analysis of Human, Nonhuman Primate, and Nonprimate Mammalian Studies," *Personality and Individual Differences* 7:519–552 (1986).

61 Diana Fishbein, "The Psychobiology of Female Aggression," *Criminal Justice and Behavior* 19:99–126 (1992).

62 Spencer Rathus, *Psychology*, 3rd ed. (New York: Holt, Rinehart & Winston, 1987), p. 88.

63 See, generally, Katharina Dalton, *The Premenstrual Syndrome* (Springfield, IL: Charles C. Thomas, 1971).

64 Fishbein, "Selected Studies on the Biology of Antisocial Behavior."

65 B. Harry and C. Balcer, "Menstruation and Crime: A Critical Review of the Literature from the Clinical Criminology Perspective," *Behavioral Sciences and the Law* 5:307–322 (1987).

66 Julie Horney, "Menstrual Cycles and Criminal Responsibility," *Law and Human Nature* 2:25–36 (1978).

67 Lee Ellis, "Evolutionary and Neurochemical Causes of Sex Differences in Victimizing Behavior: Toward a Unified Theory of Criminal Behavior and Social Stratification," *Social Science Information* 28:605–636 (1989).

68 Lee Ellis, "The Victimful-Victimless Crime Distinction and Seven Universal Demographic Correlates of Victimful Criminal Behavior," *Personality and Individual Differences* 9:525–548 (1988).

69 Kathleen Pajer, "What Happens to 'Bad' Girls?: A Review of the Adult Outcomes of Antisocial Adolescent Girls," *American Journal of Psychiatry* 155:862–870 (1998).

70 Jan ter Laak, Martijn de Goede, Liesbeth Aleva, Gerard Brugman, Miranda van Leuven, and Judith Hussmann, "Incarcerated Adolescent Girls: Personality, Social Competence, and Delinquency," *Adolescence* 38:251–265 (2003).

71 Dorothy Espelage, Elizabeth Cauffman, Lisa Broidy, Alex Piquero, Paul Mazerolle, and Hans Steiner, "A Cluster-Analytic Investigation of MMPI Profiles of Serious Male and Female Juvenile Offenders," *Journal of the American Academy of Child and Adolescent Psychiatry* 42:770–777 (2003).

72 Kristen McCabe, Amy Lansing, Ann Garland, and Richard Hough, "Gender Differences in Psychopathology, Functional Impairment, and Familial Risk Factors Among Adjudicated Delinquents," *Journal of the American Academy of Child and Adolescent Psychiatry* 41:860–867 (2002).

73 Paul Frick, Amy Cornell, Christopher Barry, Doug Bodin, and Heather Dane, "Callous-Unemotional Traits and Conduct Problems in the Prediction of Conduct Problem Severity, Aggression, and Self-Report of Delinquency," *Journal of Abnormal Child Psychology* 31:457–470 (2003).

74 Alex Mason and Michael Windle, "Gender, Self-Control, and Informal Social Control in Adolescence: A Test of Three Models of the Continuity of Delinquent Behavior," *Youth & Society* 33:479–514 (2002).

75 Thomas, *The Unadjusted Girl.*

76 David Farrington, "Juvenile Delinquency," in John Coleman, ed., *The School Years* (London: Routledge, 1992), p. 133.

77 Ibid.

78 Ruth Morris, "Female Delinquents and Relational Problems," *Social Forces* 43:82–89 (1964).

79 Cowie, Cowie, and Slater, *Delinquency in Girls*, p. 27.

80 George Calhoun, Janelle Jurgens, and Fengling Chen, "The Neophyte Female Delinquent: A Review of the Literature," *Adolescence* 28:461–471 (1993).

81 Angela Dixon, Pauline Howie, and Jean Starling, "Trauma Exposure, Posttraumatic Stress, and Psychiatric Comorbidity in Female Juvenile Offenders," *Journal of the American Academy of Child and Adolescent Psychiatry* 44:798–806 (2005).

82 Veronica Herrera and Laura Ann McCloskey, "Sexual Abuse, Family Violence, and Female Delinquency: Findings From a Longitudinal Study," *Violence and Victims* 18:319–334 (2003).

83 Julie Messer, Barbara Maughan, and David Quinton, "Precursors and Correlates of Criminal Behaviour in Women," *Criminal Behaviour and Mental Health* 14:82–107 (2004).

84 Emily Gaarder and Joanne Belknap, "Tenuous Borders: Girls Transferred to Adult Court," *Criminology* 40:481–518 (2002).

85 Ibid., p. 20.

86 Joan Moore, *Going Down to the Barrio: Homeboys and Homegirls in Change* (Philadelphia: Temple University Press, 1991), p. 93.

87 Ibid., p. 101.

88 Gaarder and Belknap, "Tenuous Borders."

89 D. Wayne Osgood, Janet Wilson, Patrick O'Malley, Jerald Bachman, and Lloyd Johnston, "Routine Activities and Individual Deviant Behaviors," *American Sociological Review* 61:635–655 (1996).

90 Jennifer Kerpelman and Sondra Smith-Adcock, "Female Adolescents' Delinquent Activity: The Intersection of Bonds to Parents and Reputation Enhancement," *Youth & Society* 37:176–200 (2005).

91 Freda Adler, *Sisters in Crime* (New York: McGraw-Hill, 1975).

92 Ibid., pp. 10–11.

93 Rita James Simon, "Women and Crime Revisited," *Social Science Quarterly* 56:658–663 (1976).

94 Ibid., pp. 660–661.

95 Roy Austin, "Women's Liberation and Increase in Minor, Major, and Occupational Offenses," *Criminology* 20:407–430 (1982).

96 Joanne Belknap and Kristi Holsinger, "The Gendered Nature of Risk Factors for Delinquency," *Feminist Criminology* 1:48–71 (2006).

97 Darrell Steffensmeier and Dana Haynie, "Gender, Structural Disadvantage, and Urban Crime: Do Macrosocial Variables Also Explain Female Offending Rates?" *Criminology* 38:403–438 (2000); Beth Bjerregaard and Carolyn Smith, "Gender Differences in Gang Participation and Delinquency," *Journal of Quantitative Criminology* 9:329–350 (1993).

98 Julia Schwendinger and Herman Schwendinger, *Rape and Inequality* (Beverly Hills, CA: Sage, 1983).

99 For a review of feminist theory, see Sally Simpson, "Feminist Theory, Crime and Justice," *Criminology* 27:605–632 (1989).

100 Victoria Titterington, "A Retrospective Investigation of Gender Inequality and Female Homicide Victimization," *Sociological Spectrum* 26:205–236 (2006).

101 Simpson, "Feminist Theory, Crime and Justice." p. 611.

102 Messerschmidt, *Masculinities and Crime.*

103 Center for Research on Women, *Secrets in Public: Sexual Harassment in Our Schools* (Wellesley, MA: Wellesley College, 1993).

104 Belknap, Holsinger, and Dunn, "Understanding Incarcerated Girls."

105 Kathleen Daly and Meda Chesney-Lind, "Feminism and Criminology," *Justice Quarterly* 5:497–538 (1988).

106 Jane Siegel and Linda Williams, "The Relationship Between Child Sexual Abuse and Female Delinquency and Crime: A Prospective Study," *Journal of Research in Crime & Delinquency* 40:71–94 (2003).

107 James Messerschmidt, *Capitalism, Patriarchy, and Crime* (Totowa, NJ: Rowman and Littlefield, 1986); for a critique of this work, see Herman Schwendinger and Julia Schwendinger, "The World According to James Messerschmidt," *Social Justice* 15:123–145 (1988).

108 John Hagan, A. R. Gillis, and John Simpson, "The Class Structure and Delinquency: Toward a Power-Control Theory of Common Delinquent Behavior," *American Journal of Sociology* 90:1151–1178 (1985); John Hagan, John Simpson, and A. R. Gillis, "Class in the Household: A Power-Control Theory of Gender and Delinquency," *American Journal of Sociology* 92:788–816 (1987).

109 Meda Chesney-Lind, "Judicial Enforcement of the Female Sex Role: The Family Court and the Female Delinquent," *Issues in Criminology* 8:51–59 (1973).

110 Thomas J. Gamble, Sherrie Sonnenberg, John Haltigan, and Amy Cuzzola-Kern, "Detention Screening: Prospects for Population Management and the Examination of Disproportionality by Race, Age, and Gender," *Criminal Justice Policy Review* 13:380–395 (2002); Kimberly Kempf-Leonard and Lisa Sample, "Disparity Based on Sex: Is Gender-Specific Treatment Warranted?" *Justice Quarterly* 17:89–128 (2000).

111 Meda Chesney-Lind and Randall Shelden, *Girls, Delinquency, and Juvenile Justice* (Belmont, CA: West/Wadsworth, 1998).

[112] John MacDonald and Meda Chesney-Lind, "Gender Bias and Juvenile Justice Revisited: A Multiyear Analysis," *Crime and Delinquency* 47:173–195 (2001).

[113] Meda Chesney-Lind and Vickie Paramore, "Are Girls Getting More Violent? Exploring Juvenile Robbery Trends," *Journal of Contemporary Criminal Justice* 17:142–166 (2001).

[114] Belknap, Holsinger, and Dunn, "Understanding Incarcerated Girls." 125. Carol Pepi, "Children Without Childhoods: A Feminist Intervention Strategy Utilizing Systems Theory and Restorative Justice in Treating Female Adolescent Offenders," *Women and Therapy* 20:85–101 (1997).

[115] Holly Hartwig and Jane Myers, "A Different Approach: Applying a Wellness Paradigm to Adolescent Female Delinquents and Offenders," *Journal of Mental Health Counseling* 25:57–75 (2003).

[116] Ibid.

[117] Jill Leslie Rosenbaum and Meda Chesney-Lind, "Appearance and Delinquency: A Research Note," *Crime and Delinquency* 40:250–261 (1994).

[118] Sealock and Simpson, "Unraveling Bias in Arrest Decisions."

[119] Chesney-Lind and Shelden, *Girls, Delinquency, and Juvenile Justice,* p. 243.

Chapter 7. The Family and Delinquency

[1] Tracy Harachi, Charles Fleming, Helene White, Margaret Ensminger, Robert Abbott, Richard Catalano, and Kevin Haggerty, "Aggressive Behavior Among Girls and Boys During Middle Childhood: Predictors and Sequelae of Trajectory Group Membership," *Aggressive Behavior* 32:279–293 (2006).

[2] Rolf Loeber and Magda Stouthamer-Loeber, "Development of Juvenile Aggression and Violence," *American Psychologist* 53:250 (1998).

[3] Callie Harbin Burt, Ronald Simons, and Leslie Simons, "A Longitudinal Test of the Effects of Parenting and the Stability of Self-Control: Negative Evidence for the General Theory of Crime," *Criminology* 44:353–396 (2006).

[4] Joan McCord, "Family Relationships, Juvenile Delinquency, and Adult Criminality," *Criminology* 29:397–417 (1991); Scott Henggeler, ed., *Delinquency and Adolescent Psychopathology: A Family Ecological Systems Approach* (Littleton, MA: Wright–PSG, 1982).

[5] For a general review of the relationship between families and delinquency, see Alan Jay Lincoln and Murray Straus, *Crime and the Family* (Springfield, IL: Charles C. Thomas, 1985); Rolf Loeber and Magda Stouthamer-Loeber, "Family Factors as Correlates and Predictors of Juvenile Conduct Problems and Delinquency," in Michael Tonry and Norval Morris, eds., *Crime and Justice,* vol. 7 (Chicago: University of Chicago Press, 1986), pp. 29–151.

[6] David Farrington, "Juvenile Delinquency," in John Coleman, ed., *The School Years* (London: Routledge, 1992), pp. 139–140.

[7] Ruth Inglis, *Sins of the Fathers: A Study of the Physical and Emotional Abuse of Children* (New York: St. Martin's Press, 1978), p. 131.

[8] National Vital Statistics Report, *Births, Marriages, Divorces, and Deaths: Provisional Data for 2005,* Volume 54, Number 20, July 21, 2006. Available at: www.cdc.gov/nchs/data/nvsr54/nvsr54_20.pdf (accessed November 21, 2006).

[9] See Joseph J. Costa and Gordon K. Nelson, *Child Abuse and Neglect: Legislation, Reporting, and Prevention* (Lexington, MA: Heath, 1978), p. xiii.

[10] Tamar Lewin, "Men Assuming Bigger Role at Home, New Survey Shows," *New York Times,* 15 April 1998, p. A18.

[11] U.S. Census Bureau, *Children's Living Arrangements and Characteristics: March 2005,* Detailed Tables for Current Population Report. Available at: www.census.gov/population/www/socdemo/hh-fam/cps2005.html (accessed November 25, 2006).

[12] Terence P. Thornberry, Carolyn A. Smith, Craig Rivera, David Huizinga, and Magda Stouthamer-Loeber, "Family Disruption and Delinquency," *Juvenile Justice Bulletin* (Washington, DC: Office of Juvenile Justice and Delinquency Prevention, September 1999).

[13] *U.S. Pregnancy Rate Down from Peak; Births and Abortions on the Decline.* Press release (Washington, DC: Department of Health and Human Services, October 31, 2003); *HHS Report Shows Teen Birth Rate Falls to New Record Low in 2001.* Press release (Washington, DC: Department of Health and Human Services, June 6, 2002).

[14] *Kids Count Survey 1998.* News release. (Baltimore, MD: Annie E. Casey Foundation, May 5, 1998).

[15] *Kids Count Survey 2006* (Baltimore, MD: Annie E. Casey Foundation, 2006). Available at: www.aecf.org/kidscount/sld/index.jsp (accessed September 25, 2006).

[16] Christopher Sullivan, "Early Adolescent Delinquency: Assessing the Role of Childhood Problems, Family Environment, and Peer Pressure," *Youth Violence and Juvenile Justice* 4:291–313 (2006).

[17] Loeber and Stouthamer-Loeber, "Family Factors," pp. 39–41.

[18] Paul Howes and Howard Markman, "Marital Quality and Child Functioning: A Longitudinal Investigation," *Child Development* 60:1044–1051 (1989).

[19] Andre Sourander, Henrik Elonheimo, Solja Niemelä, Art-Matti Nuutila, Hans Helenius, Lauri Sillanmäki, Jorma Piha, Tuulk Tamminen, Kirsti Kumpulkinen, Irma Moilanen, and Frederik Almovist, "Childhood Predictors of Male Criminality: A Prospective Population-Based Follow-up Study From Age 8 to Late Adolescence," *Journal of the American Academy of Child & Adolescent Psychiatry* 45:578–586 (2006).

[20] Barbara Dafoe Whitehead, "Dan Quayle Was Right," *Atlantic Monthly* 271:47–84 (1993).

[21] C. Patrick Brady, James Bray, and Linda Zeeb, "Behavior Problems of Clinic Children: Relation to Parental Marital Status, Age, and Sex of Child," *American Journal of Orthopsychiatry* 56:399–412 (1986).

[22] Scott Henggeler, *Delinquency in Adolescence* (Newbury Park, CA: Sage, 1989), p. 48.

[23] Thornberry, Smith, Rivera, Huizinga, and Stouthamer-Loeber, *Family Disruption and Delinquency.*

[24] Sheldon Glueck and Eleanor Glueck, *Unraveling Juvenile Delinquency* (Cambridge, MA: Harvard University Press, 1950); Ashley Weeks, "Predicting Juvenile Delinquency," *American Sociological Review* 8:40–46 (1943).

[25] Jackson Toby, "The Differential Impact of Family Disorganization," *American Sociological Review* 22:505–512 (1957); Ruth Morris, "Female Delinquency and Relation Problems," *Social Forces* 43:82–89 (1964); Roland Chilton and Gerald Markle, "Family Disruption, Delinquent Conduct, and the Effects of Sub-Classification," *American Sociological Review* 37:93–99 (1972).

[26] For a review of these early studies, see Thomas Monahan, "Family Status and the Delinquent Child: A Reappraisal and Some New Findings," *Social Forces* 35:250–258 (1957).

[27] Clifford Shaw and Henry McKay, *Report on the Causes of Crime: Social Factors in Juvenile Delinquency,* vol. 2 (Washington, DC: U.S. Government Printing Office, 1931), p. 392.

[28] John Laub and Robert Sampson, "Unraveling Families and Delinquency: A Reanalysis of the Gluecks' Data," *Criminology* 26:355–380 (1988); Lawrence Rosen, "The Broken Home and Male Delinquency," in M. Wolfgang, L. Savitz, and N. Johnston, eds., *The Sociology of Crime and Delinquency* (New York: Wiley, 1970), pp. 489–495.

[29] Christina DeJong and Kenneth Jackson, "Putting Race into Context: Race, Juvenile Justice Processing, and Urbanization," *Justice Quarterly* 15:487–504 (1998).

[30] Robert Johnson, John Hoffman, and Dean Gerstein, *The Relationship Between Family Structure and Adolescent Substance Abuse* (Washington, DC: Office of Applied Studies, Substance Abuse and Mental Health Services Administration, 1996).

[31] Sara McLanahan, "Father Absence and the Welfare of Children," Working paper (Chicago: John D. and Catherine T. MacArthur Research Foundation, 1998).

[32] Cesar Rebellon, "Reconsidering the Broken Homes/Delinquency Relationship and Exploring Its Mediating Mechanism(s)," *Criminology* 40:103–135 (2002).

[33] Ronald Simons, Kuei-Hsiu Lin, Leslie Gordon, Rand Conger, and Frederick Lorenz, "Explaining the Higher Incidence of Adjustment Problems Among Children of Divorce Compared with Those in Two-Parent Families," *Journal of Marriage and the Family* 61:131–148 (1999).

[34] En-Ling Pan and Michael Farrell, "Ethnic Differences in the Effects of Intergenerational Relations on Adolescent Problem Behavior in U.S. Single-Mother Families," *Journal of Family Issues* 27:1137–1158 (2006).

[35] Sara Jaffee, Terrie Moffitt, Avshalom Caspi, and Alan Taylor, "Life with (or Without) Father: The Benefits of Living with Two Biological Parents Depend on the Father's Antisocial Behavior," *Child Development* 74:109–117 (2003).

36 Judith Smetena, "Adolescents' and Parents' Reasoning About Actual Family Conflict," *Child Development* 60:1052–1067 (1989).

37 F. Ivan Nye, "Child Adjustment in Broken and Unhappy Unbroken Homes," *Marriage and Family* 19:356–361 (1957); idem, *Family Relationships and Delinquent Behavior* (New York: Wiley, 1958).

38 Michael Hershorn and Alan Rosenbaum, "Children of Marital Violence: A Closer Look at the Unintended Victims," *American Journal of Orthopsychiatry* 55:260–266 (1985).

39 Peter Jaffe, David Wolfe, Susan Wilson, and Lydia Zak, "Similarities in Behavior and Social Maladjustment Among Child Victims and Witnesses to Family Violence," *American Journal of Orthopsychiatry* 56:142–146 (1986).

40 Veronica Herrera, "Equals in Risk? The Differential Impact of Family Violence on Male and Female Delinquency." Paper presented at the American Society of Criminology meeting, San Diego, November 1997. Henggeler, *Delinquency in Adolescence*, p. 39.

41 Diana Formoso, Nancy Gonzales, and Leona Aiken, "Family Conflict and Children's Internalizing and Externalizing Behavior: Protective Factors," *American Journal of Community Psychology* 28:175–199 (2000).

42 Jill Leslie Rosenbaum, "Family Dysfunction and Female Delinquency," *Crime and Delinquency* 35:31–44 (1989).

43 Paul Robinson, "Parents of 'Beyond Control' Adolescents," *Adolescence* 13:116–119 (1978).

44 Loeber and Stouthamer-Loeber, "Development of Juvenile Aggression and Violence," p. 251.

45 Carolyn Smith, Sung Joon Jang, and Susan Stern, "The Effect of Delinquency on Families," *Family and Corrections Network Report* 13:1–11 (1997).

46 Amato and Keith, "Parental Divorce and the Well-Being of Children."

47 Christopher Kierkus and Douglas Baer, "A Social Control Explanation of the Relationship Between Family Structure and Delinquent Behaviour," *Canadian Journal of Criminology,* 44:425–458 (2002).

48 John Paul Wright and Francis Cullen, "Parental Efficacy and Delinquent Behavior: Do Control and Support Matter?" *Criminology* 39:677–706 (2001).

49 Carter Hay, "Parenting, Self-Control, and Delinquency: A Test of Self-Control Theory," *Criminology* 39:707–736 (2001).

50 Sonia Cota-Robles and Wendy Gamble, "Parent-Adolescent Processes and Reduced Risk for Delinquency: The Effect of Gender for Mexican American Adolescents," *Youth & Society* 37:375–392 (2006).

51 Roslyn Caldwell, Jenna Silverman, Noelle Lefforge, and Clayton Silver, "Adjudicated Mexican-American Adolescents: The Effects of Familial Emotional Support on Self-Esteem, Emotional Well-Being, and Delinquency," *American Journal of Family Therapy* 32:55–69 (2004); Robert Vermeiren, Jef Bogaerts, Vladislav Ruchkin, Dirk Deboutte, and Mary Schwab-Stone, "Subtypes of Self-Esteem and Self-Concept in Adolescent Violent and Property Offenders," *Journal of Child Psychology and Psychiatry* 45:405–411 (2004).

52 Jacinta Bronte-Tinkew, Kristin Moore, and Jennifer Carrano, "The Father-Child Relationship, Parenting Styles, and Adolescent Risk Behaviors in Intact Families," *Journal of Family Issues* 27:850–881 (2006).

53 Bill McCarthy and John Hagan, "Mean Streets: The Theoretical Significance of Situational Delinquency Among Homeless Youth," *American Journal of Sociology* 98:597–627 (1992).

54 Carolyn Smith, Alan Lizotte, Terence Thornberry, and Marvin Krohn, "Resilience to Delinquency," *Prevention Researcher* 4:4–7 (1997).

55 Jennifer Wainright and Charlotte Patterson, "Delinquency, Victimization, and Substance Use Among Adolescents With Female Same-Sex Parents," *Journal of Family Psychology* 20:526–530 (2006).

56 Sung Joon Jang and Carolyn Smith, "A Test of Reciprocal Causal Relationships Among Parental Supervision, Affective Ties, and Delinquency," *Journal of Research in Crime and Delinquency* 34:307–336 (1997).

57 Gerald Patterson and Magda Stouthamer-Loeber, "The Correlation of Family Management Practices and Delinquency," *Child Development* 55:1299–1307 (1984); Gerald R. Patterson, *A Social Learning Approach: Coercive Family Process,* vol. 3 (Eugene, OR: Castalia, 1982).

58 Christopher Ellison and Darren Sherkat, "Conservative Protestantism and Support for Corporal Punishment," *American Sociological Review* 58:131–144 (1993).

59 Eric Slade and Lawrence Wissow, "Spanking in Early Childhood and Later Behavior Problems: A Prospective Study of Infants and Young Toddlers," *Pediatrics* 113:1321–1330 (2004).

60 Murray Straus, "Discipline and Deviance: Physical Punishment of Children and Violence and Other Crime in Adulthood," *Social Problems* 38:101–123 (1991).

61 Murray A. Straus, "Spanking and the Making of a Violent Society: The Short- and Long-Term Consequences of Corporal Punishment," *Pediatrics* 98:837–843 (1996).

62 Ibid.

63 Loeber and Stouthamer-Loeber, "Development of Juvenile Aggression and Violence," p. 251.

64 Nathaniel Pallone and James Hennessy, "Brain Dysfunction and Criminal Violence," *Society* 35:21–27 (1998).

65 Nye, *Family Relationships and Delinquent Behavior.*

66 Laurence Steinberg, Ilana Blatt-Eisengart, and Elizabeth Cauffman, "Patterns of Competence and Adjustment Among Adolescents from Authoritative, Authoritarian, Indulgent, and Neglectful Homes: A Replication in a Sample of Serious Juvenile Offenders," *Journal of Research on Adolescence* 26:47–58 (2006).

67 Lisa Broidy, "Direct Supervision and Delinquency: Assessing the Adequacy of Structural Proxies," *Journal of Criminal Justice* 23:541–554 (1995).

68 James Unnever, Francis Cullen, and Robert Agnew, "Why Is 'Bad' Parenting Criminogenic? Implications from Rival Theories," *Youth Violence and Juvenile Justice* 4:3–33 (2006).

69 Jennifer Beyers, John Bates, Gregory Pettit, and Kenneth Dodge, "Neighborhood Structure, Parenting Processes, and the Development of Youths' Externalizing Behaviors: A Multilevel Analysis," *American Journal of Community Psychology* 31:35–53 (2003).

70 Jang and Smith, "A Test of Reciprocal Causal Relationships Among Parental Supervision, Affective Ties, and Delinquency"; Linda Waite and Lee Lillard, "Children and Marital Disruption," *American Journal of Sociology* 96:930–53 (1991).

71 Jennifer Beyers, John Bates, Gregory Pettit, and Kenneth Dodge, "Neighborhood Structure, Parenting Processes, and the Development of Youths' Externalizing Behaviors: A Multilevel Analysis," *American Journal of Community Psychology* 31:35–53 (2003).

72 Thomas Vander Ven and Francis Cullen," *Crime & Delinquency* 50:272–292 (2004); Thomas Vander Ven, Francis Cullen, Mark Carrozza, and John Paul Wright, "Home Alone: The Impact of Maternal Employment on Delinquency," *Social Problems* 48:236–257 (2001).

73 Douglas Downey, "Number of Siblings and Intellectual Development," *American Psychologist* 56:497–504 (2001); idem, "When Bigger Is Not Better: Family Size, Parental Resources, and Children's Educational Performance," *American Sociological Review* 60:746–761 (1995).

74 G. Rahav, "Birth Order and Delinquency," *British Journal of Criminology* 20:385–395 (1980); D. Viles and D. Challinger, "Family Size and Birth Order of Young Offenders," *International Journal of Offender Therapy and Comparative Criminology* 25:60–66 (1981).

75 Vander Ven, Cullen, Carrozza, and Wright, "Home Alone: The Impact of Maternal Employment on Delinquency."

76 For an early review, see Barbara Wooton, *Social Science and Social Pathology* (London: Allen and Unwin, 1959).

77 Daniel Shaw, "Advancing Our Understanding of Intergenerational Continuity in Antisocial Behavior," *Journal of Abnormal Child Psychology* 31:193–199 (2003).

78 Donald J. West and David P. Farrington, eds., "Who Becomes Delinquent?" in *The Delinquent Way of Life* (London: Heinemann, 1977); Donald J. West, *Delinquency: Its Roots, Careers, and Prospects* (Cambridge, MA: Harvard University Press, 1982).

79 David Farrington, "Understanding and Preventing Bullying," in Michael Tonry, ed., *Crime and Justice,* vol. 17 (Chicago: University of Chicago Press, 1993), pp. 381–457.

80 Carolyn Smith and David Farrington, "Continuities in Antisocial Behavior and Parenting Across Three Generations," *Journal of Child Psychology and Psychiatry* 45:230–247 (2004).

81 Joseph Murray and David Farrington, "Parental Imprisonment: Effects on Boys' Antisocial Behaviour and Delinquency Through the Life-Course," *Journal of Child Psychology & Psychiatry* 46:1269–1278 (2005).

[82] John Paul Wright and Kevin Beaver, "Do Parents Matter in Creating Self-Control in Their Children? A Genetically Informed Test of Gottfredson and Hirschi's Theory of Low Self-Control," *Criminology* 43:1169–1202 (2005).

[83] Leonore Simon, "Does Criminal Offender Treatment Work?" *Applied and Preventive Psychology* Summer 1–22 (1998).

[84] Nancy Day, Lidush Goldschmidt, and Carrie Thomas, "Prenatal Marijuana Exposure Contributes to the Prediction of Marijuana Use at Age 14," *Addiction* 101:1313–1322 (2006).

[85] Philip Harden and Robert Pihl, "Cognitive Function, Cardiovascular Reactivity, and Behavior in Boys at High Risk for Alcoholism," *Journal of Abnormal Psychology* 104:94–103 (1995).

[86] Laub and Sampson, "Unraveling Families and Delinquency," p. 370.

[87] Anne Dannerbeck "Differences in Parenting Attributes, Experiences, and Behaviors of Delinquent Youth with and without a Parental History of Incarceration," *Youth Violence and Juvenile Justice* 3:199–213 (2005).

[88] David P. Farrington, Gwen Gundry, and Donald J. West, "The Familial Transmission of Criminality," in Alan Lincoln and Murray Straus, eds., *Crime and the Family* (Springfield, IL: Charles C. Thomas, 1985), pp. 193–206.

[89] Abigail Fagan and Jake Najman, "Sibling Influences on Adolescent Delinquent Behaviour: An Australian Longitudinal Study," *Journal of Adolescence* 26:546–558 (2003).

[90] David Rowe and Bill Gulley, "Sibling Effects on Substance Use and Delinquency," *Criminology* 30:217–232 (1992); see also David Rowe, Joseph Rogers, and Sylvia Meseck-Bushey, "Sibling Delinquency and the Family Environment: Shared and Unshared Influences," *Child Development* 63:59–67 (1992).

[91] Richard Gelles and Claire Pedrick Cornell, *Intimate Violence in Families*, 2nd ed. (Newbury Park, CA: Sage, 1990), p. 33.

[92] Lois Hochhauser, "Child Abuse and the Law: A Mandate for Change," *Harvard Law Journal* 18:200 (1973); see also Douglas J. Besharov, "The Legal Aspects of Reporting Known and Suspected Child Abuse and Neglect," *Villanova Law Review* 23:458 (1978).

[93] C. Henry Kempe, F. N. Silverman, B. F. Steele, W. Droegemueller, and H. K. Silver, "The Battered-Child Syndrome," *Journal of the American Medical Association* 181:17–24 (1962).

[94] Brian G. Fraser, "A Glance at the Past, a Gaze at the Present, a Glimpse at the Future: A Critical Analysis of the Development of Child Abuse Reporting Statutes," *Chicago-Kent Law Review* 54:643 (1977–1978).

[95] National Center for Injury Prevention and Control. Available at: www.cdc.gov/ncipc/factsheets/cmfacts.htm (accessed November 15, 2006).

[96] See, especially, Inglis, *Sins of the Fathers*, ch. 8.

[97] William Downs and Brenda Miller, "Relationships Between Experiences of Parental Violence During Childhood and Women's Self-Esteem," *Violence and Victims* 13:63–78 (1998).

[98] Ruth S. Kempe and C. Henry Kempe, *Child Abuse* (Cambridge, MA: Harvard University Press, 1978), pp. 6–7.

[99] Fred Rogosch and Dante Cicchetti, "Child maltreatment and emergent personality organization: perspectives from the Five-Factor Model," *Journal of Abnormal Child Psychology* 32:123–145 (2004).

[100] Wendy Fisk, "Childhood Trauma and Dissociative Identity Disorder," *Child and Adolescent Psychiatric Clinics of North America* 5:431–447 (1996).

[101] National Center for Injury Prevention and Control. Available at: www.cdc.gov/ncipc/factsheets/cmfacts.htm (accessed November 15, 2006).

[102] National Center for Shaken Baby Syndrome. Available at: www.dontshake.com (accessed November 15, 2006).

[103] Mary Haskett and Janet Kistner, "Social Interactions and Peer Perceptions of Young Physically Abused Children," *Child Development* 62:679–690 (1991).

[104] Catherine Grus, "Child Abuse: Correlations with Hostile Attributions," *Journal of Developmental & Behavioral Pediatrics* 24:296–298 (2006).

[105] Kim Logio, "Gender, Race, Childhood Abuse, and Body Image among Adolescents," *Violence Against Women* 9:931–955 (2003).

[106] Jeanne Kaufman and Cathy Spatz Widom, "Childhood Victimization, Running Away, and Delinquency," *Journal of Research in Crime and Delinquency* 36:347–370 (1999).

[107] N. N. Sarkar and Rina Sarkar, "Sexual Assault on Woman: Its Impact on Her Life and Living in Society," *Sexual & Relationship Therapy* 20:407–419 (2005).

[108] Michael Wiederman, Randy Sansone, and Lori Sansone, "History of Trauma and Attempted Suicide among Women in a Primary Care Setting," *Violence and Victims* 13:3–11 (1998); Susan Leslie Bryant and Lillian Range, "Suicidality in College Women Who Were Sexually and Physically Abused and Physically Punished by Parents," *Violence and Victims* 10:195–215 (1995); William Downs and Brenda Miller, "Relationships between Experiences of Parental Violence During Childhood and Women's Self-Esteem," *Violence and Victims* 13:63–78 (1998); Sally Davies-Netley, Michael Hurlburt, and Richard Hough, "Childhood Abuse as a Precursor to Homelessness for Homeless Women with Severe Mental Illness," *Violence and Victims* 11:129–142 (1996).

[109] Jane Siegel and Linda Williams, "Risk Factors for Sexual Victimization of Women," *Violence Against Women* 9:902–930 (2003).

[110] Michael Miner, Jill Klotz Flitter, and Beatrice Robinson. "Association of Sexual Revictimization with Sexuality and Psychological Function," *Journal of Interpersonal Violence* 21:503–524 (2006).

[111] Lana Stermac and Emily Paradis, "Homeless Women and Victimization: Abuse and Mental Health History Among Homeless Rape Survivors," *Resources for Feminist Research* 28:65–81 (2001).

[112] Murray Straus, Richard Gelles, and Suzanne Steinmentz, *Behind Closed Doors: Violence in the American Family* (Garden City, NY: Anchor Books, 1980); Richard Gelles and Murray Straus, "Violence in the American Family," *Journal of Social Issues* 35:15–39 (1979).

[113] Gelles and Straus, "Violence in the American Family," p. 24.

[114] Richard Gelles and Murray Straus, *The Causes and Consequences of Abuse in the American Family* (New York: Simon & Schuster, 1988); see also Murray A. Straus and Glenda Kaufman Kantor, "Trends in Physical Abuse by Parents from 1975 to 1992: A Comparison of Three National Surveys." Paper presented at the annual meeting of the American Society of Criminology, Boston, November 1995.

[115] Murray A. Straus and Anita K. Mathur, "Social Change and Trends in Approval of Corporal Punishment by Parents from 1968 to 1994," in D. Frehsee, W. Horn, and K. Bussman, eds., *Violence Against Children* (New York: Aldine de Gruyter, 1996), pp. 91–105.

[116] Data in this section comes from U.S. Department of Health and Human Services, Administration for Children and Families. Available at: www.childwelfare.gov/can/index.cfm (accessed Sept. 25, 2006).

[117] Richard Estes and Neil Alan Weiner, *The Commercial Sexual Exploitation of Children in the U.S., Canada and Mexico* (Philadelphia: University of Pennsylvania, 2001).

[118] Lisa Jones and David Finkelhor, *The Decline in Child Sexual Abuse Cases* (Washington, DC: Office of Juvenile Justice and Delinquency Prevention, 2001).

[119] Carolyn Webster-Stratton, "Comparison of Abusive and Nonabusive Families with Conduct-Disordered Children," *American Journal of Orthopsychiatry* 55:59–69 (1985); Brandt F. Steele and Carl B. Pollock, "A Psychiatric Study of Parents Who Abuse Infants and Small Children," in Ray Helfer and C. Henry Kempe, eds., *The Battered Child* (Chicago: University of Chicago Press, 1968), pp. 103–145.

[120] Brandt F. Steele, "Violence Within the Family," in Ray E. Helfer and C. Henry Kempe, eds., *Child Abuse and Neglect: The Family and the Community* (Cambridge, MA: Ballinger, 1976), p. 13.

[121] William Sack, Robert Mason, and James Higgins, "The Single-Parent Family and Abusive Punishment," *American Journal of Orthopsychiatry* 55:252–259 (1985).

[122] Blair Justice and Rita Justice, *The Abusing Family* (New York: Human Sciences Press, 1976); Nanette Dembitz, "Preventing Youth Crime by Preventing Child Neglect," *American Bar Association Journal* 65:920–923 (1979).

[123] Douglas Ruben, *Treating Adult Children of Alcoholics: A Behavioral Approach* (New York: Academic Press, 2000).

[124] Martin Daly and Margo Wilson, "Violence Against Stepchildren," *Current Directions in Psychological Science* 5:77–81 (1996).

[125] Ibid.

[126] Margo Wilson, Martin Daly, and Atonietta Daniele, "Familicide: The Killing of Spouse and Children," *Aggressive Behavior* 21:275–291 (1995).

[127] Richard Gelles, "Child Abuse and Violence in Single-Parent Families: Parent Absence and Economic Deprivation," *American Journal of Orthopsychiatry* 59:492–501 (1989).

128 Susan Napier and Mitchell Silverman, "Family Violence as a Function of Occupation Status, Socioeconomic Class, and Other Variables." Paper presented at the American Society of Criminology meeting, Boston, November 1995.

129 Robert Burgess and Patricia Draper, "The Explanation of Family Violence," in Lloyd Ohlin and Michael Tonry, eds., *Family Violence* (Chicago: University of Chicago Press, 1989), pp. 59–117.

130 Ibid., pp. 103–104.

131 *Troxel et vir. v. Granville*, No. 99-138 (June 5, 2000).

132 452 U.S. 18, 101 S.Ct. 2153 (1981); 455 U.S. 745, 102 S.Ct. 1388 (1982).

133 For a survey of each state's reporting requirements, abuse and neglect legislation, and available programs and agencies, see Costa and Nelson, *Child Abuse and Neglect*.

134 Linda Gordon, "Incest and Resistance: Patterns of Father-Daughter Incest, 1880–1930," *Social Problems* 33:253–267 (1986).

135 P.L. 93B247 (1974); P.L. 104B235 (1996).

136 Barbara Ryan, "Do You Suspect Child Abuse? The Story of 2-Year-Old Dominic James Made Headlines Not Only Because of His Tragic Death, But Because Criminal Charges Were Lodged Against a Nurse for Failing to Report His Suspicious Injuries. A Cautionary Tale," *RN* 66:73–76 (2003).

137 Robin Fretwell Wilson, "Children at Risk: The Sexual Exploitation of Female Children After Divorce," *Cornell Law Review* 86:251–327 (2001).

138 Sue Badeau and Sarah Gesiriech, *A Child's Journey Through the Child Welfare System* (Washington, DC: The Pew Commission on Children in Foster Care, December 13, 2003); Shirley Dobbin, Sophia Gatowski, and Margaret Springate, "Child Abuse and Neglect," *Juvenile and Family Court Journal* 48:43–54 (1997).

139 PBS Frontline, Innocence Lost the Plea. Available at: www.pbs.org/wgbh/pages/frontline/shows/innocence/etc/other.html (accessed November 15, 2006); For an analysis of the accuracy of children's recollections of abuse, see Candace Kruttschnitt and Maude Dornfeld, "Will They Tell? Assessing Preadolescents' Reports of Family Violence," *Journal of Research in Crime and Delinquency* 29:136–147 (1992).

140 Ibid.

141 Debra Whitcomb, *When the Victim Is a Child* (Washington, DC: National Institute of Justice, 1992), p. 33.

142 *White v. Illinois*, 502 U.S. 346; 112 S.Ct. 736 (1992).

143 Myrna Raeder, "*White's* Effect on the Right to Confront One's Accuser," *Criminal Justice*, Winter 2–7 (1993).

144 *Coy v. Iowa*, 487 U.S. 1012 (1988).

145 *Maryland v. Craig*, 110 S.Ct. 3157 (1990).

146 *Walker v. Fagg*, 400 S.E. 2d 708 (Va. App. 1991).

147 Cesar Rebellon and Karen Van Gundy, "Can Control Theory Explain the Link Between Parental Physical Abuse and Delinquency? A Longitudinal Analysis," *Journal of Research in Crime and Delinquency* 42:247–274 (2005).

148 Gelles and Straus, "Violence in the American Family."

149 National Center on Child Abuse and Neglect, Department of Health, Education, and Welfare, *1977 Analysis of Child Abuse and Neglect Research* (Washington, DC: U.S. Government Printing Office, 1978), p. 29.

150 Steele, "Violence Within the Family," p. 22.

151 L. Bender and F. J. Curran, "Children and Adolescents Who Kill," *Journal of Criminal Psychopathology* 1:297 (1940), cited in Steele, "Violence Within the Family," p. 21.

152 W. M. Easson and R. M. Steinhilber, "Murderous Aggression by Children and Adolescents," *Archives of General Psychiatry* 4:1–11 (1961), cited in Steele, "Violence Within the Family," p. 22; see also J. Duncan and G. Duncan, "Murder in the Family: A Study of Some Homicidal Adolescents," *American Journal of Psychiatry* 127:1498–1502 (1971); C. King, "The Ego and Integration of Violence in Homicidal Youth," *American Journal of Orthopsychiatry* 45:134–145 (1975); James Sorrells, "Kids Who Kill," *Crime and Delinquency* 23:312–326 (1977).

153 Jose Alfaro, "Report of the Relationship Between Child Abuse and Neglect and Later Socially Deviant Behavior." Unpublished paper (Albany, NY: New York State Government, n.d.), pp. 175–219.

154 Cathy Spatz Widom, "Child Abuse, Neglect, and Violent Criminal Behavior," *Criminology* 27:251–271 (1989).

155 Cathy Spatz Widom, "The Cycle of Violence." *Science* 244:160–166 (April 14, 1989).

156 Michael Maxfield and Cathy Spatz Widom, "Childhood Victimization and Patterns of Offending Through the Life Cycle: Early Onset and Continuation." Paper presented at the American Society of Criminology meeting, Boston, November 1995.

157 Jane Siegel and Linda Meyer Williams, "Violent Behavior Among Men Abused as Children." Paper presented at the American Society of Criminology meeting, Boston, November 1995; Jane Siegel and Linda Meyer Williams, "Aggressive Behavior Among Women Sexually Abused as Children." Paper presented at the American Society of Criminology meeting, Phoenix, 1993 (rev. version).

158 David Skuse, Arnon Bentovim, Jill Hodges, Jim Stevenson, Chriso Andreou, Monica Lanyado, Michelle New, Bryn Williams, and Dean McMillan, "Risk Factors for Development of Sexually Abusive Behaviour in Sexually Victimised Adolescent Boys: Cross Sectional Study," *British Medical Journal* 317:175–180 (1998).

159 Carolyn Smith and Terence Thornberry, "The Relationship Between Childhood Maltreatment and Adolescent Involvement in Delinquency," *Criminology* 33:451–477 (1995).

160 Widom, "Child Abuse, Neglect, and Violent Criminal Behavior," p. 267.

161 Bruce Rind, Philip Tromovitch, and Robert Bauserman, "A Meta-Analytic Examination of Assumed Properties of Child Sexual Abuse Using College Samples," *Psychological Bulletin* 124:22–53 (1998).

162 Matthew Zingraff, "Child Maltreatment and Youthful Problem Behavior," *Criminology* 31:173–202 (1993).

163 Timothy Ireland, Carolyn Smith, and Terence Thornberry, "Developmental Issues in the Impact of Child Maltreatment on Later Delinquency and Drug Use," *Criminology* 40:359–401 (2002).

164 Ibid.

165 Kristi Holsinger and Alexander Holsinger, "Differential Pathways to Violence and Self-Injurious Behavior: African American and White Girls in the Juvenile Justice System," *Journal of Research in Crime and Delinquency* 42:211–242 (2005).

Chapter 8. Peers and Delinquency: Juvenile Gangs and Groups

1 For a general review, see Scott Cummings and Daniel Monti, *Gangs: The Origin and Impact of Contemporary Youth Gangs in the United States* (Albany: SUNY Press, 1993); this chapter also makes extensive use of George Knox et al., *Gang Prevention and Intervention: Preliminary Results from the 1995 Gang Research Task Force* (Chicago: National Gang Crime Research Center, 1995).

2 Paul Perrone and Meda Chesney-Lind, "Representations of Gangs and Delinquency: Wild in the Streets?" *Social Justice* 24:96–117 (1997).

3 John Hagedorn, "Gangs," in Karen Christianson and David Levinson, Editors, *The Encyclopedia of Community* (Thousand Oaks, CA: Sage, 2003), pp. 517–522.

4 Spencer Rathus, *Understanding Child Development* (New York: Holt, Rinehart & Winston, 1988), p. 462.

5 Peggy Giordano, "The Wider Circle of Friends in Adolescence," *American Journal of Sociology* 101:661–697 (1995).

6 Thomas Berndt and T. B. Perry, "Children's Perceptions of Friendships as Supportive Relationships," *Developmental Psychology* 22:640–648 (1986).

7 Annette La Greca and Hannah Moore Harrison, "Adolescent Peer Relations, Friendships, and Romantic Relationships: Do They Predict Social Anxiety and Depression?" *Journal of Clinical Child & Adolescent Psychology* 34:49–61 (2005).

8 Shari Miller-Johnson, Philip Costanzo, John Coie, Mary Rose, Dorothy Browne, and Courtney Johnson, "Peer Social Structure and Risk-Taking Behaviors Among African-American Early Adolescents," *Journal of Youth and Adolescence* 32:375–384 (2003).

9 John Coie and Shari Miller-Johnson, "Peer Factors in Early Offending Behavior." In Rolf Loeber and David Farrington (eds.), *Child Delinquents* (Thousand Oaks, CA: Sage, 2001), pp. 191–210.

10 Ibid.

11 Judith Rich Harris, *The Nurture Assumption: Why Children Turn Out the Way They Do* (New York: Free Press, 1998).

12 Ibid., p. 463.

13 Albert Reiss, "Co-Offending and Criminal Careers," in Michael Tonry and Norval Morris, eds., *Crime and Justice,* vol. 10 (Chicago: University of Chicago Press, 1988).

14 Robert Agnew and Timothy Brezina, "Relational Problems with Peers, Gender, and Delinquency," *Youth and Society* 29:84–111 (1997).

15 Maury Nation and Craig Anne Heflinger, "Risk Factors for Serious Alcohol and Drug Use: The Role of Psychosocial Variables in Predicting the Frequency of Substance Use Among Adolescents," *American Journal of Drug & Alcohol Abuse* 32:415–433 (2006).

16 Kevin Beaver and John Paul Wright, "Biosocial Development and Delinquent Involvement," *Youth Violence and Juvenile Justice* 3:168–192 (2005).

17 Richard Felson and Dana Haynie, "Pubertal Development, Social Factors, and Delinquency Among Adolescent Boys," *Criminology* 40:967–989 (2002).

18 Brett Johnson Solomon, "Other-Sex Friendship Involvement among Delinquent Adolescent Females," *Youth Violence and Juvenile Justice* 4:75–96 (2006).

19 See Travis Hirschi, *Causes of Delinquency* (Berkeley: University of California Press, 1969).

20 James Short and Fred Strodtbeck, *Group Process and Gang Delinquency* (Chicago: Aldine de Gruyter, 1965).

21 Kate Keenan, Rolf Loeber, Quanwu Zhang, Magda Stouthamer-Loeber, and Welmoet Van Kammen, "The Influence of Deviant Peers on the Development of Boys' Disruptive and Delinquent Behavior: A Temporal Analysis," *Development and Psychopathology* 7:715–726 (1995).

22 John Cole, Robert Terry, Shari-Miller Johnson, and John Lochman, "Longitudinal Effects of Deviant Peer Groups on Criminal Offending in Late Adolescence." Paper presented at the American Society of Criminology meeting, Boston, November 1995.

23 Terence Thornberry and Marvin Krohn, "Peers, Drug Use, and Delinquency," in David Stoff, James Breiling, and Jack Maser, eds., *Handbook of Antisocial Behavior* (New York: Wiley, 1997), pp. 218–233; Thomas Dishion, Deborah Capaldi, Kathleen Spracklen, and Fuzhong Li, "Peer Ecology of Male Adolescent Drug Use," *Development and Psychopathology* 7:803–824 (1995).

24 Mark Warr, "Age, Peers, and Delinquency," *Criminology* 31:17–40 (1993).

25 Sara Battin, Karl Hill, Robert Abbott, Richard Catalano, and J. David Hawkins, "The Contribution of Gang Membership to Delinquency Beyond Delinquent Friends," *Criminology* 36:93–116 (1998).

26 Mark Warr, "Life-Course Transitions and Desistance from Crime," *Criminology* 36:502–536 (1998).

27 Stephen W. Baron, "Self-Control, Social Consequences, and Criminal Behavior: Street Youth and the General Theory of Crime," *Journal of Research in Crime and Delinquency* 40:403–425 (2003).

28 Daneen Deptula and Robert Cohen, "Aggressive, Rejected, and Delinquent Children and Adolescents: A Comparison of Their Friendships," *Aggression & Violent Behavior* 9:75–104 (2004).

29 David Farrington and Rolf Loeber, "Epidemiology of Juvenile Violence," *Child and Adolescent Psychiatric Clinics of North America* 9:733–748 (2000).

30 Peggy Giordano, Stephen Cernkovich, and M. D. Pugh, "Friendships and Delinquency," *American Journal of Sociology* 91:1170–1202 (1986).

31 Well-known movie representations of gangs include *The Wild Ones* and *Hell's Angels on Wheels*, which depict motorcycle gangs, and *Saturday Night Fever*, which focused on neighborhood street toughs; see also David Dawley, *A Nation of Lords* (Garden City, NY: Anchor, 1973).

32 For a recent review of gang research, see James Howell, "Recent Gang Research: Program and Policy Implications," *Crime and Delinquency* 40:495–515 (1994).

33 Walter Miller, *Violence by Youth Gangs and Youth Groups as a Crime Problem in Major American Cities* (Washington, DC: U.S. Government Printing Office, 1975).

34 Ibid., p. 20.

35 Malcolm Klein, *The American Street Gang: Its Nature, Prevalence, and Control* (New York: Oxford University Press, 1995), p. 30.

36 Irving Spergel, *The Youth Gang Problem: A Community Approach* (New York: Oxford University Press, 1995).

37 Ibid., p. 3.

38 Christopher Adamson, "Defensive Localism in White and Black: A Comparative History of European-American and African-American Youth Gangs," *Ethnic & Racial Studies*, 23:272–298 (2000).

39 Frederick Thrasher, *The Gang* (Chicago: University of Chicago Press, 1927).

40 National Youth Gang Center, 2003. Available at: www.iir.com/nygc/faq.htm#q1 (accessed December 4, 2006).

41 Irving Spergel, *Street Gang Work: Theory and Practice* (Reading, MA: Addison-Wesley, 1966).

42 Miller, *Violence by Youth Gangs*, p. 2.

43 Miller, *Violence by Youth Gangs*, pp. 1–2.

44 Ibid.

45 Felix Padilla, *The Gang as an American Enterprise* (New Brunswick, NJ: Rutgers University Press, 1992), p. 3.

46 Pamela Irving Jackson, "Crime, Youth Gangs, and Urban Transition: The Social Dislocations of Postindustrial Economic Development," *Justice Quarterly* 8:379–897 (1991); Moore, *Going Down to the Barrio*, pp. 89–101.

47 Arlen Egley, Jr., and Christina E. Ritz, *Highlights of the 2004 National Youth Gang Survey* (Washington, DC: Office of Juvenile Justice and Delinquency Prevention, 2006).

48 William Julius Wilson, *The Truly Disadvantaged* (Chicago: University of Chicago Press, 1987).

49 Ibid.

50 Egley, Jr., and Ritz, *Highlights of the 2004 National Youth Gang Survey*.

51 Cheryl Maxson, *Gang Members on the Move*. Bulletin, Youth Gang Series (Washington, DC: Office of Juvenile Justice and Delinquency Prevention, 1998).

52 Ibid.

53 This section relies heavily on James Howell, The *Impact of Gangs on Communities* (Washington, DC: Office of Juvenile Justice and Delinquency Prevention, 2006.).

54 Arian Campo-Flores, "The Most Dangerous Gang in the United States," *Newsweek,* March 28, 2006; Ricardo Pollack, "Gang Life Tempts Salvador Teens," BBC News. Available at: http://news.bbc.co.uk/1/hi/world/americas/4201183.stm (accessed April 3, 2006).

55 Fagan, "The Social Organization of Drug Use and Drug Dealing Among Urban Gangs."

56 Ibid.

57 National Youth Gang Center, "Are Today's Youth Gangs Different from Gangs in the Past?" Available at: www.iir.com/nygc/faq.htm (accessed December 4, 2006).

58 Lewis Yablonsky, *The Violent Gang* (Baltimore: Penguin, 1966), p. 109.

59 James Diego Vigil, *Barrio Gangs* (Austin: Texas University Press, 1988), pp. 11–19.

60 Mark Warr, "Organization and Instigation in Delinquent Groups," *Criminology* 34:11–37 (1996).

61 Knox et al., *Gang Prevention and Intervention*, p. vii.

62 Ibid.

63 Wilson, *The Truly Disadvantaged*.

64 Ibid.

65 John Hagedorn, "The Global Impact of Gangs," *Journal of Contemporary Criminal Justice* 21:153–169 (2005).

66 Finn-Aage Esbensen and David Huizinga, "Gangs, Drugs and Delinquency in a Survey of Urban Youth," *Criminology* 31:565–587 (1993); Finn-Aage Esbensen, "Race and Gender Differences between Gang and Nongang Youths: Results from a Multisite Survey" *Justice Quarterly* 15:504–525 (1998).

67 Cheryl Maxson and Monica Whitlock, "Joining the Gang: Gender Differences in Risk Factors for Gang Membership," In C. Ronald Huff, ed., *Gangs in America III* (Thousand Oaks, CA: Sage, 2002), pp. 19–35.

68 Mars Eghigian and Katherine Kirby, "Girls in Gangs: On the Rise in America," *Corrections Today* 68:48–50 (2006).

69 Ibid.

70 Mark Fleisher and Jessie Krienert, "Life-Course Events, Social Networks, and the Emergence of Violence Among *Female* Gang Members," *Journal of Community Psychology* 32:607–622 (2004).

71 Karen Joe Laidler and Geoffrey Hunt, "Violence and Social Organization in Female Gangs," *Social Justice* 24:148–187 (1997); Moore, *Going Down to the Barrio*; Anne Campbell, *The Girls in the Gang* (Cambridge, MA: Basil Blackwell, 1984).

72 Karen Joe Laidler and Meda Chesney-Lind, "'Just Every Mother's Angel': An Analysis of Gender and Ethnic Variations in Youth Gang Membership," *Gender and Society* 9:408–430 (1995).

73 Jody Miller, *One of the Guys: Girls, Gangs, and Gender* (New York: Oxford University Press, 2001).

74 Ibid.

[75] Fleisher and Krienert, "Life-Course Events, Social Networks, and the Emergence of Violence Among *Female* Gang Members."

[76] Joan Moore, James Diego Vigil, and Robert Garcia, "Residence and Territoriality in Chicano Gangs," *Social Problems* 31:182–194 (1983).

[77] Mark Warr, "Organization and Instigation in Delinquent Groups," *Criminology* 34:11–37 (1996).

[78] Malcolm Klein, "Impressions of Juvenile Gang Members," *Adolescence* 3:59 (1968).

[79] Scott Decker, Tim Bynum, and Deborah Weisel, "A Tale of Two Cities: Gangs and Organized Crime Groups," *Justice Quarterly* 15:395–425 (1998).

[80] National Youth Gang Survey data. Available at: www.iir.com/NYGC/faq.htm#q12 (accessed September 20, 2006).

[81] National Youth Gang Center, 2003 data. Available at: www.iir.com/nygc/faq.htm#q6 (accessed December 4, 2006).

[82] The following description of ethnic gangs leans heavily on the material developed in National School Safety Center, *Gangs in Schools*, pp. 11–23.

[83] Spergel, *The Youth Gang Problem*, pp. 136–137.

[84] Know Gangs. Available at: www.knowgangs.com/gang_resources/black_gangster_disciples/bgd_001.htm (accessed October 10, 2006).

[85] Decker, Bynum, and Weisel, "A Tale of Two Cities."

[86] Thomas Winfree Jr., Frances Bernat, and Finn-Aage Esbensen, "Hispanic and Anglo Gang Membership in Two Southwestern Cities," *Social Science Journal* 38:105–118 (2001).

[87] Los Angeles County Sheriff's Department, *Street Gangs of Los Angeles County.*

[88] James Diego Vigil and Steve Chong Yun, "Vietnamese Youth Gangs in Southern California," in C. Ronald Huff, ed., *Gangs in America* (Newbury Park, CA: Sage Publications, 1990), pp. 146–163.

[89] Anthony Braga, Jack McDevitt, and Glenn Pierce, "Understanding and Preventing Gang Violence: Problem Analysis and Response Development in Lowell, Massachusetts," *Police Quarterly* 9:20–46 (2006).

[90] See Glazier, "Small Town Delinquent Gangs."

[91] For a review, see Lawrence Trostle, *The Stoners, Drugs, Demons and Delinquency* (New York: Garland, 1992).

[92] Esbensen, "Race and Gender Differences Between Gang and Nongang Youths."

[93] Darlene Wright and Kevin Fitzpatrick, "Violence and Minority Youth: The Effects of Risk and Asset Factors on Fighting Among African American Children and Adolescents," *Adolescence* 41:251–262 (2006); Terence Thornberry and James H. Burch, *Gang Members and Delinquent Behavior* (Washington, DC: Office of Juvenile Justice and Delinquency Prevention, 1997).

[94] G. David Curry, Scott Decker, and Arlen Egley Jr., "Gang Involvement and Delinquency in a Middle School Population," *Justice Quarterly* 19:275–292 (2002).

[95] Uberto Gatti, Richard Tremblay, Frank Vitaro, and Pierre McDuff, "Youth Gangs, Delinquency, and Drug Use: A Test of the Selection, Facilitation, and Enhancement Hypotheses," *Journal of Child Psychology & Psychiatry* 46:1178–1190 (2005).

[96] Malcolm Klein, Cheryl Maxson, and Lea Cunningham, "Crack, Street Gangs, and Violence," *Criminology* 4:623–650 (1991); Mel Wallace, "The Gang-Drug Debate Revisited." Paper presented at the annual meeting of the American Society of Criminology, New Orleans, November 1992.

[97] Kevin Thompson, David Brownfield, and Ann Marie Sorenson, "Specialization Patterns of Gang and Nongang Offending: A Latent Structure Analysis," *Journal of Gang Research* 3:25–35 (1996).

[98] Sara Battin, Karl Hill, Robert Abbott, Richard Catalano, and J. David Hawkins, "The Contribution of Gang Membership to Delinquency Beyond Delinquent Friends," *Criminology* 36:93–116 (1998).

[99] National Youth Gang Survey, 2001.

[100] Geoffrey Hunt, Karen Joe Laidler, and Kristy Evans, "The Meaning and Gendered Culture of Getting High: Gang Girls and Drug Use Issues," *Contemporary Drug Problems* 29:375 (2002).

[101] Terence P. Thornberry and James H. Burch, *Gang Members and Delinquent Behavior;* James C. Howell, "Youth Gang Drug Trafficking and Homicide: Policy and Program Implications," *Juvenile Justice Journal* 4:3–5 (1997).

[102] Terence Thornberry, Marvin Krohn, Alan Lizotte, Carolyn Smith, and Kimberly Tobin, *Gangs and Delinquency in Developmental Perspective* (New York: Cambridge University Press, 2003).

[103] Michael Vaughn, Matthew Howard, and Lisa Harper-Chang, "Do Prior Trauma and Victimization Predict Weapon Carrying Among Delinquent Youth?" *Youth Violence and Juvenile Justice* 4:314–327 (2006).

[104] Terence Thornberry, Marvin Krohn, Alan Lizotte, Carolyn Smith, and Kimberly Tobin, *Gangs and Delinquency in Developmental Perspective* (New York: Cambridge University Press, 2003).

[105] Howell, The Impact of Gangs on Communities, p. 3.

[106] Ibid.

[107] Ibid.

[108] James C. Howell, "Youth Gang Drug Trafficking and Homicide: Policy and Program Implications," *Juvenile Justice Journal* 4:3–5 (1997).

[109] Beth Bjerregaard and Alan Lizotte, "Gun Ownership and Gang Membership," *Journal of Criminal Law and Criminology* 86:37–53 (1995).

[110] Ibid.

[111] Pamela Lattimore, Richard Linster, and John MacDonald, "Risk of Death Among Serious Young Offenders," *Journal of Research in Crime and Delinquency* 34:187–209 (1997).

[112] Decker, "Collective and Normative Features of Gang Violence."

[113] Gini Sykes, *8 Ball Chicks: A Year in the Violent World of Girl Gangsters* (New York: Doubleday, 1998), pp. 2–11.

[114] H. Range Hutson, Deirdre Anglin, and Michael Pratts Jr., "Adolescents and Children Injured or Killed in Drive-By Shootings in Los Angeles," *New England Journal of Medicine* 330:324–327 (1994); Miller, *Violence by Youth Gangs*, pp. 2–26.

[115] Herbert Block and Arthur Niederhoffer, *The Gang: A Study in Adolescent Behavior* (New York: Philosophical Library, 1958).

[116] Ibid., p. 113.

[117] Knox et al., *Gang Prevention and Intervention*, p. 44.

[118] James Diego Vigil, "Group Processes and Street Identity: Adolescent Chicano Gang Members," *Ethos* 16:421–445 (1988).

[119] James Diego Vigil and John Long, "Emic and Etic Perspectives on Gang Culture: The Chicano Case," in C. Ronald Huff, ed., *Gangs in America* (Newbury Park, CA: Sage, 1990), p. 66.

[120] Albert Cohen, *Delinquent Boys* (New York: Free Press, 1955), pp. 1–19.

[121] Irving Spergel, *Racketville, Slumtown, and Haulburg: An Exploratory Study of Delinquent Subcultures* (Chicago: University of Chicago Press, 1964).

[122] Malcolm Klein, *Street Gangs and Street Workers* (Englewood Cliffs, NJ: Prentice-Hall, 1971), pp. 12–15.

[123] Vigil, *Barrio Gangs.*

[124] Vigil and Long, "Emic and Etic Perspectives on Gang Culture," p. 61.

[125] David Brownfield, Kevin Thompson, and Ann Marie Sorenson, "Correlates of Gang Membership: A Test of Strain, Social Learning, and Social Control," *Journal of Gang Research* 4:11–22 (1997).

[126] John Hagedorn, Jose Torres, and Greg Giglio, "Cocaine, Kicks, and Strain: Patterns of Substance Use in Milwaukee Gangs," *Contemporary Drug Problems* 25:113–145 (1998).

[127] Spergel, *The Youth Gang Problem*, pp. 4–5.

[128] Ibid.

[129] Jon Gunnar Bernburg, Marvin Krohn, and Craig Rivera, "Official Labeling, Criminal Embeddedness, and Subsequent Delinquency: A Longitudinal Test of Labeling Theory," *Journal of Research in Crime and Delinquency* 43:67–88 (2006).

[130] Yablonsky, *The Violent Gang*, p. 237.

[131] Ibid., pp. 239–241.

[132] Klein, *The American Street Gang.*

[133] Thornberry, Krohn, Lizotte, Smith, and Tobin, *Gangs and Delinquency in Developmental Perspective.*

[134] Mercer Sullivan, *Getting Paid: Youth Crime and Work in the Inner City* (Ithaca, NY: Cornell University Press, 1989), pp. 244–245.

[135] Finn-Aage Esbensen and David Huizinga, "Gangs, Drugs, and Delinquency in a Survey of Urban Youth," *Criminology* 31:565–587 (1993); G. David Curry and Irving Spergel, "Gang Involvement and Delinquency Among Hispanic and African-American Adolescent Males," *Journal of Research in Crime and Delinquency* 29:273–291 (1992).

[136] Padilla, *The Gang as an American Enterprise,* p. 103.

[137] Kathleen MacKenzie, Geoffrey Hunt, and Karen Joe-Laidler, "Youth Gangs and Drugs: The Case of Marijuana," *Journal of Ethnicity in Substance Abuse* 4:99–134 (2005).

[138] Terence Thornberry, Marvin Krohn, Alan Lizotte, and Deborah Chard-Wierschem, "The Role of Juvenile Gangs in Facilitating Delinquent Behavior," *Journal of Research in Crime and Delinquency* 30:55–87 (1993).

[139] Spergel, *The Youth Gang Problem*, pp. 93–94.

[140] Miller, *One of the Guys.*

[141] Ibid., p. 93.

[142] L. Thomas Winfree Jr., Teresa Vigil Backstrom, and G. Larry Mays, "Social Learning Theory, Self-Reported Delinquency, and Youth Gangs: A New Twist on a General Theory of Crime and Delinquency," *Youth and Society* 26:147–177 (1994).

[143] Karen Joe Laidler and Geoffrey Hunt, "Violence and Social Organization in Female Gangs," *Social Justice* 24:148–187 (1997).

[144] Chanequa Walker-Barnes and Craig A. Mason "Delinquency and Substance Use Among Gang-Involved Youth: The Moderating Role of Parenting Practices," *American Journal of Community Psychology* 34:235–250 (2004).

[145] Jerome Needle and W. Vaughan Stapleton, *Reports of the National Juvenile Justice Assessment Centers, Police Handling of Youth Gangs* (Washington, DC: Office of Juvenile Justice and Delinquency Prevention, 1983).

[146] National Youth Gang Center, *National Youth Gang Survey Analysis* (2006). Available at: www.iir.com/nygc/nygsa/ (accessed September 20, 2006).

[147] Scott Armstrong, "Los Angeles Seeks New Ways to Handle Gangs," *Christian Science Monitor*, 23 April 1988, p. 3.

[148] Barry Krisberg, "Preventing and Controlling Violent Youth Crime: The State of the Art," in Ira Schwartz, ed., *Violent Juvenile Crime* (Minneapolis: University of Minnesota, Hubert Humphrey Institute of Public Affairs, n.d.).

[149] For a revisionist view of gang delinquency, see Hedy Bookin-Weiner and Ruth Horowitz, "The End of the Youth Gang," *Criminology* 21: 585–602 (1983).

[150] Quint Thurman, Andrew Giacomazzi, Michael Reisig, and David Mueller, "Community-Based Gang Prevention and Intervention: An Evaluation of the Neutral Zone," *Crime and Delinquency* 42:279–296 (1996).

[151] Michael Agopian, "Evaluation of the Gang Alternative Prevention Program." Paper presented at the American Society of Criminology meeting, Boston, November 1995.

[152] Charles Katz and Vincent Webb, *Policing Gangs in America* (New York: Cambridge University Press, 2006).

[153] James Houston, "What Works: The Search for Excellence in Gang Intervention Programs." Paper presented at the American Society of Criminology meeting, Boston, November 1995.

[154] Curry and Spergel, "Gang Involvement and Delinquency Among Hispanic and African-American Adolescent Males."

[155] Hagedorn, "Gangs, Neighborhoods, and Public Policy."

Chapter 9. Schools and Delinquency

[1] Alexander Vazsonyi and Lloyd Pickering, "The Importance of Family and School Domains in Adolescent Deviance: African American and Caucasian Youth," *Journal of Youth and Adolescence* 32:115–129 (2003).

[2] See, generally, Richard Lawrence, *School Crime and Juveniles* (New York: Oxford University Press, 1998).

[3] U.S. Office of Education, *Digest of Educational Statistics* (Washington, DC: U.S. Government Printing Office, 1969), p. 25.

[4] Kenneth Polk and Walter E. Schafer, eds., *Schools and Delinquency* (Englewood Cliffs, NJ: Prentice-Hall, 1972), p. 13.

[5] Gary LaFree and Richard Arum, "The Impact of Racially Inclusive Schooling on Adult Incarceration Rates Among U.S. Cohorts of African Americans and Whites Since 1930," *Criminology* 44:73–103 (2006).

[6] Andrea Livingston, *The Condition of Education 2006 in Brief* (Washington, DC: National Center for Education Statistics, 2006).

[7] Lynn Karoly, M. Rebecca Kilburn, and Jill Cannon, *Early Childhood Interventions: Proven Results, Future Promise* (Santa Monica, California, Rand Corporation, 2005).

[8] Ibid.

[9] National Center For Education statistics, National Event Dropout Rates. Available at: http://nces.ed.gov/pubs2006/dropout/02.asp (accessed December 4, 2006).

[10] National Center for Education Statistics, *Averaged Freshman Graduation Rates (AFGR) for Public School Students*. Available at: http://nces.ed.gov/pubs2006/dropout/06.asp (accessed December 4, 2006).

[11] Jay Teachman, Kathleen Paasch, and Karen Carver, "Social Capital and the Generation of Human Capital," *Social Forces* 75:1343–1360 (1997).

[12] Spencer Rathus, *Voyages in Childhood* (Belmont, CA: Wadsworth, 2004).

[13] Sherman Dorn, *Creating the Dropout* (New York: Praeger, 1996).

[14] Karoly, Kilburn, and Cannon, *Early Childhood Interventions: Proven Results, Future Promise.*

[15] For reviews see Bruce Wolford and LaDonna Koebel, "Kentucky Model for Youths at Risk," *Criminal Justice* 9:5–55 (1995); J. David Hawkins, Richard Catalano, Diane Morrison, Julie O'Donnell, Robert Abbott, and L. Edward Day, "The Seattle Social Development Project," in Joan McCord and Richard Tremblay, eds., *The Prevention of Antisocial Behavior in Children* (New York: Guilford Press, 1992), pp. 139–160.

[16] Eugene Maguin and Rolf Loeber, "Academic Performance and Delinquency," in Michael Tonry, ed., *Crime and Justice: A Review of Research*, vol. 20 (Chicago: University of Chicago Press, 1995), pp. 145–264.

[17] Terence Thornberry, Alan Lizotte, Marvin Krohn, Margaret Farnworth, and Sung Joon Jang, "Testing Interactional Theory: An Examination of Reciprocal Causal Relationships Among Family, School, and Delinquency," *Journal of Criminal Law and Criminology* 82:3–35 (1991).

[18] Carolyn Smith, Alan Lizotte, Terence Thornberry, and Marvin Krohn, "Resilience to Delinquency," *Prevention Researcher* 4:4–7 (1997); Matthew Zingraff, Jeffrey Leiter, Matthew Johnsen, and Kristen Myers, "The Mediating Effect of Good School Performance on the Maltreatment-Delinquency Relationship," *Journal of Research in Crime and Delinquency* 31:62–91 (1994).

[19] Lyle Shannon, *Assessing the Relationship of Adult Criminal Careers to Juvenile Careers: A Summary* (Washington, DC: U.S. Government Printing Office, 1982).

[20] Marvin Wolfgang, Robert Figlio, and Thorsten Sellin, *Delinquency in a Birth Cohort* (Chicago: University of Chicago Press, 1972).

[21] Ibid., p. 94.

[22] Bureau of Justice Statistics, *Prisons and Prisoners* (Washington, DC: U.S. Government Printing Office, 1982), p. 2.

[23] Martin Gold, "School Experiences, Self-Esteem, and Delinquent Behavior: A Theory for Alternative Schools," *Crime and Delinquency* 24:294–295 (1978).

[24] Paul Bellair and Thomas McNulty, "Beyond the Bell Curve: Community Disadvantage and the Explanation of Black-White Differences in Adolescent Violence," *Criminology* 43:1135–1168 (2005).

[25] Michael Gottfredson and Travis Hirschi, *A General Theory of Crime* (Stanford, CA: Stanford University Press, 1990); J. D. McKinney, "Longitudinal Research on the Behavioral Characteristics of Children with Learning Disabilities," *Journal of Learning Disabilities* 22:141–150 (1990).

[26] Richard Felson and Jeremy Staff, "Explaining the Academic Performance-Delinquency Relationship," *Criminology* 44:299–320 (2006).

[27] Albert K. Cohen, *Delinquent Boys* (New York: Free Press, 1955); see also Kenneth Polk, Dean Frease, and F. Lynn Richmond, "Social Class, School Experience, and Delinquency," *Criminology* 12:84–95 (1974).

[28] Jackson Toby, "Orientation to Education as a Factor in the School Maladjustment of Lower-Class Children," *Social Forces* 35:259–266 (1957).

[29] John Paul Wright, Francis Cullen, and Nicolas Williams, "Working While in School and Delinquent Involvement: Implications for Social Policy," *Crime and Delinquency* 43:203–221 (1997).

[30] Polk, Frease, and Richmond, "Social Class, School Experience, and Delinquency," p. 92.

[31] Delos Kelly and Robert Balch, "Social Origins and School Failure," *Pacific Sociological Review* 14:413–430 (1971).

[32] Lance Hannon, "Poverty, Delinquency, and Educational Attainment: Cumulative Disadvantage or Disadvantage Saturation?" *Sociological Inquiry* 73:575–595 (2003).

[33] Jeannie Oakes, *Keeping Track: How Schools Structure Inequality* (New Haven, CT: Yale University Press, 1985), p. 48.

[34] Delos Kelly, *Creating School Failure, Youth Crime, and Deviance* (Los Angeles: Trident Shop, 1982), p. 11.

[35] Travis Hirschi, *Causes of Delinquency* (Berkeley: University of California Press, 1969), pp. 113–124, 132.

[36] *Learning into the 21st Century, Report of Forum 5* (Washington, DC: White House Conference on Children, 1970).

[37] Jane Sprott, Jennifer Jenkins, and Anthony Doob, "The Importance of School: Protecting At-Risk Youth From Early Offending," *Youth Violence and Juvenile Justice* 3:59–77 (2005); Patricia Jenkins, "School Delinquency and the School Social Bond," *Journal of Research in Crime and Delinquency* 34:337–367 (1997).

[38] Richard Lawrence, "Parents, Peers, School and Delinquency." Paper presented at the American Society of Criminology meeting, Boston, November 1995.

[39] Gary Gottfredson, Denise Gottfredson, Allison Payne, and Nisha Gottfredson, "School Climate Predictors of School Disorder: Results from a National Study of Delinquency Prevention in Schools," *Journal of Research in Crime & Delinquency* 42:412–444 (2005).

[40] National Institute of Education, U.S. Department of Health, Education and Welfare, *Violent Schools–Safe Schools: The Safe Schools Study Report to the Congress,* vol. 1 (Washington, DC: U.S. Government Printing Office, 1977).

[41] National Center for Education Statistics, Indicators of School Crime and Safety, 2006. Available at: http://nces.ed.gov/programs/crimeindicators/index.asp?ShowFileName=Exec_Summ.asp (accessed December 4, 2006).

[42] Ben Brown and William Reed Benedict, "Bullets, Blades, and Being Afraid in Hispanic High Schools: An Exploratory Study of the Presence of Weapons and Fear of Weapon-Associated Victimization Among High School Students in a Border Town," *Crime & Delinquency* 50:372–395 (2004).

[43] Christine Kerres Malecki and Michelle Kilpatrick Demaray, "Carrying a Weapon to School and Perceptions of Social Support in an Urban Middle School," *Journal of Emotional and Behavioral Disorders,* 11:169–178 (2003).

[44] Pamela Wilcox and Richard Clayton, "A Multilevel Analysis of School-Based Weapon Possession," *Justice Quarterly* 18:509–542 (2001).

[45] Mark Anderson, Joanne Kaufman, Thomas Simon, Lisa Barrios, Len Paulozzi, George Ryan, Rodney Hammond, William Modzeleski, Thomas Feucht, Lloyd Potter, and the School-Associated Violent Deaths Study Group, "School-Associated Violent Deaths in the United States, 1994–1999," *Journal of the American Medical Association* 286:2695–2702 (2001).

[46] Bryan Vossekuil, Marisa Reddy, Robert Fein, Randy Borum, and William Modzeleski, *Safe School Initiative: An Interim Report on the Prevention of Targeted Violence in Schools* (Washington, DC: United States Secret Service, 2000).

[47] Gary Gottfredson and Denise Gottfredson, *Victimization in Schools* (New York: Plenum Press, 1985), p. 18.

[48] Joan McDermott, "Crime in the School and in the Community: Offenders, Victims, and Fearful Youth," *Crime and Delinquency* 29:270–283 (1983).

[49] Ibid.

[50] Rami Benbenishty and Ron Avi Astor, *School Violence in Context: Culture, Neighborhood, Family, School and Gender* (New York: Oxford University Press, 2005).

[51] Lisa Hutchinson Wallace and David May, "The Impact of Parental Attachment and Feelings of Isolation on Adolescent Fear of Crime at School," *Adolescence* 40:457–474 (2005).

[52] Robert Brewer and Monica Swahn, "Binge Drinking and Violence," *JAMA: Journal of the American Medical Association* 294:16–20 (2005).

[53] Tomika Stevens, Kenneth Ruggiero, Dean Kilpatrick, Heidi Resnick, and Benjamin Saunders, "Variables Differentiating Singly and Multiply Victimized Youth: Results From the National Survey of Adolescents and Implications for Secondary Prevention," *Child Maltreatment* 10:211–223 (2005); James Collins and Pamela Messerschmidt, "Epidemiology of Alcohol-Related Violence," *Alcohol Health and Research World* 17:93–100 (1993).

[54] Nancy Weishew and Samuel Peng, "Variables Predicting Students' Problem Behaviors," *Journal of Educational Research* 87:5–17 (1993).

[55] Ibid.

[56] Daryl Hellman and Susan Beaton, "The Pattern of Violence in Urban Public Schools: The Influence of School and Community," *Journal of Research in Crime and Delinquency* 23:102–127 (1986).

[57] Peter Lindstrom, "Patterns of School Crime: A Replication and Empirical Extension," *British Journal of Criminology* 37:121–131 (1997).

[58] June L. Arnette and Marjorie C. Walsleben, *Combating Fear and Restoring Safety in Schools* (Washington, DC: Office of Juvenile Justice and Delinquency Prevention, 1998).

[59] Sheila Heaviside, Cassandra Rowand, Catrina Williams, Elizabeth Burns, Shelley Burns, and Edith McArthur, *Violence and Discipline Problems in U.S. Public Schools: 1996–97* (Washington, DC: United States Government Printing Office, 1998).

[60] Crystal A. Garcia, "School Safety Technology in America: Current Use and Perceived Effectiveness," *Criminal Justice Policy Review* 14:30–54 (2003).

[61] Mike Kennedy, "Fighting Crime by Design," *American School & University,* 73:46–47 (2001).

[62] National Center for Education Statistics, *Indicators of School Crime and Safety 2006,* Available at: http://nces.ed.gov/programs/crimeindicators/table_20_1.asp (accessed January 3, 2007).

[63] Bruce Jacobs, "Anticipatory Undercover Targeting in High Schools," *Journal of Criminal Justice* 22:445–357 (1994).

[64] Darcia Harris Bowman, "Curbing Crime," *Education Week,* 4/7/2004, Vol. 23, Issue 30.

[65] Stuart Tremlow, "Preventing Violence in Schools," *Psychiatric Times* 21:61–65 (2004).

[66] Allison Ann Payne, Denise Gottfredson, and Gary Gottfredson, "Schools as Communities: The Relationships Among Communal School Organization, Student Bonding, and School Disorder," *Criminology* 41:749–777 (2003).

[67] Glenn Cook, "Education Debates Return to the Headlines as Midterms Near," *American School Board Journal* 193:6–7 (2006).

[68] Stuart Yeh, "Reforming Federal Testing Policy to Support Teaching and Learning," *Educational Policy* 20:495–524 (2006).

[69] U.S. Senate Subcommittee on Delinquency, *Challenge for the Third Century,* p. 95.

[70] *New Jersey v. T.L.O.,* 469 U.S. 325, 105 S.Ct. 733 (1985).

[71] *People v. Overton,* 24 N.Y.2d 522, 301 N.Y.S.2d 479, 249 N.E.2d 366 (1969); Brenda Walts, "*New Jersey v. T.L.O.:* Questions the Court Did Not Answer About School Searches," *Law and Education Journal* 14:421 (1985).

[72] *Vernonia School District 47J v. Acton,* 115 S.Ct. 2394 (1995); Bernard James and Jonathan Pyatt, "Supreme Court Extends School's Authority to Search," *National School Safety Center News Journal* 26:29 (1995).

[73] Michael Medaris, *A Guide to the Family Educational Rights and Privacy Act* (Washington, DC: Office of Juvenile Justice and Delinquency Prevention, 1998).

[74] Ibid.

[75] 393 U.S. 503, 89 S.Ct. 733 (1969).

[76] Ibid.

[77] *Bethel School District No. 403 v. Fraser,* 478 U.S. 675, 106 S.Ct. 3159, 92 L.Ed.2d 549 (1986).

[78] *Hazelwood School District v. Kuhlmeier,* 484 U.S. 260, 108 S.Ct. 562, 98 L.Ed.2d 592 (1988).

[79] Terry McManus, "Home Web Sites Thrust Students into Censorship Disputes," *New York Times,* 13 August 1998, p. E9.

[80] *Santa Fe Independent School District, Petitioner v. Jane Doe,* individually and as next friend for her minor children, Jane and John Doe et al., No. 99-62 (June 19, 2000).

[81] *Good News Club et al. v. Milford Central School,* No. 99-2036 (2001).

[82] *Elk Grove Unified School District v. Newdow,* No. 02-1624 (2004).

[83] Ibid.

[84] *Ingraham v. Wright,* 430 U.S. 651, 97 S.Ct. 1401 (1977).

[85] *Goss v. Lopez,* 419 U.S. 565, 95 S.Ct. 729 (1976).

Chapter 10. Drug Use and Delinquency

[1] Lloyd D. Johnston, Patrick M. O'Malley, Jerald G. Bachman, and John E. Schulenberg, *Teen Drug Use Continues Down in 2006, Particularly Among Older Teens; But Use of Prescription-Type Drugs Remains High,* (Ann Arbor, MI: university of Michigan News and Information Services December 21, 2006) Table 1.

[2] Peter Greenwood, "Substance Abuse Problems Among High-Risk Youth and Potential Interventions," *Crime and Delinquency* 38:444–458 (1992).

[3] Office of Applied Studies, Substance Abuse and Mental Health Services Administration, "Youth Violence and Illicit Drug Use," *The NSDUH Report* 5 (Washington, DC: Author, 2006).

[4] Gary M. McClelland, Linda A. Teplin, and Karen M. Abram, *Detection and Prevalence of Substance Use Among Juvenile Detainees* (Washington, DC: Office of Juvenile Justice and Delinquency Prevention, 2004), pp. 4, 6.

[5] Jonathan G. Tubman, Andrés G. Gil, and Eric F. Wagner, "Co-Occurring Substance Use and Delinquent Behavior during Early Adolescence: Emerging Relations and Implications for Intervention Strategies," *Criminal Justice and Behavior* 31:463–488 (2004).

[6] Dennis Coon, *Introduction to Psychology* (St. Paul, MN: West, 1992), p. 178.

[7] Alan Neaigus, Aylin Atillasoy, Samuel Friedman, Xavier Andrade, Maureen Miller, Gilbert Ildefonso, and Don Des Jarlais, "Trends in the Noninjected Use of Heroin and Factors Associated with the Transition to Injecting," in James Inciardi and Lana Harrison, eds., *Heroin in the Age of Crack-Cocaine* (Thousand Oaks, CA: Sage, 1998), pp. 108–130.

[8] Johnston, O'Malley, Bachman, and Schulenberg, *Teen Drug Use Continues Down in 2006, Particularly Among Older Teens; But Use of Prescription-Type Drugs Remains High,* Tables 1, 2.

[9] "Drugs—The American Family in Crisis," *Juvenile and Family Court* 39:45–46 (Special issue, 1988).

[10] Federal Bureau of Investigation, *Crime in the United States, 2004* (Washington, DC: U.S. Government Printing Office, 2005), Tables 29, 38.

[11] Henrick J. Harwood, *Updating Estimates of the Economic Costs of Alcohol Abuse in the United States: Estimates, Update Methods, and Data.* Report prepared by the Lewin Group for the National Institute of Alcohol Abuse and Alcoholism (Rockville, MD: U.S. Department of Health and Human Services, 2000), Table 3.

[12] D. J. Rohsenow, "Drinking Habits and Expectancies About Alcohol's Effects for Self Versus Others," *Journal of Consulting and Clinical Psychology* 51:75–76 (1983).

[13] Spencer Rathus, *Psychology,* 4th ed. (New York: Holt, Rinehart & Winston, 1990), p. 161.

[14] National Drug Intelligence Center, *Methamphetamine Drug Threat Assessment* (Johnstown, PA: Author, 2005), p. 10.

[15] Mary Tabor, "'Ice' in an Island Paradise," *Boston Globe,* 8 December 1989, p. 3.

[16] Johnston, O'Malley, Bachman, and Schulenberg, *Monitoring the Future: National Results on Adolescent Drug Use: Overview of Key Findings, 2005,* Table 2.

[17] National Drug Intelligence Center, *Methamphetamine Drug Threat Assessment* (Johnstown, PA: Author, 2005), p. 8.

[18] Dana Hunt, Sarah Kuck, and Linda Truitt, *Methamphetamine Use: Lessons Learned* (Cambridge, MA: Abt Associates Inc., 2005), pp. iv, v.

[19] Fox Butterfield, "Fighting an Illegal Drug Through Its Legal Source," *New York Times,* 30 January 2005, p. A18; Kate Zernike, "Potent Mexican Meth Floods In as States Curb Domestic Variety," *New York Times,* 23 January 2006.

[20] Paul Goldstein, "Anabolic Steroids: An Ethnographic Approach." Unpublished paper (Narcotics and Drug Research, Inc., March 1989).

[21] Centers for Disease Control and Prevention, "Use of Cigarettes and Other Tobacco Products Among Students Aged 13–15 Years—Worldwide, 1999–2005," *Morbidity and Mortality Weekly Report* 55:553–556 (2006).

[22] Joe Nocera, "If It's Good for Philip Morris, Can It Also Be Good for Public Health?" *New York Times Magazine* (June 18):46–53, 70, 76–78 (2006).

[23] Clete Snell and Laura Bailey, "Operation Storefront: Observations of Tobacco Retailer Advertising Compliance with Tobacco Laws," *Youth Violence and Juvenile Justice* 3:78–90 (2005).

[24] Johnston, O'Malley, Bachman, and Schulenberg, *Teen Drug Use Continues Down in 2006, Particularly Among Older Teens; But Use of Prescription-Type Drugs Remains High,* Table 1.

[25] Ibid., Table 2.

[26] Ibid., p. 4.

[27] Steven P. Kurtz, James A. Inciardi, Hilary L. Surratt, and Linda Cottler, "Prescription Drug Abuse Among Ecstasy Users in Miami," *Journal of Addictive Diseases* 24:1–16 (2005); Ronnie Garrett, "Legal Highs: When the Drug Is Legal, What Can Law Enforcement Do?" *Law Enforcement Technology* 32:34–39, 42–44, 46.

[28] *PRIDE Questionnaire Report for Grades 6 Thru 12: 2004–05 National Summary* (Bowling Green, KY: PRIDE Surveys, August 17, 2006), Tables 2.9, 2.10.

[29] Department of Health and Human Services, *Results from the 2004 National Survey on Drug Use and Health: National Findings* (Rockville, MD: Department of Health and Human Services, Substance Abuse and Mental Health Services Administration, Office of Applied Studies, 2005).

[30] Ibid., p. 14.

[31] Ibid., pp. 23–24.

[32] Ibid., p. 17; Office of National Drug Control Policy, *Girls and Drugs: A New Analysis: Recent Trends, Risk Factors, and Consequences* (Washington, DC: Office of National Drug Control Policy, Executive Office of the President, 2006), Figure 3.

[33] Office of National Drug Control Policy, *Girls and Drugs: A New Analysis: Recent Trends, Risk Factors, and Consequences,* pp. 1–3.

[34] Diana C. Noone, "Drug Use Among Juvenile Detainees," in *Arrestee Drug Abuse Monitoring: 2000 Annual Report* (Washington, DC: National Institute of Justice, 2003), p. 135.

[35] McClelland, Teplin, and Abram, *Detection and Prevalence of Substance Use Among Juvenile Detainees.*

[36] Julia Yun Soo Kim, Michael Fendrich, and Joseph Wislar, "The Validity of Juvenile Arrestees' Drug Use Reporting: A Gender Comparison," *Journal of Research in Crime and Delinquency* 37:419–432 (2000).

[37] G. E. Vallant, "Parent-Child Disparity and Drug Addiction," *Journal of Nervous and Mental Disease* 142:534–539 (1966).

[38] Charles Winick, "Epidemiology of Narcotics Use," in D. Wilner and G. Kassenbaum, eds., *Narcotics* (New York: McGraw-Hill, 1965), pp. 3–18.

[39] Delbert Elliott, David Huizinga, and Scott Menard, *Multiple Problem Youth: Delinquency, Substance Abuse, and Mental Health Problems* (New York: Springer-Verlag, 1989).

[40] Peter Reuter, Robert MacCoun, and Patrick Murphy, *Money from Crime: A Study of the Economics of Drug Dealing in Washington, D.C.* (Santa Monica, CA: Rand, 1990).

[41] Thomas Dishion, Deborah Capaldi, Kathleen Spracklen, and Fuzhong Li, "Peer Ecology of Male Adolescent Drug Use," *Development and Psychopathology* 7:803–824 (1995).

[42] C. Bowden, "Determinants of Initial Use of Opioids," *Comprehensive Psychiatry* 12:136–140 (1971).

[43] Terence Thornberry and Marvin Krohn, "Peers, Drug Use, and Delinquency," in David Stoff, James Breiling, and Jack Maser, eds., *Handbook of Antisocial Behavior* (New York: Wiley, 1997), pp. 218–233.

[44] Richard Cloward and Lloyd Ohlin, *Delinquency and Opportunity: A Theory of Delinquent Gangs* (New York: Free Press, 1960).

[45] Denise Kandel and Mark Davies, "Friendship Networks, Intimacy, and Illicit Drug Use in Young Adulthood: A Comparison of Two Competing Theories," *Criminology* 29:441–471 (1991).

[46] James Inciardi, Ruth Horowitz, and Anne Pottieger, *Street Kids, Street Drugs, Street Crime: An Examination of Drug Use and Serious Delinquency in Miami* (Belmont, CA: Wadsworth, 1993), p. 43.

[47] D. Baer and J. Corrado, "Heroin Addict Relationships with Parents During Childhood and Early Adolescent Years," *Journal of Genetic Psychology* 124:99–103 (1974).

[48] Timothy Ireland and Cathy Spatz Widom, *Childhood Victimization and Risk for Alcohol and Drug Arrests* (Washington, DC: National Institute of Justice, 1995).

[49] See S. F. Bucky, "The Relationship Between Background and Extent of Heroin Use," *American Journal of Psychiatry* 130:709–710 (1973); I. Chien, D. L. Gerard, R. Lee, and E. Rosenfield, *The Road to H: Narcotics Delinquency and Social Policy* (New York: Basic Books, 1964).

[50] J. S. Mio, G. Nanjundappa, D. E. Verlur, and M. D. DeRios, "Drug Abuse and the Adolescent Sex Offender: A Preliminary Analysis," *Journal of Psychoactive Drugs* 18:65–72 (1986).

[51] G. T. Wilson, "Cognitive Studies in Alcoholism," *Journal of Consulting and Clinical Psychology* 55:325–331 (1987).

[52] John Hagedorn, Jose Torres, and Greg Giglio, "Cocaine, Kicks, and Strain: Patterns of Substance Use in Milwaukee Gangs," *Contemporary Drug Problems* 25:113–145 (1998).

[53] For a thorough review, see Karol Kumpfer, "Impact of Maternal Characteristics and Parenting Processes on Children of Drug Abusers." Paper presented at the American Society of Criminology meeting, Boston, November 1995.

[54] D.W. Goodwin, "Alcoholism and Genetics," *Archives of General Psychiatry* 42:171–174 (1985).

[55] Ibid.

[56] Patricia Dobkin, Richard Tremblay, Louise Masse, and Frank Vitaro, "Individual and Peer Characteristics in Predicting Boys' Early Onset of Substance Abuse: A Seven-Year Longitudinal Study," *Child Development* 66:1198–1214 (1995).

57 Ric Steele, Rex Forehand, Lisa Armistead, and Gene Brody, "Predicting Alcohol and Drug Use in Early Adulthood: The Role of Internalizing and Externalizing Behavior Problems in Early Adolescence," *American Journal of Orthopsychiatry* 65:380–387 (1995).

58 Ibid., pp. 380–381.

59 Jerome Platt and Christina Platt, *Heroin Addiction* (New York: Wiley, 1976), p. 127.

60 Rathus, *Psychology,* p. 158.

61 Eric Strain, "Antisocial Personality Disorder, Misbehavior, and Drug Abuse," *Journal of Nervous and Mental Disease* 163:162–165 (1995).

62 Dobkin, Tremblay, Masse, and Vitaro, "Individual and Peer Characteristics in Predicting Boys' Early Onset of Substance Abuse."

63 J. Shedler and J. Block, "Adolescent Drug Use and Psychological Health: A Longitudinal Inquiry," *American Psychologist* 45:612–630 (1990).

64 Greenwood, "Substance Abuse Problems Among High-Risk Youth and Potential Interventions," p. 448.

65 John Wallace and Jerald Bachman, "Explaining Racial/Ethnic Differences in Adolescent Drug Use: The Impact of Background and Lifestyle," *Social Problems* 38:333–357 (1991).

66 Marvin Krohn, Terence Thornberry, Lori Collins-Hall, and Alan Lizotte, "School Dropout, Delinquent Behavior, and Drug Use," in Howard Kaplan, ed., *Drugs, Crime, and Other Deviant Adaptations: Longitudinal Studies* (New York: Plenum Press, 1995), pp. 163–183.

67 B. A. Christiansen, G. T. Smith, P.V. Roehling, and M. S. Goldman, "Using Alcohol Expectancies to Predict Adolescent Drinking Behavior After One Year," *Journal of Counseling and Clinical Psychology* 57:93–99 (1989).

68 Inciardi, Horowitz, and Pottieger, *Street Kids, Street Drugs, Street Crime,* p. 135.

69 Ibid., p. 136.

70 Mary Ellen Mackesy-Amiti, Michael Fendrich, and Paul Goldstein, "Sequence of Drug Use Among Serious Drug Users: Typical vs. Atypical Progression," *Drug and Alcohol Dependence* 45:185–196 (1997).

71 The following sections lean heavily on Marcia Chaiken and Bruce Johnson, *Characteristics of Different Types of Drug-Involved Youth* (Washington, DC: National Institute of Justice, 1988).

72 Ibid., p. 100.

73 Inciardi, Horowitz, and Pottieger, *Street Kids, Street Drugs, Street Crime.*

74 Robert MacCoun and Peter Reuter, "Are the Wages of Sin $30 an Hour? Economic Aspects of Street-Level Drug Dealing," *Crime and Delinquency* 38:477–491 (1992).

75 Steven D. Levitt and Sudhir A. Venkatesh, "An Economic Analysis of a Drug-Selling Gang's Finances," *Quarterly Journal of Economics* 115:755–789 (2000), Table III.

76 Ibid., Table II.

77 Chaiken and Johnson, *Characteristics of Different Types of Drug-Involved Youth,* p. 12.

78 John Hagedorn, "Neighborhoods, Markets, and Gang Drug Organization," *Journal of Research in Crime and Delinquency* 31:264–294 (1994).

79 Chaiken and Johnson, *Characteristics of Different Types of Drug-Involved Youth,* p. 14.

80 Eric Baumer, Janet Lauritsen, Richard Rosenfeld, and Richard Wright, "The Influence of Crack Cocaine on Robbery, Burglary, and Homicide Rates: A Cross-City, Longitudinal Analysis," *Journal of Research in Crime and Delinquency* 35:316–340 (1998).

81 Ibid.

82 James Inciardi, "Heroin Use and Street Crime," *Crime and Delinquency* 25:335–346 (1979); idem, *The War on Drugs* (Palo Alto, CA: Mayfield, 1986); see also W. McGlothlin, M. Anglin, and B. Wilson, "Narcotic Addiction and Crime," *Criminology* 16:293–311 (1978); George Speckart and M. Douglas Anglin, "Narcotics Use and Crime: An Overview of Recent Research Advances," *Contemporary Drug Problems* 13:741–769 (1986); Charles Faupel and Carl Klockars, "Drugs-Crime Connections: Elaborations from the Life Histories of Hard-Core Heroin Addicts," *Social Problems* 34:54–68 (1987).

83 Eric Baumer, "Poverty, Crack, and Crime: A Cross-City Analysis," *Journal of Research in Crime and Delinquency* 31:311–327 (1994).

84 Marvin Dawkins, "Drug Use and Violent Crime Among Adolescents," *Adolescence* 32:395–406 (1997); Robert Peralta, "The Relationship Between Alcohol and Violence in an Adolescent Population: An Analysis

of the Monitoring the Future Survey." Paper presented at the American Society of Criminology meeting, San Diego, November 1997; Helene Raskin White and Stephen Hansell, "The Moderating Effects of Gender and Hostility on the Alcohol-Aggression Relationship," *Journal of Research in Crime and Delinquency* 33:450–470 (1996); D. Wayne Osgood, "Drugs, Alcohol, and Adolescent Violence." Paper presented at the annual meeting of the American Society of Criminology, Miami, 1994.

85 Fox Butterfield, "Justice Department Ends Testing of Criminals for Drug Use," *New York Times,* 28 January 2004.

86 *Preliminary Data on Drug Use and Related Matters Among Adult Arrestees and Juvenile Detainees, 2002* (Washington, DC: Arrestee Drug Abuse Monitoring Program, National Institute of Justice, 2003), Tables 2, 3.

87 McClelland, Teplin, and Abram, *Detection and Prevalence of Substance Use Among Juvenile Detainees,* Tables 2–4.

88 David Cantor, "Drug Involvement and Offending of Incarcerated Youth." Paper presented at the American Society of Criminology meeting, Boston, November 1995.

89 B. D. Johnson, E. Wish, J. Schmeidler, and D. Huizinga, "Concentration of Delinquent Offending: Serious Drug Involvement and High Delinquency Rates," *Journal of Drug Issues* 21:205–229 (1991); see also Jonathan G. Tubman, Andrés G. Gil, and Eric F. Wagner, "Co-Occurring Substance Use and Delinquent Behavior During Early Adolescence: Emerging Relations and Implications for Intervention Strategies," *Criminal Justice and Behavior* 31:463–488 (2004).

90 W. David Watts and Lloyd Wright, "The Relationship of Alcohol, Tobacco, Marijuana, and Other Illegal Drug Use to Delinquency Among Mexican-American, Black, and White Adolescent Males," *Adolescence* 25:38–54 (1990).

91 For a general review of this issue, see Helene Raskin White, "The Drug Use–Delinquency Connection in Adolescence," in Ralph Weisheit, ed., *Drugs, Crime and Criminal Justice* (Cincinnati: Anderson, 1990), pp. 215–256; Speckart and Anglin, "Narcotics Use and Crime"; Faupel and Klockars, "Drugs-Crime Connections."

92 Delbert Elliott, David Huizinga, and Susan Ageton, *Explaining Delinquency and Drug Abuse* (Beverly Hills, CA: Sage, 1985).

93 David Huizinga, Scott Menard, and Delbert Elliott, "Delinquency and Drug Use: Temporal and Developmental Patterns," *Justice Quarterly* 6:419–455 (1989).

94 See Evelyn H. Wei, Rolf Loeber, and Helene Raskin White, "Teasing Apart the Developmental Associations Between Alcohol and Marijuana Use and Violence," *Journal of Contemporary Criminal Justice* 20:116–183 (2004).

95 Jason A. Ford, "The Connection Between Heavy Drinking and Juvenile Delinquency During Adolescence," *Sociological Spectrum* 25:629–650 (2005).

96 Graham Farrell, "Drugs and Drug Control," in Graeme Newman, ed., *Global Report on Crime and Justice* (New York: Oxford University Press, 1999), p. 177.

97 *1998 International Narcotics Control Strategy Report* (Washington, DC: U.S. Department of State, February 1999).

98 Clifford Krauss, "Neighbors Worry About Colombian Aid," *New York Times,* 25 August 2000, pp. A3, A13.

99 Juan Forero with Tim Weiner, "Latin America Poppy Fields Undermine U.S. Drug Battle," *New York Times,* 8 August 2003, p. A1.

100 Carlotta Gall, "Another Year of Drug War, and the Poppy Crop Flourishes," *New York Times*, 17 February 2006; "Drugs and Security," *New York Times,* 4 December 2005, D14.

101 Gall, "Another Year of Drug War, and the Poppy Crop Flourishes."

102 *National Drug Threat Assessment 2003* (Washington, DC: National Drug Intelligence Center, U.S. Department of Justice, 2003).

103 Farrell, "Drugs and Drug Control," pp. 179–180.

104 "Operation Webslinger Targets Illegal Internet Trafficking of Date-Rape Drug," *U.S. Customs Today* 38 (2002).

105 Gardiner Harris, "Two Agencies to Fight Online Narcotics Sales," *New York Times,* 18 October 2003.

106 National Drug Intelligence Center, *Methamphetamine Drug Threat Assessment,* Figure 10.

107 Fox Butterfield, "Home Drug-Making Laboratories Expose Children to Toxic Fallout," *New York Times Magazine,* 23 February 2004.

108 Mark Moore, *Drug Trafficking* (Washington, DC: National Institute of Justice, 1988).

[109] Howard H. Snyder and Melissa Sickmund, *Juveniles Offenders and Victims: 2006 National Report* (Pittsburgh, PA: National Center for Juvenile Justice, 2006), pp. 168, 178–182.

[110] Christopher L. Ringwalt, Susan Ennett, Amy Vincus, Judy Thorne, Louise Ann Rohrbach, and Ashley Simons-Rudolph, "The Prevalence of Effective Substance Use Prevention in U.S. Middle Schools," *Prevention Science* 3:257–265 (2002).

[111] Denise C. Gottfredson, David B. Wilson, and Stacy S. Najaka, "School-Based Crime Prevention," in Lawrence W. Sherman, David P. Farrington, Brandon C. Welsh, and Doris Layton MacKenzie, eds., *Evidence-Based Crime Prevention* (New York: Routledge, 2006, rev. ed.), Table 4.9; see also Phyllis L. Ellickson, Daniel F. McCaffrey, Bonnie Ghosh-Dastidar, and Douglas L. Longshore, "New Inroads in Preventing Adolescent Drug Use: Results from a Large-Scale Trial of Project ALERT in Middle Schools," *American Journal of Public Health* 93:1830–1836 (2003).

[112] *Partnership Attitude Tracking Study: Teens, 2004* (Washington, DC: Office of National Drug Control Policy, 2005), pp. 12, 24.

[113] Department of Health and Human Services, *Results from the 2004 National Survey on Drug Use and Health: National Findings*, p. 65.

[114] Lori K. Holleran, Margaret A. Taylor-Seehafer, Elizabeth C. Pomeroy, and James Alan Neff, "Substance Abuse Prevention for High-Risk Youth: Exploring Culture and Alcohol and Drug Use," *Alcoholism Treatment Quarterly* 23:165–184 (2005).

[115] Brandon C. Welsh and Akemi Hoshi, "Communities and Crime Prevention," in Lawrence W. Sherman, David P. Farrington, Brandon C. Welsh, and Doris Layton MacKenzie, eds., *Evidence-Based Crime Prevention* (New York: Routledge, 2006, rev. ed.), pp. 184–186.

[116] Steven P. Schinke, Mario A. Orlandi, and Kristen C. Cole, "Boys and Girls Clubs in Public Housing Developments: Prevention Services for Youth at Risk," *Journal of Community Psychology, Office of Substance Abuse Prevention, Special Issue* (1992), p. 120.

[117] Ibid., pp. 125–127.

[118] Substance Abuse and Mental Health Services Administration, Office of Applied Studies, *Treatment Episode Data Sets (TEDS). Highlights—2004* (Rockville, MD: National Admissions to Substance Abuse Treatment Services, DASIS Series: S-31, DHHS Publication No. (SMA) 06-4140, 2006).

[119] Scott W. Henggeler, Sonja K. Schoenwald, Charles M. Borduin, Melisa D. Rowland, and Phillippe B. Cunningham, *Multisystemic Treatment of Antisocial Behavior in Children and Adolescents* (New York: Guilford Press, 1998).

[120] Scott W. Henggeler, W. Glenn Clingempeel, Michael J. Brondino, and Susan G. Pickrel, "Four-Year Follow-Up of Multisystemic Therapy with Substance-Abusing and Substance-Dependent Juvenile Offenders," *Journal of the American Academy of Child and Adolescent Psychiatry* 41:868–874 (2002).

[121] Eli Ginzberg, Howard Berliner, and Miriam Ostrow, *Young People at Risk: Is Prevention Possible?* (Boulder, CO: Westview Press, 1988), p. 99.

[122] James C. Howell, *Preventing and Reducing Juvenile Delinquency: A Comprehensive Framework* (Thousand Oaks, CA: Sage, 2003), p. 139.

[123] Ginzberg, Berliner, and Ostrow, *Young People at Risk: Is Prevention Possible?*

[124] Donnie W. Watson, Lorrie Bisesi, Susie Tanamly, and Noemi Mai, "Comprehensive Residential Education, Arts, and Substance Abuse Treatment (CREASAT): A Model Treatment Program for Juvenile Offenders," *Youth Violence and Juvenile Justice* 1:388–401 (2003).

[125] Steven R. Donziger, ed., *The Real War on Crime: The Report of the National Criminal Justice Commission* (New York: HarperPerennial, 1996), pp. 201, 202.

[126] Charlotte Allan and Nat Wright, "Harm Reduction: The Least Worst Treatment of All: Tackling Drug Addiction Has Few Easy Solutions," *Student British Medical Journal* 12:92–93 (2004), p. 92.

[127] Ibid., p. 92.

[128] Ibid., p. 92; see also Erik K. Laursen and Paul Brasler, "Is Harm Reduction a Viable Choice for Kids Enchanted with Drugs?" *Reclaiming Children and Youth* 11:181–183 (2002).

[129] Donziger, *The Real War on Crime*, p. 201.

[130] Snyder and Sickmund, *Juvenile Offenders and Victims: 2006 National Report*, pp. 163, 169.

[131] Eric L. Jensen, Jurg Gerber, and Clayton Mosher, "Social Consequences of the War on Drugs: The Legacy of Failed Policy," *Criminal Justice Policy Review* 15:100–121 (2004).

[132] Kathryn Ann Farr, "Revitalizing the Drug Decriminalization Debate," *Crime and Delinquency* 36:223–237 (1990).

[133] Reuter, MacCoun, and Murphy, *Money from Crime*, pp. 165–168.

New Directions in Preventing Delinquency: Secondary Prevention Efforts: Family and Community

[1] James C. Howell, ed., *Guide for Implementing the Comprehensive Strategy for Serious, Violent, and Chronic Juvenile Offenders* (Washington, DC: Office of Juvenile Justice and Delinquency Prevention, U.S. Department of Justice, 1995), p. 90.

[2] MENTOR United States, *Mentoring in America, 2005* (Alexandria, VA: Author, 2006); Joan McCord, Cathy Spatz-Widom, and Nancy A. Crowell, eds., *Juvenile Crime, Juvenile Justice* (Washington, DC: National Academy Press, Panel on Juvenile Crime: Prevention, Treatment, and Control, 2001), p. 147.

[3] Andrew Hahn, "Extending the Time of Learning," in Douglas J. Besharov, ed., *America's Disconnected Youth: Toward a Preventive Strategy* (Washington, DC: Child Welfare League of America Press, 1999).

[4] Andrew Hahn, *Evaluation of the Quantum Opportunities Program (QOP): Did the Program Work?* (Waltham, MA: Brandeis University, 1994).

[5] Jean Baldwin Grossman and Joseph P. Tierney, "Doest Mentoring Work? An Impact Study of the Big Brothers Big Sisters Program," *Evaluation Review* 22:403–426 (1998), p. 405.

[6] Ibid., p. 422.

[7] David L. DuBois, Bruce E. Holloway, Jeffrey C. Valentine, and Harris Cooper, "Effectiveness of Mentoring Programs for Youth: A Meta-Analytic Review," *American Journal of Community Psychology* 30:157–197 (2002); Brandon C. Welsh and Akemi Hoshi, "Communities and Crime Prevention," in Lawrence W. Sherman, David P. Farrington, Brandon C. Welsh, and Doris Layton MacKenzie, eds., *Evidence-Based Crime Prevention* (New York: Routledge, 2006, rev. ed.); McCord, Widom, and Crowell, *Juvenile Crime, Juvenile Justice.*

[8] Denise C. Gottfredson, Gary D. Gottfredson, and Stephanie A. Weisman, "The Timing of Delinquent Behavior and Its Implications for After-School Programs," *Criminology and Public Policy* 1:61–86 (2001), p. 61.

[9] Ibid., p. 63.

[10] Steven P. Schinke, Mario A. Orlandi, and Kristin C. Cole, "Boys and Girls Clubs in Public Housing Developments: Prevention Services for Youth at Risk," *Journal of Community Psychology* Special Issue:118–128 (1992), p. 120.

[11] Ibid., pp. 125–127.

[12] Denise C. Gottfredson, Stephanie A. Gerstenblith, David A. Soulé, Shannon C. Womer, and Shaoli Lu, "Do After School Programs Reduce Delinquency?" *Prevention Science* 5:253–266 (2004), pp. 263–264.

[13] Gottfredson, Gerstenblith, Soulé, Womer, and Shaoli, "Do After School Programs Reduce Delinquency?"; Welsh and Hoshi, "Communities and Crime Prevention"; David P. Farrington and Brandon C. Welsh, *Saving Children from a Life of Crime: Early Risk Factors and Effective Interventions* (New York: Oxford University Press, 2007).

[14] Denise C. Gottfredson and David A. Soulé, "The Timing of Property Crime, Violent Crime, and Substance Abuse Among Juveniles," *Journal of Research in Crime and Delinquency* 42:110–120 (2005).

[15] McCord, Widom, and Crowell, *Juvenile Crime, Juvenile Justice*, pp. 150–151.

[16] Peter Z. Schochet, John Burghardt, and Steven Glazerman, *National Job Corps Study: The Impacts of Job Corps on Participants' Employment and Related Outcomes* (Washington, DC: Employment and Training Administration, U.S. Department of Labor, 2001), p. xxv.

[17] Lynn A. Curtis, *The State of Families: Family, Employment, and Reconstruction: Policy Based on What Works* (Milwaukee, WI: Families International, 1995).

[18] Schochet, Burghardt, and Glazerman, *National Job Corps Study.*

[19] David A. Long, Charles D. Mallar, and Craig V. D. Thornton, "Evaluating the Benefits and Costs of the Job Corps," *Journal of Policy Analysis and Management* 1:55–76 (1981).

[20] Sheena McConnell and Steven Glazerman, *National Job Corps Study: The Benefits and Costs of the Job Corps* (Washington, DC: Employment and Training Administration, U.S. Department of Labor, 2001).

[21] Clifford R. Shaw and Henry D. McKay, *Juvenile Delinquency and Urban Areas: A Study of Rates of Delinquents in Relation to Differential Characteristics of Local Communities in American Cities* (Chicago: University of Chicago Press, 1942).

[22] Lawrence F. Murray and Steven Belenko, "CASASTART: A Community-Based, School-Centered Intervention for High-Risk Youth," *Substance Use and Misuse* 40:913–933 (2005).

[23] Adele V. Harrell, Shannon E. Cavanagh, and Sanjeev Sridharan, *Evaluation of the Children At Risk Program: Results 1 Year After the End of the Program* (Washington, DC: NIJ Research in Brief, 1999).

[24] Richard F. Catalano, Michael W. Arthur, J. David Hawkins, Lisa Berglund, and Jeffrey J. Olson, "Comprehensive Community- and School-Based Interventions to Prevent Antisocial Behavior," in Rolf Loeber and David P. Farrington, eds., *Serious and Violent Juvenile Offenders: Risk Factors and Successful Interventions* (Thousand Oaks, CA: Sage, 1998), p. 281.

[25] James C. Howell and J. David Hawkins, "Prevention of Youth Violence," in Michael Tonry and Mark H. Moore, eds., *Youth Violence: Crime and Justice: A Review of Research,* vol. 24 (Chicago: University of Chicago Press, 1998), pp. 303–304.

[26] Tracy W. Harachi, J. David Hawkins, Richard F. Catalano, Andrea M. Lafazia, Brian H. Smith, and Michael W. Arthur, "Evidence-Based Community Decision Making for Prevention: Two Case Studies of Communities That Care," *Japanese Journal of Sociological Criminology* 28:26–38 (2003).

[27] J. David Hawkins, Richard F. Catalano, and Associates, *Communities That Care: Action for Drug Abuse Prevention* (San Francisco: Jossey-Bass, 1992).

[28] Catalano, Arthur, Hawkins, Berglund, and Olson, "Comprehensive Community- and School-Based Interventions to Prevent Antisocial Behavior."

[29] Abraham Wandersman and Paul Florin, "Community Interventions and Effective Prevention," *American Psychologist* 58:441–448 (2003).

[30] Bryan J. Vila, "Human Nature and Crime Control: Improving the Feasibility of Nurturant Strategies," *Politics and the Life Sciences* 16:3–21 (1997).

[31] Richard A. Mendel, *Prevention or Pork? A Hard-Headed Look at Youth-Oriented Anti-Crime Programs* (Washington, DC: American Youth Policy Forum, 1995), p. 1.

[32] David R. Offord, Helena Chmura Kraemer, Alan E. Kazdin, Peter S. Jensen, and Richard Harrington, "Lowering the Burden of Suffering from Child Psychiatric Disorder: Trade-Offs Among Clinical, Targeted, and Universal Interventions," *Journal of the American Academy of Child and Adolescent Psychiatry* 37:686–694 (1998).

Chapter 11. The History and Development of Juvenile Justice

[1] Robert M. Mennel, "Origins of the Juvenile Court: Changing Perspectives on the Legal Rights of Juvenile Delinquents," *Crime and Delinquency* 18:68–78 (1972).

[2] Anthony Salerno, "The Child Saving Movement: Altruism or Conspiracy?" *Juvenile and Family Court Journal* 42:37 (1991).

[3] Frank J. Coppa and Philip C. Dolce, *Cities in Transition: From the Ancient World to Urban America* (Chicago: Nelson Hall, 1974), p. 220.

[4] Robert Mennel, "Attitudes and Policies Toward Juvenile Delinquency," in Michael Tonry and Norval Morris, eds., *Crime and Justice,* vol. 5 (Chicago: University of Chicago Press, 1983), p. 198.

[5] Anthony M. Platt, *The Child Savers: The Invention of Delinquency* (Chicago: University of Chicago Press, 1969).

[6] Ibid.

[7] Sanford J. Fox, "Juvenile Justice Reform: A Historical Perspective," *Stanford Law Review* 22:1187 (1970).

[8] Robert S. Pickett, *House of Refuge—Origins of Juvenile Reform in New York State, 1815–1857* (Syracuse, NY: Syracuse University Press, 1969).

[9] Mennel, "Origins of the Juvenile Court," pp. 69–70.

[10] Ibid., pp. 70–71.

[11] Salerno, "The Child Saving Movement," p. 37.

[12] Platt, *The Child Savers.*

[13] Randall Shelden and Lynn Osborne, " 'For Their Own Good': Class Interests and the Child Saving Movement in Memphis, Tennessee, 1900–1917," *Criminology* 27:747–767 (1989).

[14] U.S. Department of Justice, Juvenile Justice and Delinquency Prevention, *Two Hundred Years of American Criminal Justice: An LEAA Bicentennial Study* (Washington, DC: Law Enforcement Assistance Administration, 1976).

[15] Beverly Smith, "Female Admissions and Paroles of the Western House of Refuge in the 1880s: An Historical Example of Community Corrections," *Journal of Research in Crime and Delinquency* 26:36–66 (1989).

[16] Fox, "Juvenile Justice Reform," p. 1229.

[17] Elizabeth Pleck, "Criminal Approaches to Family Violence, 1640–1980," in Lloyd Ohlin and Michael Tonry, eds., *Family Violence* (Chicago: University of Chicago Press, 1989), pp. 19–58.

[18] Elizabeth Pleck, *Domestic Tyranny: The Making of Social Policy Against Family Violence from Colonial Times to the Present* (New York: Oxford University Press, 1987), pp. 28–30.

[19] Linda Gordon, *Family Violence and Social Control* (New York: Viking, 1988).

[20] Theodore Ferdinand, "Juvenile Delinquency or Juvenile Justice: Which Came First?" *Criminology* 27:79–106 (1989).

[21] *In re Gault,* 387 U.S. 1, 87 S.Ct. 1428, 18 L.Ed.2d 527 (1967).

[22] Mary Odem and Steven Schlossman, "Guardians of Virtue: The Juvenile Court and Female Delinquency in Early 20th-Century Los Angeles," *Crime and Delinquency* 37:186–203 (1991).

[23] John Sutton, "Bureaucrats and Entrepreneurs: Institutional Responses to Deviant Children in the United States, 1890–1920," *American Journal of Sociology* 95:1367–1400 (1990).

[24] Ibid., p. 1383.

[25] Margueritte Rosenthal, "Reforming the Juvenile Correctional Institution: Efforts of the U.S. Children's Bureau in the 1930s," *Journal of Sociology and Social Welfare* 14:47–74 (1987); see also David Steinhart, "Status Offenses" in *The Future of Children: The Juvenile Court* (Los Altos, CA: David and Lucile Packard Foundation, Center for the Future of Children, 1996).

[26] For an overview of these developments, see Theodore Ferdinand, "History Overtakes the Juvenile Justice System," *Crime and Delinquency* 37:204–224 (1991).

[27] N.Y. Fam. Ct. Act, Art. 7, Sec. 712 (Consol. 1962).

[28] *Kent v. United States,* 383 U.S. 541, 86 S.Ct. 1045, 16 L.Ed.2d 84 (1966); *in re Gault,* 387 U.S. 1, 87 S.Ct. 1428, 18 L.Ed.2d 527 (1967): Juveniles have the right to notice, counsel, confrontation, and cross-examination, and to the privileges against self-incrimination in juvenile court proceedings. *In re Winship,* 397 U.S. 358, 90 S.Ct. 1068, 25 L.Ed.2d 368 (1970): Proof beyond a reasonable doubt is necessary for conviction in juvenile proceedings. *Breed v. Jones,* 421 U.S. 519, 95 S.Ct. 1779, 44 L.Ed.2d 346 (1975): Jeopardy attaches in a juvenile court adjudicatory hearing, thus barring subsequent prosecution for the same offense as an adult.

[29] Public Law 90-351, Title I—Omnibus Safe Streets and Crime Control Act of 1968, 90th Congress, June 1968.

[30] National Advisory Commission on Criminal Justice Standards and Goals, *A National Strategy to Reduce Crime* (Washington, DC: U.S. Government Printing Office, 1973).

[31] Juvenile Justice and Delinquency Prevention Act of 1974, Public Law 93-415 (1974). For a critique of this legislation, see Ira Schwartz, *Justice for Juveniles—Rethinking the Best Interests of the Child* (Lexington, MA: D.C. Heath, 1989), p. 175.

[32] For an extensive summary of the Violent Crime Control and Law Enforcement Act of 1994, see *Criminal Law Reporter* 55:2305–2430 (1994).

[33] Shay Bilchik, "A Juvenile Justice System for the 21st Century," *Crime and Delinquency* 44:89 (1998).

[34] For a comprehensive view of juvenile law see, generally, Joseph J. Senna and Larry J. Siegel, *Juvenile Law: Cases and Comments,* 2nd ed. (St. Paul, MN: West, 1992).

[35] For an excellent review of the juvenile process, see Adrienne Volenik, *Checklists for Use in Juvenile Delinquency Proceedings* (Washington, DC: American Bar Association, 1985); see also Jeffrey Butts and Gregory Halemba, *Waiting for Justice—Moving Young Offenders Through the Juvenile Court Process* (Pittsburgh, PA: National Center for Juvenile Justice, 1996).

[36] Howard N. Snyder and Melissa Sickmund, *Juvenile Offenders and Victims: 2006 National Report* (Pittsburgh, PA: National Center for Juvenile Justice, 2006), p. 152.

[37] Fox Butterfield, "Justice Besieged," *New York Times,* 21 July 1997, p. A16.

38 National Conference on State Legislatures, *A Legislator's Guide to Comprehensive Juvenile Justice, Juvenile Detention, and Corrections* (Denver: National Conference on State Legislators, 1996).

39 James C. Howell, Marion R. Kelly, James Palmer, and Ronald L. Mangum, "Integrating Child Welfare, Juvenile Justice, and Other Agencies in a Continuum of Services," *Child Welfare* 83:143–156 (2004).

40 David P. Farrington and Brandon C. Welsh, *Saving Children from a Life of Crime: Early Risk Factors and Effective Interventions* (New York: Oxford University Press, 2007).

41 Ibid.

42 Ibid; see also Peter W. Greenwood, *Changing Lives: Delinquency Prevention as Crime-Control Policy* (Chicago: University of Chicago Press, 2006); Steve Aos, Roxanne Lieb, Jim Mayfield, Marna Miller, and Annie Pennucci, *Benefits and Costs of Prevention and Early Intervention Programs for Youth* (Olympia, WA: Washington State Institute for Public Policy, 2004).

43 Eliana Garces, Duncan Thomas, and Janet Currie, "Longer-Term Effects of Head Start," *American Economic Review* 92:999–1012 (2002).

44 Anne K. Duggan, Amy Windham, Elizabeth McFarlane, Loretta Fuddy, Charles Rohde, Sharon Buchbinder, and Calvin Sia, "Hawaii's Health Start Program of Home Visitation for At-Risk Families: Evaluation of Family Identification, Family Engagement, and Service Delivery," *Pediatrics* 105:250–259 (2000); Ned Calonge, "Community Interventions to Prevent Violence: Translation into Public Health Practice," *American Journal of Preventive Medicine* 28:4–5 (2005).

45 *Youth Violence: A Report of the Surgeon General* (Rockville, MD: U.S. Department of Health and Human Services, 2001).

46 Michael Garringer, with Mark Fulop and Vikki Rennick, *Foundations of Successful Youth Mentoring: A Guidebook for Program Development* (Washington, DC: Office of Juvenile Justice and Delinquency Prevention, 2003).

47 James C. Howell, *Preventing and Reducing Juvenile Delinquency: A Comprehensive Framework* (Thousand Oaks, CA: Sage, 2003), p. 248; see also Shelley Zavlek, *Planning Community-Based Facilities for Violent Juvenile Offenders as Part of a System of Graduated Sanctions* (Washington, DC: OJJDP Juvenile Justice Bulletin, 2005).

48 Peter W. Greenwood, "Juvenile Crime and Juvenile Justice," in James Q. Wilson and Joan Petersilia, eds., *Crime: Public Policies for Crime Control* (Oakland, CA: Institute for Contemporary Studies Press, 2002), pp. 90–91.

49 "Drug Court Activity Update: Composite Summary Information" (Washington, DC: Bureau of Justice Assistance Drug Court Clearinghouse at American University, June 15, 2006); "Summary of Juvenile/Family Drug Court Activity by State and County" (Washington, DC: Bureau of Justice Assistance Drug Court Clearinghouse at American University, July 10, 2006).

50 *Juvenile Drug Courts: Strategies in Practice* (Washington, DC: Bureau of Justice Assistance, 2003).

51 David B. Wilson, Ojmarrh Mitchell, and Doris Layton MacKenzie, "A Systematic Review of Drug Court Effects on Recidivism" (Alexandria, VA: Administration of Justice, George Mason University, 2006).

52 Nancy Rodriguez and Vincent J. Webb, "Multiple Measures of Juvenile Drug Court Effectiveness: Results of a Quasi-Experimental Design," *Crime and Delinquency* 50:292–314 (2004).

53 Barry C. Feld, "Criminology and the Juvenile Court: A Research Agenda for the 1990s," in Ira M. Schwartz, ed., *Juvenile Justice and Public Policy—Toward a National Agenda* (New York: Lexington Books, 1992), p. 59.

54 Barry C. Feld, "Juvenile and Criminal Justice Systems' Responses to Youth Violence," in Michael Tonry and Mark H. Moore, eds., *Youth Violence: Crime and Justice: A Review of Research,* vol. 24 (Chicago: University of Chicago Press, 1998), p. 222.

55 Robert O. Dawson, "The Future of Juvenile Justice: Is It Time to Abolish the System?" *Journal of Criminal Law and Criminology* 81:136–155 (1990); see also Leonard P. Edwards, "The Future of the Juvenile Court: Promising New Directions in the Center for the Future of Children," in *The Future of Children: The Juvenile Court* (Los Altos, CA: David and Lucile Packard Foundation, Center for the Future of Children, 1996).

56 Peter W. Greenwood, *Changing Lives*, p. 183.

57 Ibid., pp. 193–194.

58 Hunter Hurst, "Juvenile Court: As We Enter the Millennium," *Juvenile and Family Court Journal* 50:21–27 (1999).

59 Snyder and Sickmund, *Juvenile Offenders and Victims: 2006 National Report*, p. 113.

60 Franklin E. Zimring, *American Youth Violence* (New York: Oxford University Press, 1998); Franklin E. Zimring, *American Juvenile Justice* (New York: Oxford University Press, 2005).

61 Shay Bilchik, "A Juvenile Justice System for the 21st Century," *Crime and Delinquency* 44:89 (1998).

62 Patricia Torbet and Linda Szymanski, *State Legislative Responses to Violent Crime: 1996–97 Update* (Washington, DC: Office of Juvenile Justice and Delinquency Prevention, 1998).

63 Snyder and Sickmund, *Juvenile Offenders and Victims: 2006 National Report*, p. 111.

64 Stacy C. Moak and Lisa Hutchinson Wallace, "Legal Changes in Juvenile Justice: Then and Now," *Youth Violence and Juvenile Justice* 1:289–299 (2003), p. 292.

65 Hurst, "Juvenile Court: As We Enter the Millennium," p. 25.

66 Joan McCord, Cathy Spatz Widom, and Nancy A. Crowell, eds., *Juvenile Crime, Juvenile Justice* (Washington, DC: National Academy Press, Panel on Juvenile Crime: Prevention, Treatment, and Control, 2001), p. 224.

67 Melissa M. Moon, Francis T. Cullen, and John Paul Wright, "It Takes a Village: Public Willingness to Help Wayward Youths," *Youth Violence and Juvenile Justice* 1:32–45 (2003).

68 McCord, Spatz Widom, and Crowell, *Juvenile Crime, Juvenile Justice*, p. 152.

69 Greenwood, *Changing Lives*.

70 Snyder and Sickmund, *Juvenile Offenders and Victims: 2006 National Report*, p. 113.

71 Alida Merlo, Peter Benekos, and William Cook, "The Juvenile Court at 100 Years: Celebration or Wake?" *Juvenile and Family Court Journal* 50:7 (1999).

72 Simon M. Fass and Chung-Ron Pi, "Getting Tough on Juvenile Crime: An Analysis of Costs and Benefits," *Journal of Research in Crime and Delinquency* 39:363–399 (2002).

Chapter 12. Police Work with Juveniles

1 This section relies on sources including Malcolm Sparrow, Mark Moore, and David Kennedy, *Beyond 911: A New Era for Policing* (New York: Basic Books, 1990); Daniel Devlin, *Police Procedure, Administration, and Organization* (London: Butterworth, 1966); Robert Fogelson, *Big City Police* (Cambridge, MA: Harvard University Press, 1977); Roger Lane, *Policing the City, Boston 1822–1885* (Cambridge, MA: Harvard University Press, 1967); Roger Lane, "Urban Police and Crime in Nineteenth-Century America," in Norval Morris and Michael Tonry, eds., *Crime and Justice,* vol. 2 (Chicago: University of Chicago Press, 1980), pp. 1–45; J. J. Tobias, *Crime and Industrial Society in the Nineteenth Century* (New York: Schocken Books, 1967); Samuel Walker, *A Critical History of Police Reform: The Emergence of Professionalism* (Lexington, MA: Lexington Books, 1977); idem, *Popular Justice* (New York: Oxford University Press, 1980); President's Commission on Law Enforcement and the Administration of Justice, *Task Force Report: The Police* (Washington, DC: U.S. Government Printing Office, 1967), pp. 1–9.

2 See, generally, Walker, *Popular Justice*, p. 61.

3 Law Enforcement Assistance Administration, *Two Hundred Years of American Criminal Justice* (Washington, DC: U.S. Government Printing Office, 1976).

4 August Vollmer, *The Police and Modern Society* (Berkeley: University of California Press, 1936).

5 O. W. Wilson, *Police Administration,* 2nd ed. (New York: McGraw-Hill, 1963).

6 Wesley G. Skogan, ed., *Community Policing: Can It Work?* (Belmont, CA: Wadsworth, 2004).

7 See Wesley G. Skogan and Kathleen Frydl, eds., *Fairness and Effectiveness in Policing: The Evidence* (Washington, DC: The National Academies Press, 2004); David Weisburd and Anthony A. Braga, eds., *Police Innovation: Contrasting Perspectives* (New York: Cambridge University Press, 2006).

8 Skogan and Frydl, *Fairness and Effectiveness in Policing*; Joel Wallman and Alfred Blumstein, "After the Crime Drop," in Alfred Blumstein and Joel Wallman, eds., *The Crime Drop in America*, 2nd ed. (New York: Cambridge University Press, 2006, rev. ed.); Lawrence W. Sherman, "Fair and Effective Policing," in James Q. Wilson and Joan Petersilia, eds., *Crime: Public Policies for Crime Control* (Oakland, CA: Institute for Contemporary Studies, 2002); Steven D. Levitt, "Understanding Why Crime Fell in the 1990s: Four Factors That Explain the Decline and Six That Do Not," *Journal of Economic Perspectives* 18:163–190 (2004).

9 Yolander Hurst, James Frank, and Sandra Lee Browning, "The Attitudes of Juveniles Toward the Police: A Comparison of Black and White Youth," *Policing* 23:37–53 (2000).

10 Terrance J. Taylor, K. B. Turner, Finn-Aage Esbensen, and L. Thomas Winfree, Jr., "'Coppin' an Attitude: Attitudinal Differences Among Juveniles Toward Police," *Journal of Criminal Justice* 29:295–305 (2001).

11 Yolander G. Hurst, M. Joan McDermott, and Deborah L. Thomas, "The Attitudes of Girls Toward the Police: Differences by Race," *Policing* 28:578–593 (2005), pp. 585–586.

12 Adam M. Watkins, "Examining the Disparity Between Juvenile and Adult Victims in Notifying the Police: A Study of Mediating Variables," *Journal of Research in Crime and Delinquency* 42:333–353 (2005).

13 Denise C. Herz, "Improving Police Encounters with Juveniles: Does Training Make a Difference?" *Justice Research and Policy* 3:57–77 (2001).

14 Donald Black and Albert J. Reiss, Jr., "Police Control of Juveniles," *American Sociological Review* 35:63 (1970); Richard Lundman, Richard Sykes, and John Clark, "Police Control of Juveniles: A Replication," *Journal of Research on Crime and Delinquency* 15:74 (1978).

15 American Bar Association, *Standards Relating to Police Handling of Juvenile Problems* (Cambridge, MA: Ballinger, 1977), p. 1.

16 Samuel Walker, *The Police of America* (New York: McGraw-Hill, 1983), p. 133.

17 Karen A. Joe, "The Dynamics of Running Away: Deinstitutionalization Policies and the Police," *Juvenile Family Court Journal* 46:43–45 (1995).

18 Mary Dodge, "Juvenile Police Informants: Friendship, Persuasion, and Pretense," *Youth Violence and Juvenile Justice* 4:234–246 (2006), p. 234.

19 Ibid., p. 244.

20 Richard J. Lundman, *Prevention and Control of Juvenile Delinquency*, 3rd ed. (New York: Oxford University Press, 2001), p. 23.

21 FBI, *Crime in the United States, 2004* (Washington, DC: U.S. Government Printing Office, 2005), p. 290.

22 See Franklin E. Zimring, *American Juvenile Justice* (New York: Oxford University Press, 2005), chapter 8.

23 Lawrence W. Sherman and John E. Eck, "Policing for Crime Prevention," in Lawrence W. Sherman, David P. Farrington, Brandon C. Welsh, and Doris Layton MacKenzie, eds., *Evidence-Based Crime Prevention* (New York: Routledge, 2006, rev. ed.), p. 321; for "hot spots" policing, see also Skogan and Frydl, *Fairness and Effectiveness in Policing*; Anthony A. Braga, "The Effects of Hot Spots Policing on Crime," *Annals of the American Academy of Political and Social Science* 578:104–125 (2001).

24 Christopher S. Koper and Evan Mayo-Wilson, "Police Crackdowns on Illegal Gun Carrying: A Systematic Review of Their Impact on Gun Crime," *Journal of Experimental Criminology* 2:227–261 (2006).

25 Linda Szymanski, *Summary of Juvenile Code Purpose Clauses* (Pittsburgh: National Center for Juvenile Justice, 1988); see also, for example, GA Code Ann. 15; Iowa Code Ann. 232.2; Mass. Gen. Laws, ch. 119, 56.

26 Samuel M. Davis, *Rights of Juveniles—The Juvenile Justice System*, rev. (New York: Clark-Boardmen, June 1989), Sec. 3.3.

27 National Council of Juvenile and Family Court Judges, *Juvenile and Family Law Digest* 29:1–2 (1997).

28 See Fourth Amendment, U.S. Constitution.

29 *Chimel v. Cal.*, 395 U.S. 752, 89 S.Ct. 2034 (1969).

30 *United States v. Ross*, 456 U.S. 798, 102 S.Ct. 2157 (1982).

31 *Terry v. Ohio*, 392 U.S.1, 88 S.Ct. 1868 (1968).

32 *Bumper v. North Carolina*, 391 U.S. 543, 88 S.Ct. 1788 (1968).

33 *Miranda v. Arizona*, 384 U.S. 436, 86 S.Ct. 1602 (1966).

34 *Commonwealth v. Gaskins*, 471 Pa. 238, 369 A.2d 1285 (1977); *In re E.T.C.*, 141 Vt. 375, 449 A.2d 937 (1982).

35 *People v. Lara*, 67 Cal.2d 365, 62 Cal.Rptr. 586, 432 P.2d 202 (1967).

36 *West v. United States*, 399 F.2d 467 (5th Cir. 1968).

37 *Fare v. Michael C.*, 442 U.S. 707, 99 S.Ct. 2560 (1979).

38 *California v. Prysock*, 453 U.S. 355, 101 S.Ct. 2806 (1981).

39 See, for example, Larry Holtz, "*Miranda* in a Juvenile Setting—A Child's Right to Silence," *Journal of Criminal Law and Criminology* 79:534–556 (1987).

40 Kenneth C. Davis, *Discretionary Justice: A Preliminary Inquiry* (Baton Rouge: Louisiana State University Press, 1969); H. Ted Rubin, *Juvenile Justice: Police, Practice, and Law* (Santa Monica, CA: Goodyear, 1979).

41 Joseph Goldstein, "Police Discretion Not to Invoke the Criminal Process: Low-Visibility Decisions in the Administration of Justice," *Yale Law Journal* 69:544 (1960).

42 Victor Streib, *Juvenile Justice in America* (Port Washington, NY: Kennikat, 1978).

43 Herbert Packer, *The Limits of the Criminal Sanction* (Palo Alto, CA: Stanford University Press, 1968).

44 Black and Reiss, "Police Control of Juveniles"; Richard J. Lundman, "Routine Police Arrest Practices," *Social Problems* 22:127–141 (1974); Robert E. Worden and Stephanie M. Myers, *Police Encounters with Juvenile Suspects* (Albany: Hindelang Criminal Justice Research Center and School of Criminal Justice, State University of New York, 2001).

45 Nathan Goldman, *The Differential Selection of Juvenile Offenders for Court Appearance* (Washington, DC: National Council on Crime and Delinquency, 1963).

46 Irving Piliavin and Scott Briar, "Police Encounters with Juveniles," *American Journal of Sociology* 70:206–214 (1964); Theodore Ferdinand and Elmer Luchterhand, "Inner-City Youth, the Police, Juvenile Court, and Justice," *Social Problems* 8:510–526 (1970).

47 Paul Strasburg, *Violent Delinquents: Report to Ford Foundation from Vera Institute of Justice* (New York: Monarch, 1978), p. 11; Robert Terry, "The Screening of Juvenile Offenders," *Journal of Criminal Law, Criminology, and Police Science* 58:173–181 (1967).

48 Joan McCord, Cathy Spatz Widom, and Nancy A. Crowell, eds., *Juvenile Crime, Juvenile Justice* (Washington, DC: National Academy Press, Panel on Juvenile Crime: Prevention, Treatment, and Control, 2001), p. 163.

49 Worden and Myers, *Police Encounters with Juvenile Suspects*.

50 FBI, *Crime in the United States, 2004*, Table 68.

51 Douglas Smith and Christy Visher, "Street-Level Justice: Situational Determinants of Police Arrest Decisions," *Social Problems* 29:167–178 (1981).

52 Douglas Smith and Jody Klein, "Police Control of Interpersonal Disputes," *Social Problems* 31:468–481 (1984).

53 Goldman, *The Differential Selection of Juvenile Offenders for Court Appearance*, p. 25; Norman Werner and Charles Willie, "Decisions of Juvenile Officers," *American Journal of Sociology* 77:199–214 (1971).

54 Skogan and Frydl, *Fairness and Effectiveness in Policing*, pp. 301–303; Sherman, "Fair and Effective Policing," pp. 404–405.

55 Raymond Paternoster, Ronet Bachman, Robert Brame, and Lawrence W. Sherman, "Do Fair Procedures Matter? The Effect of Procedural Justice on Spouse Assault," *Law and Society Review* 31:163–204 (1997).

56 Skogan and Frydl, *Fairness and Effectiveness in Policing*, p. 7.

57 Aaron Cicourel, *The Social Organization of Juvenile Justice* (New York: Wiley, 1968).

58 Piliavin and Briar, "Police Encounters with Juveniles," p. 214.

59 David Klinger, "Demeanor or Crime? Why 'Hostile' Citizens Are More Likely to Be Arrested," *Criminology* 32:475–493 (1994).

60 Richard Lundman, "Demeanor or Crime? The Midwest City Police–Citizen Encounters Study," *Criminology* 32:631–653 (1994); Robert Worden and Robin Shepard, "On the Meaning, Measurement, and Estimated Effects of Suspects' Demeanor Toward the Police." Paper presented at the American Society of Criminology meeting, Miami, November 1994.

61 James Fyfe, David Klinger, and Jeanne Flaving, "Differential Police Treatment of Male-on-Female Spousal Violence," *Criminology* 35:455–473 (1997).

62 Dale Dannefer and Russel Schutt, "Race and Juvenile Justice Processing in Police and Court Agencies," *American Journal of Sociology* 87:1113–1132 (1982); Smith and Visher, "Street-Level Justice: Situational Determinants of Police Arrest Decisions"; see also, Ronald Weitzer, "Racial Discrimination in the Criminal Justice System: Findings and Problems in the Literature," *Journal of Criminal Justice* 24:309–322 (1996); Ronald Weitzer and Steven A. Tuch, "Perceptions of Racial Profiling: Race, Class, and Personal Experience," *Criminology* 40:435–456 (2002).

63 Richard J. Lundman and Robert L. Kaufman, "Driving While Black: Effects of Race, Ethnicity, and Gender on Citizen Self-Reports of Traffic Stops and Police Actions," *Criminology* 41:195–220 (2003).

64 Dan M. Kahan and Tracey L. Meares, "The Coming Crisis of Criminal Procedure," *Georgetown Law Journal* 86:1153–1184 (2000).

65 Randall Kennedy, *Race, Crime and the Law* (New York: Vintage, 1998).

66 Terence Thornberry, "Race, Socioeconomic Status, and Sentencing in the Juvenile Justice System," *Journal of Criminal Law and Criminology* 70:164–171 (1979); Dannefer and Schutt, "Race and Juvenile Justice Processing in Police and Court Agencies"; Jeffrey Fagan, Ellen Slaughter, and Eliot Hartstone, "Blind Justice? The Impact of Race on the Juvenile Justice Process," *Crime and Delinquency* 33:224–258 (1987).

67 Donna M. Bishop and Charles E. Frazier, "The Influence of Race in Juvenile Justice Processing," *Journal of Research in Crime and Delinquency* 25:242–261 (1988).

68 Ibid., p. 258; see also Howard N. Snyder and Melissa Sickmund, *Juvenile Offenders and Victims: 2006 National Report* (Pittsburgh, PA: National Center for Juvenile Justice, 2006), p. 163.

69 Merry Morash, "Establishment of a Juvenile Record: The Influence of Individual and Peer Group Characteristics," *Criminology* 22:97–112 (1984).

70 Meda Chesney-Lind, "Judicial Enforcement of the Female Sex Role: The Family Court and Female Delinquency Issues," *Criminology* 8:51–71 (1973); idem, "Young Women in the Arms of Law," in L. Bowker, ed., *Women, Crime, and the Criminal Justice System*, 2nd ed. (Lexington, MA: Lexington Books, 1978).

71 Donna Bishop and Charles Frazier, "Gender Bias in Juvenile Justice Processing: Implications of the JJDP Act," *Journal of Criminal Law and Criminology* 82:1162–1186 (1992).

72 Meda Chesney-Lind and Randall G. Shelden, *Girls, Delinquency, and Juvenile Justice*, 3rd ed. (Belmont, CA: Wadsworth, 2004), p. 35.

73 Douglas Smith, "The Organizational Context of Legal Control," *Criminology* 22:19–138 (1984); see also Stephen Mastrofski and Richard Ritti, "Police Training and the Effects of Organization on Drunk Driving Enforcement," *Justice Quarterly* 13:291–320 (1996).

74 John Irwin, *The Jail: Managing the Underclass in American Society* (Berkeley: University of California Press, 1985).

75 Darlene Conley, "Adding Color to a Black and White Picture: Using Qualitative Data to Explain Racial Disproportionality in the Juvenile Justice System," *Journal of Research in Crime and Delinquency* 31:135–148 (1994).

76 Robert Sampson, "Effects of Socioeconomic Context of Official Reaction to Juvenile Delinquency," *American Sociological Review* 51:876–885 (1986).

77 Eric Fritsch, Tory Caeti, and Robert Taylor, "Gang Suppression Through Saturation Patrol, Aggressive Curfew, and Truancy Enforcement: A Quasi-Experimental Test of the Dallas Anti-Gang Initiative," *Crime and Delinquency* 45:122–139 (1999).

78 Matthew J. Hickman and Brian A. Reaves, *Local Police Departments, 2003* (Washington, DC: Bureau of Justice Statistics, 2006), p. 20.

79 Finn-Aage Esbensen, D. Wayne Osgood, Terrance J. Taylor, Dana Peterson, and Adrienne Freng, "How Great Is G.R.E.A.T.? Results from a Longitudinal Quasi-Experimental Design," *Criminology and Public Policy* 1:87–118 (2001).

80 Finn-Aage Esbensen and D. Wayne Osgood, "Gang Resistance Education and Training (G.R.E.A.T.): Results from the National Evaluation," *Journal of Research in Crime and Delinquency* 36:194–225 (1999).

81 Esbensen, Osgood, Taylor, Peterson, and Freng, "How Great Is G.R.E.A.T.?"

82 Yale University Child Study Center, *Community Outreach Through Police in Schools* (Washington, DC: Office for Victims of Crime Bulletin, 2003), p. 2.

83 Ibid., p. 3.

84 For an analysis of this position, see George Kelling and James Q. Wilson, "Broken Windows: The Police and Neighborhood Safety," *Atlantic Monthly* 249:29–38 (1982).

85 Robert Trojanowicz and Hazel Harden, *The Status of Contemporary Community Policing Programs* (East Lansing: Michigan State University Neighborhood Foot Patrol Center, 1985).

86 Hickman and Reaves, *Local Police Departments, 2003*, p. 20.

87 Ibid., p. 20.

88 Terence Dunworth, *National Evaluation of the Youth Firearms Violence Initiative* (Washington, DC: NIJ Research in Brief, 2000), pp. 1, 4.

89 Ibid., p. 8.

90 See Anthony A. Braga, *Gun Violence Among Serious Young Offenders* (Washington, DC: Office of Community Oriented Policing Services, U.S. Department of Justice, 2004).

91 *Project Safe Neighborhoods: America's Network Against Gun Violence* (Washington, DC: Bureau of Justice Assistance Program Brief, 2004).

92 Susan Guarino-Ghezzi, "Reintegrative Police Surveillance of Juvenile Offenders: Forging an Urban Model," *Crime and Delinquency* 40:131–153 (1994).

93 See David Weisburd and John E. Eck, "What Can Police Do to Reduce Crime, Disorder, and Fear?" *Annals of the American Academy of Political and Social Science* 593:42–65 (2004), p. 57, Table 1.

94 Michael D. Reisig and Roger B. Parks, "Community Policing and Quality of Life," in Wesley G. Skogan, ed., *Community Policing: Can It Work?* (Belmont, CA: Wadsworth, 2004).

95 The President's Crime Prevention Council, *Preventing Crime and Promoting Responsibility: 50 Programs that Help Communities Help Their Youth* (Washington, DC: U.S. Government Printing Office, 1995).

96 Mark H. Moore, "Problem-Solving and Community Policing," in Michael Tonry and Norval Morris, eds., *Modern Policing. Crime and Justice: A Review of Research*, vol. 15 (Chicago: University of Chicago Press, 1992), p. 99.

97 Anthony A. Braga, *Problem-Oriented Policing and Crime Prevention* (Monsey, NY: Criminal Justice Press, 2002), p. 10.

98 Moore, "Problem-Solving and Community Policing," p. 120.

99 Debra Cohen, *Problem-Solving Partnerships: Including the Community for a Change* (Washington, DC: Office of Community Oriented Policing Services, 2001), p. 2.

100 David Sheppard, Heath Grant, Wendy Rowe, and Nancy Jacobs, *Fighting Juvenile Gun Violence* (Washington, DC: OJJDP Juvenile Justice Bulletin, 2000), p. 2.

101 Ibid., p. 10.

102 Cohen, *Problem-Solving Partnerships*, p. 2.

103 Ibid., pp. 5–7.

104 Kelly Dedel Johnson, *Underage Drinking. Problem-Specific Guides Series*, No. 27 (Washington, DC: Office of Community Oriented Policing Services, 2004).

Chapter 13. Juvenile Court Process: Pretrial, Trial, and Sentencing

1 Kelly Dedel, "National Profile of the Organization of State Juvenile Corrections Systems," *Crime and Delinquency* 44:507–525 (1998). Herein cited as National Profile.

2 Howard N. Snyder and Melissa Sickmund, *Juvenile Offenders and Victims: 2006 National Report* (Pittsburgh, PA: National Center for Juvenile Justice, 2006), p. 157.

3 Ibid., pp. 161, 163.

4 *Powell v. Alabama* 287 U.S. 45, 53 S.Ct. 55, 77, L.Ed.2d 158 (1932); *Gideon v. Wainwright* 372 U.S. 335, 83 S.Ct. 792, 9 L.Ed.2d 799 (1963); *Argersinger v. Hamlin* 407 U.S. 25, 92 S.Ct. 2006, 32 L.Ed.2d 530 (1972).

5 See Judith B. Jones, *Access to Counsel* (Washington, DC: Office of Juvenile Justice and Delinquency Prevention, 2004).

6 For a review of these studies, see T. Grisso, "The Competence of Adolescents as Trial Defendants," *Psychology, Public Policy, and Law* 3:3–32 (1997).

7 Christine Schnyder Pierce and Stanley L. Brodsky, "Trust and Understanding in the Attorney–Juvenile Relationship," *Behavioral Sciences and the Law* 20:89–107 (2002).

8 Ibid., p. 102.

9 Melinda G. Schmidt, N. Dickon Reppucci, and Jennifer L. Woolard, "Effectiveness of Participation as a Defendant: The Attorney–Juvenile Client Relationship," *Behavioral Sciences and the Law* 21:175–198 (2003).

10 Ibid., p. 193.

11 George W. Burruss, Jr. and Kimberly Kempf-Leonard, "The Questionable Advantage of Defense Counsel in Juvenile Court," *Justice Quarterly* 19:37–67 (2002).

12 Lori Guevara, Cassia Spohn, and Denise Herz, "Race, Legal Representation, and Juvenile Justice: Issues and Concerns," *Crime and Delinquency* 50:344–371 (2004), pp. 362–364.

13 Howard Davidson, "The Guardian *ad litem*: An Important Approach to the Protection of Children," *Children Today* 10:23 (1981); Daniel Golden, "Who Guards the Children?" *Boston Globe Magazine*, 27 December 1992, p. 12.

14 Chester Harhut, "An Expanded Role for the Guardian *ad litem*," *Juvenile and Family Court Journal* 51:31–35 (2000).

15 Steve Riddell, "CASA: Child's Voice in Court," *Juvenile and Family Justice Today* 7:13–14 (1998).

16 American Bar Association, *A Call for Justice: An Assessment of Access to Counsel and Quality of Representation in Delinquency Proceedings* (Washington, DC: ABA Juvenile Justice Center, 1995).

17 Douglas C. Dodge, *Due Process Advocacy* (Washington, DC: Office of Juvenile Justice and Delinquency Prevention, 1997); see also Jones, *Access to Counsel*.

18 "ABA President Says New Report Shows 'Conveyor Belt Justice' Hurting Children and Undermining Public Safety." News release (Washington, DC: American Bar Association, October 21, 2003).

19 James Shine and Dwight Price, "Prosecutor and Juvenile Justice: New Roles and Perspectives," in Ira Schwartz, ed., *Juvenile Justice and Public Policy* (New York: Lexington Books, 1992), pp. 101–133.

20 James Backstrom and Gary Walker, "A Balanced Approach to Juvenile Justice: The Work of the Juvenile Justice Advisory Committee," *The Prosecutor* 32:37–39 (1988); see also *Prosecutors' Policy Recommendations on Serious, Violent, and Habitual Youthful Offenders* (Alexandria, VA: American Prosecutors' Institute, 1997).

21 Leonard P. Edwards, "The Juvenile Court and the Role of the Juvenile Court Judge," *Juvenile and Family Court Journal* 43:3–45 (1992); Lois Haight, "Why I Choose to Be a Juvenile Court Judge," *Juvenile and Family Justice Today* 7:7 (1998).

22 National Council of Juvenile and Family Court Judges, *Juvenile Delinquency Guidelines: Improving Court Practice in Juvenile Delinquency Cases* (Reno, NV: Author, 2005), p. 24.

23 *Standards for Juvenile Detention Facilities* (Laurel, MD: American Correctional Association, 1991).

24 National Profile, p. 514.

25 Madeline Wordes and Sharon Jones, "Trends in Juvenile Detention and Steps Toward Reform," *Crime and Delinquency* 44:544–560 (1998).

26 Robert Shepard, *Juvenile Justice Standards Annotated: A Balanced Approach* (Chicago: American Bar Association, 1997).

27 Leslie Kaufman, "Child Detention Centers Criticized in New Jersey," *New York Times*, 23 November 2004.

28 Dylan Conger and Timothy Ross, "Project Confirm: An Outcome Evaluation of a Program for Children in the Child Welfare and Juvenile Justice Systems," *Youth Violence and Juvenile Justice* 4:97–115 (2006).

29 Snyder and Sickmund, *Juvenile Offenders and Victims*, p. 168.

30 Ibid., pp. 169–170, 191.

31 Bohsiu Wu and Angel Ilarraza Fuentes, "The Entangled Effects of Race and Urban Poverty," *Juvenile and Family Court Journal* 49:41–51 (1998).

32 Katherine E. Brown and Leanne Fiftal Alarid, "Examining Racial Disparity of Male Property Offenders in the Missouri Juvenile Justice System," *Youth Violence and Juvenile Justice* 2:107–128 (2004), p. 116.

33 Ibid., p. 119.

34 James Maupin and Lis Bond-Maupin, "Detention Decision Making in a Predominantly Hispanic Region: Rural and Non-Rural Differences," *Juvenile and Family Court Journal* 50:11–21 (1999).

35 Earl Dunlap and David Roush, "Juvenile Detention as Process and Place," *Juvenile and Family Court Journal* 46:1–16 (1995).

36 "OJJDP Helps States Remove Juveniles from Jails," *Juvenile Justice Bulletin* (Washington, DC: U.S. Department of Justice, 1990).

37 *The Jail Removal Initiative: A Summary Report* (Champaign, IL: Community Research Associates, 1987).

38 Mark Soler, James Bell, Elizabeth Jameson, Carole Shauffer, Alice Shotton, and Loren Warboys, *Representing the Child Client* (New York: Matthew Bender, 1989), sec. 5.03b.

39 *Schall v. Martin*, 467 U.S. 253 (1984).

40 Jeffrey Fagan and Martin Guggenheim, "Preventive Detention for Juveniles: A Natural Experiment," *Journal of Criminal Law and Criminology,* 86:415–428 (1996).

41 Snyder and Sickmund, *Juvenile Offenders and Victims*, p. 177.

42 Leona Lee, "Factors Influencing Intake Disposition in a Juvenile Court," *Juvenile and Family Court Journal* 46:43–62 (1995).

43 Deborah A. Chapin and Patricia A. Griffin, "Juvenile Diversion," in Kirk Heilbrun, Naomi E. Sevin Goldstein, and Richard E. Redding, eds., *Juvenile Delinquency: Prevention, Assessment, and Intervention* (New York: Oxford University Press, 2005); see also Edwin E. Lemert, "Diversion in Juvenile Justice: What Hath Been Wrought?" *Journal of Research in Crime and Delinquency* 18:34–46 (1981).

44 Don C. Gibbons and Gerald F. Blake, "Evaluating the Impact of Juvenile Diversion Programs," *Crime and Delinquency Journal* 22:411–419 (1976); Richard J. Lundman, "Will Diversion Reduce Recidivism?" *Crime and Delinquency Journal* 22:428–437 (1976); B. Bullington, J. Sprowls, D. Katkin, and M. Phillips, "A Critique of Diversionary Juvenile Justice," *Crime and Delinquency* 24:59–71 (1978); Thomas Blomberg, "Diversion and Accelerated Social Control," *Journal of Criminal Law and Criminology* 68:274–282 (1977); Sharla Rausch and Charles Logan, "Diversion from Juvenile Court: Panacea or Pandora's Box?" in J. Klugel, ed., *Evaluating Juvenile Justice* (Beverly Hills, CA: Sage, 1983), pp. 19–30.

45 Arnold Binder and Gilbert Geis, "Ad Populum Argumentation in Criminology: Juvenile Diversion as Rhetoric," *Criminology* 30:309–333 (1984).

46 Mark Ezell, "Juvenile Diversion: The Ongoing Search for Alternatives," in Ira M. Schwartz, ed., *Juvenile Justice and Public Policy* (New York: Lexington Books, 1992), pp. 45–59.

47 Alison Evans Cuellar, Larkin S. McReynolds, and Gail A. Wasserman, "A Cure for Crime: Can Mental Health Treatment Diversion Reduce Crime Among Youth?" *Journal of Policy Analysis and Management* 25:197–214 (2006).

48 Peter W. Greenwood, *Changing Lives: Delinquency Prevention as Crime-Control Policy* (Chicago: University of Chicago Press, 2006), chapter 8; Franklin E. Zimring, *American Juvenile Justice* (New York: Oxford University Press, chapter 4).

49 Zimring, *American Juvenile Justice*, p. 47.

50 Albert W. Alschuler, "The Prosecutor's Role in Plea Bargaining," *University of Chicago Law Review* 36:50–112 (1968); Joyce Dougherty, "A Comparison of Adult Plea Bargaining and Juvenile Intake," *Federal Probation*, June 1988, pp. 72–79.

51 Sanford Fox, *Juvenile Courts in a Nutshell* (St. Paul, MN: West, 1985), pp. 154–156.

52 See Darlene Ewing, "Juvenile Plea Bargaining: A Case Study," *American Journal of Criminal Law* 6:167 (1978); Adrienne Volenik, *Checklists for Use in Juvenile Delinquency Proceedings* (Chicago: American Bar Association, 1985); Bruce Green, "Package Plea Bargaining and the Prosecutor's Duty of Good Faith," *Criminal Law Bulletin* 25:507–550 (1989).

53 Joseph Sanborn, *Plea Negotiations in Juvenile Court.* Ph.D. thesis (Albany: State University of New York, 1984); Joseph Sanborn, "Philosophical, Legal, and Systematic Aspects of Juvenile Court Plea Bargaining," *Crime and Delinquency* 39:509–527 (1993).

54 Snyder and Sickmund, *Juvenile Offenders and Victims*, p. 186.

55 Patrick Griffin, *Trying and Sentencing Juveniles as Adults: An Analysis of State Transfer and Blended Sentencing Laws* (Pittsburgh, PA: National Center for Juvenile Justice, 2003), pp. 2–3, Table 1.

56 Ibid., p. 8, Table 5.

57 Ibid., p. 10, Table 6.

58 *Kent v. United States,* 383 U.S. 541, 86 S.Ct. 1045, 16 L.Ed.2d 84 (1966); *Breed v. Jones,* 421 U.S. 519, 95 S.Ct. 1179, 44 L.Ed.2d 346 (1975).

59 Barry Feld, "The Juvenile Court Meets the Principle of the Offense: Legislative Changes in Juvenile Waiver Statutes," *Journal of Criminal Law and Criminology* 78:471–534 (1987); Paul Marcotte, "Criminal Kids," *American Bar Association Journal* 76:60–66 (1990); Dale Parent et al., *Transferring Serious Juvenile Offenders to Adult Courts* (Washington DC: U.S. Department of Justice, National Institute of Justice, 1997).

60 Richard Redding, "Juvenile Offenders in Criminal Court and Adult Prison: Legal, Psychological, and Behavioral Outcomes," *Juvenile and Family Court Journal* 50:1–15 (1999); Craig A. Mason, Derek A. Chapman, Chang Shau, and Julie Simons, "Impacting Re-Arrest Rates Among Youth Sentenced in Adult Court: An Epidemiology Examination of the Juvenile Sentencing Advocacy Project," *Journal of Clinical Child and Adolescent Psychology* 32:205–214 (2003); David L. Myers, "The Recidivism of Violent Youths in Juvenile and Adult Court: A Consideration of Selection Bias," *Youth Violence and Juvenile Justice* 1:79–101 (2003).

61 Benjamin Steiner, Craig Hemmens, and Valerie Bell, "Legislative Waiver Reconsidered: General Deterrent Effects of Statutory Exclusion Laws Enacted Post-1979," *Justice Quarterly* 23:34–59 (2006).

62 Griffin, *Trying and Sentencing Juveniles as Adults*, p. 9.

63 Thomas Grisso, Laurence Steinberg, Jennifer Woolard, Elizabeth Cauffman, Elizabeth Scott, Sandra Graham, Fran Lexcon, N. Dickon Repucci, and Robert Schwartz, "Juveniles' Competence to Stand Trial: A Comparison of Adolescents' and Adults' Capacities as Trial Defendants," *Law and Human Behavior* 27:333–363 (2003); Darla M. Burnett, Charles D. Noblin, and Vicki Prosser, "Adjudicative Competency in a Juvenile Population," *Criminal Justice and Behavior* 31:438–462 (2004).

64 Megan C. Kurlycheck and Brian D. Johnson, "The Juvenile Penalty: A Comparison of Juvenile and Young Adult Sentencing Outcomes in Criminal Court," *Criminology* 42:485–517 (2004), p. 498.

65 Redding, "Juvenile Offenders in Criminal Court and Adult Prison," p. 11; see also Richard E. Redding, "The Effects of Adjudicating and Sentencing Juveniles as Adults: Research and Policy Implications," *Youth Violence and Juvenile Justice* 1:128–155 (2003).

66 Emily Gaarder and Joanne Belknap, "Tenuous Borders: Girls Transferred to Adult Court," *Criminology* 40:481–517 (2002).

67 Redding, "Juvenile Offenders in Criminal Court and Adult Prison."

68 Howard N. Snyder and Melissa Sickmund, *Juvenile Offenders and Victims: 1999 National Report* (Washington, DC: U.S. Department of Justice, Office of Juvenile Justice and Delinquency Prevention, 1999), p. 177.

69 See Mason, Chapman, Shau, and Simons, "Impacting Re-Arrest Rates Among Youth Sentenced in Adult Court"; Myers, "The Recidivism of Violent Youths in Juvenile and Adult Court."

70 James Howell, "Juvenile Transfers to the Criminal Justice System: State of the Art," *Law and Policy* 18:17–60 (1996).

71 Snyder and Sickmund, *Juvenile Offenders and Victims*, pp. 186–187; Jeffrey Fagan, Martin Forst, and T. Scott Vivona, "Racial Determinants of the Judicial Transfer Decision: Prosecuting Violent Youth in Criminal Court," *Crime and Delinquency* 33:359–386 (1987); J. Fagan, E. Slaughter, and E. Hartstone, "Blind Justice: The Impact of Race on the Juvenile Justice Process," *Crime and Delinquency* 53:224–258 (1987); J. Fagan and E. P. Deschenes, "Determinants of Judicial Waiver Decisions for Violent Juvenile Offenders," *Journal of Criminal Law and Criminology* 81:314–347 (1990); see also James Howell, "Juvenile Transfers to Criminal Court," *Juvenile and Family Justice Journal* 6:12–14 (1997).

72 Snyder and Sickmund, *Juvenile Offenders and Victims*, pp. 176, 186.

73 Gerard Rainville and Steven K. Smith, *Juvenile Felony Defendants in Criminal Courts: Survey of 40 Counties, 1998* (Washington, DC: U.S. Department of Justice, Office of Juvenile Justice and Delinquency Prevention).

74 Snyder and Sickmund, *Juvenile Offenders and Victims*, p. 187. Available at: http://ojjdp.ncjrs.gov/ojstatbb/nr2006/downloads/chapter6.pdf (accessed December 5, 2006).

75 Barry Feld, "Delinquent Careers and Criminal Policy," *Criminology* 21:195–212 (1983).

76 Howard N. Snyder, Melissa Sickmund, and Eileen Poe-Yamagata, *Juvenile Transfers to Criminal Court in the 1990s: Lessons Learned from Four Studies* (Washington, DC: U.S. Department of Justice, Office of Juvenile Justice and Delinquency Prevention, 2000).

77 Rainville and Smith, *Juvenile Felony Defendants in Criminal Courts.*

78 Sanjeev Sridharan, Lynette Greenfield, and Baron Blakley, "A Study of Prosecutorial Certification Practice in Virginia," *Criminology and Public Policy* 3:605–632 (2004).

79 Franklin E. Zimring, "Treatment of Hard Cases in American Juvenile Justice: In Defense of the Discretionary Waiver," *Notre Dame Journal of Law, Ethics, and Policy* 5:267–280 (1991); Lawrence Winner, Lonn Kaduce, Donna Bishop, and Charles Frazier, "The Transfer of Juveniles to Criminal Courts: Reexamining Recidivism Over the Long Term," *Crime and Delinquency* 43:548–564 (1997).

80 Rainville and Smith, *Juvenile Felony Defendants in Criminal Courts.*

81 Institute of Judicial Administration, American Bar Association Joint Commission on Juvenile Justice Standards, *Standards Relating to Adjudication* (Cambridge, MA: Ballinger, 1980).

82 Joseph B. Sanborn Jr., "The Right to a Public Jury Trial—A Need for Today's Juvenile Court," *Judicature* 76:230–238 (1993). In the context of delinquency convictions to enhance criminal sentences, see Barry C. Feld, "The Constitutional Tension Between *Apprendi* and *McKeiver*: Sentence Enhancement Based on Delinquency Convictions and the Quality of Justice in Juvenile Courts," *Wake Forest Law Review* 38:1111–1224 (2003).

83 Linda Szymanski, *Juvenile Delinquents' Right to Counsel* (Pittsburgh, PA: National Center for Juvenile Justice, 1988).

84 *In re Winship*, 397 U.S. 358, 90 S.Ct. 1068 (1970).

85 *McKeiver v. Pennsylvania*, 403 U.S. 528, 91 S.Ct. 1976 (1971).

86 See, generally, R. T. Powell, "Disposition Concepts," *Juvenile and Family Court Journal* 34:7–18 (1983).

87 Fox, *Juvenile Courts in a Nutshell*, p. 221.

88 This section is adapted from Jack Haynes and Eugene Moore, "Particular Dispositions," *Juvenile and Family Court Journal* 34:41–48 (1983); see also Grant Grissom, "Dispositional Authority and the Future of the Juvenile Justice System," *Juvenile and Family Court Journal* 42:25–34 (1991).

89 Barry Krisberg, Elliot Currie, and David Onek, "What Works with Juvenile Offenders," *American Bar Association Journal on Criminal Justice* 10:20–24 (1995).

90 Snyder and Sickmund, *Juvenile Offenders and Victims*, p. 177.

91 Ibid., p. 174.

92 Ibid., p. 174.

93 Anthony Platt, *The Child Savers: The Invention of Delinquency* (Chicago: University of Chicago Press, 1969); David Rothman, *Conscience and Convenience: The Asylum and the Alternative in Progressive America* (Boston: Little, Brown, 1980).

94 Joseph Goldstein, Anna Freud, and Albert Solnit, *Beyond the Best Interests of the Child* (New York: Free Press, 1973).

95 See, for example, *in Interest on M.P.* 697 N.E. 2d 1153 (Il. App. 1998); *Matter of Welfare of CAW* 579 N.W. 2d 494 (MN. App. 1998).

96 See, for example, *Matter of Willis Alvin M.* 479 S.E. 2d. 871 (WV 1996).

97 Simon Singer and David McDowall, "Criminalizing Delinquency: The Deterrent Effects of NYJO Law," *Law and Society Review* 22: Sections 21–37 (1988).

98 Washington Juvenile Justice Reform Act of 1977, ch. 291;Wash. Rev. Code Ann. Title 9A, Sec. 1–91 (1977).

99 Griffin, *Trying and Sentencing Juveniles as Adults*, p. 3, Table 1.

100 *Roper v. Simmons*, 125 S.Ct. 1183 (2005).

101 Erica Goode, "Young Killer: Bad Seed or Work in Progress?" *New York Times*, 25 November 2003.

102 Adam Liptak, "Court Takes Another Step in Reshaping Capital Punishment," *New York Times*, 2 March 2005.

103 *Roper v. Simmons*, 125 S.Ct. 1183 (2005).

104 Victor L. Streib, *The Juvenile Death Penalty Today: Death Sentences and Executions for Juvenile Crimes, January 1, 1973–September 30, 2003* (Ada, OH: Claude W. Pettit College of Law, Ohio Northern University, October 6, 2003), p. 3; see also Stuart Banner, "When Killing a Juvenile Was Routine," *New York Times*, 6 March 2005, part 4, p. 4.

105 Victor L. Streib, *The Juvenile Death Penalty Today: Death Sentences and Executions for Juvenile Crimes, January 1, 1973–September 30, 2003*; see also Snyder and Sickmund, *Juvenile Offenders and Victims*, p. 239.

106 Steven Gerstein, "The Constitutionality of Executing Juvenile Offenders, *Thompson v. Oklahoma*," *Criminal Law Bulletin* 24:91–98 (1988); *Thompson v. Oklahoma*, 108 S.Ct. 2687 (1988).

107 109 S.Ct. 2969 (1989); for a recent analysis of the *Wilkins* and *Stanford* cases, see the note in "*Stanford v. Kentucky* and *Wilkins v. Missouri*: Juveniles, Capital Crime, and Death Penalty," *Criminal Justice Journal* 11:240–266 (1989).

108 Victor Streib, "Excluding Juveniles from New York's Impendent Death Penalty," *Albany Law Review* 54:625–679 (1990).

109 Erica Goode, "Young Killer: Bad Seed or Work in Progress?" *New York Times*, 25 November 2003.

110 Peter J. Benekos and Alida V. Merlo, "Juvenile Offenders and the Death Penalty: How Far have Standards of Decency Evolved?" *Youth Violence and Juvenile Justice* 3:316–333 (2006), p. 324.

111 Paul Piersma, Jeanette Ganousis, Adrienne E. Volenik, Harry F. Swanger, and Patricia Connell, *Law and Tactics in Juvenile Cases* (Philadelphia: American Law Institute, American Bar Association, Committee on Continuing Education, 1977), p. 397.

112 J. Addison Bowman, "Appeals from Juvenile Courts," *Crime and Delinquency Journal* 11:63–77 (1965).

113 *In re Gault*, 387 U.S. 1 87 S.Ct. 1428 (1967).

114 *Davis v. Alaska*, 415 U.S. 308 (1974); 94 S.Ct. 1105.

115 *Oklahoma Publishing Co. v. District Court*, 430 U.S. 97 (1977); 97 S.Ct. 1045.

116 *Smith v. Daily Mail Publishing Co.*, 443 U.S. 97, 99 S.Ct. 2667, 61 L.Ed.2d 399 (1979).

117 Linda Szymanski, *Confidentiality of Juvenile Court Records* (Pittsburgh, PA: National Center for Juvenile Justice, 1989).

118 Ira M. Schwartz, *Justice for Juveniles: Rethinking the Best Interests of the Child* (Lexington, MA: D. C. Heath, 1989), p. 172.

119 Richard E. Redding, "Use of Juvenile Records in Criminal Court," *Juvenile Justice Fact Sheet* (Charlottesville, VA: Institute of Law, Psychiatry, and Public Policy, University of Virginia, 2000).

Chapter 14. Juvenile Corrections: Probation, Community Treatment, and Institutionalization

1 Charles Murray and Louis B. Cox, *Beyond Probation* (Beverly Hills, CA: Sage, 1979).

2 Robert Shepard Jr., ed., *Juvenile Justice Standards, A Balanced Approach* (Chicago: American Bar Association, 1996).

[3] George Killinger, Hazel Kerper, and Paul F. Cromwell Jr., *Probation and Parole in the Criminal Justice System* (St. Paul, MN: West, 1976), p. 45; National Advisory Commission on Criminal Justice Standards and Goals, *Corrections* (Washington, DC: U.S. Government Printing Office, 1983), p. 75.

[4] Ibid.

[5] Jerome Miller, *Last One Over the Wall: The Massachusetts Experiment in Closing Reform Schools* (Columbus: Ohio State University Press, 1998).

[6] Bureau of Justice Statistics, *Report to the Nation on Crime and Justice* (Washington, DC: U.S. Government Printing Office, 1988), pp. 44–45; Peter Greenwood, "What Works with Juvenile Offenders: A Synthesis of the Literature and Experience," *Federal Probation* 58:63–67 (1994).

[7] Howard N. Snyder and Melissa Sickmund, *Juvenile Offenders and Victims: 2006 National Report* (Pittsburgh, PA: National Center for Juvenile Justice, 2006), pp. 174–175. Available at: http://ojjdp.ncjrs.gov/ojstatbb/nr2006/downloads/chapter6.pdf (accessed December 5, 2006).

[8] Emily Gaarder, Nancy Rodriguez, and Marjorie S. Zatz, "Criers, Liars, and Manipulators: Probation Officers' Views of Girls," *Justice Quarterly* 21:547–578 (2004).

[9] Charles Puzzanchera, Anne L. Stahl, Terrence A. Finnegan, Howard N. Snyder, R. Poole, and Nancy Tierney, *Juvenile Court Statistics 1997* (Washington, DC: Office of Juvenile Justice and Delinquency Prevention, 2000).

[10] *In re J.G.* 692 N.E. 2d 1226 (IL App. 1998).

[11] *In Re Michael D.,* 264 CA Rptr 476 (CA App. 1989).

[12] *Morrissey v. Brewer,* 408 U.S. 471, 92 S.Ct. 2593, 33 L.Ed.2d 484 (1972); *Gagnon v. Scarpelli,* 411 U.S. 778, 93 S.Ct. 1756, 36 L.Ed.2d 655 (1973).

[13] William A. Reese, Russell L. Curtis, and James R. Whitworth, "Dispositional Discetion of Disparity: The Juvenile Probation Officer's Role in Delinquency Processing," *Journal of Applied Behavioral Science* 24:81–100 (1988).

[14] Richard Lawrence, "Reexamining Community Corrections Models," *Crime and Delinquency* 37:449–464 (1991).

[15] See Matthew J. Giblin, "Using Police Officers to Enhance the Supervision of Juvenile Probationers: An Evaluation of the Anchorage CAN Program," *Crime and Delinquency* 48:116–137 (2002).

[16] See Richard G. Wiebush, "Juvenile Intensive Supervision: The Impact on Felony Offenders Diverted from Institutional Placement," *Crime and Delinquency* 39:68–89 (1993); James Byrne, "The Control Controversy: A Preliminary Examination of Intensive Probation Supervision Programs in the United States," *Federal Probation* 50:4–16 (1986).

[17] For a review of these programs, see James Austin, Kelly Dedel Johnson, and Ronald Weitzer, *Alternatives to the Secure Detention and Confinement of Juvenile Offenders* (Washington, DC: OJJDP Bulletin, 2005), pp. 18–19.

[18] James Ryan, "Who Gets Revoked? A Comparison of Intensive Supervision Successes and Failures in Vermont," *Crime and Delinquency* 43:104–118 (1997).

[19] Sheldon X. Zhang and Lening Zhang, "An Experimental Study of the Los Angeles County Repeat Offender Prevention Program: Its Implementation and Evaluation," *Criminology and Public Policy* 4:205–236 (2005).

[20] Jodi Lane, Susan Turner, Terry Fain, and Amber Sehgal, "Evaluating an Experimental Intensive Juvenile Probation Program: Supervision and Official Outcomes," *Crime and Delinquency* 51:26–52 (2005).

[21] Angela A. Robertson, Paul W. Grimes, and Kevin E. Rogers, "A Short-Run Cost-Benefit Analysis of Community-Based Interventions for Juvenile Offenders," *Crime and Delinquency* 47:265–284 (2001).

[22] Richard Ball and J. Robert Lilly, "A Theoretical Examination of Home Incarceration," *Federal Probation* 50:17–25 (1986); Joan Petersilia, "Exploring the Option of House Arrest," *Federal Probation* 50:50–56 (1986); Annesley Schmidt, "Electronic Monitors," *Federal Probation* 50:56–60 (1986); Michael Charles, "The Development of a Juvenile Electronic Monitoring Program," *Federal Probation* 53:3–12 (1989).

[23] Sudipto Roy, "Five Years of Electronic Monitoring of Adults and Juveniles in Lake County, Indiana: A Comparative Study on Factors Related to Failure," *Journal of Crime and Justice* 20:141–160 (1997).

[24] Marc Renzema and Evan Mayo-Wilson, "Can Electronic Monitoring Reduce Crime for Moderate to High-Risk Offenders?" *Journal of Experimental Criminology* 1:215–237 (2005).

[25] Anne Seymour and Trudy Gregorie, "Restorative Justice for Young Offenders and Their Victims," *Corrections Today* 64:90–92 (2002), p. 90.

[26] Heather Strang and Lawrence W. Sherman, "Restorative Justice to Reduce Victimization," in Brandon C. Welsh and David P. Farrington, eds., *Preventing Crime: What Works for Children, Offenders, Victims, and Places* (New York: Springer, 2006), p. 148; see also Lawrence W. Sherman, Heather Strang, Caroline Angel, Daniel Woods, Geoffrey C. Barnes, Sarah Bennett, and Nova Inkpen, "Effects of Face-to-Face Restorative Justice on Victims of Crime in Four Randomized, Controlled Trials," *Journal of Experimental Criminology* 1:367–395 (2005).

[27] Ibid., pp. 152–156.

[28] Nancy Rodriguez, "Restorative Justice, Communities, and Delinquency: Whom Do We Reintegrate?" *Criminology and Public Policy* 4:103–130 (2005).

[29] Andrew J. DeAngelo, "Evolution of Juvenile Justice: Community-Based Partnerships Through Balanced and Restorative Justice," *Corrections Today* 67:105–106 (2005); Dennis Mahoney, Dennis Romig, and Troy Armstrong, "Juvenile Probation: The Balanced Approach," *Juvenile and Family Court Journal* 39:1–59 (1988).

[30] Gordon Bazemore, "On Mission Statements and Reform in Juvenile Justice: The Case of the Balanced Approach," *Federal Probation* 61:64–70 (1992); Gordon Bazemore and Mark Umbreit, *Balanced and Restorative Justice* (Washington, DC: Office of Juvenile Justice and Delinquency Prevention, 1994).

[31] Office of Juvenile Justice and Delinquency Prevention, *The 8% Solution.* Fact sheet (Washington, DC: U.S. Department of Justice, Office of Juvenile Justice and Delinquency Prevention, 2001).

[32] Ibid., pp. 1–2.

[33] Peter R. Schneider and Matthew C. Finkelstein, eds., *RESTTA National Directory of Restitution and Community Service Programs* (Washington, DC: Office of Juvenile Justice and Delinquency Prevention, U.S. Department of Justice, 1998).

[34] Gordon Bazemore, "New Concepts and Alternative Practice in Community Supervision of Juvenile Offenders: Rediscovering Work Experience and Competency Development," *Journal of Crime and Justice* 14:27–45 (1991).

[35] Anne Schneider, "Restitution and Recidivism Rates of Juvenile Offenders: Results from Four Experimental Studies," *Criminology* 24:533–552 (1986).

[36] Shay Bilchik, *A Juvenile Justice System for the 21st Century* (Washington, DC: Office of Juvenile Justice and Delinquency Prevention, 1998).

[37] Schneider and Finkelstein, *RESTTA National Directory of Restitution and Community Service Programs,* Tables 12, 15.

[38] Anne Schneider, "Restitution and Recidivism Rates of Juvenile Offenders," *Directory of Restitution Programs* (Washington, DC: OJJDP Juvenile Justice Clearinghouse, 1996). This directory contains information on more than five hundred restitution programs across the country.

[39] Shelley Zavlek, *Planning Community-Based Facilities for Violent Juvenile Offenders as Part of a System of Graduated Sanctions* (Washington, DC: OJJDP Bulletin, 2005), p. 5; Peter W. Greenwood, "Juvenile Crime and Juvenile Justice," in James Q. Wilson and Joan Petersilia, eds., *Crime: Public Policies for Crime Control* (Oakland, CA: Institute for Contemporary Studies, 2002), pp. 90–91.

[40] Sharon F. Mihalic, Abigail Fagan, Katherine Irwin, Diane Ballard, and Delbert Elliott, *Blueprints for Violence Prevention* (Washington, DC: OJJDP Report, 2004).

[41] Patricia Chamberlain and John B. Reid, "Comparison of Two Community Alternatives to Incarceration," *Journal of Consulting and Clinical Psychology* 66:624–633 (1998).

[42] *Children in Custody 1975–1985: Census of Public and Private Juvenile Detention, Correctional, and Shelter Facilities* (Washington, DC: U.S. Department of Justice, 1989), p. 4.

[43] For a detailed description of juvenile delinquency in the 1800s, see J. Hawes, *Children in Urban Society: Juvenile Delinquency in Nineteenth-Century America* (New York: Oxford University Press, 1971).

[44] D. Jarvis, *Institutional Treatment of the Offender* (New York: McGraw-Hill, 1978), p. 101.

[45] Margaret Werner Cahalan, *Historical Corrections Statistics in the United States, 1850–1984* (Washington, DC: U.S. Department of Justice, 1986), pp. 104–105.

[46] Clemons Bartollas, Stuart J. Miller, and Simon Dinitz, *Juvenile Victimization: The Institutional Paradox* (New York: Wiley, 1976), p. 6.

47 LaMar T. Empey, *American Delinquency—Its Meaning and Construction* (Homewood, IL: Dorsey, 1978), p. 515.

48 Edward Eldefonso and Walter Hartinger, *Control, Treatment, and Rehabilitation of Juvenile Offenders* (Beverly Hills, CA: Glencoe, 1976), p. 151.

49 Ibid., p. 152.

50 M. Rosenthal, "Reforming the Justice Correctional Institution: Efforts of U.S. Children's Bureau in the 1930s," *Journal of Sociology and Social Welfare* 14:47–73 (1987).

51 Peter W. Greenwood, *Changing Lives: Delinquency Prevention as Crime-Control Policy* (Chicago: University of Chicago Press, 2006), chapter 8; Franklin E. Zimring, *American Juvenile Justice* (New York: Oxford University Press), chapter 4.

52 National Conference on State Legislatures, *A Legislator's Guide to Comprehensive Juvenile Justice, Juvenile Detention, and Corrections* (Denver: National Conference on State Legislatures, 1996).

53 Ibid.

54 Howard N. Snyder and Melissa Sickmund, *Juvenile Offenders and Victims: 2006 National Report* (Pittsburgh, PA: National Center for Juvenile Justice, 2006), chapter 7.

55 Snyder and Sickmund, *Juvenile Offenders and Victims*, pp. 198–199.

56 Ibid., p. 201.

57 Ira Schwartz, Marilyn Jackson-Beck, and Roger Anderson, "The 'Hidden' System of Juvenile Control," *Crime and Delinquency* 30:371–385 (1984).

58 Rebecca Craig and Andrea Paterson, "State Involuntary Commitment Laws: Beyond Deinstitutionalization," *National Conference of State Legislative Reports* 13:1–10 (1988).

59 Robert Pear, "Many Youths Reported Held Awaiting Mental Help," *New York Times*, 8 July 2004.

60 Richard Lezin Jones and Leslie Kaufman, "New Jersey Youths Out of Foster Homes End Up in Detention," *New York Times*, 31 May 2003.

61 Melissa Sickmund, *Juvenile Residential Facility Census, 2002: Selected Findings* (Washington, DC: OJJDP Bulletin, 2006), p. 2; see also Snyder and Sickmund, *Juvenile Offenders and Victims*, p. 223.

62 Ibid., p. 9.

63 John M. Broder, "Dismal California Prisons Hold Juvenile Offenders: Report Documents Long List of Mistreatment," *New York Times*, 15 February 2004, p. A12.

64 Snyder and Sickmund, *Juvenile Offenders and Victims*, pp. 209, 215.

65 Gail A. Wasserman, Peter S. Jensen, Susan J. Ko, Joseph Cocozza, Eric Trupin, Adrian Angold, Elizabeth Cauffman, and Thomas Grisso, "Mental Health Assessments in Juvenile Justice: Report on the Consensus Conference," *Journal of the American Academy of Child and Adolescent Psychiatry* 42:752–761 (2003).

66 Gail A. Wasserman, Susan J. Ko, and Larkin S. McReynolds, *Assessing the Mental Health Status of Youth in Juvenile Justice Settings* (Washington, DC: OJJDP Bulletin, 2004), p. 1.

67 Deborah Shelton, "Patterns of Treatment Services and Costs for Young Offenders with Mental Disorders," *Journal of Child and Adolescent Psychiatric Nursing* 18:103–112 (2005).

68 Wasserman, Jensen, Ko, Cocozza, Trupin, Angold, Cauffman, and Grisso, "Mental Health Assessments in Juvenile Justice: Report on the Consensus Conference," p. 752.

69 Snyder and Sickmund, *Juvenile Offenders and Victims*, p. 213.

70 Michael J. Leiber and Kristan C. Fox, "Race and the Impact of Detention on Juvenile Justice Decision Making," *Crime and Delinquency* 51:470–497 (2005).

71 Snyder and Sickmund, *Juvenile Offenders and Victims*, p. 212.

72 Rodney L. Engen, Sara Steen, and George S. Bridges, "Racial Disparities in the Punishment of Youth: A Theoretical and Empirical Assessment of the Literature," *Social Problems* 49:194–220 (2002).

73 Snyder and Sickmund, *Juvenile Offenders and Victims*, p. 211.

74 John F. Chapman, Rani A. Desai, Paul R. Falzer, and Randy Borum, "Violence Risk and Race in a Sample of Youth in Juvenile Detention: The Potential to Reduce Disproportionate Minority Confinement," *Youth Violence and Juvenile Justice* 4:170–184 (2006).

75 Heidi M. Hsia, George S. Bridges, and Rosalie McHale, *Disproportionate Minority Confinement: 2002 Update: Summary* (Washington, DC: Office of Juvenile Justice and Delinquency Prevention, 2004).

76 Ibid., pp. 16–17.

77 See David M. Halbfinger, "Care of Juvenile Offenders in Mississippi Is Faulted," *New York Times*, 1 September 2003.

78 Snyder and Sickmund, *Juvenile Offenders and Victims*, p. 206.

79 Bartollas, Miller, and Dinitz, *Juvenile Victimization*, sec. C.

80 Christopher Sieverdes and Clemens Bartollas, "Security Level and Adjustment Patterns in Juvenile Institutions," *Journal of Criminal Justice* 14:145 (1986).

81 Snyder and Sickmund, *Juvenile Offenders and Victims*, p. 206.

82 Several authors have written about this sexual double standard. See E. A. Anderson, "The Chivalrous Treatment of the Female Offender in the Arms of the Criminal Justice System: A Review of the Literature," *Social Problems* 23:350–357 (1976); G. Armstrong, "Females Under the Law: Protected but Unequal," *Crime and Delinquency* 23:109–120 (1977); Meda Chesney-Lind, "Judicial Enforcement of the Female Sex Role: The Family Court and the Female Delinquent," *Issues in Criminology* 8:51–59 (1973); idem, "Juvenile Delinquency: The Sexualization of Female Crime," *Psychology Today* 19:43–46 (1974); Allan Conway and Carol Bogdan, "Sexual Delinquency: The Persistence of a Double Standard," *Crime and Delinquency* 23:131–135 (1977); Meda Chesney-Lind and Randall G. Shelden *Girls, Delinquency, and the Juvenile Justice System*, 3rd ed. (Belmont, CA: Wadsworth, 2004).

83 Snyder and Sickmund, *Juvenile Offenders and* Victims, p. 209.

84 Kristi Holsinger and Alexander M. Holsinger, "Differential Pathways to Violence and Self-Injurious Behavior: African American and White Girls in the Juvenile Justice System," *Journal of Research in Crime and Delinquency* 42:211–242 (2005).

85 See Emily Gaarder and Joanne Belknap, "Tenuous Borders: Girls Transferred to Adult Court," *Criminology* 40:481–518 (2002).

86 Leslie Acoca, "Outside/Inside: The Violation of American Girls at Home, on the Streets, and in the Juvenile Justice System," *Crime and Delinquency* 44:561–589 (1998).

87 Barbara Bloom, Barbara Owen, Elizabeth Piper Deschenes, and Jill Rosenbaum, "Improving Juvenile Justice for Females: A Statewide Assessment in California," *Crime and Delinquency* 48:526–552 (2002), p. 548.

88 For a historical analysis of a girls' reformatory, see Barbara Brenzel, *Daughters of the State* (Cambridge, MA: MIT Press, 1983).

89 Ilene R. Bergsmann, "The Forgotten Few Juvenile Female Offenders," *Federal Probation* 53:73–79 (1989).

90 *Justice by Gender: The Lack of Appropriate Prevention, Diversion, and Treatment Alternatives for Girls in the Justice System: A Report* (Chicago: American Bar Association and National Bar Association, 2001), pp. 27–29.

91 Doris Layton MacKenzie, "Reducing the Criminal Activities of Known Offenders and Delinquents: Crime Prevention in the Courts and Corrections," in Lawrence W. Sherman, David P. Farrington, Brandon C. Welsh, and Doris Layton MacKenzie, eds., *Evidence-Based Crime Prevention* (New York: Routledge, 2006, rev. ed.), p. 352.

92 Patrick A. Langan and David J. Levin, *Recidivism of Prisoners Released in 1994* (Washington, DC: Bureau of Justice Statistics, 2002)

93 David Farabee, *Rethinking Rehabilitation: Why Can't We Reform Our Criminals?* (Washington, DC: American Enterprise Institute, 2005); for a rebuttal of this view, see James M. Byrne and Faye S. Taxman, "Crime (Control) Is a Choice: Divergent Perspectives on the Role of Treatment in the Adult Corrections System," *Criminology and Public Policy* 4:291–310 (2005).

94 Mark W. Lipsey and David B. Wilson, "Effective Intervention for Serious Juvenile Offenders: A Synthesis of Research," in Rolf Loeber and David P. Farrington, eds., *Serious and Violent Juvenile Offenders: Risk Factors and Successful Interventions* (Thousand Oaks, CA: Sage, 1998).

95 Steve Aos, Roxanne Lieb, Jim Mayfield, Marna Miller, and Annie Pennucci, *Benefits and Costs of Prevention and Early Intervention Programs for Youth* (Olympia, WA: Washington State Institute for Public Policy, 2004); Brandon C. Welsh, "Monetary Costs and Benefits of Correctional Treatment Programs: Implications for Offender Reentry," *Federal Probation* 68:9–13 (2004).

96 Michael F. Caldwell, Michael Vitacco, and Gregory J. Van Rybroek, "Are Violent Delinquents Worth Treating: A Cost-Benefit Analysis," *Journal of Research in Crime and Delinquency* 43:148–168 (2006).

97 Louise Sas and Peter Jaffe, "Understanding Depression in Juvenile Delinquency: Implications for Institutional Admission Policies and Treatment Programs," *Juvenile and Family Court Journal* 37:49–58 (1985–1986).

98 See, generally, William Glasser, "Reality Therapy: A Realistic Approach to the Young Offender," in Robert Schaste and Jo Wallach, eds., *Readings in Delinquency and Treatment* (Los Angeles: Delinquency Prevention Training Project, Youth Studies Center, University of Southern California, 1965); see also Richard Rachin, "Reality Therapy: Helping People Help Themselves," *Crime and Delinquency* 16:143 (1974).

[99] Helen A. Klein, "Toward More Effective Behavior Programs for Juvenile Offenders," *Federal Probation* 41:45–50 (1977); Albert Bandura, *Principles of Behavior Modification* (New York: Holt, Rinehart & Winston, 1969); H. A. Klein, "Behavior Modification as Therapeutic Paradox," *American Journal of Orthopsychiatry* 44:353 (1974).

[100] Thomas J. Dishion, Joan McCord, and François Poulin, "When Interventions Harm: Peer Groups and Problem Behavior," *American Psychologist* 54:755–764 (1999); Joan McCord, "Cures That Harm: Unanticipated Outcomes of Crime Prevention Programs," *Annals of the American Academy of Political and Social Science* 587:16–30 (2003).

[101] Larry Brendtero and Arlin Ness, "Perspectives on Peer Group Treatment: The Use and Abuses of Guided Group Interaction/Positive Peer Culture," *Child and Youth Services Review* 4:307–324 (1982).

[102] Elaine Traynelis-Yurek and George A. Giacobbe, "Communication Rehabilitation Regime for Incarcerated Youth: Positive Peer Culture," *Journal of Offender Rehabilitation* 26:157–167 (1998).

[103] Bruno Bettelheim, *The Empty Fortress* (New York: Free Press, 1967).

[104] Doris Layton MacKenzie, "Reducing the Criminal Activities of Known Offenders and Delinquents: Crime Prevention in the Courts and Corrections," p. 355; Doris Layton MacKenzie, "Evidence-Based Corrections: Identifying What Works," *Crime and Delinquency* 46:457–471 (2000).

[105] Thomas Castellano and Irina Soderstrom, "Therapeutic Wilderness Programs and Juvenile Recidivism: A Program Evaluation," *Journal of Offender Rehabilitation* 17:19–46 (1992).

[106] MacKenzie, "Reducing the Criminal Activities of Known Offenders and Delinquents," p. 355.

[107] Sandra Jo Wilson and Mark W. Lipsey, "Wilderness Challenge Programs for Delinquent Youth: A Meta-Analysis of Outcome Evaluations," *Evaluation and Program Planning* 23:1–12 (2003).

[108] Jerald Burns and Gennaro Vito, "An Impact Analysis of the Alabama Boot Camp Program," *Federal Probation* 59:63–67 (1995).

[109] Ronald Corbett and Joan Petersilia, eds., "The Results of a Multi-Site Study of Boot Camps," *Federal Probation* 58:60–66 (1995).

[110] David B. Wilson and Doris Layton MacKenzie, "Boot Camps," in Brandon C. Welsh and David P. Farrington, eds., *Preventing Crime: What Works for Children, Offenders, Victims, and Places?* (New York, Springer, 2006), p. 80, Table 2.

[111] Ibid., p. 80.

[112] Ibid., p. 80; Doris Layton MacKenzie, *What Works in Corrections: Reducing the Criminal Activities of Offenders and Delinquents* (New York: Cambridge University Press, 2006), p. 294.

[113] MacKenzie, "Reducing the Criminal Activities of Known Offenders and Delinquents," p. 348.

[114] Dale G. Parent, *Correctional Boot Camps: Lessons Learned from a Decade of Research* (Washington, DC: National Institute of Justice, 2003).

[115] Anthony Salerno, "Boot Camps—A Critique and Proposed Alternative," *Journal of Offender Rehabilitation* 20:147–158 (1994).

[116] Joanne Ardovini-Brooker and Lewis Walker, "Juvenile Boot Camps and the Reclamation of Our Youth: Some Food for Thought," *Juvenile and Family Court Journal* 51:12–28 (2000).

[117] Morton Birnbaum, "The Right to Treatment," *American Bar Association Journal* 46:499 (1960).

[118] See for example, *Matter of Welfare of CAW* 579 N.W. 2d 494 (MN App. 1998).

[119] *Inmates of the Boys' Training School v. Affleck*, 346 F. Supp. 1354 (D.R.I. 1972).

[120] Ibid., p. 1343.

[121] *Nelson v. Heyne*, 491. F. 2d 353 (1974).

[122] *Morales v. Turman*, 383 F. Supp. 53 (E.D. Texas 1974).

[123] *Pena v. New York State Division for Youth*, 419 F. Supp. 203 (S.D.N.Y. 1976).

[124] *Ralston v. Robinson*, 102 S.Ct. 233 (1981).

[125] Patricia Puritz and Mary Ann Scali, *Beyond the Walls: Improving Conditions of Confinement for Youth in Custody* (Washington, DC: Office of Juvenile Justice and Delinquency Prevention, 1998).

[126] Joan McCord, Cathy Spatz Widom, and Nancy A. Crowell, eds., *Juvenile Crime, Juvenile Justice.* (Washington, DC: National Academy Press, Panel on Juvenile Crime: Prevention, Treatment, and Control, 2001), p. 194.

[127] David M. Altschuler and Rachel Brash, "Adolescent and Teenage Offenders Confronting the Challenges and Opportunities of Reentry," *Youth Violence and Juvenile Justice* 2:72–87 (2004), p. 72.

[128] Daniel P. Mears and Jeremy Travis, "Youth Development and Reentry," *Youth Violence and Juvenile Justice* 2:3–20 (2004), p. 3

[129] Edward J. Latessa, "Homelessness and Reincarceration: Editorial Introduction," *Criminology and Public Policy* 3:137–138 (2004).

[130] Joan Petersilia, *When Offenders Come Home: Parole and Prisoner Reentry* (New York: Oxford University Press, 2003).

[131] Margaret Beale Spencer and Cheryl Jones-Walker, "Intervention and Services Offered to Former Juvenile Offenders Reentering Their Communities: An Analysis of Program Effectiveness," *Youth Violence and Juvenile Justice* 2:88–97 (2004), p. 91.

[132] Pamela K. Lattimore, "Reentry, Reintegration, Rehabilitation, Recidivism, and Redemption," *The Criminologist* 31:1, 3–6 (2006), p. 1.

[133] David M. Altschuler and Troy L. Armstrong, "Juvenile Corrections and Continuity of Care in a Community Context: The Evidence and Promising Directions," *Federal Probation* 66:72–77 (2002).

[134] David M. Altschuler and Troy L. Armstrong, "Intensive Aftercare for High-Risk Juveniles: A Community Care Model" (Washington, DC: Office of Juvenile Justice and Delinquency Prevention, 1994).

[135] David M. Altschuler and Troy Armstrong, "Reintegrating Juvenile Offenders: Translating the Intensive Aftercare Program Model into Performance Standards." Paper presented at the American Society of Criminology meeting, San Francisco, November 2000.

[136] See *Morrissey v. Brewer*, 408 U.S. 471, 92 S.Ct. 2593, 33 L.Ed.2d 484 (1972).

New Directions in Preventing Delinquency: Tertiary Prevention Efforts: The Role of the Juvenile Justice System

[1] Irvin Waller, *Less Law, More Order: The Truth About Reducing Crime* (Westport, CT: Praeger, 2006).

[2] Peter W. Greenwood, *Changing Lives: Delinquency Prevention as Crime-Control Policy* (Chicago: University of Chicago Press, 2006); Franklin E. Zimring, *American Juvenile Justice* (New York: Oxford University Press, 2005).

[3] Barry C. Feld, "Juvenile and Criminal Justice Systems' Responses to Youth Violence," in Michael Tonry and Mark H. Moore, eds., *Youth Violence: Crime and Justice: A Review of Research*, vol. 24 (Chicago: University of Chicago Press, 1998), p. 222.

[4] Greenwood, *Changing Lives*, chapter 8.

[5] See David Weisburd and Anthony A. Braga, eds., *Police Innovation: Contrasting Perspectives* (New York: Cambridge University Press, 2006).

[6] Anthony A. Braga, David M. Kennedy, Elin J. Waring, and Anne Morrison Piehl, "Problem-Oriented Policing Deterrence and Youth Violence: An Evaluation of Boston's Operation Ceasefire," *Journal of Research in Crime and Delinquency* 38:195–225 (2001).

[7] David Sheppard, Heath Grant, Wendy Rowe, and Nancy Jacobs, *Fighting Juvenile Gun Violence* (Washington, DC: Office of Juvenile Justice and Delinquency Prevention, Juvenile Justice Bulletin, 2000), p. 2.

[8] Arthur L. Kellerman, Dawna Fuqua-Whitley, and Constance S. Parramore, *Reducing Gun Violence: Community Problem Solving in Atlanta* (Washington, DC: National Institute of Justice, 2006); George E. Tita, K. Jack Riley, Greg Ridgeway, and Peter W. Greenwood, *Reducing Gun Violence: Operation Ceasefire in Los Angeles* (Washington, DC: National Institute of Justice, 2005).

[9] Jeffrey A. Butts, Janeen Buck, and Mark B. Coggeshall, *The Impact of Teen Court on Young Offenders* (Washington, DC: Urban Institute, 2002).

[10] Peter W. Greenwood, "Juvenile Crime and Juvenile Justice," in James Q. Wilson and Joan Petersilia, eds., *Crime: Public Policies for Crime Control* (Oakland, CA: Institute for Contemporary Studies, 2002), pp. 90–91.

[11] Doris Layton MacKenzie, *What Works in Corrections: Reducing the Criminal Activities of Offenders and Delinquents* (New York: Cambridge University Press, 2006).

[12] Rolf Loeber and David P. Farrington, "Never Too Early, Never Too Late: Risk Factors and Successful Interventions for Serious and Violent Juvenile Offenders," *Studies on Crime and Crime Prevention* 7:7–30 (1998).

Glossary

abandonment: Parents physically leave their children with the intention of completely severing the parent-child relationship.

abuse: Any physical, emotional, or sexual trauma to a child, including neglecting to give proper care and attention, for which no reasonable explanation can be found.

academic achievement: Being successful in a school environment.

active speech: Expressing an opinion by speaking or writing; freedom of speech is a protected right under the First Amendment to the U.S. Constitution.

addict: A person with an overpowering physical or psychological need to continue taking a particular substance or drug.

addiction-prone personality: The view that the cause of substance abuse can be traced to a personality that has a compulsion for mood-altering drugs.

adjudicatory hearing: The fact-finding process wherein the juvenile court determines whether there is sufficient evidence to sustain the allegations in a petition.

adolescent-limited: Offender who follows the most common delinquent trajectory, in which antisocial behavior peaks in adolescence and then diminishes.

advisement hearing: A preliminary protective or temporary custody hearing in which the court will review the facts, determine whether removal of the child is justified, and notify parents of the charges against them.

aftercare: Transitional assistance to juveniles equivalent to adult parole to help youths adjust to community life.

age of onset: Age at which youths begin their delinquent careers; early onset is believed to be linked with chronic offending patterns.

aging-out process (also known as desistance or spontaneous remission): The tendency for youths to reduce the frequency of their offending behavior as they age; aging out is thought to occur among all groups of offenders.

alcohol: Fermented or distilled liquids containing ethanol, an intoxicating substance.

anabolic steroids: Drugs used by athletes and body builders to gain muscle bulk and strength.

anesthetic drugs: Nervous system depressants.

anomie: Normlessness produced by rapidly shifting moral values; according to Merton, anomie occurs when personal goals cannot be achieved using available means.

appellate process: Allows the juvenile an opportunity to have the case brought before a reviewing court after it has been heard in juvenile or family court.

arrest: Taking a person into the custody of the law to restrain the accused until he or she can be held accountable for the offense in court proceedings.

at-risk youths: Young people who are extremely vulnerable to the negative consequences of school failure, substance abuse, and early sexuality.

authority conflict pathway: Pathway to delinquent deviance that begins at an early age with stubborn behavior and leads to defiance and then to authority avoidance.

bail: Amount of money that must be paid as a condition of pretrial release to ensure that the accused will return for subsequent proceedings; bail is normally set by the judge at the initial appearance, and if unable to make bail the accused is detained in jail.

balanced probation: Programs that integrate community protection, accountability of the juvenile offender, competency, and individualized attention to the juvenile offender; based on the principle that juvenile offenders must accept responsibility for their behavior.

balancing-of-the-interests approach: Efforts of the courts to balance the parents' natural right to raise a child with the child's right to grow into adulthood free from physical abuse or emotional harm.

barrio: A Latino word meaning neighborhood.

battered child syndrome: Non-accidental physical injury of children by their parents or guardians.

behavior modification: A technique for shaping desired behaviors through a system of rewards and punishments.

behaviorism: Branch of psychology concerned with the study of observable behavior rather than unconscious processes; focuses on particular stimuli and responses to them.

best interests of the child: A philosophical viewpoint that encourages the state to take control of wayward children and provide care, custody, and treatment to remedy delinquent behavior.

bifurcated process: The procedure of separating adjudicatory and dispositionary hearings so different levels of evidence can be heard at each.

biosocial theory: The view that both thought and behavior have biological and social bases.

bipolar disorder: A psychological condition producing mood swings between wild elation and deep depression.

blended families: Nuclear families that are the product of divorce and remarriage, blending one parent from each of two families and their combined children into one family unit.

boot camps: Programs that combine get-tough elements with education, substance abuse treatment, and social skills training.

broken home: Home in which one or both parents is absent due to divorce or separation; children in such an environment may be prone to antisocial behavior.

chancery courts: Court proceedings created in fifteenth-century England to oversee the lives of highborn minors who were orphaned or otherwise could not care for themselves.

child abuse: Any physical, emotional, or sexual trauma to a child, including neglecting to give proper care and attention, for which no reasonable explanation can be found.

child savers: Nineteenth-century reformers who developed programs for troubled youth and influenced legislation creating the juvenile justice system; today some critics view them as being more concerned with control of the poor than with their welfare.

Children's Aid Society: Child-saving organization that took children from the streets of large cities and placed them with farm families on the prairie.

chivalry hypothesis (also known as paternalism hypothesis): The view that low female crime and delinquency rates are a reflection of the leniency with which police treat female offenders.

choice theory: Holds that youths will engage in delinquent and criminal behavior after weighing the consequences and benefits of their actions; delinquent behavior is a rational choice made by a motivated offender who perceives that the chances of gain outweigh any possible punishment or loss.

chronic juvenile offenders (also known as chronic delinquent offenders, chronic delinquents, or chronic recidivists): Youths who have been arrested four or more times during their minority and perpetuate a striking majority of serious criminal acts; this small group, known as the "chronic 6 percent," is believed to engage in a significant portion of all delinquent behavior; these youths do not age out of crime but continue their criminal behavior into adulthood.

classical criminology: Holds that decisions to violate the law are weighed against possible punishments and to deter crime the pain of punishment must outweigh the benefit of illegal gain; led to graduated punishments based on seriousness of the crime (let the punishment fit the crime).

cliques: Small groups of friends who share intimate knowledge and confidences.

cocaine: A powerful natural stimulant derived from the coca plant.

cognitive theory: The branch of psychology that studies the perception of reality and the mental processes required to understand the world we live in.

collective efficacy: A process in which mutual trust and a willingness to intervene in the supervision of children and help maintain public order creates a sense of well-being in a neighborhood and helps control antisocial activities.

community policing: Police strategy that emphasizes fear reduction, community organization, and order maintenance rather than crime fighting.

community service restitution: Offenders assist some worthwhile community organization for a period of time.

community treatment: Using nonsecure and non-institutional residences, counseling services, victim restitution programs, and other community services to treat juveniles in their own communities.

complaint: Report made by the police or some other agency to the court that initiates the intake process.

conditions of probation: Rules and regulations mandating that a juvenile on probation behave in a particular way.

conduct disorder: A psychological disorder characterized by difficulty following rules and behaving in a socially acceptable way.

confidentiality: Restricting information in juvenile court proceedings in the interest of protecting the privacy of the juvenile.

continuity of crime: The idea that chronic juvenile offenders are likely to continue violating the law as adults.

controversial status youth: Aggressive kids who are either highly liked or intensely disliked by their peers and who are the ones most likely to become engaged in antisocial behavior.

co-offending: Committing criminal acts in groups.

cottage system: Housing in a compound of small cottages, each of which accommodates twenty to forty children.

covert pathway: Pathway to a delinquent career that begins with minor underhanded behavior, leads to property damage, and eventually escalates to more serious forms of theft and fraud.

crack: A highly addictive crystalline form of cocaine containing remnants of hydrochloride and sodium bicarbonate; it makes a crackling sound when smoked.

crackdown: A law enforcement operation that is designed to reduce or eliminate a particular criminal activity through the application of aggressive police tactics, usually involving a larger than usual contingent of police officers.

criminal atavism: The idea that delinquents manifest physical anomalies that make them biologically and physiologically similar to our primitive ancestors, savage throwbacks to an earlier stage of human evolution.

critical feminists: Hold that gender inequality stems from the unequal power of men and women and the subsequent exploitation of women by men; the cause of female delinquency originates with the onset of male supremacy and the efforts of males to control females' sexuality.

critical theories: The view that inter-group conflict, borne out of the unequal distribution of wealth and power, is the root cause of delinquency.

crowds: Loosely organized groups who share interests and activities.

cultural deviance theory: Links delinquent acts to the formation of independent subcultures with a unique set of values that clash with the mainstream culture.

cultural transmission: The process of passing on deviant traditions and delinquent values from one generation to the next.

culture conflict: When the values of a subculture clash with those of the dominant culture.

culture of poverty: View that lower-class people form a separate culture with their own values and norms, which are sometimes in conflict with conventional society.

custodial interrogation: Questions posed by the police to a suspect held in custody in the prejudicial stage of the juvenile justice process; juveniles have the same rights against self-incrimination as adults when being questioned.

dark figures of crime: Incidents of crime and delinquency that go undetected by police.

deinstitutionalization: Removing juveniles from adult jails and placing them in community-based programs to avoid the stigma attached to these facilities.

delinquent: Juvenile who has been adjudicated by a judicial officer of a juvenile court as having committed a delinquent act.

designer drugs: Lab-made drugs designed to avoid existing drug laws.

detached street workers: Social workers who go out into the community and establish close relationships with juvenile gangs with the goal of modifying gang behavior to conform to conventional behaviors and help gang members get jobs and educational opportunities.

detention hearing: A hearing by a judicial officer of a juvenile court to determine whether a juvenile is to be detained or released while proceedings are pending in the case.

determinate sentence: Specifies a fixed term of detention that must be served.

developmental theory: The view that criminality is a dynamic process, influenced by social experiences as well as individual characteristics.

differential association theory: Asserts that criminal behavior is learned primarily in interpersonal groups and that youths will become delinquent if definitions they learn in those groups that are favorable to violating the law exceed definitions favorable to obeying the law.

disaggregated: To break down a variable into its constituent parts in order to better understand its association with another variable.

discretion: Use of personal decision making and choice in carrying out operations in the criminal justice system, such as deciding whether to make an arrest or accept a plea bargain.

disorganized neighborhood: Inner-city areas of extreme poverty where the critical social control mechanisms have broken down.

disposition: For juvenile offenders, the equivalent of sentencing for adult offenders; juvenile dispositions should be more rehabilitative than retributive.

disposition hearing: The social service agency presents its case plan and recommendations for care of the child and treatment of the parents, including incarceration and counseling or other treatment.

diversion: Officially halting or suspending a formal criminal or juvenile justice proceeding at any legally prescribed processing point after a recorded justice system entry, and referral of that person to a treatment or care program or a recommendation that the person be released.

drop out: To leave school before completing the required program of education.

drug courts: Courts whose focus is providing treatment for youths accused of drug-related acts.

due process: Basic constitutional principle based on the concept of the primacy of the individual and the complementary concept of limitation on governmental power; safeguards the individual from unfair state procedures in judicial or administrative proceedings; due process rights have been extended to juvenile trials.

early onset: The view that kids who begin engaging in antisocial behaviors at a very early age are the ones most at risk for a delinquency career.

egalitarian families: Husband and wife share power at home; daughters gain a kind of freedom similar to that of sons and their law-violating behaviors mirror those of their brothers.

ego identity: According to Erik Erikson, ego identity is formed when persons develop a firm sense of who they are and what they stand for.

electronic monitoring: Active monitoring systems consist of a radio transmitter worn by the offender that sends a continuous signal to the probation department computer; passive systems employ computer-generated random phone calls that must be answered in a certain period of time from a particular phone.

extraversion: Impulsive behavior without the ability to examine motives and behavior.

familicide: Mass murders in which a spouse and one or more children are slain.

family group homes: A combination of foster care and group home; they are run by a single family rather than by professional staff.

Federal Bureau of Investigation (FBI): Arm of the U.S. Department of Justice that investigates violations of federal law, gathers crime statistics, runs a comprehensive crime laboratory, and helps train local law enforcement officers.

final order: Order that ends litigation between two parties by determining all their rights and disposing of all the issues.

foster care programs: Placement with families who provide attention, guidance, and care.

free will: The view that youths are in charge of their own destinies and are free to make personal behavior choices unencumbered by environmental factors.

gang: Group of youths who collectively engage in delinquent behaviors.

gateway drug: A substance that leads to use of more serious drugs; alcohol use has long been thought to lead to more serious drug abuse.

gender-schema theory: A theory of development that holds that children internalize gender scripts that reflect the gender-related social practices of the culture. Once internalized, these gender scripts predispose the kids to construct a self-identity that is consistent with them.

general deterrence: Crime control policies that depend on the fear of criminal penalties, such as long prison sentences for violent crimes; the aim is to convince law violators that the pain outweighs the benefit of criminal activity.

general strain theory: Links delinquency to the strain of being locked out of the economic mainstream, which creates the anger and frustration that lead to delinquent acts.

general theory of crime (GTC): A developmental theory that modifies social control theory by integrating concepts from biosocial, psychological, routine activities, and rational choice theories.

gentrified: The process of transforming a lower-class area into a middle-class enclave through property rehabilitation.

graffiti: Inscriptions or drawings made on a wall or structure and used by delinquents for gang messages and turf definition.

group homes: Nonsecured, structured residences that provide counseling, education, job training, and family living.

group therapy: Counseling several individuals together in a group session.

guardian *ad litem:* A court-appointed attorney who protects the interests of the child in cases involving the child's welfare.

guided group interaction (GGI): Through group interactions a delinquent can acknowledge and solve personal problems with support from other group members.

hallucinogens: Natural or synthetic substances that produce vivid distortions of the senses without greatly disturbing consciousness.

harm reduction: Efforts to minimize the harmful effects caused by drug use.

hashish: A concentrated form of cannabis made from unadulterated resin from the female cannabis plant.

hearsay: Out-of-court statements made by one person and recounted in court by another; such statements are generally not allowed as evidence except in child abuse cases wherein a child's statements to social workers, teachers, or police may be admissible.

heroin: A narcotic made from opium and then cut with sugar or some other neutral substance until it is only 1 to 4 percent pure.

hot spot: A particular location or address that is the site of repeated and frequent criminal activity.

house arrest: Offender is required to stay home during specific periods of time; monitoring is done by random phone calls and visits or by electronic devices.

House of Refuge: A care facility developed by the child savers to protect potential criminal youths by taking them off the street and providing a family-like environment.

identity crisis: Psychological state, identified by Erikson, in which youth face inner turmoil and uncertainty about life roles.

impulsive: Lacking in thought or deliberation in decision making. An impulsive person lacks close attention to details, has organizational problems, is distracted and forgetful.

in loco parentis: In the place of the parent; rights given to schools that allow them to assume parental duties in disciplining students.

indeterminate sentence: Does not specify the length of time the juvenile must be held; rather, correctional authorities decide when the juvenile is ready to return to society.

individual counseling: Counselors help juveniles understand and solve their current adjustment problems.

informant: A person who has access to criminal networks and shares information with authorities in exchange for money or special treatment under conditions of anonymity.

inhalants: Volatile liquids that give off a vapor, which is inhaled, producing short-term excitement and euphoria followed by a period of disorientation.

intake: Process during which a juvenile referral is received and a decision made to file a petition in juvenile court to release the juvenile, to place the juvenile under supervision, or to refer the juvenile elsewhere.

Intensive Aftercare Program (IAP): A balanced, highly structured, comprehensive continuum of intervention for serious and violent juvenile offenders returning to the community.

interactional theory: A developmental theory that attributes delinquent trajectories to mutual reinforcement between delinquents and significant others over the life course—family in early adolescence, school and friends in mid-adolescence, and social peers and one's own nuclear family in adulthood.

interstitial group: Delinquent group that fills a crack in the social fabric and maintains standard group practices.

intra-family violence: An environment of discord and conflict within the family; children who grow up in dysfunctional homes often exhibit delinquent behaviors, having learned at a young age that aggression pays off.

juvenile court judge: A judge elected or appointed to preside over juvenile cases whose decisions can only be reviewed by a judge of a higher court.

juvenile defense attorneys: Represent children in juvenile court and play an active role at all stages of the proceedings.

juvenile delinquency: Participation in illegal behavior by a minor who falls under a statutory age limit.

juvenile intensive probation supervision (JIPS): A true alternative to incarceration that involves almost daily supervision of the juvenile by the probation officer assigned to the case.

juvenile justice process: Under the *parens patriae* philosophy, juvenile justice procedures are informal and nonadversarial, invoked for juvenile offenders rather than against them; a petition instead of a complaint is filed; courts make findings of involvement or adjudication of delinquency instead of convictions; and juvenile offenders receive dispositions instead of sentences.

juvenile justice system: The segment of the justice system including law enforcement officers, the courts, and correctional agencies that is designed to treat youthful offenders.

juvenile officers: Police officers who specialize in dealing with juvenile offenders; they may operate alone or as part of a juvenile police unit in the department.

juvenile probation officer: Officer of the court involved in all four stages of the court process—intake, predisposition, postadjudication, and postdisposition—who assists the court and supervises juveniles placed on probation.

juvenile prosecutor: Government attorney responsible for representing the interests of the state and bringing the case against the accused juvenile.

klikas: Subgroups of same-aged youths in Hispanic gangs that remain together and have separate names and a unique identity in the gang.

labeling theory: Posits that society creates deviance through a system of social control agencies that designate (or label) certain individuals as delinquent, thereby stigmatizing them and encouraging them to accept this negative personal identity.

latent trait: A stable feature, characteristic, property, or condition, such as defective intelligence or impulsive personality, that makes some people delinquency-prone over the life course.

latent trait theory: The view that delinquent behavior is controlled by a "master trait," present at birth or soon after, that remains stable and unchanging throughout a person's lifetime.

Law Enforcement Assistance Administration (LEAA): Unit in the U.S. Department of Justice established by the Omnibus Crime Control and Safe Streets Act of 1968 to administer grants and provide guidance for crime prevention policy and programs.

learning disabilities (LD): Neurological dysfunctions that prevent an individual from learning to his or her potential.

least detrimental alternative: A program that will best foster a child's growth and development.

least restrictive alternative: A program with the least restrictive or secure setting that will benefit the child.

legalization of drugs: Decriminalizing drug use to reduce the association between drug use and crime.

liberal feminism: Asserts that females are less delinquent than males because their social roles provide them with fewer opportunities to commit crimes; as the roles of girls and women become more similar to those of boys and men, so too will their crime patterns.

life course persister: One of the small group of offenders whose delinquent career continues well into adulthood.

life course theory: A developmental theory that focuses on changes in behavior as people travel along the path of life and how these changes affect crime and delinquency.

mandatory sentences: Sentences are defined by a statutory requirement that states the penalty to be set for all cases of a specific offense.

marijuana: The dried leaves of the cannabis plant.

masculinity hypothesis: View that women who commit crimes have biological and psychological traits similar to those of men.

meta-analysis: An analysis technique that synthesizes results across many programs over time.

milieu therapy: All aspects of the environment are part of the treatment, and meaningful change, increased growth, and satisfactory adjustment are encouraged.

minimal brain dysfunction (MBD): Damage to the brain itself that causes antisocial behavior injurious to the individual's lifestyle and social adjustment.

***Miranda* warning:** Supreme Court decisions require police officers to inform individuals under arrest of their constitutional rights; warnings must also be given when suspicion begins to focus on an individual in the accusatory stage.

monetary restitution: Offenders compensate crime victims for out-of-pocket losses caused by the crime, including property damage, lost wages, and medical expenses.

multisystemic treatment (MST): Addresses a variety of family, peer, and psychological problems.

nature theory: The view that intelligence is inherited and is a function of genetic makeup.

near-groups: Clusters of youth who, outwardly, seem unified but actually have limited cohesion, impermanence, minimal consensus of norms, shifting membership, disturbed leadership, and limited definitions of membership expectations.

need for treatment: The criteria on which juvenile sentencing is based. Ideally, juveniles are treated according to their need for treatment and not for the seriousness of the delinquent act they committed.

negative affective states: Anger, depression, disappointment, fear, and other adverse emotions that derive from strain.

neglect: Passive neglect by a parent or guardian, depriving children of food, shelter, health care, and love.

neuroticism: A personality trait marked by unfounded anxiety, tension, and emotional instability.

nuclear family: A family unit composed of parents and their children; this smaller family structure is subject to great stress due to the intense, close contact between parents and children.

nurture theory: The view that intelligence is determined by environmental stimulation and socialization.

Office of Juvenile Justice and Delinquency Prevention (OJJDP): Branch of the U.S. Justice Department charged with shaping national juvenile justice policy through disbursement of federal aid and research funds.

oppositional defiant disorder (ODD): A psychological condition with symptoms including an ongoing pattern of uncooperative, defiant, and hostile behavior toward authority figures that seriously interferes with day-to-day functioning.

orphan train: A practice of the Children's Aid Society in which urban youths were sent West for adoption with local farm couples.

overt pathway: Pathway to a delinquent career that begins with minor aggression, leads to physical fighting, and eventually escalates to violent delinquency.

parens patriae: The power of the state to act on behalf of the child and provide care and protection equivalent to that of a parent.

parental efficacy: Families in which parents are able to integrate their children into the household unit while at the same time helping assert their individuality and regulate their own behavior.

Part I offenses (also known as index crimes): Offenses including homicide and non-negligent manslaughter, forcible rape, robbery, aggravated assault, burglary, larceny, arson, and motor vehicle theft; recorded by local law enforcement officers, these crimes are tallied quarterly and sent to the FBI for inclusion in the UCR.

Part II offenses: All crimes other than Part I offenses; recorded by local law enforcement officers, arrests for these crimes are tallied quarterly and sent to the FBI for inclusion in the UCR.

passive speech: A form of expression protected by the First Amendment, but not associated with actually speaking words; examples include wearing symbols or protest messages on buttons or signs.

paternalistic family: A family style wherein the father is the final authority on all family matters and exercises complete control over his wife and children.

petition: Document filed in juvenile court alleging that a juvenile is a delinquent, a status offender, or a dependent and asking that the court assume jurisdiction over the juvenile.

plea bargaining: The exchange of prosecutorial and judicial concessions for a guilty plea by the accused; plea bargaining usually results in a reduced charge or a more lenient sentence.

pledge system: Early English system in which neighbors protected each other from thieves and warring groups.

Poor Laws: English statutes that allowed the courts to appoint overseers for destitute and neglected children, allowing placement of these children as servants in the homes of the affluent.

positive peer culture (PPC): Counseling program in which peer leaders encourage other group members to modify their behavior and peers help reinforce acceptable behaviors.

power-control theory: Holds that gender differences in the delinquency rate are a function of class differences and economic conditions that influence the structure of family life.

precocious sexuality: Sexual experimentation in early adolescence.

predatory crimes: Violent crimes against persons and crimes in which an offender attempts to steal an object directly from its holder.

prestige crimes: Stealing or assaulting someone to gain prestige in the neighborhood; often part of gang initiation rites.

pretrial conference: The attorney for the social services agency presents an overview of the case, and a plea bargain or negotiated settlement can be agreed to in a consent decree.

preventive detention: Keeping the accused in custody prior to trial because the accused is suspected of being a danger to the community.

probable cause: Reasonable ground to believe the existence of facts that an offense was committed and that the accused committed that offense.

probation: Nonpunitive, legal disposition of juveniles emphasizing community treatment in which the juvenile is closely supervised by an officer of the court and must adhere to a strict set of rules to avoid incarceration.

problem behavior syndrome (PBS): A cluster of antisocial behaviors that may include family dysfunction, substance abuse, smoking, precocious sexuality and early pregnancy, educational underachievement, suicide attempts, sensation seeking, and unemployment, as well as delinquency.

problem-oriented policing: Law enforcement that focuses on addressing the problems underlying incidents of juvenile delinquency rather than the incidents alone.

procedural justice: An evaluation of the fairness of the manner in which an offender's or another group's problem or dispute was handled by police.

pseudomaturity: Characteristic of life course persisters, who tend to engage in early sexuality and drug use.

psychodynamic theory: Branch of psychology that holds that the human personality is controlled by unconscious mental processes developed early in childhood.

psychopathic personality (also known as sociopathic or antisocial personality): A person lacking in warmth, exhibiting inappropriate behavior responses, and unable to learn from experience; the condition is defined by persistent violations of social norms, including lying, stealing, truancy, inconsistent work behavior, and traffic arrests.

psychotherapy: Highly structured counseling in which a therapist helps a juvenile solve conflicts and make a more positive adjustment to society.

public defender: An attorney who works in a public agency or under private contractual agreement as defense counsel to indigent defendants.

reality therapy: A form of counseling that emphasizes current behavior and requires the individual to accept responsibility for all of his or her actions.

reentry: The process and experience of returning to society upon release from a custody facility post-adjudication.

reform schools: Institutions in which educational and psychological services are used in an effort to improve the conduct of juveniles who are forcibly detained.

relative deprivation: Condition that exists when people of wealth and poverty live in close proximity to one another; the relatively deprived are apt to have feelings of anger and hostility, which may produce criminal behavior.

representing: Tossing or flashing gang signs in the presence of rivals, often escalating into a verbal or physical confrontation.

residential programs: Residential, nonsecure facilities such as a group home, foster home, family group home, or rural home where the juvenile can be closely monitored and develop close relationships with staff members.

resource dilution: A condition that occurs when parents have such large families that their resources, such as time and money, are spread too thin, causing lack of familial support and control.

restorative justice: Non-punitive strategies for dealing with juvenile offenders that make the justice system a healing process rather than a punishment process.

review hearings: Periodic meetings to determine whether the conditions of the case plan for an abused child are being met by the parents or guardians of the child.

right to treatment: Philosophy espoused by many courts that juvenile offenders have a statutory right to treatment while under the jurisdiction of the courts.

role conflicts: Conflicts police officers face that revolve around the requirement to perform their primary duty of law enforcement and a desire to aid in rehabilitating youthful offenders.

role diffusion: According to Erik Erikson, role diffusion occurs when youths spread themselves too thin, experience personal uncertainty, and place themselves at the mercy of leaders who promise to give them a sense of identity they cannot develop for themselves.

routine activities theory: The view that crime is a "normal" function of the routine activities of modern living; offenses can be expected if there is a motivated offender and a suitable target that is not protected by capable guardians.

rural programs: Specific recreational and work opportunities provided for juveniles in a rural setting such as a forestry camp, a farm, or a ranch.

school failure: Failing to achieve success in school can result in frustration, anger, and reduced self-esteem, which may contribute to delinquent behavior.

search and seizure: The U.S. Constitution protects citizens from any search and seizure by police without a lawfully obtained search warrant; such warrants are issued when there is probable cause to believe that an offense has been committed.

sedatives: Drugs of the barbiturate family that depress the central nervous system into a sleeplike condition.

self-control: Refers to a person's ability to exercise restraint and control over his or her feelings, emotions, reactions, and behaviors.

self-fulfilling prophecy: Deviant behavior patterns that are a response to an earlier labeling experience; youths act out these social roles even if they were falsely bestowed.

self-labeling: The process by which a person who has been negatively labeled accepts the label as a personal role or identity.

self-reports: Questionnaire or survey technique that asks subjects to reveal their own participation in delinquent or criminal acts.

shelter care: A place for temporary care of children in physically unrestricting facilities.

situational crime prevention: A crime prevention method that relies on reducing the opportunity to commit criminal acts by making them more difficult to perform, reducing their reward, and increasing their risks.

skinhead: Member of European American supremacist gang, identified by a shaved skull and Nazi or Ku Klux Klan markings.

social bond: Ties a person to the institutions and processes of society; elements of the bond include attachment, commitment, involvement, and belief.

social capital: Positive relations with individuals and institutions, as in a successful marriage or a successful career, that support conventional behavior and inhibit deviant behavior.

social control: Ability of social institutions to influence human behavior; the justice system is the primary agency of formal social control.

social control theories: Posit that delinquency results from a weakened commitment to the major social institutions (family, peers, and school); lack of such commitment allows youths to exercise antisocial behavioral choices.

social development model (SDM): A developmental theory that attributes delinquent behavior patterns to childhood socialization and pro- or antisocial attachments over the life course.

social disorganization: Neighborhood or area marked by culture conflict, lack of cohesiveness, a transient population, and insufficient social organizations; these problems are reflected in the problems at schools in these areas.

social investigation report (also known as predisposition report): Developed by the juvenile probation officer, this report includes clinical diagnosis of the juvenile and the need for court assistance, relevant environmental and personality factors, and other information to assist the court in developing a treatment plan.

social learning theories: Posit that delinquency is learned through close relationships with others, assert that children are born "good" and learn to be "bad" from others.

social learning theory: The view that behavior is modeled through observation either directly through intimate contact with others or indirectly through media; interactions that are rewarded are copied, whereas those that are punished are avoided.

social structure theories: Those theories that suggest that social and economic forces operating in deteriorated lower-class areas, including disorganization, stress, and cultural deviance, push residents into criminal behavior patterns.

socialization: The process of learning the values and norms of the society or the subculture to which the individual belongs.

Society for the Prevention of Cruelty to Children (SPCC): First established in 1874, these organizations protected children subjected to cruelty and neglect at home or at school.

specific deterrence: Sending convicted offenders to secure incarceration facilities so that punishment is severe enough to convince them not to repeat their criminal activity.

status offense: Conduct that is illegal only because the child is under age.

stigmatized: People who have been negatively labeled because of their participation, or alleged participation, in deviant or outlawed behaviors.

stimulants: Synthetic substances that produce an intense physical reaction by stimulating the central nervous system.

strain: A condition caused by the failure to achieve one's social goals.

substance abuse: Using drugs or alcohol in such a way as to cause physical harm to oneself.

suppression effect: A reduction of the number of arrests per year for youths who have been incarcerated or otherwise punished.

systematic review: A type of review that uses rigorous methods for locating, appraising, and synthesizing evidence from prior evaluation studies.

teen courts: Courts that make use of peer juries to decide nonserious delinquency cases.

tracking: Dividing students into groups according to their ability and achievement levels.

trait theory: Holds that youths engage in delinquent or criminal behavior due to aberrant physical or psychological traits that govern behavioral choices; delinquent actions are impulsive or instinctual rather than rational choices.

tranquilizers: Drugs that reduce anxiety and promote relaxation.

transfer process: Transferring a juvenile offender from the jurisdiction of juvenile court to adult criminal court.

transitional neighborhood: Area undergoing a shift in population and structure, usually from middle-class residential to lower-class mixed use.

truant: Being out of school without permission.

truly disadvantaged: According to William Julius Wilson, those people who are left out of the economic mainstream and reduced to living in the most deteriorated inner-city areas.

turning points: Critical life events, such as career and marriage, that may enable adult offenders to desist from delinquency.

underachievers: Those who fail to meet expected levels of school achievement.

underclass: Group of urban poor whose members have little chance of upward mobility or improvement.

Uniform Crime Report (UCR): Compiled by the FBI, the UCR is the most widely used source of national crime and delinquency statistics.

utilitarian: A person who believes that people weigh the benefits and consequences of their future actions before deciding on a course of behavior.

victim service restitution: Offenders provide some service directly to the crime victim.

victimization: A person who has suffered direct, or threatened, physical, emotional, or financial harm as a result of being the target of a criminal act.

waiver (also known as bind over or removal): Transferring legal jurisdiction over the most serious and experienced juvenile offenders to the adult court for criminal prosecution.

watch system: Replaced the pledge system in England; watchmen patrolled urban areas at night to provide protection from harm.

wayward minors: Early legal designation of youths who violate the law because of their minority status; now referred to as status offenders.

widening the net: Phenomenon that occurs when programs created to divert youths from the justice system actually involve them more deeply in the official process.

wilderness probation: Programs involving outdoor expeditions that provide opportunities for juveniles to confront the difficulties of their lives while achieving positive personal satisfaction.

writ of habeus corpus: Judicial order requesting that a person detaining another produce the body of the prisoner and give reasons for his or her capture and detention.

zero tolerance policy: Mandating specific consequences or punishments for delinquent acts and not allowing anyone to avoid these consequences.

Name Index

Myers, David, 402n60
Myers, Jane, 387nn115, 116
Myers, Kristen, 393n18
Myers, Stephanie, 294, 400nn44, 49

N

Nagin, Daniel, 375nn36, 37, 39, 382nn14, 18, 25, 383nn52, 70
Najaka, Stacy, 397n111
Najman, Jake, 389n89
Nalla, Mahesh, 380n76
Nanjundappa, G., 395n50
Napier, Susan, 390n128
Nas, Coralijn, 378n169
Nation, Maury, 219, 391n14
Neaigus, Alan, 395n7
Neal, Stephen, 386n57
Needle, Jerome, 393n145
Needleman, Herbert, 376n85
Neff, James Alan, 397n114
Nelson, Gordon, 387n9
Ness, Arlin, 406n101
Ness, Robert, 376n85
Neumark-Sztainer, Dianne, 219
New, Michelle, 390n158
Newcomb, Michael, 382n20
Newman, Graeme, 372n52, 378n176, 396n96
Ngo, Jennifer, 143
Nicewander, W. Alan, 117, 383n54
Nickoletti, Patrick, 371n24
Niederhoffer, Arthur, 198, 392nn115, 116
Niemelä, Solja, 387n19
Nieuwbeerta, Paul, 374n13
Nilsson, L-L., 377n152
Noblin, Charles, 402n63
Nocera, Joe, 395n22
Nofziger, Stacey, 379n4
Noone, Diana, 395n34
Nores, Milagros, 384n13
Noriega, Manuel, 247
Novak, Kenneth, 375n63
Novak, Scott, 250
Nurge, Dana, 302
Nuutila, Art-Matti, 387n19
Nye, F. Ivan, 156, 159, 372nn14, 21, 373nn47, 48, 388nn37, 65

O

Oakes, Jeannie, 393n33
Obradovic, Jelena, 384n83
O'Brien, Robert, 25, 375n34
O'Connor, Sandra Day, 172
Odem, Mary, 398n22
O'Donnell, Julie, 393n15
O'Donovan, Michael, 376n110
Offord, David, 398n32
Ohlin, Lloyd, 199, 380n73, 390nn129, 130, 395n44, 398n17
Oken, Emily, 376n84
Olds, David, 384nn2, 3
Olsen, Virgil, 373n48
Olson, Jeffrey, 398nn24, 28
Olweus, Dan, 218, 219
O'Malley, Patrick, 236, 371n22, 372n15, 373n26, 374n119, 386n89, 394n1, 395nn8, 16, 24–26
Onek, David, 403n89
Opler, Mark, 376n85
Orbuch, Terri, 383nn39, 47

Orlandi, Mario, 397nn10, 11, 116, 117
Orlebeke, Jacob, 376n94
Orme, Nicholas, 9, 371n34
Ormrod, Richard, 133, 385n5
Orobio de Castro, Bram, 378n169
Osborn, Denise, 375n30
Osborne, Lynn, 263, 398n13
Osgood, D. Wayne, 117, 374nn19, 68, 379n29, 383n54, 386nn58, 89, 396n84, 401nn79–81
Ostresh, Erik, 381n97
Ostrow, Miriam, 397nn121, 123
O'Sullivan, Ryan, 235
Ouimette, Paige Crosby, 377n141
Ousey, Graham, 379nn33, 34
Owen, Barbara, 405n87
Owen, Michael, 376n110

P

Paasch, Kathleen, 393n11
Packer, Herbert, 400n43
Padilla, Felix, 200, 391n45, 392n136
Pahlke, E., 211
Pajer, Kathleen, 386n57, 386n69
Pallone, Nathaniel, 388n64
Palmer, James, 399n39
Palmer, Julie, 379n3
Pan, En-Ling, 387n34
Papillo, Angela Romano, 381n102
Paradis, Emily, 389n111
Paramore, Vickie, 147, 387n113
Pardini, Dustin, 384n83
Parent, Dale, 402n59, 406n114
Parker, Aaliyah, 2
Parker, Karen, 373n31, 379nn31, 37, 380n47
Parks, Roger, 401n94
Parramore, Constance, 302, 406n8
Parsons, Thomas, 385nn15, 17
Partelow, L., 211
Paschall, Mallie, 373n38
Patchin, Justin, 379n5
Paternoster, Raymond, 295, 374n22, 375n48, 381nn91, 116, 383nn46, 52, 400n55
Paterson, Andrea, 405n58
Patterson, Charlotte, 388n55
Patterson, Gerald, 379n19, 382n29, 384n7, 388n57
Paulozzi, Len, 394n45
Paulson, Amanda, 318
Payne, Allison, 394nn39, 66
Payne, Gary, 380nn67, 69
Payne, Monique, 379n44
Peake, Philip, 377n155
Pear, Robert, 405n59
Pearson, Sarah, 281
Peel, Robert, 285, 286
Pelham, Molina, Jr., 63
Peng, Samuel, 394nn54, 55
Penn, Joseph, 275
Pennucci, Annie, 384n4, 399n42, 405n95
Pepi, Carol, 387n114
Pepler, D. J., 385n20
Peralta, Robert, 396n84
Perel, James, 386n57
Perez, Cynthia, 382nn1, 24, 28
Perkins, Craig, 374n86
Perlmutter, M., 377n162
Perrone, Paul, 390n2
Perry, Cheryl, 219

Perry, David, 377n156
Perry, Louise, 377n156
Perry, T. B., 390n6
Persons, W. S., 375n75
Perusse, Daniel, 377n121
Petechuk, David, 41
Petersilia, Joan, 360, 399nn8, 48, 404nn22, 39, 406nn10, 109, 130
Peterson, Dana, 401nn79, 81
Peterson, David, 381n102
Peterson, Eric, 47
Peterson, Ruth, 379n28, 380n55
Petraitis, John, 374n9
Petras, Hanno, 382nn11
Petrosino, Anthony, 250
Pettit, Gregory, 380n57, 388nn69, 71
Phelps, Charles, 384n3
Phillips, Julie, 372n6, 373nn40, 42, 43
Phillips, M., 402n44
Pi, Chung-Ron, 399n72
Piaget, Jean, 377n158
Piaget, Jen, 71
Pickering, Lloyd, 380n84, 383n71, 393n1
Pickett, Robert, 398n8
Pickrel, Susan, 397n120
Piehl, Anne Morrison, 302, 406n6
Pierce, Christine Schnyder, 401nn7, 8
Pierce, Glenn, 392n89
Piersma, Paul, 403n111
Piha, Jorma, 387n19
Pihl, Robert, 389n85
Piliavin, Irving, 400nn46, 58
Piquero, Alex, 375n55, 377nn140, 163, 380nn69, 70, 382nn8, 17, 383nn63, 72, 384nn87–89, 386n71
Platt, Anthony, 100, 263, 371n44, 372n58, 381n124, 398nn5, 6, 12, 403n93
Platt, Christina, 396n59
Platt, Jerome, 396n59
Pleck, Elizabeth, 371nn46, 47, 372nn49, 51, 398nn17, 18
Ploeger, Matthew, 374n23, 385n21
Plomin, Robert, 378n180
Podboy, J. W., 376n101
Podolski, Cheryl-Lynn, 73
Poe-Yamagata, Eileen, 403n76
Pogarsky, Greg, 54, 375nn36, 37, 39, 48, 55, 383n70
Polk, Kenneth, 393nn4, 27, 30
Pollock, Carl, 389n119
Polsenberg, Christina, 385n44
Pomeroy, Elizabeth, 397n114
Poole, R., 404n9
Pope, Carl, 373n44, 385n44
Porterfield, A. L., 372n9
Potter, Lloyd, 394n45
Pottieger, Anne, 395n46, 396nn68, 69, 73
Poulin, François, 406n100
Powell, R. T., 403n86
Powlen, Dave, 55
Pranis, Kay, 381n132
Pratt, Travis, 378n166, 383n72, 384n92
Pratts, Michael, Jr., 392n114
Price, Dwight, 310, 402n19
Prinz, Ronald, 382n12
Prosser, Vicki, 402n63
Proulx, Jean, 382n10
Pruitt, B. E., 378nn174, 177
Prysock, Randall, 292–293

Subject Index

CODAC Family Health Promotion (FHP) program, 129–30
"code of the streets," 92
cognitive behavioral treatment, 344
cognitive theory, 67, 71–73, 76, 77, 79
cohort studies, 173–74
collateral review, 332
collective efficacy, 89, 123
Colombian drug cartels, 247–48
Colorado IAP, 365
Columbia University's Center for the Promotion of Mental Health in Juvenile Justice, 353
Columbine High School tragedy, 57–58, 277
Commonwealth Fund, 133
Communities That Care (CTC), 257
community
    community cohesion, 88–89
    gangs and the, 189
    high-intensity community supervision, 314
    influence on chronic offending, 41
    neighborhood deterioration, 83, 86–89, 94, 105, 185
    routine activities theory, 51
    school crime, 220, 222
    social capital and change in, 116, 118, 119
    socialization influenced by, 86, 93–94
community-based treatment programs
    aftercare and reentry, 343, 364, 365
    community policing, 287, 288, 294, 298, 300–301
    Community Resources Against Street Hoodlums (CRASH), 204
    community service, 328
    comprehensive, 257, 314
    DDAP case-management model, 315
    drug control strategies, 251
    gangs and, 183, 203–4
    overview on, 336–38, 341, 369
    prevention programs, 95, 102, 257
    restitution, 104–5, 345, 346, 348
    See also probation
Community Outreach Through Police in Schools Program, 300
community release. See probation
Community Resources Against Street Hoodlums (CRASH), 204
community treatment. See community-based treatment programs
competency to withstand trial, 323
complaint, 318
Comprehensive Employment Training Act of 1973, 103
Comprehensive Residential Education, Arts, and Substance Abuse Treatment (CREASAT) programs, 252
concentric zones, 86
concurrent jurisdiction, 320
conduct disorder (CD), 62, 69, 112
confidentiality in juvenile proceedings, 333
consent decree, 316
conservation camps, 349–50
constitutionally masculinized, 139
contemporary trait theory, 59, 138–40, 148
continuing a case, 325
continuity of crime. See persistence
control. See prevention; social control; treatment and rehabilitation

controversial status youth, 179–80
COPS (Office of Community Oriented Policing Services), 300–301, 303
corporal punishment, 158–59, 164, 228
corrections. See community-based treatment programs; institutions/institutionalization; probation
correlates of delinquency
    age, 37–38
    gender, 32–34
    race, 24, 34–36
    social class and, 36–37
    time and place, 32
    See also personal traits/social characteristics
cottage system, 349
counseling
    aftercare and, 363
    by defense attorneys, 308
    group therapy, 251, 337, 340, 358
    intensive, 340
    treatment and, 2, 132, 251, 337, 357–58
county attorney, 309–11, 334
County Health Department Maternal Child Health (MCH) nurses, 128
court. See juvenile court
Court-Appointed Special Advocates (CASA), 308, 309, 311
court-ordered school attendance, 328
covert pathway to crime, 113–14, 120
Coy v. Iowa, 172
CPS (Child Protection Services), 164–65, 168
crack cocaine
    decline in use of, 6
    gangs and, 197, 245
    gateway drugs and, 242
    motivated offenders and, 52
    overview on, 232–33
    prediction on maturation of "crack babies," 27
    tie to violent delinquency rate, 25
crackdowns, 57
Craig, Maryland v., 172
CRASH (Community Resources Against Street Hoodlums), 204
CREASAT (Comprehensive Residential Education, Arts, and Substance Abuse Treatment) programs, 252
Creating the Dropout (Dorn), 212
Crime and Human Nature (Wilson, Herrnstein), 117
Crime in the Making (Sampson, Laub), 114
crime rate trends
    data sources, 22–23, 26–28, 31–32, 44
    drug use today, 236–38
    factors shaping, 24–25, 31
    gender and, 132–33, 136–37, 144
    gun ownership and, 25, 32, 44
    overview on, 23, 26, 27, 44
    race and, 34
    unreported crimes and, 28
    See also arrests
criminal atavism, 58
criminal court. See adult justice system
CRIPA (Civil Rights of Institutionalized Persons Act) of 1980, 362
Crips gang, 181, 183, 193, 194, 204
critical feminist views, 145–48
critical theories, 99–101, 104–5, 145–46, 343, 345

crowds, 179
cruel and unusual punishment, 331–32
"crystal"/"crystal meth," 234–35, 243
CSDD (Cambridge Study in Delinquent Development), 160
CTC (Communities That Care), 257
cultural deviance theory, 91–94, 101, 105
cultural transmission, 86, 87
cultural values, 32, 86, 91–93, 124, 136
cultural view. See social structure theories
culture of poverty, 85
curfews, 17, 18
custodial interrogation, 292–93

D

Daily Mail Publishing Co., Smith v., 333
D.A.R.E. (Drug Abuse Resistance Education), 249–50
"dark figures of crime," 29
data sources, 22–23, 26–28, 31–32, 44
    See also self-report surveys
date-rape drug (GHB), 248
David and Lucile Packard Foundation, 152
Davis v. Alaska, 333
day-center electronic monitoring, 314
DDAP (Detention Diversion Advocacy Program), 314, 315
death penalty, 331–32
decarceration, 342, 350
"decent values," 92
decision making, 49–50, 69, 77, 111, 164
Decisions to Actions, 77
defense attorney, 307–8, 322, 334
deinstitutionalization, 103, 276
"Deinstitutionalizing Status Offenders" (Holden, Kapler), 16
delinquency, concept of, 12–14
delinquency, study of, 6–8, 18
delinquency control squads, 286
Delinquency in a Birth Cohort (Wolfgang, Figlio, Sellin), 39, 214
delinquency in schools
    bullying, 218–20
    causes of, 220
    reducing, 221–22
    school shootings, 57–58, 217–19
    surveys on, 216–17
Delinquency Prevention Act of 1974, 268
delinquent act and the offender, 118–20
Denver IAP program, 365
Department of Social Services, Lassiter v., 167
depression
    antisocial behavior, 69
    child abuse, 163, 164
    inadequate diet, 60
    school failure, 215
    substance abuse, 233, 238
    violent youths, 68, 219
Des Moines Independent Community School District, Tinker v., 225
designer drugs, 235, 248
desistance from crime, 37–38, 43, 117–19, 123
detached street workers, 203
detention, 270, 311–15, 319, 324
Detention Diversion Advocacy Program (DDAP), 314, 315
determinate sentence, 330

socialization (continued)
  general theory of crime and, 122, 124
  peers and, 179
  schools and, 209, 215, 228
  twin studies and, 65
  See also social process theories
society, critical theory on, 99–100
Society for the Prevention of Cruelty to
  Children (SPCC), 264–65
Society for the Prevention of Pauperism, 261
sociobiology, 59
sociocultural view of gangs, 199, 201
socioeconomic factors
  and choice theory, 48–49, 57, 79
  and chronic offending, 41
  developmental view and, 124
  disparity between rich and poor, 84, 100
  drug use and, 239, 241
  family stress and, 153
  gangs and, 184, 187–89, 204–5
  influencing crime rate trends, 24, 27, 32,
    35–36, 44
  law enforcement organizational bias, 297
  life transition disruptions and, 109
  and social structure theories, 86
  trait theory and, 76–77
  unemployment, 24, 36, 85, 87–88, 112,
    204–5
  See also poverty
sociological views
  critical theory, 99–101, 104–5, 145–46
  delinquency prevention, 101–5
  overview on, 83
  social factors, 83–85
  See also social process theories; social struc-
    ture theories
sociopathic personality, 74–75, 241
source control, drug, 247–49
Southwest Texas gangs, 188–89
Southwestern Pennsylvania Costs of Services
  in Medicaid Study, 130
SPCC (Society for the Prevention of Cruelty
  to Children), 264–65
specific deterrence, 54–55, 57, 79
Spectrum Wilderness Program, 360
spontaneous remission, 37–38, 43, 117,
  118–19, 123
standard of proof, 325
Stanford v. Kentucky, 331
state attorney, 309–11, 334
state comparison of juvenile custody rates, 351
state laws
  child abuse cases, 168–71, 175
  conditions of probation, 340–41
  on disposition, 327–28, 330–31
  increasing social control, 18–19
  status offenses, 14
  waiver, 12–13, 269, 275, 278, 320–21, 330
state training schools, 272
statistics. See data sources
status, 136, 189, 209
status offenders
  aiding, 16
  characterization of, 14–15, 268
  deinstitutionalization of, 314, 350
  detention of, 312–14, 319, 356
  diversion of, 317
  divorce and, 155
  gender and, 140, 147, 355

history of incarceration, 262, 263, 267
  and the juvenile justice system, 15–17, 19
  neurosis and, 68
  probation as disposition, 340
  reforming laws, 16–18
statutory exception, 333
statutory exclusion policies, 320
statutory limit, 12–13, 269, 275, 278, 320–21,
  330
steroids, 235
stigmatization
  and family deviance, 161
  prevention programs and, 258
  reducing, 12, 13, 103, 327
  as reinforcing delinquency, 105
  residential treatment programs, 252
  social reaction theories and, 98–99
  status offense categories and, 15, 19
  treatment and, 78, 252
stimulants, 234–35
strain theory, 89–91, 94, 101, 105
"street family," 120
street values, 92
stress
  drug use and, 240
  in families, 152, 153, 156, 161
  maltreated children and, 164, 166, 167
  and mental illness, 70
  strain and, 91
structural view. See social structure theories
substance abuse
  addiction-prone personality, 241
  ADHD and, 63
  antisocial personality and, 75
  child abuse link, 163, 166
  defined, 231
  early puberty in females and, 139
  and family deviance, 161
  by gang members, 197
  Intensive Aftercare Program and, 365
  learning disabilities and, 62, 63
  linked rap music, 3
  prevalence of, 231
  primary prevention programs, 129
  and problem behavior syndrome, 112
  runaways and, 2
  school violence and, 220
  status offender, 17
  treatment, 251–52
  trend of rejecting hard drugs, 6
  See also alcohol abuse; cigarette smoking;
    drug abuse
suicidal behavior
  amongst monozygotic twin pairs, 65
  at-risk youths and, 3
  child abuse and, 163, 164
  and problem behavior syndrome, 112
  school shooting and, 217–19
  statistics on, 7
  status offender high rate of, 17
suitable targets, 51–52
supervision, 159–60, 363–64
suppression effect, 338
Supreme Court. See U.S. Supreme Court
surrogate court, 306
susceptibility rationale, 63
suspending judgment, 327
Swedish bullying intervention program, 218–19
Synar Amendment of 1992, 235–36

"Take Charge of Your Life" (prevention
  program), 250
target-hardening techniques, 56
targeting drug dealers, 249
teachers
  at-risk students and, 111
  as crime victims, 217
  prevention programs involving, 125
  routine activities theory and, 51
  socialization influenced by, 93–94, 96
  use of corporal punishment, 228
teen courts, 260, 277, 279–81, 369
teen pregnancy
  birthrates, 6
  dropping out, 212
  female gang members and, 191
  and the Prenatal/Early Infancy Project, 128
  and problem behavior syndrome, 112
  substance abuse during, 63, 111
  unwed mothers, 152
television, and teen violence, 2–3, 25, 70–71
territory, and gangs, 186–88, 190–91, 195,
  197
tertiary prevention efforts, 127, 368–69
testosterone, 61, 139
theft, 23, 33, 110, 113, 114, 133
Thompson v. Oklahoma, 331
thrill seeking. See risk taking
timeline of juvenile justice ideology, 273
Tinker v. Des Moines Independent Community
  School District, 225
Title III of the JJDPA, 16
T.L.O., New Jersey v., 224
totality of the circumstances doctrine, 292
tracking, academic, 216
Trafficking Victims Protection Act of 2003, 143
trait theory
  contemporary trait theory, 59, 138–40, 148
  embraced by conservatives, 78
  evaluating, 76–77
  gender and, 138–40, 148
  and latent trait view, 117–18
  maltreatment and delinquency, 173
  origins of, 58–59
  overview on, 47–48, 58, 79
  and prevention, 77–78
  primary prevention programs, 129
  See also biosocial theory; psychological
    theory
tranquilizers, 234
transfer. See waiver
transitional neighborhoods, 86, 87
treatment and rehabilitation
  versus adult "punishment," 13, 277
  aftercare and reentry, 362–66
  boot camps, 360
  child abuse and family, 168
  of chronic juvenile offenders, 42
  cognitive, 72–73, 344
  counseling, 2, 132, 251, 337, 357–58
  delinquent females and, 355–56
  as disposition, 328
  diversion and, 316–17
  drug control strategies, 2, 251–52
  educational/vocational/recreational
    programs, 341, 358–59
  "get tough" policies and, 7–8, 19
  group treatment techniques, 358

increasing social control, 18–19
and the juvenile justice system, 267,
271–72
legal responsibility of youth and, 13–14
legal right to, 360–62, 366
prevention and, 77–78, 127, 369
public support of, 7
resulting in stigmatization, 78
shift away from, 52
of status offenders, 15–17
two major categories of, 337–38
wilderness programs, 359–60
wrap-around approach, 151
See also community-based treatment programs; institutions/institutionalization;
probation; restitution/restorative justice
trial, 13, 270, 271, 313, 325–30, 333
Troxel v. Granville, 167
truancy, 75, 110, 113, 140, 212, 328
truly disadvantaged, 85
"turf violations," gang, 186–88, 197
Turman, Morales v., 361
turning points, 114–15
TV, and teen violence, 2–3, 25, 70–71
twin studies, 65, 241

U

UCLA's Comprehensive Residential Education,
Arts, and Substance Abuse Treatment
(CREASAT) programs, 252
UCR (Uniform Crime Report), 22–23, 28,
31–32
Unadjusted Girl, The (Thomas), 140
underachievers, 213
underclass, 85, 93, 185, 200
unemployment, 24, 36, 85, 87–88, 112, 204–5
Uniform Crime Report (UCR), 22–23, 28,
31–32
United States, Kent v., 321–23
United States attorney, 309–11, 334
University of Michigan's Institute for Social
Research (ISR), 30, 137
"unruly child." *See* status offender
urban-rural delinquency rates, 83
urbanization, 280, 291
U.S. Census Bureau, 42–44, 47
U.S. Children's Bureau, 267, 350
U.S. Constitution
Eighth Amendment, 228, 314, 331, 361
Fifth Amendment, 269, 291, 318, 321–23,
326
First Amendment, 225–27, 333
Fourteenth Amendment, 228, 318, 323, 326,
329, 361
Fourth Amendment, 224–25, 269, 291, 303
Sixth Amendment, 325
U.S. Department of Education, 6, 209, 250
U.S. Department of Health and Human
Services, 164, 165, 168
U.S. Department of Justice, 42–44, 235, 245,
353
See also OJJDP
U.S. Department of Labor, Job Corps, 256–57,
274
U.S. Food and Drug Administration, 232, 236,
248
U.S. Secret Service, school shooting profile,
218–19
U.S. Supreme Court

child abuse and protection cases, 167,
171–72, 175
on the death penalty, 8, 331–32, 334
on detention, 315, 318
due process rights, 326–27, 329, 334
fairness in waiver process, 321–23
on juvenile justice system, 266–68, 280
on police operations, 286, 291–93
on privacy, 333
right to treatment cases, 361
school search and seizure practices, 224,
226–27
utilitarian philosophy, 48

V

values
cultural, 32, 86, 91–93, 124, 136
socialization and, 94, 96, 97
vandalism, 55, 57, 58
Vernonia School District 47J v. Acton, 224, 227
vicarious liability, 19
victim service restitution, 346
victimless crimes, 28
Victims of Child Abuse Act of 1990, The, 171
victims/victimization
African Americans, 42, 297
at-risk youths and, 3, 41
data sources, 42
detention and, 314, 324
female, 145, 147
high cost of, 42
NCVS (National Crime Victimization
Survey), 42–44
prevention and treatment, 302
restitution made to, 104, 328, 345, 346
school bullying/violence, 218, 220
and self-control, 122
sentencing and, 7–8
strain and, 91
substandard living conditions and, 5
and their criminals, 43
views of police and, 287
video games, violent and sexually explicit, 8, 25
videotaped testimony, 171, 172
Vietnamese gangs, 195–96
violence/violent acts
by abused/neglected children, 70, 141, 164, 174
crime rate trends, 23, 31
detention centers and, 312
environmental factors and, 5, 32, 83
gangs, 187–89, 191, 196–98
gender and, 32, 33, 137, 139, 140
intra-family, 47, 156
limitations of choice theory and, 58
in the media, 2–3, 70–73 76
mental "scripts" and, 71–72
neurological dysfunction and, 61
overt pathway to crime and, 113, 114
police and, 289–90
poverty and, 87
prevention programs, 257
and problem behavior syndrome, 112
race and, 36
schools and, 216–17, 223
and self reports, 31
social learning theory and, 70
statistics on juvenile, 7
substance abuse and, 233–34, 245
victimization surveys, 43

"violence begetting violence" cycle, 158–59
and waiver to adult court, 14, 321, 324
See also aggression
*Violent Crime Control and Law Enforcement Act
of 1994*, 268
Violent Schools–Safe Schools (study), 216
Virginia IAP, 365
vocational treatment programs, 341, 358–59
Volunteer Court-Appointed Special Advocates
(CASA), 308, 309, 311

W

Wade, Roe v., 24
Wah Ching, Chinese gang, 195
waiver (transfer)
future of juvenile justice and, 277–79
"get-tough" policies and, 278, 321
and the juvenile justice process, 14, 270–71,
310, 320–25
plea bargaining and, 320
pros and cons of, 53, 334
statistics on, 320, 321, 324, 352
statutory limit and, 12–13, 269, 275, 278,
320–21
War on Drugs, 252
warrantless search, 291, 292
watch system, 285
wayward minors, 15
wealth distribution, 84, 100
weapons
gang members use of, 194, 197
influencing crime rate trends, 25, 32, 44
in schools, 217–19
statistics on carrying, 7
vicarious liability and, 19
Youth Firearms Violence Initiative (YFVI),
300–301
weather, and crime trends, 32
Wellesley v. Wellesley, 10
West Coast gang graffiti, 192
White v. Illinois, 172
widening the net, 317
wilderness probation, 359–60
Wilkins v. Missouri, 331
work. *See* employment
working poor, 92
wrap-around approach, 151
Wright, Ingraham v., 228
writ of habeas corpus, 332

Y

YFVI (Youth Firearms Violence Initiative),
300–301
YINS (youth in need of supervision), 15
youth. *See* children/childhood
Youth Challenge, 96
youth courts, 260, 277, 279–81, 369
Youth Development and Delinquency
Prevention Administration, 268
Youth Firearms Violence Initiative (YFVI),
300–301
youth in need of supervision (YINS), 15
youth services programs, 202
YouthBuild U.S.A., 274

Z

zero tolerance policy, 221

Credits

This page constitutes an extension of the copyright page. We have made every effort to trace the ownership of all copyrighted material and to secure permission from copyright holders. In the event of any question arising as to the use of any material, we will be pleased to make the necessary corrections in future printings. Thanks are due to the following authors, publishers, and agents for permission to use the material indicated.

Chapter 1. 1: © Larry Towell/Magnum Photos; **5:** © Lara Jo Regan/Getty Images; **8:** © Tim Boyle/Getty Images; **11:** © Bettmann/Corbis; **15:** © AP Images/*Salem News*/Paul Bilodeau; **16:** © AP Images/Lauren Greenfield/VII; **17:** © AP Images/Rogelio V. Solis.

Chapter 2. 21: © Jim Goldberg/Magnum Photos; **26:** © AP Images/Michael Dwyer; **30:** © AP Images/David Kidwell; **33:** © AP Images/WSB-TV Channel 2; **35:** © AP Images/Steve Yeater; **38:** © Bill Aaron/PhotoEdit; **43:** © Sarasota County Sheriff's Office via Getty Images.

Chapter 3. 46: © Mika/zefa/Corbis; **49:** © AP Images/*The Knoxville News Sentinel*/Michael Patrick; **53:** © AP Images/Lauren Greenfield/VII; **55:** © AP Images/*The Charlotte Observer*/Jason E. Miczek; **56:** © AP Images/*Daily Press*/Sangjib Min; **63:** © AP Images/Lauren Greenfield/VII; **74:** © AP Images/*The Post Crescent*/Kirk Wagner; **78:** © AP Photo/*East Valley Tribune*/Andrew T. Sawyer.

Chapter 4. 81: © Christopher Anderson/Magnum Photos; **84:** © Alex Webb/Magnum Photos; **88:** © AP Images/Mike Derer; **91:** © AP Images/Dan Rosenstrauch, Pool; **93:** © AP Images/*Kitsap Sun*/James Branaman; **96:** © AP Images/*Roswell Daily Record*/Andrew Poertner; **102:** © AP Images/*Powell Tribune*/Gib Mathers.

Chapter 5. 107: © Danny Lyon/Magnum Photos; **111:** © AP Images/Gary Kazanjian; **115:** © Jennifer Dunlop/Alamy; **120:** © AP Images/*The Beaver County Times*/Sylvester Washington Jr.; **123:** © AP Images/Damian Dovarganes.

Chapter 6. 131: © Manoocher Geghati/AFP/Getty Images; **134:** © ACE Stock Limited/Alamy; **135:** © Ed Quinn/Corbis; **138:** © Richard Lord/PhotoEdit; **141:** © Cleo Photography/PhotoEdit. All rights reserved.; **146:** © AP Images/Matt Slocum.

Chapter 7. 150: © Eli Reed/Magnum Photos; **155:** © Chislain and Marie David de Lossy/The Image Bank/Getty Images; **158:** © AP Images/Steve Helber; **160:** © AP Images/Consignment Gallery release via Bedford, N.H. Police Department; **162:** American Humane Society; **166:** © AP Images/*Columbus Dispatch*/Tom Dodge; **168:** © AP Images/Tony Dejak, Pool; **171:** © Charles Gupton/Stone/Getty Images.

Chapter 8. 177: © Matt Cardy/Getty Images; **180:** © Janine Wiedel Photolibrary/Alamy; **183:** © JP Laffont/Sygma/Corbis; **185:** © AP Images/Reed Saxon; **190:** © Nancy Siesel; **195:** © A. Ramey/PhotoEdit, Inc.; **197:** © Lyndsay Russell/Alamy; **202:** © Robert Nickelsberg/Getty Images.

Chapter 9. 207: © David McNew/Getty Images; **212:** © AP Images/Adam Hunter; **214:** © AP Images/Damian Dovarganes; **216:** © AP Images/Jane Hwang; **221:** © David McNew/Getty Images; **223:** © Karen Bleier/AFP/Getty Images; **225:** © AP Images/Reed Hoffman/*Democrat and Chronicle*.

Chapter 10. 230: © Brent Stirton/Getty Images; **232:** © Michael Newman/PhotoEdit; **235:** © AP Images/*New Haven Register*/Arnold Gold; **239:** © Jim Goldberg/Magnum Photos; **240:** © Michelle D. Bridwell/PhotoEdit; **242:** © Joel Gordon; **247:** © Jeff Greenberg/PhotoEdit; **249:** © AP Images/*The Herald*/Lauren Tagliatela.

Chapter 11. 259: © Jeff Greenberg/Alamy; **262:** American Correctional Association; **264:** Stock Montage, Inc.; **276:** © AP Images/Daniel R. Patmore; **279:** © AP Images/*The Daily News*/Randy Davey.

Chapter 12. 284: © Alex Webb/Magnum Photos; **286:** © Claudet/Getty Images; **288:** © Cleve Bryant/PhotoEdit; **291:** © AP Images/Donovan Quintero; **296:** © Michael A. Dwyer/Stock, Boston; **299:** Bureau of Justice Assistance U. S. Department of Justice.

Chapter 13. 305: © Larry Kolvoord/The Image Works; **307:** © Shelley Gazin/Corbis; **312:** © Joel Gordon; **316:** © AP Images/Will Shilling; **319:** © AP Images/Jeff T. Green; **326:** © AP Images; **330:** © AP Photo/*Daytona Beach News-Journal*/David Tucker.

Chapter 14. 336: © Joel Gordon; **340:** © AP Images/Peter Pereira-Pool; **343:** © John Birdsall/The Image Works; **349:** From the Collection of the Rochester Public Library Local History Division; **355:** © Joel Gordon; **359:** © Joel Gordon; **362:** © AP Images/Chris Goodenow.

TO THE OWNER OF THIS BOOK:

I hope that you have found *Juvenile Delinquency: The Core,* Third Edition useful. So that this book can be improved in a future edition, would you take the time to complete this sheet and return it? Thank you.

School and address: _____

_____

Department: _____

Instructor's name: _____

1. What I like most about this book is: _____

_____

_____

2. What I like least about this book is: _____

_____

_____

3. My general reaction to this book is: _____

_____

_____

4. The name of the course in which I used this book is: _____

_____

5. Were all of the chapters of the book assigned for you to read? _____

   If not, which ones weren't? _____

6. In the space below, or on a separate sheet of paper, please write specific suggestions for improving this book and anything else you'd care to share about your experience in using this book.

_____

_____

_____

_____

_____

_____

BUSINESS REPLY MAIL
FIRST-CLASS MAIL   PERMIT NO. 34   BELMONT CA

POSTAGE WILL BE PAID BY ADDRESSEE

Attn: Carolyn Henderson Meier, Criminal
Justice Editor

Wadsworth/Thomson Learning
10 Davis Dr
Belmont CA 94002-9801

OPTIONAL:

Your name: _____ Date: _____

May we quote you, either in promotion for *Juvenile Delinquency: The Core,* Third Edition
or in future publishing ventures?

Yes: _____ No: _____

Sincerely yours,

Larry J. Siegel, Brandon C. Welsh